Electrical Injuries
Engineering, Medical and Legal Aspects

Second Edition

Robert E. Nabours, Ph.D., PE
Raymond M. Fish, Ph.D., M.D., FACEP
Paul F. Hill, Esq.

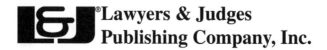

Lawyers & Judges
Publishing Company, Inc.

Lawyers & Judges Publishing Company, Inc.

P.O. Box 30040 • Tucson, AZ 85751-0040
(800) 209-7109 • FAX (800) 330-8795
e-mail: sales@lawyersandjudges.com

Library of Congress Cataloging-in-Publication Data

Nabours, Robert E.
 Electrical injuries : engineering, medical and legal aspects / Robert E. Nabours, Raymond M. Fish, Paul F. Hill.-- 2nd ed.
   p. cm.
Includes bibliographical references and index.
 ISBN 1-930056-71-0 (hardcover)
 1. Electrical injuries. I. Fish, Raymond M. II. Hill, Paul F. III. Title.
RA1091.N33 2004
617.1'2--dc22

ISBN 1-930056-71-0
Printed in the United States of America
10 9 8 7 6 5 4 3 2 1

2003021270

www.lawyersandjudges.com

Contents

3. Electrical Codes and Standards

4. An Introduction to Basic Electrical Systems

5. The Effects of Electrical Energy on Humans

Part 2
Medical Evidence of Electrical Injuries
Raymond M. Fish, Ph.D., M.D., FACEP

11.Basic Bioengineering Relavent to Electrical Accidents

12. Electrical Stimulation of the Heart

25. More Power-Line Accidents and Some Miscellaneous Cases

26. Trespassing Adults and Minors

27. Liability for Power Surges, Outages and Fires

Preface

This new edition of *Electrical Injuries* contains updated and expanded material in Parts 1 and 3 as well as the rearrangement of Part 2 that now concentrates on the medical evidence of electrical injuries and minimizes material of a general bioengineering and medical nature.

Raymond M. Fish and Leslie A. Geddes have recently published a new book titled: *Medical and Bioengineering Aspects of Electrical Injuries.* Their new book and the second edition of this book offer a complete synopsis of known electrical injury causes and effects on humans and property.

Some of the subjects and material that have been added and updated include

- recent U.S. Supreme Court rulings on expert testimony vis-à-vis the *Daubert* and *Kumho* cases
- electrical codes and standards
- NESC interpretations—Internet access to current data
- information on arc-fault circuit interrupters (AFCIs)
- information on ground-fault-forced cables (GFFCs)
- discussion on the art of utility protective relaying
- information on static discharge hazard during gasoline refueling
- additional information on electrical arcs
- expansion of Chapter 9 ("Lightning" including a section on ball lightning and a section on lightning-related injuries)
- three new forensic engineering case studies in Chapter 10
- thirty-one new legal case summaries in Part 3
- improved and expanded subject index

Chapter 39 of the first edition, "Power Lines and Cancer Litigation: Is it Junk Science?" has been omitted because there is no active litigation at this time. Readers with an interest in this subject should refer to the first edition and to Section 5.7 of this edition.

We are confident that our readers will find this new edition of *Electrical Injuries: Engineering, Medical, and Legal Aspects* a welcome addition to their technical library on this subject.

Robert E. Nabours, Editor

Introduction

Electrical injuries, personal and property damage, are a significant peril that humans face in the modern environment. Electrical energy, both natural and man-made, can be of great benefit as well as an extensive danger to humans, animals and nonliving material.

The effects of electrical energy such as product failure, fire, direct personal contact, exposure to ionizing and non-ionizing radiation, induction charge effects, and illumination can cause injury.

Electrical engineers invoke the practical application of mathematical and scientific principles of electricity for the benefit of mankind. When an injury has allegedly been caused by electricity, forensic electrical engineers are often asked to serve as expert witnesses to address the technical issues of a legal conflict by the respective sides in the discord.

Part 1 of this book is intended to explain the relationship between attorneys and electrical engineers in their symbiotic roles as they serve the judicial system. The goal herein is to introduce electrical engineers to forensic engineering, legal terminology, voluntary standards, electrical codes and regulations. Attorneys are introduced to a few basic concepts of electrical engineering and both professions are made aware of the potential injuries that can result from electrical energy gone astray. Reconstruction of electrical accidents in principle and by case studies is illustrated.

Part 2 of the book addresses the medical evidence of electrical injuries, particularly the detailed effects on various body parts caused by electricity. There is frequently a question of the medical condition of a person who alleges an electrical causation for their injury. It is essential to a scientific evaluation of cause and effect that the medical aspects of accident reconstruction are in agreement with the engineering reconstruction of the accident.

Specific medical case studies are presented to illustrate conditions that have resulted from electrical accidents. The use of medical records and medical research are emphasized in the accident reconstruction process. A number of specific electrical energy sources that have led to personal injury are discussed and case histories are cited for injury etiology.

Part 3 of the book emphasizes the legal aspects of electrical injuries using actual case citations to illustrate the legal principles involved with electricity. Product liability and strict liability of electricity as viewed by various legal jurisdictions are discussed. A wide variety of accidents involving power lines are presented on a case-by-case basis.

Electric utility liability for power supply quality is illustrated with multiple case studies. Recent case settlements and verdicts are presented.

In its entirety, this book presents a complete summary of electrical injury issues for the electrical injury litigator and technical investigator.

Robert E. Nabours, Editor

Part 1

Forensic Electrical Engineering

Robert E. Nabours, Ph.D., PE

Chapter 1

The Forensic Electrical Engineer

1.1 The Engineering Expert Witness

A forensic engineer has several professional roles to fulfill. To this end, the forensic electrical engineer must

- exercise a high level of technical competence in electrical engineering,
- have the ability to serve the client as a technical consultant and specifically to be capable as an expert witness, and
- possess and demonstrate the necessary professional qualifications to testify as an expert in court.

Not all electrical engineers can or want to provide these essential functions of a forensic electrical engineer.

The procedures of the U.S. courts are adversarial in nature and many engineers choose to avoid conflict, particularly when an opposing litigant or another expert calls their judgment or technical ability into question.

It is also not sufficient for an engineer to be both technically competent and willing to testify. The court must first qualify the engineer as an expert. In most judicial proceedings, an expert must have "special knowledge, skill, experience, training or education relating to the nature of the case"[1] and it is the providence of the judge to rule on an expert's qualifications. Although an engineer is not required by law to hold a professional license in order to testify as an expert, in practice, this is often a minimum requirement. First of all, most states require an engineering license before an engineer can provide services to the public. Secondly, the professional status afforded to the engineer who has established his technical ability through professional licensing is likely to produce credibility and weight to his testimony in the courtroom.

The National Society of Professional Engineers (NSPE) has undertaken to study the specialty of forensic engineering, and in 1980 published "Guidelines for Forensic Engineering." Shortly thereafter, in 1982, three prominent professional engineers (PEs) formed the National Academy of Forensic Engineers (NAFE).[2] (NAFE is a chartered affinity group of NSPE with headquarters at 174 Brady Avenue, Hawthorne, NY 10532.)

The NAFE seeks to improve the practice, elevate the standards, and advance the cause of forensic engineering. Membership in the Academy is limited to registered professional engineers who are members of NSPE and also members in an acceptable grade of a recognized major technical engineering society.[3] For electrical engineers, this would be the Institute of Electrical and Electronics Engineers (IEEE). Candidates for membership in the NAFE are required to demonstrate actual experience in forensic engineering, including testimony under oath subject to cross-examination. Recommendations are required from practicing attorneys or senior claims managers familiar with the candidate's forensic experience. In furtherance of its goals, NAFE holds meetings and conducts seminars at the biannual meetings of the NSPE that are held throughout the U.S. The NAFE publishes two issues of the *Journal* each year that include learned papers presented at the meetings and seminars.

Since the *Journal of the NAFE* was first published in 1984, there have been 285 articles published on various aspects of forensic engineering including ethical considerations of the profession. There are currently over 630 members of NAFE; moreover, with correspondents, international affiliates, and honorary designations, the organization's participation includes nearly 700 individuals.

1.2 The Forensic Electrical Engineer's Clients

In the author's experience, over a thirty-five-year-period of practice, the first clients and by far the greatest number of clients have been attorneys. At first, these were largely plaintiffs' attorneys; but as time progressed, the mix between plaintiffs' cases and defense cases has become about equal. In most of these cases, the attorney representing one of the parties in a lawsuit directly contacted this expert. The initial contact by an attorney will usually explore the possibility of any conflict of interest in the case or between the parties involved and determine the willingness and capability of the expert to handle the assignment.

Plaintiffs' attorneys are initially interested in determining whether, in the expert's opinion, liability exists on the part of a potential defendant or defendants. A defendant's attorney may seek the expert's help in answering these same questions but, because a lawsuit has usually already been filed, will wish to explore the existence and gathering of possible evidence that will be beneficial to his client as a defense.

The ensuing preliminary investigation and report by the electrical engineering expert must be thoroughly and objectively prepared. The result of this preliminary work will usually serve to tell the attorney (client) whether (1) they have a case, (2) they have a case but with considerable technical difficulty, or (3) they have no case at all.[4]

The actual parties in these litigations or potential lawsuits are plaintiffs who typically believe they have suffered injury by electrical product failure, contact with electrical energy, fire of electrical origin, failures of electrical systems, professional malpractice, or inadequate illumination. The defendants in such charges of liability include manufacturers, design professionals, contractors and installers of electrical equipment or systems, electric and communication utilities, transportation companies, owners of structures, owners of industrial plants and facilities, government agencies, and insurance companies.

Insurance companies are the second largest class of clients in the author's practice. Ordinarily, a direct contact from an insurance company originates from a senior claims adjustor and the most frequent question to be answered is, "Did electricity cause the accident?" This includes fire, product failure, and personal injury. The insurance company may be interested in the possible subrogation of a claim, or it may anticipate a lawsuit against one of its insured; consequently, the expert is retained even before a lawyer is contacted. Fires of suspected electrical origin are the most numerous type of case directly referred to the author by insurance companies.

A third and fourth ranking of clients by number of cases referred would be the courts and individuals. The court may appoint an expert to serve as a "friend of the court" in which case the expert is not a witness for either plaintiff or defendant. The expert may be paid jointly and equally by the parties to the lawsuit in such cases.

On occasion, the author has been retained directly by an individual to conduct a preliminary investigation regarding the efficacy of a potential litigation. Certain individuals or parties apparently prefer to examine the engineering electrotechnical aspects of a liability question before they retain a lawyer.

1.3 The Forensic Electrical Engineer's Function
A. Preliminary investigation
As has already been stated, the first work of the forensic electrical engineer is to conduct a preliminary investigation of the case. This investigation may include a review of all fact witness statements or depositions, examination of photographs and evidence, a possible visitation to the site of the incident, a review of other experts' reports and depositions, and research for applicable codes and standards. If the client has only recently begun to assemble a file on the case, there may be little or none of the material cited above available to review.

It is frequently necessary in early discovery for the expert to suggest how and what material needs to be gathered in order to prepare a thorough analysis of the incident. Occasionally, the expert should recognize the initial information regarding a potential litigation as decisively negative, and it is incumbent upon the forensic engineer to be forthright in expressing this opinion.

B. Detailed technical investigation
Following a preliminary investigation, resulting in a realistic basis for proceeding with the litigation, the detailed technical work of case preparation begins. It is now the expert's job to recommend and conduct any mathematical analyses, physical experiments, or field investigations that will assist the client in solidifying their case. It is also necessary for an

objective technical investigation to anticipate the preparation of the other attorneys' experts and to prepare to accept or refute other technical explanations for the incident.

There are scientific literature databases available for computer searches both online and through university and general libraries that can greatly enhance the investigator's preparation of opinions and rebuttal of opposition opinion. These reference sources are extremely useful in complicated technical cases involving complex scientific issues.

An important part of an expert's job is to recognize their own limitations in knowledge and training that may need supplementation by other experts. There should be no disgrace brought upon an expert who says, "I don't know the answer" or "That is beyond my area of expertise."

Comprehensiveness (i.e., the extensive understanding of many things) is a valuable asset for a consulting forensic engineer. However, an expert's ego has no place in the courtroom. A NAFE engineer expressed it very well when he wrote, "The difference between a comprehensivist and a specialist is that the comprehensivist has a practical working knowledge of many areas of engineering and knows enough about several specialties outside of his own that he can recognize the need for other specialists and work with them."[5]

During the conduct of field investigations, experiments, and evidence examination, photographs and videotapes are valuable adjuncts to the forensic engineer's notes and observations. The ability to fully use these photographic tools for supplementing the investigation is a good reason for comprehensiveness by the expert.

The attorney will obtain additional information from sources not directly available to the engineering expert as the technical investigation progresses. A close working relationship with the attorney will allow the expert to be aware of these information sources and to obtain copies of relevant materials. Examples of such information are police reports, fire and insurance investigation reports, weather reports, subpoenaed manufacturer's data, depositions, and answers to interrogatories.

Electrical cases frequently require a hypothetical explanation. The forensic electrical engineer, therefore, must utilize the scientific method for hypothesis testing in order to present a quantum of proof to the court that weighs heavily in favor of the proposed explanation for the incident.

This has been found to be particularly true of electrical product failure and fire cases.

All possible hypotheses must be considered and the least likely eliminated by objective scientific and mathematical analysis. The most likely postulated explanation for the incident will require a preponderance of rigorous proof that can be explained to the court and made understandable to the jury. The reduction of frequently complicated mathematical and scientific facts to a format that can be understood by the layman is a challenge for an engineer, even to one who has experience in teaching beginning engineering students.

C. Final report

After the available facts have all been ascertained and the technical investigation completed, a final report can be prepared by the expert. The report should include references to all sources relied upon in reaching the conclusions and opinions expressed by the forensic engineer. The report should be discussed between the attorney and the engineer prior to committing the work in writing. Frequently, the attorney will request that the engineer avoid a written final report since it will then be subject to discovery by the other litigants. Most material in the engineer's case file is discoverable by all parties to the law suit; therefore, all notes, calculations, or other work products by the engineer should be prepared with such ultimate disclosure in mind.

If the final report and expert's conclusions are favorable to the attorney's case, the expert will usually then be identified and disclosed to the other litigants and, in some cases, the court may compel such disclosure. Should the results of the engineer's investigation not support the attorney's case, the engineer may or may not be listed or called upon to testify at trial. Whether or not the engineer is named as a witness, the results of the engineer's work on the case should be treated with confidentiality and should not be revealed to anyone except the client or his attorney, unless legally asked by opposing counsel or ordered to do so by the court or client attorney. If required by subpoena to testify in deposition or at trial, the engineer must, of course, answer fully and truthfully all questions posed to the best of his or her ability. Frequently, in the author's experience, the technical investigation produces very strong evidence that may be used to persuade the other litigants to settle the case out of court.

Occasionally, the facts discovered about the alleged liability of a party have been so persuasive that the attorney has requested the author to prepare an affidavit to support a motion for summary judgment requesting a directed verdict by the court. The adverse party for summary judgment can use this process, of course, in the reverse to resist such motions.

D. Discovery

Attorneys customarily use two processes to formally inquire into the opposing counsels' case: the interrogatory and the deposition. Interrogatories are written questions submitted by an attorney to the opposing attorney requesting written answers under oath by a litigant. The forensic engineer is frequently asked to help prepare technical questions for the interrogatories. Such questions are discussed by the engineer and the attorney to assist the lawyer in understanding the technical aspects of the case and to properly word the questions in order to increase the likelihood of receiving a useful response. These technical questions may be referred to the engineer for assistance in preparing the answers. Again, the engineer and attorney will discuss the questions or answers to improve the lawyer's understanding of the details of the case and to avoid answers that do not specifically reply to the question.

A deposition is testimony taken under oath outside the court. At a deposition, the questions from an attorney to a witness and the answers thereto are taken down by a court reporter who then produces a written verbatim record. An expert is notified by subpoena or by informal arrangement through the office of the client attorney that his or her deposition will be taken at a certain time. On that date, the expert, client attorney, opposing attorney, and court reporter meet to conduct the deposition. There may be several attorneys, and sometimes, when the lawyers are in agreement, other experts present during a deposition.

A deposition is the equivalent of court testimony and all statements taken by deposition can be ruled admissible by the judge during a trial. The intended purpose of a deposition is for the opposing attorney to discover what the witness will testify to at trial. In reality, depositions are used for many other purposes including: an exploration of the other attorney's case, an appraisal of the expert's capability and credibility as a witness, and an attempt to create ambiguity in the expert's testimony that can later be used to discredit the witness before a jury.

Frequently, in the author's experience about 75 percent of the time, a deposition is taken, but the case never goes to trial. Sometimes, this is because of the strength or weakness of the case that is exposed during the deposition leading to a settlement out of court.

In other instances, the expert's deposition is taken by the opposition attorney to convince their client that the case is unlikely to be won in court.

Giving a deposition is a critical point in the expert's preparation of a case. The art of testifying in deposition has been explored by forensic engineers[6,7] and attorneys[8] in numerous publications and is too lengthy a subject to pursue adequately in this text.

E. Testifying at trial

In order to prepare for testimony in court, the expert should thoroughly review all work done during the technical investigation, all depositions taken by other experts that bear upon the planned testimony, and all reports and depositions given by the engineer. The attorney and engineer should meet prior to trial to discuss the planned testimony and to be sure that both anticipate the opposing party's examination. It is also important to discuss the opposing attorney's strategy for trial as far as known. The client attorney may have prior experience with the other attorney that can be helpfully shared with the expert.

During the technical investigation and at the conclusion of the discovery process, the engineer and attorney should have decided what exhibits would be useful at trial. Certain graphs, charts, or blowups of mathematical calculations can be prepared by or at the direction of the engineer. Photographic enlargements and physical evidence are also frequently offered as exhibits. The engineer should study all exhibits prior to his or her court testimony, both those offered by the client and those of the opposition.

The direct examination is usually straightforward with questions asked of the expert by the client attorney. The attorney will review the expert's qualifications including education, training, and experience. Then the forensic engineer will be asked to explain the investigation, theories, experiments, and analyses of the technical aspects of the case. Finally, the expert will be asked for his or her conclusions and opinions based upon these facts.

The direct examination may include questions regarding the work of other experts and the engineer's opinions of the validity of that work. A professional, objective, and impersonal critique of the other expert's work is often helpful in convincing the jury of an engineer's credibility and honesty.

Following the direct examination, the other attorney will conduct a cross-examination. The cross examination can be a stressful experience for both the engineer and the attorney. Very few attorneys will be as technically qualified as the expert in their field, and questions posed indiscriminately of an expert can produce answers that are ruinous to the attorney's case. On the other hand, it is the attorney's job to offer as strong an opposition to an expert's damaging opinions as can be found and most qualified attorneys are prepared for this exercise by their scientific consultants.

In some cases, the attorney will directly attack an expert's qualifications or attempt to show bias by the expert in favor of the expert's client or case. If an expert has a conscious or subconscious bias in favor of his client, a competent cross-examination will undoubtedly make this clear. An engineer may have a justifiable bias toward their own work and opinions, but they cannot serve effectively as a forensic expert if they are biased toward the client or case.[9]

Other subjects for the cross examination of an expert are errors in assumptions, incorrect facts, judgment errors, inconsistent testimony in prior cases, and errors in engineering technology or science. Note: All of these targets for cross-examination can be essentially eliminated by the expert through careful preparation of the technical work on the case.

Fact witnesses may give certain facts that can be taken by the engineer at face value and often used as a predicate for hypothetical opinions. Such facts should be given credibility in proportion to their consistency with other witness observations, their agreement with the physical laws of nature, and the perceived bias or truthfulness of the witness. Other facts are developed by the technical investigation, and these are, and generally should be, subject to analytic verification in most cases.

Checking and rechecking the work can best avoid errors in engineering technology or science. Often a review by a colleague or another expert with a different specialty will be appropriate when the analytical or scientific work is complicated or critically dependent upon assumptions.

As was the case with testifying in deposition, testifying under cross-examination is a subject with too much detail to explore further in this text.

Following cross-examination, the client attorney may ask additional questions of the expert under redirect examination. Only the subject matter brought out under cross-examination is permitted to be addressed under redirect. The attorney can use redirect to allow the expert to expand or clarify answers given under cross-examination; however, a good cross-examination will rarely give the expert this opportunity. This is an excellent opportunity (and offers the only one) for the engineer to clarify brief answers given to convoluted hypothetical questions posed by the other attorney and to explain unrealistic assumptions contained therein.

As a matter of policy, the author retains a permanent file of all original work on forensic cases. Material that was furnished by others and can reasonably be expected to exist elsewhere is purged from the file after sufficient time has transpired to be assured that the case has not been appealed.

F. *Daubert* and *Kumho*

The U.S. Supreme Court has heard three cases that have generated considerable attention in the scientific and engineering professions regarding testifying at trial since 1993: *Daubert*,[10] *Joiner*[11] and *Kumho*[12] were all reviewed by the Court with respect to admissibility of expert witness testimony.

The decisions that the Court applied to the admissibility of expert testimony in these cases have influenced the presentation of engineering reports and potential testimony at trial.

The Court has made it clear that the trial judge in federal and most state courts must be an evidentiary gatekeeper with the obligation to insure that *all* expert testimony is reliable in *all* aspects.[13] In both the Daubert and Joiner cases, the decision was limited to that portion of Fed. R. Evid. 702 that refers to "scientific" knowledge and was applied to the kinds of scientific theories and methodologies that involved complex questions of epidemiology.[14]

In the *Kumho Tire* case, the Court seemed less absorbed in formulating general rules for assessing the reliability of expert testimony or in singling out testability as the preeminent factor of concern and more concerned about directing judges to concentrate on "the particular circumstances of the particular case at issue."[15]

An *amicus curaie* brief filed by the NAFE in *Kumho* was the only one cited by the Supreme Court in its decision.[16] In *Kumho* the Court essentially determined in favor of the NAFE recommendations. The one universal "factor" to measure admissibility of expert testimony is the comparison of the experts "methodology" used in court to the methods used in the everyday practice.[17] The bottom line is that no engineering expert can expect to give his or her opinion simply because they are "qualified".[18] The expert must document as best they can, that all aspects of their opinion are reliable.

Attention to the details set forth in Sections 1.3.B and C regarding the technical investigation and final report with particular emphasis on hypothesis testing should demonstrate to the judge the admissibility and reliability of the engineer's opinions. The judge however, without interfering with the jury's role as trier of fact, must determine whether purported scientific and engineering evidence is "reliable" and will "assist the trier of fact".[19]

Endnotes

1. D. G. Sunar, *The Expert Witness Handbook: A Guide for Engineers* (San Carlos, CA: Professional Publications, Inc., 1985), 2.

2. Marvin M. Specter, "Recollections of Ten Years of NAFE," *Journal of the NAFE* 9(2):1–20 (1992).

3. National Academy of Forensic Engineers, *NAFE Directory*, 2nd ed. (Hawthorne, NY: NAFE, 2003), Introduction.

4. Marvin M. Specter, "The Benefit of Negative Opinion," *Journal of the NAFE*, 3(2):15 (1986).

5. Bill E. Forney, "The Forensic Engineer as the Comprehensivist," *Journal of the NAFE* 3(2):87 (1986).

6. Sunar, *Expert Witness Handbook,* 18–27.

7. Robert L. Bleyl, "The Forensic Engineer on the Witness Stand Under Cross-Examination Attack," *Journal of the NAFE* 2(2):15–19 (1985).

8. Thomas A. Bratten, "The Forensic Engineer on Cross-examination," *Journal of the NAFE* 4(1)1:67–78, 1987.

9. Ibid., 70.

10. *Daubert v. Merrell Dow Pharmaceuticals, Inc.*, 509 U.S. 579, 113 S. Ct. 2786, 125 L. Ed. 2d 469 (1993).

11. *General Electric Company v. Joiner*, 118 S. Ct. 512; 139 L. Ed. 2d 508 (1997).

12. *Kumho Tire Co. v. Carmichael*, 119 S. Ct. 1167, 143 L. Ed. 2d 238 (1999).

13. David V. Scott, *NAFE and Kumho Amicus Curiae Brief of NAFE, Decision of U.S. Supreme Court, Update Following Decision* (Hawthorne, NY: NAFE, January 2001), 47.

14. Margaret A. Berger, "The Supreme Court's Trilogy on the Admissibility of Expert Testimony," in *Reference Manual on Scientific Evidence* (Washington, DC: Federal Judicial Center, 2000), 11–15.

15. Ibid., 21.

16. National Academy of Forensic Engineers (NAFE), *NAFE and Kumho Amicus Curiae Brief of NAFE, Decision of U.S. Supreme Court, Update Following Decision* (Hawthorne, NY: NAFE, January 2001), v.

17. Ibid., 59.

18. Ibid., 60.

19. Stephen Berger, "Introduction," *Reference Manual on Scientific Evidence* (Washington, DC: Federal Judicial Center, 2000), 5.

Chapter 2

Standards and the Law

2.1 Terminology

Electrical codes and standards will be presented in detail in Chapter 3. Throughout that chapter there will be terminology used that needs definition to assure that a precise meaning is conveyed. The following terms are defined in the context of standardization.

standard. Commonly used and accepted as an authority;[1] a document setting forth requirements normally dictated by customary practices in industry, science or technology.[2]

code. A systematic collection of regulations and rules of conduct or procedure;[1] a body of recommendations of good practice to satisfy certain considerations (e.g., safety, quality, economy or performance).[2]

recommended practice. A standards document that provides information on good engineering practice;[2] advised or counseled procedure for conducting an engineering activity (e.g., design, analysis or synthesis).

guides. A standards document that provides alternative information that comprises good engineering practice.[2]

national standard. A standard that has been adopted by a recognized national standards body, such as the American National Standards

Institute (ANSI);[2] a standard that is recognized and used nationally by preference. [2] See Section 3.1.

2.2 Legality and Liability

The question of legality of a standard can be separated into two considerations. First, is the standard acceptable under U.S. laws relating to price fixing and trade restraints? The Federal Trade Commission and Department of Justice are concerned with this aspect of the creation or adoption of standards. A national standard such as that adopted by ANSI is extremely unlikely to violate these precepts. Standards created by participants who follow an unprejudiced and fair development practice leading to an equitable resolution of the economic, safety, quality, and performance requirements for a product, process, or procedure are also unlikely to have their work questioned legally.

Second, has the standard been enacted into law? Unless the standard has been enacted into law by a governmental body having jurisdiction in the matter, it is not a mandatory legal requirement, the breach of which imposes liability; but rather, it may and frequently does become a measure by which the jury may evaluate "good practice." When the standard does not strictly govern the behavior of a party, the question may revert to a jury who may interpret the nonconformance with a recognized and customary practice in the industry (i.e., a standard) to be sufficient cause for liability.

Certainly in most cases, standards are essential to the law. As previously discussed, even when a standard does not carry the force of statutory liability in a litigation, the violation of a standard may and often does persuade a jury to find for the plaintiff. Standards may also be a strong defense for the defendant. Compliance with both adopted standards and non-adopted, but widely accepted standards, can frequently resolve a liability issue in favor of the party in compliance, often without the necessity and expense of a trial. Today, the National Electrical Safety Code (NESC; see Section 3.3) and the National Electrical Code (NEC; see Section 3.2) are viewed by most U.S. courts as dispositive so that most legal-electric issues and juries therein are frequently instructed accordingly.

2.3 A Brief History of Electrical Standards

Throughout this text, standards have been treated in the legal sense. We have focused on the use of electrical standards for the establishment of a norm of conduct under the law.

Standards are essential in any scientific endeavor for the avoidance of conflict and needless duplication of research. A new technology first develops the standards necessary to scientific measurement and communication of research and study. Later, as engineers apply the technology, the need for safety standards, codes, specifications, and laws become essential to the practical use of the technology. The development of standards in electrical science began in the U.S. around 1880. There were early problems to be resolved regarding basic definitions and measurements for such phenomena as self-induction, resistance of conductors, and electromotive force. It was not until 1896 that a first conference on standard electrical rules was held, which produced the Underwriter's Rules that eventually led to the National Electrical Code.

In 1897, the standard of luminous intensity (candlepower) was adopted. Then in 1898 and 1899, the first American Institute of Electrical Engineers (AIEE) product standards committees were formed to address the subjects of generators, motors, and transformers.

In 1901, the U.S. Congress established a national bureau for standardization which became known as the National Bureau of Standards (NBS) which greatly affected the growth of electrical technology in the U.S. Progressively, the process of standardization moved from basic scientific standards to technical standards; after World War I, the process of standardization moved into manufacturing.

2.4 International Electrical Standards

International electrical standards were begun in 1904 at St. Louis and have now evolved into the International Electrotechnical Commission (IEC). The International Electrotechnical Commission (IEC) has membership comprised of national committees from forty-two nations. The technical work of the IEC is done in technical committees (TCs). Currently, there are seventy-eight TCs, many of which are subdivided into subcommittees.

The generation of IEC standards begins in a working group created by a TC. Leading experts in the field of work are selected from the individuals offered by the national committees. These experts participate in the working group as individuals, not as representatives of their national committees.

The working group develops a draft for a proposed standard that is forwarded to the IEC central office in Geneva and circulated to all national committees. Comments on the document may be referred back to the working group, and the process repeated until the TC decides that a draft is ready for final ballot. A 20-percent negative vote by the national committees will defeat adoption of the proposed standard. Eventually, if a draft has been accepted, after all editorial changes are resolved and another ballot taken, the document becomes an IEC standard.

The U.S. participates intimately in the IEC through the U.S. National Committee (USNC). The USNC is now a part of ANSI and is run by an executive committee of elected officers with an ANSI staff member acting as secretary. Each member of the executive committee assumes responsibility for a selected number of IEC TCs through a group of individuals called technical advisers (TAs). The TA is responsible for organizing a committee of experts, usually an existing committee in the U.S. This can be an existing ANSI committee or a committee from some other organization such as an engineering society, manufacturer's organization, or a special committee appointed for the specific TC area.

The *Commission Internationale de l'Eclairage* (CIE) was formed in 1913 to deal with illumination. The Illuminating Engineering Society of North America (IESNA) is a member of the CIE and has worked closely with the international organization to standardize and improve the art and science of illumination.

The CIE has approved a system that can identify and designate color, tint and shade by instrumentation, eliminating visual judgment. The standard instrument used to measure color, or more specifically the radiant power at various wavelengths, is called a spectrophotometer.[3] This system has resulted in a specification for light sources that allows their color rendering properties to be compared analytically.

Among other standards developed by or approved by the CIE are luminaire classifications, spectral luminous efficiency values, and standard illuminants.

2.5 Voluntary Standards

Standards that are developed by the voluntary activities of professional societies (e.g., the Institute of Electrical and Electronic Engineers, Inc. [IEEE]; see Section 3.4), trade associations (e.g., the National Electrical Manufacturer's Association [NEMA]; see Section 3.6) or other organizations (e.g., Underwriters Laboratories [UL]; see Section 3.7) are, effectively, the approved recommendations of these organizations. Unless these standards are adopted by governmental bodies as regulatory provisions or incorporated into laws and statutes by Congress, state legislatures, or local governments, they have no mandatory legal force. (See Section 2.2, "Legality and Liability.")

Conformance to a standard can neither be presumed nor is conformance mandatory unless prescribed by law. Many standards are developed by manufacturers for reasons other than safety of the consumer or the public in general. Trade association standards are frequently adopted to represent the technical quality of products for warranty limitation purposes.

The effectiveness of the voluntary standards system in the U.S. is largely because of the activities of ANSI. Those standards that are independently developed by multiple organizations are not adopted as national standards by ANSI without a thorough review of the various proposals for technical accuracy, fairness, and conflict. Only standards that are technologically sound and for which the need can be established become ANSI designated national standards.

Endnotes

1. *Webster's II: New Riverside University Dictionary* (Boston: Riverside Publishing Company, 1988).

2. Donald G. Fink and H. Wayne Beaty, eds., *Standard Handbook for Electrical Engineers*, 13th ed. (NY: McGraw-Hill, 1993), 28-6 to 28-8.

3. Louis Erhardt, *Radiation Light and Illumination: A Recreation*, from the original text by Charles P. Steinmetz (Camarillo, CA: Camarillo Reproduction Center, 1977), 70–76.

Chapter 3

Electrical Codes and Standards

3.1 American National Standards Institute (ANSI)

The American National Standards Institute (ANSI) coordinates and promotes the development of standards. It also approves as American National Standards, documents that have been prepared in accordance with its regulations. ANSI evolved from the American Engineering Standards Committee (AESC) which was formed in 1919 as a result of development by the American Institute of Electrical Engineers (AIEE—founded in 1884). ANSI is now headquartered at 1430 E. Broadway, New York, NY 10018. The AIEE has since merged with the Institute of Radio Engineers (IRE—founded in 1912) to form the Institute of Electrical and Electronics Engineers (IEEE—formed in 1963).

Standards developed and approved by other organizations may be approved by ANSI, in which case the standards carry the identification numbers of both organizations. Such standards are available from either organization. ANSI also appoints committees for standards development that are organized and administered by other organizations. Generally such committees are formed to coordinate the work of a large number of organizations. Standards developed by ANSI committees will carry only an ANSI number. ANSI standards of interest to forensic electrical engineers include the following:

- ANSI/IEEE Std. 141-1993, IEEE Recommended Practice for Electric Power Distribution for Industrial Plants, IEEE Red Book.
- ANSI/IEEE Std. 142-1991, IEEE Recommended Practice for Grounding of Industrial and Commercial Power Systems, IEEE Green Book.
- ANSI/IEEE Std. 241-1990, (R1997) IEEE Recommended Practice for Electrical Power Systems in Commercial Buildings, IEEE Gray Book.
- ANSI/IEEE Std. 242-2001, IEEE Recommended Practice for Protection and Coordination of Industrial and Commercial Power Systems, IEEE Buff Book.
- ANSI/IEEE Std. 399-1997, IEEE Recommended Practice for Power Systems Analysis, IEEE Brown Book.
- ANSI/IEEE Std. 446-1995, IEEE Recommended Practice for Emergency and Standby Power Systems for Industrial and Commercial Applications, IEEE Orange Book.
- ANSI/IEEE Std. 493-1997, IEEE Recommended Practice for the Design of Reliable Industrial and Commercial Power Systems, IEEE Gold Book.
- ANSI/IEEE Std. 602-1996, IEEE Recommended Practice for Electric Systems in Health Care Facilities, IEEE White Book.
- ANSI/IEEE Std. 739-1995, IEEE Recommended Practice for Energy Conservation and Cost Effective Planning in Industrial Facilities, IEEE Bronze Book.
- ANSI/IEEE Std. 1100-1999, IEEE Recommended Practice for Powering and Grounding Sensitive Electronic Equipment, IEEE Emerald Book.
- IEEE Std. 902-1998, IEEE Guide for Maintenance, Operation and Safety of Industrial and Commercial Power Systems, IEEE Yellow Book.

- ANSI/IEEE Std. 1015-1997, IEEE Recommended Practice for Applying Low-Voltage Circuit Breakers Used in Industrial and Commercial Power Systems, IEEE Blue Book.
- ANSI/IEEE Std. 100-1996, IEEE Standard Dictionary of Electrical and Electronic Terms.
- ANSI/NFPA 70-2002, National Electrical Code.
- ANSI C2-2002, National Electrical Safety Code.
- ANSI/IEEE Std. C95.1-1999, Standard for Safety Levels with Respect to Human Exposure to Radio Frequency Electromagnetic Fields, 3 kHz to 300 GHz—Supplement.

3.2 National Electrical Code (NEC and NFPA)

The National Fire Protection Association (NFPA) has acted as sponsor for the National Electrical Code (NEC) since 1911. The NEC is periodically reviewed and revised to reflect changes in both technology and hazard recognition within the electrical industry. The NEC Committee includes representatives from all phases of electrical technology (e.g., manufacturers, contractors, electrical building inspectors, utilities, engineering organizations, fire underwriters, and independent testing laboratories). NFPA is located at Batterymarch Park, Quincy, MA 02269.

The NEC has been published since 1897 with periodic superseding editions. The 2002 edition is the latest edition, with a 2005 revision currently in process. The purpose of the NEC is the practical safeguarding of persons and property from hazards arising from the use of electricity.

The NEC covers[1]

- installations of electric conductors and equipment for public and private buildings and structures,
- installations of conductors and equipment that connect to the supply of electricity (utility service),
- installations of other outside conductors and equipment on the premises, and
- installations of optical fiber cable.

The NEC does not cover[1]

- installations in ships, watercraft other than floating buildings, railway rolling stock, aircraft, or automotive vehicles other than mobile homes and recreational vehicles;
- installations underground in mines and self-propelled mobile surface mining machinery and its attendant electrical trailing cable;
- installations of railways for generation, transformation, transmission, or distribution of power used exclusively for operation of rolling stock or installations used exclusively for signaling and communications purposes;
- installations of communications equipment under the exclusive control of communications utilities located outdoors or in building spaces used exclusively for such installations; or
- installations under the exclusive control of electric utilities for the purpose of communications or metering; or for the generation, control, transformation, and distribution of electric energy located in buildings used exclusively by utilities for such purposes or located outdoors on property owned or leased by the utility; or on public highways, streets, roads and so on, or outdoors by established rights on private property.

The intent of the NEC is to cover all premises wiring or wiring other than utility owned metering equipment, on the load side of the service point of buildings, structures, or any other premises not owned or leased by the utility. Also, it covers installations in buildings used by the utility for purposes other than listed above, such as office buildings, warehouses, garages, machine shops, and recreational buildings that are not an integral part of a generating plant, substation, or control center.[2]

The NFPA publishes extensively on the subject of fire safety. Besides the NEC, there are other NFPA products of interest to electrical engineers including:

- *The NEC Handbook*, edited by Mark W. Earley, Richard H. Murray and John M. Caloggero.
- *Electrical Installations in Hazardous Locations*, Peter J. Schram and Mark W. Earley.

- *American Electricians' Handbook*, Terrell Croft and Wilford J. Summers, McGraw-Hill.

There are also NFPA codes and standards published in pamphlet editions:

- NFPA 70B, "Electrical Equipment Maintenance."
- NFPA 70E, "Electrical Safety Requirements for Employee Workplaces."
- NFPA 72, "National Fire Alarm Code."
- NFPA 73, "Residential Electrical Maintenance Code for One- and Two-Family Dwellings."
- NFPA 75, "Protection of Electronic Computer/Data Processing Equipment."
- NFPA 77, "Static Electricity."
- NFPA 79, "Electrical Standard for Industrial Machinery."
- NFPA 110, "Emergency and Standby Power Systems."
- NFPA 111, "Stored Energy Emergency and Standby Power Systems."
- NFPA 262, "Method of Test for Flame Travel and Smoke of Wire and Cables for Use in AirHandling Spaces."
- NFPA 496, "Purged and Pressurized Enclosures for Electrical Equipment."
- NFPA 497, "Classification of Flammable Liquids, Gases or Vapors and of Hazardous (Classified) Locations for Electrical Installations in Chemical Process Areas."
- NFPA 499, "Classification of Combustible Dusts and of Hazardous (Classified) Locations for Electrical Installations in Chemical Process Areas."
- NFPA 780, "Standard for the Installation of Lightning Protection Systems," 1997.
- NFPA 850, "Fire Protection for Electric Generating Plants and High Voltage Direct Current Converter Stations."
- NFPA 851, "Fire Protection for Hydroelectric Generating Plants."
- NFPA 921, "Guide for Fire and Explosion Investigations," 1998.

The NFPA also publishes special topics references, brochures and videos.

3.3 National Electrical Safety Code (ANSI and IEEE)

The National Electrical Safety Code (NESC), ANSI C2-2002, is developed by the American National Standards Committee C2 and published by the IEEE. IEEE headquarters are at 345 East 47th St., New York, NY 10017. The NESC work began in 1913 with the publication by the National Bureau of Standards of NBS Circular 49 and was continued by NBS until H81, American Standard C2.2-1960 was issued in November 1961. Work was again commenced in 1970 by the ANSI C2 Committee, resulting in the publication by the IEEE of ANSI C2-1973. (Ref. NESC C2-1990, corrected edition, 3rd printing. Foreword.) The IEEE has published eight updated editions of the NESC since 1973.

The purpose of the NESC is the practical safeguarding of persons (both utility employees and the public) during the installation, operation, or maintenance of electric supply and communication lines and associated equipment.

The NESC rules cover supply and communication lines, equipment, and associated work practices employed by an electric supply, communication, railway, or similar utility in the exercise of its function as a utility. They cover similar systems under the control of qualified persons, such as those associated with an industrial complex or utility interactive system.

The NESC covers utility facilities and functions from the point of origin of the utility's supply of electrical energy or communication signals through the utility system to the point of delivery to a customer's facilities. In the case of an electric supply utility, this is the point of metering the customer's electric service. For a communications utility, this is the customer's antenna, receiver, or line termination point.

NESC rules do not cover installations in mines, ships, railway rolling equipment, aircraft, or automotive equipment, or utilization wiring except as necessary for the installation and maintenance of electric supply stations and underground electric supply and communication lines as covered by Parts 1 and 3 of the code.[3]

The membership of ANSI Committee C2 includes representatives from the utilities, insurance groups, railroads, public transit association,

National Safety Council, electrical inspectors, area power administrations, and the Canadian Standards Association.

The IEEE publishes Interpretations of the NESC prepared by a representative committee acting upon requests for interpretations of the rules contained in the code. Seven volumes of interpretations have been published to date, beginning with the period from 1961–1977 inclusive and concluding with the 1994–1997 inclusive period. Interim editions of Interpretations are collected and published on a regular basis by the IEEE. A complete collection 1943–1999 of interpretations is available from the IEEE. Current interpretations are available on the Internet from http://standards.ieee.org/nesc/interpretations.

3.4 IEEE Standards

The IEEE publishes numerous standards relating to the various fields in electrical and electronics engineering. Many of these standards are recognized and designated as ANSI Standards. Some have also been approved by the Canadian Standards Association and are CSA designated. Besides the ANSI/IEEE standards cited in the ANSI Section 3.1 of this text, the IEEE publishes standards in the areas of aerospace and electronics, broadcasting and communications, computers, power engineering, instrumentation and measurement, insulators and insulation, magnetics, motors and generators, nuclear power, recording, symbols and units, and electrical transmission and distribution.

IEEE standards are developed through ballot within the technical committees, and final approval is required by a standards board consisting of leading experts in a broad range of electro technology. The IEEE is the largest engineering society in the world (over 250,000 members). Membership is available to qualified individuals in engineering and science. No company memberships are offered.

3.5 Electronic Industries Association (EIA)

The EIA was originally formed in 1925 and since that time it has absorbed several electronic industry associations. Standards are developed by committees which operate under divisional panels representing various segments of the industry: consumer electronics, distributor products, communications, industrial electronics, component parts, solid state products, electron tubes, and government electronics. EIA is located at 2001 Eye St. NW, Washington, DC 20006.

Among EIA services are activities such as compiling statistics, developing standards that are usually submitted to ANSI, presenting consensus views and recommendations, and representing the industry in governmental agencies and public hearings. The EIA publishes a consumer electronics annual review and the standards and engineering Publications.

3.6 National Electrical Manufacturers Association (NEMA)

NEMA was formed in 1926 and has grown to a membership of more than 550 companies engaged in the manufacture of electrical products for such fields as construction, power electronics, industrial electrical equipment, insulation, lighting, and wire and cable. NEMA is located at 2101 L St. NW, Washington, DC 20037.

NEMA technical committees are comprised of engineers who represent member companies that develop product standards. These standards take into consideration the realistic economic and technological factors that are essential to practical standardization in a manufacturing industry. Standards are adopted by consensus of the membership with final approval by the NEMA Codes and Standards Committee.

NEMA generates four classifications of standards:

- **NEMA standard**. Defines a commercial product subject to repetitive manufacture.
- **Suggested standard for future design**. Suggests an approach to product improvement or development.
- **Authorized engineering information**. Explains data or information in conjunction with NEMA standards.
- **Official standards proposal**. Standards draft for adoption submitted to some other organization (e.g., ANSI).

ANSI has appointed NEMA as the secretariat organization for a number of standards committees including

- insulated wire and cable,
- dry cells and batteries,

- attachment plugs and receptacles,
- low voltage fuses, rated for less than 600 volts,
- industrial control apparatus,
- insulators for electric power lines,
- switchgear,
- transformers, regulators and reactors,
- capacitors,
- surge arresters, and
- preferred voltage ratings for AC systems and equipment.

3.7 Underwriters Laboratories (UL)

Underwriters Laboratories (UL) was founded in 1894. UL is an independent not-for profit organization originally engaged in testing products for electrical and fire hazards for insurance companies. Today, the scope of UL has expanded to include the investigation and testing of materials, devices, products, equipment, constructions, methods and systems for hazards to life and property. UL headquarters are at 333 Pfingsten Rd., Northbrook, IL 60062.

Engineering Services of UL evaluates appliances, rebuilt motors and generators, and electrical construction materials and wiring used to distribute power inside buildings and structures (i.e., electrical systems covered by the NEC). Approved (listed) products are given a UL label or mark. UL also lists (publishes) a directory of companies who have demonstrated the ability to produce certain products conforming to its requirements. UL submits its standards to ANSI for adoption as national standards.

3.8 Government Regulatory Standards
A. Consumer Products Safety Commission (CPSC)

The Consumer Products Safety Commission (CPSC) was established by Congress in 1972. In connection with its primary function, which is the prevention of injuries associated with consumer products, the CPSC compiles a consumer product hazard index that ranks such products by severity and frequency of accidents. The CPSC publishes regulations that result from the development of safety standards for various types of products, which in the electrical field include electric toys, TV sets and appliances.

Upon a determination of the need for a standard by CPSC, a notice is published in the *Federal Register*. Interested persons or organizations are invited to submit standards for consideration toward this need. After the CPSC has evaluated such submissions, the Commission will publish the accepted standard as a regulation in the *Federal Register*.

B. Federal Communications Commission (FCC)

The Federal Communications Commission (FCC) was begun in the late 1920s as the Federal Radio Commission (FRC) to deal with the problems that were being created by radio frequency interference and frequency overlaps occurring in a growing broadcasting industry. The FCC Act of 1934 converted the FRC into the Federal Communication Commission. Since 1934, the FCC has grown to become one of the government's most extensive bureaucratic agencies, with sections for broadcasting, safety and special radio services, cable television, field operations and common carrier (telecommunications).

FCC Rules are developed after a convoluted process of initiation, evaluation, notices of inquiry or proposed rule making, docket issuance, comment and reply evaluation, report and orders, public petitions for reconsideration and modifications.[4] The commission cooperates with many organizations including the IEEE, the EIA, ANSI, the International Radio Consultative Committee (CCIR), the Federal Telecommunications Standards Committee (FTSC), and the Law Enforcement Standards Laboratory (LESL).

C. Nuclear Regulatory Commission (NRC)

The Nuclear Regulatory Commission (NRC) was established in 1974 when the Atomic Energy Commission functions of regulation, research, and development were separated.

The NRC provides regulatory guides that specify how an applicant for an NRC license may satisfy the Commission's safety criteria. The regulatory guide is not mandatory as a result of its issuance. The NRC attempts to cooperate and work with a voluntary standards system developed by leading organizations involved in nuclear power standards, such as ANSI, American Society of Mechanical Engineers (ASME), American Society of Testing Materials (ASTM) and IEEE.

In-house, the NRC develops basic standards that define a level of risk judged acceptable to the public; the NRC also develops standards on assumptions for evaluating the consequences of nuclear plant accidents.

D. Occupational Safety and Health Administration (OSHA)

The Occupational Safety and Health Administration (OSHA) was established as a division of the U.S. Department of Labor by Congress in 1970. OSHA's primary function is the prevention of injuries in the workplace. Like the CPSC, OSHA uses the *Federal Register* to both solicit comments and publish proposed rules and, after multiple review and final approval, to publish the standard as an OSHA regulation.

Many of OSHA's regulations and rules are taken directly from such ANSI standards as the NEC and the NESC. OSHA has promulgated rules for the operations of cranes and other forms of high profile equipment in proximity to overhead power lines. Violation of OSHA regulations can, in many jurisdictions, result in the imposition of legal liability as discussed in Chapter 2.

3.9 Uniform Building Code (UBC)

The UBC is intended to develop better building construction and greater public safety by uniformity in building laws.[5] The UBC was first enacted by the ICBO in 1927. The code has been revised at approximately three-year intervals since first enacted. The UBC is published by the International Conference of Building Officials (ICBO), 5360 S. Workman Mill Rd., Whittier, CA 90601.

The UBC cites related publications for user knowledge of code enforcement and administration of a building inspection program. Among the related publications cited by the UBC is the National Electrical Code (NEC) that the UBC describes as "the electrical code for the majority of states, counties and cities in the United States."

The ICBO, the International Association of Plumbing and Mechanical Officials (IAPMO), the International Association of Electrical Inspectors, the Pacific Coast Electrical Association and NEMA have promulgated an administrative document, The Uniform Administrative Code, to enable the UBC to be used by code enforcement agencies throughout the nation. Electrical systems specified as minimum standard requirements under the UBC are generally covered by other standards (e.g., the Uniform Fire Code and the NEC).

3.10 State and Local Standards

Individual governmental bodies exercising legal jurisdiction over electrical installations and utilities as well as insurance underwriters may choose to adopt all, some, or none of the national standards that have been cited herein; however, the legal implications for such actions are significant.

Predominantly, the states and local governments in the U.S. have chosen to adopt the widely accepted standards as promulgated by ANSI, particularly the NEC and the NESC. Many states have their own codes for electrical work that are modeled after the NEC with certain exceptions, usually enacting more conservative or restrictive requirements. The state of California, for example, through the Public Utility Commission (PUC), has its own code for electric utilities. PUC general order No. 95 covers overhead lines and G.O. No. 128 deals with underground facilities.

State regulations, which are in conflict with parallel federal regulations are preempted, and the courts will apply the applicable federal regulations. However, the degree of a standard is not always clearly defined and frequently an engineering opinion is necessary to assist a court or judicial hearing in its interpretation of standards.

Most states have commissions or regulatory bodies responsible for the regulation of public utilities that operate within the state. Frequently, in the case of electric power and communication utilities, the state utility commissions adopt the NESC as the minimum standard of operation for the applicable utility.

3.11 The Illuminating Engineering Society of North America (IESNA)

The Illuminating Engineering Society of North America (IES) was founded in 1906 for the purpose of disseminating knowledge relating to the art and science of illumination. A lighting handbook was first published by the IES in 1949. Since then, the IES has periodically updated and expanded its handbook to accommodate its research and application activities. The IESNA is headquartered at 120 Wall St. 17th Floor, New York, NY 10005.

In 1926, the IES created a committee on roadway lighting, publishing *The Principles of Street Lighting* in 1928. This committee's work continued and resulted in the *American Standard Practice for Street and Highway Lighting*, published in 1947. The first ANSI standard for roadway lighting was published in 1972 and has evolved to include the American National Standard Practice for Roadway Lighting, RP-8 1996 which is a part of the U.S. Department of Transportation, Federal Highway Administration's *Roadway Lighting Handbook*. See Chapter 8, "Illumination" and its references.

The purpose of the standard practice is to serve as a basis for design of fixed lighting for roadways, bikeways and pedestrian ways. It is not intended as, nor does it establish, a legal standard for roadway lighting systems.[6] The adoption of the IES standard practice by governmental agencies, however, creates a legal standard, and certainly the principles of design recommended by the standard practice represent state-of-the-art engineering for lighting systems. At the very least, the IES standard practice is an accepted standard for good lighting.

The IES *Lighting Handbook* is currently published in one volume with two sections, a reference section and an applications section. The Lighting Handbook treats the subject matter of terminology, physics of light, light and vision, measurements, luminaire design, day lighting, light sources, lighting calculations, lighting applications, and codes and regulations. Importantly, the IES has published recommendations for illuminance (density of incident light energy) for a broad classification of visual activities.

Endnotes

1. American National Standards Institute (ANSI), *ANSI/NFPA 70, National Electrical Code: 2002* (Quincy, MA: National Fire Protection Association), Art. 90-2, 70-1, 2.

2. Ibid., (FPN), 70-2.

3. ANSI C2-1990, *National Electrical Safety Code: 2002*, Sec. 1.011, Scope, 45.

4. Donald G. Fink and H. Wayne Beaty, eds., *Standard Handbook for Electrical Engineers*, 13th ed. (NY: McGraw-Hill, 1993), 29-16, 17.

5. International Conference of Building Officials (ICBO), *Uniform Building Code* (Whittier, CA: International Conference of Building Officials), pt. 1, ch. 1, sec. 102, Purpose.

6. *Roadway Lighting*, ANSI/IES (NY: Illuminating Engineering Society, 2000), 3.

Chapter 4

An Introduction to Basic Electrical Systems

4.1 Electrical-Hydraulic Analogy

The purpose of this part of the book is to explain the function of electrical engineering as applied to legal proceedings. To convey this message effectively, it is helpful if the non-electrical engineer reader has a fundamental understanding of electricity as frequently encountered in our modern world.

The author has found that electrical terms such as voltage, current and resistance are difficult to understand for someone who is not schooled in these abstract concepts. Most people are comfortable, however, with ideas that associate with familiar things, and it is for this reason that the electrical-hydraulic analogy is presented. A word of caution: there are pitfalls inherent in the use of analogies, and the reader is admonished not to depend strictly upon the comfort that this analogy offers.

The basis of the electrical-hydraulic analogy is that electrical current is analogous to water flow. Electrical current is the flow of electrical charge, primarily electrons within a material. Water flow is the motion of water molecules within a pipe. Water flow is measured in units such as gallons per minute (GPM). Electrical current is measured in amperes (amps).

35

The hydraulic force that produces water flow is pressure, and the analogous force that produces current is called electrical pressure. Water pressure is measured in pounds per square inch and electrical pressure is measured in volts.

As water flows through a pipe, it encounters roughness of the pipe surfaces and is restricted by the pipe cross section. This interference with

Table 4.1 Electrical-Hydraulic Analogy	
Electrical System Element	**Hydraulic System Element**
Generator	Pump
Voltage (Volts)	Pressure (PSI)
Current (amps)	Water flow (GPM)
Resistance of wire (ohms)	Friction of water
Wire size (AWG)	Pipe size (I.D.)
Switch (On/Off)	Valve (On/Off)
Electrons	Water

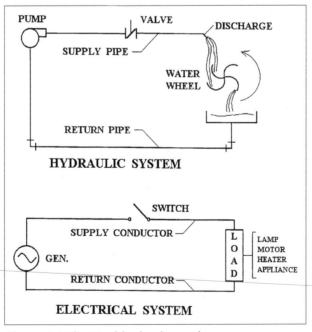

Figure 4.1 Electrical-hydraulic analogy

water flow through the pipes or other conveyances causes an energy loss. Analogously, when electrons move through the atomic structure of a material, they encounter collisions and interferences from other atomic particles that produce a loss of energy. The resistance of an electrical material is measured in ohms. Resistance is used to account for the energy loss that occurs when current flows through a material.

The end product of water flow may be used for filling a tank, irrigating a lawn, or perhaps turning a water turbine for generating electricity. The practical end product of an electrical current flow may be for energizing a light bulb, creating heat, or powering a motor.

4.2 Ohm's Law

Perhaps the most satisfactory part of basic electrical science is that the real world behaves in a highly predictable manner if one is able to discover the applicable mathematical model and the parameters that apply to the case being considered. Electrical engineers with a modicum of humility are frequently amazed to find that Ohm's law is universally upheld by nature. Ohm's law may be stated in several equivalent forms:

$$V \text{ (volts)} = I \text{ (amps)} \times R \text{ (ohms)} \qquad \text{(Equation 4.1)}$$

$$I \text{ (amps)} = \frac{V \text{ (volts)}}{R \text{ (ohms)}} \qquad \text{(Equation 4.2)}$$

$$R \text{ (ohms)} = \frac{V \text{ (volts)}}{I \text{ (amps)}} \qquad \text{(Equation 4.3)}$$

Basically, Ohm's law states that when an electrical pressure of one volt is applied across a material whose resistance is one ohm, there will be one amp flowing through the material. Since there is current flow in a conducting material when a voltage is impressed across it, there will be energy lost as the current passes through the conductor.

The rate of energy loss in a material conducting current is called power and is expressed in watts. Power can be expressed in terms of voltage, current, and resistance.

$$P \text{ (watts)} = [I \text{ (amps)}]^2 R \text{ (ohms)} \qquad \text{(Equation 4.4)}$$

$$P \text{ (watts)} = \frac{[V \text{ (volts)}]^2}{R \text{ (ohms)}} \qquad \text{(Equation 4.5)}$$

The power equation states that when one amp flows through a material having a resistance of one ohm, there will be one watt of power dissipated within the material. Another way of saying this is that when one volt is applied across a conductor having one ohm of resistance, there is one watt of power lost in the conducting process that ensues. One last relationship also exists for purely resistive materials such that power can be expressed as

$$P \text{ (watts)} = V \text{ (volts)} \times I \text{ (amps)}. \qquad \text{(Equation 4.6)}$$

4.3 Basic Electrical Circuits

For electrical energy to be usefully applied, there are three fundamental components necessary:

- a source of electrical energy (e.g., a generator, a battery, or other energy converter);
- a transmitting means for carrying the energy from the source to the end use, such as wires or other conductors of energy; and
- an end-use element, usually called a load (e.g., a light bulb, an appliance, or a motor).

An electrical circuit incorporates each of these components. All basic electrical circuits can be treated as series circuits, parallel circuits, or a combination thereof.

In the simple series circuit, the current flow I is the same through each component. As shown in Figure 4.2, the current I (amps) which flows in the supply and return wires is the same current I which flows through the load and is the same current furnished by and returned to the generator.

Consider that, otherwise, there would be an accumulation of electrons somewhere which would eventually break through an electrical component similar to water breaking through a dam, creating a physical avalanche of current (a flood) not unlike a lightning strike. Since we know that such a phenomenon does not occur with ordinary current flow through a circuit in its normal mode of operation, we must reject this as a reasonable possibility.

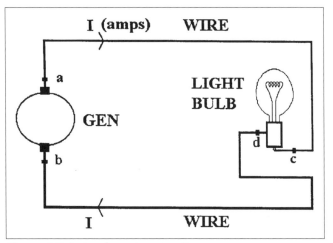

Figure 4.2 *A simple series circuit*

It is the electrical pressure of the generator expressed in volts that causes the current I to flow through the wires and the load. Electrical engineers represent the elements of this simple series circuit schematically as shown in Figure 4.3.

In Figure 4.3, the generator is schematically implied to supply an alternating current voltage (AC). The resistances of the supply and return conductors and the load are schematically represented by the resistor symbol shown on the right. The values for the various  electrical parameters of the circuit are shown algebraically by the symbols $V, R_W/2, R_L$ and I.

The total force or electrical pressure that produces a current flow through the wires and load must be divided among the component parts of the circuit. In accordance with Ohm's law, Equation 4.1, we may state that the supply pressure (voltage) is equal to the sum of the pressure losses (voltage drops) around the series loop.

$$V = I\frac{R_W}{2} + IR_L + I\frac{R_W}{2}$$ (Equation 4.7)

On combining terms algebraically, we have

$$V = I(R_W + R_L)$$ (Equation 4.8)

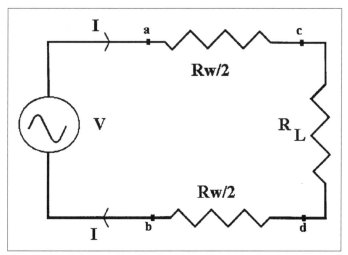

Figure 4.3 *Schematic of a simple series circuit*

A practical example of the application of Equation 4.8 is a residential electrical circuit where a 100-watt light bulb is supplied by 100 feet of copper wire (fifty feet each way from the source). In this example, the electrical parameters are $V = 120$ volts, $R_W = 0.314$ ohms (14 AWG wire), and $R_L = 144$ ohms.

Solving Equation 4.8 for I gives:

$$I = \frac{V}{R_W + R_L} = \frac{120}{0.314 + 144} = 0.8315 \text{ amp} \qquad \text{(Equation 4.9)}$$

Using Ohm's law Equation 4.4 to verify the power delivered to the load, we find that

$$P = I^2 \times R_L = (0.8315)^2 \times 144 = 99.56 \text{ watts.} \qquad \text{(Equation 4.10)}$$

How can this be correct if the light bulb is rated at 100 watts? The answer lies in the fact that the light bulb is rated at 100 watts for a voltage of 120 volts. Since there is a small resistance in the wires of the circuit, there is some energy lost in heat as the current passes through these wires. There is then a voltage loss (pressure drop) between the source and the load. According to Ohm's law, the voltage drop in the wires is given by

$$V_D = I \times R_W = 0.8315 \times 0.314 = 0.261 \text{ volt.} \qquad \text{(Equation 4.11)}$$

The voltage at the supply V_{ab} = 120 volts is, therefore, reduced to a voltage at the load of

$$V_{cd} = V_{ab} - V_D = 120 - 0.261 = 119.74 \text{ volts.} \quad \text{(Equation 4.12)}$$

If this corrected voltage is applied at the load in Ohm's law Equation 4.5, we find that

$$P_L = \frac{V_{cd}^2}{R_L} = \frac{(119.74)^2}{144} = 99.57 \text{ watts.} \quad \text{(Equation 4.13)}$$

which agrees within 0.01 watt of our previous calculation, Equation 4.10. Mathematically, Ohm's law is upheld. Experimentally, a circuit having these parameters will produce physically measurable results for current, voltage, and power that agree closely with these calculations.

A simple parallel circuit is shown schematically in Figure 4.4.

In this schematic representation, we have neglected the usually small resistances of the wires and only considered the relatively larger resistances of the loads. This representation is generally accurate when analyzing branch power circuits for supplying energy to residential and commercial users within a structure.

The principles of analysis for the parallel circuit are similar to those used for the series circuit; again, electrons will not accumulate without limit in some element of the circuit. Therefore, the current furnished by the generator must be returned to the generator.

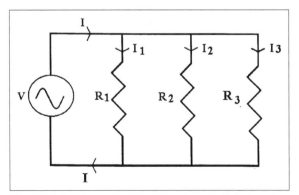

Figure 4.4 *Schematic of a simple parallel circuit*

Electrical engineers like to jest that electrical utilities have an ideal business: they loan the electricity to the customer and instantaneously get all of it (electrons) returned undamaged so that they can reloan the same electricity with interest. Actually the electrons furnished by the utility have greater energy (measured in kilowatt-hours) than do the returning electrons, which flow back to the utility's generators with zero net energy. The utility's generators then convert mechanical energy into electrical energy, thereby raising the energy of the electrons before they are resupplied to the customer. It is for this added energy value that the utilities charge.

A parallel circuit is most eloquently analyzed by recognizing that the supply current from the source must equal the sum of the parallel path currents furnished to the loads. Mathematically we have

$$I = I_1 + I_2 + I_3 .$$ (Equation 4.14)

Applying Ohm's law, Equation 4.2, to Equation 4.14 gives

$$I = \frac{V}{R_1} + \frac{V}{R_2} + \frac{V}{R_3} .$$ (Equation 4.15)

By algebraic combination we have

$$I = V \frac{R_2 R_3 + R_1 R_3 + R_1 R_2}{R_1 R_2 R_3} .$$ (Equation 4.16)

While Equation 4.16 can be used to calculate the total current that is supplied to these three loads, the simplest method of analysis for parallel loads is to sum their individual current requirements. Since the voltage is assumed to be the same for each load, by Ohm's law (Equation 4.2) and using Equation 4.6 for resistive circuits, it is easiest to sum the power requirements of the individual loads and then divide by the supply voltage to determine the total current I.

Our electrical systems are by practice and by code usually designed and constructed so that the supply voltage V remains essentially constant throughout the circuit. We are then relatively accurate in performing calculations based upon power requirements for loads rather than resistances. An example follows.

Calculate the line current required to supply ten 100-watt light bulbs connected in parallel at a rated voltage of 120 volts. The total load is first found:

$$P_L = 10 \times 100 = 1,000 \text{ watts.} \qquad \text{(Equation 4.17)}$$

Then by Equation 4.6 we obtain

$$I = \frac{P_L}{V} = \frac{1,000}{120} = 8.333 \text{ amps.} \qquad \text{(Equation 4.18)}$$

Taking into consideration the wire resistance and placement of the loads, an accurate analysis for this example will be made. We can then compare the accurate analysis with the approximation obtained by Equation 4.18. Assume that the ten loads are located at 10, 20, 30, . . . , 90, and 100 feet from the source respectively. Then the total voltage drop to the furthest load can be shown to be

$$V_D = 2.841 \text{ volts.} \qquad \text{(Equation 4.19)}$$

(The voltage drop in this example was calculated using a proprietary program "Feeder Design" which was developed by the author's company Nabours' Software. For information about this software, contact the editor.)

Since we assumed that the loads were equally spaced from the source, this total drop occurs in ten equal increments, and we can calculate the voltage at each load by the relationship

$$V_n = 120 - n\frac{(2.841)}{10} \qquad \text{(Equation 4.20)}$$

where $n = 1, 2, \ldots, 10$.

The current through each load can then be calculated, and the total current becomes

$$I = \sum_{n=1}^{10} \left[\frac{120 - n(0.2841)}{144} \right]. \qquad \text{(Equation 4.21)}$$

Evaluation of this summation for the ten load currents gives

$$I = 8.225 \text{ amps.} \qquad \text{(Equation 4.22)}$$

The error between the more accurate value of I, Equation 4.22 and the approximate calculation for I, Equation 4.18 is

$$|\Delta I| = |8.225 - 8.333| = 0.108 \text{ amp.} \qquad \text{(Equation 4.23)}$$

This is a 1.3 percent error, sometimes worth the more complex, time-consuming and accurate calculations.

4.4 Alternating Current Circuits

An AC electrical generator creates an electromotive force (voltage) from the interaction of magnetic fields as the rotor or rotating part of the generator mechanically passes the stator or stationary part of the generator. The power necessary to rotate the generator is converted by this magnetic field interaction from a mechanical source of energy, such as water from a dam or steam from a boiler, to an electrical source of energy.

Because the rotor windings or conductors of a generator pass cyclically in uniform rotational motion past the stator, the voltage produced by this motion can be described mathematically and confirmed by experiment to be a sinusoidal function of time as expressed by Equation 4.24

$$v(t) = V_m \sin \omega t \qquad \text{(Equation 4.24)}$$

where ω is the equivalent angular rotation rate of the generator in radians per second, t is time in seconds, and V_m is the maximum voltage in volts. In the United States ω is 377 radians per second, which engineers refer to as 60 hertz (60 Hz), or 60 CPS AC in older terminology. A plot of $v(t)$ for V_m = 169.7 volts, Equation 4.24 is shown in Figure 4.5.

The time required for one complete cycle of this voltage waveform is designated as T, where T is 1/60th of a second (0.0167 sec). There are sixty complete cycles per second from zero through positive values back through zero then through negative values and returning to zero. This voltage variation, because it has both a positive and negative characteristic, causes the current which flows in an electrical circuit to also vary sinusoidally such that

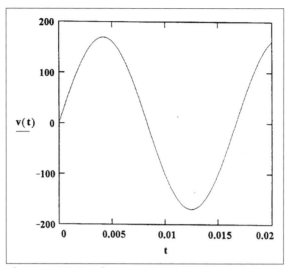

Figure 4.5 *AC voltage versus time; t = 0 + Δ through 0.02; v(t) = 169.7 sin(377t)*

$$i(t) = I_m \sin \omega t .$$
(Equation 4.25)

Ohm's law, Equation 4.1, governs the heating effect of an AC current flowing through resistance; however, the voltage value that should be used in this equation is not immediately obvious. By using the calculus, we can show that the appropriate voltage to use for calculating the effective heating of an AC voltage is

$$V = \sqrt{\frac{1}{T} \int_0^T v(t)^2\, dt} .$$
(Equation 4.26)

After substituting Equation 4.24 for $v(t)$, Equation 4.26 evaluates as

$$V = \frac{V_m}{\sqrt{2}} \cong (0.707)V_m .$$
(Equation 4.27)

This is called the effective voltage or RMS AC voltage. "RMS" stands for "root-mean-squared," which is what the calculus expression Equation 4.26 represents.

Similarly, we find that the effective AC current is given by

$$I = \frac{I_m}{\sqrt{2}} \cong (0.707)I_m. \qquad \text{(Equation 4.28)}$$

Effective values V and I are then used in the Ohm's law equations for the mathematics of AC circuit analysis. As a matter of fact, we have already used the RMS values of voltage and current in our previous examples of circuit analysis.

It is important to recognize that when we have a typical 120-volt AC electrical supply, the peak voltage for this source is given from Equation 4.27 by

$$V_m = \sqrt{2}V \qquad \text{(Equation 4.29)}$$

or

$$V_m = (1.414)(120) = 169.7 \text{ volts.} \qquad \text{(Equation 4.30)}$$

Generalized AC circuit analysis is more complex than the purely resistive circuit analysis, which has been discussed previously. In generalized circuits, it is necessary to consider two additional parameters when dealing with AC electricity.

The first element is termed inductance. Inductance is an electrical parameter which is applied like resistance, but which accounts for the storage of electrical energy in magnetic fields which are created whenever current is changing within a material. The inductive circuit element is represented by a resistive-like term called "inductive reactance" and is expressed mathematically by the following steady-state equation:

$$V_L = (I)(X_L). \qquad \text{(Equation 4.31)}$$

Electrical engineers use the term steady state to refer to the circuit conditions that eventually obtain following the initial excitation of a circuit, for example, by closing a switch. In steady state, AC currents and voltages behave sinusoidally as in Equations 4.24 and 4.25.

In Equation 4.31, V_L is the voltage across the inductive element (inductor), I is the current through the inductor, and X_L is the inductive reactance. X_L is given by

$$X_L = j\omega L \qquad \text{(Equation 4.32)}$$

where ω is again the sinusoidal radian angular frequency, L is the value of the inductance expressed in henries (H), and j is the imaginary unit $\sqrt{-1}$.

The second element is termed capacitance. Capacitance is an electrical parameter that is also used like resistance. However, it accounts for the storage of electrical energy in electric fields; these electrical fields are created whenever a net electrical charge is stored temporarily within a material. The capacitive circuit element is represented by a resistance-like term called capacitive reactance, and it is expressed mathematically by the following steady-state equation:

$$V_C = (I)\,(X_C).$$
(Equation 4.33)

In Equation 4.33, V_C is the voltage across the capacitive element (capacitor), I is the current through the capacitor, and X_C is the capacitive reactance. X_C is given by

$$X_C = \frac{1}{j\omega C}$$
(Equation 4.34)

where ω and j are as in the previous Equation 4.32 and C is the value of the capacitance expressed in farads (F).

A simple series circuit having all three energy elements is shown in Figure 4.6.

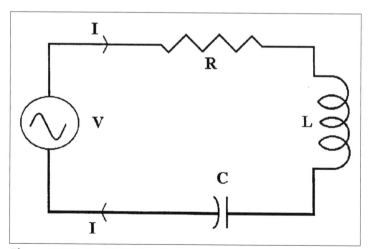

Figure 4.6 Series RLC circuit

The analysis of this circuit requires the use of complex numbers and phasors, which are beyond the scope of this text. However, the results of such an analysis are important, and therefore, the following example is given.

Let V be a 120-volt 60-Hz source, let $R = 1.5$ ohms, $L = 1.99$ millihenries, and $C = 17,680$ microfarads. These units have been chosen to be typical of values encountered in power circuits. The use of Ohm's law, similarly to the derivation of Equation 4.7, gives

$$V = I(R) + I(X_L) + I(X_C).$$
(Equation 4.35)

Finding X_L by Equation 4.32 and X_C by Equation 4.34 and substituting in Equation 4.35 we have

$$120 = I(1.5 + 0.75j - 0.15j) = I(1.5 + 0.6j).$$
(Equation 4.36)

Solving for I we have

$$I = \frac{120}{1.5 + 0.6j}.$$
(Equation 4.37)

Using complex number theory the RMS current I may be expressed as

$$I = 74.28 \angle -21.8°.$$
(Equation 4.38)

Equation (4.38) can be converted by using phasor theory to a sinusoidal equation as

$$i(t) = (105.05) \sin(\omega t - 0.38).$$
(Equation 4.39)

The -21.8 degrees and its equivalent of -0.38 radians (rad) represent the fact that for this circuit, the current lags the voltage by this angular value, or by the time duration of $(0.38/377)$ which is approximately one millisecond. A plot of $v(t)$ and $i(t)$ for this circuit is shown in Figure 4.7.

An important effect of the reactive circuit elements, inductance, and capacitance on AC circuit behavior lies in the resulting time displacement of current with respect to voltage. The use of Equation 4.6 is not valid for such circuits. In fact, the correct version of Equation 4.6 for AC power circuits is

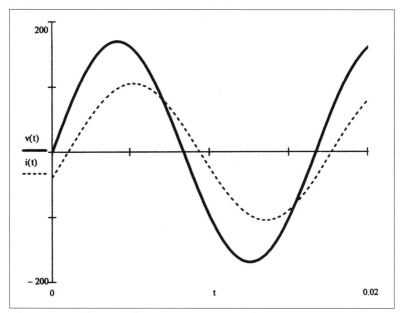

Figure 4.7 *Voltage and current versus time for RLC series circuit; t = 0 + Δ through 0.02; v(t) = 169.7 sin(377t); i(t) = 105.05 sin(377t − 0.38)*

$$P \text{ (watts)} = (V)(I)p_f \qquad \text{(Equation 4.40)}$$

where p_f is the abbreviation for power factor. Power factor is defined as

$$p_f = \cos \theta \qquad \text{(Equation 4.41)}$$

where θ = the angle between $v(t)$ and $i(t)$.

For the example just considered, starting with Equation 4.35, the power factor is

$$p_f = \cos(-21.80) = 0.9285. \qquad \text{(Equation 4.42)}$$

By Equation 4.40, the power dissipated in the series circuit we have analyzed should be

$$P = (120)(74.28)(0.9285) = 8,276.6 \text{ watts.} \qquad \text{(Equation 4.43)}$$

This assertion can be checked using Ohm's law, which states that the power dissipated in the resistance of this circuit, is given by

$$P = I^2R = (74.28)^2 (1.5) = 8,276.3 \text{ watts.} \quad \text{(Equation 4.44)}$$

Depending upon the algebraic sign of the phase angle θ, the current in an AC circuit may either lag or lead the voltage. Physically, it is impossible for $|\theta|$ to be greater than 90 degrees; therefore, we have

$$0 \leq p_f \leq 1.0. \quad \text{(Equation 4.45)}$$

Equation 4.45 states that the dissipated power in an AC circuit is always less than or equal to the apparent power for the circuit, where apparent power is defined as

$$P_{app} = (V)(I). \quad \text{(Equation 4.46)}$$

Apparent power is measured in volt-amps not watts.

4.5 Common Electrical Power Systems

Residential electrical systems in the United States today are almost always furnished power by the local utility at 120/240V 1Ø 60 Hz AC. [Note: "120/240V 1Ø 60 Hz AC" refers to 120/240-volt, single-phase, 60-hertz alternating current.] The electrical utility supplies this voltage by transforming from a single-phase (1Ø) high-voltage distribution circuit to the lower utilization voltage. The usual transformer arrangement for this process is called the Edison connection as shown in Figure 4.8.

The utility may choose to use a lower or higher primary (PRI) voltage, but the 120/240volt secondary voltage has been standard since 1982.[1]

The Edison connection permits the user to supply loads of 120 volts by connecting the load from either of the hot legs, H_1 or H_2, to neutral (N). By connecting between H_1 and H_2, a 240-volt load may be served. The grounded neutral at the center tap of the transformer's secondary enhances the safety of the system and establishes a stable reference for the secondary and primary electrical voltages.

If someone contacts either hot leg and a grounded conducting material, a 120-volt shock may result. The grounded neutral generally prevents a higher voltage contact and shock. However, if a person makes contact

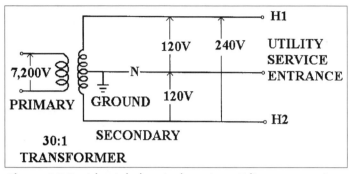

Figure 4.8 *Residential electrical service—Edison connection*

with both hot legs, say with the right and left hands, there will be 240 volts across his or her body. The effect of these contacts will be treated in detail later in this text.

The Edison connection has been referred to as a 115/230V 1Ø system, or even in older terminology as 110/220V 1Ø, but these systems are all the same configuration. The actual voltage supplied by the utility may vary. If the primary voltage were lower than 7,200 volts by say 10 percent (i.e., 6,480 volts), then by the transformer voltage conversion ratio (30:1), the secondary voltage would be lower by 10 percent (i.e., 108/216 volts). ANSI Standards have been established for the allowable voltage variation by U.S. utilities to assure the customer of a relatively stable supply voltage and, therefore, ensure the reliable operation of electrical products and appliances.

The most common commercial U.S. electrical system for the past forty or more years is the 120/208V Y 3Ø supply, called the 120/208-volt Wye system. This system is shown schematically for the three-phase secondary transformer windings in Figure 4.9.

The voltage relationships in a three-phase power system are best explained using phasor theory; however, one may think in terms of stationary vectors as shown in Figure 4.10.

For the two vectors, OA and OB, shown in Figure 4.10, the magnitude of the vector AB can be found using trigonometry:

$$\left| \overline{AB} \right| = \left| \overline{OA} \right| \sqrt{\left(\frac{3}{2} \right)^2 + \left(\frac{\sqrt{3}}{2} \right)^2} = \sqrt{3} \left| \overline{OA} \right|. \qquad \text{(Equation 4.47)}$$

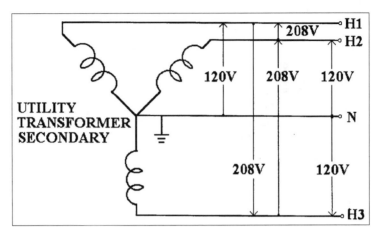

Figure 4.9 *120/208 V Y ("wye") commercial power system*

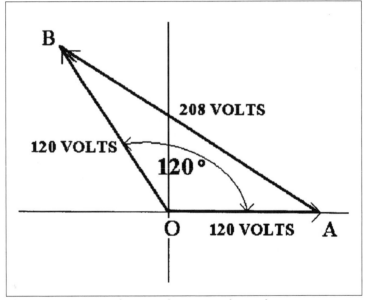

Figure 4.10 *Vectors for two phases in a three-phase wye system*

In the case where the magnitudes of OA and OB are both 120 volts, then the magnitude of $AB = \sqrt{3} \times 120$ volts = 207.8 volts. This is rounded to 208 volts for describing this power system as a 120/208V Y. The reader is encouraged to verify the preceding calculations and to examine the other vector relationships between the three-phase voltages in the wye system.[2]

Industrial power systems generally use power at a higher voltage than do commercial users. The 277/480V Y system is commonly found in U.S. industrial plants. Note that $480 \approx \sqrt{3} \times 277$.

In some cases of very large industrial power systems, even higher utilization voltages are found (e.g., 4,160Y/2,400V and 12,470Y/7,200V systems are used). Although these systems are wye connected, they are conventionally designated in reverse numerical order compared to the lower voltage wye systems. These voltage connections are also frequently utilized by electrical utilities for their overhead and underground distribution systems. The phase-to-phase voltage is again $\sqrt{3}$ times the phase-to-neutral voltage.

There are still other types of three-phase voltage systems in use in the U.S. and around the world. The most common U.S. variation is the delta system. Frequently, commercial and small industrial users are supplied with a 120/240V Δ 3Ø 4W system as shown in Figure 4.11.

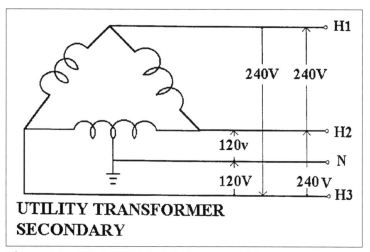

Figure 4.11 *120/240 V Δ 3Ø 4W commercial power system*

In this 4W delta system, the transformer winding with its center tap connected to neutral behaves like an Edison connection; however, because of the connections with the other windings this system can also be used to supply three-phase 240-volt loads. There are many reasons for using three-phase power systems, some of which are given below.

- The energy delivered by a three-phase system can be furnished with one-third less current per conductor than a single-phase system, assuming the same voltage and load characteristics. Therefore, three-phase systems can generally use smaller, less costly wiring than single-phase systems. Even when the difference in number of conductors (three versus two) is considered, a three-phase circuit will have one-sixth of the total line loss that a single phase circuit will have with the same size line conductors, voltage and load.[3]
- The neutral current (fourth wire) in a three-phase wye system with balanced loads is zero. Therefore, under balanced or nearly balanced load conditions, there is zero or little energy loss due to the neutral or return current. Three-phase motor loads require only three conductors for their supply in a wye or delta system.
- Three-phase motors use electrical energy at a constant rate; therefore, the torque production of a three-phase motor is constant, not pulsating, as is the case with single-phase motors. Such motors run smoother with less bearing wear, are quieter, and last longer.
- Large horsepower motors are only produced in three-phase rather than single-phase because of their lower internal copper losses. Therefore, commercial and industrial users with requirements for large HP motors require three-phase power.
- Electrical utilities have established service requirements that specify load limits by class of service. Single-phase 120/240-volt service is available for smaller loads, up to about 150kW. For larger loads, the utilities require three-phase, and specify what voltage will be furnished according to the load size. A large load user is, therefore, required to accept three-phase service from the serving utility.[4]

4.6 Wiring Methods and Materials

Fixed wiring for branch circuit residential applications may consist of separately enclosed conductors in metallic or nonmetallic conduit (pipe), electrical metallic tubing (EMT) or surface metallic or nonmetallic raceway. By far, however, the most common method of fixed wiring for residences is nonmetallic-sheathed cable, also known by the trade name of Romex. Commercial and industrial wiring systems are almost uniformly constructed using individual conductors enclosed in metallic raceways including rigid metal conduit, EMT wire way, cable tray, flexible metal conduit, and armored cable.

Conductors for the fixed wiring used in construction are manufactured in a wide variety of sizes (diameters) and insulation types. Wires are available in single and multiple conductor stranding, with the larger American wire gauge (AWG) sizes having only multiple stranding. Wire above #8 AWG, which is about one-eighth inch in diameter, is stranded so that the cables will be flexible enough to be pulled through conduit and will curve where the conduit bends. Construction wiring varies in size from #18 AWG (0.04 in. dia.) through 28 sizes up to 2,000 kcmil conductor (1.63 in. dia.)[5]. The notation "kcmil" is read thousand circular mils.

Ultimately, it is the rated temperature of a conductor's insulation that determines the maximum ampacity of the wire. The current carrying capacity of a conductor, called ampacity, is a function of the temperature developed by $I^2 \times R$ loss of electrical energy into heat within the wire. Refer to Section 7.3 for further information on conductor heating due to current flow. For most applications, the National Electrical Code (NEC) has specified ampacities[6] for conductors, and these values are generally accepted as national standards. The subject of codes and standards is treated in Chapter 3 of this text.

The operating temperature developed by a current carrying conductor is a function of several factors, including the conductor material, that is, metal, the type and thickness of insulation, the type of installation (e.g., within conduit, in free air or directly buried in earth), the ambient temperature, and the mutual heating effect from other nearby conductors.

General wiring conductors for building construction are manufactured using copper, aluminum, or copper-clad aluminum. They are available as bare wire and with insulation. The types of insulation available include plastics, mineral insulation material, rubbers, silicone asbestos, plastic-asbestos, and varnished fibers. The NEC recognizes insulation temperature ratings for general wiring of 60°C, 75°C, 85°C, 90°C, 125°C, 150°C, 200°C and 250°C. For most construction, fixed wiring insulation ratings of 60°C, 75°C, and 90°C are used.

Modern electrical wiring is usually moisture- and heat-resistant thermoplastic insulated PVC (polyvinyl chloride). This is the most popular choice for contemporary wire insulation because of cost and availability.

The distribution of electrical energy from the utility service to the various loads requires the separation of wiring into "branches" (branch circuits) that emanate from a distribution center. A distribution center contains circuit breakers or fuses to protect the branch circuit conductors from overloads or short circuits. A distribution center may consist of a panelboard, multiple fused switches, or a combination of such arrangements. A schematic for a three-phase four-wire circuit breaker panelboard is shown in Figure 4.12.

In Figure 4.12, H_1, H_2 and H_3 are the three hot legs from a 120/208V 3Ø 4W service. These service voltages are available for use from the panelboard in several variations.

A 120-volt circuit can be created by connecting a branch circuit from any individual single pole breaker to the load and to the neutral as shown by connections a-b. A 208V 1Ø circuit will be formed when connections c-d are made from a two pole breaker to a 208-volt load. Making connections e-f-g from a three-pole breaker to a three-phase load can form a 208V 3Ø circuit. Whether or not a neutral is used, a separate grounding

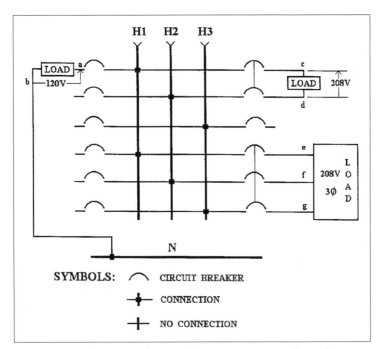

Figure 4.12 *Schematic diagram for a 3Ø 4W panelboard*

conductor is frequently installed along with the supply conductors in order to electrically ground equipment or appliances to the service ground.

4.7 Protection Devices

Overcurrent protection of the wires that emanate from a branch circuit distribution center can be realized with either fuses or circuit breakers. Fuses are thermal acting components whose fusible material is responsive to the heat produced by excess current, melting open and deenergizing the conductor upon overload. Fusible elements are made from bismuth, cadmium, and tin in various proportions to set the overcurrent limit and affect the opening of the circuit under extreme current conditions such as overloads or faults. Fuses are capable of interrupting specified current at a specified voltage rating. If either the voltage or current exceeds the specified ratings, a fuse may catastrophically fail under overcurrent conditions, rupturing or exploding. The maximum interrupting current specification for a fuse is termed the interrupting rating or interrupting capacity (IC). Typical ICs for fuses are 10kA, 100kA and 200kA, where kA = 1,000 amps.

Older Edison-base fuses were available in 15-, 20-, 25-, 30-, 35-, 40- and 50-amp ratings. These fuses no longer meet the NEC requirements but are available for replacement only.

Type-S fuses are designed to make tampering or bridging difficult. They are installed with adapters to fit the Edison base socket. After installation, the adapter cannot be removed without damaging the socket. Edison base fuses will not fit into the adapters and larger fuses cannot be installed in a lower rated adapter. Pennies will not fit into the adapters to by-pass the fuses.

Circuit breakers are automatically operated mechanical switching devices, usually of the thermal-magnetic type. The thermal element provides operation for lower current overloads, up to approximately twenty times the device rating. The magnetic element operates very fast (usually less than twenty milliseconds) for massive faults. Breakers are rated both for their normal current limit and for their ability to operate safely under high fault current. When the fault current exceeds the IC of the breaker, the breaker may not clear the circuit or it may fail catastrophically. Typical modern circuit breakers have interrupting capacities from 10kA to 200kA.

Circuit breakers are operable mechanically as switches and can be re-set after automatic operation unless damaged by excessive fault current. Normal residential breakers are available in 10 to 225 amp ratings with eighteen ratings in between. Ten-kilo amps is the most common interrupt-ing capacity. Commercial and industrial circuit breakers are available in sizes from 100 to 4,000 amps.

Different manufacturers use various means to visually indicate that the breaker has automatically tripped, such as position of the toggle handle, or a red flag in a view window integral with the breaker housing. None of these indicators or their absence can be taken as positive proof that the breaker has automatically tripped.

Both fuses and circuit breakers have operating characteristics that are described by current-versus-time plots. Neither device will open the cir-cuit instantaneously upon being subjected to an excess current. The time required for a fuse or circuit breaker to operate and open the circuit varies inversely with the current. This means that as the current increases in magnitude, the operating time for the protective device decreases. Table 4.2 gives typical operating times for generic fuses and circuit breakers versus current expressed in multiples of the device rating.

Special purpose circuit breakers are available for the protection of personnel rather than wiring. The ground-fault-interrupter (GFI) and the appliance-leakage current-interrupter (ALCI) are designed to protect against electrical shock. The arc-fault circuit-interrupter (AFCI), by de-

Table 4.2
Typical Operating Times for Generic Fuses and Circuit Breakers

Current multiple of rating	Fuse operating time(s)	Circuit breaker operating time(s)
1×		
2×	8	60
3×	2.2	20
5×	0.4	5
10×	< 0.1	1
15×	–	< 0.03

fault, also protects against electrical shock from exposed wire created by an arcing fault in an extension cord.

GFI protection, which for personnel operates at 4 to 6 milliamps (mA), is sensitive to the flow of current between an energized conductor and ground no matter what that path may be including ground wire, metallic conduit, metallic water pipe, or metallic building material. Beginning on January 1, 1991, for hand-held hair dryers, UL 859 has required the use of (1) an integral ground-fault circuit interrupter (GFCI), or (2) an integral immersion detection circuit interrupter (IDCI), or (3) an integral protection device of another type that de-energizes all current carrying parts when the appliance is immersed in water *having an electrically conductive path to ground.* U.L. has termed all such integral ground-fault interrupters for appliances "appliance leakage current interrupters" (ALCI) and requires this protection to activate when the appliance leakage current to ground is in the range of 4 to 6 mA.

The GFI device is not sensitive to phase-to-phase or phase-to-neutral faults (i.e., from one hot leg H_1 to the other H_2 or from one hot leg H_1 to neutral N). When such faults occur on a GFI protected circuit, the GFI device does not reduce the shock and fire hazards. Only the basic level of circuit breaker or fuse protection is effective under phase-to-phase or phase-to-neutral faulting on a GFI protected circuit. For most residential receptacle, lighting, and appliance branch circuits, the probability of phase-to-phase faulting is low. There remains, however, a potential for such faults to occur even on a GFI protected circuit.

Manufacturers of ground fault circuit interrupters recommend that these devices be checked on a regular basis, as often as once a month. The GFI is equipped with a "test" button that connects a resistor between hot leg and ground to produce a ground fault current of not more than 6 mA which should immediately trip the breaker to de-energize the down stream circuit. A "reset" button, which pops out under test, is used with the GFI to restore power to the circuit following the test. Some manufacturers recommend testing the down stream devices or loads to be sure that the power has been interrupted even after the reset button pops out.

A recent development of a device termed the arc-fault circuit-interrupter (AFCI) has prompted a change in the NEC requiring that such devices be used to protect the branch circuits that supply receptacle outlets in dwelling unit bedrooms.[7] An AFCI is a "smart" circuit breaker that uses a microcomputer chip to identify the current waveform signature of a detected arc fault. The AFCI is intended to protect not only the branch circuit wiring to the receptacle, but also to protect the load wiring plugged into the receptacle that frequently includes extension cords that are subject to failure from mechanical stress. When arcing faults occur in two-wire extension cords they may persist intermittently thereby destroying the cord insulation and exposing an energized wire. AFCIs can react to such arcing faults to deenergize the circuit and the cord.

Ground-fault-forced cables (GFFCs) have recently been proposed that convert a line-to-line fault into a line to ground fault, allowing detection and protection of such wiring by ordinary ground fault protective devices (GFCIs). The use of such cable, particularly for extension and appliance cords would serve to reduce the personnel danger created when a fault is self-extinguishing and leaves an exposed conductor energized to create a shock hazard. GFFCs would also reduce the fire hazard created by an arcing fault between the cable conductors.[8]

In the accident case study 10.14 reviewed in Chapter 10 of this book, the use of a GFFC for the hair dryer cord would have in great likelihood saved the life of the woman who was electrocuted in her bathtub.

4.8 Common Appliances and Equipment

Electric heating equipment includes air heaters and water heaters, both fixed and portable. Portable residential air heaters are generally rated 120 volts and less than 16 amps (1,800 watts or less), and often include a fan for air circulation across the heating coils. Commercial air heaters are available in much higher wattage and use larger fans for air circulation.

Air heaters may present a personnel or fire hazard if they are improperly located near combustibles or receive an inadequate air supply. UL listing indicates that suitable safeguards have been employed by the manufacturer against fire hazards resulting from appliance contact with draperies, furniture, carpeting, bedding and similar household combustibles. The operation of such a heater in an explosive or highly combustible atmosphere may be extremely hazardous.

Water heaters, including immersion heaters and high temperature kitchen sink units, are hazardous when operated without water or immersion in liquid. Heater element failure usually results in an open circuit, which is a fail-safe mode; however, a short-to-ground failure may produce a high resistance fault that can persist without activating the circuit protection. Such faults are likely to produce extended arcing or glowing at the fault point.

Ranges and built-in cooking units are similar to air heaters, except that the heating elements are usually encased in a steel sheath and frequently designed to operate by direct contact with a cooking utensil. Such heating elements can produce surface temperatures approaching 1,200°F, and human contact is dangerous. Naturally, contact with combustibles represents an extreme fire hazard. The author has observed an oven heating element, rated 3.410 watts at 240 volts, fail by shorting to the grounded sheath. The element exhibited sustained arcing without tripping the 50-amp circuit breaker. No incipient fire hazard existed, however, because the hot particles from the arc were confined to the interior of the oven. The situation could have been different if the faulted element had been a surface cooking unit.

Motor-operated appliances in residences include refrigerators, dishwashers, garbage disposals, trash compactors, ventilating hoods and fans, washers, dryers, and room air conditioning units. Many of these motor-operated appliances also have heating coils or elements in conjunction.

The branch circuits to such appliances are subject to possible long-term overloads because of frequent starting of the motors, which produces short-term high current inrush, lugging of the motors or stalling, which also increases the line current draw, and increased line current caused by low voltage conditions.

A motor is basically a constant power device for constant mechanical load, so that input power is given by Equation (4.48)

$$P \text{ (watts)} = (V)(I) \, p_f \qquad \text{(Equation 4.48)}$$

and the effect of reduced terminal voltage to a motor will be increased line current such that power remains constant. If the voltage becomes too low, the motor will stall or the line current will become too high and the circuit protection should operate.

Branch circuit wire size for motors is critical in order to avoid excessive heating of the conductors. The NEC, Art. 430 requires that single motor supply conductors be sized for the full load amperes of the motor on the circuit plus 25 percent. Certain exceptions are made for motors that will not operate continuously with load under any condition of use. In addition to this requirement, safe electrical design and construction practice is to select wire sizes that will avoid voltage drop in excess of 3 percent for the branch circuit and 5 percent from service entrance to the motor.[9]

The local utility power supply must also remain close to the nominal service voltage and should be within the ANSI standard supply range of 114 volts to 126 volts for a 120-volt nominal supply under most operating conditions (i.e., –5 percent to +5 percent, a band of 10 percent centered on 120 volts). These standards and practices establish the minimum motor terminal voltage as 108 volts for a 120-volt system.

Most residential light fixtures are either incandescent or fluorescent. Both types may present a fire hazard due to excessive heat generation or arcing. An incandescent lamp (light bulb) operates by creating visible electromagnetic radiation (light) from a super-heated tungsten filament that is encased in an evacuated or inert gas-filled glass bulb. The incandescent lamp is a resistive load similar to a heater. Voltage variations, high or low, to an incandescent lamp cause current variations in approximately direct proportion according to Ohm's law Equation (4.2).

$$I \text{ (amps)} = \frac{V \text{ (volts)}}{R \text{ (ohms)}} \qquad \text{(Equation 4.49)}$$

As voltage is reduced, lamp current, wattage and light output are reduced, and lamp life is increased. Conversely, if voltage is increased, lamp current, wattage and light output increase, and lamp life is reduced. The resistance of an incandescent lamp filament varies with its heat dissipation; therefore, Ohm's law does not strictly hold since R is not a constant but a function of current, I. These relationships are summarized in Table 4.3 in percent of rated value.

Incandescent light fixtures are rated for maximum lamp wattage. Although a standard base lamp socket used in a fixture may be rated 250 W, 250 V, the light fixture manufacturer may caution the user to limit the lamp wattage to a lesser value. This is done to avoid excessive heat transfer from the lamp to the fixture components, including wire and housing. High utility voltages can produce excessive temperatures within a light fixture, even though properly lamped, and can create a fire hazard.

Table 4.3
Incandescent Lamp Life, Output, Current and Power versus Voltage

voltage (%)	Rated lamp life (%)	Rated light output (%)	current (%)	watts (%)
85	850	58	92	78
90	400	70	94	84
95	200	84	97	92
100	100	100	100	100
105	50	119	103	107
110	30	137	105	116
115	16	160	108	124

Fortunately, lamp life decreases more rapidly than lamp wattage and heat output increase, so that sustained high utility voltage usually burns out incandescent lamps before it creates fires. Note that incandescent lamps produce relatively high bulb surface temperatures even when operating at rated voltage and wattage. Fluorescent lamps, on the other hand, are not high temperature light sources. The potential hazard for fire in fluorescent light fixtures resides in the ballast and wiring components of the fixture. Cold cathode (fluorescent) lamps require a ballast which accomplishes two functions: (1) it provides a high voltage, 400- to 1,000-volt transient (kick), to start the lamp by striking an arc, and (2) it limits the lamp current to a safe level that will not cause the gas in the fluorescent tube to burn itself out immediately after the arc is struck.

Older fluorescent ballast circuits usually had a transformer, a capacitor and perhaps an inductor with the associated wiring. These components were encased in a metal can, the ballast housing, which was filled with an asphaltic-sand potting compound. The potting compound served as an insulator for both heat and electricity, as well as a sound deadening material. The heat produced within the ballast, which can cause the case to approach 90°C (194°F), must be transferred to the surrounding environment in order for the wiring and components within the fixture and ballast to operate safely. Since 1978, the NEC has required all except simple reactor ballasts to have thermal protection integral within the ballast. Such fixtures are termed Class P and are required to be so labeled. Before class-P fluorescents were being produced, a large number of fires were traced to malfunctioning and overheated fluorescent ballasts. Since 1978, the incidence of fires attributed to fluorescent fixtures has fallen dramatically. Modern commercial and some residential fluorescent fixtures use solid-state electronic ballasts that operate much more efficiently than core-coil ballasts, generating less heat and reducing the fire hazard.

Radios, television sets, stereo systems, and computers have all become frequently used appliances in our residences. These appliances neither behave electrically like simple resistive loads nor have the characteristics of motors. All such appliances produce operating heat and must be properly ventilated to avoid fire hazards.

Television sets and computers, in addition to heat, also operate with cathode ray tubes that require high-voltage electronic circuits. High voltage, in excess of 600 volts, can stress insulation, causing wiring to fail internally in the appliance and can produce arcing. Usually, the protective devices within such appliances de-energize failing circuits and avoid fires; however, misapplications, dirty conditions, and the proximity to combustibles can lead to fire.

The high technology engineering and relative cost of electronic appliances when compared to hair dryers, clothing irons and toasters, for example, tends to preclude the catastrophic failure of such products. Nevertheless, electronic appliances, even the highest quality, can and have caused fires.

Products such as toasters, toaster-ovens, coffee makers, hair dryers, hair curlers, heating pads, and electric blankets all belong to the same classification of small heating appliances. The previous discussion of heating equipment has implications regarding these appliances. The elevated temperature surfaces of such products must obviously be guarded from personal contact or close proximity to combustibles.

The electrical shock hazard of hand-held equipment is pronounced; and since 1971, the NEC has recognized this electrocution hazard by requiring ground fault interrupting (GFI) circuit breakers and receptacles for certain work place and residential locations where water is likely to be present. Since 1978, all residential bathrooms have been required to have GFI protected receptacles.

Endnotes

1. Institute of Electrical and Electronics Engineers, Inc. (IEEE), *IEEE Red Book*, 6th ed., ANSI/IEEE Std. 141-1986 (NY: Institute of Electrical and Electronics Engineers, 1986).

2. Egon Brenner and Mansour Javid, *Analysis of Electric Circuits* (NY: McGraw-Hill, 1959), ch. 17.

3. Ernst A. Guillemin, *Introductory Circuit Theory* (NY: John Wiley, 1953), 388–392.

4. Tucson Electric Power Co., *Electric Service Requirements*, 2003 ed. (Tucson, AZ: Tucson Electric Power Co., 2003).

5. American National Standards Institute (ANSI), *National Electrical Code: 2002*, ANSI/NFPA 70 (Quincy, MA: National Fire Protection Association, 2002), Art. 310.

6. Ibid., Art. 210.19 (A)(1) (FPN#4), 310.15(B)(FPN) and 215.2 (A)(4) (FPN#3).

7. Ibid., Art. 210.12 (B).

8. Guiseppe Parisi and Robert E. Nabours, "Arc Fault Protection of Branch Circuits, Cords and Connected Equipment" (paper presented at the IEEE Industrial and Commercial Power Systems Technical Conference, May 2003, ICPS-03-15).

9. ANSI, *National Electrical Code: 2002,* Art. 215.2(A)(4)(FPN #2)

Chapter 5

The Effects of Electrical Energy on Humans

5.1 Introduction

Electrical energy exists on earth today due to both natural and man-made phenomenon. The presence of natural electrical energy was undoubtedly first recognized by the manifestation of lightning. The devastating effects of nature's power as evidenced by lightning must have been awesome to the earth's first cognizant life forms and was likely identified as a product of the gods who ruled the earth's environs and dictated man's existence on this planet.

    The first practical relevancy of electrical energy to man was probably lightning-produced fire which prehistoric humans adapted for useful purposes. Throughout the history of man's evolution and increasing recognition of electrical phenomenon, many observations and curious inquiries must have arisen. Imagine the first human's discovery that an inanimate object, human hair, would move untouched toward a bone comb or that two pieces of rock would rotate untouched in mysterious ways when brought close to one another. These discoveries and inquiries are the essence of a mystery that even today continues to challenge mankind's ability to explain the phenomenon of electricity.

The Greeks, who observed that electricity had at least two forms, positive and negative, and that these forms tended to attract or repel one another according to their polarity, first studied electricity scientifically.

Humans also recognized magnetism by this time and understood that certain natural materials not only possessed the properties of expulsion and attraction between themselves, but also exhibited a tendency to align their axes in relation to the earth, so as to always exhibit a geometrically directional preference.

The work of Coulomb in 1785 first quantified the electrostatic force that existed between charged bodies. In the early nineteenth century, Orsted observed that a magnetic field exists in the space that surrounds a wire carrying an electrical current, and André Ampère found that magnetic forces exist between two current carrying wires. In 1831, Faraday announced his discovery of electromagnetic induction,[1] and formulated a mathematical law for the voltage induced in a conductor due to a time varying magnetic field. Faraday's discoveries formed the theoretical basis for electric transformer operation and for modern mathematical analysis of induction currents. It was not, however, until the later part of the nineteenth century that scientists discovered electromagnetic waves and that the propagation of such waves was proposed as a model for the transference of electrical energy through space. (See Section 8.2.)

Electrical energy, both natural and man-made, affects life on the planet earth. Electricity has become all-pervasive in the modern human lifestyle. Principally humankind has found electricity to be an extremely useful and life enriching form of energy; it is readily available, economically feasible at least in developed countries, and highly versatile.

There are negative aspects, however, to the widespread applications of man-made electricity. On the negative side, electrical energy can be extremely dangerous whether in the form of lightning, high-voltage power lines, household wiring and electrical appliances, industrial tools and processes, or electromagnetic radiation. Three known mechanisms by which electrical energy can interact with the human body are:

- direct contact current or close-proximity arcing-current flow from an energized source of electricity through the body,
- directly induced current flow within the body caused by close proximity to time varying electrical energy sources, and
- electromagnetic waves—both ionizing and non-ionizing—that produce biological effects in humans.

Each of these mechanisms will be treated in detail in the following sections of this chapter.

5.2 Direct Contact Effects of Electricity on Humans

During the bodily contact with an electrical energy source of the type found throughout the U.S. in homes, offices, and commercial and industrial buildings, it is the passage of 60-hertz electrical current through tissue and organs which can produce adverse physiological effects upon the body.

The flow of current can be related to the voltage across the body by Ohm's law:

$$I = \frac{V}{R}$$ (Equation 5.1)

where I is expressed in amperes, V in volts, and R in ohms. Resistance of the body (R) is a function of several factors including:

- **skin condition**. Abraded or broken skin offers a lower resistance path between the epidermal skin and the vascular corium and deep tissues. Perspiration, water, saliva and blood can all reduce the surface resistance of skin contact. Calloused skin and the presence of keratin in the skin increase resistance.
- **contact resistance**. Firm contact pressure between the skin and an energized conductor can reduce resistance. Conversely, light pressure increases contact resistance.
- **area of contact**. The resistance of skin contact is lowered as the contact area is increased and the heating effect of current flow varies in-

versely with the area of contact between energized conductor and the skin.

Typical values of resistance used to estimate electrical current flow through the human body vary from 500 ohms to 2,000 ohms or more when the various factors stated above are taken into consideration[2]; see Table 5.3 and Section 11.1.C. Journeymen electricians have frequently been known to lick their fingers before touching a 120-volt conductor to test it for an energized condition. Evidently their hands are heavily calloused and their "startle reaction" is much less sensitive than that of the average person.

To place this in numerical perspective, the current flows shown in Table 5.1 are calculated for a 120-volt RMS contact between both hands, one to an energized conductor and the other to a grounded surface.

Table 5.1
RMS Current Flow versus Resistance for 120-V RMS

R (ohms)	I (milliamps)
500	240
1,000	120
1,500	80
2,000	60

The first recorded death from commercial electricity was in 1879, when a stage carpenter in Lyon, France, was killed by electrocution from a 250-volt Siemens dynamo.[3] The first electrical execution took place at the state prison in Auburn, New York, on August 6, 1890. A convicted murderer named William Kemmler, who had taken an axe to his lover Matilda "Tillie" Ziegler, was sentenced to die in one of the first three electric chairs constructed for that purpose.

Inexperience at the time led to the condemned man receiving a fifteen-second shock at an unrecorded current magnitude. The medical doctors, prison officials and witnesses to this execution were greatly disturbed that Mr. Kemmler did not immediately die after this attempted electrocution. A second shock was administered for a "considerably longer time," and the prisoner finally died. An account of the witnesses' reactions to these proceedings reported that

The witnesses may have nearly wanted to die too, after this cruel surprise. The electrocution, complete with heaving chest, gurgles, foaming mouth, bloody sweat, burning hair and skin, and smell of feces, made a stunning impact on them. Many who had pulled political strings to secure a witness seat regretted doing so.[4]

Despite the public condemnations of the process that quickly followed this first execution by electrical current, even the severest critics agreed that it appeared painless, the discharge apparently rendering the victim unconscious well before he could feel pain.

The effect of current upon the human body has since then been studied scientifically by Dalziel[5]. The factors influencing ventricular fibrillation, which is the most common form of death arising from electrical contact, are body weight, current magnitude, and shock duration. Dalziel found empirically that the following equation, known as "the Dalziel equation," can predict the ventricular fibrillation (v-f) current for man:

$$I = \frac{k}{\sqrt{t}} \qquad \text{(Equation 5.2)}$$

where I is expressed in milliamps, t in seconds and k is an empirical constant varying according to body weight from about 116 to 185. The lower values of k apply to children, and a 155-pound man would have a k value of approximately 165. The valid range of time for Equation. 5.2 is from 8.3 milliseconds to about 5 seconds. This calculated current would produce v-f in about one out of 200 individuals. Tests have also indicated that this threshold v-f current equation holds for t as long as 20 or 30 seconds[6]. The threshold v-f current predicted by Equation 5.2 is valid for intact individuals who make ordinary hand-to-hand or trans-thoracic touching contact with energized conductors. An individual in a hospital with a catheter or instrument probe penetrating the skin will have a much lower v-f current.

Dalziel[7,8] has concluded from studying accidents involving impulse shocks (i.e., current pulses of brief duration), that an electrical impulse having an upper limit of 50 joules represents the safe level for such shocks to humans. The duration of the impulse in these studies was approximately 0.2 second with an off period of approximately 0.8 second.

The joule (J) is a metric measure of energy equal to one newton-meter that is also equal to one watt-second. When the voltage and current are in-phase, one watt equals one volt-ampere. For the durations of impulse shock described above, the energy delivered by a 60-Hz AC source is essentially given by volts times amps times seconds. Therefore, for a 120-volt RMS source and a 500-ohm load, the shock duration of 0.2 second represents 5.8 joules of energy and should be well below the limit of safe exposure. As a practical matter, UL has established standards for electric fence controllers that generally follow these guidelines. The maximum shock energy allowed for an electric fence is 3.2 joules. (See Section 6.5 for an additional discussion of electric fences.)

If the effects of increasing current through the body are examined, we find that the ranges shown in Table 5.2 prevail.

The let-go limit represents the maximum current flowing through the hands or hand of an individual for which the involuntary contraction of the muscles of the hand can still be overcome by the voluntary commands from the brain. For current above the let-go value, the brain can no longer control the contraction of the hand, and an individual cannot turn loose from a conductor or wire. For continuous contact with 60-Hz AC electricity, it has also been determined that ventricular fibrillation occurs at a threshold of approximately 10 to 50 joules with current in the range from 20 to 250 mA (milliamperes). (See Table 15.3 for additional discussion).

Physical evidence of electrical contact can include skin trauma such as burns. See Chapter 16. The estimated lowest current that can produce noticeable first or second-degree burns in a small area of the skin is 100 A for one second.[9] Burns caused by the direct heating effect of electrical current (I^2R) frequently conform in size and shape to the metallic conductor of contact. In a study of 220 electrocutions of which 50 percent were caused by contact at less than 1,000 volts, 45 percent of these had no perceptible electrical burns. In contrast, of the 50 percent of the contacts at higher than 1,000 volts, only 4 percent had no perceptible burns.[10]

The current through the human body depends upon the resistance of the path taken by the current flow through the body. It is also the case that at about 600 volts, the resistance of the skin ceases to be a factor. The epidermal layer of tissue is punctured at these higher voltages just as capacitor insulation is punctured by excessive voltage stress across the insulation between plates.

Table 5.2
Effects of Various Amounts of Current in Man

Ranges are approximate and depend on a number of factors. The amount of current needed depends on the subject factors (including health, medications, sex and weight), duration of current flow and current path (e.g., head to foot).

Effect	Current Path	Minimum Current (milliamperes, 60 Hz rms AC)
ventricular fibrillation	through an electrode wire or fluid-filled catheter to the inside surface of a cardiac ventricle	0.06 to 0.43
tingling sensation, minimal perception	through intact skin	0.5 to 2
pain threshold	through intact skin	1 to 4
inability to let go; tetanic contractions of forearm muscles tighten grasp, decreasing contact resistance	from hand, through forearm muscles, into the trunk (other pathways will stimulate other muscular contractions)	6 to 22
respiratory arrest; can be fatal if prolonged	through the chest	18 to 30
ventricular fibrillation	through the chest	70[1] to 4,000
ventricular standstill (asystole); in effect, a defibrillation; when the current stops, sinus rhythm may resume, sometimes with persistent respiratory arrest	through the chest	>2,000 (>2 amperes)

1. A minimum value for a 50-kg man with current applied for three seconds; for the most sensitive 0.5 percent of the population (Dalziel and Lee, 1968, p. 476).

Reproduced with permission from Fish and Geddes, *Medical and Bioengineering Aspects of Electrical Injuries* (Tucson, AZ: Lawyers & Judges Publishing Co., Inc, 2003).

At voltages greater than 600 volts, only the internal body resistance impedes the flow of current. At around 2,400 volts, burning becomes a major effect whereas at lower voltages respiratory arrest (asphyxiation) and ventricular fibrillation usually manifest.

Some typical human resistance values for various skin-contact conditions are shown in Table 5.3.[11]

Electricity produced by technological means has been called in the literature "technical electricity," which includes all man-made forms of

Table 5.3		
Some Typical Human Resistance Values		
Condition	Resistance (in)	
	Dry	Wet
finger touch	40,000–1,000,000	4,000–15,000
hand holding wire	5,000–50,000	3,000–6,000
finger-thumb grasp	10,000–30,000	2,000–5,000
hand holding pliers	5,000–10,000	1,000–3,000
palm touch	3,000-8,000	1,000–2,000
hand around 1.5-inch pipe (or drill handle)	1,000–3,000	500–1,500
two hands around 1.5-inch pipe	500–1,500	250–750
hand immersed		200–500
foot immersed		100–300
human body internal,excluding skin	200–1,000	

electricity, principally the electricity produced by utilities, but also medical forms such as electroshock therapy, See Section 5.3.

The specific physiology of individuals accounts in part for the variable effects of current, however the path that current flow takes through the body is a major determinant in the degree of injury sustained.

Certain human organs, for example the tongue and eyes, are more sensitive to threshold detection of current levels of 1 mA or less, than are more muscular or heavily epidermal parts such as the hands and feet. Respiratory muscle contractions are observed when currents of 20 to 40 mA at 60 Hz pass through the body from extremity contacts. If continued, such currents can produce insufficient breathing with oxygen starvation (hypoxia or anoxia) of the heart muscle or brain leading to ventricular fibrillation. Such currents producing respiratory insufficiency can also lead to loss of consciousness and (if prolonged) brain injury.

When human electrical shock is produced by subcutaneous contact, as possible in operating rooms or intensive care facilities where catheters or implant transducers are used, as little current as 20 microamperes passing through the heart (20 μA = 20/1,000,000 of an ampere) can induce cardiac arrhythmia leading to ventricular fibrillation. Standards have been formulated to require 20 μA limitation for input circuit isolation on 120 volt systems in electromedical apparatus.[12]

Extremity contacts from hand-to-hand or hand-to-foot produce much more current flow through the thoracic region of the body around the heart muscle and lungs than foot-to-foot contacts. It has been estimated that ten to twenty-five times more current can be tolerated during electrical shock with foot-to-foot contacts before damaging current levels are produced in the thoracic region.[13]

At current levels in the range of over two amperes, the heart may stop (asytole), preventing ventricular fibrillation, and then resume beating spontaneously when the current stops. Death may not ensue at these high current levels if the exposure duration is brief enough. Legal electrocution was carried out in the state of Illinois where 7.5 amps, 60 Hz, 2,300 volts was applied for seven seconds, followed by the same current and frequency but at 550 volts for 52 seconds. This cycle was repeated a second time to complete the execution.[14]

Visible skin burn evidence of electrical shock (usually central pallor with charring surrounded by redness) is caused by the I^2R heating of body tissue and varies according to the following factors (See also Section 16.1).

- **voltage**. High voltage direct contact or arcing contact (above 600 volts) is likely to break the outer skin layer, reducing resistance and increasing current flow. Lower voltages require virtually direct contact since the arcing distance through air at low voltage is very small, on the order of less than 1 mil (0.001 inch) at 120 volts. Lower voltage contacts will result in less current flow and generally much less skin burn.

- **contact resistance**. Low contact pressure with a minute air gap between skin and conductor allows some arcing which increases contact resistance and burn trauma. Tightly held contact with an energized metallic conductor decreases contact resistance and usually reduces I^2R heating of the skin contact area. If skin epidermis is cracked or broken substantially, the increasing current that may ensue can be such that I^2R increases faster than R decreases and a net increase in I^2R heating effect will occur. Area of contact inversely affects contact resistance, large area contacts having less resistance than small.

- **skin conditions**. As already stated, penetration of the epidermal layer by voltage or prior skin condition reduces contact resistance. Perspiration or saline body fluids on the skin surface markedly reduces electrical resistance, perhaps by a factor of fifteen or twenty, compared to dry skin resistance. Dirt or foreign material on the skin can produce an effect in either way, depending upon the electrical properties of the foreign material. Grease or oil for example lowers skin resistance.

- **contact duration**. Since the total heat energy dissipated by the skin is I^2R multiplied by the time of current flow, long duration contact generally increases burn trauma. With increased heat dissipation, skin charring may increase contact resistance sufficiently to decrease current more rapidly than R increases, in which case the net I^2R heating decreases. Thermodynamic considerations such as heat transfer to the surrounding environment, or to the blood flow of the body, can become critical factors in the resultant skin burn conditions.

- **bodily current path**. The current passes through the body as if it were a multi-resistance three-dimensional network with current division inversely proportional to path resistance. Highly saline body fluids offer the lowest electrical resistance while bone and cartilage present the greatest. The vascular and nerve systems therefore conduct most of the shock current through the body along with muscle tissue. Path resistance is also increased by overall length; extremity contacts tend to distribute most of the current along the shortest, highest conductive paths between contacts.

- **metabolic acidosis**. An increased amount of acid produced by the cell metabolism process can occur due to heavy physical exertion before or during shock and increases the severity of shock.[15]

The estimated minimum current necessary to produce first-degree skin burns is 100 mA for from 1 second to 9 seconds for a skin area of 1 sq cm.[16,17] Mazer gives the lower estimate and the upper estimate is given by Wright and Davis. In a model contact having 1 square cm contact points for a depth of 1 cm, Wright and Davis conclude that it requires exposure of the skin to 50°C for 20 seconds to produce first-degree burns. Since the fibrillation time at 100 mA is given by the Dalziel equation (5.2) as between 1 and 3.4 seconds, it is likely that most shock victims have already been in ventricular fibrillation before the skin heating has reached temperatures sufficient to cause burns. Wright and Davis therefore conclude that low-voltage "electrical burns are postmortem, in the sense of not requiring blood circulation for their expression."

In high-voltage shock contacts, the current produced is so large, on the order of several amperes, that even for an exposure of 0.1 second sufficient heat energy will be transferred to the contact to raise the skin temperature far beyond the 50°C required for first-degree burns. High-voltage shock therefore almost always produces electrical burns while low voltage shocks do not. If the victim of the low-voltage contact remains in contact with the energized conductor and ground for an extended period of time perhaps due to loss of consciousness and slumping against the contact, then electrical burns can occur.

Deep tissue trauma is more likely to be associated with electrical burns than thermal, but thermal contact produces greater skin damage. In high-voltage contacts arcing is frequently involved and clothing may become ignited, producing thermal burns as well as electrical trauma. In arcing explosions, which frequently occur in electrical power equipment at less than 1,000 volts, the hot expanding gases and superheated metal particles surrounding the arc can produce thermal burns and leave hot metal fragment imprints on the skin. Flash burns and eye trauma frequently result from electrical arcing accidents. Mazer explores further the subject of electrical burn marks on human skin, including the detection of conductor metals, iron, copper, aluminum and zinc in tissue.[18] See Section 16.1.F on skin metallization.

Neurological effects of electrical shock are frequently delayed, with the onset requiring from a few days to twenty-four months. In such cases, damage to the endothelial cells of blood vessels by the electrical current may produce altered blood flow, leading to delayed fibrosis of the perineural and neural tissue of the nervous system.[19]

Electrical shock can cause immediate effects such as loss of consciousness with possible retrograde amnesia. Shock victims have reported altered sensory perception such as loss of hearing or tinnitus (ringing in the ear) and visual aberrations experienced during the accident.[20] A sense of suspension or slowing down of time is frequently reported. The current path does not usually involve the head as a direct contact point in these cases. Hand-to-hand or hand-to-foot contacts most frequently produce these symptoms.

When low-voltage shock does produce prolonged blackout, cerebral sequelae are more likely.[21] Panse suggests that even when the head lies outside the most direct path of current flow, loss of consciousness is prima facie evidence of brain involvement. He further postulates that anoxic effects on respiration and cardiac involvement may be responsible.

Immediate post-accident clinical symptoms such as cerebral edema, headaches, and swelling of the tongue are indications of cerebral involvement in the shocking process. Cerebral convulsion has been observed as long as four weeks after peripheral electrical contact at 500 volts AC.[22]

Even when neurological anomalies are not present a day after the trauma; EEGs can indicate definite deviations from normal. The EEG should be regarded as a useful diagnostic aid in electrical injury cases, particularly when pathological clinical signs in the central nervous system are absent. Panse and others[23] have voiced the opinion that EEGs should be recorded above all immediately after electric trauma. However, modern emergency procedures according to Dr. Fish do not follow this recommendation.

Electric cataracts frequently result when the head is involved as a contact point, particularly at high voltage. Thermoelectric damage due to radiation generally is responsible for electric cataract formation.[24]

Table 5.4 is based on a similar construction presented by Panse.[25]

5.3 Electroconvulsive Therapy (EST or ECT)
by Raymond M. Fish

Electroshock therapy (EST or ECT) as originally devised consists of the application of electric current through the head to elicit loss of consciousness and seizures. Several minutes after the seizure, the patient awakens and then may sleep for several hours.

A. Types of electric current used to induce seizures
Stimuli have varied over the years, using different wave forms (sine, square, pulse), voltages, currents, polarities (positive, negative, both), duration of cycles or pulses, intervals between pulses or cycles, and the total stimulus duration. A "usual commercial" electroconvulsive therapy instrument has been described as an AC sine wave of 200 peak volts, 600

Table 5.4
Typical Physical Effects Produced by Utility Electricity
for Low Voltage (< 1,000 V) and High Voltage (> 1,000V)

Less than 30 V

Low-voltage lighting, telephone and other communication circuits. Power-limited. Protection from harmful electric shock by normal contact renders these systems of minimal physical danger to the body.

Low-voltage systems can be dangerous if they are capable of furnishing lethal current (e.g., 30 volts across 1,000 ohms produces 30 mA). Communication systems can produce noticeable shock, but are generally power limited such that the probability of lethal shock is minimal.

Lightning induced voltages on low-voltage communication circuits can be lethal. Power system circuits can make inadvertent electrical contact with communication conductors, raising the voltage to lethal levels.

30 to 1,000 V

DC current is somewhat less dangerous than AC current. The average DC let-go current is 74 mA.

Instant death

Current path generally from contact point to contact point.

Current above about 10 mA can prevent let-go. Current above about 20 mA can cause ventricular fibrillation if prolonged respiratory arrest and systemic hypoxia occurs, with the exposure time decreasing as the current increases.

Above 70 mA, ventricular fibrillation can result from electrical stimulation of the heart if current flows for a long enough time.

On survival

Possible organic and or functional cardiac damage. No, or usually brief, loss of consciousness. Possible cerebral involvement. Altered sensory perception during the shock. Headaches, cerebral edema, swelling of the tongue, metallic taste.

Lasting effects

Rare, but typical. Spinal atrophic sequelae

Hand-to hand contact via the middle and lower cervical cord, often mild and followed by gradual recovery. In very rare cases, amyotrophic lateral sclerosis with its slowly progressive evolvement.

Table 5.4 (continued)

More than 1,000 V
Current usually greater than 250 mA. Heart stops and may resume beating if exposure time is brief. More than a few seconds usually causes death.

Instant death
Frequently due to burns of severest degree, including charring and calcination. Head contact can boil the brain. Death not infrequently caused by abscess formation under the skull and frequently by complications due to fourth-degree burns at the extremities and kidney damage by the release of toxic myoglobin.

Also frequently caused by untreated ventricular fibrillation that starts promptly or by respiratory arrest continuing after a brief period of asytole despite resumption of a normal heart rhythm.

On survival
With head contact the bony skullcap provides a relative barrier to current and heat to the brain. Often marked and severe encephalopathic involvement. Focalized damage is not infrequent.

With peripheral contact, electrothermic damage in the region of the spinal cord and irreparable damage to nerves of the extremities.

Electrothermic burns to the forehead and face frequently cause cataracts.

---

mA peak current, and a stimulus duration of 0.75 second (Weaver et al. 1977). A voltage of 130 volts AC applied for 0.3 second has also been used (Kelly 1954).

The induction of seizures by very brief current pulses was studied by Cronholm and Ottosson (1963). Bifronto-temporal electrodes were used to induce seizures for EST. A stimulus of 0.1 millisecond long pulses at a rate of 15 to 50 pulses per second was used. The peak current was 0.7 or 0.8 amp. Seizures were induced when the stimulus length in seconds was twice the age in decades (such as, four seconds for a twenty-year-old). Seizure duration was 35 to 207 seconds.

Valentine, Keddie and Dunne (1968) describe EST machines that put out 200 to 300 volts AC for several seconds and another machine that put out 260 volts for one second. Unidirectional (one voltage polarity, or pulsed DC) stimuli were also studied, as were bidirectional (positive and negative pulsed) stimuli. After the shock was applied, spontaneous respirations resumed in 41 to 98 seconds, and consciousness returned in 97 to

480 seconds. The time periods varied depending on the various electrode positions. Spontaneous respirations came first; the recovery of consciousness tended to take at least twice as long.

B. Complications
1. Orthopedic complications

Fractures, dislocations, and fat emboli were formerly occasional complications of electroshock therapy. These complications are much less common with the use of anesthesia and paralysis. The most common fractures that occur with electroconvulsive therapy are vertebral, followed by scapular, humeral and femoral neck, and pelvic bone fractures. Dislocations have been reported of the ankle, shoulder, elbow, and mandible (Somogyi and Tedeschi 1977).

A report of fractures and dislocations complicating electroconvulsive therapy between 1942 and 1952 in one hospital described fifty-three fractures and dislocations that occurred in 2,200 patients undergoing 37,000 convulsions (Kelly 1954). There was one dislocated jaw. There were fractures of the spine (twenty-one), neck of femur (fifteen), upper humerus (fifteen), and coracoid process (one). Four of the persons with spinal fractures had more than one vertebra fractured. Fractures occurred anywhere from the fourth thoracic vertebra to the fifth lumbar vertebra. There was no spinal cord damage. There were no deaths due to spinal fracture.

The 1954 paper by Kelly describes the method used to produce convulsions at that time: The patient lies on a bed on a firm mattress. A small pillow is placed under the lower thoracic spine. One nurse controls the shoulders, one nurse the thighs, and the third places a gag in the mouth and controls the jaw. Electrodes are placed on the temple, which gives 130 volts for 0.3 second.

2. Spinal fractures in seizures not associated with ECT or electric shock

Spinal fractures can occur with grand mal seizures in general, not just those caused by electric shock. For example, Youssef et al. (1995) describe a seizure-induced lumbar burst in thirty-five-year-old man who had a seizure while lying on a couch. He had lumbar burst fractures of L1 and L2. McCullen and Brown (1994) report a thoracic burst fracture and bilateral proximal humerus fractures secondary to a seizure. Computed tomography of the spine showed T7 to have a burst component with 15 percent spinal canal compromise. There were wedging deformities of T6 and T8.

Although they do occur, spinal fractures in patients with epileptic seizures are rare. A study of 1,656 emergency department patients, with seizures uncomplicated by other traum, revealed no spinal injuries. There were three nonspinal fractures associated with the seizures. The authors of the study question the routine use of spinal immobilization in all seizure patients (McArthur and Rooke 1995).

Kelly (1954) cites a number of old studies that looked at the presence of healed spinal fractures in patients with chronic epilepsy. The incidence was close to 10 percent, varying significantly from study to study. It is likely that many patients of that era had poorly controlled epilepsy. Not all fractures were necessarily due to the seizures themselves; fractures may have occurred in some patients because of secondary trauma (such as falling from a raised object or from a height). The person having the seizure would not necessarily remember such occurrences.

3. Cardiac deaths

It was reported in 1970 that several hundred deaths had occurred following electroshock therapy (McKenna et al. 1970). Most of these had occurred in elderly patients who had coronary artery disease. Cardiac dysrhythmias following electroconvulsive therapy are thought to be due to vagal or sympathetic origin. Unless controlled ventilation is provided during the treatment, there will be development of some degree of hypoxia (low arterial oxygen), hypercapnia (high arterial carbon dioxide), and respiratory acidosis (low pH due to insufficient respirations).

Pretreatment with atropine can prevent the bradycardia (slow heart rate) and cardiac standstill associated with vagal stimulation. The most common abnormalities seen with electroconvulsive therapy are premature ventricular contractions (PVC), frequently with bigeminy or trigeminy (a premature ventricular beat on the EKG every other or every third beat). Monitoring has detected these premature ventricular contractions in as many as 43 percent of normal patients, and in 78 percent of patients with organic heart disease. The peak incidence of dysrhythmias is after the seizure and prior to the onset of adequate spontaneous breathing. The premature ventricular contractions are usually self-limited, but it is thought that the R-on-T phenomenon may occur in some patients, producing ventricular fibrillation (McKenna et al. 1970). With the R-on-T phenomenon, the PVC comes during a portion of the T-wave when initiation of ventricular fibrillation is more likely.

4. Electroconvulsive therapy in pregnancy

When it was done, the incidence of fetal damage from insulin-induced coma was 35.5 percent. In contrast, several reports reviewed by Repke and Berger (1984) indicate that electroconvulsive therapy is safe in pregnant women. It is necessary, however, to avoid hypoxia and hypotension. In a case reported in this paper, there was a period of hypotension following a patient's first electroconvulsive therapy treatment. This was avoided by better hydration before her following treatments. Real-time ultrasonography was done during some of the treatments, and no problems were detected.

5. Cerebral hypoxia and other brain injury during electroconvulsive therapy

During convulsions, the brain's need for oxygen increases. Simultaneously, respiration decreases greatly or stops, and there is intense muscle activity in the body. The expected hypoxia can be prevented by muscle paralysis and artificial ventilation (Posner et al. 1969).

Brain injury during seizures can be due to prolonged hypoglycemia, hypoxia, hypotension, and secondary trauma (such as falls). These factors are generally avoided during modern electroconvulsive therapy. Therefore, recent studies have not found evidence of injury to brain cells following electroconvulsive therapy (Devanand 1995).

A 1994 article reviewed 159 studies that searched for alteration of brain structure following ECT. It was concluded that ECT did not alter brain structure (Devanand, 1994). The articles included CT, MRI, and autopsy-based reviews of patients.

6. Reports of safety of ECT

A 1985 Consensus Conference report sponsored by the National Institute of Mental Health made the following points: The commonly quoted overall mortality rate for electroconvulsive therapy in the first few decades of its use was 0.1 percent. At the time of this report, mortality rates varied from 2.9 deaths per 10,000 patients (0.029 percent) to 4.5 deaths per 100,000 patients (0.0045 percent). In the earlier days of electroconvulsive therapy, complications such as fractures were relatively common. At the time of this study, there was a complication rate of about one per 1,300. Complications did include laryngospasm, tooth damage, vertebral compression fractures, status epilepticus (persistent seizures), peripheral nerve palsy, skin burns, and prolonged apnea (NIH 1985).

A 1993 editorial in the *New England Journal of Medicine* made the following points. In the treatment of certain types of severe depression, electroconvulsive therapy is more firmly established than ever. It is most effective in treating depression with delusions and psychomotor retardation with up to 90 percent of psychotically depressed patients responding. Acute mania also responds to treatment, but medications are usually effective in those cases. There is also evidence that some patients with schizophrenia do respond to electroconvulsive therapy, especially if the onset is acute and confusion and mood disturbance are present. Catatonia also benefits from electroconvulsive therapy. Catatonia is a condition with episodes of physical rigidity or stupor that can occur in association with a variety of mental disorders. Electroconvulsive therapy does not give permanent relief, with many cases requiring long-term treatment, including medication and more electroconvulsive therapy treatments. Brain imaging studies suggest that there is no damage to the brain after electroconvulsive therapy. There is transient cognitive impairment after electroconvulsive therapy, especially loss of memory for events shortly before and during treatment. Stimulus intensity and electrode placement are variables that can be changed to bring different response rates and changes in the short-term cognitive side effects (Potter and Rudorfer 1993).

C. Making ECT safer and more effective

The article "Optimizing Electroconvulsive Therapy" describes various measures taken to make electroconvulsive therapy safer and more effective (Fink 1994). The following points are explained.

- Unilateral electrode placement elicited fewer cognitive complaints and was as effective as bilateral placement.
- The risk of fracture is reduced by muscle paralysis, using curare starting in 1941 and succinylcholine since 1951.

- Barbiturates or other medications are used to block awareness of paralysis and inhibition of breathing.
- Ventilation with high concentrations of oxygen before, during, and after the seizure markedly reduces the effects of the seizures on cognition and memory (see also Lew 1986).
- Treatment optimization includes monitoring the patient's heart rate, blood pressure, and pulse (finger) oximetry.
- Anticholinergic drugs (atropine or glycopyrrolate) are given in patients with systemic disorders especially cardiovascular disorders.

5.4 Power Line Contact Accidents

Electrical utility systems are intended to supply electrical energy to consumers with utilization equipment that can vary in size and energy requirements from milliwatts (10^{-3} watts) to megawatts (10^6 watts).

In order to generate, transmit, and distribute electrical energy efficiently, U.S. utilities have established standards promulgated by such organizations as the IEEE, ANSI, NEMA, and UL. An essential part of these standards for electrical systems of power distribution is the system voltage within which the characteristics of the electrical equipment and components are designed to operate.

These "nominal voltage ratings" are expressed in terms of the root-mean-square or rms phase-to-phase voltages, which are close to the actual voltage levels at which the system normally operates. Each voltage class has a maximum and minimum standard that has been established to ensure reliable and satisfactory operation of the equipment and electrical components under normal system operating conditions without derating.

As a general classification, U.S. utility standards refer to low, medium, and high voltage systems. Low voltages are nominal system voltages of less than 1,000 volts, medium voltages are from 1,000 to 100,000 volts, and high voltages are equal to or greater than 100,000 volts. A different classification of low and high voltage systems is utilized by the National Electrical Code (NEC), wherein low voltage refers to less than 50 volts, medium voltages are from 50 to 600 volts, and high voltages are greater than 600 volts.

A typical utility generation, transmission, and distribution system with nominal voltages shown in parenthesis for the various portions of the system is shown in Figure 5.1.

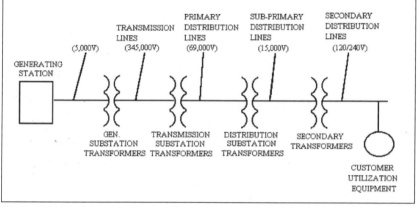

Figure 5.1 *Typical electrical utility generation, transmission and distribution system*

From the previous discussion of electrical contact effects on humans, it is obvious that all of the voltages used in a typical utility electrical energy supply system are hazardous. Furthermore, these electrical systems represent an extremely dangerous form of energy that surrounds our modern lifestyles.

In order to safeguard the public and utility employees from direct contact with the hazardous electrical energy voltages utilized in the system, the National Electrical Safety Code (NESC) originated in 1913 at the National Bureau of Standards. This code has now become ANSI C2, published by the IEEE. (See Chapter 2 for further discussion of electrical codes and standards.)

The NESC contains rules that are designed to provide for "the practical safeguarding of persons during the installation, operation, and maintenance of electrical supply and communication lines and associated equipment."

In particular, the NESC sets forth rules that deal with types of construction and methods of installation, including strength of materials, clearances involving overhead lines, line insulation, safety during installation and maintenance, and rules for systems operation.

Direct human contact with bare conductor energized overhead power lines is usually fatal if the person is "grounded" (i.e., also in direct contact with the earth). If a person could jump high enough to grasp a 345,000-volt transmission line and hold on without touching another energized conductor or a grounded surface, they could hang there without harm just as a bird can sit on the line without being electrocuted. So long as there is no appreciable conduction of current through the body, there is no danger. That is to say if the value of R in Equation 5.1 is infinite, or very large, although $V = 345,000$ volts, I is virtually 0. Unfortunately, when direct or even close contact occurs with a high voltage line, R is usually not large enough to limit I to a safe value, so death or serious injury results.

Typical line clearances above ground where truck traffic[26] is likely to occur are specified in the NESC, Table 232-1, depending upon the supply voltage as shown in Table 5.5.

Many cases of contact with overhead utility lines result from high profile vehicles moving too close to a line. Although the NESC, OSHA, and other standards recommend maintaining a safe clearance from overhead power lines, workers continue to fail to observe these safety recommendations and overhead line contacts are one of the prevalent forms of construction/industrial accidents.

Data from the National Institute for Occupational Safety and Health (NIOSH) indicate that electrocutions during the period 1980–89 averaged fifteen per year by contact between cranes and similar boomed vehicles and energized, overhead power lines. From 1982 through 1994, NIOSH found that twenty-nine out of 226 onsite investigations of work-related electric shock (which resulted in thirty-one fatalities) involved crane contact with overhead power lines. Nearly half of the incidents occurred in the construction industry. Since the investigations conducted involved only sixteen states, these fatalities represent only a portion of the crane-related electrocutions during this period.

Table 5.5
Typical Line Clearances as Specified in the NESC (Ø = Phase)

Supply Voltage	Line Clearance
240 V (ø to ø) or 120 V to ground	16.0 feet
15 kV (ø to ø) or 8.7 kV to ground	18.5 feet
69 kV (ø to ø) or 40 kV to ground	19.1 feet
345 kV (ø to ø) or 199 kV to ground	24.4 feet

A study conducted by OSHA showed that for the period from 1985–89 there were 113 electrocutions involving cranes out of 580 work-related electrocutions occurring in the construction industry.

Contacts with overhead power lines continue to occur for many reasons. Studies by human factors scientists[27] have confirmed that it is difficult to visually judge accurately the clearance between a crane boom or hoist cable and an overhead line. Visual conditions that contribute to this difficulty include sunlight, bright skies, overcast skies, and interference by trees and buildings. It is also difficult for a person to observe accurately more than one visual target at a time.

ANSI Standard B30.5-1994, 5-3.4.5, provides the guidelines for operating cranes near energized overhead power lines shown in Table 5.6.

Note that in the case of a 345-kV overhead transmission line, the NESC permits a minimum clearance above ground of 24.4 feet, which means that any vehicle over 4.4 feet high cannot pass under the line at its point of minimum clearance without encroaching within 20 feet of the conductor. Obviously, a hazard may not exist if a uniformly contoured vehicle with a maximum height of less than 24.4 feet passes under such a transmission line.

As a practical matter, most transmission lines are constructed well in excess of the NESC minimum clearances so that most high-profile vehicles such as semitrailer trucks can safely pass under the lines where they

---

Table 5.6
ANSI Guidelines for Operating Cranes Near
Energized Overhead Power Lines

Power line voltage Phase-to-phase (kV)	Minimum safe clearance (feet)
50 or less	10
Above 50 to 200	15
Above 200 to 350	20
Above 350 to 500	25
Above 500 to 750	35
Above 750 to 1000	45

cross highways. While a semitrailer truck may be 13.5 feet high, if the highway crossing clearance of a 345-kV line is 31 feet, then the truck's trailer will pass under the line with 17.5 feet of clearance.

On the other hand, an urban distribution line at 15 kV can be as little as 18.5 feet above a street crossing subject to truck traffic, and now a semi-truck's 13.5-foot trailer passes under the line with as little as five feet of clearance. So long as the vehicle's profile does not equal or exceed 13.5 feet, there may be adequate clearance from this class of line, but a higher profile trailing load such as a sailboat with an 18-foot fixed mast height cannot safely pass under a 15 kV overhead line that has been constructed at the code minimum of 18.5 feet above grade. Most states have enacted laws governing the dimensions of tractor-trailer trucks and such regulations are generally consistent with the NESC minimum clearances. Other types of high profile vehicles and equipment are not so regulated, and the majority of power line contacts occur between such vehicles or equipment and the lower clearance power lines. (See the typical line clearances from the NESC, Table 232-1, as quoted in this chapter.)

Overhead electric supply lines are required by the National Electrical Safety Code (NESC) to satisfy rules for installation and maintenance that include requirements for spacing, clearances, and strength of construction. The rules are interactive in the sense that the requirements overlap one another in establishing a design condition. An example of this interaction within the rules for safety in the NESC follows.

Example. The construction of a specific line includes a requirement for maintaining a minimum vertical clearance above a roadway as specified in NESC Sec. 23 of 19.75 feet. Additionally, the conductor span is to be 300 feet and the location and weather conditions require a conductor loading under Rule 250 for heavy loading. The electrical load for the conductor and material inventory for the utility has determined that 3/0 ACSR, aluminum-conductor steel-reinforced is to be used as the conductor.

3/0 ACSR cable consists of 6×0.1672-inch diameter strands of aluminum and 1×0.1672 strand of steel having an overall diameter of 0.502 in. and a rated breaking strength of 6,620 pounds. The cable weighs 230.8 pounds per 1,000 feet.

Under rule 251, the NESC requires an assumed conductor loading where the vertical load is determined by the conductor's own weight plus the weight of any supported equipment and the weight of 0.5 inch of radial ice covering. Ice is assumed to weigh 57 pounds per cubic foot. The horizontal load on the conductor is to be taken as 4 pounds per square foot on the projected area of the ice covered conductor and supported equipment.

The total design load on the conductor is the resultant of the vertical and horizontal loads plus a constant of 0.30 pound per foot. The conductor tension is to be computed from this total loading.

The tension on a conductor supported from two fixed points located at the same elevation can be calculated for most practical cases by the parabolic approximation to the theoretically correct catenary form of the conductor curve between supports. The parabolic equation for conductor tension is

$$t = \frac{wS^2}{8d} \, .$$

The parabolic equation for tension is accurate to about 0.5 percent for sags up to 6 percent of the span and is about 2 percent too small for a sag of 10 percent of the span.

Rule 261.H of the NESC requires that the conductor tension calculated under the assumed loading of Rule 251 shall not exceed 60 percent of the ultimate breaking strength of the cable. An analysis of the conductor tension vs sag for this example shows that for any sag less than $d_b =$ 3.65 feet, the conductor design tension will exceed the requirements of Rule 261.H.

Combining the d_b requirement with the vertical clearance requirement results in a specified minimum mounting height for the conductor supports at each end of this span.

$$\text{mounting height (MH)} = d_b + \text{vertical clearance}$$

$$MH = 3.65 + 19.75 = 23.4 \text{ feet.}$$

For poles with crossarms as supporting structures, the crossarm mounting position on the pole and the pole burial depth will determine the minimum pole length that can be used to satisfy the mounting height requirement. For a typical construction, the MH requirement for this example will dictate a minimum pole length of 30 feet with a standard burial

depth (BD) of 5.5 feet. This pole size, burial depth, and crossarm are all standard in the electrical utility industry.

$$\text{pole length} = MH + BD + 0.75 \text{ feet} = 29.65 \text{ feet.}$$

This example illustrates the need for the forensic electrical engineer to analyze the line construction for compliance with the NESC. Satisfying the vertical clearance minimum requirement by excessively reducing the sag can cause the construction to violate the maximum tension requirement.

Overhead power line contacts have been reported for numerous types of equipment and work situations including cranes, truck-mounted booms, excavators, power shovels, pumpcrete trucks with booms, scaffolds, forklifts, ladders, drilling rigs, house-moving equipment, concrete floats, paint brush extensions, TV antennas, and tree trimming equipment.

A center for hazard information, located in Arizona,[28] publishes a newsletter that tracks some reported equipment power line contacts. Unfortunately, there is no nationwide agency currently employing a system for comprehensively collecting data that identifies the hazard, equipment involved, and safeguard applications in effect.

There are a number of safeguards that will assist in the avoidance of injury or death due to power line contact. *The single most effective preventive solution to hazardous contact with power lines is de-energization.* By correctly de-energizing and grounding the lines, there is no voltage present on the conductors; therefore, no danger exists due to contacting the lines with a conductive path. This obvious solution is generally not practical since it will interrupt service to all consumers downstream from the point of de-energization. If the lines must be de-energized for an appreciable time period so that work can take place near the lines, serious disruption of service to consumers will result. Some types of consumers, such as hospitals, cannot tolerate an extended interruption of commercial electrical service without dangerously affecting their function.

Other solutions that can be effective and practical are

- temporary insulation of the lines using cover-up sleeving or rubber blankets,

- relocation of the power lines, and
- underground placement of the lines.

Each of these first four solutions requires the cooperation of the electrical utility and are usually reimbursable at the contractor's expense.

In the case of high-voltage (> 100,000 V) overhead lines, such as transmission lines, the use of temporary insulation, such as cover-up sleeving or rubber blankets on the conductors, is not practical. No available temporary insulation materials will reliably provide enough isolation between the energized line and ground to ensure a safe level of leakage current through contact with a grounded conducting material, a portion of which is assumed to be a human body.

In the vast majority of power line contact injuries and deaths, low- or medium voltage lines are involved simply because there is more exposure to the public with these lines than with high voltage lines.[29] This exposure factor makes the first four solutions as stated above both effective and practical in substantially reducing the hazard of overhead power-line contact.

There are still other safeguards that are important to recognize that have been used effectively to improve the safety of persons working near energized overhead power lines. Some of these safeguard procedures are

- mapping on the ground identifying the danger zones of vehicle approach,
- using spotters to assist the crane or high profile vehicle operator for line contact avoidance, and
- equipment isolation guards and alarms.

Ground mapping by crane operators and job workers can be particularly effective in accidental contact prevention. For a typical 15-kV line, layout on the ground of a fifteen-foot distance on each side of each power pole and marking a continuous line from these points pole to pole can be used to set up a barricade line using saw horses and banner tape. Because the power line conductors are supported by cross arms usually not exceeding ten feet in length, the conductors are generally located within a ten foot wide space centered on the power poles. By establishing a thirty-foot-wide corridor for the danger zone, a safe separation from the overhead line of approximately ten feet is designated on the ground on each side of the line. See Figure 5.2 for an illustration of this process.

With the danger zone mapped on the ground, cranes or other high-profile equipment can be placed so that any configuration of the boom or other parts of the equipment cannot make line contact. No equipment or material should be placed or stored within the danger zone.

The movement of high-profile equipment near power lines can be monitored using spotters who are designated ground operating personnel and whose only job is to observe the relationship between the vehicle and the overhead conductors. Spotters can immediately issue a warning or stop order when the high profile portion of the vehicle encroaches within the minimum safe clearance for the line.

Among the equipment safeguards that are presently available for use in avoidance of power line contact are insulated links, proximity alarms, nonconductive taglines, boom guards, and nonconductive remote controls for operator protection. It is important to recognize that most high-profile vehicle contacts with overhead power lines create a hazard for the workmen on the ground rather than the vehicle operator, unless the operator is out of the vehicle on the ground controlling the operation.

Insulated links are isolation devices used to couple the hoist cable of a crane to its lift hook. These devices are usually rated to withstand contact at up to 50 kV, but are tested at 100 kV for negligible leakage at manufacture. Because they are capable of isolating the load material from electri-

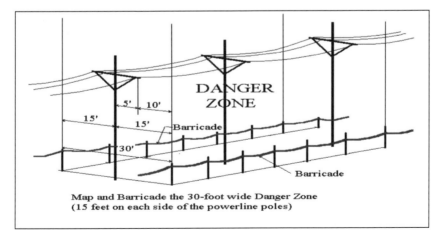

Map and Barricade the 30-foot wide Danger Zone
(15 feet on each side of the powerline poles)

Figure 5.2 Mapping a danger zone

cal contact by the crane's hoist cable, they can be effective in protecting a ground workman from electrical contact when handling the load. The crane body is not isolated however, so the insulated link does not prevent contact between the crane boom or hoist cable from energizing the machine's body.

Proximity alarms are electronic receivers designed to detect the electrostatic field that exists in the space around an energized power line. By audibly and visually providing an alarm to the operator, a crane can be operated to maintain a set clearance from an energized line. A number of federal and military agencies, as well as private high-profile vehicle owners, have successfully used proximity alarms to identify and avoid contact with energized power lines. Prior to using a proximity alarm device, field testing should be conducted with observed known clearances at the site to verify the sensitivity settings of the alarm and to determine if any interference or blocking from adjacent structures and materials impedes the effective operation of the alarm.

Nonconductive taglines (lines attached to the lift hook or load) can be used to protect the ground workmen from conduction of current from the crane to the load. Again, these devices do not isolate the crane body from being energized or from ground.

Boom guards and insulated boom cages can be effective in preventing certain types of direct contact between the crane's boom and a power line, but they cannot prevent contact between the hoist cable and the line. Insulated booms are used for lift trucks specifically designed to bring utility workers in an insulated bucket close to power lines. Even when working from an insulated boom truck, utility workers use additional protection when working on energized (live) lines. Section 44 of the NESC sets forth rules for the safety of supply employees who must work on live lines.

Remote controls for high-profile vehicles are available using nonconductive connections between the hand-held control carried by an operator outside the machine and the vehicle. If conductive control wiring is used, the operator standing on the ground is also in electrical continuity with the vehicle body and in extreme danger if energized line contact is made. By using radio signals from a remote transmitter to a receiver in the vehicle, control of the machine can be accomplished without placing the remote operator in conductive electrical contact with the vehicle. Other methods such as pneumatic controls and fiber optic controls are also available for nonconductive remote control of high-profile machinery.

A typical scenario for a crane accident occurs when the metal conducting structure of the crane and its support vehicle contact an energized overhead power line. In conjunction with the contact, a workman standing on the ground and either touching the vehicle or holding a conductive tagline or remote control is severely shocked or electrocuted by providing a conductive path from the energized metal structure of the crane to ground through his or her body. The operator of the crane, situated within the cab of the equipment, is isolated from the ground fault current path and escapes injury if he remains inside the cab. By moving the crane away from the line contact following the accident, the operator can now safely exit the equipment to ground without danger of electrocution.

A complication to overhead line contacts with equipment, where the contact is maintained for a period of more than a few seconds, occurs when the power line contacted has an automatic reclosing circuit breaker in the circuit. The "recloser" will usually de-energize the conductor contacted within a few milliseconds, but then it will re-energize the line perhaps four times before locking out or discontinuing to reclose. Unless the equipment has been moved away from the contact during this reclosing period of operation, the ground fault remains and any personnel making contact with the equipment while standing on the ground is in great danger for several seconds or even a minute, until the fourth reclosing operation has de-energized the line.

Electrical utilities use reclosers in order to avoid "nuisance outages" or power interruptions that are due to momentary line faults that quickly clear and do not represent a continuing overload to the circuit. Such faults are created when birds ground the line across an insulator, or tree branches are wind blown into momentary contact with the line. Such faults are usually self-clearing and the recloser operation generally reestablishes power without danger to the public or the utilities' equipment.

In this engineer's opinion, *whenever a working entity must approach energized electrical utility facilities, any potentially involved automatic reclosers should be set for instantaneous operation only (i.e., no reclosing action).*

Additionally, when a utility company is aware of work occurring in proximity to its overhead lines, the standards of care for safety set forth by the NESC and OSHA require that the utility act in concert with the working entity to avoid hazardous line contact. Most U.S. electrical utilities have established internal safety rules and procedures for advising and assisting the outside workmen who must approach energized utility equipment. If practical, the utility should offer one of the first four preventive solutions to hazardous contact as set forth in this section.

Since most power lines operate at greater than 1,000 volts, a significant arc flash hazard exists for any grounded material or person that approaches too close to the energized open conductor of a power line. An arc flash is created when the air space separating the high voltage conductor form the grounded material becomes small enough for an electrical discharge (arc) to occur through the air space. This arc flash is similar to a lightning discharge as described in Section 9.2, but has considerably less current and voltage.

The insulation breakdown process that initiates an arc flash is identical to the process described in Section 7.2, and the temperatures created are sufficient to melt or vaporize most metals. The super heated gases and metal particles expelled during an arc flash can cause fatal burns as much as five feet away.[30]

Protective clothing and other devices can be used to prevent injury from arc flashes. These issues are discussed in IEEE 1584, ASTM 1506, and NFPA 70E. In the case of electric utility linemen working close to energized power lines, the NESC has specific safety rules for employers and employees that specify the minimum approach distance to live parts. When working on live (energized) lines and equipment linemen are instructed to neither approach nor bring any conductive object without a suitable insulating handle closer to the energized part than as specified in NESC Rule 441. The **rubber glove work method** supplemented with insulating sleeves or coverings of protective equipment, is required when linemen work on energized lines or parts.

The reader is directed to Section 16.1.C.2 for medical material on arc flash injuries.

5.5 Directly Induced Current Flow within the Human Body

The presence of a time varying electromagnetic field (EMF) in proximity to a material that conducts electricity will result in free charge displacement due to the electric field (E field) forces on such charges and conduction currents due to the magnetic field (H field) forces on the moving charges within the material. The human body has both free and moving electrical charges that exist within the cellular structure of the body tissue and organs. Therefore, when an external EMF of sufficient strength is present in the human environment, there will be displacement and conduction charge motion induced within the body.

The calculations of electrical induction on inanimate objects is a precise science utilizing well-established mathematical models and subject to experimental verification. Such calculations for induction in the human body are not, however, easily made, nor subject to simple experimental verification. Mathematical models for the body in proximity to an EMF source are subject to a great many simplifying assumptions and idealizations. Nevertheless, such calculations can be performed, yielding results that provide engineers and biomedical scientists with meaningful insight about the physical effects of such induction on the human body.

All energized electrical power lines have electric and magnetic fields associated with their supply of electrical energy. An electrical power line is energized by a voltage source at the generating (sending) end of the line and connected through conductors to the load at the other (receiving) end of the line. In order for energy to be transferred from the generator to the load, an electric and a magnetic field must be formed in relationship to each other and as physically determined by the power line conductors, including their geometry.

The generator produces the line's electric field and the magnetic field is formed when the load is connected. The current that flows in the line conductors is a result of the energy transfer occurring due to the electric and magnetic field interactions, but the current flow in the conductors is not transferring power to the load. Rather, the line current causes a loss (I^2R) in the conductors. In order to minimize the line losses in a power line, the current must be held to reasonable values and the resistance of the line must be economically minimized.

The significant fact about the power line EMF phenomenon is that the energy flows through the air surrounding the line, truly creating an electrical power corridor in space. The line conductors serve as an energy guide for the directional transfer of power from source to load. Anything that resides within this EMF corridor will be subject to the effects of the energy transfer taking place in the space around the power lines. If the material residing within the corridor has an electrical nature, electrical charge within the body of the material may be displaced or realigned. It is ultimately the effect of such electrical activity that scientists are searching for as biological effects of power-line EMFs.

More than 1,500,000 circuit miles (one way distance from source to load, not one way distance times the number of conductors) of overhead high voltage commercial electric power lines now exist throughout the U.S. (Using data from the EEI (1994) for circuit miles of OH electric lines from 22 kV to 143 kV, the author estimated at least the same number of circuit miles to exist from 5 kV to 22 kV.) More than 200,000 miles of these circuits operate at voltages from 143 kV to 765 kV (transmission lines) and over 600,000 miles operate at between 22 kV and 143 kV. Research transmission lines have been operated as high as 1500 kV.

The EMFs of overhead power lines, 5 kV to 1000 kV, vary with distance from the conductors and with the shielding effects of structures and natural landscape features such as trees and hills. Some examples of the maximum electric fields at ground level found near power lines are given in Table 5.7.

These electric fields are reduced by increasing distance from the lines. For example, a 115-kV transmission line (TL) with 2-kV/m maximum field will produce a field of approximately 200 V/m at 65 meters (213 feet) from the center line of the TL corridor.

The magnetic fields associated with a power line can be related to the line currents flowing within the conductors and, as is the case with electric fields, these magnetic fields will also decrease with increasing distance

Table 5.7
Examples of the Maximum Electric Fields at Ground Level
Found Near Power Lines

Line Voltage (kV)	Max. Field at Ground Level (kV/m)
23	0.050
115	2.0
345	5.6
500	8.0

from the line. An example TL with line currents of 2,000 amps and line conductors at 18.5 m above the ground will produce a maximum magnetic field of 0.18 gauss (G) at ground level directly under the line. This field will decrease to approximately 0.02 G at a distance of 80 meters (262 feet) from the center of the line. (The gauss is a unit of magnetic flux density that measures the ability of electric currents to produce magnetic induction forces at a point.)

The Electric Power Research Institute (EPRI) has set forth a set of six characterizing parameters that are of importance when considering the electric field induction on objects in proximity to high-voltage energized power line conductors.[31] They are:

1. the short-circuit current I_{sc}, which is the current that is induced in a zero impedance path from object to ground,
2. the voltage V_{og}, which is the voltage that is induced between object and ground and depends upon the impedance between the object and ground,
3. the impedance between object and ground given by $Z_{og} = V_{og}/I_{sc}$,
4. the capacitance between the object and ground, C_{og},
5. the spark-discharge capacitance to ground, C_s, which has a negligible series resistance in the spark-discharge time of 1 microsecond, and
6. the maximum energy stored per half-cycle in the object.

$$J = \frac{1}{2}C_s(\sqrt{2}V_{og})^2 = C_s(V_{og}^2) \qquad \text{(Equation 5.3)}$$

The EPRI has also published tables for use in applying these parameters to various objects including people, horses, vehicles, houses and other structures in uniform electric fields.

An important effect of induced voltage on an inanimate object in the vicinity of an electromagnetic field is the contact by humans standing on the ground with the object after it becomes energized. If the V_{og} of the object is high and the Z_{og} of the object is high with respect to the impedance between human contact and ground, then the current flow through the person can be hazardous.

Most objects that are in close proximity (within three meters) to high-voltage power lines are low impedance structures such as metal towers or wooden poles, so that Z_{og} is low. Even if a person standing on the ground touches such a structure, the current flow through the human is insignificant (see parameter 3 above).

The danger from high-voltage overhead power lines to people standing under the lines due to induced voltage or current is minimal so long as a third factor such as a very large inanimate object in the vicinity of the line does not enter into the situation. If an ungrounded large object is affected by induction from a high-voltage power line and a human makes contact with the object while standing on the ground, then it is possible for an electrical current to flow through the person with an adverse effect.

Formulas for electric field induced short-circuit currents I_{sc}, are given in the EPRI *Transmission Line Reference Book*[32] (Tables 8.8.2 and 8.8.3), for a number of geometric shapes and specifically those shown in Table 5.8 below.

For each of these objects, in a 7-kV/m electric field, short-circuit currents can be calculated as shown in Table 5.9.

Table 5.8
Formulas for Electric Field Induced Short-Circuit Currents

h in meters, E in V/m

cow	$I_{sc} = 17.5 \times 10^{-9} \times h^2 \times E$
	$C_s = 200$ pF
people	$I_{sc} = 5.4 \times 10^{-9} \times h^2 \times E$
	$C_s = 140$ pF
large school bus	$I_{sc} = 3.9 \times 10^{-7} \times E$
	$C_s = 1,800$ pF

Table 5.9
Short-Circuit Currents in a 7-kV/m Electric Field

cow	$I_{sc} = 0.17$ mA
person	$I_{sc} = 0.13$ mA
large school bus	$I_{sc} = 2.73$ mA

In the case of the large school bus, when stopped on dry pavement under and perpendicular to a 500-kV transmission line, if a person standing on the ground with wet shoes or on wet grass were to make hand contact with the bus, there would be a current passing through the body of 2.73 mA. This is a large enough current to startle 20 percent of adult men, and in fact exceeds the perceptible current threshold for almost all humans. Obviously, in this example the electric field-induced effect on humans is undesirable but not life threatening, unless the startle reaction creates an inadvertent danger such as stepping backward into traffic or tripping.

A greater danger from the startle reaction caused by electric field-induced voltages on persons lies in the spark discharge current that occurs slightly before full contact. is made by a person who reaches out to touch a grounded object. The voltage from person-to-ground V_{oc}, is determined in a spark discharge situation by the electric field, the individual's position, and the impedance to ground. In the case of very high impedance to ground, the voltage to ground is

$$V_{oc} = \frac{I_{oc}}{\omega C} \qquad \text{(Equation 5.4)}$$

where C is derived from EPRI measured data, Figure 8.10.14,[33] and I_{sc} for people is given in the data above.

$$I_{sc} = 5.4(10^{-9})h^2 E \qquad \text{(Equation 5.5)}$$

where h = height of person in meters and E = electric field intensity at ground level in V/m.

For the I_{sc} calculated in the previous example with a 7-kV/m electric field and $h = 1.855$ meters ($h = 6$ feet) we have a typical V_{oc} of

$$V_{oc} = \frac{0.13(10^{-3})}{377(160)(10^{-12})} = 2,155 \text{ Vrms} \qquad \text{(Equation 5.6)}$$

This is a peak voltage at discharge of $(2,155) \sqrt{2} = 3,048$ V. To place this high voltage in perspective, the DC voltages attained by people walking on carpet in a very dry environment typically range from 4 kV up to 8 kV. Everyone has probably experienced the startle effect that results from the discharge of the accumulated static electric charges at these DC voltages.

A significant difference in the AC-induced spark discharge situation lies in the possibly repetitive nature of the discharges for slowly made or brushing contacts. Such spark discharges are undoubtedly more startling than experienced in a static carpet-induced single discharge.

Magnetic fields at power line frequencies may cause significant voltages to be induced in objects whose length is considerable and oriented parallel to the power line. Such objects as metal fences, pipes and wires are known to exhibit large induced voltages when placed parallel and in close proximity to overhead power lines. Many years ago, farmers discovered that by coiling a number of turns of wire under an overhead transmission line crossing their farms that they could steal electrical power and electrify their barns. Unfortunately, some of these attempts to obtain free electrical power burnt the barns down or electrocuted someone or some animal.

We cannot readily calculate the induced voltage in a conductor from a measurement of the magnetic field strength, or magnetic flux density $B = \mu H$ in gauss. Rather, it is the magnetic potential, M, which is analogous to space potential that is used to calculate electric field-induced voltages and currents, and which determines the voltage induced in an object due to the magnetic field effect. These quantities are related by Equation 5.7.

$$H = \frac{B}{\mu} = \frac{1}{\mu} \times \frac{\partial M}{\partial r} \qquad \text{(Equation 5.7)}$$

The voltage induced in a parallel object is given by

$$V_a = j(\omega)M \qquad \text{(Equation 5.8)}$$

where V_a is volts per meter of the object's length, $\omega = (2\pi)f$, where f is the frequency (Hz) of the magnetic field, and M is the magnetic potential of the object a.[34]

Comparisons between magnetic field-induced current and electric field-induced current in the human body have been made using a circular cross-sectional model for body elements.[35] These comparisons show that for an electric field of 10 kV/m and a magnetic field of 0.5 G, values chosen as representing maximums known to exist under high-voltage power lines, that the electric-induced currents are at least ten times greater than the magnetic induced currents. To conclude from this fact that magnetic fields are of less biological importance to humans and animals than electric fields due to power lines is at best premature at this time and at worst, nonscientific.

As will later be discussed in this book, the preponderance of experimental evidence that has been developed during the past twenty-five years indicates that electromagnetic field effects on biological systems may not be insignificant in our environment and that we should proceed with caution with respect to human exposure to EMFs at all frequencies. As long ago as 1972, Robert O. Becker, M.D.[36] wrote that the concept that electromagnetic forces might have any effect upon living organisms, other than the thermal effect due to Joule heating, was for many years rejected by the organized biomedical community. But under the weight of experimental evidence, this attitude has changed.

5.6 Effects of Ionizing Electromagnetic Radiation

Ionizing radiation is any electromagnetic (EM) or particulate radiation capable of ionizing matter, directly or indirectly. Ionization is the process or the result of any process whereby a neutral atom or molecule acquires a positive or negative charge.

An example of ionizing radiation is found in the photon energy emitted by the sun as this electromagnetic energy passes through air. Another example of ionizing radiation is the emission of both ionizing electromagnetic energy in the form of gamma rays and alpha and beta particles from radioactive materials.

Most alpha particles are emitted at energy states that correspond to approximately 3,000 megahertz (MHz), or at the lower range of the SHF radio band (just above the UHF band). Gamma rays start at about 1,015 MHz and hard x-rays can be as high in frequency as gamma rays. Microwave radiation refers rather loosely to EM energy propagated at frequencies from about 1,000 MHz upward[37,38] to about 40×103 MHz. [1,000 MHz = 103×106 Hz = 109 Hz = 1 gigahertz (GHz)]. Ionizing radiation starts at 7.9×108 MHz or for wavelengths less than 3,800 Å (angstroms)

(1 Å = 10^{-10} m = 10^{-8} cm. Note that wavelength in meters is given by 300 divided by frequency in MHz.).

Ionizing radiation (IR) as well as particle radiation has been recognized since the late nineteenth century as a potential health hazard to biological systems, specifically humans and animals. From the beginning, research biomedical scientists identified the dependence of dosage and duration of IR exposure in assessing the risk of hazardous health effects.[39]

Measures of ionizing radiation have evolved from the early units of the **rad** and **rem**. The rad is an absorbed radiation unit equivalent to 100 ergs per gram of absorber.[40] The rem is equivalent to the rad in units, but was introduced later to account for the biological effects of frequency and particulate radiation that differ from x-rays and gamma rays. The SI unit currently used is the sievert (Sv) which is a dose equivalent that takes into account quality factor (Q) and the product of other multiplying factors (N) stipulated by the International Commission on Radiological Protection. One sievert is equal to 100 rems, and is the dose equivalent of one joule per kilogram of exposed material.[41]

One sievert is generally considered the threshold above which exposure to IR causes greatly increasing damage to the body, including radiation sickness and radiation dermatitis, cataracts or failure of various organs. Some of the health effects of IR occur many years after exposure, typically five to fifteen years for leukemia, and forty years or longer for skin, lung, breast and other cancers.[42] The International Commission on Radiological Protection has determined that the total risk of death from IR exposure is about 1 percent of the exposed population per sievert of absorbed radiation.

5.7 Effects of Non-Ionizing Electromagnetic Radiation

The relationship between non-ionizing electromagnetic radiation (EMFs) and humans was not recognized as a quantitative problem until approximately fifty years after d'Arsonval established the use of electromagnetic radiation in medicine in 1890.[43] It was not until 1941 that a scientific team conceived and developed the first true radio frequency dosimetry by quantifying the temperature rise in exposed tissues in terms of a volume-normalized energy rate of absorption. This early work was surprisingly close to the presently used mass-normalized specific absorption rate (SAR) expressed in watts per kilogram.[44]

From the mid- through the late 1960s, laboratory bioeffects research by Guy,[45, 46] Justesen[47] and Gandhi[48] resulted in improved understanding of animal orientation with respect to incident electromagnetic waves and their energy absorption. Other environmental factors, such as temperature and humidity, in addition to dosimetric quantities were found to be of importance.[49] In 1979, Durney et al. developed an empirical formula for broad-band SAR calculations applicable to humans and animals.[50]

Experimental work with microwave radiation was believed as recently as 1961 to have shown that the chief effect of microwave energy on living tissue is to produce heating.[51] However, there was then, and is much more so today, a growing body of research that suggests many more complex interactions by the human body with microwave EMFs.

W. Ross Adey and others have, since the early 1960s, investigated cerebral tissue interactions with environmental electromagnetic fields.[52] The research by Adey and his associates at the UCLA Brain Institute and Department of Anatomy has clearly shown altered electrochemical effects on the central nervous system due to weak VHF (30–300 MHz) fields, amplitude modulated at brain wave frequencies.[53] Other researchers have observed effects of weak fields at 1–100 MHz radio frequencies on blood cell chaining.[54]

Russian scientists have reported central nervous system (CNS) effects at very low microwave power levels, below 10 mW/cm^2.[55-57] As a result of this research, the Soviet government in the mid-1970s established safe exposure levels for microwave radiation 1,000 times lower than the U.S. level at that time of 10 mW/cm^2.

The U.S. safety standards for human exposure to microwave energy have evolved from the 10 mW/cm^2 value considered safe for continuous exposure at all frequencies from 10 MHz to 100 GHz, based upon thermal considerations of maximum allowable core temperature rise in the body, to a frequency-dependent standard which thermally accounts for the increased absorption of the body particularly near body resonance frequencies of approximately 30 to 300 MHz.[58] The latest recommended standards are specified in the current version of ANSI C95.[59]

ANSI C95.1-1991, IEEE *Standard for Safety Levels with Respect to Human Exposure to Radio Frequency Electromagnetic Fields, 3 kHz to 300 GHz* includes recommendations to prevent general EMF harmful effects to humans but is not intended to apply to the exposure of medical patients as practiced by the healing arts.[60]

The current recommended standards are based upon the concept of **maximum permissible exposure** (MPE) in two classes of environments: controlled and uncontrolled. An uncontrolled environment is a location where exposed individuals have no knowledge or control of their exposure. Areas such as homes or workplaces, where there are no expectations of exposure beyond those specified in C95.1-1991 Table 2, p. 15, are classified as uncontrolled environments. A controlled environment, on the other hand, is a location where exposed individuals are placed as a result of their employment and where the individual is aware of the potential for such exposure. Such areas of exposure are limited by C95.1-1991, Table 1, p. 13.

In brief summary of the recommended MPEs for these environments the following limits are stated:

- The maximum MPE for all frequencies is an E field strength of 614 V/m and the minimum MPE is 27.5 V/m.
- The maximum MPE for all frequencies is an H field strength of 163 A/m (2.05 G) and the minimum MPE is 0.0729 A/m (916 mG).
- The maximum averaging time for either E or H field strengths as previously stated is thirty minutes and the minimum is six minutes for frequencies up to 15 GHz. (Averaging time is a concept designed to determine whether an exposure is in compliance with the MPE. Any exposure exceeding the averaging time is termed a continuous exposure, and is considered harmful to humans.)
- The maximum MPE for both E and H fields are specified for the lowest frequencies, (i.e., 3 kHz to 100 kHz).

C95.1-1991 has also specified recommendations for maximum induced and contact radio frequency currents (3 kHz to 100 MHz) in humans that basically are given in Table 5.10 for uncontrolled environments.

The maximum recommendations for controlled environments are given in Table 5.11.

A method for calculation of the total MPE in an environment that includes multiple sources of electromagnetic radiation is presented in Appendix C of that IEEE publication. There is also a section of the standard

Table 5.10
Maximum Recommendations for Uncontrolled Environments

Frequency range	Max. current (mA)	Contact through each foot
0.003–0.1 MHz	$450 \times f$	$450 \times f$
0.1–100 MHz	45	45

where f = frequency in MHz for the range.

Table 5.11
Maximum Recommendations for Controlled Environments

Frequency range	Max. current (mA)	Contact through each foot
0.003–0.1 MHz	$1,000 \times f$	$1,000 \times f$
0.1–100 MHz	100	100

where f = frequency in MHz for the range.

which recommends procedures for measuring electric and magnetic fields and presents cautionary advisory information to the engineer which is intended to standardize and improve the data gathering accuracy of such field measurements.[61] Included in C95.1-1991 is an extensive bibliography of sixty citations and a list of 321 papers comprising the initial database for the standard.

5.8 Effects of Extremely Low Frequency EMFs

Biological effects of electric and magnetic fields at extremely low frequencies (ELF) below about 300 Hz, such as power frequencies of 50 and 60 Hz, have generated scientific curiosity and research since the late nineteenth century. Before this however, the first scientific observations of the relationship between biological systems and man-made electricity were published by Stephen Gray in England in the *1731 Philosophical Transactions* in a paper entitled "Experiments Concerning Electricity." Gray used static electricity to electrify a human subject. By the mid-1700s, DC electricity was being generated with Leyden jar batteries greatly increasing the interest in biological experimentation with DC. There were then a number of physicians, and unfortunately outright charlatans, who were crudely using this new source of energy to treat afflictions in humans.

In 1786 Galvani discovered, during the dissection of a frog, that an electrical force somehow existed within the frog's leg muscles. From that time on, physicians and biologists have recognized and investigated the electrical properties of living tissue. It was not until 1941, however, when Szent-Gyorgyi, a physician and biochemist, proposed a startling hypothesis that the biological structure of protein was sufficiently structured to function as a crystalline lattice and therefore that semiconduction could exist in living systems.[62] This was a particularly advanced hypothesis considering that Shockley, Bardeen, and Brattain would not actually produce a working semiconductor transistor until after World War II and that Shockley did not publish the theory of the p-n junction semiconductor until 1949.[63]

Simultaneously, during WWII, there was a new science of "cybernetics" being developed at MIT and Harvard that dealt with communication and control, whether in man or machine. Scientists began to apply these advanced concepts to neurophysiology and to the complex problem of modeling the brain function. Biologists finally recognized that the simple nerve impulse or action potential was not the sole basis for all nervous system functions. These radical concepts were further extended to the central nervous system (CNS), and soon investigators began to experiment with electrically influenced growth and regeneration of bone tissue.[64]

The effects of EMFs at ELF on animals have been generally recognized by today's scientific community to include a wide range of biological systems: the central nervous system (CNS), [65] psychological behavior,[66,67] migration, navigation and communication,[68] melatonin production by the pineal gland,[69] growth and development,[70] and tissue regeneration.[71]

Specifically the question of EMF effects at power line frequencies on humans has been the subject of scientific research since the 1960s when the U.S. Navy began project Sanguine, an extremely large antenna proposed for communication with submarines during underwater operations. Sanguine utilized frequencies in the same range as commercial AC power lines and created similar magnetic field intensities, but had an electric field about one-millionth the strength of a typical transmission line. The

Navy, in compliance with the National Environmental Policy Act, initiated experimental studies at various universities and medical research laboratories to assess the effect of such EMFs. Ultimately, many of these studies reported positive effects in which the fields produced specific changes in the biological system being studied.

Also during the 1960s, scientists in the U.S.S.R. conducted studies on overhead high-voltage lines and their biological effects. The Russian EMF work included epidemiological studies which led the Soviet Ministry of Electricity in 1970 to establish rules limiting the duration of exposure to EMFs for electrical workers.[72-75] Continuing Soviet research resulted in the adoption of additional EMF exposure regulations in 1975.[76]

In the U.S., research on the EMF effects of overhead power lines began in 1967 with the John Hopkins studies that were sponsored by the electrical utility industry. Although the 1967 studies found reduced sperm counts in linemen and stunted growth in the male offspring of exposed mice, these animal studies were not continued.[77] The studies on linemen were continued and eventually reported as negative.[78] In 1972, the Electric Power Research Institute (EPRI) was founded and it took over almost all responsibility for utility industry and DOE-sponsored EMF research. EPRI has continued to sponsor research in biological effects.

The independent epidemiological work of Nancy Wertheimer and Ed Leeper at the University of Colorado in 1976–77 was the first study to indicate a possible connection between ELF-EMF exposure and human cancer.[79] This study was published in 1979 in the *American Journal of Epidemiology*, and was almost immediately refuted by a Rhode Island study by Fulton published in the same journal in 1980.[80] Some in the utility industry were also quick to criticize the Wertheimer and Leeper research and, despite a detailed letter to the editor regarding the Rhode Island study that gives several explanations for the different results, the industry generally continued to ignore the Colorado study in favor of the negative result study.[81] In 1982, a Swedish epidemiological study confirmed the Colorado study.[82] In 1987, the IEEE reported that Leonard Sagan, program manager for radiation studies at EPRI, called a New York State study that appeared to link exposure to EMFs with leukemia and other types of cancer in children "well conceived and conducted."[83] Additional epidemiological studies were conducted in Los Angeles and published in 1991 by a team of researchers from the University of Southern California School of Medicine that seem to confirm the Colorado study.[84]

The earth has a natural electromagnetic environment that varies in frequency from 0 Hz (DC) to several thousand kilohertz (kHz). At 50 to 60 Hz frequencies the earth's background EMF strength is on the order of 10^{-4} V/m (0.0001 volts per meter) and 10^{-8} G (0.00000001 gauss) for electric and magnetic fields respectively.[85]

The widespread use of electrical energy in our modern world has greatly increased the EMF exposure beyond that of nature. Typically the 60 Hz EMF strengths inside a single-family residence in the U.S. will be on the order of 1–10 V/m and 50 mG.[86]

Field strengths near residential appliances, however, can be as high as 300 V/m (20 cm above a rotisserie with a reversed plug) and 1.12 G (3 cm above a 1000 W stove coil).[87] It should be noted that these levels of exposure for humans would usually be very brief and would require extremely close proximity to the appliance. However, certain other home appliances can produce high EMFs and are subject to extended human exposure time, such as electric blankets and waterbed heaters, where the fields can be as high as 250 V/m and 1.0 G.

Section 5.5 stated the effects of overhead power lines (OHPL) on environmental EMFs. In summary, OHPL create electric fields in the vicinity of the lines that can be as high as 10 kV/m at ground level[88] and can produce magnetic fields of 0.5 G.[89] If a person lived openly under such an OHPL, they would be exposed to electric and magnetic fields that are 2,000 times and ten times greater, respectively, than the usual electric and magnetic fields found inside a residence.

As recently as 1991, the scientific community was not in general agreement concerning the possible health effects of exposure to residential EMFs. At that time, public concern regarding possible health risks from residential exposures to low-strength, low frequency electric and magnetic fields produced by power lines and electric appliances had become widespread. As a result, Congress asked the National Academy of Sciences (NAS) to review the research literature on the effects from exposure to these fields.[90]

The National Research Council convened a committee of sixteen scientists to conduct this review. The members of the committee, all eminent in their respective fields, represented a wide range of specialties; neurobiology, epidemiology, neurochemistry, electrical and biomedical engineering, neurological genetics, physics, chemistry, biophysics, biochemistry, neuroendrocrinology, psychology, electromagnetic physiology, statistics, nuclear chemistry, and oncology. In 1997 the committee published a report that concluded:

> Specifically, no conclusive and consistent evidence shows that exposures to residential electric and magnetic fields produce cancer, adverse neurobehavioral effects, or reproductive and developmental effects.
>
> At extreme levels well above those normally encountered in residences, electrical and magnetic fields can produce biological effects (promotion of bone healing is an example), but these effects do not provide a consistent picture of a relationship between the biologic of these fields and health hazards.[91]

For nearly fifty years there has been no question that higher frequency EMFs, both ionizing and non-ionizing, can produce harmful biological effects to humans. Private agencies and governments worldwide that set limits on the exposure of humans and animals to such EMFs have established safety standards. Although the agreement on threshold levels for these safety standards is not uniform, such standards are intended to reasonably minimize the risk of health hazards due to electromagnetic radiation.

The EM spectrum below the range of non-ionizing frequencies where wavelength is large in proportion to body dimensions cannot produce heating by inducing electric currents within the bodies of humans and animals. Consequently, no exposure limits have been set for radio frequency EM fields below 3 kHz (wave lengths of 328 kft.). Refer to Section 5.7 for specific recommended exposure limits for non-ionizing EMFs and to Section 5.6 for specific exposure limits and risk for ionizing radiation.

There are sources of high-ELF EMFs in our modern environment that greatly exceed the levels included in the study of residential exposures previously cited. Open transmission power lines, workplace devices such as electric furnaces, welders and large motor-operated machines can produce electric and magnetic fields as large as 10 kV/m and 100 G.[92] In the author's opinion, prolonged exposure to such extreme EMFs should be treated with prudent avoidance until further research establishes conclusive evidence that such exposures are not health hazards to a reasonable degree of risk. The cost of prudent avoidance in these extreme cases of EMF strength should not be great and will mitigate the risk to human health while scientists search for answers to the question of ELF EMF exposure at high levels of field strength.

In order to avoid high-level EMF emission in the workplace, the sources can be shielded in many cases and workers can be equipped with exposure-reducing clothing and apparel. Product design for emission field control is ultimately the most effective EMF hazard prevention method for human protection, just as double-insulated and ground-fault protected tools have been proven the most effective electrical shock prevention methods for both the general public and the work force. Certain manufacturers of high-level EMF producing products, such as video data terminals, have already elected to shield their products, thereby greatly reducing the magnetic fields emitted.

Endnotes

1. Ernst Weber and Frederik Nebeker, *The Evolution of Electrical Engineering: A Personal Perspective* (NY: IEEE Press, 1994), 32–33.

2. William M. Mazer, *Electrical Accident Investigation Handbook* (Glen Echo, MD: Electrodata Inc., 1987), vol. 2, ch. 7, 7.4.2.5.

3. Theodore Bernstein, *Theories of the Causes of Death from Electricity in the Late Nineteenth Century*, reprint no. 1863 (University of Wisconsin, Engineering Experiment Station), 267.

4. James F. Penrose, "Inventing Electrocution," *American Heritage of Invention & Technology* 9(4):35–44 (1994).

5. C. F. Dalziel, "Reevaluation of Lethal Electric Currents," *IEEE Transactions on Industry and General Applications* IGA-4(5):467–476 (1968).

6. Theodore Bernstein, "Effects of Electricity and Lightning on Man and Animals," (American Society for Testing and Materials [ASTM], 1973), authorized reprint from the *Journal of Forensic Sciences* 18(1):8.

7. C. F. Dalziel, "A Study of the Hazards of Impulse Currents," *AIEE Transactions* 72(3):1032–1053 (1953).

8. Bernstein, *Theories of the Causes of Death*, 9.

9. Mazer, *Electrical Accident Investigation Handbook*, 7.4.2.0.

10. R. K. Wright, M.D. and J. H. Davis, M.D., *The Investigation of Electrical Deaths: A Report of 220 Fatalities* (American Academy of Forensic Sciences, 1979), 515.

11. R. H. Lee, "Electrical Safety in Industrial Plants," *IEEE Spectrum,* June 1971.

12. Institute of Electrical and Electronic Engineers (IEEE), *The White Book,* IEEE Std. 602-1986 (NY: Institute of Electrical and Electronic Engineers, 1985), 373.

13. Mazer, *Electrical Accident Investigation Handbook*, 7.3.2.0.

14. Theodore Bernstein, *Effects of Electricity and Lightning on Man and Animals*, reprint no. 1636 (University of Wisconsin, Engineering Experimental Station, 1973), 10.

15. Mazer, *Electrical Accident Investigation Handbook*, 7.4.2.1.

16. Ibid., 7.4.2.0.

17. Wright, *Investigation of Electrical Deaths*, 518.

18. Mazer, *Electrical Accident Investigation Handbook*, 7.4.2.6.5 to 7.4.2.6.6.

19. Ibid., 7.4.2.7.39.

20. Freidrich Panse, "Die Shädigungen des Nervensystems durch technische Elektrizikät," *Monatsschrift für Psychiatrie und Neurologie* 78:193–213 (1931).

21. Ibid., 699.

22. Ibid., 700.

23. Ibid., 701.

24. Ibid., 712.

25. Ibid., 720.

26. For the purpose of this rule, trucks are defined as any vehicle exceeding eight feet in height.

27. Lorna Middendorf and Robert Cunitz, "Problems in the Perception of Overhead Power Lines," *Hazard Prevention, Journ. of the Systems Safety Society* 21(2) (1985).

28. Center for Hazard Information, David V. MacCollum, P.E., Editor in Chief, P.O. Box 3962, Sierra Vista, AZ, 85636-3962.

29. It is estimated that in 1992 there were more than 475,000 miles of OH electric lines in the U.S. operating at from 5kV to 22kV. See Section 5.4.

30. R. H. Lee, "The Other Electrical Hazard: Electric Arc Blast Burns," *IEEE Transactions on Industry Applications* IA-18:246–251 (1982).

31. Electric Power Research Institute, *EPRI Transmission Line Reference Book 345 kV and Above,* 2nd ed. (Palo Alto, CA: Electric Power Research Institute, 1982), 348.

32. Ibid., 355–356.

33. Ibid., 372.

34. Ibid., 365.

35. Ibid., 380.

36. Robert O. Becker M.D., "Electromagnetic Forces and Life Processes," *Technology Review* 75(2).

37. *CRC Handbook of Chemistry and Physics*, 73d ed., David R Lide, ed. (Boca Raton: CRC Press, 1992–93) 10–298.

38. *IEEE Standard Dictionary of Electrical and Electronics Terms*, ANSI/IEEE Std. 100-1984, 547.

39. A. W. Guy, "Quantitation of Electromagnetic Fields in Biological Systems," in *Biological Effects in Electromagnetic Radiation*, John M. Osepchuck, ed. (NY: IEEE Press, 1983), 1–5.

40. IEEE, *IEEE Standard Dictionary*, 716.

41. Ibid., 836.

42. The American Medical Association, *Home Medical Encyclopedia* (NY: Random House, 1989), 846.

43. Guy, "Quantitation of Electromagnetic Fields," 1.

44. Ibid., 1.

45. A. W. Guy and J. F. Lehmann, "On Determination of an Optimum Microwave Diathermy Frequency for a Direct Contact Applicator." *IEEE Trans. Bio-Med. Eng.* BME-13:76–87 (1966).

46. A. W. Guy et al., "Studies on Therapeutic Heating by Electromagnetic Energy," in *Thermal Problems in Biotechnology* (NY: ASME, 1968), 26–45.

47. D. R. Justesen and N. W. King, "Behavioral Effects of Low Level Microwave Irradiation in the Closed Space Situation," in: *Proc. Biological Effects and Health Implications of Microwave Radiation Symp.*, (PB 193898), Richmond, VA, September 1969.

48. O. P. Gandhi, "Frequency and Orientation Effect on Whole Animal Absorption of Electromagnetic Waves," *IEEE Trans. Bio-Med. Eng.* BME-22:536–542 (1975).

49. W. W. Mumford, "Heat Stress Due to RF Radiation," *Proc. IEEE* 57:171–178 (1969).

50. C. H. Durney et al., "An Empirical Formula for Broad-Band SAR Calculations of Prolate Spheroidal Models of Humans and Animals," *IEEE Trans. Microwave Tech.* MTT-27:758–763 (1979).

51. W. W. Mumford, "Some Technical Aspects of Microwave Radiation Hazards," *Proc. IRE* 49:429 (1961).

52. W. R. Adey "Evidence for Cooperative Mechanisms in the Susceptibility of Cerebral Tissue to Environmental and Intrinsic Electric Fields," in *Biological Effects of Electromagnetic Radiation*, John M. Osepchuk, ed. (NY: IEEE Press, 1983), 108–116.

53. S. M. Bawin, L. K. Kaczmarek and W. R. Adey, "Effects of Modulated VHF Fields on the Central Nervous System," *Ann. N. Y. Acad. Sci.* 247:74–81 (1985).

54. C. C. Johnson, and A. W. Guy, "Non-Ionizing Electromagnetic Wave Effects in Biological Materials and Systems," *Proc. IEEE* 60:693 (1972).

55. Yu A. Kholodov, "The Effect of an Electromagnetic Field on the Central Nervous System," ASTIA Doc. 284 123 (Washington, DC: Library of Congress, 1962).

56. Yu A. Kholodov, "Effect of a UHF Electromagnetic Field on the Electrical Activity of a Neuronally Isolated Region of the Cerebral Cortex," ATF P 65-68 (Washington, DC: Library of Congress, 1964).

57. Yu A. Kholodov, "The Effect of Electromagnetic and Magnetic Fields on the Central Nervous System," NASA Technical Translation, TTF-465, 1967.

58. A. W. Guy, "Non-Ionizing Radiation Dosimetry and Interaction," in *Biological Effects of Electromagnetic Radiation*, J. M. Osepchuk, ed. (NY: IEEE Press, 1983), 530–531.

59. Institute of Electrical and Electronic Engineers, *IEEE Standard for Safety Levels with Respect to Human Exposure to Radio Frequency Electromagnetic Fields, 3 kHz to 300 GHz*, ANSI/IEEE C95.1-1991 (NY: IEEE, 1992).

60. Ibid., 9.

61. Ibid., 29–32.

62. R. O. Becker and Andrew A. Marino, *Electromagnetism and Life* (Albany: State University of NY Press, 1982), 21.

63. W. Shockley, *Bell System Tech. Jour.* 28:435 (1949).

64. Becker, *Electromagnetism and Life*, 40–56.

65. H. A. Hansson, "Purkinje Nerve Cell Changes Caused by Electric Fields: Ultrastructural Studies on Long-Term Effects on Rabbits," *Medical Biology* 59:103–110 (1981).

66. W. R. Gibson and W. F. Moroney, *The Effects of Extremely Low Frequency Magnetic Fields on Human Performance*, AD A005898, NAMRL-1195 (Pensacola, FL: Naval Aerospace Medical Research Laboratory, 1974).

67. J. R. Hamer, "Effects of Low-level Low-frequency Electric Fields on Human Reaction Time," *Commun. Behavioral Biology* 2(A):217 (1968).

68. Becker, *Electromagnetism and Life*, 70–74.

69. Taylor Moore, "Sharpening the Focus on EMF Research," *IEEE Power Engineering Review* 12(8):8 (1992).

70. Jose M. R. Delgado et al., "Embryological Changes Induced by Weak, Extremely Low-Frequency, Electromagnetic Fields," *Journal Anat. (Gr. Brit.)* 533–550 (1982).

71. R. O. Becker and J. A. Spadaro, "Electrical Stimulation of Partial Limb Regeneration in Mammals," *Bull. N.Y. Acad. Med.* 48:627.

72. N. A. Solov'ev, "The Biological Effect of the Electric Component of a Low Frequency Electromagnetic Field (Literature Survey)," *Medical Technology News,* Moscow, VNIIMIO, No. 5:86–94 (1962).

73. Yu I. Novitskiy et al.,"Radio Frequencies and Microwaves: Magnetic and Electric Fields," in *Foundations of Space Biology and Medicine*, Vol. 2, Part 1 (Moscow: Academy of Sciences, 1970; Washington, DC: NASA Technical Translation TT-F-14, 021, Nov. 1971).

74. Yu L. Dumanskiy, V. Ya Akimenko and Ye V. Prokhvatilo, *Biological Effects of Low Frequency and Static Electromagnetic Fields* (Moscow: USSR Ministry of Health, 1977).

75. V. P. Korobkova et al., "Influence of the Electric Field in 500 and 750 kV Switchyards on Maintenance Staff and Means for Its Protection," in *Proceedings of the International Conference on Large High Tension Systems* (Paris, 1972).

76. Yu I. Lyskov and Yu S. Emma, "Electrical Field as a Parameter Considered in Designing Electric Power Transmission of 750–1150 kV: The Measuring Methods, the Design Practices, and Direction of Further Research," in *Proceedings of the Symposium of EHV Power Transmission* (Washington, DC: Joint American-Soviet Committee on Cooperation in the Field of Energy, Feb. 1975).

77. Andrew A. Marino and Robert O Becker, "High Voltage Lines: Hazards at a Distance," *Environment* 20(9) (1978).

78. M. L. Singewald, O. P. Langworthy, and W. B. Kouwenhoven, "Medical Follow-Up Study of High Voltage Linemen Working in AC Electric Fields," *IEEE Trans. on Power Apparatus and Systems* PAS-92:1307–1309 (1973).

79. N. Wertheimer and E. Leeper, "Electrical Wiring Configurations and Childhood Cancer," *Am. J. Epidemiol.* 109:273 (1979).

80. J. P. Fulton et al., "Electrical Wiring Configurations and Childhood Leukemia in Rhode Island," *Am. J. Epidemiol.* 111:292 (1980).

81. N. Wertheimer and E. Leeper, "Electrical Wiring Configurations and Childhood Leukemia in Rhode Island," *Am. J. Epidemiol.* 111:461 (1980).

82. L. Tomenius, L. Hellstrom and B. Enander, "Electrical Constructions and 50 Hz Magnetic Field at the Dwellings of Tumor Cases (0–18 years of age) in the County of Stockholm" (paper presented at the Symposium on Occupational Health and Safety in Mining and Tunneling, Prague, June 21–25, 1982).

83. "Spectral Lines," *IEEE Spectrum* 24(9):25 (1987).

84. Taylor Moore, "Sharpening the Focus on EMF Research," *IEEE Power Engineering Review* August 1992, 7.

85. A. R. Sheppard and M. Eisenbud, *Biological Effects of Electric and Magnetic Fields of Extremely Low Frequency* (NY: New York University Press, 1977), 2-1.

86. A. R. Sheppard and M. Eisenbud, *Biological Effects*, 3-3,4.

87. Electric Power Research Institute, *EPRI Transmission Line Reference Book,* 348.

88. Electric Power Research Institute, *EPRI Transmission Line Reference Book,* 347.

89. Electric Power Research Institute, *EPRI Transmission Line Reference Book,* 342–343.

90. National Research Council (U.S.). Committee on the Possible Effects of Electromagnetic Fields on Biologic Systems, *Possible Health Effects of Exposure to Residential Electrical and Magnetic Fields* (Washington, DC: National Academy Press, 1997), 1.

91. Ibid., 2

92. *Proceedings of the Scientific Workshop on the Health Effects of Electric and Magnetic Fields on Workers*, NTIS, PB92-131721 (U.S. Dept. of Commerce, 1991), 49.

References for Section 5.3

Cronholm, B. and J. O. Ottosson, "Ultrabrief Stimulus Technique in Electroconvulsive Therapy," *Journal of Nervous and Mental Diseases* (137):117–123 (1963)

Devanand, D. P., "Does Electroconvulsive Therapy Damage Brain Cells?" *Seminars in Neurology* 15(4):351–357 (1995).

Devanand, D. P. et al., "Does ECT Alter Brain Structure?" *American Journal of Psychiatry* 151(7):957–970 (1994).

Fink, M., "Optimizing Electroconvulsive Therapy," *L'Encephale* 20:297–302 (1994).

Kelly, J. P., "Fractures Complicating Electro-Convulsive Therapy and Chronic Epilepsy," *J. Bone Joint Surgery* 36B:70–9 (1954).

Lew, J. K. L., R. F. Eastely and C. D. Hanning, "Oxygenation during Electroconvulsive Therapy," *Anaesthesia* 41:1092–1097 (1986).

McArthur, C. L. and C. T. Rooke, "Are Spinal Precautions Necessary in All Seizure Patients?" *American Journal of Emergency Medicine* 13(5):512–513 (1995).

McCullen, G. M. and C. C. Brown, "Seizure-Induced Thoracic Burst Fractures: A Case Report," *Spine* 19(1):77–79 (1994).

McKenna, G. et al., "Cardiac Arrhythmias during Electroshock Therapy: Significance, Prevention, and Treatment," *Amer. J. Psychiat.* 127:530–533 (1970).

"NIH Consensus Conference," *JAMA* 254(15):2103–2108 (1985).

Posner, J. B., F. Plum and A. V. Poznak, "Cerebral Metabolism during Electrically Induced Seizures in Man," *Arch. Neurol.* 20:388–395 (1969).

Potter, W. Z. and M. V. Rudorfer, "Electroconvulsive Therapy: A Modern Medical Procedure," *New England Journal of Medicine* 328(12):882–883 (1993).

Repke, J. T. and N. G. Berger, "Electroconvulsive Therapy in Pregnancy," *Obstetrics & Gynecology* 63(3-Supplement):39S–41S (1984).

Somogyi, E. and C. G. Tedeschi, "Injury by Electrical Force," in *Forensic Medicine: A Study in Trauma and Environmental Hazards*, vol. 1: *Mechanical*

Trauma, Tedeschi, C. G., W. G. Eckert and L. G. Tedeschi, eds. (Philadelphia: W. B. Saunders, 1977) 645–76.

Valentine, M., K. M. G. Keddie and D. Dunne, "A Comparison of Techniques in Electro-Convulsive Therapy," *Brit. J. Psychiat* 114:989–996 (1968).

Weaver, L. A. et al., "A Comparison of Standard Alternating Current and Low-energy Brief Pulse Electrotherapy," *Biological Psychiatry* 12(4):525–543 (1977).

Youssef, J. A., G. M. McCullen and C. C. Brown. "Seizure-Induced Lumbar Burst Fracture," *Spine* 20(11):1301–1303 (1995).

Chapter 6

Electrical Products and Failures

Synopsis

6.1 Introduction

All products will eventually fail. Nothing that can be made by man will last forever. The applicable definition of "failure" given in the dictionary[1] is

> 1. The condition or fact of not achieving the desired end or ends . . .
> 3. Insufficiency or inadequacy. 4. A cessation of proper functioning.
> 5. Nonperformance of what is requested or expected . . . 7. A decline in strength or effectiveness.

Electrical products fail under these definitions for many reasons: they wear out (e.g., light bulbs or heaters), or they cease to perform their intended function, (e.g., motors or generators), or they loose their effectiveness with age, (e.g., insulation, switches, or personal computers).

The failure of an electrical product can produce many effects such as property damage, personal injury, system safety degradation, or loss of adequate function. Reliable, dependable, electrical products are the goal of electrical manufacturers, system designers and engineers who seek to provide a technology that will be useful to mankind. Electrical products are frequently subjected to reliability analysis and life cycle testing in order to predict their ability to perform dependably.

Because electrical products are used both as end products and as components in other products, it is the purpose herein to describe the function, operation, design, and possible failure mechanisms of several types of frequently used electrical products, without specifically stating how the electrical product's failure contributes to a total product failure. The conclusion in regard to total product failure is left open to interpretation.

6.2 Insulators

Two electrically charged bodies which have a voltage potential difference between them are termed "insulated" from one another when they are separated by a dielectric substance that offers a high resistance to the passage of current between the bodies. An "ideal insulator" has an infinite resistance. Practical insulators have resistance through their material structure that limits the current that can pass through the insulator at operating voltages to an insignificant level.

An example of the application of practical insulation is the plastic PVC insulation used for many wiring applications such as 600 volt rated building wire. Dielectric strength of an insulator is defined as the maximum potential gradient that the material can withstand without rupture. Dielectric strength is frequently expressed as volts per unit of material thickness. For plasticized PVC insulation, the dielectric strength is 425–1,300 V/mil (short time).[2] This translates as a withstand voltage of over 19 kV DC for typical 600-volt, 45-mil thick wire insulation.

In order to break down or rupture such insulation in its originally manufactured form, a sustained (5-minute) overvoltage of more than 9 kV DC would be required.[3] The NEMA standard AC test voltage for this class of insulated wire or cable is 3 kV for five minutes or five times the rated voltage (RMS) of the wire. Breakdown of insulator material appears not only to require sufficient dielectric stress but also a minimum amount of energy.

Practical dielectric strength is affected by material defects, exposure to the service environment, thermal aging, and partial discharges (corona). For unidirectional voltage pulses having rise times of less than a few microseconds, there is a time lag of breakdown, which results in an apparent higher strength for very short pulses.[4] Organic resinous insulating materials, including PVC, are subject to deterioration due to thermal aging. Increasing temperature usually accelerates such effects; the so-called "ten-degree rule" has been classically used to predict the influence of temperature on the useful life of insulating systems. The rule states that for every ten degrees rise in operating temperature, the life of the insulating material would be halved.[5]

Electrical engineers have observed for years that low-voltage small electrical equipment failed essentially from temperature deterioration of the insulation while large systems, such as turbo generators and large motors, are prone to fail more due to electrical and mechanical stresses than temperature.[6]

Electrical insulation must satisfy not only the electrical application requirements but also the mechanical and environmental conditions of the application. Thermal conditions, moisture, and surface dirt contamination can degrade the integrity of insulation. Aged insulation frequently fails primarily due to mechanical stress.

In Chapter 7, the effects of current flow in an electrical conductor are discussed and the resultant heating effect on the conductor's insulation is analyzed. It is temperature degradation that frequently leads to insulation failure under predictable electrical operating conditions such as over voltage swells, surges, and transients. Extremely high voltage and current transients caused by lightning can damage almost any insulation system and can be the primary cause of wiring insulation failure.

Other than lightning, most power disturbances in residential and commercial building wiring systems are limited in magnitude to less than 6 kV and are of extremely short duration (less than a microsecond) at voltages greater than 1 kV.[7] It is therefore highly unlikely that supply voltage transients are the primary cause of insulation breakdown in unaged and unstressed building wiring. Sustained high-voltage stress by the supply can and has caused building wiring failures, but the duration of such a high voltage condition must be fairly long (several minutes). There is usually damage to the connected loads such as appliances or motors as well as damage to the building wire.

Sensitive electronic equipment is highly susceptible to damage from moderate supply voltage transients and surge protection for such equipment is discussed in Chapter 9. Moderately high voltages can damage such equipment by insulation breakdown of the internal wiring, but more often by directly rupturing semiconductor junctions or integrated circuit material layers.

In summary, before there should be suspected damage to building wire and cable insulation due to power transient surge voltage, widespread damage of sensitive electronic equipment and other electrical equipment or appliances should be found. Sustained over voltage conditions by the supply utility will produce early failures in incandescent lamps and motor burnouts throughout the building.

6.3 Switches

An electrical switch is a device designed to close or open, or both, one or more electric circuits. Simply stated, an "ideal switch" is either open (prevents current flow) or closed (allows current to flow unimpeded).

A mechanical switch is actuated by manual, electrical or other suitable means to cause the movable contacts of the switch to close or open. These contacts are connected to two points in an external electric circuit between which a current is intended to flow or must be prevented from flowing.

As an example the switch S, shown schematically in the circuit of Figure 6.1, can turn the light bulb (lamp) on (when closed) or off (when open).

Nonmechanical switching devices operate by means other than by separable mechanical contacts. There are numerous types of solid state devices, which are used to switch electronic signals, and there are power electronic solid state devices available that can switch large currents at high voltages in power systems.

An electric switch fails or at least operates non-ideally when it does not perform the "ideal switch" operations as previously stated. If the switch contacts do not have zero or very low resistance when closed, then the current flow will be impeded and the lamp in Figure 6.1 may glow dimly instead of brightly. If the switch contacts do not have infinite or very high resistance when open, then the lamp may not turn off or continue to glow dimly when it is supposed to be off.

Mechanically, if the switch actuation is not positive, in other words, sufficient to close or open the contacts, then the operation may be intermittent or random and therefore unexpected. The design of mechanical switches almost always uses springs or tension producing mechanisms to

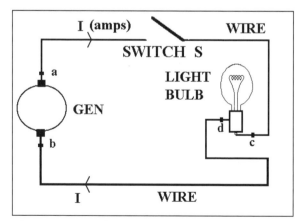

Figure 6.1 Switched circuit

force the switch contacts together and to hold them apart. These forcing mechanisms act to increase contact pressure under closing and to accelerate the motion of the contacts when the switch operates in either direction.

Contact pressure is important in achieving low resistance. Acceleration during opening and closing operations serves to reduce electrical arcing at the contacts. Arcing during both opening and closing is an unavoidable consequence of completing or breaking the electric current flowing through or changing the voltage appearing across the contacts.

Normal arcing at switch contacts eventually causes material loss or deposition at the contact surfaces much as arc welding produces a loss or gain of material between the rod and the work material, depending upon the flow of molten metal during the high temperature created by the arcing process. If the reader is old enough to have worked with mechanical-electrical auto ignition systems, he or she may remember the distributor points (contacts) and their condition after several thousand miles of operation. At one time, automotive mechanics used to file the distributor points to restore them to a relative flat surface and try to correct mistiming of the distributor spark.

The eventual change from smooth to irregular contact surfaces, after millions of electrical switching operations, creates increased contact resistance and therefore increased contact heating due to the I^2R effect and increasing material destruction. Eventually, the switch may fail to provide the ideal zero resistance when closed or infinite resistance when open.

Good switch design employs a sliding or rolling action during closing and opening to self-clean the contact surfaces and help to break any welding attachment of the contacts. Contact material has a major effect on contact resistance, and the use of gold and silver plating of contact surfaces is employed to improve (lower) the contact resistance.

Switches can contribute to electrical product failure in many ways depending upon their use in the product's function. Safety interlocks or emergency stop switch failure can be obvious contributors or proximate causes for accidents involving machinery.

Limit switch or proximity switch failure may cause a control system to malfunction creating a hazardous operating condition in machinery or equipment.

A general principal in product safety for electrical products is to provide high or low limit control to prevent the product from exceeding the safe range of operation prescribed by the product's design and intended use. High limit temperature switches or sensors, high-speed cut-off switches, travel limit switches, and fusing or circuit breakers to prevent excessive circuit current, are all examples of limit control safety features related to electrical product design.

Since switch operation depends upon an external signal (mechanical, electrical, thermal, pneumatic and so forth) to cause the switch contacts to move, the investigation of a suspected switch failure must include these signal sources and their affect on the suspect switch. Very clearly, if an actuator arm is broken or inoperative, the switch will not react to the intended actuator motion. The electrical connections to a switch, which create the switch circuit function, must also be investigated before the switch alone can be suspected of failure.

The switch is a type of electrical product that is frequently used as a component in complex automation systems. In order to predict the automation system's reliability resulting from the use of this component, the automation product engineer uses the switch manufacturer's specifications, which include environmental, electrical, and mechanical testing specifications, to determine the component's suitability for the application and to predict the resultant system reliability.

Examples of the use of mechanical switches include manual control, key operated safety interlocks, travel or motion detection, level sensing and control, and emergency stopping. Typical switch component specifications[8] include temperature range of operation, vibration resistance, shock resistance, mechanical life, rated voltage and current, contact resistance, and repeatability of operation. To ensure safe operation of machinery, machine designers often incorporate an electrical interlock switch or limit switch that prevents machine operation whenever a hazard to the operator exists. A nonworking or failed switch in such products can become the cause of a serious or fatal accident. Such alleged component failures are the basis for many product failure litigations, and if proven, probably represent the most compelling evidence for product failure that can be presented in such cases.

It is essential to recognize that product failure, in the sense of loss of operator protection from dangerous machinery, can be caused not only by component failure but also by circumvention of component function within the machine system.[9] Unless forensic engineering investigation of

the suspect machinery can support a hypothesis of switch failure, including component suitability and application, the question of circumvention
of the protection remains unanswered.

Because human factors and human nature can sometimes be at odds in
machine accidents, the forensic engineer cannot ignore the clever machine operator who has discovered that disabling an electrical interlock
allows faster machine operation, and therefore, personal job enhancement. Hazard [10] has expressed it well: "No system has yet been devised
that will withstand the efforts of mischievous hands."

In the beginning of an investigation of a switch product-related accident, the forensic engineer often learns that the product operated unex-
pectedly, which was one of the dictionary definitions of "failure" given at
the beginning of this chapter. One can conclude, therefore, that (1) the
switch did not operate correctly, because of either an electrical or mechanical malfunction, or (2) a circumvention or tampering of the switch
has occurred.

Regardless of the investigator's supposition of what may be causing a
switch to fail, the switch should never be dissected until all interested parties in the case have reviewed the protocol for disassembly and testing and
are present to witness the activity.[11]

6.4 Relays

Electromechanical relays are switching devices that operate as a result of
electromagnetic, electrostatic, or electrothermic forces created by input
signals. They respond to input signals by physical movement of mechanical parts such as contacts or plungers. Solid state relays use solid state
analog components in their logic elements.

The most basic of uses for relays is to switch an electric circuit. A
relatively low level signal can be used to activate the electromagnetic coil
of a relay in order to switch a high level (current or voltage) circuit,
thereby isolating the low level control circuit from the high level controlled circuit. Relays are used extensively in motor control systems for
starting, braking, reversing, speed control, and protection.

Relays are used to provide many forms of electric circuit protection,
including overload, ground-fault detection and interruption, undervolt-
age, overvoltage, reverse-current, power and phase-rotation protection.

In electric utility power systems protective relaying is used to disconnect a faulty part of the system thereby deenergizing (tripping) that part of the power system and preventing damage to the remaining parts. A protective relay uses the current and voltage information obtained from instrument transformers in the utility power delivery circuits to actuate a warning signal or activate the trip circuit of a high-voltage circuit breaker.

There are a number of causes for the failure or breakdown of a power system. Faults or short circuits can occur between wires as a result of the breakdown of the insulation protecting them. The failure of insulation in power systems (which for bare conductor overhead power lines includes isolation by air) can be due to many factors such as the environment (wind, ice and sleet; large birds bridging the insulators; lightning; interfering trees; contact by high profile vehicles).

There are three characteristics associated with a protective relay that effect its ability to perform adequately: sensitivity, selectivity, and speed.

Sensitivity of a relay refers to the minimum current or voltage required causing the relay to operate. Conditions of operation while under minimum generating capability will produce a fault with the least current and therefore impose the greatest requirement for sensitivity of a relay.

Selectivity refers to the ability of a relay to recognize a fault in a certain part or parts of the system and trip a minimum number of circuit breakers to clear the fault while ignoring breakers in other parts of the system that should not be deenergized. The design of protective relaying for selectivity is an engineering art that requires the selection of relay types and arranging of their location within the electric circuits of the power system.

Speed of a relay/circuit breaker operation is essential to protecting against the potential damage caused by a short circuit or fault. The speed of operation also has a direct effect on power system synchronism and stability.[12]

Modern microprocessor-based relays are available that are capable of optimizing the three characteristics of protective relaying previously discussed as well as providing reclosing, instrumentation and fault data storage.

Modern thermal-magnetic molded case circuit breakers operate as protective relays for lower voltage systems by using thermal sensors (bimetals), hydraulic-magnetic release mechanisms, and/or electronics to provide inverse-time delay to overloads. Larger frame breakers are usually provided with field-adjustable trip levels to facilitate user flexibility in protection selection.

Environmental factors, such as temperature, pressure, humidity, and so forth can adversely affect relay and circuit breaker operation. Circuit breakers are rated to carry a specified load current without interruption over a range of ambient temperature, pressure (or altitude), rated voltage and frequency.

Molded case circuit breakers, by far the largest class of such products, are addressed by UL Standard 489, under which they are required to carry 100 percent of their nameplate current continuously in free air when connected to specified cables at 25°C. Enclosed circuit breakers (e.g., molded case circuit breakers in a metal enclosure such as a box or panelboard) are rated under UL Standard 489 to carry 100 percent of their rated value intermittently (up to 3 hours maximum) and 80 percent continuously in free air when connected to specified cables at 25°C.

Group mounted circuit breakers may require derating of the circuit breaker and cable in room ambient temperatures exceeding 25°C. Molded case circuit breakers are typically available for operation in open or enclosed constructions at 10–50°C. Ambient compensated circuit breakers are capable of operating satisfactorily at higher temperatures than uncompensated devices.

Design altitude for G.E. circuit breakers is 0 to 6,000 feet.[13] At altitudes above 6,000 feet, the thin air affects the heat transfer of the breaker as well as its interrupting capacity, so breakers are derated by an additional 4 percent at altitudes from 6,000 to 10,000 feet.

Application factors such as excessive load break operations; overload tripping, or severe load cycling can adversely affect breaker life.

Specialized forms of relay construction include definite purpose contactors and motor starters. Definite purpose contactors are relays, usually with multiple pole contacts, designed for specific loads such as switching lighting, heating, air conditioning, and service equipment. Motor starters are used to start and stop motors used for machinery and many other industrial applications.

Industrial control relays are also manufactured to provide timing functions for the output switching contacts such as On delay, Off delay, interval timing, repeat cycle operation, and cycle one-shot operation.

These relays are available in field programmable configurations that permit the user to customize the control function. They are manufactured with motor drives, electronic timing and control functions, and pneumatic timing. Many versions of these products include analog and digital displays (alpha numeric forms) with LED status displays available in miniature constructions.[14]

All of the comments previously made regarding the operation, reliability, and potential failure mechanisms for switches apply to electromechanical relays. In addition, since electromechanical relays utilize an input signal to activate a movable contact output, relays can fail or operate unsatisfactorily because of insufficient pickup energy, damaged or open magnetic coils, contact chatter, and electromagnetic interference.

6.5 Electric Fences
by Raymond M. Fish

Electric fences derive their electricity from a power source that may be referred to as a controller, energizer, fence charger, or power unit. The controller may be powered from standard household power lines (120 VAC in the United States), or may be battery operated. The battery may be charged from household power, sunlight, or other means.

Most fence controllers put out short pulses of high voltage about once a second. The output of the controller may be as much as 10,000 volts (pulse voltage). The minimum effective voltage for dairy cows, pigs and horses is 700 volts. For longhaired cattle, sheep, and goats, it is 2,000 volts. One or more fence wires are energized by being connected to one output of the controller (Eftink and Buckingham 1987).

A. Grounding
The ground lead of the controller needs to be connected to a good ground. An 8-foot-long, 0.75-inch galvanized pipe driven almost its full length into the soil is recommended. For dry or frozen ground or very long fences, more than one such pipe may be needed. Using a power line ground can divert lightning striking the power line to the controller and fence, or from the fence to farm wiring. Water hydrants are often insufficient grounds because of the plastic pipes used in water systems. Water

pipe grounds might also cause electric current to leak to livestock watering systems (Eftink and Buckingham 1987).

B. Sparks from electric fences

The high voltage on electric fences can cause sparks when animals or plants come close to or touch the fence. Fire could result if there are flammable vapors nearby. In one case, gasoline was being used to kill bumblebees on a farm, and the gasoline exploded in flames. Action was brought against the farm owner, the manufacturer, and the seller of the electric fence charger used in the area. In this case, one of the injured used a match just prior to the explosion and fire. The fence charger produced a voltage pulse fifty times a minute. The pulse was 10,000 volts and lasted 1/4,000 of a second. With a resistance of 500 ohms (an estimate of the average wire fence resistance), the charger could produce a spark over a one-quarter inch gap (103 Ill.App.3d 154, 158, 430 N.E.2d 670, 674).

C. Fence controllers with continuous AC output

Some fence controllers put out a 60-Hz, several-thousand-volt AC signal. The signal is a somewhat distorted sine wave obtained from a transformer that incorporates means of limiting the current. The current in some models is limited to 10 mA (milliamperes).

D. Respiratory arrest and death from continuous AC fence current

In one case, a three-year-old, thirty-five-pound child was standing with his legs against an electric fence wire and his hands holding a nearby chain link fence. He became unconscious and was pulled from the fence. He was visibly cyanotic (blue). An ambulance was called, and the child was given CPR and was brought to a hospital. However, he could not be resuscitated.

Analysis of this case involves referring to the work of Dalziel (1956), who presented data on "let-go" currents. An adult grasping a conductor will not be able to let go if the current is above a certain level. The person cannot let go because the forearm muscles are stimulated into a forceful sustained contraction, causing the hands to hold on to the electrical conductors. For 60 Hz AC, the let-go current was determined for a number of adults and the "safe" limits estimated. Safe was taken to mean that 99.5

percent of adults would be able to let go, and 0.5 percent (one of two hundred adults) would not be able to let go. Safe let-go currents for 60 Hz AC are 9 mA for men and 6 mA for women. Breathing is "difficult" for currents of 23 mA in men and 15 mA in women, according to Dalziel.

The average let-go threshold (as contrasted with the safe threshold listed just above) is 16 mA for men and 10.5 mA for women for 60 Hz AC. At 10,000 Hz, the average let-go threshold is 75 mA for men and 50 mA for women (Dalziel 1956). The muscles of respiration (intercostal, pectoral, and diaphragmatic) may be stimulated into a continuous, forced contraction along with the forearm muscles. This respiratory paralysis will happen if the current is approximately 18 to 40 milliamperes for the adult (Cabanes 1985; Dalziel and Lee 1968; Lee 1965; Dalziel 1968).

Paralysis of the muscles of respiration with continued circulation of the blood eventually leads to hypoxia and cyanosis. In contrast, persons dying of ventricular fibrillation without preceding hypoxia will usually not be cyanotic (Polson et al. 1985). In a child who was one-quarter the weight of an adult, it is likely that 10 mA of 60-Hz AC current flowing from hands to legs would cause the child to be: (1) unable to let go, and (2) unable to breathe. This would lead to the child being stuck to the fence and being cyanotic, as occurred in this case.

Currents actually needed to cause respiratory paralysis and cardiac arrhythmias in children have not been measured experimentally, and probably never will be. Estimates of the currents needed to cause ventricular fibrillation for persons or animals of various weights have been estimated from animal experiments (Yu et al. 1998).

For a three-second 50 to 60-Hz electric shock, the current required to cause ventricular fibrillation is directly proportional to the weight. This applies to the maximum nonfibrillating current limit (Yu et al. 1998, fig. 4, p. 32). It has been suggested that the direct proportionality of fibrillation current to weight occurs when comparing different species; but within any one type of animal, the fibrillation current is proportional to the square root of the weight (Reilly 1998).

The maximum current that can be applied for five seconds without causing ventricular fibrillation in 99.5 percent of 50-kilogram (110-pounds) adults is $51.9 = 116 / \sqrt{5}$ milliamperes (Dalziel and Lee 1968, pages 473, 476). The ratio of weights for this case is thus $35/110 = 0.318$. The square root of this ratio is 0.564. For a thirty-five-pound child, the maximum current that would not cause ventricular fibrillation would be 16.5 milliamperes assuming the linear relationship. It would be 29.3 milliamperes assuming the square root relationship.

The current expected to cause respiratory paralysis current would be lower. For adults respiratory paralysis will happen if the current is on the order of 18 to 40 milliamperes for a limb-to-limb current pathway in an adult (Cabanes 1985; Dalziel and Lee 1968; Lee 1965; Dalziel 1968). If the direct proportionality between required current and weight associated with ventricular fibrillation also applies to respiratory paralysis, the current needed to cause respiratory paralysis in a thirty-five-pound child would be 5.72 to 12.7 milliamperes. With the square root relationship it would be 10.2 to 22.6 milliamperes.

In the case example, the child was noted to be cyanotic. This means that respiratory paralysis preceded the onset of cardiac arrest. This agrees with the calculations in that the fence controller limiting current (10 milliamperes) was not enough to cause ventricular fibrillation (16.5 to 29.3 milliamperes), but was enough to cause respiratory paralysis (5.72 to 12.7 milliamperes), assuming a linear relationship. Respiratory arrest might also occur assuming the square root relationship (10.2 to 22.6 milliamperes), taking into account the fact that the calculations probably have an uncertainty of more than plus or minus 10 percent.

6.6 Microwave Oven Injuries
by Raymond M. Fish

Burns and nerve injury cased by microwave energy can resemble that caused by electrical current flow through the body. This section compares the injuries caused by these different sources.

Microwave ovens can be associated with injury in several ways. Liquids and solid foods may be overheated. Microwave radiation can leak out and affect nearby persons. Microwaves may interfere with pacemakers and other electronic devices. If used to heat blood, microwave ovens can cause hemolysis (break down of red blood cells) and hyperkalemia (high potassium) in the blood. Safety devices should prevent operation of microwave ovens if the door is open. There have been two reported cases of small children being placed in microwave ovens, an unfortunate form of child abuse.

A. Nerve injury from microwave radiation

Fleck (1983) reported a five-second exposure of both arms from a microwave oven with its door open. There was a pulsating, burning sensation in all fingers during exposure and redness of the dorsum of both hands and forearms. Electromyographic evaluation four years later showed denervation of median, ulnar, and radial nerves in both arms.

B. Steam burns

Steam burns may result when containers such as popcorn bags are opened (Budd 1992). This has led to burns of the cornea and eyelids (De Respinis and Frohman 1990).

C. Burns caused by microwave energy

1. Water content influences heating

Microwave energy will heat tissues based on the water content of the tissue. Thus, muscle will be burned more than subcutaneous fat. In contrast, subcutaneous fat will be burned more than deeper muscle with burns caused by radiant heat, contact immersion, and chemicals. These later agents first contact the outermost tissues and have lesser effect the deeper they penetrate.

2. Non-uniform heating

Microwave ovens heat deep inside food more than on the surface. In contrast, most other ovens heat from the outside with the center of foods remaining colder. Food and the containers of food may feel cool, but the inside of the food may be extremely hot. This is true of solid foods and infant formula bottles (Budd 1992). Oral and other burns may result because of this non-uniform heating.

3. Comparison of microwave and other types of burns

Microwave burns are similar to some electrical burns (and different than conventional oven burns) in that there is often deep injury. With microwaves, there may be burning of the skin and deep muscles, with little damage to the intermediate subcutaneous tissues (Alexander 1987). Microwaves may give more heating in areas of poor blood supply and at tissue interfaces. Furthermore, with microwave burns, there may be a delay between time of injury and signs of skin damage or pain (Budd 1985).

4. Histology

Microwave burns tend to be sharply demarcated. The burns will be expected to be on those parts of the body that were closer to the microwave-emitting device, often in the top of the oven (Surrell 1987). Full thickness skin biopsy at the junction of normal and burned skin should show layered tissue sparing. Such sparing is seen with microwave burns, but not seen with flame, contact, chemical immersion, or electrical burns. Microscopic nuclear streaming that is characteristic of electrical burns will not be seen with microwave burns (see Chapter 16).

D. Case reports of children put in microwave ovens

There were two cases reported of children being put in a microwave oven. The first child needed skin grafts and had no long term adverse effects. The other child required amputations of parts of one leg and one hand (Alexander et al. 1987). Morbidity was due to thermal effects.

The first child was a five-week-old female who was brought to the emergency department by her mother with multiple full-thickness burns totaling 11 percent of the body surface area. The child was alert and irritable. The left hand had full thickness, circumferential burns of all fingers, and full thickness burns of the palmar and volar surfaces. A large, sharply demarcated full thickness burn extended over the left abdomen and left chest. There were also sharply demarcated circumferential full thickness burns on all of the right toes and dorsum of the right foot. There were partial-thickness burns on both anterior upper thighs. The mother said the child had been near the microwave oven, but never in it.

The second child was brought to the emergency department by a teenage baby-sitter with a five-inch by seven-inch second- and third-degree burns of the mid-back. The baby-sitter eventually admitted placing the child in the microwave oven for about sixty seconds. The child had multiple skin grafts. At the time of the article, the child was ten years old and seemed to have no emotional, cognitive or physical effects. Computerized tomography of the head was normal and there were no cataracts.

E. Investigation and treatment of possible microwave burns

The source of microwaves (usually an oven) should be examined for malfunctions and modifications. It should be determined if the victim could have fit into the oven. Biopsy, as described above, can be done to establish the nature of the burn if not otherwise clear. Signs of deeper tissue damage should be sought. For example, stenotic (narrowed) segments of burned bowel may lead to obstruction (Surrell et al. 1987). Thoracic damage may be investigated by chest x-ray. Serum CPK and urine dipstick testing can investigate deep muscle damage. Clinical examination and monitoring are advisable though no guidelines have been established.

6.7 Stun Guns, TASERs® and Related Devices
by Raymond M. Fish

Stun guns, shock batons, TASERs and electric cattle prods (goads) generate high voltages that can be used for self-defense, as weapons, and to control violent people (Robinson 1990). At least, one hundred companies around the world are marketing stun guns and related devices. This section discusses experimental results and clinical reports concerning stun guns and TASERs. Physiological effects of the devices on people will be discussed.

The approval of such devices by governmental agencies has been criticized. Such approval has been based, at least in some instances, on theoretical calculations rather than testing on humans or animals (O'Brien 1991).

A. Stun guns
1. Construction
Stun guns are hand-held devices that usually contain a 9-volt battery and two pairs of electrodes. The outer pair of electrodes are spaced about two inches apart and point forward; these can be pressed against the skin of an attacker. The outer electrodes may be sharp, so as to cause penetration of the skin. The inner pair of electrodes are usually spaced less than an inch apart and are pointed towards each other; arcing of current occurs between the inner electrodes (Robinson 1990). In the stun gun, a capacitor is charged slowly and then is rapidly discharged. A step-up transformer or other circuitry raises the voltage.

2. Output characteristics
Voltage pulses of up to 50 kV (50,000 volts) at repetition rates between 5 and 20 pulses per second are produced by some stun guns. Pulse

duration can vary from 20 nanoseconds to 20 microseconds (Roy and Podgorski 1989; Welsh 1997). Two different modes of operation commonly occur. If stun gun electrodes are in contact with the skin, a relatively slow rising current waveform will result. This resembles a damped sinusoid with a rise time of a few microseconds and a current of up to 3.8 amperes. If electrodes are separated from the skin by a thick layer of clothing, an electrical discharge (spark over) gives a somewhat triangular pulse with a rise time of a few nanoseconds. At an air gap of 3 mm, the current spike can have a duration of 20 nanoseconds and a peak current of 190 amperes (Roy and Podgorski 1989). These characteristics and numbers vary greatly depending on the circuitry of particular devices and conditions of use.

B. TASERs: Construction and output

The TASER (Thomas A. Swift's Electric Rifle) fires two barbed darts connected to a gun by wires. A small gunpowder charge or compressed gas gives the barbs an initial muzzle velocity of 55 meters/second. The TASER is primarily used by police. Some models have been classified as a firearm by the federal government and have been designated a weapon by some courts. The maximum range is about 18 feet, and the wires are connected to a source of 10 to 15 pulses per second of 50,000 volts. The cassette of the TASER can be removed and replaced by extendible 12-inch electrodes, allowing the TASER to function as a stun gun (Burdett-Smith 1997).

C. Effects on animals and people

Stun gun effects have been described depending on the length of discharge. For up to 0.5 second, the victim is startled and repelled. One to 2 seconds of current discharge will cause the victim to lose the ability to stand. Discharges of 3 to 5 seconds will leave the victim immobilized, dazed, and weak for five to fifteen minutes (Robinson 1990). Effects vary greatly, depending on characteristics of the particular device, placement of electrodes, distance between electrodes, and the condition of the person being TASERed. Thus, expected effects may not occur in some cases.

1. Cardiac arrest

Experiments were conducted by Roy and Podgorski (1989) on pigs. It is thought that the response of a pig's heart to electrical stimulus is similar to that of the human heart. Two normal Yorkshire pigs, weighing 40 and 52 kg were used, with a stun gun being applied to the intact chest, the exposed pericardium, or the intact chest of an animal with an implanted pacemaker. The animals were anesthetized with valium, Ketamine and fluothane. The following occurred.

- When the stun gun was discharged through three layers of operating room towels (to simulate clothing) over the animal's skin, the blood pressure dropped to near zero. Lack of blood pressure persisted as long as the stun gun was on. A normal rhythm and blood pressure returned when the gun was turned off.
- When the stun gun was applied to the chest of an animal with an implanted pacemaker, ventricular fibrillation resulted. This was probably because of the current carried to the heart by the pacemaker leads rather than by any effect on the pacemaker itself.

2. Additional TASER effects

The patient shot with a TASER will likely be immobilized with two to three seconds of applied current; this will occur even if there is no skin contact or penetration because the current can pass through two inches of clothing. Treatment of patients shot with a TASER includes treatment for the condition that caused them to be shot, such as toxic psychosis. Other injuries and conditions related to the person's current state (often trauma and drug use) must also be addressed. Several patients have had cardiac arrest, or respiratory arrest followed by cardiac arrest, within five to twenty-five minutes of being shot with the TASER (Ordog et al. 1987). Such cases are usually complicated by concurrent drug use, trauma due to struggling or pre-existing heart disease.

Theoretical complications of TASER use may arise if the eye or a blood vessel is penetrated, or there is secondary trauma from a fall. Reported injuries include contusions, abrasions, lacerations, mild rhabdomyolysis (muscle breakdown with breakdown products going into the blood and kidneys) and testicular torsion (Ordog et al. 1987).

Stun guns produce a superficial inflammatory response (skin lesions) without significant tissue destruction. The lesions may initially be red and slightly raised, but usually become flat and do not scar. Postinflammatory loss of pigment may develop and is more noticeable in people with dark or tanned skin (Frechette and Rimsza 1992).

D. Debate concerning lethal effects

Many of those who die after having a TASER applied to them have been taking illicit drugs. Such substances have been associated with deaths in the absence of the application of electricity. On the other hand, many people who have had toxic concentrations of drugs and chemicals in their systems have died by other means (Dix and Calaluce 1998), or have not died at all. To determine the relevance of drugs, application of electricity, physical trauma, and other factors, each case must be carefully examined, taking into account (if possible) the times events took place and autopsy findings.

The use of TASERs to control violent people is usually safer than alternative methods (Ordog et al. 1987).

6.8 Electronic Devices

Nearly all modern electronic circuits employ semiconductor technology, either in the form of discrete components such as transistors and diodes, or in the form of solid state integrated circuits (ICs) that utilize microchips to fabricate complex electronic circuits. ICs with more than one million devices per chip are currently being produced and one billion device chips are projected to arrive shortly after the turn of the century.

The semiconductor evolution that began shortly after World War II with the Bell Laboratories invention of the transistor, has taken us with breakneck speed from vacuum technology electronics to personal computers, hand-held cellular telephones, VCRs and a truly staggering array of consumer, commercial and industrial products. The first cost of semiconductor devices is only part of the explanation for this revolution in electronics. More important than initial price, these products are less expensive to own and operate due to reduced energy and maintenance costs; moreover, they are highly reliable.

Vacuum devices require a power supply with voltage in the 100- to 1,000-plus-volt class, and the most widely used types depend upon a thermionic emission of electrons from a heated cathode. Older electrical engineers have been known to refer to vacuum tubes as "Watt-sucking fire bottles" because of their input power and environmental heat dissipation requirements. Any one who has replaced a tube in an old radio or TV set can recall the requirement for turning off the power to let the tubes cool down before touching them with a bare hand. There was also considerable personal electrical shock risk involved in approaching the energized circuitry of a vacuum tube electronic product.

Most semiconductor devices and circuits operate with power supplies in the 1- to 50-volt class at less than 10 watts of input power. Modern PCs may require up to 500-watt power supplies, but the power supply is handling multiple loads including cooling fans, lights, hard disk drives and peripherals. The DC output voltage of such supplies is typically ±5 volts and ±12 volts at total load currents of less than 22 amps.

Modern semiconductors use materials such as silicon and gallium arsenide that have a relatively small number of electrons in their conduction band (upper energy level), a number that can be easily changed by doping (adding impurities). Conductors, on the other hand, have a large number of free electrons and are not sensitive to doping.

The weak fields in semiconductors cause the charge carriers, electrons, and holes (missing electrons) to be easily affected such that conduction of current in the material is sensitive to small magnitude and polarity changes by an externally applied signal. Semiconductors are called n or p-type depending upon the majority charge carrier, n-type for electrons, p-type for holes. By applying a properly polarized external signal, it is possible to inject minority carriers into the majority carrier region from the external source, but it is impossible to alter the charge density of the material by injecting majority carriers. This process, termed carrier injection, was discovered by Bell Laboratories scientists in 1949[15] and is the origin of the transistor principle.

A three terminal semiconductor, bipolar npn or pnp transistor, can be operated such that a low input power signal can be used to produce an increased change in the output power level. When operated in this mode, the semiconductor becomes a signal amplifier and forms one of the most important components in electronic circuits.

ICs utilize a silicon or gallium arsenide wafer to form a continuous substrate on or within which are placed interconnected circuit elements such as transistors, diodes, resistors, capacitors, inductors, and conductors. The patterning and arrangement of these circuit elements determines the ICs function. Microprocessors and DRAMS (memory) are examples of the highest-order ICs.

Semiconductors are theoretically capable of operating forever unless some external force such as high ambient temperature or extreme electrical stressor damages them. When operated within their design limitations, semiconductors are non-aging. For example, they do not use up material such as crystalline atomic structure and electrons. However, because of their sensitivity to electrical signals, semiconductors are easily damaged, and even low level electrical disturbances can destroy junctions and perforate material stratum to cause the device to fail.

6.9 Sensors—General

A sensor is an electrical system element that responds quantitatively to a physical condition or property such as temperature, pressure, velocity, distance, electric or magnetic fields, illumination, radiation and so on. Analog sensors produce an electrical signal (i.e., voltage, current, resistance) that is continuous and varying in proportion to the measured physical property. Sensors can also act as switches by operating contacts when a physical quantity reaches a certain value or set point.

Analog sensors are frequently used as the primary detectors in automatic control systems where they perform the initial conversion to an electrical signal that is compared to a standard representing the desired performance of the physical condition to be controlled. In closed-loop control systems with feedback, any measured (sensed) deviation from the standard is fed back into the control system in a manner such that it will reduce the deviation of the controlled quantity from the standard.

A closed-loop control system can be shown schematically as in Figure 6.2.

The sensor in Figure 6.2 converts a physical condition to an electrical signal that can be directly compared to the reference electrical signal. The resulting error signal is converted by the control system to a proportional change in the desired physical condition. When the physical condition matches (becomes equal to) the reference, the error is zero and no change is made to the physical condition.

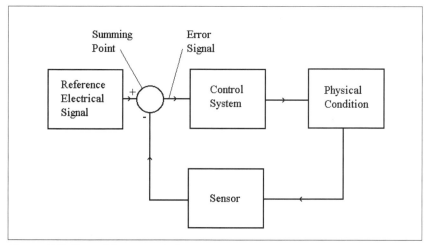

Figure 6.2 *Closed-loop control system*

In an analog (continuous) closed-loop control system, the error signal is continuous and the physical condition is continuously adjusted. In a sampled data closed-loop control system if the rate is slow, the adjustments in the physical condition will be slow and additional error can be created. This is to say that a sampled data control system must have a sampling rate that is high enough in relation to the changing physical condition to adequately characterize the condition within desired error bounds.

A third type of automatic control system has become technically and economically feasible because of advances in modern digital computer technology. Not only can the continuous system be digitized in time (sampled data), but the magnitude of the continuous signals can be converted to digital code for data-processing and decision making by a computer. The control system is then referred to as a digital control system that generically includes

- a controlled physical condition,
- control elements,
- digital-to-analog converters (D/A),
- analog-to-digital converters (A/D), and a
- digital computer or data processor (PC).

When a sensor is used as the primary detector in an automatic control system, the performance of the control system is dependent upon the accuracy of conversion by the sensor. For example, a thermostatically controlled oven may use a variable component setting to establish the standard temperature which is then compared to the sensor measured temperature (voltage, current or resistance). If the sensor conversion from temperature to electrical parameter is inaccurate, then the comparison of this signal to the standard is flawed and an erroneous differential error signal is fed back to the heating control for the oven. The result of this sensor malfunction may be to create a runaway heating increase causing the oven temperature to increase without limit. The proximate cause of this oven product failure is a faulty sensor leading to a control system failure, not a failure in the heat-producing element of the product.

6.10 Thermal Sensors

The oldest form of temperature sensor, which has been in use since the early part of this century, is the bimetal switch or filled Bourdon tube used to make or break a contact (switch). Most residential thermostats today use the bimetal switch that has the advantages of being low in cost and having relatively high reliability. The disadvantages of the bimetal switch are its limited accuracy, sensing range, and low vibration tolerance; also, the bimetal switch is not an analog device, so it cannot provide a continuous signal proportional to the measured temperature.

The thermocouple is an analog sensing device consisting of two different metal wires joined at one end. A voltage is developed between the open-end of the wires due to the thermoelectric or Seebeck effect when the junctions are at different temperatures. By connecting the open end of the wires to a properly scaled milliammeter, temperature is converted to current. The thermocouple, in addition to providing an analog output, has improved accuracy and wider temperature sensing range than the bimetal switch. Its disadvantages are varying calibration depending upon wire length and the need to use the same wire material for the entire length of the thermocouple. Connecting a group of thermocouples in series aiding creates a thermopile. The thermopile can be used to measure radiant energy (heat) or to act as a source of electric energy.

Other modern forms of heat radiation sensors include the resistance temperature detector (RTD), the thermistor, and pyroelectric materials. The RTD is a resistor made of a material for which the electrical resistivity is a known function of the temperature. A common form of the RTD is the copper-constantan thermometer.

The thermistor is an electronic device that makes use of the change of resistivity of a semiconductor with change in temperature. Pyroelectric materials are polar dielectrics in which internal dipole moment is temperature dependent. They are used to detect infrared radiation in such devices as intruder alarms, energy conservation control systems, pollution monitors, fire and flame detectors, and thermal imaging devices like night vision binoculars. The major advantages of these materials, in comparison with competing infrared detectors, are that no cooling is necessary, they are inexpensive, and they consume little power.

6.11 Pressure Sensors

The most common pressure sensor is the metal wire strain gage that is created by fixing wire to an immovable anchor at one end and to a deformable element at the other. The wire's resistance varies in proportion to its length, which is constant for constant temperature. Using a cantilever beam structure where the free end of the beam moves in response to acceleration force one can also use the metal wire strain gage to measure acceleration.

Piezoelectric sensors are used to measure pressure, for example, in strain gauges, vibration sensors, and accelerometers. Piezoresistors are produced from semiconductors that produce a change in resistance when subjected to strain force. A piezoelectric crystal is a material that becomes electrically polarized when mechanically strained. Such crystals are used in microphones and loudspeakers since the crystal responds reciprocally; in other words, applied pressure creates electric voltage and an externally applied voltage will create a mechanical displacement of the crystal material.

6.12 Light Sensors

The most commonly used modern device for visible light detection is the photodiode. A p-n junction semiconductor diode will respond to incident light radiation by producing an externally measurable current. The current is proportional to the light intensity and also depends upon the frequency of the incident light. Since the p-n junction responds reciprocally—an applied external current can create a light output—photodiodes are also used as light-emitting diodes and can generate specific wavelengths by design of the material used for the diode compound.

Photovoltaic cells directly convert radiant energy into small electrical current and voltage. PV cells are also called solar cells that are produced as large area semiconductor p-n junction diodes. Photovoltaic applications range from sensors for instrumentation and control to electric power sources having capacities from milliwatts to megawatts.

Photoemissive tubes are vacuum or gas tube devices that use a photocathode that emits electrons when irradiated. They have excellent short-term stability and high speed response. Modern semiconductor devices are largely replacing tube sensors for many applications.

Photo tubes have been used for many years to detect objects in automatic door controls. Solid state photoelectric sensors have largely supplanted tube sensors because they are less expensive, have higher reliability, and can be packaged for miniature and micro applications. Solid state PE sensors also operate at much lower voltage and power levels than vacuum tube sensors so that sensor power supply costs, size, and input power requirements are reduced.

Photomultiplier tubes are the most sensitive of light sensors, but they require high voltage power supplies ranging from 700 to 3,000 volts. They can be used to detect very low light levels and for measurement of the statistical properties of light by detecting the arrival of individual photons.[16]

6.13 Chemical Sensors

Ion-selective electrodes (ISEs) are used to measure the concentration of a specific ion in a multiple-ion solution. A membrane that selectively generates a potential dependent upon the ion of interest is used. The pH electrode uses a sodium glass membrane that has a high exchange rate for H+. The electric potential that develops across the membrane when the glass tube with the membrane closing one end is immersed in a test solution can be measured with respect to a reference electrode placed in the same test solution. This potential difference is proportional to log (H^+) and a one pH unit change corresponds to a factor of ten change in molar concentration of H^+.

6.14 Biosensors

Most biosensors require multiple transduction mechanisms to produce an electrical output. Two examples are the immunosensor and the enzyme sensor. When used for glucose sensing, the enzyme sensor involves two chemical-to-chemical transductions and a chemical-to-electrical transduction.[17]

6.15 Smart Sensors

Smart sensors utilize smart materials that have inherent intelligence and self-adaptive capabilities to external stimuli.[18] Fiber-optic based sensors, for example, are based on changes in optical effects such as refractive index, optical absorption, luminescence, and chromic properties caused by changes in the environment in which the fiber is imbedded. Strain, thermal, and electromagnetic properties of the environment are transduced by such sensors. Other forms of smart sensors include pizeoelectric-based sensors, magnetostriction-based, shape-memory-based, electromagnetics-based, and electroacoustic smart sensors.[19]

Endnotes

1. *Webster's II: New Riverside University Dictionary* (Boston: Riverside Publishing Company, 1988).

2. H. S. Adams, "Problems in Insulated Wire and Cable in Space-Vehicle Systems," *Electrotechnology* 72(3):13 (1963).

3. National Electrical Manufacturers Association (NEMA), Std. Publ. No. WC 5, *Thermoplastic Insulated Wire and Cable for theTransmission and Distribution of Electrical Energy,* ICEA Pub. No. S-61-402 (Washington, DC: National Electrical Manufacturers Association, 1993), 15.

4. Donald G. Fink and H. Wayne Beaty, eds., *Standard Handbook for Electrical Engineers* (NY: McGraw-Hill, 1993), 4-125.

5. Emanuel L. Brancato, "An Update on Multifactor Aging," *Electrical Insulation Magazine*, September-October 1998, 23.

6. Ibid., 23.

7. Institute of Electrical and Electronics Engineers, Inc. (IEEE), *IEEE Recommended Practice on Surge Voltages in Low-Voltage AC Power Circuits*, ANSI C 62.41-1991 (NY: IEEE, 1991).

8. *Telemecanique Automation Controls Catalog* (White Plains, NY: Square D Company, 1992).

9. Irving F. Hazard, "The Circumvention and Failure of Electrical Interlock Switches," *Journal of the National Academy of Forensic Engineers* 11(1):23–46 (1994).

10. Ibid., 32.

11. Ibid., 38.

12. General Electric Co., *The Art of Protective Relaying*, (Philadelphia: General Electric Co., Power Systems Management Business Dept., 1972), GET-1206A.

13. General Electric Company, *General Electric Specifier's Guide,* EESG 1-F-60 0291, 1991 (Plainsville, CT: General Electric Company, 1991), 31.

14. W. W. Grainger, Inc., *Grainger 2003 Catalog*, http://www.grainger.com.

15. W. Shockley, G. L. Pearson and J. R. Hayes, "Hole Injection in Germanium-Qualitative Studies and Filamentary Transistors," *Bell System Technical Journal* 28:344–366 (1949).

16. Richard C. Dorf, ed., *The Electrical Engineering Handbook* (Boca Raton: CRC Press, 1993), 755.

17. Ibid., 1159.

18. Ibid., 1173–1174.

19. Ibid., 1182–1183.

References for Section 6.5

Cabanes, J., "Physiological Effects of Electric Currents on Living Organisms, More Particularly Humans," in *Electrical Shock Safety Criteria: Proceedings of the First International Symposium on Electrical Shock Safety Criteria,* Bridges, J. E. et al., eds. (NY: Pergamon Press, 1985), 7–24.

Dalziel, C. F. and W. R. Lee, "Lethal Electric Currents," *1968. IEEE Spectrum* (6):44–50 (1969).

Dalziel, C. F., "Effects of Electrical Shock on Man," *IRE Transactions on Medical Electronics* PGME-5:44–62 (1956).

Dalziel, C. F., "Reevaluation of Lethal Electric Currents," *IEEE Transactions on Industry and General Applications* IGA-4(5):467–476 (1968).

Eftink, B. and F. Buckingham. "Successful Farming Tests the Imported Fences," *Successful Farming* 85:48–50 (1987).

Lee, W. R., "The Mechanisms of Death from Electric Shock," *Medicine, Science, and the Law* 5(1):23–28 (1965).

Polson, C. J., D. J. Lee and B. Knight, *The Essentials of Forensic Medicine*, 4th ed. (NY: Pergamon Press, 1985), 281.

Reilly, J. Patrick, *Electrical Stimulation and Electropathology* (NY: Springer, 1998), 221.

Yu, L., M. Chow and J. Bowen, "Safety and Ground Fault Protection in Electrical Systems," *WEE Industry Applications Magazine* March-April 1998, 32–36; IEEE, previously published as "Permissible Body Current Limit," in *IEEE Guide for Safety in AC Substation Grounding* (NY: IEEE Press, 1986), 31–33.

References for Section 6.6

Alexander, R. C., J. A. Surrell and S. D. Chole. "Microwave Oven Burns to Children: An Unusual Manifestation of Child Abuse," *Pediatrics* 79(2):255–260 (1987).

Budd, R., "Burns Associated with the Use of Microwave Ovens," *Journal of Microwave Power and Electromagnetic Energy* 27(3):160–163 (1992).

Budd, R. A., "Can Microwave/Radio-frequency Radiation (RFR) Burns Be Distinguished from Conventional Burns?" *Journal of Microwave Power and Electromagnetic Energy* 20(1):9–11 (1985).

De Respinis, P. A. and L. P. Frohman, "Microwave Popcorn: Ocular Injury Caused by Steam," [letter] *New England Journal of Medicine* 323(17):1212 (1990).

Fleck, H., "Microwave Oven Burn," *Bulletin of the New York Academy of Medicine* 59:313–317 (1983).

Surrell, J. A. et al., "Effects of Microwave Radiation on Living Tissue," *Journal of Trauma* 27(8):935–939 (1987).

References for Section 6.7

Burdett-Smith, Peter, "Stun Gun Injury," *Journal of Accident and Emergency Medicine* 14:402–404 (1997).

Dix, J. and R. Calaluce, *Guide to Forensic Pathology* (St. Louis: Jay Dix, 1998), 67, 71–72.

Frechette, A. and M. E. Rimsza, "Stun Gun Injury: A New Presentation of the Battered Child Syndrome," *Pediatrics* 89(5):898–901 (1992).

O'Brien, D. J. "Electronic Weaponry: A Question of Safety," *Annals of Emergency Medicine* 20:583–587 (1991).

Ordog G. J. et al., "Electronic Gun (Taser) Injuries," *Annals of Emergency Medicine* 16:73–78 (1987).

Robinson, M. N., C. G. Brooks and G. D. Renshaw, "Electric Shock Devices and Their Effects on the Human Body," *Med. Sci. Law* 30:285–300 (1990).

Roy, O. Z. and A. S. Podgorski, "Tests on a Shocking Device: The Stun Gun," *Medical & Biological Engineering & Computing* 27:445–448 (1989).

Chapter 7

Fires of Electrical Origin

7.1 Introduction

For an electrical energy source to be the proximate cause for a fire, electrical energy must be converted into sufficient heat energy that is then transmitted to a quantity of combustible material. Naturally an atmosphere with an adequate oxygen supply is necessary for the fire to perpetuate.

Usually investigators in fire cause and origin, such as fire technicians and fire department arson investigators, are the first on the scene. They seek to agree on an area of damage and possibly on a point of origin for the fire. Subsequently, and before an electrical causation theory can be advanced, there must be confirmed electrical energy present within the structure and specifically within the area of origin or at the point of origin of the fire. The determination of what specific electrical equipment, material, and system was involved, and what conditions were necessary to initiate the fire constitutes the rigorous scientific basis of investigation leading to the advancement of an electrical causation theory. The possibility of an electrical origin must then be ranked along with other possibilities for the most probable causation to be concluded.

In order to prove electrical causation the point of initial combustion must be in relatively close proximity to a source of electrically heated material unless arcing is the suspected proximate cause. Heat transfer between an electrically heated material and a combustible is essential for electrical fire initiation. If arcing is the suspected origin, then the initial point of combustion may be somewhat more removed from the electrical source; however, a physically acceptable path for sparks or heated metal explosions from the arc must exist unless the arcing occurs in an incendiary atmosphere.

Vague theories of conductor overheating or arcing of wiring in the area of origin without specific evidence and a scientific explanation for the cause of such defects will not survive the logical scrutiny of technical electrical experts or attorneys. Such statements as "Since electricity was the only energy source in the area of origin, it must have started the fire," will not suffice.

7.2 Electrical Ignition—Arcs

An electrical arc is a result of the breakdown of insulation between two conductors of different potential voltages. As the breakdown begins, stray electrons are drawn under the force of the electrical field between the two conductor surfaces from one to the other. If the field intensity is great enough, these stray electrons will gain enough energy between molecular collisions to ionize the material separating the conductors which further liberates electrons to produce additional ionization: the ensuing chain reaction or electron avalanche results in an arc.

A round figure for the electric field intensity necessary to create an arcing breakdown between 10-cm (diameter) spherical electrodes in air (at 760 mm Hg, 25°C) is 75,000 DC volts per inch. This decreases to 20 kV per inch for needlepoint electrodes.[1] The minimum voltage differential necessary to produce an electrical arc between flat plate conductors in air has been determined experimentally to be approximately 350 volts with 0.01mm (0.39 mil) separation.[2,3] Increasing the separation requires increased voltage for arcing to occur; for example, at 1 mm, the arcing voltage is 4,500 volts. The arcing voltage is reduced when the gas between the conductors has greater conductivity than air, such as when vaporized carbonaceous materials are created during a fire. In a fire, we find that electrical arcing between conductors can occur with as little as 100-V peak between conductors.

During the arcing process, which follows the same physical principles as arc welding, temperatures from 6,000°F to more than 23,000°F can be created.[4] Such heat can melt or vaporize most metals and the violent striking and restriking of the arc can eject small super heated sparks from the metallic materials.

Vaporized copper in an electrical arc can expand about 30,000 times its solid state volume.[5] Electric arcs can readily start fires when combustibles are nearby. However, for the arcing to begin either the insulation between the conductors must fail or the applied voltage difference must exceed the breakdown potential of the insulation. In most fires, the electric wiring is exposed to heat in the range from 400 to 2,000°F[6,7] and the insulation fails either by becoming soft and flowing off the conductor or by burning in the fire. If the wiring remains energized during the fire, there is frequently evidence of arcing found in the wiring. Such arcing evidence by itself cannot indicate that the fire was caused electrically.

All switching devices can create normal electrical arcs at their contacts during the making or breaking process. This includes ordinary toggle switches, thermostats, relays, and motor starters. If an explosive atmosphere is present in a space where a switching device will be operated, the possibility of arc ignition of the atmosphere is likely. Fortunately, we have few spaces in our environment where explosive atmospheres are ordinarily present and where such explosive hazards exist; the NEC mandates certain types of electrical equipment and installation methods to reduce the possibility of an electrically produced explosion.

Chapter 5 stated that many commonly used products utilize high-voltage circuits in their operation. Television sets, personal computers, fluorescent and high-intensity discharge light fixtures, neon signs, and neon light fixtures all incorporate high-voltage circuits for their operation, some in excess of 6,000 volts. High voltages stress insulation, particularly 600-V rated conductor insulation, and a circuit failure in such products may lead to high voltage-induced arcing which can produce a fire. Such products are arcing causation suspects if found within the area of origin in a fire.

Static electrical charges results when usually nonconductive materials come into contact and then separate. The transfer of electrons between bodies results in one becoming negatively charged by gaining electrons and the other becoming positively charged by giving up electrons. The equal but oppositely charged bodies then create an electric field in the space between them and if the insulative gap between them is small enough, an electrical energy release will occur, producing a static spark. In order to "feel static shock," about 4000 volts must exist between the body and the grounded material.

Common sources of static electricity are (1) contact of footwear with floor coverings while moving, (2) moving small bodies of material on conveyor belts, in pneumatic tubes or through troughs, (3) discharging of liquids from a constricted opening in a hose or pipe with moisture or small particulates present, (4) moving vehicles with nonconductive wheels or tires, (5) nonconductive moving belts such as power drives or conveyors, (6) thunderstorms (see Chapter 9 on lightning) and (7) electromagnetic field induction (see Chapter 5).

The electrical energy available in a static discharge can be expressed as

$$E = C \frac{V^2}{2} \qquad \text{(Equation 7.1)}$$

where E is the energy in joules, C is the capacitance of the charged body in farads and V is the voltage across the gap between bodies in volts.

Only when the arc energy equals or exceeds the minimum ignition energy of an exposed fuel will an ignition occur. Not all of the stored energy expressed by Equation 7.1 is dissipated in the arc. Some of this available static electrical energy is expended in heating of the material surfaces (electrodes). Experimental results have shown that arc voltages of at least 1,500 volts are required to ignite common flammable gases. Minimum ignition energies for gases begin at approximately 0.02 millijoules.[8] Dusts and fibers require 10 to 100 times more discharge energy than gases and vapors for ignition by arcs in optimum air mixtures.[9]

Static electrical discharge from the human operators of motor vehicles during the commercial refueling process have resulted in explosions of the gasoline vapor that accumulates near the gas tank filler tube.[10] Automotive batteries can produce electrical arcs, particularly when fully charged and shorted by low impedance from energized-to-ground terminals. Loss of metal in the arc area is indicative of a sustained arcing condition and other symptoms are likely to occur simultaneously such as headlight flicker and engine stalling.

Lead acid automotive and vehicle batteries are sources of hydrogen and oxygen gas generation during normal operation, and such gases are vented to the atmosphere. Excessive charging rates can create substantial heat and explosive gas concentrations. Internal as well as external arcing can produce gas ignition and an explosion. Hydrogen explosions involving lead acid storage batteries generally take place in battery charging rooms that are inadequately ventilated.

Harry S. Dixon has proposed a more likely scenario for battery explosions.[11] Dr. Dixon advances "BLEVE" as the most logical explanation for the explosion of mobile equipment batteries under heavy discharge conditions such as starting motor operation. "BLEVE" stands for boiling liquid expanding vapor explosions, which result from the superheating of the liquid electrolyte in the battery case to the point that it suddenly flashes into the vapor or steam stage with an attendant large increase in volume; in the case of water, this increase is approximately 1,500 times. This large volumetric increase within the battery can produce forces that cause the battery case to explode.

7.3 Electrical Ignition—Overheating

Electrical current flowing through any material creates heat according to the relationship $P = I^2R$. When the resistance of a material is expressed in ohms and current is expressed in amps, the power is expressed in rate of heat energy transfer to the material in watts. Watts can be expressed in Btu per hour by the conversion factor 1 watt = 3.412 Btu/hr.

The current flowing in an electrical conductor such as a branch circuit wire or feeder cable produces joule heating of the conductor which is uniformly distributed along the length of the wire. If the heat generated is not dissipated by conduction, convection, and radiation to the surrounding environment at a rate sufficient to stabilize the conductor temperature at a value below the maximum recommended service temperature of the wire insulation, the insulation can be damaged, particularly if the overheating is prolonged. Maximum service temperatures for thermoplastic polymers range from 65°C to 260°C or 149°F to 500°F.[12] The NEC publishes maximum operating temperatures for general service conductors in Article 310.

Electrical current heating at a poor connection can generate high temperature. Poor electrical connections are defined as series electrical contact points that exhibit high resistance. Very small contact areas and insufficient pressure are frequently the cause of poor electrical connections;

although corrosion and contamination of the conductor contact surfaces can also be a cause for poor connections.

As little as 12 amps flowing through a contact with 0.1 ohm of resistance can create a temperature rise in excess of 700°F at the connection.[13,14] When such a connection is formed by a poor wiring splice or an insufficiently torqued screw connector at a wiring device, the localized heating may cause damage to the adjacent wiring insulation or electrical components. This can lead to arcing or fire initiation by heat energy transfer to combustibles.

The fire investigator who suspects electricity as a cause must take care to consider all possible current paths within the electrical system. A poorly grounded system may cause fault current to return through normally non-current-carrying paths that are not immediately obvious. A well grounded electrical system with adequate ground conductor sizing and good electrical continuity from service entrance to the branch circuit loads will not be capable of starting a fire due to return path overheating.

An overheated conductor or connection may not produce arcing, but the transfer of heat to adjacent combustibles can produce a fire. Since current flow must always complete a circuit returning to the source, it is sometimes the case that metallic electrical conduits, metallic water pipes, metal structures, and even metal decorations attached to a building carry all or portions of the return current to the service. These conditions usually arise when a ground fault occurs in older inadequately grounded systems. Since most of these return paths have significantly higher resistance than copper wire, the heat generated in such material will be appreciable even with modest electrical fault current. For example, 2 amps flowing through a 60-ohm resistance generates heat at a rate of 240 watts (819 Btu/hr). As little as 5 watts per square cm is sufficient to ignite many combustibles.[15]

Electrical current flows through parallel paths inversely as their resistance, such that the low resistance grounding conductor path takes most of the current and the high resistance inadvertent path takes very little. For example, let the total circuit resistance of a branch circuit that normally conducts 12 amps equal 10 ohms, of which the supply and return conductors together have 0.3 ohms of resistance. Now if an alternate parallel path to the return conductor is created which has 10 ohms of resistance, this path will carry only about 0.2 amp and generate heat at a rate of less than 0.4 watt.

Most common types of appliance and extension cords used in the U.S. use two and three conductor all plastic, parallel, flexible cords. Appendix 7A presents an analysis of the temperature rise for No. 18 through No. 10 AWG cords in the three types of NEC recognized type SPT constructions[16] for the case of current carrying two- and three-conductor cords in air.

Analyses are also made for the cases of No. 16 AWG cords (1) lying on a hardwood floor in air and (2) under carpet. A comparative analysis is also made for the case of three-conductor (with ground) No. 18 AWG cord in air. The plots of temperature increase above 30°C (86°F) ambient, as a function of current for these cords, are given for each of the cases analyzed in Appendix 7A.

The results derived indicate that these cords should be derated for ambient temperatures in excess of the NEC standard of 30°C (86°F). This information should be of interest to fire investigators who must consider the possibility of appliance or extension cord conductors overheating. The safe current carrying capacity of a No. 16 2/C cord lying on a hardwood floor under carpet with a rubber pad is shown in Appendix 7A, Figure 7.5 to be approximately 7 amps, not 13 amps as given by the NEC in Table 400-5(A). In the author's opinion, it was not intended by the NEC that flexible appliance or extension cords be used under carpet or rugs; however, experience shows that users of such cords continue to place these conductors under such floor coverings.

Flexible cords not smaller than No.18 are permitted under the NEC Art. 400.13 to be considered as protected against overcurrent by 20-ampere circuits; similarly No. 16 cord and larger are protected against overcurrent by 30-ampere circuits. Based upon the data derived in Appendix 7A, *the maximum overcurrent protection of 30 amps for a No. 16 cord lying on a hardwood floor under carpet would exceed the safe current carrying capacity of the cord by 429 percent. In most residential wiring circuits with 20-amp circuit breakers, it would be exceeded by 286 percent.*

Numerous types of electrical heating products are in use and many are used within residential, commercial, and industrial structures. Chapter 5 noted the fire hazard of heating appliances and equipment in general. Whenever heating products are located within the suspected area of fire origin, they should become targets for detailed investigation. Space heating appliances are generally protected with guards to prevent direct contact with combustibles; however, long-term exposure of cellulose materials, such as wood and cotton fiber, in close proximity to heaters can pyrolyze these materials. This would reduce their ignition temperatures, and eventually cause a fire when an ambient condition change, such as exposure to direct sunlight, adds to the temperature rise of the combustible.

Unintended electrically produced heat from products such as incandescent lamps is also capable of creating fires. Over-wattage lamping of incandescent fixtures has caused heat buildup in fixtures with subsequent direct ignition of combustible structural materials or destruction of conductor insulation leading to arcing or smoldering ignition.

The surface temperatures of an incandescent lamp (light bulb) can exceed 450°F.[17] The NEC requires surface mounted incandescent light fixtures installed in clothes closets to maintain a clearance of at least 12 inches to any combustible material stored within the closet.[18]

Unfortunately, people do not always arrange their storage within the closets to maintain these mandated minimum clearances; in addition, until 1990, exposed incandescent lamps were permitted. Combustible materials stored within clothes closets that can come into direct contact with bare incandescent lamps represent a serious fire hazard.

During the 1950s and into the 1970s, many fires were reported as beginning at aluminum wiring connections, particularly where No. 8 AWG or smaller aluminum conductors were terminated at switch or receptacle terminals.

Potential fire hazards are created when aluminum, which is softer and has about a one-third greater temperature coefficient of expansion than copper, is joined with copper or copper alloys such as brass. The hazard exists because as the electrical connection is made, pressure deforms the aluminum material more severely than copper and subsequently normal heat generated by current flow at the connection causes the aluminum to expand more than the copper, which further deforms the aluminum. Repetitions of the heating and cooling process as the current flow varies causes the aluminum-to-copper connection to loosen thereby increasing the connection resistance and producing increased heating. The process is accumulative and becomes a fire danger when the loosened connection grows excessively hot or electrical arcing begins.

Before 1965, the NEC did not specifically recognize the problems associated with electrically connecting copper and aluminum materials. The NEC now requires connections between the dissimilar metals to be made with devices identified as suitable for the purpose and conditions of use. Older installations may not use such connecting devices at pressure terminals, pressure splicing connectors, or soldering lugs. The fire hazard remains for such constructions.

Motor vehicle (MV) fires, in contrast to structural fires, are more likely to produce extensive damage. Burn or damage patterns in such cases should be applied with caution in reconstruction of the fire.

Electrical ignition sources in MV fires include batteries, as mentioned in Section 7.2, as well as other electrical components used in modern motor vehicles such as electrically operated windows, seats, tops, heaters, antennas, relays, and fuel pumps.

External electrical energy can be a source of MV fires where commercial power facilities are used to provide electrical hookups for recreational vehicles (RVs), trailers, or cab and engine heaters. Battery chargers in RVs are frequently connected to commercial power by electrical hookups when the vehicles are stored or parked. Fires have allegedly started when chargers have been overloaded or relays have overheated during these operations.

7.4 Physical Evidence

The physical evidence of overheating of wires is usually distinguishable from arcing by its greater extent of conductor involvement. Both phenomena can produce beading of conductors. However, overheated conductors, either from fire or high current, frequently show necking, reduced cross section, and offsets in cross section, and beads with pointed ends. Refer to the photographs in NFPA 921, pages 112–114.

Overheated wire will show damage to the insulation from internally generated heat throughout the length of the overloaded conductors, even outside the areas of fire involvement, (provided the conductors have all been subject to the same ambient temperature conditions and electrical overload). Internal heating of insulated wire displays signs including loose, sagging or swollen insulation, and charring on the inside, not outside, of the insulation. Multiple points of origin along the suspected circuit and charring where the circuit wiring passes through or near wood or other cellulose materials are signs of electrically overheated conductors.

Overheated wire generally requires the following conditions for ignition:

- a complete energized circuit,
- an overload or fault condition which causes excessive current,
- defeated, malfunctioning, or improper overcurrent protection on the circuit, and
- adequate combustibles at the points of origin.

Arcing of conductors at residential voltages may produce clean gouges with melted copper edges or severed conductors with beaded ends. Near the arc mark, the conductor is generally not melted. Stranded conductors are less likely to exhibit cavities due to arcs. Occasionally, there will be splattered metal on nearby metallic surfaces, such as outlet or junction boxes from the arc. Arcing evidence is generally similar whether in copper or aluminum wiring.

Melting from fire can eliminate arcing evidence or other evidence present at the beginning of the fire. Smaller gauge stranded copper wire used in flexible cords and solid aluminum wire with its lower melting temperature (1,220°F) are subject to destruction in many fires. The total loss of considerable sections of solid copper conductor is not accountable during most structural fires unless sustained arcing has been present. The melting temperature of copper (1,985°F) is generally higher than the heat produced by the fire. Unless unusual combustibles have entered into the fire process, solid copper is not destroyed but remains largely intact. The author has observed considerable destruction of heavy copper wire and bus bars in fires and explosions that have involved sustained electrical arcing, but for which there were no evident sources of high heat from the surrounding combustibles.

Arcing may not activate the circuit protection because it can be intermittent—starting and stopping at irregular short intervals—yet not lasting continuously long enough to activate the thermal element of the protective device. See Section 4.7 on AFCIs and GFFCs. Intermittent arcing can permit a number of arcing evidence locations to be found after an extensive fire. Unless the arcing evidence is in an area of suspected origin, it should be eliminated as a possible cause and recognized as a result of the fire.

Insulation failure is one of the most common problems in electrical systems. The principal causes of insulation failure are heat, moisture, and dirt. Insulation can also fail because of chemical stress, mechanical damage, ultraviolet radiation (sunlight), and excessive voltage.

Since abnormal arcing must be initiated by either the failure of insulation or the occurrence of an excessive voltage that stresses the insulation, the evidence of one of these conditions should be sought when arcing is the suspected cause.

Insulation failure can occur due to manufacturing defects that should appear shortly after the electrical system is first energized or tested. Good insulation can also be damaged by poor electrical construction techniques or by outside forces. A history of the building from initial construction through remodeling is useful when searching for possible insulation failure explanations.

The NEC rates conductor insulation for voltage and maximum operating temperature characteristics. Typical residential wire is rated 600 V, 60°C (140°F). If #10 AWG Cu 60°C conductor, 30°C rated at 30 amps, were located adjacent to a furnace where the ambient temperature was 50°C (122°F), the wire ampacity would be derated by the NEC to $0.58 \times 30 = 17.4$ amps because of the operating temperature in excess of 30°C (86°F).

For No.12 AWG NMC Cu wire in an uncooled attic space in Tucson, Arizona, the summer ambient temperature being typically 110°F to 115°F (avg. 45°C), the wire would be derated to $0.71 \times 25 = 17.8$ amps, and the continuous load on such wire should not exceed $0.8 \times 17.8 = 14.2$ amps. If the wiring has been in service for ten or twenty years with frequent, continuous (three hours or more) loading at over 15 amps, there has probably been insulation deterioration due to excessive temperature rise. Such wiring, when subjected to a temporary overload of say 60 amps, which might last as long as 20 seconds before a 20-amp breaker would operate, could develop an insulation failure at a weak point and arcing would result.

Excessive voltage can break down solid insulation by tunneling through the insulation at a material anomaly. A short-term overvoltage condition or transient in the voltage waveform can initiate this break down. The magnitude of voltage excess required to initiate insulation breakdown depends upon many factors such as age, deterioration, moisture, heat, and structural damage to the insulation. Thermoplastic-insulated PVC wire for 0-to-600-volt circuits (phase to phase) is specified by NEMA, ICEA standards[19] to be tested at AC voltages from 1.5 to 7.0 kV depending upon conductor size and insulation thickness. When tested by the manufacturer using the DC spark test, the cable is tested for faults at 10.5 kV for #8 through #2 AWG conductor sizes. The voltage is applied between the outside surface of the cable and the conductors for not less than 0.05 second in the spark test.

Unless the owner of the structure has experienced other high voltage problems such as widespread early incandescent lamp failure or unusual failure of electronic equipment, it is difficult to postulate and more difficult yet to prove that an alleged cause was insulation failure due to excessive voltage. A site power quality survey can be used, if the fire destruction is not too great, to determine the quality of the serving utility electrical power and the possible internally generated power disturbances that could contribute to an insulation failure.

Circuits having personnel ground-fault circuit protection (i.e., GFCI breaker or device protection) are unlikely to fail by short-circuiting to ground in a manner that produces a fire. The very sensitive detection of ground current, 4 to 6 milliamperes, by GFCIs prevents overheating of conductors or high energy arcing to be produced under such faulting conditions. However, should a line-to-neutral or a line-to-line fault occur on a GFCI protected circuit, the GFCI will not protect the wiring from overheating or arcing. See Section 4.7 for a discussion of GFCIs. The ordinary circuit breaker must protect under these types of faults. If initial faulting of line-to-neutral or line-to-line progresses such that ground-fault current becomes involved, then GFCI protection will be effective but, depending upon the time required for this involvement to occur, a fire may already be produced.

Chapter 16 of NFPA 921[20] contains an extensive discussion of the management of a major fire investigation. Also included in 921, Chapter 9, are detailed recommendations on preserving, processing, and handling evidence. The subject of investigative photographs is included in Chapter 8 of NFPA 921. One cannot stress too strongly the value of extensive photographs as early in the investigation as possible. Even when the investigator does not recognize an important clue, the information is often available from a later examination of the photographs and only available from the photographs because of the altered fire scene or totally demolished evidence. Early investigators should *take numerous photographs* including multiple views of the same area or component.

7.5 Incendiary Electrical Fires

The starting of an electrical fire in a manner that makes it appear accidental is difficult to accomplish, generally requiring a knowledgeable technician to create an apparent natural ignition within the electrical system or its connected loads. Crude electrical incendiary fires are easily created however, and most often take the form of placing a heating appliance against combustibles. The post-fire evidence of such crudely started electrical fire is usually found by the early fire investigators and requires minimal scientific knowledge of electricity for verification.

Attempts at electrical arson by creating loose connections or bad splices may be effective fire instigators, but they behave randomly and without reliable time predictability. This makes such fire generators undesirable to the criminal who usually requires a highly reliable and extensive fire initiation method.

Another form of contrived fire creation is the sabotaged appliance, which is difficult for the layman to accomplish without leaving an evidence trail that is apparent to a trained investigator. The use of electrically fired pyrotechnic devices is a reliable and predictable fire starter; however, natural ignition post-fire evidence is extremely difficult to fake with such methods.

The combination of an electrical arc and an explosive gas is a reliable and predictable arson method, but the violent explosive nature of the fire always produces the extensive, thorough fire investigation that the arsonist usually seeks to avoid.

In summary, electrical arson is seldom the choice of the fire-starting criminal because it is either too easily discovered or because its successful achievement is too difficult. Nevertheless, the criminal mind is devious and often brilliant, and arsonists will create fires of electrical origin, some with ingenious methods. Fire investigators, particularly forensic electrical engineers, should remain vigilant in pursuing causation discovery to prevent undetected arson using electrical energy.

The professional forensic electrical engineer is frequently called upon to provide expertise in fire investigation when the generalist in fire cause and origin cannot offer a scientifically acceptable electrical explanation for the fire or when an electrical cause is suspected but unproven.

By employing the principles of physics and electrical engineering, the engineer-investigator can arrive at plausible scientific explanations for many fires. This expertise is important in facilitating the legal system to adjudicate the liability for the fire. In Chapter 10, actual fire case studies are used to illustrate these principles.

Appendix 7A

Introduction

The National Electrical Code (NEC), NFPA 70-2002, contains specifications for the allowable current carrying capacity (ampacity) of flexible cords and cables. See NEC Table 400.5(A). These specifications are based upon certain conditions as stated in the NEC. In 400.5, the NEC states that in no case shall the limiting temperature of the conductors be exceeded. The limiting temperature for a conductor is defined to be the maximum continuous operating temperature of the conductor insulation.[21]

Adjustment factors for other loading conditions are permitted by the NEC to be calculated under engineering supervision by Section 310.15(C). In this section, a general formula is given which relates conductor temperature, ambient temperature, and ampacity based upon the classic Neher-McGrath paper.[22]

The application of this general formula is treated in the NEC Appendix B, wherein typical ampacities are calculated for multiple conductors and multiconductor cables of insulation types used for general fixed systems wiring. There is no similar information provided in the NEC for the case of flexible cords and cables used with general use equipment or as portable extension cords. Moreover, the application of the Neher-McGrath equation requires a knowledge or estimate of the temperature rise due to dielectric loss, an evaluation of conductor skin and proximity effects, and knowledge of the effective thermal resistance between conductor and surrounding ambient. These factors enter into the physical models necessary to analyze conductor ampacity for multiple cables in ducts and underground duct banks in general power systems, especially at voltages above 120 volts to ground. However, they unnecessarily complicate the thermal analysis for smaller wire gauge general use flexible cords and cables in air.

Thermodynamic analysis

Steady-state heat conduction through a homogeneous material can be shown to follow Fourier's law, which states that

$$Q = -kA\frac{dt}{dL} \qquad \text{(Equation 7.A1)}$$

where Q = heat transferred across the material with surface area A, t = temperature, L = thickness of the homogeneous material and k = thermal conductivity.

For solids, particularly metals, k is relatively constant with temperature.

For heat transfer through a curved wall, specifically a cylinder of finite thickness, Fourier's equation (Equation 7.A1) can be written as

$$Q = k2\pi rz\left[-\frac{dt}{dr}\right] \qquad \text{(Equation 7.A2)}$$

where z is the length of the cylinder and $2\pi rz$ is the differential surface area. The temperature change across differential element dr is $-dt$, the negative sign denoting a decreasing temperature as r increases.[23]

Separating variables and integrating gives

$$Q = \int_{r_i}^{r_o} \frac{dr}{r} = 2\pi kz \int_{t_a}^{t_b} -dt \qquad \text{(Equation 7.A3)}$$

$$Q = \ln\left[\frac{r_o}{r_i}\right] = 2\pi kz(t_a - t_b) \qquad \text{(Equation 7.A4)}$$

$$Q = \frac{2\pi kz(t_a - t_b)}{\ln\left(\frac{r_o}{r_i}\right)} \qquad \text{(Equation 7.A5)}$$

where r_o is the outside radius, r_i is the inside radius, t_a is the inside temperature and t_b is the outside temperature of the cylinder.

A useful substitution for analyzing heat transfer through cylindrical materials is the logarithmic mean area, where

$$A_m \equiv \frac{A_o - A_i}{\ln(A_o - A_i)}.$$

(Equation 7.A6)

It is easily shown that the logarithmic mean area as defined by Equation 7.A6 is equivalent to Equation 7.A7 where each cylinder is z (1 foot) in length:

$$A_m = \frac{2\pi(r_o - r_i)}{\ln\left(\dfrac{r_o}{r_i}\right)}.$$

(Equation 7.A7)

Combining Equations 7.A5, 7.A6 and 7.A7, one may write as the heat flow through the cylindrical material

$$Q = \frac{kA_m(t_a - t_b)}{r_o - r_i}$$

(Equation 7.A8)

where k is typically expressed in Btu per hr.-ft.-°C.

In the analysis of heat transfer from a metallic conductor (wire) through the insulation surrounding the wire into the air surrounding the conductor and insulation, two additional terms are required to account for the temperature change which occurs due to conduction, convection, and radiation from the insulation surface into the air.[24]

There is a thin film of air on the surface of the conductor that produces a temperature drop due to conduction and convection from the temperature t_b at the insulation surface to the cooler ambient air temperature t_c. For a given temperature drop across this film of air, there will be a flow of a quantity of heat Q_c due to conduction and convection, frequently expressed in Btu per hour per square foot of surface for one degree F temperature differential. In equation form, this is

$$Q_c = h_c A(t_b - t_c).$$

(Equation 7.A9)

In addition to this flow of heat due to conduction and convection, there will be heat flow due to radiated heat from the surface of the insulation. In equation form, the radiated heat flow is

$$Q_r = h_r A(t_b - t_c). \qquad \text{(Equation 7.A10)}$$

The total heat flow at the insulation surface is the sum of these terms, $Q_c + Q_r$, and this total must equal the total heat flow Q from the conductor. Equations 7.A8, 7.A9 and 7.A10 form the basis for determining the temperature differential between the wire and the air surrounding the conductor. Combining Equations 7.A8, 7.A9 and 7.A10 we have

$$\Delta T = (t_a - t_b) + (t_b - t_c) = t_a - t_c = Q\left[\frac{r_o - r_i}{kA_m} + \frac{1}{Ah_c} + \frac{1}{Ah_r}\right]. \qquad \text{(Equation 7.A11)}$$

The total quantity of heat flow input to the conductor configuration is given by

$$Q = I^2 R \qquad \text{(Equation 7.A12)}$$

where Q is expressed in watts per foot of conductor length, I is in amps, and R is in ohms per foot of conductor length. Note that 1 watt = 3.413 Btu per hour. The temperature differential ΔT is given by substituting for Q in Equation 7.A11:

$$\Delta T = I^2 R(3.413)\left[\frac{r_o - r_i}{kA_m} + \frac{1}{Ah_c} + \frac{1}{Ah_r}\right] \qquad \text{(Equation 7.A13)}$$

Dimensional analysis shows that the first term in Equation 7.A13 gives temperature differential in degrees C and that the second and third terms in Equation 7.A13 express temperature differential in degrees F. This is due to the units used to express k, h_c and h_r respectively.

Expressing Equation 7.A13 in Celsius temperature units gives

$$\Delta T = I^2 R(3.413)\left[\frac{r_o - r_i}{kA_m} + \frac{5}{9}\left[\frac{1}{A(h_c + h_r)}\right]\right] \qquad \text{(Equation 7.A14)}$$

Define the bracketed quantity in Equation 7.A14 to be

$$\gamma \equiv \left[\frac{r_o - r_i}{kA_m} + \frac{5}{9}\left[\frac{1}{A(h_c + h_r)} \right] \right].$$
(Equation 7.A15)

The conductor wire resistance R in Equation 7.A14 may be expressed as a function of ΔT as follows

$$R = R_c(1 + \alpha \Delta T)$$
(Equation 7.A16)

where R_c is the electrical resistance of the conductor wire at t_c in ohms per foot, α is the temperature coefficient of resistivity of the wire at t_c, and $\Delta T = t_a - t_c$ where t_c is the temperature of the wire caused by the I^2R heating of the conductor.

Substituting Equations 7.A15 and 7.A16 into Equation 7.A14 gives

$$\Delta T = I^2 R_c(1 + \alpha \Delta T)(3.143)\gamma.$$
(Equation 7.A17)

Combining terms and solving for ΔT yields

$$\Delta T = \frac{I^2 R_c(3.143)\gamma}{1 - I^2 R_c \alpha(3.143)\gamma}.$$
(Equation 7.A18)

The factor γ in Equation 7.A17 was defined by Equation 7.A15 and is the critical term in a determination of temperature rise for an appliance or extension cord-carrying current. The three thermal conductance terms k, h_c, and h_r are empirical parameters whose values are referenced in Appendix 7A for various materials and assumptions.

The remaining terms, r_o, r_i, A_m, and A are all physical parameters of the cord construction being determined by the conductor (wire) gage and the cord insulation thickness. In the practical application of Equation 7.A15, it is expedient to rewrite the definition for γ in the following equivalent form:

$$\gamma \equiv \frac{\ln\left(\dfrac{r_o}{r_1}\right)}{2\pi k} + \frac{5}{9}\left[\frac{1}{2\pi\left(\dfrac{r_o}{12}\right)(h_c + h_r)}\right] \qquad \text{(Equation 7.A19)}$$

where r_o and r_i are the outside radius of the cord and the outside radius of the conductor (wire) respectively, expressed in inches.

Specific applications

The determination of a value for γ as defined by Equation 7.A15 requires a knowledge of the physical parameters r_o, r_i, k, h_c and h_r. The first two parameters are properties of the wire gauge and insulation thickness, while the latter three parameters are properties of the insulation material and the surface exchange of heat from the insulation material into air and the surrounding enclosure.

Appendix 7B discusses the evaluation of the three parameters k, h_c and h_r. The values for r_o and r_i may be obtained from various references including the NEC.[25]

The derivation of Equation 7.A15 and 7.A19 has assumed that the cord is of single conductor construction, so that the entire insulation and wire circumference per unit length are areas that transfer heat to the surrounding enclosure. In practice, most flexible cord sets are of multiple conductor construction, with the most common appliance and extension cords being two or three conductor cords. The effect of this bundling of conductors into a single cord is such that the effective areas of heat transfer are reduced, both from the wire and from the insulation surface. Appendix 7C is an analysis of a typical cord construction to determine these effective heat conduction areas for two current carrying wires in a single cord.

The most common types of appliance and extension cords used in the U.S. are two and three conductor-type SPT all-plastic-parallel-flexible cords. Generally, these cords are constructed from polyvinyl chloride (PVC) plastic insulation extruded over copper wire. There are three types of SPT all-plastic-parallel cord recognized by the NEC as designated by SPT-1, -2 and -3.[26] Depending upon the type of cord, these insulations vary in thickness from 30 mils to 110 mils for wire sizes from No. 20 AWG to No. 10 AWG.

Figure 7.1 is a plot of the solution to Equation 7.A18 for temperature rise versus current for a 2/C #18 AWG Cu SPT cord with the various insulation thickness of 30, 45 and 60 mils for SPT-1, -2 and -3 cords, respectively. It is notable that the heating effect on the cord wire, due to current, decreases with increasing insulation thickness. This is because γ decreases as r_o increases (see Equation 7.A19), and ΔT varies directly with γ (see Equation 7.A17).

Since the continuous operating temperature for type TW PVC cord insulation is 60°C, any temperature rise for the wire exceeding 30°C with respect to a 30°C ambient will exceed the continuous temperature rating of the insulation. The NEC ampacity rating[27] for two-conductor #18 cord is 10 amps, a current that is predicted by this analysis to produce a temperature rise of 24°C, 20°C, and 17°C for the three SPT insulation thicknesses, respectively. This analysis indicates that #18 2/C SPT-1 cord is limited, under the assumed conditions, to a maximum continuous ampacity of 11 amps at 30°C ambient. The NEC rating of 10 amps would appear to be conservative in this respect.

Figure 7.2 is a plot of conductor temperature rise versus current for a 2/C #16 AWG Cu SPT cord with the two available insulation thicknesses of 45 and 60 mils for SPT-2 and -3 cords, respectively. Again, note that the heating effect on the cord wire, due to current, decreases with increasing insulation thickness.

The NEC ampacity rating for two-conductor #16 cord is 13 amps,[28] a current that is predicted by this analysis to produce a temperature rise of 19°C and 17°C for the two SPT insulation thicknesses, respectively. The NEC rating is conservative with respect to the maximum continuous operating temperature for the PVC insulation predicted by this analysis.

Figure 7.3 is a plot of cord heating versus current for 2/C #14, #12, and #10 AWG Cu SPT-3 cords with the various NEC specified insulation thicknesses of 80, 95, and 110 mils for these cords in each gauge, respectively.

The NEC ampacity ratings for #14, #12, and #10 2/C cords are 18, 25, and 30 amps, respectively.[29] These currents are predicted by this analysis to produce temperature rises of 16°C, 17°C, and 13°C for the three conductor sizes, respectively. Again, the NEC ratings are conservative with respect to the maximum continuous operating temperature for the PVC insulation as predicted by this analysis.

Text continues on page 176.

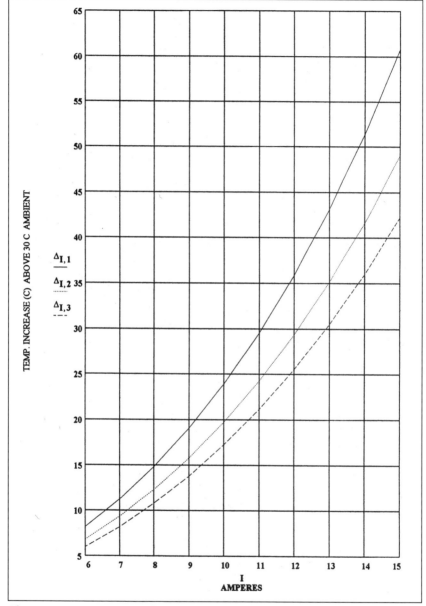

Figure 7.1 *2/C #18 AWG heat versus current*

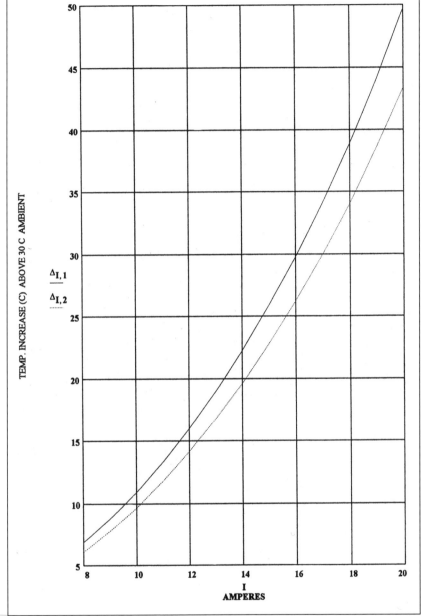

Figure 7.2 *2/C #16 AWG heat versus current*

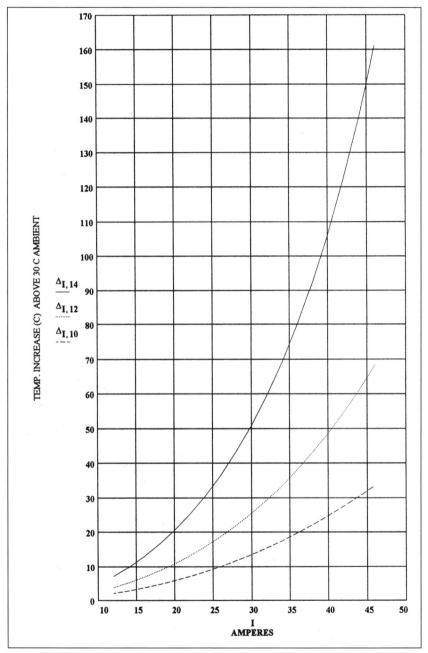

Figure 7.3 *2/C #14, 12 and 10 heating*

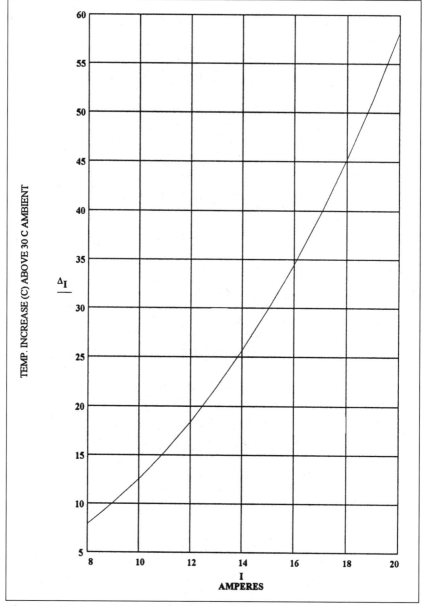

Figure 7.4 #16 cord heating, hardwood floor

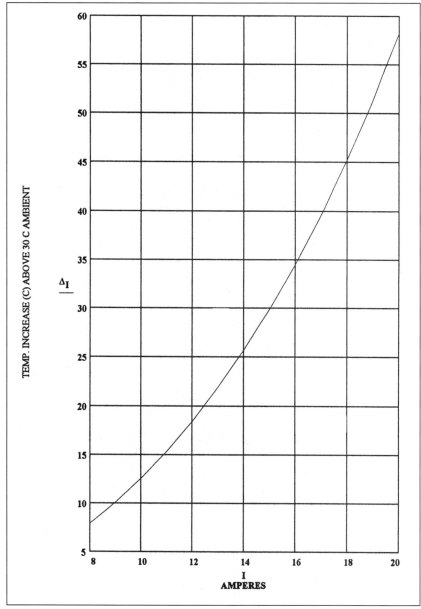

Figure 7.5 *#16 cord heating under carpet*

Figure 7.4 is a plot of cord heating versus current for 2/C #16 AWG Cu SPT-2 cord lying on a hardwood floor. The cord heating is greater under these conditions than that for a cord totally surrounded by air since the thermal conductivity of the hardwood floor is less than the surface convection and radiation heat transfer for that portion of the cord insulation surface in contact with the floor. Although the cord heating is greater when lying in contact with a hardwood floor, the NEC ampacity of 13 amps for #16 AWG 2/C Cu cord is still acceptable and should not result in operational temperatures that exceed the continuous insulation temperature when operating in a 30°C ambient environment.

Figure 7.5 is a plot of cord heating versus current for 2/C #16 AWG Cu SPT-2 cord lying on a hardwood floor under a carpet with a rubber pad. The cord heating is greater under these conditions than that for a cord totally surrounded by air since the thermal conductivity of the hardwood floor and carpet is significantly less than the surface convection and radiation heat transfer for the cord completely surrounded by air.

The safe current carrying ampacity of #16 2/C cord under these conditions is approximately 7 amps, not the 13 amps given by the NEC in Table 400-5(A).

Figure 7.6 depicts the construction cross section of a three-conductor #18 AWG SPT-2 cord in air. In this case, the third conductor is a non-cur-

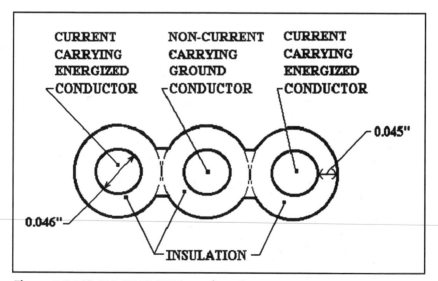

Figure 7.6 *3/C #18 AWG SPT-2 cord section*

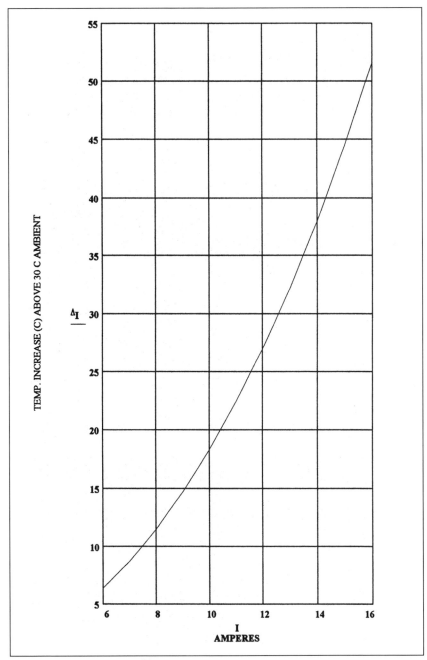

Figure 7.7 *#18 3/C cord heating*

rent-carrying ground wire which rather than contributing heat to the system acts as a heat sink by removing heat energy through conduction to the wall outlet ground plug and ground wire for the fixed wiring in the structure. In the analysis of this case, we have assumed that the fixed wiring ground is at ambient room air temperature and that the current carrying heat producing conductors have an 85 percent effective conduction area for heat removal to the air and a 15 percent effective heat conduction area through insulation to the ground conductor.

Figure 7.7 is a plot of cord heating versus current for the 3/C #18 AWG SPT-2 cord. Because of the increased heat conduction provided by the ground conductor, the NEC-rated value of 10 amps for this cord produces a temperature rise of 18.3°C. This is approximately 1.4°C less than the rise created by 10 amps , the NEC-rated value of 10 amps for this cord produces a temperature rise of 18.3°C. This is approximately 1.4°C less than the rise created by 10 amps.

Appendix 7B

In order to apply Equation 7.A19 to typical appliance or extension cords, the values of the parameters k, h_c and h_r must be determined.

Various references can be found for the thermal conductivities of electrical insulating materials. The NEC, in Appendix B, gives typical values of thermal resistivity Rho $(\rho) = 1/k$:

polyethylene (PE) = 450
polyvinyl chloride (PVC) = 650
rubber and rubber-like = 500
paper insulation = 550

where ρ is expressed in units of °C-cm per watt.

These values of thermal resistivity can be converted into the appropriate units for thermal conductivity, k, as follows.

Let $k = K \times (1/\rho)$ or $K = r \times k$. Using dimensional analysis we have that

$$K = \frac{C° - cm}{watts} \frac{Btu}{hr. - ft. - C°} = \frac{Btu - cm}{watts - hr. - ft.}. \quad \text{(Equation 7.B1)}$$

Since 1 watt = 3.41304 Btu per hour and 1 cm = 0.032808 feet we can determine the numerical value for K as

$$K = \frac{3.41304}{0.032808} = 104.31.$$
(Equation 7.B2)

Note that dimensionally

$$k = \frac{Btu - cm}{watts - hr. - ft.} \frac{watts}{C° - cm} = \frac{Btu}{hr. - ft. - C°}.$$
(Equation 7.B3)

The NEC table of thermal resistivities can then be expressed in conductivity (k) values:

polyethylene (PE) = 0.2312
polyvinyl chloride (PVC) = 0.1600
rubber and rubber-like = 0.2081
paper insulation = 0.1891

where k is expressed in units of Btu per hr.-ft.°C. These thermal conductivity values are in close agreement with the values published by Fink and Beaty.[30]

The American Society of Heating, Refrigerating and Air-Conditioning Engineers (ASHRAE) has published in its *Handbook of Fundamentals* equations for calculation of natural convection heat transfer coefficients of surfaces in air.[31] Assuming that the conductor cords of interest are from 18 AWG to 10 AWG in size, the value of h_c calculated from the ASHRAE equations is between 1.31 and 1.89 with median value $h_c = 1.60$ Btu per square ft.-hr.-°F.

V. M. Faire[32] has also published an equation for the surface coefficient of natural convection in atmospheric air:

$$h_c = (0.27)\left(\frac{\Delta t}{D_o}\right)^{0.25}$$
(Equation 7.B4)

where D_o is the outside diameter of the cord in feet and Δt is the temperature differential between the cord surface and the surrounding air in degrees F. For an assumed Δt of 54°F, the median Δt for cord surface temperatures between 86°F (30°C) and 194°F (90°C) with ambient air at 86°F, the values of h_c calculated from Equation 7.B4 are between 1.32 and 1.79 with median value $h_c = 1.56$ Btu per square ft.-hr.-°F.

In view of the close agreement between these two sources, the author has elected to use the value $h_c = 1.58$ for the coefficient of natural convection at the surface of the cords considered in this analysis.

For the case of thermal coefficient of radiation, where the radiating body is small and inside a large enclosure, the Stefan-Boltzmann law for blackbody radiation obtains and the expression for Q_r becomes

$$Q_r = (0.173)\varepsilon_1 A\left[\left(\frac{T_1}{100}\right)^4 - \left(\frac{T_2}{100}\right)^4\right]$$
(Equation 7.B5)

where Q_r is expressed in Btu per hr.

In Equation 7.B5 T_1 is the surface temperature of the hot body radiator, T_2 is the temperature of the walls of the space enclosing the hot body with the temperatures expressed in Rankine degrees and ε_1 is the emissivity of the surface.

Substituting for $T_1 = t_b + 460$ and for $T_2 = t_c + 460$ in Equation 7.B5, gives

$$Q_r = (0.173)\varepsilon_1 A 10^{-8}\left[(t_b + 460)^4 - (t_c + 460)^4\right].$$
(Equation 7.B6)

For $t_c = 86°F$ (30°C) and 86°F $\leq t_b \leq$ 194°F (90°C), Equation 7.B6 can be closely approximated by the linear relationship

$$Q_r \approx (1.5069)\varepsilon_1 A(t_b - t_c).$$
(Equation 7.B7)

Substituting this Equation 7.B7 into Equation 7.A10 from Appendix 7A, h_r becomes

$$h_r = 1.5069\varepsilon_1$$
(Equation 7.B8)

where h_r is expressed in Btu per hr.-sq.ft.-°F.

For cords that are black or of a very dark color, the emissivity ε_1 is close to unity and can be taken as 0.92. For lighter colored cords, even white, Faires[33] indicates that at temperatures near 200°F, $\varepsilon_1 \sim 0.92$.

Appendix 7C

The commercially available flexible cords used as examples in the specific calculations given in this chapter are assumed to be all-plastic parallel two- or three conductor cord sets as designated by the NEC, Table 400.4, Type SPT. When three conductor cords are used, the third conductor is for grounding purposes only and not ordinarily current carrying, see Note 6 to NEC Table 400.4.

In order to determine the effective areas for heat flow in a two current-carrying conductor parallel cord set, the geometry shown in Figure 7.8 is assumed.

r_i = outside radius of the conductor (wire),
r_o = outside radius of the insulator, and
θ = angle of effective heat conduction from each conductor in the cord.

From the construction of Figure 7.8, wherein the two conductors are assumed to be tangent at their respective outside insulation surfaces, the

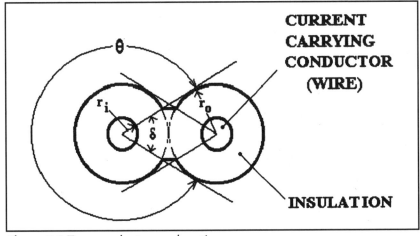

Figure 7.8 Two-conductor cord section

length of the arc on the outside circumference of the conductor subtended by δ is given by

$$S = (r_o)\delta.$$ (Equation 7.C1)

Also, from Figure 7.8, we have the relationship

$$\frac{\delta}{2} = \arctan\left(\frac{r_o}{2r_o}\right).$$ (Equation 7.C2)

Substituting Equation 7.C2 into 7.C1 for δ gives

$$S = r_o(2)\tan^{-1}\left(\frac{r_o}{2r_0}\right) = 2r_o\tan^{-1}\left(\frac{1}{2}\right) = 2r_o(0.1476)\pi.$$ (Equation 7.C3)

The total outside circumference of each conductor is $2\pi r_o$, therefore the effective heat conduction area of the two-conductor cord becomes

$$A_{eff} = 2\pi r_o - S = 2\pi r_o(0.8524).$$ (Equation 7.C4)

Thus, approximately 85 percent of the areas A_m and A, are effective in allowing heat transfer from the conductors since both areas are subtended by the same angle θ, as expressed in Equation 7.A14. Since γ for a single conductor cord as defined by Equations 7.A15 and 7.A19 is inversely proportional to these areas, γ must be increased by a multiplier of $(1/0.85) = 1.18$ in the case of a two conductor cord.

Endnotes

1. *CRC Handbook of Chemistry and Physics*, 73rd ed., David R. Lide, ed. (Boca Raton: CRC Press, 1992–93), 15–34.

2. National Fire Protection Association, *Guide for Fire and Explosion Investigations,* 1995 ed., NFPA 921 (Quincy, MA: National Fire Protection Association), pt. 14-8.4.

3. Bernard Beland, "Examination of Electrical Conductors Following a Fire," *NFPA Fire Technology*, November 1980, 252–258.

4. National Fire Protection Association, *Manual for the Determination of Electrical Fire Causes*, 1988 ed., NFPA 907M (Quincy, MA: National Fire Protection Association), pt. 12-2.1.

5. William M. Mazer, *Electrical Accident Investigation Handbook*, with 1996 Supplement (Glen Echo, MD: Electrodata, Inc.), 1.1.5.2.

6. P. D. Gandhi, "Temperature and Velocity Correlations in Room Fires for Estimating Sprinkler Actuation Times," *NFPA Fire Technology* 31(2):137–157 (1995).

7. Beland, "Examination of Electrical Conductors," 252–258.

8. NFPA, *Manual for the Determination of Electrical Fire Causes*, tables 3-3.4 and 13-13.2.

9. Ibid., pt. 14-8.4.

10. Robert E. Nabours, "Static Discharge Hazard in Explosive Atmospheres," ICPS-03-12 (presented at the IEEE Industrial & Commercial Power Systems Technical Conference, Clearwater, Florida, May 2003).

11. Harry S. Dixon, "Storage Battery Explosions: Hydrogen or 'Bleve'?" *Journal of the National Academy of Forensic Engineers* 1(1):13–18 (1984).

12. W. Tillar Shugg, *Handbook of Electrical and Electronic Insulating Materials* (NY: Van Nostrand Reinhold, 1986), table 2-14.

13. Robert E. Nabours, "Heat and Arcing Fire Causation at Conduit Connections," *Journal of the National Academy of Forensic Engineers* 10(1):63–76 (1993).

14. Mazer, *Electrical Accident Investigation Handbook*, 1.3.4.1.

15. Mazer, *Electrical Accident Investigation Handbook*, 1.1.5.3.

16. American National Standards Institute (ANSI), *National Electrical Code: 2002,* ANSI/NFPA 70 (Quincy, MA: National Fire Protection Association, 2002), table 400.4.

17. Illuminating Engineering Society (IES), *IES Lighting Handbook,* Reference Volume (NY: Illuminating Engineering Society, 1981), fig. 8-10, p. 8-8.

18. ANSI, *National Electrical Code: 2002*, Art. 410.8.

19. National Electrical Manufacturers Association (NEMA), *NEMA Standards,* publication No. WC 5, ICEA publication No. S-61-402 (Washington, DC: National Electrical Manufacturers Association, 1993).

20. NFPA, *Manual for the Determination of Electrical Fire Causes,* 124–129.

21. ANSI, *National Electrical Code: 2002*, Art. 310.10.

22. J. H. Nehr and M. H., McGrath, "The Calculation of the Temperature Rise and Load Capability of Cable Systems," *AIEE Transactions on Power Apparatus and Systems* 76:752–764 (1957).

23. Virgil Moring Faires, *Applied Thermodynamics* (NY: MacMillan Co., 1952), 430.

24. American Society of Heating, Refrigerating and Air Conditioning Engineers, Inc., *ASHRAE Handbook of Fundamentals*, (NY: American Society of Heating, Refrigerating and Air Conditioning Engineers, Inc., 1976), ch. 2.

25. ANSI, *National Electrical Code: 2002*, tables 8 and 400.4.

26. Ibid., table 400.4.

27. Ibid., table 400.5(A).

28. Ibid., table 400.5(A).

29. Ibid., table 400.5(A).

30. Donald G. Fink and H. Wayne Beaty, eds., *Standard Handbook for Electrical Engineers*, 13th ed. (NY: McGraw-Hill, 1993), tables 4-64, -65, and -68.

31. ASHRAE, *ASHRAE Handbook*, 39–41.

32. Faires, *Applied Thermodynamics*, 463.

33. Ibid., 440–441.

Chapter 8

Illumination

8.1 Introduction

The subject of illumination in forensic science is related to a question that frequently arises in matters of litigation: "Was there sufficient light for a person to see in order to avoid placing themselves or others in a dangerous or harmful situation?"

The forensic electrical engineer can be qualified by education and training to "shed some light" on this subject. First of all, one should recognize that light is a form of electromagnetic radiation, occurring at certain frequencies, which can be detected by human optical nerves and processed by the brain to provide an individual with information about their environment. Since we are dealing with electromagnetic energy, we are discussing the fundamental energy form of study and application by electrical engineers. Because not all electrical engineers are experts in illumination engineering, it requires additional study beyond what is presented in the usual electrical engineering curriculum to become proficient in this area of science. Illuminating engineers are responsible for the optimal design of the visual environment, without waste of material or energy.

Artificial lighting, most of which is created by the conversion of electrical energy into light energy, is a part of what an electrical engineer must understand. The practicing electrical design engineer must therefore be able to deal with illumination in a scientific manner in order to design and specify lighting systems that will be useful to mankind. The subject of light—and more specifically illumination—therefore becomes an integral part of an electrical engineer's practice if the engineer is designing electrical systems for products, structures, or areas that people will utilize.

8.2 Physics of Light

The electromagnetic theory of visible radiant energy as advanced by James Clerk Maxwell in 1865 was based upon the following postulates.[1]

- Luminous bodies emit light in the form of radiant energy.
- Radiant energy is propagated in the form of electromagnetic waves.
- Electromagnetic waves stimulate the retina of the eye that converts visible radiant energy into electrical signals that are sent to the brain.

In 1887, Heinrich Hertz demonstrated in the laboratory the validity of Maxwell's theory and proceeded to show that electric radiation had rectilinear properties, was capable of being reflected, refracted, and polarized. Therefore, such radiation was astonishingly like light radiation although differing in wavelength and frequency. These contributions led to the adoption of the term hertz (Hz) for "cycles per second."[2]

Visible radiation wavelengths fall in the range from 760 to 380 nanometers (10^{-9} meters) which corresponds to 3.94 to 7.89 $\times$ 1,014 Hz since $c = \lambda v$, where c is the velocity of light, v is the radiation frequency in Hz, and λ is the radiation wavelength. Human vision is greatest at 555 nanometers, which corresponds to yellow-green colored light. The visible wavelengths of radiation comprise only a tiny fraction of the electromagnetic spectrum which includes electric, radio, microwave, infrared, ultraviolet, x-ray, gamma, and cosmic radiation, a spectrum of frequencies from 1 to 10^{24} Hz.

Sir Isaac Newton advanced another theory describing radiant energy two hundred years before Maxwell's electromagnetic theory. Newton's theory of light, known as the corpuscular theory, postulates that radiant energy is emitted in discrete particles which Max Planck later termed photons. These quanta emissions of energy were assigned a magnitude h, where h = 6.626×10^{-34} joule seconds (Planck's constant), and v = velocity of the particle in m/sec. Later, a unified theory was proposed by de Broglie and Heisenberg having the following premises:

- Moving bodies of mass m have an associated wave of radiant energy whose wavelength is given by $\lambda = h/(mv)$.
- It is impossible to determine simultaneously all of the properties that are distinctive of a wave or a corpuscle.

The second premise is known as the Heisenberg uncertainty principle.

It is accepted in modern physics that light, and radiation in general, are a form of energy describable by both particle and wave theories, and that the radiant energy travels at a very high speed of 3×10^8 meters per second, in a vacuum. Gamma and cosmic radiation are more often measured in terms of power or energy rather than frequency and wavelength.

Electromagnetic radiant energy results when electrically charged particles are accelerated. Particle acceleration can be accomplished by oscillations of electric and magnetic fields. Such oscillations may be generated by the rotation of a conductor in a magnetic field (i.e., an electrical generator), by electronic circuits, or by heating. Radiation may be caused by electric arcs, as in lightning, by electron bombardment, or by radioactivity.

Radiation by luminescent sources is produced when the excitation of single valence electrons results in these electrons returning to their quiescent or intermediate orbits with the resulting energy loss by the atomic structure appearing as a photon of radiation. In gaseous materials, line spectra such as those produced by mercury or sodium arcs, result. In crystalline solids or organic materials, relatively narrow bands of emission, usually in the visible spectrum, are produced. Luminescence is the phenomenon of light production employed in fluorescent and vapor lamps, and in light-emitting diodes (LEDs).

Luminescent radiation differs from incandescent radiation where the high temperature heat energy release of many electrons associated with numerous atoms results in a continuous spectrum of radiation from dark red to bluish color. A tungsten filament lamp produces visible light radiation in nearly the same proportions that exist in sunlight.[3] Most modern incandescent lamps have tungsten or tungsten alloy filaments. Metal halide lamps are a variation of the tungsten filament lamp which incorporates a halogen gas in the bulb to decelerate the loss of tungsten, which normally evaporates off the filament when operating at incandescence, thereby extending the life of the lamp and improving the average lamp efficacy.

8.3 Visual Environment and Visibility

The amount of illumination or intensity of light principally determines the ability of a person to "see." What "seeing" means is a subject of considerable scientific inquiry. The illumination required for an average adult individual with normal eyesight to read printed material of a certain size and contrast on certain background with specified error is one definition of adequate illumination. Notice that this definition includes a number of terms such as "average," "normal," "certain," and "error." If the idea that a definition of adequate illumination for all seeing tasks is not easily made precise, such as the definition of an ampere or a volt, this is correct. Some of the terms used in illumination science are important to define as follows.

- **illumination**. The act of illuminating or state of being illuminated, exposed to visible radiation energy.
- **luminance**. Informal, brightness; luminous radiative flux leaving, passing through, or arriving at a surface.
- **illuminance**. The density of luminous flux incident on a surface.
- **contrast**. The relationship between the luminance of an object and its immediate background.
- **footcandle**. The illuminance on a surface one square foot in area on which there is a uniformly distributed flux of one lumen.

The ability to "see" an object depends on many factors. The principal determinants are:[4]

- luminance (brightness) of the object
- luminance of the background
- spectral distribution
- contrast (determined by 1, 2 and 3 above)
- size
- duration of observation

- temporal frequency characteristics
- location relative to the line of sight
- movement in the field of view
- non-uniformities of luminance in the object and the background

Studies of individual observers have taught us many things about illumination. We know that moonlight of approximately 0.01 footcandle intensity is adequate for fairly good acuity, but color perception is not possible. Well-defined objects and good contrast allow an individual to perceive considerable detail at this low level of illumination. Comprehension time is longer than at higher levels of illumination and shadows create too low an intensity for recognition of detail. Motion aids discrimination of objects at these low levels of illumination as long as such motion is not too rapid.[5]

At about 0.1 footcandle of illumination, human vision changes from scotopic (rod vision) to photopic (cone vision) and color becomes apparent with some suddenness. Foveal vision becomes predominant. Any major dominating motion at the edge of the visual field will instantly direct attention. Acuity improves with contrast in both intensity and color. Ease and speed of visual comprehension improve as illumination increases up to about 1,000 footcandles or even more under controlled conditions. At extremely high intensity, most people have decreased visual ability and bright sunlight (3,000 footcandles) can cause physical discomfort in many individuals.[6]

The human eye is capable of responding to luminance through a range of ten to eleven logarithmic units[7]—in other words, about 100,000,000,000 times (100 billion to one).

Illumination is not the total determinant of our ability to see, however. Beside the human physiological and psychological components affecting the visual task, there are other physical factors in the environment, which determine whether "seeing" is accomplished. Some of these factors are listed below:

- **Contrast** is the basic element that provides useful information to inform us about luminous discontinuities and gradients in the visual field. This function has been studied in great detail and can be quantified in terms of individual probabilities for detection in a specified time duration of a small round test object on a uniform background with varying background luminance (brightness). Typical testing uses a four-minute disk exposed for 0.2 second. Contrast detection varies with exposure duration and retinal illuminance.

- **Visual acuity** is a term used to describe the visibility of fine details in a multi-stimuli visual field. This varies individually of course, but also with exposure duration and luminance.

- **Temporal resolution** expresses the visual system's ability to respond to contrasts in time rather than space. Because targets can appear to move either by eye movements or by movement of the object itself, recognition is related to the periodicity and duration of flashing targets; and in some cases, recognition is related to the luminance. For flashes at frequencies between 2 and 20 hertz, an intermittent stimulus may appear brighter than the same stimulus as a constant target. This is known as brightness enhancement.[8]

- **Temporal contrast** can also be known as "flicker" and a knowledge of flicker effects is important when considering such problems as fluorescent lamp flicker, flashing signal detection, and animated visual fields.

- **Color discrimination** is related to contrast, but expresses the human observer's ability to distinguish between structure-free patches of light of the same size and shape but different colors (frequencies). Threshold illuminance for colored light signals is about the same as white light; however, from 0.5 to 3.0 log units, greater illumination is required to permit identification of color.[9]

The color of a light source can be expressed as color temperature when the chromaticity (purity) falls on the blackbody locus. Color temperature relates to the color of a completely radiating (blackbody) source and of light sources that match the color of such a body.[10] Figure 8.1, taken from the IES HB, plots the preferred color temperature of light sources at various illuminance levels.

Inherent to the subject of illumination and "seeing" is the consideration of human performance capabilities relative to the visual task.[11] Human factors evaluations are essential to a forensic illumination engineer's scientific approach to accident reconstruction.

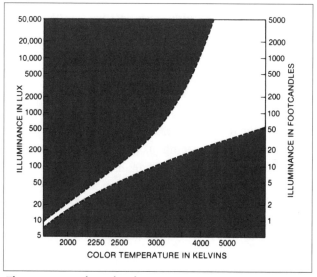

Figure 8.1 *Preferred color temperatures at various illuminance levels*

Accident reconstruction must be based upon a reasonable range of individual performance under the subject conditions, including illumination physics and human reaction to the visual environment.

The preceding discussion of human "seeing" should indicate to the reader that recommended illumination levels must be recognized as guides, not absolute values. The Illuminating Engineering Society of North America (IES) is the leading scientific society concerned with illuminating engineering in the United States and has been in existence since 1906. The IES publishes recommendations for illuminance for a broad classification of visual activities. Included in the IES recommendations are lighting for safety, emergency lighting, roadway, walkway, bikeway and area lighting, aviation and transportation lighting, lighting of swimming pools, theaters, offices, industrial tasks, commercial, residential, educational, institutional and public building lighting.

8.4 Lighting Design

The design of an illumination system requires not only engineering but also art. Lighting design is not confined to the utilitarian purpose of providing an adequate degree of visibility for seeing tasks and objects. The humanistic aspects of good lighting design can be found in the use of light sources, luminaries, and techniques to achieve subtle enhancement of spaces used by people.

Many examples of good, and unfortunately, bad lighting design can be found in our homes, gardens, offices and public places. Good lighting provides not only the requisite illumination for the seeing function in a particular environment such as task lighting, but enhances the observer's subconscious feelings for the space. Bad lighting both fails to provide the requisite illumination for the seeing task and it offends our sense of well-being and contentment with the environment.

Lighting design is a process of analysis and synthesis that seeks to illuminate an environment used and enjoyed by people. Good design will provide both the quantity and quality of illumination necessary to satisfy the severity of the seeing tasks while providing comfort by minimizing visual fatigue. The selection and placement of light sources, luminaries, equipment and lighting system components requires the designer exercise professional judgment, personal taste, and considered choice among the available solutions.

The design for adequate quantity of illumination should consider the extensive recommendations of the IES found in its *Handbook*. Inherent in the design process for quantity of illumination is the consideration of lighting installation maintenance or lack thereof. It is necessary to use light loss factors in planning a lighting system so that the expected uncontrollable depreciation in initial illumination will not reduce the illuminance of the space to unacceptable levels.

Factors that contribute to the overall loss of light are[12]

- luminaire ambient temperature,
- voltage to luminaire,
- ballast factor,
- luminaire surface depreciation,
- environment changes,
- lamp and ballast burnouts,
- lamp lumen depreciation, and
- luminaire dirt depreciation.

The design of a lighting system must consider these factors in order to select the initial design illumination, or the actual illumination will degrade with use, and eventually may become unacceptable.

A numerical example of this process serves to illustrate as follows.

If it is expected that the luminaries will be cleaned on a schedule every eighteen months, that 50 percent of the lamps will be replaced on a schedule every eighteen months, and that lamp burnouts will not be replaced as they occur, it may result that at the end of eighteen months of operation, the light output is 67 percent of the initial design light output. If the recommended minimum illuminance for the area/activity is 20 footcandles (fc), then the initial design must be for 30 fc after the temperature and voltage loss factors have been applied. Unless ambient temperature and voltage are changing with time, the system always has these as constant loss factors affecting the light output from the luminaires. If the combined effect of temperature and voltage is a loss factor of 5 percent, then the initial design must be for 31.6 fc (30/0.95).

8.5 Slips, Falls and Safety

Frequently encountered personal injury litigation related to the subject of adequate illumination involves slips, falls and safety. In addition to the recommended minimums or adequate ranges of illumination found in the IES standards, there are guidelines for brightness (luminance) ratios within areas that detract from human visual acuity. The subjects of disability glare, veiling reflections, and reflected glare are also a part of the engineering and scientific illumination factors considered by illumination engineers.

Disability glare results in reduced visual performance and visibility. It is often accompanied by discomfort. Another term for disability glare is "veiling luminance," which refers to the reduction in contrast of an image caused by scattered light, since this effect can be simulated by adding a uniform "veil" of luminance to the object. A commonly encountered source of disability glare is that from oncoming automobile headlights.[13]

Reflected glare is produced by regular reflections superimposed upon diffuse reflections from a viewed object that partially or totally obscure the details seen by effectively reducing the contrast. The reflection of an incandescent lamp in a polished metal surface is an example of a type of reflected glare that can be annoying, distracting, and even disabling to the viewer.[14]

Veiling reflections are created when light is reflected from specular or semi-matte surfaces that physically reduce the contrast of the visual task. The effect is prevalent in the work place and can greatly affect the visual task performance of reading print or handwriting on paper or viewing a video display terminal.[15]

In most cases, the IES recommends illumination levels based upon the visual tasks to be performed in the space. It suggests that the lighting designer include multiple level lighting systems, segregation of visual tasks, nonuniform lighting systems, and uniform lighting systems as viable considerations for optimal lighting design. The IES recommends minimum illuminance levels, but suggests a wide variation of possible illuminance levels as reasonable accommodations for human visual performance.[16]

In the case of illuminance levels for safety, absolute minimums are recommended for safety in any situation where safety is related to seeing conditions.[17] IES recommendations also address other factors affecting a visually safe environment, such as excessive glare and uncontrolled large differences in illuminance.

Indoor lighting conditions are possible to field evaluate using photometric instruments to measure illuminance and luminance. Investigative observations are useful to discover glare-producing sources within the visual field. Care must be taken, however, to recreate the precise lighting environment that existed at the time of the accident, including all light reflecting objects (humans included) that were present. Daylight can also be a contributing factor to the environment. The contribution of daylight to an interior space is a function of building fenestration and the geometrical position of the sun as well as the sky conditions at the time. Thorough research of the lighting environment is necessary to accurately reconstruct these conditions.

8.6 Vehicular Accidents

Vehicular accidents frequently are caused by, or have lighting as, a contributing factor. The IES and the U.S. Department of Transportation have jointly authored an American National Standard for Roadway Lighting that is a part of the U.S. Department of Transportation, Federal Highway

Administration's *Roadway Lighting Handbook.* The design of roadway lighting systems using pavement luminance (brightness) is the presently recommended criteria for design of modern highway lighting systems in contrast to the previously used method of design for illuminance. The IES Roadway Lighting Committee is currently reviewing recommended practice RP-8-98, *American National Standard Practice for Roadway Lighting*, with respect to the inclusion of a third criteria for roadway lighting based upon the work of W. Adrian, who has proposed a design metric termed small target visibility (STV).[18]

While the object of a fixed lighting system for highways is to supplement the headlights of vehicles, making the roadway and objects related thereto more visible, there are more miles of non-lighted highways in the U.S. than there are lighted. Thus, there are more vehicular accidents which involve questions of adequate vehicle headlight illumination than accidents which question the fixed roadway lighting system.

A forensic illumination investigation of a vehicular accident must consider daylight conditions or nighttime conditions. The investigation should include both the fixed lighting system (if present) and the vehicular headlights as possible contributing factors to the question of driver visibility and reaction as accident producing factors. The adequacy of warning or directional signage and sign visibility can also be considerations in vehicular accidents. Time/motion studies with visual acquisition and reaction times are frequently necessary to reconstruct vehicular accidents. The placement of roadway barriers and their visual identification under artificial lighting, as well as day lighting conditions, are important factors in many accident investigations.

Nighttime vehicular accident investigation frequently raises the question of whether the vehicle was operating with headlights turned on. Besides eye witnesses, the physical evidence can frequently be used to answer this question. For example, if even one of the head lamps has reasonably survived the accident, the condition of the lamp filament can sometimes be used to determine whether the lamp was energized at the time of the accident. The effectiveness of an automobile's headlights can be an important factor in the contribution to an accident. Proper alignment of the headlights, use of high or low beam settings, age and type of headlights are all important factors in accident reconstruction. Even the physical attitude of the automobile is important in lighting of the roadway. An overloaded or custom modified vehicle may have the headlight system altered to reduce the effectiveness of the illumination.

Other traffic conditions are equally important in vehicular accident investigations. Oncoming traffic can cause disability glare with distraction or impairment of the operator's function. The geometry of the roadway is crucial to lighting investigation and a thorough examination and reconstruction of the three dimensional roadway conditions at the accident site is usually necessary. An accurate survey of these conditions should be obtained by using a competent land surveyor working closely with the forensic lighting engineer.

Roadway lighting conditions are controlled by many environmental factors such as

- location of all light sources, fixed and moving,
- type, age, and condition (dirt accumulation) of light sources,
- type, age, and condition of road surface including dry or wet environments, and
- geometrical position of viewer, which is essential to a determination of veiling luminance.

Lighting measurements are frequently used in accident investigation to field determine the actual visual environment or in the laboratory to verify light source photometrics. Portable instruments are used to field measure illuminance and luminance. The advantage of actual field measurements, when available, is considerable in comparison to calculated values since many assumptions or known parameters are required to perform accurate hand or computer calculations of illuminance, luminance, or small target visibility.

In a vehicular accident investigation, the determination of target level of contrast, at which a reasonably alert driver would detect it, is the most important factor in evaluating the illumination contribution to the accident.

Dr. Paul L. Olson has devoted two chapters[19] to the important subject of driver perception-response time in vehicular accidents. He distinctly points out that perception-response time is likely to be critically influenced by driver expectation or preconditioned anticipation of action by another driver.

An example, given by Olson, of this change to relatively straightforward data on perception-response time measurement is "the case of the driver who simply blows the stop sign." The offending vehicle may be detected upon approach with no expectation or suspicion by the other driver who has the right-of-way, but eventually the combination of forward speed and proximity to the intersection will cause the driver on the through street to realize that the other vehicle is not going to stop. This delayed identification of the hazard results in an increased total time for perception-response beyond the available data from research on perception-response time.

Many factors can affect perception-response time, such as the expectancy example given. These include driver fatigue, age, sex and use of chemicals such as alcohol and other drugs.

The function of a vehicle's lighting system is not only to provide illumination for the driver to see, but importantly to allow the vehicle to be seen. It seems that too often individuals choose to operate their motor vehicles without lights because they believe that they can see adequately. This is most common at sunset or at sunrise when the ambient light is marginal. At these times, it is also difficult to see unlighted vehicles. An individual may believe that he can see adequately to drive, but that belief does not ensure that other observers can readily see an unlighted vehicle.

Highway product safety experts have long recognized that automotive headlight operation at all times is a significant factor in motor vehicle accident reduction. Several automobile manufacturers have chosen within the past few years to incorporate automatic headlight and taillight operation into their products. Since 1978, California has required motorcycles to have both headlight and taillights on when operated on state highways. The U.S. Department of Transportation requires motorcycles that operate on the interstate highway system to operate with lights on at all times.

Automatic lighting controls are no guarantee against vehicle accidents due to visibility. The control system may fail, the lamps may burn out, the control system may be circumvented, and other factors such as environmental conditions can defeat the safety enhancement of automatic identification lighting.

A case investigated by this engineer involved a motorcycle with an automatic lighting system that was rendered inoperative during driving by the random operation of a circuit breaker. Investigation revealed that the main circuit breaker was operating prematurely under normal load current due to engine heat. The product was defective in that the main circuit breaker was located too close to high temperature engine components and was not compensated by design or selection to avoid tripping at normal load current.

The motorcycle in this case could be started and operated with the lights on until the engine temperature reached a critical value, whereupon both lights and engine would shut off when the circuit breaker opened. Unfortunately for the operator, the motorcycle would continue to move with the engine off and without lights for some distance, depending upon speed before the electrical system failure. During a period of operation on a city street near sundown, such a failure occurred and an automobile turned left into the path of the motorcycle. The automobile driver claimed never to have seen the approaching motorcycle.

8.7 Emergency Lighting

The Uniform Building Code (UBC) requires exits to be illuminated at any time a building is occupied except within individual dwellings, guest rooms, and sleeping rooms. In the event of failure of the normal power supply system, illumination is required to be provided automatically from an emergency system for certain occupancies.[20] Storage batteries or on-site generation in accordance with the National Electrical Code (NEC) can provide the emergency power supply for exit lighting.[21]

The emergency power supply source is required to be available within not more than ten seconds following failure of the normal supply and to supply and maintain the total load for a period of not less than one and one-half hours in the case of batteries. In the case of on-site generation utilizing internal combustion engine-generator sets, the system is required to have an on-site fuel supply capable of two hours full-demand operation of the emergency system.[22]

The *IES Handbook* gives the recommended practice for design of egress route emergency lighting wherein minimum illuminance, uniformity, visibility of hazards and the location of egress luminaries are discussed.[23] Escape route identification, including exit signage and illumination thereof are also found in the *IES Handbook*. Additional references to emergency lighting are to be found in NFPA 101, the *Life Safety Code*.[24]

8.8 Nighttime Photography

Photography can be a powerful form of visual presentation in court. Daytime photographs are usually easy to take and even an unskilled photographer can prepare such evidence, as it would appear under daytime levels of illumination.

Lighting installation photography using color film requires some special considerations.[25] Fluorescent with incandescent fill light, for example, produces a noticeable color mismatch in the photograph. Because all films are designed to respond to a continuous spectrum, high intensity discharge lamps such as high-pressure sodium, metal halide, mercury, and low-pressure sodium, which have discontinuous line spectrums, will produce an unrealistic color on the film. Lamp and film manufacturers can generally provide recommendations for the use of suitable filters for obtaining a realistic color balance.

Again, Paul L. Olson, has devoted a chapter to the subject of problems with the use of nighttime photography as evidence in court. He identifies the following major concerns with the use of nighttime photographs as evidence:[26]

- distortion of contrast
- field of view of the camera
- lack of motion (fixed photo) as in a traffic collision
- protracted viewing of the photograph by the jury
- preconditioning of the jury who view a photograph when they know what to look for and where it will be located

An important principle in color photography when used for presentation, as evidence is that the eye readily accepts illumination of mixed color temperature, but photographic film does not![27]

Endnotes

1. Illuminating Society of North America, *IES Lighting Handbook*, 8th ed. (NY: Illuminating Society of North America, 1993), 3.

2. Louis Erhardt, *Radiation, Light and Illumination* (Camarillo, CA: Camarillo Reproduction Center, 1977), 5.

3. Ibid., 15.

4. IES, *Lighting Handbook*, 82.

5. Erhardt, *Radiation*, 309.

6. Ibid., 310.

7. Paul F. Olson, *Forensic Aspects of Driver Perception and Response* (Tuscon, AZ: Lawyers & Judges Publishing Co., Inc., 1996), 32.

8. IES, *Lighting Handbook*, 97.

9. Ibid., 96.

10. Ibid., 99, 108.

11. Olson, *Forensic Aspects*, 9–10.

12. IES *Lighting Handbook*, Application Volume, 1981, 4–21.

13. IES, *Lighting Handbook*, 79.

14. IES *Lighting Handbook*, Application Volume, 1981, 2–26.

15. IES, *Lighting Handbook*, 83–84.

16. Ibid., Ch. 11.

17. Ibid., 899.

18. W. Adrian, "Visibility of Targets: Model for Calculation," *Lighting Research and Technology* 21(4):181–188 (1989).

19. Olson, *Forensic Aspects*, 171–205.

20. International Conference of Building Officials, *Uniform Building Code*, 1991 ed. (Whittier, CA: International Conference of Building Officials), sec. 3313.

21. National Fire Protection Association, *National Electrical Code*, 1996 ed. (Quincy, MA: National Fire Protection Association), article 700.

22. Ibid., Art. 700-12.

23. IES, *Lighting Handbook*, 889–892.

24. National Fire Protection Association, *Life Safety Code,* NFPA 101 (Quincy, MA: National Fire Protection Association).

25. IES, *Lighting Handbook*, 707–710.

26. Olson, *Forensic Aspects*, 145–154.

27. IES, *Lighting Handbook*, 709.

Chapter 9

Lightning

9.1 Introduction

Benjamin Franklin was the first to scientifically inquire about the nature of lightning in 1752. This was neither his first nor his only contribution to electrical physics. In 1747, he had, along with the independent work of William Watson in England, simultaneously reached the same conclusion regarding the electrical characteristic of matter. Both scientists originated the theory of conservation of charge: the total charge of an insulated system remains constant.

Franklin's experiment with lightning was extremely dangerous. He flew a kite with a metallic tip using hemp line during a thunderstorm. At the end of the line, he attached a metal key, to which a nonconducting silk string was attached which he held in his hand. When he held his knuckles near the key, he could draw sparks from it. Two subsequent experimenters who tried this were killed.[1]

9.2 Physics of Lightning

Lightning can occur whenever natural atmospheric conditions are favorable for the separation of electric charge, most often during the formation of thunderclouds (cumulonimbus clouds), but also during dust and snowstorms and within the gases emitted by an erupting volcano.[2] Lightning can also occur on clear days, possibly giving rise to the expression "a bolt from the blue." Lightning can take many forms, including bead or chain lightning, ball lightning (also called globe lightning) and as a glowing phenomenon known as Saint Elmo's Fire, which is a corona discharge commonly seen on aircraft extremities when flying in dry snow or in the vicinity of thunderstorms.[3] (See Section 9.4 for additional information on ball lightning.)

On May 14, 1998, smoke drifted north from extensive forest fires in Mexico apparently triggering intense thunderstorms from Texas to North Dakota. There were more than 43,000 cloud-to-ground lightning strikes recorded within twenty hours on this date, an average of 2,150 strikes per hour, or more than three times the normal rate of lightning strikes for this area.

The usual cloud-to-ground lightning observed from the earth is initiated by separation and accumulation of electrical charges within the cloud and transfers some 20 to 30 coulombs of negative cloud charge to the earth during the flash.[4] A coulomb is a unit of electric charge equivalent to 6.24 × 10^18 elementary charge units (electrons).

An 1885 theory that explains the separation of charges within a cloud is known as the **precipitation theory**[5] and is based upon the observation that the gravitational field accelerates large water droplets toward the earth while smaller droplets can remain suspended in air and rise as warmer air moves upward within the cloud. Experiments have shown that collisions between these oppositely moving droplets result in a net negative charge transfer to the large droplets, and of course, a net positive charge to the smaller droplets. Conservation of charge requires that as the lower portions of the cloud become negatively charged, the upper portions will become equally positively charged.

A second, more recently formulated theory explaining the process of cloud charge separation is the **convection theory**.[6] Both upward and downward air currents (drafts) exist within clouds that serve as carriers for ionized air molecules. Cosmic rays emitted by the sun that impinge on air molecules generate both positive and negative charged ions creating the ionized air. The negative ions attach themselves to water droplets and ice particles that are moved by gravity or downward drafts to lower altitudes. As part of the convection theory, the earth's surface is included as a contributor to the cloud's charge formation. Sharp objects on the earth's surface produce corona discharges when influenced by high-intensity electric fields that are created by the charged overhead clouds. These discharges create positive ions in the cloud that are transported to higher altitudes by upward drafts in the cloud. This results in even greater accumulation of negative charge in the lower portions of the cloud.

The modern theory of charge separation in clouds is somewhat more complex than either precipitation or convection theory alone provides. Current scientific opinion is that a tripole separation of charge occurs in thunderclouds, with the upper part of the cloud charged positive, the lower part charged negative and a third smaller layer of positive charges accumulating somewhere in the lower middle portions of the cloud.

As thunderclouds pass over the ground they cause a net positive ground charge to appear at the earth's surface that moves in synchronism with the cloud. When the electric field intensity becomes great enough in the cloud, it starts a preliminary breakdown and a particular form of electric discharge occurs.[7] These discharges are termed **pilot streamers**. A second form of discharge then occurs called a **stepped leader**.[8] The step leader discharges are discrete luminous steps approximately 50 meters long and propagate downward from the cloud toward the ground at speeds of 105 to 106 meters per second (m/s). Within 10 to 20 ms, the stepped leaders reach a point above the earth where the resulting electrical field intensity rises above the critical breakdown potential of the air separation and an upward-going discharge is initiated. This begins the **attachment process**. A high intensity discharge then occurs through the ionized air channel established by the step leaders. This discharge is extremely luminous and is observed as a bolt of lightning. The upward propagating potential discontinuity is known as a **return stroke**. The completion of this first return stroke, which requires about 100 µs, does not typically end the flash.[9] Several more leader-return strokes may ensue before the flash is complete.

Another less common form of cloud-to-ground lightning is the positive flash where positive charge accumulation is conducted to the earth. Positive flashes generally have only one return stroke that is preceded by a pulsating rather than a stepped leader.[10] The currents produced in positive flashes are usually much larger than negative flashes, typically being in the range above 100 kA. Positive flashes represent from 1 to 20 percent of all lightning produced by summer thunderstorms and as much as 50 percent of winter lightning storms.[11]

Only cloud-to-ground lightning has been described herein since this form of nature's electrical activity impacts power and communication systems on the ground as well as creates a serious hazard to life. Other forms of lightning include in-cloud, cloud-to-cloud, and cloud-to-air. These forms of atmospheric lightning are of concern to aircraft safety and can adversely affect broadcast communications, but seldom are life-threatening. An important exception to this observation is the case of aircraft involvement with atmospheric lightning that causes a fuel explosion. Currently, all major aircraft are designed with safeguards to prevent lightning from producing an electrical discharge that could ignite fuel tanks or lines. The metal skin of an aircraft is an excellent shield and diverting conductor for the lightning current which prevents enclosed electrical and mechanical systems as well as passengers from being adversely affected.

The voltage between thundercloud and ground prior to a lightning discharge is estimated to be from 10 MV to 1,000 MV (MV = 1 million volts).[12] The voltage of concern to lightning protection engineers is, however, determined by the stroke current times the impedance. Stroke current is by itself of importance since high current implies high magnetic field strength and greater coupling of energy to nearby objects. The reader will find additional discussion of electromagnetic fields in Chapter 5.

9.3 Characteristics of Lightning

From many studies conducted around the world, scientists have developed a statistical profile for lightning strokes occurring between thundercloud and ground. A summary of these findings follows.[13]

Crest of stroke current: 1 to 200 kA
    90 percent exceed 18 kA
    10 percent exceed 84 kA
    average crest magnitude = 47 kA

Time to reach crest of stroke: 0 to 6 μs
    90 percent exceed 0.65 μs
    10 percent exceed 3.35 μs
    average time to reach crest = 1.65 μs

Number of leader-return strokes: 1 to 50
    21 percent six-or-more-strokes lightning
    36 percent single-stroke lightning
    mean value of multiple strokes = 3

Electrical engineering simulations of lightning have widely accepted the use of the "Standard Lightning Impulse" as specified according to ANSI C68.1-1968 as a 1.2/50 waveform that is shown in Figure 9.1.

The standard lightning impulse has a front rise time of 1.2 μs and a decay time to half value of 50 μs. The crest magnitude can be adjusted to represent the previously shown crest statistics. This waveform is acceptable both as a high-voltage, laboratory-generated function and as a com-

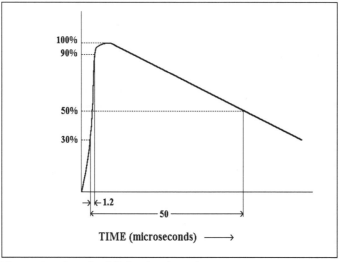

Figure 9.1 *Standard lightning impulse*

puter model for the lightning waveform. Although all lightning strokes do not follow this exact waveform, its adoption standardizes the high-voltage testing of lightning protection devices and procedures and allows computer modeling to subject the mathematical model of a system to standard testing for response.

9.4 Ball Lightning and Related Phenomena
Raymond M. Fish

Ball lightning and similar phenomena have been reported by thousands of people over the last several hundred years. While ball lightning is most often associated with thunderstorms, it does occur near arcing of man-made power sources and can be produced in the laboratory. Some injuries have resulted from ball lightning.

Ball lightning refers to a single luminous globe while multiple luminous balls are called bead lightning. Bead lightning is most often the residue of a cloud-to-cloud or cloud-to-ground lightning stroke. Bead lightning looks like a string of pearls or series of luminous balls separated by dark regions and remains visible for about a second (Barry 1980).

A. Incidence

The appearance of ball lightning is infrequent and apparently random. The mysterious fireballs have been sighted not only by laypersons but also by professional scientists (Singer 1991).

Ball lightning usually occurs during thunderstorms, often related to the occurrence of ordinary lightning. Hundreds of observations from Japan, however, contain ten times as many cases in fair weather as in rain or storm (Singer 1991; Ohtsuki and Ofuruton 1991; Barry and Singer 1988).

B. Properties observed

Ball lightning can float slowly and enter buildings, causing problems for nearby structures and persons. The balls can move against the direction of winds and penetrate windowpanes without making a hole in the glass. Such properties have been demonstrated with artificially produced ball lightning. Ball lightning appears as a bright or flaming globe with various possible colors, including orange, red-orange, intense white, blue, green, or yellow. The typical size of the ball is 25 to 30 cm in diameter, with a range of 1 cm to over 10 meters having been reported. Shapes other than globes do occur (Uman 1984). Persons who were close to the balls have received burns while others reported absence of warmth. Combustible materials have been ignited. The balls may disappear silently or with an explosion (Singer 1991; Radada and Trueba 1996; Uman 1984).

Ball lightnings usually have a lifetime under five seconds; though, a small number of reports have indicated that lifetimes of over a minute can occur. They may move horizontally, vertically, or remain motionless in mid-air. They may seem to spin and to bounce off of solid objects including the ground. Hissing sounds have been reported as well as sharp and repugnant odors. Ball lightnings sometimes seem to be attracted to metallic objects and may move along wire fences or telephone lines. They can enter houses through screens or chimneys. They also may seem to enter houses through glass windowpanes or originate from telephones. They have been reported in all-metal enclosures such as an airplane (Uman and Lowke 1968; Uman 1984).

C. Ball lightning associated with man-made electric power sources

There have been a number of reports of ball lightning-like phenomena being initiated accidentally in high power electrical equipment (Uman, 1984). One such report involved discharge of current from a 260-volt DC source across a circuit breaker in a submarine (Silberg 1965).

D. Experimentally produced ball lightning

Laboratory experiments have produced fireballs that resemble ball lightning (Singer 1991). These have been produced in three different experimental settings:

- globes formed in dilute mixtures of fuel gas in air,
- radio-frequency gas discharges, and
- luminous spheres produced by electric discharge from metal wires.

Plasma fireballs resembling ball lightning have been produced by setting off electric discharges in an atmosphere-containing aerosol with varying concentrations of ethane, methane or both. Plasma fireballs have also been produced in a natural atmosphere by microwave interference (interaction of two microwave signals). The latter fireballs exhibited properties similar to eyewitness observations of ball lightning, including motion against the wind and the ability to pass through a wall intact (Ohtsuki and Ofuruton 1991).

E. Types of ball lightning

There are probably several types of ball lightning. There are a number of theories and models that explain various types of ball lightning. A few general ideas concerning this complex subject are listed below, derived from the discussion by Uman (1984):

- Ball lightning theories fall generally into one of two general classes, depending on whether the energy source is inside or outside of the ball.
- Internally generated energy may come from
  - burning gas or
  - chemical reactions involving dust, soot, or other materials.

- External power sources for ball lightning could include current flowing from
  - cloud to ground, or from
  - another power source.
- Some forms of ball lightning may be high-density plasmas, contained by their own magnetic fields.
- Some forms of ball lightning may consist of a microwave radiation field contained within a thin spherical shell of plasma.

F. Reported injuries from ball lightning

Injuries from ball lightning have included burns, loss of consciousness, and one possible death (Barry 1980).

One possibly fatal case involved a Dr. Richmann, a scientist in 1753 using an apparatus to attract lightning to his laboratory. According to some witnesses, a ball lightning appeared in his laboratory following a lightning strike. Some witnesses say that the ball lightning moved through the air and struck Dr. Richmann on the head. Other witnesses suggest that Dr. Richmann may have been hit by the bolt of lightning (Barry 1980, 152).

Ball lightning has been reported by thousands of people over the years, and it has been produced in the laboratory. It has interesting and varied properties; there are probably several different phenomena leading to different types of ball lightning. Injuries have been reported, but the number of persons who have made physical contact with this form of energy appears to be small.

An especially descriptive layman's report of ball lightning follows.

On June 27, 2001 . . . it was very cloudy and we could hear thunder very far. I saw I very bright light in my home and it went through the hallway and then disappeared. My husband was outside and then suddenly I heard a very loud explosion. I checked to see if my chidren [sic] were all right and then I looked through my living room window and saw my husband lying face down on the ground. I ran outside and turned him over to see that he wasn't breathing anymore. I lowered his arms on the side of his body and replaced his head straight to help him breath. I then ran back inside and tried to dial 911 but my phone was dead. Luckily we had an old dial phone in my daughter's room that was still working. The peramedics [sic] were at home within 10 minutes and they gave my hus-

band oxygen. His eyes were bloodshot and his breathing was extremely slow. His face was swollen, his nose was broken with all the skin torn off. There was a burnt hold [sic] in his chin. Today he has many medical problems such as a large tumor to his pancreas and many other tumors to his gall bladder. The doctors don't know what to do because they have never seen such a case . . . .
(Labelle 2002)

Dr. Fish comments, "Some are probably acute injuries; the cancers reported are probably unrelated."

9.5 Life Safety

In the U.S. alone, about 150 people are killed each year and several hundred are injured due to lightning, a death rate exceeding that caused by hurricanes and tornadoes.[14] A direct lightning flash with a human or animal is almost always fatal, particularly when the electrical stroke enters at the head. Lightning strokes that have been survived are probably due to marginal involvement such that only a fraction of the electromagnetic energy discharged actually impacted the living body. See Section 9.6 for an expanded discussion of lightning-related injuries.

Strange accounts of lightning stroke survival have arisen throughout history. There is one account of a horseback rider who awoke relatively unharmed following a lightning flash to find himself on the ground several feet from his horse, which was dead. The metal shoes on the horse were severely arc damaged by electrical discharge into the earth.

Injuries caused to survivors of lightning are similar to those caused by direct high voltage contact as discussed in Chapter 5. A significant difference between contact with high voltage technical electricity and lightning is that the former lasts at least a few tenths of a second or longer while a typical lightning flash is over in less than a few hundred microseconds, including multiple return strokes. Extreme cases of lightning occurrence have been recorded with large numbers of multiple strokes—such as forty or fifty—with duration of the lightning event lasting more than 0.5 second.[15]

If a person finds himself outside in a thunderstorm, the safest shelter is within a structure such as a large building or totally enclosed metal housing like an automobile. If in an open area like a field or golf course, the human body can be minimized as a lightning target by lying on the ground in a fetal position. Never seek shelter under a tree or next to a tall narrow projection or structure such as a radio antenna or water tower. Lightning does strike twice in the same place, and in fact, prefers sharp projections from the ground surface because these anomalies increase the electrical field intensity between ground and cloud when charge differences exist.

Persons are advised to seek shelter inside buildings, cars, or other large metallic sheathed structures, underground tunnels or caves, even city streets that have high-rise buildings nearby. The protection of a building is like an umbrella extending outward. From the top for a fifty-foot-tall building, for example, the protection is about a 45-degree angle with the vertical.[16] Avoid small-unprotected buildings such as barns and sheds, open automobiles such as convertibles, and nonmetal trailers. Buildings that have passive lightning protection, such as air terminals (lightning rods), ground terminals, interconnecting conductors, and other components necessary to form a lightning protection envelope for the structure, are generally safe locations for persons during thunderstorms. Extremely hazardous locations include high profile ground, tops of buildings, open fields, golf courses, swimming pools, lakes, and areas near fences, overhead wires, and railroad tracks.

The use of electrical appliances, telephones, plumbing fixtures or other conductive objects should be avoided during thunderstorms. Active lightning protection using surge arresters to protect the electrical systems of the structure can prevent fires and reduce the shock hazard from transmission of high voltage to the interior wiring system.

Reports of injuries and even deaths from lightning conducted by telephone system wiring are found in the literature;[17] however, more than half of these case histories are prior to 1940 and involve telephone wiring that had been modified or that did not include lightning arresters. See Section 9.6.C for more recent reports of lightning injury. Nonetheless, it is advisable to avoid the use of the telephone during thunderstorms if for no other reason than possible hearing injury due to an audible transfer of electromagnetic energy through the headset.

Protection of livestock exposed in fields is difficult, but certain precautions can be taken. Isolated trees, particularly on high ground, should be removed. Fences should be constructed with metallic posts and broken continuity to reduce the magnetic field induced voltages and currents. Wooden post fences with continuous wire are the most dangerous. Occasional metallic posts and broken wire continuity will reduce the lightning hazard substantially.

In high-profile lightning strike areas, barns should be constructed with passive lightning protection systems, Moreover, if electrical service is provided, the service entrance should be protected with lightning arresters as described in the following sections of this chapter.

9.6 Lightning-Related Injuries
Raymond M. Fish

A. Being struck by lightning is often not fatal
There are many ways to be "struck by lightning." It is likely that persons who receive a direct lightning strike will be killed, or at least be injured more severely than persons who receive an indirect strike. Indirect types of lightning strikes are described below.

In persons struck by lighting who do not die, any organ system can be injured. An intense systemic vasoconstriction often occurs, leading to cyanosis of extremities, lack of pulses, and the feeling of paresthesias or anesthesia in some extremities. This usually resolves; but if it does not, gangrene may develop and an amputation may be required (Stanley and Suss 1985). Intracranial injury can be especially disabling (Kleinschmidt-DeMasters 1995).

In one review of lightning deaths (Cooper 1980), death occurred in 30 percent of the cases. Prognosis was poor for persons with leg burns (mortality 30 percent), cranial burns (37 percent), and cardiopulmonary arrest (76 percent). Permanent sequelae were found in 74 percent of survivors.

B. Types of lightning contact

- **direct hits**. Persons hit directly by lightning may be killed or severely injured. Indirect hits, as described below, are often not as damaging.
- **stride potential**. When a lightning strike is several meters from a person, current flow from the strike creates a voltage gradient along the ground that decreases with greater distance from the strike. The

voltage is high near the strike and gradually goes to zero at a large distance from the strike. The voltage difference between a person's legs will depend on the distance each is from the strike, sometimes called the stride potential. Cows standing so as to face toward or away from the lightning strike may be electrocuted while those standing sideways to the strike may be unharmed.

- **side flashes**. Lightning may have several arms or side splashes, may seem to bounce from one object to another, or may travel along electrical wires and other objects. A side flash occurs when current splashes from a primary conductor to another object, such as occurs with a person standing under a tree that is struck by lightning (Pierce 1986; Fontanarosa 1988).

- **indirect hit case report**. An example of an indirect lightning hit was reported by Amy et al. (1985). A sixteen-year-old boy suffered 23-percent body surface area burn when lightning struck a television antenna on a nearby trailer and then arced over to him. He was thrown to the ground, and his clothing ignited and caused the burns. He had premature ventricular contractions that spontaneously resolved. He had a sixty-one day stay in the hospital for treatment of the burns, but had no other problems.

- **flash-over**. Electric current tends to travel on the outside of conductors. This effect is more pronounced for higher frequencies and short pulses of electricity (Fink and Beaty 1987, 2-25). Lightning consists of short pulses of electricity. Thus, much of the electric current from a lightning strike may travel over the surface of the body. Wet clothes would aid this process. In such cases, the clothes may be split or exploded off the relatively intact body (Pierce et al. 1986). This effect does not adequately protect all persons who are hit by lightning.

- **multiple-victim incidents**. Multiple people are often injured simultaneously by lightning because of the stride potential or side flashes (DeAtley 1991). For example, respiratory arrest was reported in an eleven-year-old boy standing thirty feet away from a lightning strike; a side flash may have hit him. Another boy 100 feet from the main lightning flash suffered unconsciousness and cardiac dysrhythmias (Kotagal 1982).

Table 9.1
Electrical Mechanisms of Telephone-Related Lightning Injury

direct strike. If a communication (telephone) line is struck by lightning, current may pass through the telephone user to ground.

indirect strike. Current and voltage surges can be electrically induced onto communication lines if nearby power lines or other
objects are struck by lightning. Again, current may pass through
the telephone user to ground.

earth potential rise (EPR). If lightning strikes the ground or is conducted to ground near a telephone user, the *local earth (ground)
near the user* is raised to a high voltage for a short time. Problems
may occur if the *user* is somehow both: (1) connected to the local
ground and (2) holding a telephone that is grounded to the telephone exchange some miles away. In this situation the person
would be between two different "grounds." One of the grounds is
being raised to a high voltage by a lightning strike

C. Telephone-related lightning injury

1. Occurrence

Though it happens infrequently, lightning can injure people using
telephones indoors. There are about eighty such injuries in Australia
yearly with no deaths being reported as of 1992. In the United States,
there are about eight injuries and one death each year (Andrews 1992).

Between 1977 and 1985, Telecom Australia received 326 reports of
telephone-related lightning injury. Of these, 42 percent involved electric
shock alone, while others involved acoustic injury with or without accompanying electrical shock. Injuries included variable periods of loss of consciousness (some with retrograde amnesia) and burns that sometimes included the auditory canal (Frayne 1987; Johnstone 1986).

2. Electrical mechanisms of telephone-related lightning injury

In Australia, at least 80 percent of telephone-related injuries are
thought to be caused by lightning impulses delivered to nearby ground or
power systems. There are three ways harmful voltage and current can
originate: direct strike, indirect strike, and earth potential rise, as de-

scribed in Table 9.1. Because the voltages associated with lightning are very high, being "connected" in the examples below may occur through arcing. The arcing to the person can be from conductors inside the telephone and from other nearby conductors connected to local ground (Andrews 1992).

3. Medical effects of telephone-related lightning injury

a. Lightning strike syndromes. In a study of 328 patients, three "lightning strike syndromes" were identified (Andrews 1992). About 40 percent of patients were in the first group, which had the least injury. Symptoms usually lasted less than twenty-four hours and related to emotional "shock," confusion, and nervousness. There were sometimes complaints of burning feelings, paresthesias (numbness or tingling), and weakness in the current path. Burns were rare.

About 50 percent of patients were in the second group. Symptoms were similar to the first group, but recovery took longer, often a few months. These patients had pain and paresthesias in the current path. The ear was affected with some deafness and tinnitus (ringing in the ear). Slowly resolving psychiatric symptoms were also reported.

The most severe symptoms occurred in group 3, comprising 10 percent of patients. They had symptoms persisting beyond three months. Symptoms were similar to group 2, though fewer reported hearing loss. Long-term symptoms included pain in the current path and a psychiatric picture resembling obsessional concern with symptoms, depression, and problems with memory, concentration, and "mental acuity." Some patients had persistent anxiety and phobic symptoms.

In a prospective study of ten patients, examination was performed as soon as possible after injury. In this study, ear symptoms were noted in some cases, but there were no ruptured tympanic membranes, which is somewhat common with outdoor injuries due to lightning. In this study, pain, tinnitus, and altered sensation were noted in 30 percent of cases. Face, neck, and arm pain were seen in 30 percent. In addition, psychiatric symptoms were seen in 60 percent (Andrews 1992, 823; Andrews and Darveniza 1991).

Signs and symptoms similar to those of a more direct lightning strike can occur in telephone-mediated lightning strike. In one case, the patient had been holding a phone to his ear. There was extensive damage to the telephone and other electrical devices. He was thrown against a wall and seemed to have a period of loss of consciousness. The patient could not remember the actual injury, but remembered lying on the floor unable to breathe or speak. He had weakness and paresthesias throughout his body, as well as a headache. Paralysis of the right leg resolved over several hours. He also had a rapid heartbeat, arborescent skin burns, tinnitus, and singed hair. Audiometric testing showed a mild left conductive hearing loss (Andrews 1992; Johnstone et al. 1986).

b. Predictors of patients likely to have more serious problems. Predictors of patients likely to have more serious problems from telephone-related lightning injury include (Andrews 1992)

- being thrown physically by the shock,
- a greater amount of power system damage at the residence, and
- early neuritic pain (pain suggestive of inflammation of a nerve).

c. Causalgia and reflex sympathetic dystrophy from telephone-mediated lightning strike. Two telephone operators developed severe causalgia after being struck by lightning through their telephone headsets. They were sitting next to each other when they were struck. Both women felt a shock going through their bodies, most of which seemed to pass from their heads to their right arms. They felt as if they had been hit with a baseball bat. Their right arms turned purple and developed a painful burning sensation immediately after the shock. Treatments included pain medications, antidepressants, physical therapy, and transcutaneous electrical nerve stimulation. Six months later, their arms were still swollen. There was persistent burning, aching, tightness, throbbing, and numbness. Pain was worsened with exposure to heat or cold. Generalized symptoms included psychological problems, dizziness and headaches. The arms and forearms were swollen, cold, and tender to the touch. Both women had allodynia, hyperpathia, dysesthesia, hyperalgesia, and vasomotor changes (see definitions below). Their right shoulder muscles were taut and tender. Their heads were slightly tilted to the right. Sympathetic blocks were done and did bring relief. Interpleural blocks were done at the right fourth intercostal space about 6 cm from the spinous process. These were repeated and accompanied by physical and occupational therapy, psychotherapy, and biofeedback. Symptoms were 90 percent relieved after one week of daily injections and both women were able to return to work (Shantha 1991).

Signs and symptoms. Definitions of some signs and symptoms found in RSD and causalgia (*Stedman's Medical Dictionary*):

Allodynia is a condition in which ordinarily nonpainful stimuli evoke pain.

Hyperpathia is an exaggerated subjective response to painful stimuli, with a continuing sensation of pain after the stimulation has ceased.

Dysesthesia has three definitions:

1. Impairment of sensation short of anesthesia.

2. A condition in which a disagreeable sensation is produced by ordinary stimuli; caused by lesions of the sensory pathways, peripheral or central.

3. Abnormal sensations experienced in the absence of stimulation.

Hyperalgesia is extreme sensitiveness to painful stimuli.

Vasomotor changes involve causing dilation or constriction of blood vessels. This can lead to visible color changes, swelling, and sensitivity to heat, cold or both.

Sudomotor changes refer to abnormalities of the autonomic (sympathetic) nerves that stimulate the sweat glands to activity.

d. Case report of paralysis, sensory symptoms, and otological disturbance. A thirty-one-year-old man was struck by lightning while using the telephone inside a private home in a semi-rural district near Melbourne, Australia (Johnstone et al. 1986). He had been holding a one-piece telephone against his left ear and was sitting on a stool with his right leg touching a dishwasher. There was a loud thunderclap, and pictures were blown off the wall in an adjacent room. The man was thrown about three feet, hit a wall, and appeared to be unconscious for a few seconds. He could not later recall the actual lightning strike, but he did remember lying on the floor being unable to breathe or speak for up to a minute. He soon became able to breathe and move his arms weakly. He felt a warm burning sensation with some paresthesias throughout his body. This was greater in his right leg which was completely paralyzed. Over an hour, strength returned to his arms and left leg. His right leg remained weak for several hours. He also had fast, regular palpitations, tinnitus in his left ear, and a headache. Physical examination showed red marks (Lichtenberg figures) that extended down the left side of his neck, spread from left to right across his trunk and down his lateral right thigh. There were associated singed body hairs. The marks faded over twenty-four hours. His left-sided tinnitus resolved over five hours. There was a mild left conductive deafness. An audiogram three months later showed a left sensorineural hearing loss of 35 decibels above 3 kHz, compared to a right-sided loss of 25 decibels.

Moreover, the telephone had extensive internal burns. Arc marks were present on the dishwasher where the man had been touching it and inside the telephone wall plug.

e. Injury attributed to "mass anxiety." Workers at the Manitoba Telephone System reported ninety-two incidents over two weeks that were thought to be caused by electric shocks. Lesser numbers of reports continued after that time. There were numbness and tingling in the limbs, face, or head, and other diffuse symptoms. There was much publicity about the alleged injuries. A panel and a committee were unable to substantiate any injury besides electrostatic shock and occupational stress. The reports started when there was a possible power failure: video display terminals had gone blank, and others had distorted displays. Three operators concurrently reported "shocks," described as a sudden tingling sensation in the arms and one side of the body. No physical signs were present (Yassi et al., 1989).

D. Thermal and mechanical shock wave injury
Lightning causes damage through several mechanisms (Craig 1986). Brief, but intense, thermal radiation is emitted from lightning; the thermal flash most often produces superficial burns. Lightning can also cause deeper burns. A mechanical shock wave produced in association with the lightning can produce tympanic membrane perforation and internal organ contusion or perforation.

E. Cardiac complications of lightning injury
Cardiac complications reported following lightning injury have included transient hypertension, tachycardia, nonspecific electrocardiographic changes, direct myocardial injury, congestive heart failure (Kleiner 1978; Chia 1981) and dysrhythmias. Dysrhythmias have included atrial fibrilla-

tion, ventricular tachycardia, and ventricular fibrillation (Craig 1986; Zeana 1984; Jackson and Parry 1980).

There are several theories of how lightning produces dysrhythmias. It is thought that lightning sometimes acts as a strong defibrillation, resulting in asystole. Sinus rhythm (a normal heart rhythm) is spontaneously restored after a short time, similar to the situation in cardiac resuscitation when a man-made defibrillator applies a few thousand volts to the chest. However paralysis of the respiratory center in the brain stem often persists following lightning strike. Unless ventilatory assistance is provided, hypoxia leads to a secondary ventricular fibrillation (Fontanarosa 1988; Pierce 1986).

1. Myocardial infarction

Myocardial infarction following lightning strike occurred in a fourteen-year-old boy. Lightning struck the bathroom in which he was seated (Amy et al. 1985). The outer wall of the bathroom was blown off by the associated explosion. The child was found semicomatose. EKG showed a subendocardial (partial wall thickness) myocardial infarction. He also had bilateral perforated tympanic membranes. He regained normal sensorium and had a normal neurological examination. He had partial thickness burns in a serpiginous pattern on the anterior and posterior aspects of the trunk. After three days, he was transferred to a burn center. The burns healed spontaneously. He was discharged with persistent, but not progressive, EKG evidence of subendocardial infarction. He also had decreased hearing due to the tympanic membrane injuries.

Another case involved a forty-one-year-old man who was holding an umbrella in his right hand when lightning struck. His first memory was of complete paralysis of both legs and right arm. He was gasping for breath. Over half an hour, he regained strength of his limbs and developed a severe burning pain in his right arm and shoulder. EKG showed an acute inferior myocardial infarction, but he made a good recovery (Jackson and Parry 1980).

2. Congestive heart failure

A previously healthy twenty-four-year-old woman was struck by lightning while walking in a field. She was unconscious for a number of minutes, but woke and was able to walk. Several hours later, she was found to be in congestive heart failure with a normal blood pressure. There were first- and second-degree burns on her left chest and abdomen. CPK and SGOT were elevated, and EKG showed deeply inverted T waves in leads II, III, AVF and V3 through V6. She made a full recovery, with an EKG six months later being normal (Chia 1981).

3. Resuscitation of patients with cardiac arrest from lightning strike

Persons suffering cardiac arrest due to lightning strike can sometimes be resuscitated and survive (Lifschultz and Donoghue 1993; Moran 1986).

The American Heart Association states: (Under "lightning strike" page 2,249): "For victims in cardiopulmonary arrest, BLS and ACLS should be instituted immediately. The goal is to oxygenate the heart and brain adequately until cardiac activity is restored."

F. Neurological sequelae of lightning strike

With lightning strike, many victims are rendered unconscious or have temporary lower extremity paralysis. Seizures may be secondary to direct CNS damage or hypoxia (Fontanarosa 1988; Craig 1986; Pierce 1986; Apelberg 1974).

Common early and reversible neurological sequelae of lightning injury include loss of consciousness or confusion, and abnormalities of motor and sensory function of one or more limbs. Paraplegia, quadriplegia and focal paralysis may development immediately, but usually resolve completely within hours to days (Levine et al. 1975). Retrograde amnesia commonly persists. Late developing hemiplegia and aphasia have been reported (Apelberg 1974). Also, later-occurring neuritis (nerve inflammation) and neuralgia (pain in the distribution of a nerve) have developed in extremities not always involved in earlier vasoconstriction (Craig 1986; Apelberg 1974). Peripheral (median) neuropathy has also been reported (Amy et al. 1985). Neuropsychiatric disorders may occur despite normal brain CT scan and EEG (Frayne 1987).

A variety of neurological problems can occur in children struck by lightning. These problems include coma with cerebral edema, inappropriate secretion of antidiuretic hormone (SIADH), seizures, cerebellar ataxia, and painful sensory disturbances. Abnormalities of memory, mood, and affect may persist for months, requiring psychiatric and neurologic follow-up (Kotagal et al. 1982).

1. Delayed onset of neurological deficit

Delayed onset of neurological deficit occurred in a thirty-one-year-old woman who sustained a 3-percent body surface area burn after lightning struck the metal umbrella she was holding in her right hand. There was an arborizing pattern of partial-thickness burns on her skin. There were also some first degree burns of the neck. Her initial neurological examination was normal, but during her nineteen-day hospital stay she developed a mild median nerve deficit which was confirmed by electromyogram (EMG) (Amy et al. 1985).

2. Transient loss of consciousness and paralysis

Loss of consciousness from lightning injury with no permanent deficit other than retrograde amnesia is often reported (Stanley and Suss 1985).

In conscious patients, transient paralysis is sometimes reported. Transient paralysis of the legs is reported more often than of the arms, and is thought to be due to electric current effects on the spinal cord. Loss of consciousness and paralysis usually resolve spontaneously (Stanley and Suss 1985). If there is structural damage to the brain or spinal cord, permanent neurological deficit may occur.

G. Vascular events following lightning injury

Vasomotor spasm is sometimes seen as a local response. Possible mechanisms include sympathetic nervous stimulation, local arterial spasm, and ischemia of peripheral nerves (Tribble 1984). Parts of extremities may repeatedly change color from white to blue to red after lightning injury. This presumably represents cycles of vasoconstriction with pallor and cyanosis, followed by hyperemia.

Severe vasoconstriction (temporary spasm of muscles that constrict blood vessels) is thought to be responsible for loss of pulse, mottling of skin, coolness of extremities, loss of sensation and paralysis due to ischemia of peripheral nerves. These signs and symptoms often spontaneously resolve. The literature has suggested that fasciotomy should be reserved for failure of peripheral circulation to return for several hours (Apelberg 1974; Currens 1945).

1. Arterial spasm and transient paralysis

Arterial spasm and transient paralysis resulting from lightning is reported by Currens (1945). In this case, a small all-metal amphibious airplane had landed, and its motor had stopped. A storm with electrical activity approached. The three occupants of the plane were on the ground, with two of them standing under the wing of the plane, about twelve inches from the closest metal of the plane. The third person was leaning against the fuselage, the right forearm and right thigh in contact with the metal of the plane. He was wearing rubber soled shoes and was standing on an asphalt runway. A few drops of rain had started when a sudden ball of fire was seen to envelop most of the airplane, accompanied by a loud sound of thunder. The two persons standing under the wing were thrown to the ground. The man in contact with the plane ended up on the ground four to six feet toward the tail of the plane. Two men who had been working on a plane fifteen yards away were thrown against the side of the plane but were not injured.

The man who had been leaning against the plane was fifty-three years old. On arrival at the hospital, he was conscious. His right arm and leg felt numb, and he could not move them. The right hand and foot were pale, cool, and dry. The right radial, ulnar, and brachial arteries were not palpable, though they were easily palpable on the left. His jaw also felt stiff. The numbness and paralysis started to resolve after about fifteen minutes. At thirty minutes past the lightning strike, faint pulses could be felt, and these become stronger over the next ten minutes. Movement, color, and sensation improved. He was able to walk within an hour of the accident. Tingling of the toes and fingers on the right continued for two days. Several hours after the accident, the patient noted pink spots over the right heel that corresponded with nails in the heel of his shoes. He felt pain in his heel for two weeks. X-ray later showed a small linear fracture of the right mandible. After the accident, the patient found four coins in his right trouser pocket that were burned and stuck together. He was able to separate two of the coins by hand. There were burned areas on the coins, but not on his trousers or skin.

One of the other two patients was a sixty-three-year-old man. He had initial hypotension: a blood pressure of 80/60 with a pulse of 60. This hypotension resolved spontaneously in two hours. The airplane showed no damage. However, there were three depressed areas in the runway, each six to eight inches long and one-fourth of an inch deep in the deepest area. One of the areas was on either side of the rear wheel where the metal came to within six inches of the ground. The other area was under the fuselage where it was about six inches off the ground.

2. Arterial spasm, hemoglobinuria, and myoglobinuria

Hemoglobinuria and myoglobinuria following lightning injury are very rare.

Arterial spasm, hemoglobinuria, and myoglobinuria after lightning strike was reported by Apelberg et al. (1974). Witnesses stated that a lightning bolt struck a nine-year-old girl directly in the chest while she was standing on a large metal playground slide. She "lit up" and then had a convulsion and unconsciousness for ten to fifteen minutes. In the hospital forty-five minutes after the injury, she was restless, hysterical, and semi-comatose. Her blood pressure was 104/70 with a pulse of 140. There were second degree burns over the anterior abdomen and thighs. Both feet were cold, mottled and cyanotic. There were no palpable pulses below the femoral arteries at the groin, and there was minimal sensation. She had pulmonary edema (possibly from IV fluid administration, thought the paper does not give enough information to determine this). Fasciotomies of the legs were considered, but she had spontaneous improvement in color and sensation over several hours. Urine hemoglobin and myoglobin were 3-plus for forty-eight hours and then returned to normal. She was discharged on the sixth post-injury day.

H. Myoglobinuria

Myoglobinuria following lightning strike was also reported by Yost and Holmes (1974). Their case involved a fourteen-year-old who was struck on the right shoulder by lightning. Defibrillation fifteen minutes later was successful. His right eardrum was ruptured. He had grossly bloody urine containing hemoglobin, myoglobin, red blood cell casts and clumps, and white blood cell clumps. His CPK rose to about 186 times the upper limits of normal. The EKG showed inverted T waves in leads 2, 3, aVf, V4R, and

V1 through V4. There was an elevated ST segment in V2. He was unresponsive at first, but within a week had no detectable physical or neurological complications except for EKG changes and a mild hearing loss in the right ear.

I. Anatomic findings in brain injury caused by lightning

Lightning can cause a variety of anatomic abnormalities of the brain, some of which do show on computed tomography and MRI of the brain. Such anatomic abnormalities include petechial hemorrhages, subarachnoid blood, fissuring and splitting apart of the cortical layers, and a dilatation of the subarachnoid space surrounding blood vessels (Stanley and Suss 1985).

J. Brain injury, as caused by lightning

The mechanisms of injury to the brain are discussed in this book Chapter 17.

The injury. An eleven-year-old boy received what appeared to be a direct lightning stroke to the head and was immediately unconscious (Stanley and Suss 1985). A medical student who witnessed the event started CPR immediately. On arrival at the hospital, blood pressure was 120/70, pulse 76, spontaneous respirations 28. Arterial blood gases were: pH 6.93, pCO_2 58 torr, pO_2 47 torr. The child was in coma with burns of the parieto-occipital scalp, left chest, left abdomen, and legs. There was hemotympanum with perforation of the left eardrum. The legs were mottled with no palpable pedal pulses initially, though these returned spontaneously. EKG showed peaked T waves. Chest x-ray showed bilateral diffuse infiltrates that were interpreted as aspiration. Computed tomography of the brain showed three discrete hematomas in the right basal ganglia.

Treatment. Treatment included a ventriculostomy for ICP (intracranial pressure) monitoring. The patient was put on a ventilator to help manage the aspiration pneumonia and also to allow decrease of intracranial pressure through controlled hyperventilation. Prophylactic phenobarbital was given. Burns were treated with sliver sulfadiazine cream and dressing changes. The ICP remained normal, and the ventriculostomy was removed on the fifth day.

Outcome. The patient's condition improved gradually. After fourteen weeks, he had mild hearing impairment bilaterally, worse on the left. He was ambulatory, but had some left hemiparesis. The hemiparesis was worse in the arm than in the leg.

K. Eye and ear injuries from lightning
See Sections 17.5 and 17.6 (eye and ear injuries).

L. Skin injury
Burns of any depth can be produced. Superficial, spidery, aborescent, erythematous markings are all characteristic of lightning injury. These superficial markings heal without scarring (Craig 1986; Apelberg 1974).

M. Fetal injuries
Pliny the Elder in his *Natural History* (year 77) recorded lightning hitting a pregnant woman; the child was killed, but the woman survived (Rackham 1938; Wagner, McCann and Clayton 1950). In a more recent study of ten cases of reported lightning injury to pregnant women who survived the injury, fetal or neonatal death occurred in five of the cases (Pierce 1986). See also Chapter 20 (maternal and fetal injuries).

N. Autopsy considerations
Lightning may cause injury due to passage of electric current through the body, and also to a blast effect transmitted by air. Although lightning can also cause deep and fatal burns, severe burns are relatively uncommon. Death from lightning may result from the passage of current through the heart or brain stem without evidence of injury to the surface of the body (Fisher 1980, 371).

Burns. The blast associated with lightning can tear clothing, giving the appearance of assault by a person. Lightning is attracted to metallic objects on a person, and these are sometimes melted. Lightning may also produce very superficial red, branching patterns on the skin. These may disappear in several hours.

Edema of the skin at points of current entry may form, possibly due to paralysis of local capillary and lymphatic vessels or nerve injury (Fisher 1980).

Autopsy findings other than burns. If death from lightning is suspected, indications in addition to characteristic skin lesions should be sought (Camps 1976). Examination of the scene of the accident may be far more important than examination of the person's body with lightning, as well as with other types of electrocutions (Fisher 1980, 375). Information that may be important includes: history of an electric storm in the area at the time, blast effects on nearby objects, areas of burning of vegetation, melted or magnetized metal objects, finding of electrical short circuits or defective wiring, and melting of nylon underclothing.

9.7 Structural Systems Protection

Passive protection for structures includes the use of air terminals (lightning rods), conductors, and ground terminals. The requirements for passive lightning protection systems are found in NFPA 780.[18] The purpose of the standard is the practical safeguarding of persons and property from hazards arising from exposure to lightning.[19] Installation requirements given in NFPA 780 cover (1) ordinary structures, (2) miscellaneous structures and special occupancies, (3) heavy metal stacks, (4) watercraft, and (5) structures containing flammable vapors, flammable gases, or liquids that can give off flammable vapors.

The basic tenet of passive lightning protection is that an enclosing system of grounded electrical conducting materials will intercept lightning flashes and dissipate the effect, so that the electromagnetic energy transfer is shunted into the earth thereby avoiding major damage to the structure. A low impedance path is constructed so that the discharge current can enter or leave the earth without following high impedance paths through building materials such as wood, brick, concrete and so on. The I^2R heating effects are minimized by these low impedance constructs and by concentrating the points of discharge attachment to the most elevated and sharpest of the structure's parts; this means that the lower parts are shielded from the flash.

The 200-year-old NFPA 780 approach to structural lightning protection recommends using Franklin rods as air terminals; these terminals are constructed as sharp pointed solid or tubular copper or aluminum rods that are placed at strategic locations along the highest portions of a structure. The effects created by these air terminals, whereby thousands of amperes of lightning current are diverted through the terminals and the ground connecting wiring from these terminals into the earth, can be severely damaging to nearby sensitive electronic equipment such as computers, telephones, energy management systems and so on.

Modern systems of lightning protection utilize the charge transfer system of preventing lightning strikes by replacing the sharp pointed Franklin rods with a multipoint discharge system or "charge transfer system" (CTS).[20] The CTS, if properly designed and installed, breaks down into corona under low potential and delays the formation of lightning streamers, thereby reducing the likelihood of direct lightning attachment.[21] By gradually transferring charge between structure and cloud, the probability of a lightning strike directly to the structure is decreased and the magnitude of discharge current is greatly reduced.

In either method of lightning protection, secondary conductors are utilized to interconnect metal parts of the structure to prevent large potential differences from occurring that would cause side flashes or spark-over discharges. Active suppression devices providing transient voltage surge suppression (TVSS) are also recommended to prevent power, communication, and interior electronic systems from both direct and induced flash currents. See Section 9.8 for further discussion of TVSS methods.

9.8 Electrical Systems Protection

Electric utility companies have recognized from the earliest days of their existence that lightning presented a severe hazard to their business physical facilities. More than 1 million miles of overhead power lines are exposed to the effects of lightning in the U.S. Several million volts can be generated by a direct lightning strike to an overhead power line, which creates an overvoltage that is proportional to the current of the stroke and the characteristic impedance of the line. It is a practical and economic impossibility to insulate overhead power lines below 230 kV to withstand these magnitudes of overvoltage.[22]

To minimize the effects of lightning on electric-utility power transmission lines (TLs), distribution lines (DLs), and equipment (such as transformers and switches), the lines and equipment are (1) shielded by passive diverting lightning protection designs, (2) effectively grounded, and (3) actively protected with lightning arresters at critical points.

The shielding system is designed to intercept lightning flashes that would otherwise directly strike lines or equipment and divert this discharge energy to the earth.

Effective grounding reduces the characteristic impedance of the shielding conductors, line towers, and materials to improve the efficiency of the diversion of destructive lightning energy into the earth.

Lightning arresters are devices placed between the normally energized parts of a utility system facilities and ground. In the case of transmission lines more than 130 kV to ground, arresters are intended to permit normal voltages, to be present on the overhead conductors and equipment without affecting the arrester. In addition, arresters also prevent large overvoltages from occurring by switching the current surge that accompanies the overvoltage condition across the arrester, through the arrester and into the earth.

Overhead power line shielding is accomplished by techniques similar to those recommended and used for structures. By placing effectively grounded continuous conductors above the energized phase conductors of a TL or DL, an umbrella of protection is created for the power lines below. Multiple shielding conductors and increased height separation between shield conductors and phase conductors improves the effectiveness of the shield.

The basic impulse insulation level (BIL) of power electrical equipment is specified in kV (kilovolts) and represents the withstand capability of an apparatus that is subjected to a standard 1.2×50 μs full wave impulse test of specified crest kV. The apparatus must withstand this test without flashover or apparent damage. Examples of the BIL ratings for liquid-filled power transformers are as follows.[23]

Transformer Insulation Class (1.2 × 50) kV (rms)	BIL kV (crest)
5.0	75
8.7	95
15.0	110
25.0	150
34.5	200
69.0	350
115.0	550
138.0	650

By coordinating these equipment capabilities with the protective characteristics of surge arresters, electrical engineers can design power systems which reliably withstand the stress of lightning produced voltage surges. In all but the extreme cases of lightning flash severity, the reliability of electrical power systems is very high. While there are approximately 10,000 forest fires per year in the U.S. because of lightning, there are relatively few power outages lasting more than a few minutes caused by lightning.

Surge arrester protection has evolved over the past ninety-plus years to improve the device characteristics. The ideal surge protector would have a protection quality index (PQI) of 1, where

$$PQI \equiv \frac{V_r}{V_p}.$$
 (Equation 9.1)

V_r in Equation 9.1 is the reseal voltage level below which the protector will not allow significant current to pass through it to ground, and V_p is the protection voltage level which is the maximum voltage allowed by the protector across its terminals. If, without a protector, lightning surge currents reach the protector location such that overvoltages greater than V_p are created then all excess surge current is diverted through the protector into the ground and the voltage across the protector is "clamped" at V_p.

The earliest and basic form of surge protection was the air or spark gap arrester. It is constructed by placing two electrodes near each other with an air gap between them. The electrodes can be rigid wires of various shapes and sizes, or one wire and a metal plate, or two metallic spheres, and so forth. Air gap arresters, even the most sophisticated of designs, generally exhibit low PQI, but they are capable of withstanding large surge currents.

The next oldest of power system arrester technologies is the gapped surge arrester which consists of a series of air gaps along with blocks of nonlinear resistors. Modern gapped arresters use silicon carbon (SiC) block resistor material to create the nonlinear resistance characteristics of the arrester. These arresters can clamp the voltage at a maximum while continuing to withstand large surge currents to ground.

The most modern active arrester technology for power systems utilizes metal-oxide solid-state varistor (MOV) construction. Typically, these devices are manufactured using highly conductive particles of a metal oxide (such as zinc oxide—ZnO) suspended in a semiconducting material. 24 MOV arresters are superior to SiC gapped arresters in their power-follow current limiting characteristics, but they are inferior to SiC arresters in their ability to limit the discharge voltage at high discharge currents (above 10 kA).

In order to improve the performance of MOV arresters at higher discharge current, the innovation of shunt spark gap construction has occurred. MOV blocks with shunt gaps have been designed to permit the air gap to spark over when the MOV discharge current increases beyond a certain value. This reduces the discharge voltage at high discharge currents below the standard MOV characteristics with attendant improvement in protection.

Power system surge arresters have been classified into four groups, starting with the highest, according to kV ratings:

- station arresters
- intermediate arresters
- distribution arresters
- secondary/industrial/commercial arresters

There is some overlap of kV ratings between the first three classes (e.g., distribution arresters are available in the range from 1 to 30 kV, in twelve ratings, and intermediate arresters are available in the range from 3 to 120 kV, in seventeen ratings). Secondary arresters are available in two ratings, 0.175 and 0.650 kV.

Historically, the protection quality of an arrester was highest for the station arresters and decreased to lowest for secondary arresters. Today however, there are MOV arresters available for use as secondary-class arresters that exhibit a very high PQI and are of the same quality as station class arresters.[25]

The discussion of electrical systems protection against lightning has so far dealt with power systems, both primary and secondary, where the system operating voltages to ground or between conductors exceeds 100 volts. Transient voltage surges caused by lightning or power systems switching can even more easily damage lower voltage communication and sensitive electronic equipment.

The telephone industry has existed for more than 150 years. This is far longer than the power industry that did not become viable until dynamos were constructed to effectively generate electricity in the 1880s. The widespread commercial use of electricity, however, was delayed until after methods for transmission were developed in 1884.[26]

In 1837, Samuel Finley Breese Morse (1791–1872) first demonstrated his working telegraph system by transmitting a message 1,700 feet. In 1856, the Western Union Telegraph Company was formed. On October 9, 1876, Alexander Graham Bell and Thomas A. Watson conducted a two-way telephone conversation between Boston and Cambridge. In 1880, the American Bell Telephone Company was created; and in 1885, American Telephone and Telegraph (AT&T) was formed to construct and operate intercity telephone lines.[27]

The need to protect telegraph and telephone equipment against lightning damage was well recognized by the mid-19th century. The earliest forms of air terminal spark gap arresters were developed during this period.

Modern telephone system surge arresters are manufactured using either gas-tube or solid-state (MOV) technology. Station class arresters are available with impulse breakdown ratings for 100 V/μs surge voltage waveforms in 300 to 750 V (gas-tube) and less than 400 V (solid-state) ratings. The holdover or power-follow limiting characteristics for these arresters are typically 150 V extinguishing in less than 150 ms. These characteristics are generally adequate to protect modern telephone wiring and telephone receiving sets from all but the most direct lightning surges.

In addition to lightning, transient overvoltages in power systems may be generated by system conditions such as switching operations and faults. The voltage and current surges that result from switching operations or faults are generally more severe in circuits operating at primary utility voltages above 115 kV than at lower primary or secondary voltages. These transients have peak magnitudes that relate to the nominal system rms operating voltage, generally being not more than a multiple of two to three times the nominal voltage. Disturbances on low voltage (less than 1,000 volts rms) power systems have been the subject of many investigations and studies[28] that have resulted in the IEEE recommended practice cited.

IEEE C62.41-1991 defines three broad categories of circuit locations or "installation categories" as follows.

A. Outlets and long branch circuits
B. Major feeders and short branch circuits
C. Outside and service entrance

Without the use of surge protective devices, the amplitude of both voltage and current are reduced by the effect of series impedance that increases from the outside to locations well within the building.

For other than direct lightning strikes at the point of service, the use of 10 kA, 4/10 μs rated secondary arresters has resulted in successful protection in location category C environments for many years. The location categories A and B are recommended to follow the guide for peak voltages and currents using the standard 0.5 μs/100 kHz ring wave test waveform.[29] Peak values of the test waveform vary from 2 to 6 kV depending upon system exposure.[30]

Sensitive electronic equipment such as solid-state PBX switching equipment, computers, fire alarm systems, energy management and control systems (EMCS), security systems, and closed-circuit television systems are all easily damaged by voltage surges. Even a 20-V surge, if it directly impacts an integrated circuit such as a PC processor, can cause irreparable damage to the equipment. In order to protect against such low electrical energy surges, additional levels of protection must be used beyond the major lightning surge protection afforded by arresters on the electrical power lines and transformers or on the telephone station service lines.

Lightning surge arresters belong to a class of protection devices called shunt protectors. They bypass or "shunt" the excess current caused by a lightning strike into the ground, diverting the excess energy by introducing a parallel path with the load. As has already been observed, the basic limitation of shunt protection is that it cannot reduce the voltage below its clamping voltage level that must be greater than the normal peak voltage required by the power or communication system. MOV shunt protectors have limiting voltages of 300 to 400 volts, and therefore, the equipment will see this magnitude of voltage. Also, there is a finite response time for

such arresters that means that very fast rising surge voltages may pass
through unlimited to the load.

Another form of surge protection is termed series protection because
it acts in-line with the load to block or shut out abnormal electrical energy
from reaching the load. An inductor or coil acts as impedance to the passage of high frequency current through it to the load. In fact, the complex
quantity called inductive impedance has a magnitude given by

$$|X_L| = 2\pi fL$$ (Equation 9.2)

where f is the frequency of the electrical signal in hertz (cycles per second)
and L is the inductance of the coil in henries. Obviously, the impedance of
an inductor increases as f increases. By using multiple elements, inductors

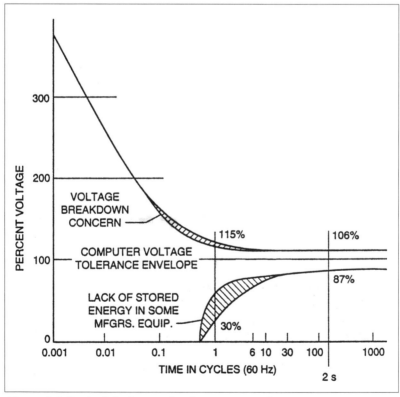

Figure 9.2 *Typical design goals of power-conscious computer
manufacturers.*

and capacitors, electrical filters can be constructed that will pass a 60-Hz AC power signal and block electrical signals at higher frequencies, thereby stopping a high frequency signal like a lightning impulse or switching surge from reaching the load.

Practical limitations such as size and cost constrain the design of series protectors and dictate a compromise form of protection for sensitive electronic equipment known as hybrid protection. By using both parallel and series protection in a "hybrid" design, reasonably economical and physically realistic protectors can be constructed. The most effective and highest quality transient voltage surge suppression (TVSS) devices use hybrid technology. Surge suppressors using the hybrid technology are commercially available for around fifty dollars, and some manufacturers offer equipment protection warranties on their products.

The application of surge protection to sensitive electronic systems requires a thorough engineering analysis of the system and the selective design of protection levels. All electrical interconnections to the sensitive electronic equipment must be protected against disturbances that can damage the equipment. Among the various disturbances to be considered are lightning, load switching, power system faulting, and nonlinear loads.

Computer manufacturers are well aware of the susceptibility of their products to damage through a hostile electrical environment. A widely published consensus design goal of computer manufacturers is expressed by Figure 9.2.[31]

The graph shown in Figure 9.2 depicts only the magnitude and duration of the voltage and does not address the subject of how rapidly the disturbance voltage is applied to the equipment. The rise time of the disturbance is important for two reasons:

- fast rising impulse disturbances have a greater possibility of coupling into adjacent circuits, and
- slowly rising disturbances can pass through series inductive blocking protection.

Lightning protection or large surge current protection is best accomplished by utilizing properly rated surge arresters at the service entrance to the building, both on the power and communications services. TVSS protective devices at distribution power panels, particularly computer

room power panels, and at the load connection terminals can further reduce any surges passed by this first line of protection. These cascaded
surge protective devices must be properly coordinated to avoid overload-
ing the downstream devices by requiring them to divert excessive surge
current.[32]

Computer networks, particularly when work stations are at remote
locations such as in separate buildings, require surge protection on the
network wiring as well as to the power and telephone connections to the
outside world. Even absent a lightning strike, the ground voltage buildup
caused by overhead thunderclouds can produce large voltage differentials
between buildings with sufficient site separation. Unless these voltage differentials are blocked or diverted from affecting the network wiring, high
surge currents can flow between buildings through ground conductors
with harmful impact on sensitive electronic equipment and even people.

Metal conductor data cable such as twisted pair single and multiple
pair shielded and unshielded cable, coaxial cable such as Ethernet or
Thinnet cable, and communication cable for intercom, security, control,
and fire alarm, are all susceptible to lightning induced transients. Minimi-
zation of the open-loop areas created by routing cable, particularly in
large facilities, will minimize coupling problems due to electrical interference (e.g., lightning or switching induced surges).[33]

IEEE recommended practice for lightning protection of metallic cable
connected equipment is to provide TVSS devices on both ends of the data
cable. Hybrid surge protectors are generally recommended. The proper
selection of a TVSS protector is dependent upon the type of signal being
used on the cable. High-quality, very fast-acting, less than 5 nanoseconds
response time, protectors for telephone, data and modem type protection
are available with clamping levels from 130 V rms decreasing in six dec-
rements to 7 V rms.[34]

The silicon avalanche diode (SAD) is a modern form of a very fast-
acting voltage-sensitive device capable of diverting multiple surges of
current and of clamping the voltage at relatively low levels. The SAD uses
a diffused junction technology capable of producing some characteristics
similar to the older Zener diodes. SADs are used by some manufacturers
together with MOVs in TVSS devices to prevent early fatigue and failure
of the MOVs. Unlike MOVs, the SAD devices will not degrade with the
number of transient surges absorbed, failing only when their energy ab-

sorption capacity is exceeded. In addition, more precise clamping levels are achievable with SADs than with MOVs alone.

The use of fiber-optic cable is highly recommended for interconnecting parts of large networks. Fiber-optic cable, unlike metallic wiring cable (even shielded cable), is unaffected by routing adjacent to power wiring since it is totally immune to electrical noise induction. It is also highly immune to electrical surge voltages and has high intersystem ground noise rejection.

System grounding is critical to the protection of electrical and electronic equipment from overvoltage damage whether lightning produced or system produced in the form of power disturbances and transients. The earth electrode subsystem is necessary to provide a facility with earth ground-reference for lightning, electrical fire, and shock hazard purposes. The earth electrode ground provides protection only from the standpoint of life safety and does not benefit the electronic signal producing equipment nor connections made thereto.[35]

It is necessary, when sensitive electronic equipment is being utilized, to establish a signal reference subsystem with an equipotential ground plane that will effectively ground signals with frequencies that can range from DC to hundreds of megahertz. Such a signal ground subsystem will assure that minimal voltage variations can exist between the signal circuits and the interconnected equipment.[36]

In all cases, the equipotential signal ground plane is required to be bonded to both the local building ground and to its grounding electrode conductor as specified in Article 250 of the NEC and in ANSI/NFPA 780.

A 1984 EPRI sponsored research program has led to the development of the National Lightning Detection Network (NLDN) which utilizes a network of electromagnetic sensors, computer systems, and satellite communications to identify the location, time, and magnitude of lightning strikes throughout the continental U.S. More than eighty electric power utilities currently use the NLDN to support their operations by preparing for storms, allowing the utility to alert, schedule and position repair crews, analyze line outages, and improve system design.[37]

The NLDN uses satellites to relay the multiple sensor information from locations throughout the country to the National Control Center (NCC) in Tucson, Arizona. The NCC computes the characteristics and location of each lightning strike and transmits the data to network users for real time display on personal computers of the lightning activity in their area. The received data gives events accurate to within 300 nanoseconds in time and within about 0.3 mile or better in location accuracy.

Electrical utilities are not the only beneficiaries of the NLDN. The U.S. Bureau of Land Management uses the network to assist in early detection and location of lightning caused fires and the FAA, military, and National Weather Service use real-time lightning data provided by the NLDN as forecasting and warning tools.[38]

Forensic electrical engineers can utilize the NLDN to verify the time of occurrence and location of lightning strikes for investigation of alleged lightning damage to property.[39] This avoids the dependence on eyewitness accounts and less specific National Weather Service reports. Damage to sensitive electronic equipment due to lightning frequently leaves few directly observable signs of the overvoltage source such as burnt, distorted or smoke marked components. A failed electronic product following a lightning storm may or may not have failed due to a lightning strike; but in the absence of lightning activity in the vicinity of the product or its power and communication supply lines, it is highly unlikely that lightning was the source of the product failure.

Endnotes

All IEEE publications are published by The Institute of Electrical and Electronics Engineers, Inc., 345 East 47th Street, New York, NY 10017-2394.

1. Grolier Electronic Publishing, *Software Toolworks Multimedia Encyclopedia* (Grolier Electronic Publishing, Inc., 1992).

2. *Encyclopaedia Britannica*, 1996.

3. Ibid.

4. Richard C. Dorf, ed., *The Electrical Engineering Handbook* (Boca Raton: CRC Press, 1993), 935.

5. Donald G. Fink and H. Wayne Beaty, eds., *Standard Handbook for Electrical Engineers*, 13th ed. (NY: McGraw-Hill, 1993), 27-7.

6. Ibid., 27-7.

7. Dorf, *Electrical Engineering Handbook*, 936.

8. D. G. Fink and H. W. Beaty, *Standard Handbook*, 27-11.

9. Dorf, *Electrical Engineering Handbook*, 936.

10. Ibid., 936.

11. Ibid., 936.

12. Fink and Beaty, *Standard Handbook*, 27-13.

13. Ibid., 27-12 to 27-14.

14. Grolier, Inc., *Software Toolworks*.

15. A. Larson, *Annual Report* (Washington, DC: Smithsonian Institution, 1905), 119.

16. National Fire Protection Association, *Standard for the Installation of Lightning Protection Systems*, NFPA 780 (Quincy, MA: National Fire Protection Association, 1995), 3-10.2.2, 780–7.

17. William M. Mazer, *Electrical Accident Investigation Handbook* (Glen Echo, MD: Electrodata, Inc., 1996), 7.4.3.4 and 7.4.3.8.

18. NFPA 780, 1-1.1, 780–4.

19. Ibid. 1-2, 780–4.

20. Donald W. Zipse, *Lightning Protection Methods: An Update and a Discredited System Vindicated* (IEEE Industrial & Commercial Power Systems Technical Conference, May 2000), 155–170.

21. Bruce A. Kaiser, "Lightning Protection: A Three-Part Approach," *Electrical Contracting & Engineering News,* March 2003, 21.

22. Fink and Beaty, *Standard Handbook*, 27-22.

23. Institute of Electrical and Electronics Engineers, Inc., *The Red Book: Recommended Practice for Electric Power Distribution for Industrial Plants*, IEEE Std. 141-1986 (NY: IEEE, 1996), table 15, p. 122.

24. Fink and Beaty, *Standard Handbook*, 27-43 to 27-48.

25. Ibid., 27-50.

26. Ernst Weber with Frederik Nebeker, *The Evolution of Electrical Engineering*, (NY: IEEE Press, 1994), 77.

27. Ibid., 44–58.

28. IEEE, *Red Book*, C 62.41-1991, 24–25.

29. Ibid., 46.

30. Ibid., 30.

31. Institute of Electrical and Electronics Engineers, Inc., *The Emerald Book: IEEE Recommended Practice for Powering and Grounding Sensitive Electronic Equipment*, IEEE Std. 1100-1992 (NY: Institute of Electrical and Electronics Engineers, Inc., 1992), 47.

32. Ibid., 88–90.

33. Ibid., 210.

34. DITEK, Diversified Technology Group, Inc., Manufacturers of surge protective devices, Largo, FL.

35. IEEE, *Emerald Book*, 90.

36. Ibid., 92.

37. R. Bernstein et al., "Lightning Detection Network Averts Damage and Speeds Restoration," *IEEE Computer Applications in Power* 9(2):12–17 (1996).

38. Ibid., 16.

39. VAISALA Group (formerly Global Atmospherics, Inc.), Tucson, AZ, www.lightningstorm.com.

References for Section 9.4

Barry, James D., *Ball Lightning and Bead Lightning. Extreme Forms of Atmospheric Electricity* (NY: Plenum Press, 1980).

Barry, James D. and Stanley Singer, "Ball Lightning: The Continuing Challenge," in *Science of Ball Lightning (Fire Ball)*, Yoshi-Hiko Ohtsuki, ed. (Singapore: World Scientific Publishing, 1988), 4.

"Labelle, Jean-Claude," "On June 27, 2001 . . . ," e-mail dated 7 February 2002, available online at the Weird Science Page Database of Ball Lightning Reports, www.amasci.com/weird/unusual/bl.html.

Ohtsuki, Yoshi-Hiko and Hideho Ofuruton, "Plasma Fireballs Formed by Microwave Interference in Air," *Nature* 350:139–141 (1991).

Rañada, Antonio F. and José L. Trueba, "Ball Lightning: An Electromagnetic Knot?" *Nature* 383:32 (1996).

Silberg, Paul A., "A Review of Ball Lightning," in *Problems of Atmospheric and Space Electricity*, S. C. Coronti, ed. (NY: American Elsevier Publishing Company, 1965), 436–454.

Singer, Stanley, "Great Balls of Fire," *Nature* 350:108–109 (1991).

Uman, Martin A., *Lightning* (NY: Dover Publications, 1984).

Uman, Martin A. and John J. Lowke, "Decaying Lightning Channels, Bead Lightning and Ball Lightning," paper presented at the Fourth International Conference on the Universal Aspects of Atmospheric Electricity, Tokyo, Japan, May, 1968.

References for Section 9.6

American Heart Association Emergency Cardiac Care Committee and Subcommittees. "Guidelines for Cardiopulmonary Resuscitation and Emergency Cardiac Care, part 1: Introduction," *JAMA* 268:2172–2183 (1992).

Amy, B. W. et al. "Lightning Injury with Survival in Five Patients," *JAMA* 253(2):243–245 (1985).

Andrews, C. J., "Telephone-Related Lightning Injury," *Medical Journal of Australia* 157:823–826 (1992).

Andrews, C. J. and M. Darveniza, "Further Identification and Treatment Modalities in Telephone Mediated Lightning Strike," in *Proceedings of the International Aerospace and Ground Conference on Lightning and Static Electricity*, conference publication 10058, W. Jafferis, ed. (Cocoa Beach, FL: NASA, 1991).

Apelberg, D. B., F. W. Masters and D. W. Robinson, "Pathophysiology and Treatment of Lightning Injuries," *Journal of Trauma* 14(6):453–460 (1974).

Camps, Francis E., Anne E. Robinson and Bernard G. B. Lucas, *Gradwohl's Legal Medicine* (Chicago: John Wright & Sons, Year Book Medical Publications, 1976).

Cherington M., "Lightning and Transportation," *Seminars in Neurology* 15(4): 362–366 (1995).

Chia, B. L., "Electrocardiographic Abnormalities and Congestive Cardiac Failure Due to Lightning Stroke," *Cardiology* 68:49–53 (1981).

Cooper, M. A., "Lightning Injuries: Prognostic Signs for Death," *Annals of Emergency Medicine* 9:134–138 (1980).

Craig, Steven R., "When Lightning Strikes," *Postgraduate Medicine* 79(4):109–124 (1986).

Currens, J. H., "Arterial Spasm and Transient Paralysis Resulting from Lightning Striking an Airplane," *Journal of Aviation Medicine* 16:275–277 (1945).

DeAtley, C., "Management of Lightning Injuries," *Rescue-EMS Magazine*, November-Deceber 1991, 16–21.

Fink, D. G. and H. W. Beaty, *Standard Handbook for Electrical Engineers*, 12th ed. (NY: McGraw-Hill, 1987), 2-25.

Fisher, R. S., "Electrical and Lightning Injuries," in *Medicolegal Investigation of Death, Guidelines for the Application of Pathology to Crime Investigation*, 2nd ed., Werner U. Spitz and Russell S. Fisher, eds. (Springfield, IL: Charles C. Thomas, 1980), 371.

Fontanarosa, P. B. "Electrical Shock and Lightning Strike," *Annals of Emergency Medicine* 22(2):378–387 (1988).

Frayne, J. H. and B. S. Gilligan, "Neurological Sequelae of Lightning Stroke," *Clinical and Experimental Neurology* 24:195–200 (1987).

Jackson, S. H. D. and D. J. Parry, "Lightning and the Heart," *British Heart Journal* 43:454–457 (1980).

Johnstone, B. R., D. L. Harding and B. Hocking, "Telephone-Related Lightning Injury," *Medical Journal of Australia* 144:707–709 (1986).

Kleiner, J. P. and J. H. Wilkin, "Cardiac Effects of Lightning Stroke," *JAMA* 240(25):2757–2759 (1978).

Kleinschmidt-DeMasters, B. K.. "Neuropathology of Lightning-Strike Injuries," *Seminars in Neurology* 15(4):323–328 (1995).

Kobernick, M., "Electrical Injuries: Pathophysiology and Emergency Management," *Annals of Emergency Medicine* 11(11):633–638 (1982).

Kotagal S. et al. "Neurologic, Psychiatric, and Cardiovascular Complications in Children Struck by Lightning," *Pediatrics* 70(2):190–192 (1992).

Levine, N. S. et al., "Spinal Cord Injury Following Electrical Accidents: Case Reports." *Journal of Trauma* 15(5):459–463 (1975).

Lifschultz, B. D. and E. R. Donoghue, "Deaths Caused by Lightning," *Journal of Forensic Sciences* 38(2):353–358 (1993).

Moran, K. T., J. N. Thupari and A. M. Munster, "Electric- and Lightning-Induced Cardiac Arrest Reversed by Prompt Cardiopulmonary Resuscitation," *JAMA* 255(16):2157 (1986).

Pierce, M. R., R. A. Henderson and J. M. Mitchell, "Cardiopuomonary Arrest Secondary to Lightning Injury in a Pregnant Woman," *Annals of Emergency Medicine* 15(5):597–599 (1986).

Rackhan, H., *Pliny's Natural History*, Book II, translated by H. Rackhan (Cambridge: Harvard University Press, 1938), 275.

Shantha, T. R,. "Causalgia Induced by Telephone-Mediated Lightning Electrical Injury and Treated by Intrapleural Block," *Anesthesia & Analgesia* 73:502–510 (1991).

Stanley, L. D. and R. A. Suss, "Intracerebral Hematoma Secondary to Lighting Stroke: Case Report and Review of the Literature," *Neurosurgery* 16(5):686–688 (1985).

Stedman's Electronic Medical Dictionary (Hagerstown, MD: Williams & Wilkins, 1996).

Tribble, C. G. et al., "Lightning Injury," *Current Concepts in Trauma Care,* spring 1984, 5–10.

Wagner, C. F., G. D. McCann, and J. M. Clayton, "Lightning Phenomena," in *Electrical Transmission and Distribution Reference Book*, 4th ed. (East Pittsburgh, PA: Westinghouse Electric, 1950).

Yassi, A. et al., "Epidemic of 'Shocks' in Telephone Operators: Lessons for the Medical Community," *Canadian Medical Association Journal* 140:816–820 (1989).

Yost, J. W. and F. F. Holmes, "Myoglobinuria Following Lightning Strike," *JAMA* 28(9):1147–1148 (1974).

Zeana, C. D., "Acute Transient Myocardial Ischemia after Lightning," *International Journal of Cardiology* 5:207–209 (1984).

Chapter 10

Case Studies

10.1 Introduction

Since 1957, this author has practiced electrical engineering, and since 1968, has provided forensic engineering services to the legal profession. During the years since 1968, the forensic engineering portion of this practice has steadily grown such that today it occupies more than 90 percent of the author's professional effort.

During this engineer's work in forensic electrical engineering, by far the greatest number of cases have dealt with electrocution or shock, 47 percent of all cases. Fires of possible electrical origin have constituted the second largest class of cases, 30 percent. The remaining 23 percent of the cases have involved in descending order, product failures, electromagnetic fields, illumination, construction, lightning, water damage to electrical equipment, and nonlethal damage due to overhead power line contact.

In the early years, most of this forensic engineering work was done for plaintiff's attorneys; however, today the cases are about equally divided between plaintiffs and defendants.

There have also been a sizable number of forensic investigations, conducted for insurance companies, utilities, and others that were performed for unidentified legal positions (i.e., neither a plaintiff nor a defendant since no law suit was contemplated).

In the following case studies, the names of litigants are omitted and generic terms will be used to describe locations, products, and features to avoid unwarranted exposure of parties to the litigations or actions involved.

10.2 A Case of Power Line Electrocution by a Rabbit

In 1982, a farmer and his two young sons were working in a field that used 30-foot-long aluminum irrigation pipes that could be coupled together to selectively carry water to the plant rows. One of the boys saw a rabbit run into a pipe section, and he called for his father to raise the pipe from one end while he and his brother waited at the low end of the pipe for the rabbit to slide out. As the man walked the pipe upward to a greater and greater height, the pipe made contact with an open overhead 13-kV power line conductor that ran beside the field inside the fence line. The electrical current which resulted from the 7,200 V to ground contact killed the man and severely injured both boys. The attorney who represented the decedent's wife and boys contacted this engineer for an opinion and investigation of liability against the electric utility that owned the power line.

In this case, the 1977 NESC was in effect, based upon the date of construction of the power line, and this edition of the code had been adopted by the state utility commission at the time. Section 232, Table 232-1, of the code requires a minimum clearance of twenty feet above grade for this class of line. The actual clearance of the subject line was twenty-two feet, four inches at point of contact, and the line was 21 feet 6 inches above grade at its minimum clearance point in the accident span. The code minimum of 20 feet is for a classification of surface underneath the conductors that is other land traversed by vehicles such as cultivated, grazing, forest, orchard and so forth. The accompanying footnote reads: "These clearances are for land cultivated or traversed by vehicles and equipment whose overall operating height is less than fourteen ft."

Although it would appear that the electric utility was in compliance with the NESC based upon Section 232, there are also more general sections of the code, such as Section 210 which states, "All electric supply and communication lines and equipment shall be of suitable design and construction for the service and conditions under which they are to be operated." Section 211 states, "All electric supply and communication lines and equipment shall be installed and maintained so as to reduce hazards to life as far as is practical."

An investigation into the operation of this farm and others in the vicinity of the subject power line showed that there was widespread use of the 30-foot-long aluminum pipes for irrigation and that such use had been common for more than fifteen years prior to this accident. The investigation also revealed that the pipes, which were about 6 inches in diameter and weigh about 100 pounds each, are easily stood on end by walking the pipe up from a horizontal to a vertical position, as the decedent was doing.

Based upon the reasonable knowledge that an electric utility which operates in such a rural agricultural area would have of the potential danger from OH line contact by this equipment, it was this engineer's opinion that the utility was in violation of Section 210 and Section 211 of the NESC by constructing and operating the 13-kV OH power line inside the irrigated field fence at less than thirty feet above grade. The specific use of the land where thirty-foot long metallic pipes were used in large numbers along with the ease in standing such pipes upright made it incumbent, in this engineer's opinion, upon the electric utility to construct its open conductor OH high-voltage power lines in a manner that would be practical and reduce the hazard to life from line contact with such equipment.

The defendant's attorney deposed the plaintiff's forensic engineer in this case, and the case was settled before trial began. It is interesting that the NESC (see Chapter 3), since the code revision of 1981, has changed Rule 210 and has deleted Rule 211. A less specific rule related to reducing hazards is now found in Section 012 that states, "All electric supply and communication lines and equipment shall be designed, operated, constructed and maintained to meet the requirements of these rules. For all particulars not specified in these rules, construction, operation, and maintenance should be done in accordance with good practice for the given local conditions." An important change in this wording is inherent in the term "should" instead of "shall", the latter meaning a mandatory requirement and the term "should" meaning a provision that is "normally and generally practical for the specified condition."[1]

The 1990 NESC further reduces the effectiveness of Rule 012 by stating that, "Where the word 'should' is used, it is recognized that, in certain instances, additional local conditions not specified herein may make these provisions impractical. When this occurs, the difference in conditions shall be appropriately recognized and Rule 012 shall be met."

If the question of what happened to the rabbit has occurred to the reader, it is this author's scientific conclusion that the rabbit survived.

10.3 A Case of the Good Samaritan Fire

In June 1979, a homeowner was in the process of having his air conditioning system repaired by a licensed air conditioning serviceman. As an adjunct to the service call, the man asked for the serviceman's help in locating an electrical problem at the residence. It seemed that the receptacles in his living room that had table lamps plugged into them and the front porch lights were not functional. After locating the correct interior panelboard, the serviceman found a tripped 15-amp circuit breaker. He demonstrated to the owner the proper procedure for resetting the breaker; however, the breaker immediately tripped off as he reset it. At this time, the serviceman instructed the owner to wait at the panelboard while he returned to the living room area in order to observe any electrical activity before he called for the owner to reset the breaker one more time.

When the owner reset the breaker the second time, the serviceman heard a loud "pop" and saw a "flash" from the side of the living room picture window near the floor. The hanging drapery beside this window then immediately burst into flame. The fire spread was extremely rapid and resulted in both localized structural and widespread smoke damage to the residence.

This engineer was contacted by the owner's insurance company three days following the fire and was requested to investigate the scene, which at that time had only been disturbed by the rural-metro fire fighters who had responded to the fire. On arrival at the residence, this engineer was given a first hand account of the events that preceded the fire from the owner. A careful examination of the debris in the area of the observed fire origin disclosed the metal remnants of a duplex receptacle and lamp cord plug along with two small portions of a phenolic plastic commonly used in electrical molded insulators that form the body of many duplex receptacles.

Two other smoked but otherwise undamaged receptacles were removed from the residence in order to compare their parts with the discovered remnants and to identify the manufacturer of the receptacle from the area of fire origin. By comparing the parts of the two undamaged receptacles with the partial remnant parts from the fire origin, it was possible to determine where the remnant parts had lost material during the fire and how much had been lost. Since the metallic parts from these receptacles are brass and copper, which melt at temperatures between 930°C and 1,083°C, it is unlikely that a fire of this type would create temperatures sufficient to destroy any of these metallic parts.

However, an electrical arc cannot only melt and vaporize such metals, but along with the eyewitness account of a "pop" and a "flash," this evidence strongly suggested that an electrical arc did indeed initiate the fire. There was also evidence of electrical arcing present as globular metal deposited and fused into one of the remnant receptacle terminal clips.

At this point in the investigation, it was apparent that an arc had occurred in the receptacle which had a lamp cord plug inserted in it and that the superheated metal particles which exploded from that arcing process had ignited the draperies which were hanging directly in front of the receptacle. Several years before this case, this engineer had been given a receptacle and plug that an engineer friend had recovered from his own kitchen following an arcing incident that startled both him and his wife. I had examined this receptacle and plug at that time and had determined that the cause of the arcing was a plug which was inserted or which had been displaced in a nonperpendicular manner into the receptacle, such that the plug prong had broken through a thin plastic barrier which was designed to separate the plug prong from the grounded metal mounting strap within the receptacle body. The energized side of the receptacle and plug thus came into contact with the ground strap and an electrical arc ensued.

This previous device failure was the basis for this engineer's theory in this fire case that an energized plug prong had come into contact with the grounded metal strap of the receptacle. Electrical arcing resulted, creating the fire. There is no way to be certain, from the available evidence, whether the receptacle failed because the plug broke through a normal plastic barrier in the device or whether the plastic barrier was defective as manufactured (i.e., a barrier that was missing or formed with inadequate material). In either situation, there is a defective product involved because such receptacles must be designed to accept without failure the normal wear and tear and variances that will occur as plugs are inserted or removed. The subject receptacle was, according to the owners, not one that was regularly used, and the table lamp had been continuously plugged into the receptacle since the last time any furniture was moved. After this engineer's report and conclusions were presented to the insurance company in this case, a subrogation lawsuit was filed against the receptacle manufacturer. Several years later, the manufacturer's attorney deposed this engineer and the case was subsequently settled out of court. Unfortunately for the air conditioning company that was servicing the residence, a lawsuit was later brought against the serviceman alleging inadequate technical skill and care for helping the home owner with his electrical problem. Despite this engineer's testimony that it is not unusual, nor beneath the standard of care expected of such technicians to reset a breaker more than once during a troubleshooting investigation, the trial against the air conditioning company and its serviceman resulted in an unfavorable jury verdict against the Good Samaritan serviceman.

10.4 A Case of a Utility's Failure to Respond to a Request for Help

In 1975, a contractor was installing approximately 1.4 miles of 8-foot-diameter storm line buried 20 to 25 feet deep along the side of a city street paralleled by a 12-kV overhead power line. During the construction project, it was necessary to build a box culvert 30 feet deep at an intersection, the construction of which required the use of sheet pilings for the excavation. The pile-driver frame was nearly 6 feet higher than the OH PL and the contractor recognized the danger as his workers were in the initial process of setting up the derrick and pile-driver frame.

The contractor then stopped that portion of the work and telephoned the electric utility to request assistance in assuring the safety of the work near the power line. A field representative from the utility visited the construction site following the contractor's request. The utility field representative observed the OH PL and construction equipment, after which he informed the contractor that the line could not be de-energized and that he should not bring his equipment within ten feet of the line. After this advice, the utility representative left the construction site.

Faced with this "Catch 22" situation, the contractor proceeded to set up the derrick and pile driver as far away as possible from the line and still allow the equipment to drive the sheet pilings. This setup placed the driver frame two feet three inches from the closest OH PL conductor. A day or so later, as the pile driver was operating, a laborer on the ground was holding onto a steel cable used to guy the driver frame when the cable moved laterally and made contact with the 7,200 volts to ground power line. The worker was electrocuted, and his widow filed a lawsuit against the utility company and the city who was the owner of the drainage line. The contractor-employer was immune from liability under a state workers' compensation law.

An investigation of the case established the following:

- Before starting construction, a pre-job conference was held between the contractor, the engineer, the city and the local water, gas, electric and telephone utility representatives. The purpose of the pre-job conference was to inform all parties involved of the project scope and timing and to review any foreseeable difficulties, interferences, or safety issues that the project presented.
- At the pre-job conference, the contractor discussed the use of a high-profile crane throughout the project to lift and place the eight-foot-diameter concrete drainage pipe sections.
- The engineer's plans and specifications for the project were furnished to all involved parties prior to the pre-job conference.
- At the pre-job conference, the electric utility representative cautioned the contractor about the hazard of working around the 138-kV OH transmission line that crossed over the street toward the north end of the project. No offer was made by the electric utility representative to assist the contractor with any problems that might involve OH PLs.
- The electric utility company's safety manual stresses the problem of crane contacts with its OH lines and emphasizes that the company places a high priority on the safety aspects of prevention of such con-

tacts. The manual strongly recommends that all crane operations near OH PLs use a trained ground spotter and that the high profile equipment be grounded by a bonding conductor to the closest available ground point.

• During the job, a conference with contractor, city inspector, and electric utility representative took place to discuss the specific problems foreseen with the box culvert construction.

• The utility's field representative, who responded to the contractor's telephone call for assistance, was not electrically trained or educated, and had only recently been transferred from the utility's gas division to its electrical division.

• After the accident, at the contractor's expense, the utility built a temporary short line called a "shoofly" around the box culvert construction area and de-energized the conductors that were adjacent to the pile driver.

• The electric utility line involved was a short (less than two miles) radial circuit that served no critical loads, for example, a hospital.

The 1973 NESC, which was in effect at the time of this accident, has three sections that apply to the conduct of the utility in this case:

210. Design and Construction. All electric supply and communication lines and equipment shall be of suitable design and construction for the service and conditions under which they are to be operated.

211. Installation and Maintenance. All electric supply and communication lines and equipment shall be installed and maintained so as to reduce hazards to life as far as practicable.

214. Isolation and Guarding.
A. Current-carrying Parts.
To promote safety to the general public and to employees not authorized to approach conductors and other current- carrying parts of electric supply lines, such parts shall be arranged so as to provide adequate clearance from the ground or other space generally accessible, or shall be provided with guards so as to isolate them effectively from accidental contact by such persons.

In deposition and later during trial, this engineer testified that in his opinion "(the electric utility) was definitely negligent in not taking positive action in concert with the contractor to increase the safety of the operation . . . and that (the utility) was in violation of the 1973 NESC Sec. 210, 211 and 214.A."

The jury awarded $1.5 million to the family of the deceased laborer. The verdict was upheld upon appeal to the state supreme court. In addition, OSHA cited the contractor for violation of state safety regulations and the contractor was fined $4,500.

10.5 A Case of Severe Electrical Shock in the Shower

In 1970, a woman was taking a shower in her bathtub when she was suddenly overcome by a sense of electrical shock apparently coming through the water spray. She passed out and evidently fell in the tub, striking a water control knob as she collapsed which allowed nearly 100 percent hot water to continue to discharge from the shower nozzle onto her body. Approximately three to five minutes later, she regained consciousness and screamed for help. Her husband responded from outside the residence and rushed her to the hospital where she was treated for second and third degree burns over a considerable portion of her body.

This engineer was contacted by the woman's attorney to investigate the electrical shock phenomenon that she apparently experienced and to identify the source of this shock. Early in review of the case, the husband reported that a 30-amp fuse supplying one leg of a 230-volt water heater was found blown after the incident. The couple also reported that they had been mildly shocked by touching the kitchen sink water faucet prior to the incident.

An engineering investigation of the residential electrical system disclosed the following:

- The water heater resistance was 2.5 ohms from line 1 of the 230-volt supply to the lower water heater element and the cold water pipes.
- Line 2 to the lower water heater element was open circuited (infinite resistance) to the cold water pipes.
- The house was grounded at the service entrance via a driven ground rod.

- The service entrance neutral was bonded to the ground connection, but not to the metallic water piping supply system.
- The metallic water supply line serving the house was electrically isolated from the main utility water lines by an insulating coupling.
- The resistance between the service entrance neutral and the residence water piping was measured at 7.1 ohms.
- The resistance from the metal shower drain fitting to the driven ground was measured at 56 ohms.
- The resistance between the metal shower drain and the bathtub showerhead was measured at 120 ohms.
- The house was wired originally around 1950 using NMC conductors without a separate ground wire and the water heater was installed in 1967 without a separate ground wire.

The lower-faulted heater element was removed and examined. An obvious electrical arc had burned near a hole in the element sheath approximately one-fifth of the distance from the shorted terminal to the open terminal. The other terminal was open circuited to the grounded sheath and to the first terminal. The element was x-rayed to verify the internal condition of the helix resistance wire and its relationship to the sheath. Using x-ray diffraction, emission spectroscopy, and certain chemical analyses of the coating on the heater element, it was determined that the coating was composed almost entirely of carbonates, the greatest portion of which was calcium carbonate in aragonite form. It was determined by serial numbers and manufacturer's records that the heater was manufactured about two and one-half years before the incident and it was found that the water heater had been in service about two years prior to the accident.

A water sample from the supply to the residence was chemically analyzed for soluble salts, hardness, pH, fluoride and nitrates.

This data was compared with other water analyses from various locations across the country in order to assess the effect of water chemicals on the expected deterioration of the immersion heater element.

An electrical circuit model was formulated to include the measured parameters from the residence electrical and plumbing systems as shown in Figure 10.1.

Various voltages were calculated assuming a wet body and water path resistance of 1,000 ohms as shown (i.e., resistance from the shower head

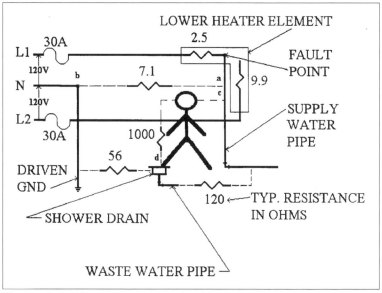

Figure 10.1 *Water heater case circuit*

through the water stream and body to the shower drain). The victim was postulated to have been subject to an initial shock of approximately

$$I = \frac{V_{CD}}{R} = \frac{57.7}{1,000} = 57.7 \text{ mA}.$$ (Equation 10.1)

This shocking current, if continued for a period of more than ten seconds, would likely produce ventricular fibrillation (v-f) in a person. Simultaneously, as the woman experienced this shock, there would be a change in the electrical circuit parameters. If the initial current flow through the head and upper torso from the shower water produced a rapid loss of consciousness, then as she fell to the floor of the tub, the path resistance through the water spray and body would increase significantly and the likelihood of v-f or electrocution would decrease. Also, as hot water was used from the storage tank, the upper heating element would activate, increasing the line current. As the arcing contact between the failing element helix and sheath lowered its resistance, the circuit current would increase beyond the fuse rating and the fuse would blow. This postulated explanation for the accident agrees in all respects with the discovered facts following the incident.

The plaintiff's attorney, in view of the early failure of an appliance that, according to the manufacturer's life cycle testing is expected to last over fifteen years, filed suit against the water heater and element manufacturer for a faulty product. The x-ray examination of the water heater element clearly showed that the helix, on both sides of the break and arcing location, was displaced from a centering location within the tube sheath. This strongly suggests a misalignment of the helix as it is loaded and the powdered magnesium oxide insulation is packed around it in the tube. Such a manufacturing defect would likely pass the final inspections, since the manufacturer was relying primarily on hi-pot (high voltage) testing to insure the insulation integrity between the helix and sheath. As the element was used, the heating and cooling of the helix in the region where a slight void or lack of MgO existed would aggravate the defect and would logically result in an early failure such as an arcing fault from the helix to the grounded metal sheath.

This case was ultimately tried. The jury awarded $550,000 to the injured party which was the largest personal injury award ever given in that state as of that time. Following trial the manufacturer, who had participated with the local REA utility in marketing the electric water heaters within the area, sent a letter to all owners informing them of the necessity to connect a separate ground wire from the appliance to the service entrance grounded neutral.

10.6 A Case of an Attractive Nuisance Substation

A utility substation is an extremely hazardous area for anyone to enter except qualified individuals. Substations are enclosed or semi-enclosed structures that contain the transformers, switches, circuit protective devices, and controls for the conversion and redistribution of electrical energy from transmission or sub transmission voltages, usually above 34 kV, to distribution voltages from 4 to 34 kV. A typical rural area substation is generally a fenced enclosure with overhead power lines entering and perhaps exiting the enclosure. Within the enclosure, the lines usually are placed on lowered structures such that open bare conductors are present at levels as low as 7 feet 8 inches above grade. (Minimum vertical clearance requirement from the 1948 NESC H30, Section 114, Table 2, for 600 volts between phases. The 1990 code requires 8 feet, 8 inches for this voltage classification.)

A rural area 69:12-kV substation, approximately 80 feet by 180 feet, became the object of interest for two eight-year-olds. A seven-foot-high chain link fence that had a three-strand barbed wire climbing guard at the top enclosed the substation. The inside of the substation was relatively open and, at the time of the accident, an employee of the utility had stored his pickup camper shell inside the locked substation fence.

The boys were attracted to the substation because of a pirate game that they regularly played using the camper shell, which was raised above grade on concrete blocks, that became their ship and hiding spot. They had played several times inside the substation, gaining entrance sometimes by climbing over the fence and wire guards and at other times by slipping under the double gate that had an eroded rain runoff space beneath it. On the day of the accident, one of the boys was using a five-foot length of broken auto antenna as a play sword. While standing next to the substation transformer, he slashed overhead with the sword and made contact with a 69-kV conductor located on the top of an insulated bushing.

The arc flash that ensued burned both boys; one boy was burned severely, but both survived.

This engineer was retained as an expert for the plaintiffs in the subsequent lawsuit. The plaintiffs' attorney had already begun an investigation and had obtained photographs showing the condition of the substation immediately following the accident, copies of the sheriff's report, and hospital records from the incident.

An engineering investigation revealed that the substation was constructed in 1971. A site inspection by this engineer approximately six months following the incident showed that the substation had an established runoff pattern under the access gates that would exceed 12 inches in height by 30 inches in width unless fill material was used to replace the erosion. Local weather reports showed that the area had received 6.5 inches of rain during the ten days before the accident.

Research into the code indicated that the applicable NESC was H30, adopted in 1948. Under H30, Section 10 Protective Arrangements of Stations and Substations, Section. 102.A, Enclosure of Rooms and Spaces, states: "Rooms and spaces shall be so arranged with fences . . . as to prevent entrance of unauthorized persons or interference by them with equipment inside . . . shall be kept locked." Also under H30, Section 102 General Requirements, Section 102 B.2. Storage and Manufacturing Pro-

cesses, the code states: "They [stations and substations] shall be used neither for the storage of material nor for manufacturing processes . . . except
those materials . . . attendant upon the production or distribution of a supply of electric energy."

Despite this engineer's opinion, expressed during deposition taken by
the defendant utility's attorney—that the utility had violated Rule 102.A.
and Rule 102.B.2. of the NESC and further had created an attractive nuisance by allowing an employee to store his camper shell in the substation—the case was tried before a jury. The jury awarded $325,000 to one
boy, of which $50,000 was for punitive damages, and $70,000 to the other,
of which $50,000 was for punitive damages.

10.7 A Case of Mobile Home Fire due to Faulty Wiring

The attorney for a mobile home manufacturing firm contacted this engineer in 1975 to investigate an alleged electrical fire that severely damaged
a mobile home. Following its initial manufacture, the subject mobile
home had been modified to allow its use as a real estate office..

The engineering investigation began by an examination of the following materials.

1. The floor plan of the subject mobile home as originally manufactured showing the basic electrical plan.
2. A sales order showing that the mobile home was to be constructed
   with a 120/240-V 100-amp electrical service.
3. An invoice of different date confirming item 2.
4. A separate floor plan with hand drawn modifications added.
5. A local fire department run report.
6. A portion of the manufacturer's quality control program showing
   electrical system testing procedures utilized during and at completion of construction.
7. A report authored by another engineer who had initially investigated
   the fire.
8. A partial copy of NFPA 501B 1973 Standard of Mobile Homes, Part
   E Electrical Systems.
9. A portion of wiring evidence approximately 2 feet in length taken
   from the subject mobile home.

10. A summary of the deposition of the millwright who modified the original mobile home to allow its use as an office.

Following an examination of this information, the engineer requested and obtained information as to the manufacture and specific product for the circuit breaker load center installed in the mobile home, an inventory of the office equipment in use at the time of the fire, photographs of the fire damaged structure taken shortly after the fire, and photographs from the original manufacturer showing the wiring as typically installed in its mobile homes. Unfortunately, the actual fire damaged mobile home was salvaged about eight months before this investigation began and, therefore, was not available for inspection by this engineer.

After all the physical evidence, photographs, plans, and statements were examined, it was this engineer's conclusion that the fire started in the vicinity of the wiring to a receptacle, specifically at a point where a wire staple had been used to secure the copper NM cable wiring to a wood stud. A distinctive V fire pattern was present from this location upward, and the depth of char, as well as other structural damage from the fire, was most severe in this area compared to the other area photographs. This area of origin also agreed with the eyewitness accounts of the fire and the fire department's opinion of an area of origin.

Because of the difference in wiring method used in the area of fire origin compared to the manufacturer's photographs, and based upon the hand drawn modifications used to describe the changes made following manufacture, it was concluded that the wiring at the point of fire origin was most likely installed after the product was originally constructed.

This case was eventually submitted for trial by jury. The verdict was entirely in favor of the defense with no damages awarded to the plaintiffs in this matter.

10.8 A Case of Careless Tree Trimming

In 1986, this engineer was retained by an attorney representing a public utility in defense of a lawsuit involving the death of a tree trimmer. The accident occurred in 1980 when a forty-nine-year-old tree trimmer in the process of trimming a palm tree came into contact with an overhead 12-kV distribution line owned by the defendant.

The decedent had apparently used a 29-foot-long aluminum ladder to ascend a tall palm tree, where he then proceeded to throw a metallic safety chain out from and around the tree. As he did this, the chain came into contact with the utility power line that was energized at 7,200 volt to ground. The subsequent arcing explosion ignited both the victim's clothes and the tree. The man lost consciousness and while still holding his gasoline chain saw, he fell to the ground.

The chain saw gasoline tank either ruptured upon striking the ground or was ignited during the arcing explosion, and the victim was severely burned across the front of his body while lying on the ground. Although the man was alive and breathing on his own after transport to the hospital, he had sustained third degree burns over 30 percent of his body and second degree burns over 17 percent of his body. The victim died two months later, presumably from the burn injuries.

The plaintiff's attorney sued the utility, the chain saw manufacturer, and the owner's of the residence alleging against the utility that it had, as quoted from the complaint:

1. carelessly, negligently, or intentionally, without due regard for the public or for persons lawfully employed in work taking them close to the wires, maintained wires without insulation;
2. failing to properly inspect and see that the wires do not touch the limbs of the trees, and in permitting the wires to touch or run close to the limbs of trees;
3. failing to warn persons, and particularly Plaintiff's Decedent, of the fact that the wires were carrying electrical current of high voltage and were dangerous;
4. failing to give warning to persons that ordinarily comes [sic] in contact with the tree near which, or through which wires ran, although Defendant power company knew that tree must be trimmed, cut, or treated.
5. failing to take reasonable precautions in the premises or to use due care, in that it failed to install prevent or maintain proper or adequate circuit breakers or fuses or other safety devices to break the electrical circuit when such lines come in contact with Decedent's tools.
6. failing to inspect or to make reasonable inspections of its lines and equipment so that the dangerous proximity of the high voltage lines

to the trees on which decedent was working would have been discovered.

7. failing to have the wires of such high and potential [sic] dangerous voltage of electricity installed underground or installed in proper conduits.

8. failing to warn the public, particularly the decedent of the extremely high voltage being carried by its wires when the voltage was so high that it would arc or jump to the equipment used in cutting trees or trimming trees in the premises.

9. maintaining the high tension electrical wires in such a manner without proper precautions in residential areas as to constitute a public and private nuisance.

The engineer's investigation revealed the following.

- The subject power line was a minimum of 27 feet 6 inches above grade in the incident span.
- The subject power line was 6 feet 6 inches north of the north face of the incident palm tree.
- The victim was a part-time tree trimmer who had on previous occasions trimmed the subject tree as well as other trees on the property where the accident occurred.
- A specific safety clearance is not specified by the 1977 NESC for separation of overhead lines and trees, but the provisions of the code in a more restrictive environment require a minimum horizontal clearance of five feet from the balconies of buildings which are accessible to pedestrians.
- In all aspects of a detailed review, the existing utility facilities were in conformance with the NESC at the time of the accident and the line was installed, operated and maintained according to reasonable standards of care within the utility industry.

Despite this engineer's affidavit and subsequent statement, that clearly supported the utility, taken by the plaintiff's attorney in deposition, the case went to trial before a jury. The jury found no liability on the part of the utility in this case.

10.9 A Case of an Exploding Bus Duct

In July 1982, an outdoor bus duct serving a newspaper production and office facility failed violently. Prior to this violent failure, one of three 3,000-A main circuit breakers had tripped shutting off power to a large portion of the facility. The owner's maintenance electricians had tried to reset this breaker serving DS-2, but it had tripped out immediately with an electrical arc flash occurring at a tie bus joint, point F1 as shown in Figures 10.2 and 10.3. Three maintenance workers were injured by the flying metal particles and superheated gas from this overhead fault. At this time, the newspaper contacted the electrical contractor, who had originally installed the system approximately ten years prior to this incident, to provide troubleshooting service and to restore power to the facility.

The contractor's electrician arrived at the site and determined that he could probably restore power to the facility by disconnecting the tie bus connection at the tee connection point A between DS-2 and DS-3, as shown in Figures 10.2 and 10.3. As the electricians were working on removing the tie bus jumpers with DS-2 de-energized, several newspaper employees were standing eight to ten feet from transformer T2 and nearly underneath the bus duct from T2 to DS2. The lead electrician was talking to a city fireman, and they were standing in the doorway to DS2 when they heard an explosion and a shower of sparks flashed across the area outside DS-2 toward T2.

Three employees of the newspaper were enveloped in the electrical fireball that erupted. One employee later died from the second- and third-degree burns sustained over 70 percent of his body. A second underwent years of skin grafts and surgery for his second- and third-degree burns over 50 percent of his body; this man never worked again. The third man was burned with second-degree injuries over 40 percent of his body and third-degree burns on one hand. He later lost a finger to these injuries. Four other employees required hospital treatment for their injuries.

The local utility was immediately notified and within minutes had disconnected the 4,160-volt circuits feeding the two 2,500-kVA transformers at the facility. The city fire department and police immediately secured the area—even the electricians were not allowed to enter, and the arson squad investigated the scene.

After the electricians were allowed to enter the area and begin their work, the contractor's lead electrician discovered that a great deal of

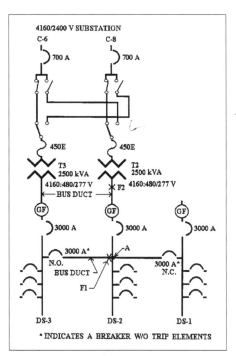

Figure 10.2 *Bus duct case circuit*

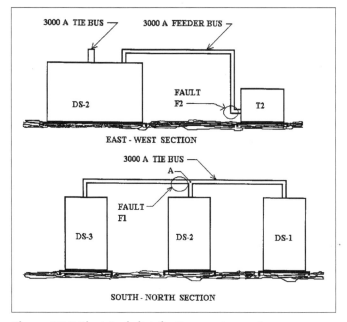

Figure 10.3 *Electrical distribution center sections*

moisture had entered the tie bus duct at fault point F1. The electrician identified this moisture as a likely cause of the faulting to ground that had originally caused the main 3,000-amp circuit breaker to DS-2 to trip. It is important to note that the bus duct from DS-2 to DS-3 was carrying no current since the 3,000-amp breaker in DS-3 was normally open (N.O.).

The attorneys representing the newspaper in the wide-ranging lawsuits that were subsequently filed retained this engineer. Nearly everyone who was involved in the design, construction, maintenance, and electrical service of the facility was named as defendants in these multiple lawsuits.

The initial engineering investigation in this case consisted of the discovery of the basic sequence of events leading up to the explosion as has already been described. The weather in the area prior to the incident had been extremely rainy; in fact, rain had fallen nearly continuously during the twelve-hour period preceding the accident. Original electrical plans for the facility construction were obtained, and detailed information was gathered regarding the protective devices, circuit breaker settings, available fault current, manufacturer's time-current curves for the fuses and circuit breakers, transformer impedances and ground fault protection. After approximately four and one-half hours, the electricians were allowed to reenter the area following the explosion, and they proceeded to remove all faulted bus duct, test all bus duct intended to remain in place with a megger (high voltage tester for insulation integrity), and to install temporary cables to serve the facility loads. It was at this time that the lead electrician discovered the high moisture content of the tie bus duct near the tee point A in Figure 10.2 and 10.3.

The available fault current from transformer T2 was estimated by the utility at 40 kA. After the electricians had disconnected the tie bus connection at point A linking DS-2 to DS-3, and with the 3,000-amp main breaker (MB) in DS-2 open, the second fault F2 occurred. At this time, the feeder bus from T2 to DS-2 was still energized, but no load current had been flowing in this bus duct for about 45 minutes since the DS-2 main breaker had last tripped.

A logical explanation for the second fault was apparent at this point in the investigation. The feeder bus duct to DS-2 had, before the DS-2 MB tripped off, been carrying the load of DS2 and DS-1, which at that time of morning was about 800 amps. This would cause the bus duct conductors to operate at a temperature of around 48°C (118°F) and would tend to drive moisture away from the conducting buses. When the load was disconnected, the bus bars would begin to cool down, approaching the outdoor ambient of about 32°C (90°F). As this cooling effect occurred, moisture would not only stop being expelled, but would be drawn to the bus bars of the duct through any porous material nearby.

In November 1982, the feeder bus duct was opened by drilling the spot welds, careful chiseling, and metal sabre saw cutting of the sheet steel enclosure that houses the multiple aluminum bus bars which are the conductors. Figure 10.4 shows the bus duct construction.

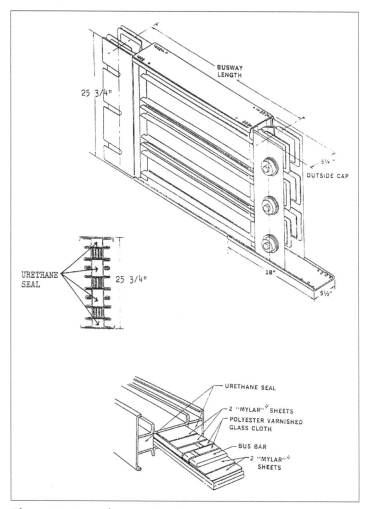

Figure 10.4 Bus duct construction

The feeder bus duct was rated by the manufacturer at 600 V, 3,000 amps, 3Ø 4 W, with full sized neutral, suitable for outdoor use having a totally-enclosed weatherproof, dust-resistant design. The fault damaged section of bus duct showed clear evidence of moisture penetration with rust deposits on structural steel and insulating materials inside the duct. The urethane foam seal material used readily absorbed and retained moisture, and this material was only separated from the bus bars by two layers of polyester varnished glass cloth. The presence of moisture within the duct enclosure was concluded as the prime factor contributing to the fault at F2.

Only the utility's overcurrent devices, the 450E primary fuses and 700-A relaying circuit breakers electrically protected the secondary bus duct feeders from T2 and T3. The 450E fuses will allow a secondary fault of 11,440 amps rms to exist for 16.67 minutes before clearing the fault and the utility substation phase overcurrent relays will allow a current of 6,100 amps rms in the secondary for at least 3.33 minutes before clearing the fault. The electric utility found that after the second fault, two phase relays on C-8 activated which, along with the existing wye-wye transformer configuration, indicated that basically a line-to-line fault finally cleared the circuit. The extensive damage to the bus duct at F2 eventually involved all three phases and the neutral, however.

Arcing faults are known to frequently exhibit low current levels due to the apparent impedance of the arc itself. Tests on aluminum conductors within steel enclosures have shown that the instantaneous current values at various arc resistances from 0.01 to 0.2 ohm can vary from 200 to 15,000 amps.[2] Obviously, the arcing can and frequently does persist at rms current levels insufficient to operate either circuit breakers or fuses. Meanwhile, the violent effects of the electrical arcing continue, creating temperatures of several thousand degrees Celsius with gas plasmas and explosions that scatter superheated metal particles that can destroy equipment and severely injure or kill bystanders.

In this case, all experts agreed with the conclusions as to the cause of both faults F1 and F2 as previously given. The client was obviously concerned with the future reliability of the feeder bus duct that had not faulted from T3 to DS-3. Although this bus duct had been high voltage tested before the utility restored power to the facility, there remained a question of the efficacy of this bus duct to withstand future moisture penetration. It was the owner's decision, based upon the engineer's recommendation, to replace all outdoor bus duct with insulated cable in rain-tight wireway. In order to provide the 3,000-A capacity of the feeder and tie bus ducts with cable in wireway, eight 500 kcmil 90°C rated copper (Cu) cables were required when derated to a maximum ambient of 45°C (113°F). (1981 NEC code-rated ampacity for this cable configuration is 2,993 amps.) The existing transformer secondaries to the buses were connected with nine short sections of 500 kcmil 75°C rated Cu cable. In accordance with the 1981 NEC Code, these cables are rated at 380 A each for an ambient temperature not to exceed 30°C and derated to 82 percent of this ampacity for ambient temperatures not to exceed 45°C. The use of nine 500 kcmil Cu 75°C rated cables provides 2,804 amps of capacity.

In order to better protect the multiple secondary paralleled feeder cables from T2 and T3 to DS-2 and DS-3, respectively, the engineer considered the following alternatives:

- installing ground fault interrupting circuit breakers in the padmounted transformer secondary compartments of T2 and T3,
- installing cable limiting in-line fuses on both ends of the secondary cables 8 limiters × 3 phases × 2 ends or 48 cable limiters per transformer and distribution center, and
- installing primary current limiting fuses rated 400E at the transformer primaries to allow in-rush currents to the transformer and to limit the maximum instantaneous peak current let-through.

The third alternative will limit the "I^2t" let-through to a secondary fault, but has the disadvantage of requiring at least 0.1 second fuse melting time at twelve times the continuous primary rating of the transformer (i.e., 4,164 A). This is a continuous secondary current of 36,084 A rms, a value too large to expect a usual arcing fault in the secondary to activate the fuses.

The first alternative was not realizable due to the transformer secondary compartment space limitations and the multiple paralleled feeder cables planned.

This leaves the second alternative, which was ultimately installed using manufacturer recommended 500 kcmil copper cable limiters that will clear a 1,500-A rms fault in five minutes and a 3,000-A rms fault in ten seconds. These potential arcing fault currents are considerably lower than the protection provided by the original system prior to the time of the accident. There is also an increased reliability associated with the main feeders to the facility's distribution centers in respect to moisture and dust induced failure.

Concurrent with this engineering design work to modify the electrical service at the newspaper, the lawsuit continued. More than two years after the accident, this engineer was still providing information regarding his investigation to attorneys for defendants and plaintiffs in the matter. The engineer's deposition was taken in early April 1983, and a trial was first set for late 1983. After several continuations of trial, all parties settled their law suits for an undisclosed amount. Knowledgeable sources in the case have estimated that the total settlement amount in these lawsuits was several million dollars.

10.10 A Case of EMF Concern for a New Power Line

In early 1982, an electric utility company requested a confirmation from the state utility commission of the state siting committee's prior approval for a two and one-half mile extension of the utility's 138-kV transmission line system to reach an existing substation presently served by a 46-kV subtransmission line. The confirmation was necessitated by an intervenor's motion for denial of the new line's siting, which was filed on behalf of the residential property owners along the proposed route of the line.

The attorney representing the property owners retained this engineer to provide expert opinion and gather evidence in support of the owners' position. Crucial to the property owners' case was an already filed motion which cited the Wertheimer and Leeper study from Colorado (as referenced in Section 5.7, Endnote 79), and which epidemiologically showed a significant increase in childhood leukemia due to EMF exposure. Both litigants were well aware of this study by 1982.

The electric utility responded to this challenge to their planned expansion of facilities in the following way:

- By citing the rules of civil procedure in the state which provide for relief from judgment because of the discovery of new evidence, which by due diligence could not have been discovered in time to move for a new trial. This argument is generated by the original hearing proceedings, held in 1981, in which the property owner's expert (not at that time this engineer) was unaware of the Wertheimer and Leeper (W-L) study.

- By introducing affidavits from two experts: an electrical engineer who is Department of Energy (DOE) and utility oriented, and a radiation biologist who was the program director for research in 60-Hz bioeffects at a university heavily subsidized by DOE and EPRI. Both experts criticized the W-L study and even went so far as to state that "[such work is] certainly not allowable in an acceptable scientific study."
- By alleging that "the purported evidence is not newly discovered, is not credible . . . would serve no purpose other than to delay . . . is an attempt by the Intervenors to confuse the issues."

Despite the somewhat intimidating testimony of these utility experts, the engineering testimony for the property owners concentrated upon the methods of acceptable statistical analysis employed by Wertheimer and Leeper and their resultant conclusions. Unfortunately, the Swedish study published in June 1982, (as referenced in Chapter 5, Note 81), which confirmed the W-L work, was not discovered by this engineer until after this hearing, but the large body of research known at this time solicited an engineering opinion which stated "there is . . . sufficient evidence of adverse biological effects due to power frequency electromagnetic fields on humans to suggest that we proceed with caution to transmit and distribute electrical energy . . . in close proximity to human habitation."

Further, this engineer criticized the close proximity of the 138-kV line to adjacent residential and institutional property, and in particular the previously approved diagonal crossing of the transmission line over an elementary school recreational yard.

The state utility commission ultimately granted the electric utility's request, but a compromise was enacted regarding the line placement over the school yard and the line was constructed such that it remains on the opposite side of the two roadways near the school property and does not cross over the playground.

10.11 A Case of an Exploding Voltmeter

In May 1987, a forty-four-year-old air conditioning mechanic was in the process of troubleshooting a 200-ton centrifugal chiller located in the basement of a high rise government complex building. The chiller had shut down and the building maintenance engineer reported that the 400-amp three-pole circuit breaker (CB) protecting the 480-volt feeder to the chiller would not reset.

Upon arriving at the job site, the air conditioning mechanic located the tripped breaker, the chiller, and its safety disconnect switch. He visually inspected the equipment and turned off the safety disconnect at the chiller. He had reason to believe that there was possibly a bad winding in the 150-hp motor driving the chiller, which he intended to check. First, he returned to the motor control center where the CB for the chiller feeder was located and used his multimeter to check the voltage at the load side of the breaker, which he found was zero (in other words, the breaker was indeed tripped off). (A multimeter is an instrument that can be used to measure voltage, current, or resistance selectively.)

Next he went back to the chiller, removed the covers to gain access to the motor electrical terminals, and checked for grounded or shorted windings using the resistance measuring capability (ohmmeter function) of his instrument. He next checked the fuses and connections at the safety disconnect switch using both the voltmeter and ohmmeter functions of the multimeter. At this point, he concluded that the motor was probably not at fault and that the safety disconnect and fuses were in good working order.

He then returned to the motor control center to check the line side of the CB for power (voltage). As he touched the first voltmeter probe to one of the line terminals, an electrical explosion occurred and he was knocked backward to the floor by the fireball which came from the CB cubicle. His clothing was on fire and another workman in the area quickly extinguished this with a hand-held fire extinguisher.

The mechanic suffered third-degree burns over 45 percent of his body that required extensive reconstructive surgery and skin grafting. He also suffered hearing loss in both ears and limited dexterity in his hands. After about three and one-half months, he was able to return to limited work in the office of his employer. After a year, he was able to return to working at his previous job as an air conditioning mechanic. The man had worked for some thirteen years as an air conditioning mechanic prior to this accident.

This engineer was contacted by the insurance carrier for the employer within a month of the accident and began an engineering investigation to determine cause. The accident site had been basically left as it was except that the electrical contractor, who had originally installed the motor control center and feeder to the chiller, had removed the CB involved and had retained it as evidence. The damaged multimeter was also available, having been taken as evidence by the mechanic's employer. This engineer also owned an exact make and model of the subject multimeter that served as an exemplar in this investigation.

The cause of the explosion was concluded by the engineer in a report issued to the insurance company within two months of the initial site examination. It was stated therein that,

> . . . it is most likely that the explosion . . . was the result of a phase-to-ground fault at the line side terminals of the . . .circuit breaker. This ground fault rapidly escalated into a phase-to-phase fault . . . and the resulting . . . explosion with expanding plasma gas and vaporized metal . . . [It is] believed that the Ohm probe tip touched grounded metal, probably the breaker operating mechanism, while the left hand voltage probe touched an energized line terminal. This placed the resistance metering circuitry of the [omitted trade name] across a 277 volt potential and caused a low resistance phase-to-ground fault. The Ohm probe is equipped with a 1 A 8AG glass body fuse rated at 250 volts or less. This fuse can safely interrupt up to 35 A at 250 volts, but will likely fail at voltages greater than 250 volts and for fault currents greater than 35 Amp. This fuse obviously failed catastrophically.

The report continued.

> At this time, I have no evidence to indicate that the breaker installation contributed to the severity of the accident or that it was a proximate cause for this accident. However, the use of washers to shim a 3/4" space in a bus connection is not acceptable practice in electrical work at these voltage and current levels. There also appears to have been a missing barrier with warning across the line terminals of the original breaker that was furnished by the manufacturer on the replacement breaker.
>
> The fuse protection for the MCC (motor control center) main disconnect and MCC feeder disconnect are not properly coordinated in that

the closest upstream device to the fault should clear the fault first, which did not occur. This lack of coordination did not, however, cause the accident nor affect the accident severity.

The catastrophic failure under the hypothesized energized phase-to-ground connection of the Ohm probe is a foreseeable event by the instrument manufacturer. In my opinion neither the design nor the warning issued with the instrument were adequate to protect the user from injury in this situation.

The engineer was deposed in May of 1989 and the case remained active until the early part of 1990 before a settlement was reached between the parties. The plaintiff mechanic received a $350,000 award for the injuries sustained as a result of this product failure.

10.12 A Case of Inadequate Illumination

In 1983, a female civilian food-service worker at a military base was assaulted while working. The worker had left the mess hall where she was employed at around 2 A.M. to carry some garbage to an outside disposal area. She was attacked by a man who "put a box cutter to her throat," cut and fondled her, and probably would have raped her if a passing car had not startled the attacker with its headlights, frightening the man away.

A lawsuit was subsequently filed against the government for failing to provide adequate protection for this employee in the workplace. The worker's attorney in order to evaluate the adequacy of the lighting in the vicinity of the assault contacted this engineer in 1985. The engineer visited the site at night and used a low level sensitive photometer to measure the illumination in the area of assault. General observations were made and recorded during this inspection regarding the surrounding light interfering structures and sources of illumination. The date of inspection was coordinated with the time of the moon to assure that moonlight was at a comparable intensity during the investigation.

The engineer issued a report to the client attorney stating the opinion that "the illumination of the trash enclosure area interior was deficient." Cited in this report were recommended standards of the IESNA for minimum levels of illuminance (footcandles) necessary to provide protective lighting and for safety. The measured illuminance behind the trash enclosure fence where the woman was attacked was less than 0.01 footcandle

(FC). In addition, the facility was operated without light sources from the building to provide illumination within the trash enclosure. The only artificial light sources contributing to the illumination within the trash enclosure came from (1) a street light approximately seventy-five feet diagonally N-W from the enclosure west wall and (2) the light emanating from the windows of a three-story residence hall approximately fifty feet north of the enclosure. The trash enclosure was surrounded on three sides by a seven-foot-high fence made of wire mesh with interwoven sheet metal visual barriers, and on the south side by the north wall of the mess hall. Within the trash enclosure were several large metal trash boxes (dumpsters) of six-foot height that offered dark hiding places.

The defense offered illuminance measurements taken with an instrument which the manufacturer stated was not intended to read less than 5 FC; and in a lighting survey report issued by the government's investigator, it was stated that "at the dumpsters, no light readings could be noted."

Despite these obvious deficiencies in the defense's case, the case was tried before a federal judge, who personally inspected the area at night, and who awarded the plaintiff $67,750 in damages from the military service responsible for the base operations.

10.13 A Case of a Misdiagnosed Electrocution

On July 4, 1974, during mid-morning, a man weighing 214 pounds and wearing shoes, trousers, leather gloves, but no shirt, was using a hand-held electric circular saw to cut firewood at his residence. The ground was wet, as it had been irrigated the day before. He had been working for about two hours at the task when he was discovered lying dead on the ground face down. The saw was under his abdomen and continuing to run with the spring guard covering the rotating blade.

At the time of its operation, the saw was connected to an electrical outlet by two extension cords. One extension cord was a three-wire cord with ground and the other cord was a two-wire cord without ground. The three-prong to two-wire adapter plug provided with the circular saw by the manufacturer was not used by the decedent.

The fire and police department investigators who responded to the accident requested a city electrician to be called to the scene to examine the electrical components for possible malfunction that could have electrocuted the man. The electrician's investigation found that the three-wire extension cord had been damaged and that there were some frayed exposed conductors visible in the cord when the insulation tape used to repair the cord was removed.

Upon completion of his resistance and continuity checks, the electrician turned on the saw and demonstrated to the other investigators that he could hold the saw in his hand and place the other hand firmly on the wet ground without being shocked. He found no indication of any voltage on the case or handle of the saw. An ammeter attached to the saw and cord indicated no abnormal current flow.

The saw, extension cords, and leather gloves were sent collectively to three different engineering testing laboratories at different times over the next six months for evaluation. The laboratory tests all indicated that:

- The case of the saw was effectively electrically connected to the ground wire and prong of the saw cord and male plug.
- The hot and neutral legs of the saw cord were isolated electrically from the saw case and ground wire by over 2 mega ohms of resistance, respectively, which is normal for this product and safe for the intended use.
- Leakage current was measured according to the UL 45 and ANSI C101.1 test procedures and standards. The maximum reading obtained was 0.04 mA. The maximum allowed by UL and ANSI is 0.5 mA. The manufacturer's specification is 0.2 mA max.
- The saw was subjected to running tests to heat the insulation and 24-hour humidity tests to introduce moisture into the insulation system. The leakage current tests were repeated, with maximum leakage current measured at 0.08 mA and no breakdown of dielectric strength.
- By using the decedent's gloves, it was found that the size and thickness of these gloves resulted, in many positions of operation, in holding the trigger switch closed even when no pressure was applied by the index finger.
- Upon removal of the insulation tape around the extension cord at two locations, a lateral cut through the insulation of all three conductors was found. The tape was old, probably installed before the incident. The method of reinsulating the extension cord was not such that it would provide a reliable and safe use of the cord since it did not

reinsulate the individual conductors adequately. With abrasion and flexure, the cord could fail electrically.

Shortly after the accident, the county medical examiner performed a postmortem examination and concluded the cause of death was electrocution. In the medical examiner's opinion, the burns on the decedent were electrical rather than thermal. He opined that electrical current had entered the body from the saw through a 3-inch-diameter burned area on the decedent's mid-abdomen and that this would likely have produced a cardiac arrhythmia or fibrillation of the heart. The examiner also found a small-elongated burn on the back of the right hand toward the thumb over the bones of the hand that go to the index and middle finger.

A lawsuit was brought in this case for products liability against the saw manufacturer and the three-wire extension cord manufacturer. It was alleged that the saw was defective in design because it was not double insulated and that the manufacturer failed to provide adequate warnings in the instructions which accompanied the saw about the danger of using the product with an ungrounded electrical supply or two wire extension cord.

Against the three-wire extension cord manufacturer, the plaintiff alleged that the cord was defective in design and manufacture because of the cuts in the insulation that had exposed bare conductor wires, and because of inadequate warnings provided with the cord concerning the danger of using the cord with such insulation damage.

The trial judge in this case granted summary judgment in favor of all defendants, and the plaintiff appealed. On appeal, the court affirmed summary judgment for the cord manufacturer, but reversed the summary judgment as to the saw manufacturer.

The court held that genuine issues of material fact existed as to defectiveness of the design of the saw, adequacy of warnings given in the instructions accompanying the saw, and as to whether the use of an ungrounded extension cord was an unforeseeable misuse of the product. There was a partial dissent by one judge who agreed with the trial court's decision in favor of the cord manufacturer, but disagreed in the reversal against the saw manufacturer. This judge's opinion was that the express instructions and warnings furnished by the saw manufacturer were unmistakably clear as to the consequences of using the saw with a two-prong extension cord. "A skull and crossbones was not required." The judge further said "since it is clear that the saw would not have been energized with an electric current if a grounded extension cord had been used, the saw was not unreasonably dangerous as a matter of law, regardless of whether there was an alternate design (double insulation) available."

This engineer was retained in January 1985 to advise the defendant saw manufacturer's attorney before the scheduled trial of the case, and to testify at trial if warranted. The engineer was furnished with the first trial depositions of three engineers and the county medical examiner, and with various reports of testing performed on the subject saw and cords. In addition, he was provided with the pleadings to the court of appeals, the decision of the court, the instructions for operation furnished with the saw, and an engineering evaluation of the case by Ralph H. Lee. (Lee Electrical Engineering, Inc. Oct. 18, 1979. Mr. Lee, who is deceased, was a recognized consulting electrical engineer, particularly in the field of lightning protection. He served as chairman of the NESC Committee, ANSI C2-1981 and 1984.)

In Lee's report, he made various estimates of the resistance of the electrical circuit through the victim in order to determine a range of reasonably probable shock current in this case. His estimates varied from 6 mA to 80 mA under differing conditions of gloves-no gloves, shoes-no shoes, and one hand-two hand contacts. He also estimated the fibrillation current for this 214-pound man at 95 mA for 0.5 percent of all individuals (i.e., greater than 95 mA for 99.5 percent of all individuals of this weight). (See Section 5.2) Lee concluded "the evidence shows that the victim died from cause [sic] other than electrocution."

This engineer's evaluation of the evidence supports this conclusion. The medical examiner was in error when he concluded that the burn was electrical because "the appearance of the burn . . . in the center . . . had the characteristic . . . dried desiccated appearance of an electrical burn as opposed to a thermo [thermal] burn." When asked in his deposition, "How would the appearance of that burn been different from a thermo [sic] burn if a hot object was held against the abdomen for a period of time?" the examiner answered, "It would vary and depend somewhat on the intensity of a thermo [sic] burn. The most remarkable difference is a marked reddening in the case of a thermo burn possibly with a blood formation or blistering and as opposed to the dry type of burn that you get with electricity in which there is no reddening or blistering." The question was then asked, "Are you saying there was no redness and blistering?" to which the answer was "Not in the center of it (a 3 inch diameter burn area) that I referred to at the margins. As I said, there was probably some thermo [sic] burn." When asked how deep the burn was, the medical examiner had no notes on that aspect and did not recall.

Mazer states in his three volume handbook on electrical accident investigation that deep subdermal injury is usually more closely associated with electrical burns than thermal burns and that thermal burns damage the skin more severely.[3] He further states that it is estimated that the lowest current that can cause a noticeable first or second-degree burn in a small area is about 100 mA flowing for about one second[4] (as has already been stated in a study cited in Chapter 5, for electrocutions by contact at less than 1,000 volts, 45 percent had no perceptible electrical burns). The reader should refer to Section 16.1C.1, on burns, of this text. "A current produced by a 110-volt AC source will rarely cause a large electrothermal injury of the skin unless the contact is maintained for a significant period of time (Damjanov and Linder, 1996, page 107)."

With respect to the possibility expressed by the medical examiner that the abdomen burn area and right hand burn area represent entrance and exit wounds for electrical contact, this is impossible if the saw case was energized as suggested, since it would be at a constant potential (with respect to ground) and there would be no electrical force to cause current to flow between abdomen and hand.

These observations, along with the engineer's opinions regarding the efficacy of double insulated hand tools versus a third wire ground were communicated in a report to the client's attorney before trial.

Rather than try the case, the manufacturer decided to settle by payment of a nominal amount to plaintiff and the file was closed in this matter.

10.14 A Case of a Faulty GFCI System

In 1993, a fifty-five-year-old woman who was also a registered nurse was bathing in her residence bathtub. Foolishly, she was also blow-drying her hair with a hand-held hair dryer. Perhaps because of her profession, she was overly trustful of the ground-fault circuit-interrupter (GFCI) protection she believed to be provided at the wall receptacle in her bathroom.

Evidently she dropped, or the hair dryer fell, into approximately 18 inches of bath water. She was subsequently electrocuted. Her husband who, while home at the time, did not check on her until he noticed the lack of sounds coming from the bathroom discovered her body.

The husband reported receiving a shock when he attempted to aid her and to remove the hair dryer from the bath water. A postmortem examination revealed electrical burns on her left leg, nearest to the discovered position of the hair dryer in the water. Electrical burns were also found inside the left wrist, on the right side of the chest, on the inside of the left arm opposite the left breast, and on the left breast next to the arm.

An electrical engineering examination was conducted on the residence electrical system, the hair dryer, and the receptacle in the bathroom that supplied the hair dryer. An upstream GFCI receptacle in an immediately adjacent bathroom protected the bathroom receptacle. The ground-fault circuit-interruption operation of the supply receptacle was found to be correct and in accordance with NFPA recommendations. At 5 mA of leakage current, the GFCI receptacle interrupted current flow in 0.1 second; in other words, within six cycles of 60-Hz current.

How then could this woman have been electrocuted? As described in Chapter 4, a ground-fault interrupting (GFI) device determines the leakage current supplied to the connected load by sensing the difference between the current flow in the hot wire of the 120-volt power conductors and the neutral wire. Normally a GFCI receptacle senses this difference because a leakage is occurring to ground from the hot wire. When a path to ground exists because of the load conditions such that at least 5 mA of leakage current flows, the GFI will trip, deenergizing the hot wire and interrupting all current flow to the load. If there is no current path to ground or a very high resistance path (more than 24,000 ohms at 120 volts) the leakage will be less than 5 mA and the conductors will remain energized, (e.g., over ten seconds at ≥30,000 ohms of leakage resistance).

The current supplied by the source in the absence of a ground fault is limited by the branch circuit breaker, which is typically a 15- or 20-amp device for a residential receptacle circuit. This current flows from the hot wire and returns through the neutral spreading out through the water mass and flowing through any material immersed in the water according to Ohm's law; that is, inversely proportional to the path resistance. So long as the total current flowing is less than the circuit breaker rating, the water will remain energized and a potentially lethal current can be delivered to a human who is immersed in the water.

Measuring the AC resistance between the metallic parts of the subject bathtub and ground at the electrical service entrance showed that this resistance was greater than 10,000 ohms.

The subject hair dryer was tested by plugging it into a GFCI receptacle and submerging it into water contained in a plastic basin. The hair dryer submersion with the switch on or off did not trip the GFCI. In fact, the hair dryer blower continued to run under water.

A test was then conducted using a plastic female mannequin with sheet metal plate probes attached to the left leg, the left breast, and to the right side of the chest. A 1,000-ohm resistor was used to simulate body resistance between each pair of plates. The mannequin was immersed in the subject bathtub filled to eighteen inches with tap water mixed with the victim's favorite bath oil. The energized hair dryer was submersed approximately 6 inches from the left leg of the mannequin. Voltages were measured between the probes and parts of the bathtub with the hair dryer on and off and with the two-prong plug forward and reversed, that is, hot and neutral conductors reversed.

Various AC voltages were recorded from 0 volts (switch off) to 104 volts from the left leg to the metallic water supply outlet to the tub. A voltage of 35 volts between the left breast and the left leg was measured with the dryer switch off and 70 volts with the switch on.

Further resistance measurements were made between the tub drain, the bathroom sink supply faucets and drain connections, the kitchen sink supply and drain connections, and the water service ground at the electrical service entrance to the house. All of these points had greater than 10,000 ohms to ground.

It was determined that the house plumbing was piped with plastic supply and ABC drain lines. These nonconductive materials defeat the electrical ground that is necessary to cause ground-fault interrupting devices to activate when the leakage path is established through water held in a plumbing appliance such as a wash basin, bathtub, water heater, or hot tub. Unless the plumbing appliance has a metallic surface in good contact with the water and in continuity with the electrical ground at the building service, a low resistance plumbing ground path will not exist.

Hand held electric appliances such as hair dryers, curling irons, electric shavers, cord connected electric toothbrushes, lighted makeup mirrors and so on, are susceptible to immersion in the water of open plumbing appliances like wash basins, bath tubs, showers and hot tubs. As previously explained, when immersed in water an electric appliance is capable of dangerously energizing the water even when the electric supply is protected by a GFI circuit breaker or device.

If the source of electricity in the water is a two conductor AC power supply without ground, the current conducted through the water returns through the neutral conductor and a differential leakage current does not exist to activate a GFI device. This dangerous condition is usually avoided when the water is in contact with ground through a metallic drainpipe fitting and or metallic water supply pipes, however with plastic pipes this ground return path is lost.

If the manufacturers of two wire hand held appliances would include a third (ground) wire that connects supply ground to a metal plate inside their appliance housing, the dangerous condition previously described would likely be avoided even with plastic piping systems. Another solution to this problem would be to construct plumbing systems with a ground conductor extended from a metallic drain fitting in all open water appliances to the electrical ground for the structure. This conductor could be separately installed or included as an integral component of the plastic pipe.

Since the building codes such as the UBC, the UPC, and the NEC now permit the use of plastic supply and waste piping systems without requiring grounding, these codes would have to be changed to solve the problem at the construction level. Also, since electrical appliance standards such as UL now permit the manufacture of two wire hand held appliances that do not activate GFI devices when submerged in ungrounded water vessels, these standards would have to be changed to solve the problem at the consumer product level.

The decedent's husband filled an action against the home builder in this case and the parties eventually reached a confidential financial settlement. However, no changes were made to the plumbing or electrical systems at the subject residence and nothing was done to rectify the grounding problem at any of the other homes built at the same time by this builder in a development of several dozen homes.

Contact with the U.S. Consumer Product Safety Commission in December of 1995, revealed that for the three year period from January 1993 through December 1995, there were four reported electrocutions in the U.S. due to hair dryers being immersed in bathtubs, one of these was the case reported here. The other three involved three two- through four-year-old children and a fourteen-year-old girl. One case simultaneously involved two children; one died and one lived. HEW estimates are that some 20,000 injuries from personal use appliances (non-shaving) out of nearly 15 million from listed consumer products occurred in the U.S. from the early 1970s through the mid-1990s.

Obviously, the incidence of death from the danger described in this case is not relatively great and therefore little is being done by the electrical industry to reduce the danger. Either of the previously suggested methods for solving the problem would be expensive to implement on a national scale.

10.15 A Case of a Faulty Control System

In 1994, a fire occurred at a coffee roaster's facility. The roaster plant had three coffee roasters and the fire began in one of the machines after the coffee beans had reached their desired roast temperature of 450°F, when the control system failed to automatically shut down the roasting process.

Plant personnel, upon discovery of the fire, manually shut down the roasting process by turning off the gas heater and forced air blower, and turning on the water spray (normally used to cool the roasted beans) to extinguish the fire within the roaster chamber.

On two prior occasions, the automatic controller lost digital readout, the gas heater did not shut off, and the water spray did not automatically turn on although two thermostats reading the roaster chamber temperature indicated that the desired bean temperature had been achieved. The process was manually terminated on these occasions before a fire resulted.

An engineering investigation of the roaster automatic control system revealed that it was intended to operate as follows.

- On "reset" of all automatic controls, manual starting of the roaster blower should produce air pressure sufficient to activate a pressure switch which energizes the high limit digital display temperature controller (HLTC), an electro-mechanical relay (e-m relay), and an analog display process temperature controller (PTC).

- Thermocouple TC-1, the sensor for the HLTC, senses the inlet air temperature to the roaster chamber. The HLTC should shut off the burner gas and close off the blower supply duct to the roaster when its set temperature is reached. This high limit set temperature is greater than the desired maximum roasting temperature for the beans and is selected to prevent excess temperature within the burner chamber and ducts to the roaster.

- Thermocouple TC-2, the sensor for the PTC, senses the temperature of the beans in the roasting chamber. This controller should signal the e-m relay to switch off the burner gas, close off the air supply to the roaster, and activate the timed water spray solenoid to cool the roasted coffee beans within the chamber.

Immediately before the fire, neither did the burner gas shut off, nor did the water spray activate when the beans reached their set temperature of 450°F. Because of the prior incidents of malfunction, a technician had replaced the e-m relay with a new unit in an attempt to correct the problem. This obviously did not solve the control problem however, and the beans continued to heat beyond their desired temperature, eventually igniting.

At the time of the fire the HLTC was set at 600°F, a safe temperature for the equipment, but too high a temperature to prevent the beans from igniting.

The PTC, HLTC, and e-m relay were removed from the control panel and tested independently and as a system. The PTC was found to operate intermittently by switching back and forth rapidly starting at 450°F and continuing until 497°F. The e-m relay tripped (set) on the first intermittent operation of the PTC at 450°F. The HLTC was found to trip (set) at approximately any set temperature from 400° to 550°F.

The wiring connections and integrity within the control panel were inspected and no breaks or loose connections were found.

This engineer rendered the following opinions and conclusions:

Since the technician replaced the e-m relay without success in correcting the control system problem and since testing did not produce a failure of the relay, it is logical to believe that some other component is responsible for the control failures. Also, since the water solenoid and burner gas solenoid are independent distinct components, it is highly improbable that both units would simultaneously fail to operate upon receipt of the proper signals from the e-m relay. It is therefore probable that the e-m relay did not receive a "set" signal from the PTC. The PTC will fail to activate the e-m relay under any of the following conditions:

A) Loss of power to the PTC by an interruption of either the hot or neutral line supply wiring to the controller.

B) Break in a wiring jumper connection required by the PTC.

C) Malfunction of the thermocouple TC-2 or wiring.

D) Malfunction of the PTC electronics.

E) Break in the wiring from the PTC to the e-m relay.

Possibilities A, B, and E were eliminated by the wiring connection and integrity inspection along with the roasting process operation that occurred prior to the fire. Testing eliminated a malfunction of the thermocouple TC-1, and the wiring was essentially eliminated by the system wiring inspection although the wiring had been cut off about four feet from the control panel in order to remove the damaged roaster elements.

A malfunction of thermocouple TC-2 could not be eliminated since the thermocouple was destroyed by the fire in the roasting chamber.

Although the testing did not produce a failure in the PTC, the intermittent operation of this component strongly suggests an electronic failure possibility. Random and intermittent electronic failures are very difficult, if not impossible to detect, and rarely can such a failure be observed by testing. All evidence was preserved so that it could be made available to interested parties should a legal action result in this case.

In this engineer's opinion, the PTC had an internal electronic problem that caused it to fail to reliably activate the e-m relay to switch off the burner gas, close the air supply, and activate the water spray timer.

The control system was redesigned and a new control and roaster system was placed in operation in 1995. It has continued to operate successfully without failure since this date.

No litigation resulted in this matter.

10.16 A Case of a Battery Explosion

In 1992, a 12-volt lead-acid automotive battery used to start and run an emergency engine-generator (e-g) set exploded and emitted acid fumes that were widely circulated, thereby causing extensive damage to a cellular telephone relaying facility.

The owner-operator of the cellular telephone facility filed suit against the manufacturer of the emergency generator set claiming, among other claims, that the e-g set battery charger and regulator was improperly designed, manufactured and maintained. The plaintiffs alleged damages of more than $600,000 to their equipment and facility.

Laboratory testing of the subject charger and regulator indicated that the regulator was continuously overcharging a fully charged battery. A second test with a new exemplar regulator showed the charger to perform properly as a "float" type charger.

An investigation of the service records for the subject e-g set disclosed that approximately ten weeks before the explosion, a field service technician performed a scheduled semiannual maintenance where he found and replaced a dead battery and set the adjustable voltage regulator at its "lowest setting." In deposition, the service technician described the lowest setting as being a fully counterclockwise (CCW) setting of the adjusting potentiometer. The manufacturer's specifications, however, state that the potentiometer is rotated CCW to increase the float voltage and CW to decrease the float voltage.

A third laboratory test was now conducted with the subject charger and regulator but with the regulator adjusted following the manufacturer's specifications. This test confirmed that a properly adjusted regulator caused the charger to perform correctly as a float type charger.

Normally a properly operating float charger for this application delivers 100 mA and maintains a battery open circuit terminal voltage of 13.3 volts. The subject charger as adjusted by the field technician was found to be delivering from 1.4 to 1.6 A into a partially discharged (12.04-volt) battery and stabilizing the battery open circuit terminal voltage at 14.4 volts.

It was further discovered from the service records that the e-g set was automatically programmed to be exercised weekly, that is, it was started, run for 10 minutes, and shut down. Also it was determined that the electrolyte level in the battery was being checked semiannually. The manufacturer's recommended interval for electrolyte monitoring was one month.

Several of the experts in this case postulated that a low electrolyte level in the battery would be further diminished during a heavy current discharge of engine starting and that the battery "BLEVED" during such an operation causing the explosion. (Refer to Chapter 7 for a detailed description of a boiling liquid expanding vapor explosion—BLEVE.)

A combination of factors in this case supported the BLEVE hypothesis:

- the high continuous charging level set by the field technician,
- the frequent (weekly) exercising of the engine (starting) and
- the lack of a regular monthly monitoring of the electrolyte level.

Each repetitive starting of the engine produced current heating of the battery plates and electrolyte. This was followed by a short (one week) period of relatively high current recharging that would accelerate the loss of electrolyte from the battery case. The BLEVE occurred when this combination of events overheated the diminished electrolyte level in the closed battery case and caused the liquid electrolyte to boil and expand catastrophically.

In this engineer's opinion, the accident was not caused by the design or manufacture of the battery charger and regulator, but rather by the field maintenance of the battery charging system and battery. The determination of this maintenance program was jointly the responsibility of the e-g set manufacturer and the owner of the facility who was paying the bill for field maintenance and elected to save money by reducing the recommended field maintenance frequency.

A jury tried this case and awarded damages and costs totaling $140,000 to the plaintiffs from the service maintenance defendant but reached a defendant's verdict in favor of the e-g manufacturer, who was awarded $7,500 in costs from the plaintiffs.

10.17 A Case of a Shocking Kitchen Appliance

In 1995, a housewife received a severe shock when she simultaneously touched a built-in electric oven and the metal surface of a built-in electric range top.

The woman reported that at the time of the shock she touched the oven door handle with her right hand and placed her left hand palm down on the cook top. She was then shocked and was unable to let go of the oven handle. She described the sensation as "the most painful thing I have ever felt in my life. It felt like an explosion had happened. It felt like someone was in my chest and had kicked me full force inside my rib cage and then [the pain] {sic} going right down my left arm." She remembers winding up in the pantry, approximately 9 feet across the room from the oven, but did not remember letting go of the oven. Her husband found her in the pantry doorway. She described her feelings then as if "my heart was flipping inside."

The day after the accident and before an engineering expert could examine the scene, the installing electricians were called back to the home. Although poorly documented, these electricians evidently used an instrument (volt meter?) to measure between the oven and the cook top. Then they worked on the oven cord and plug, put the oven back into the cabinet and told the homeowner they had fixed the problem. Later, in a deposition of the lead electrician, he stated that he found between 110 and 120 volt to ground on the oven case.

One week later, a representative of the general contractor was at the residence and, while there for other reasons, decided to operate the oven. When he turned the oven on and adjusted the controls, "an arcing sound occurred and smoke blew out of the oven." At this time, he cautioned the woman not to use the oven, saying that something was wrong.

Three weeks later a contingent of representatives for the general contractor, the electrical contractor, the appliance supplier, and an insurance adjuster videotaped an inspection of the oven at the residence and discovered a loose wire and arc marks inside the metal panel that enclosed the oven. After the wire was resoldered to its suspected terminal connection, the oven was operated and tested for voltage on the outer case to ground and no voltage was found.

This engineer subsequently concluded that when the oven was originally installed, it was not connected to the residence ground that would have prevented the oven case from being energized. It is probable that the electricians corrected the missing ground on the day following the accident and a week later, when the oven was placed in operation for the first time with the case properly grounded, the loose wire arced to the metal case.

When the woman simultaneously touched both the energized oven case (caused by the loose internal wire) and the grounded metal surface of the electric cook top, she created a path through her body and was shocked. An electrical engineer was able to recreate the fault condition and discovered that an internal source resistance of between 953 and 1799 ohms was present from the residential supply to the oven case.

It was found that an open circuit case voltage of 107.8 volts to ground was created when the loose wire touched the ungrounded oven enclosure. The available ground fault current through the woman's body was estimated at from 39 to 55 mA, which is sufficient to produce extreme muscle contractions, breathing difficulty, and if sustained for several seconds, ventricular fibrillation.

Three years after the shock, the woman reports having back pain twenty-four hours a day, severe pain in her left axilla (arm pit) and left upper arm down to the elbow.

This litigation was settled just prior to trial for $980,000, the payment being made nearly equally by the oven manufacturer and the electrical contractor.

10.18 A Case of Children Climbing Trees

In 2002 a ten-year-old boy was injured by contacting a 7,620-volt primary bare conductor that was running through a tree. The tree was a mature Magnolia located at the side of a residential street. Two boys who frequently played together in the area of the subject tree were both climbing the tree when the boy who was injured ascended to a height in the branches that brought him within a few inches of the energized power line. He was shocked by either direct or indirect contact with the power line and fell out of the tree. He had extensive injuries from the electrical current and from the fall.

A wrongful injury suit was filed on behalf of the injured boy and his parents alleging negligence on the part of the electric utility that owned and operated the power line.

The NESC in Rule 218 states "Trees that may interfere with ungrounded supply conductors should be trimmed or removed." Official interpretations to the NESC have made it clear that tree trimming is to be done for the safety of both utility employees and members of the public and *not only* to prevent abrasion and damage to overhead conductors.

In addition to the NESC requirements, the electric utility in this case had a written forestry line clearance management plan that recognized the risk of children climbing trees and contacting electric lines. The utility specifically classified and directed its line clearance standards to the climbable tree hazard by specifying that a minimum clearance of 6 feet is required in all directions from trees and branches to primary conductors. Further, the utility directed that "climbable tree conditions shall be eliminated under all circumstances."

This engineer expressed the following opinions in this case:

- The subject tree was readily climbable under the NESC definition of the term.
- The tree was a climbing attraction to children because of its size, location and readily climbable features.
- Under the utility's Overhead Construction Standards climbable trees shall be trimmed to avoid enabling a person to climb to within six feet of an energized conductor.
- The tree was not trimmed to maintain the utility's Standards and in fact had an energized conductor within two feet of the main trunk of the tree at the time of the accident.
- The utility's overhead line condition as installed, operated and maintained was not in compliance with the NESC nor in accord with the standards of good practice followed by many U.S. electric utilities. Moreover, this inherently dangerous condition was allowed to exist for from three to six or more years before this accident.

This case settled before trial and the plaintiffs received a confidential award in settlement of their claim for damages.

10.19 A Case of Interference with OH Lines by a High-Profile Vehicle

In 1999 a company was transporting a mobile or manufactured home to a residential site in a rural area. During the transport, the home became entangled with an overhead telephone line that was located at a lower height above ground than the overall height of the mobile home (MH) on its carrier.

In order to move the load past this telephone line interference, the truck driver went on top of the home to try to untangle and lift the telephone line. Above the telephone line was a single phase 14.4-kV overhead power line. The neutral for the power line was the first conductor above the telephone line and the primary phase conductor was above the neutral.

The driver somehow contacted the energized phase conductor while standing on top of the trailer and was severely burned by the electrical current that resulted. The electrical utility and telephone company were named as defendants in a lawsuit.

This engineer was retained as an expert for the defendant, the electrical utility. In the subsequent investigation it was discovered that: the highest point on the MH roof was 14 feet 11.25 inches above finished grade AFG); the telephone line was sagged to 12 feet 11 inches AFG; the power line neutral was sagged to 18 feet 8 inches AFG; and the primary phase conductor was sagged to 24 feet 4 inches AFG.

It was therefore determined that the energized conductor was 7 feet 4.75 inches above the highest part of the MH roof. Since a six-foot tall man, with average reach, cannot touch a point 1 foot 4 inches above his head while standing, it appears that either the driver jumped to reach the primary or had a conducting material in his hand that extended his reach.

With respect to the NESC, the primary phase and neutral conductor clearances in the area of the accident were found to be compliant. The telephone cable however was not in compliance with the NESC. For this accident site, the telephone cable is required to have a minimum vertical clearance AFG of 15.5 feet.

This engineer prepared an affidavit (sworn declaration) testifying to the court that the electric utility lines were within the required minimum height under the 1997 NESC. The court subsequently granted summary judgment in favor of the electric utility. The telephone company was found not guilty by a jury trial and the judge imposed court costs against the plaintiff.

10.20 A Case of Utility's Failure to Inspect

In 2000, a house painter was severely shocked when he touched a bare spot on an overhead service drop to the house he was painting. He was standing on a ladder washing the house when he received an electric shock that caused him to fall. The painter was rendered paraplegic and suffered multiple broken bones.

This engineer was retained by the plaintiff to investigate the cause for this accident and asked to opine on the electric utility's part in contribution to the hazardous condition that resulted in this worker's injuries.

The National Electrical Safety Code (NESC) has, from its inception in 1913 by the National Bureau of Standards, set forth rules for safeguarding of persons during the installation, operation and maintenance of overhead and underground electric supply and communication lines and their associated equipment. The rules contain the basic provisions that are considered necessary for the safety of employees and the public under specified conditions.

Of significance in the NESC rules for safety is the requirement for inspection and testing of lines and equipment. It has always been recognized by the codifiers of the NESC that in order to provide safeguarding of persons from the dangers of electrical energy it is necessary to continue to inspect and test the systems for delivery of this energy form to ensure that the systems remain reasonably safe for their intended use.

In the house painter case, the overhead 120/240-volt service drop to the house was originally installed twenty-seven years before this accident. At sometime during these years of exposure to the elements the insulating tape (used to cover the clamp between the utility's secondary service drop and the house service entrance cable) became frayed and disintegrated thereby exposing the energized metal conductor.

The house painter made contact with the exposed metal through one hand. He was standing on an aluminum ladder that was supported by the earth and was therefore subjected to a 120-volt induced shock current through his body to the ladder to ground.

The rules that apply to electrical utilities such as the NEC, the NESC, and the subject state administrative code require that electrical service be safe for use by the public and further state that the utility has a duty to inspect its lines and facilities to ensure their safe condition. Further, the type of electrical connection, specifically its form of insulation did not meet the standards of the utility nor the recognized codes.

A jury tried this case and the plaintiff was awarded $7.23 million. The award was reduced to $5.06 million because the jury found plaintiff 30 percent at fault.

Endnotes

1. Institute of Electrical and Electronics Engineers, Inc. (IEEE), *National Electrical Safety Code* (NY: Institute of Electrical and Electronics Engineers, Inc., 1990), 47.

2. Richard R. Conrad and Derio Dalasta, "A New Ground Fault Protective System for Electrical Distribution Circuits," *IEEE Trans. on Industry and General Applications*, May-June 1967, 222.

3. William M. Mazer, *Electrical Accident Investigation Handbook* (Glen Echo, MD: Electrodata, Inc., 1996), 7.4.1.0.

4. Ibid., 3, 7.4.2.0.

Part 2

Medical Evidence of Electrical Injuries

Raymond M. Fish, Ph.D., M.D., FACEP

Chapter 11

Basic Bioengineering Relavent to Electrical Accidents

This chapter gives a brief overview of the factors affecting severity of electrical injury, stimulation of excitable cells, and thermal injury. The topic of death from electrical injury without skin burns is discussed.

11.1 Factors Related to Electrical Injury
A. Thermal injury
Thermal injury occurs when electrical energy is converted into heat. The amount of heat energy produced is calculated by

$$Q = I^2(R)(t)$$

In the equation, Q is the energy in joules, I is the current in amps, R is the resistance to current flow in ohms, and t is the time in seconds. In reality, these quantities often change over time. Specifically, with burning, the resistance may change, which may cause changes in the current.

One watt of power being delivered for one second produces 0.24 calorie of heat. In tissue, the current usually enters the skin by making contact with an object. The area of skin touched by the object determines the area over which heating occurs. A certain current applied to a pinpoint area of skin may produce a burn; while, the same current applied over a wide area may not cause enough heating in any one area to cause a burn. It is, therefore, sometimes useful to calculate the current per unit area (the current density).

Burns can injure any area of the body. The results can be fatal from a variety of causes including destruction of vital organs, blood loss, electrolyte imbalance, and infection. High body temperature itself can be fatal. Heating of tissues can result from

- current flow through the tissue itself,
- arcing of current through the air (arcs have temperatures of thousands of degrees),
- contact with burning clothing or other hot materials,
- microwave radiation, and
- explosion of gases or other materials ignited by the electrical current or associated fire,

These mechanisms are discussed further in Chapter 16.

B. Voltages causing electrical injury

Power transmission lines in the United States are 60 Hz (cycles per second) AC. These lines sometimes carry voltages of 100,000 volts or more. Outdoor power-line residential and industrial voltages are often 7620 volts (Wright and Davis 1980). Home voltages are 120 volts, with 240 volts being available between the two separate hot wires that are present in many homes. Industrial sources and electronic equipment may provide DC sources of electricity.

Many electrical appliances operate from low-voltage sources such as a nine-volt battery, but higher voltages are generated inside the appliance, making electrical injury possible. For example, battery powered stun guns, shock batons, and cattle prods generate thousands of volts. Though the voltage is high, the current that can be drawn from this source will usually be low; or the device will only deliver very short pulses of high currents. In contrast, a microwave oven is likely to have a several-thousand-volt source that can put out large, continuous currents. There will be a potentially lethal current available from this source. Electrosurgical devices generate high voltages, usually at high (0.3 to 2 MHz) frequencies (Gilbert 1991).

Government, university, and industrial laboratories have fusion energy devices, high power lasers, and particle accelerators that store large amounts of energy that can be suddenly released. The rapid release of stored energy is the basis for fields of pulsed power and can result in very high voltages and currents (Gordon 1991). Electrophoresis experiments in biology make use of several hundreds or thousands of volts that are direct current or of various other waveforms.

C. Skin resistance

The human body has an internal resistance of 500 ohms (these numbers are all approximate, as are many measurements in medicine). Hands and feet have a minimal resistance of 1,000 ohms (Wright and Davis 1980). The resistance of dry skin varies from one individual to another, but it is often around 10,000 to 100,000 ohms. The resistance of any given contact will depend on the area of contact, pressure applied, the magnitude and duration of current flow, and moisture present. The resistance will vary with time as the skin is charred or perforated and as physiological reactions occur.

When the current is large enough to cause tissue injury, skin resistance may fall within a fraction of a second. With an initial current of 20 milliamps per square millimeter of skin contact area, resistance changes are due to swelling of the skin. Currents of 35 milliamps per square millimeter of skin contact area cause resistance changes due to blister formation. Currents of 75 milliamps per square millimeter of skin contact area will cause carbonization of the skin (Biegelmeier 1985).

When the current is not large enough to cause tissue injury, the skin resistance falls over a period of about half a second as the current becomes large enough to be felt. Nute (1985) applied an increasing voltage across electrodes on the forearms of human subjects. Initially the resistance was on the order of 100,000 ohms. At the onset of sensation, the resistance dropped to less than 10,000 ohms. The results are similar for AC and DC applied voltages. The resistance does not return to its former high value after the voltage is removed; the body retains a residual physiological change for some time after a nondestructive current. The body resistance change depends on the magnitude of the voltage and the length of time the voltage has been applied in a manner not completely understood.

Tissues differ in their resistance to the passage of electric current. Nervous tissue is the least resistant, followed by blood vessels, muscle, skin, tendon, fat and bone. The actual passage of current through the body will depend on the resistance of the various tissues (Luce and Gottlieb 1984; Chandra et al. 1990). This explains why nervous tissues are so often injured by electrical current while other tissues are relatively intact.

11.2 Stimulation of Excitable Cells

Many aspects of electrical injury are due to electrical stimulation (cellular depolarization) of tissues. The consequences of such stimulation can include stopping heart function or respirations, causing seizures and loss of consciousness, or causing a reflex movement that results in a fatal fall from a height.

Stimulation of a large mass of muscle cells may occur, as with the "let-go" phenomenon. The let-go current threshold is measured by having a person hold an electrode in each hand. Above a certain current the person cannot let go because of the repetitive (tetanic) stimulation of forearm muscles. The let-go current is between 6 and 22 mA (milliamps), depending on the size and sex of the person. Partially responsible for this phenomena is the fact that the forearm flexor muscles are stronger than the extensors. The forearm flexor muscles flex the fingers. This phenomena often keeps victims frozen to the source of electricity and causes a firmer (and lower resistance) contact to be made.

Voltages within cells. Nerve and muscle cells are called excitable cells because the voltage within the cells can be stimulated to dramatically change their intracellular voltage. There is normally a resting potential of about −90 mv (millivolts) inside of such cells. This voltage can be measured by placing an electrode outside of the cell and inserting the tip of another electrode inside the cell. If current were injected into the cell by the electrode, the potential inside the cell would change. The intracellular potential would increase or decrease, depending upon the polarity (+ or −) of the current. If the intracellular potential were moved to the cell's threshold potential (around −60 mv), the cell would depolarize. With depolarization, the intracellular voltage rises to about +20 mv within about a millisecond. It then more slowly returns to the resting potential.

The depolarization of cells has effects that depend on the function of the cell. A muscle cell would contract. A nerve cell would stimulate other nerve cells, give a signal to the brain, cause a muscle to contract, or perform another function, depending on where the nerve cell was and its connections to other cells.

The resting potential is maintained by mechanisms that keep various ions at certain concentrations inside and outside the cell membrane. The sodium and potassium ions are especially important. Factors that affect this balance can change the excitability (ease of causing depolarization) of the cell. Such factors include lack of oxygen, and electrolyte (sodium, potassium, and other) imbalances. Medications and illicit drugs can also affect the excitability of cells, leading to (or suppressing) seizures in the brain, rhythm disturbances in the heart, and spasm in the skeletal muscles.

The application of large voltages from outside the body can stimulate excitable cells by causing current flow through tissues. Muscles can be caused to contract more strongly than could be done voluntarily, leading to fractures, dislocations, and avulsion of tendons. Seizures can be induced through direct electrical stimulation of the brain and by lack of oxygen to the brain (hypoxia) caused by abnormal respiratory or cardiac function.

11.3 Death Occurring without Skin Burns

A calculation can be done to determine if a person receiving an electrical current adequate to cause ventricular fibrillation would also suffer an electrothermal skin burn. A current able to cause ventricular fibrillation at 60 hertz, 120 volts is 120 milliamps for three seconds (Dalziel and Lee 1968). It has been estimated that a skin temperature of 50°C for twenty seconds is required to cause first degree burns. Charring requires a temperature of 90°C (Wright and Davis 1980). Calculations show that the above fibrillating current will raise the tissue temperature only 5.2°C, and thus not cause an electrothermal burn.

In the model used for the above calculation, there are two contacts, each one square centimeter area. One contact is energized, the other grounded. The heating is assumed to be completely concentrated in the tissue near the contact points for a depth of one centimeter. In this model, two cubic centimeters of tissue (mostly water) are heated. The rise in temperature will, therefore, be 0.5°C for each calorie of heat delivered to the tissue (Wright and Davis 1980; Moritz and Henriques 1947).

References

Biegelmeier, P. G., "New Knowledge on the Impedance of the Human Body," in *Electrical Shock Safety Criteria: Proceedings of the First International Symposium on Electrical Shock Safety Criteria* J. E. Bridges et al., eds. (NY: Pergamon Press, 1985), 15–132.

Chandra, N. C., C. O. Siu and A. M. Munster,"Clinical Predictors of Myocardial Damage after High Voltage Electrical Injury," *Crit. Care Med.* 18(3):293–297 (1990).

Dalziel, C. F. and W. R. Lee, "Reevaluation of Lethal Electric Currents," *IEEE Transactions on Industry and General Applications* IGA-4(5):467–476 (1968).

Gilbert, T. B., M. Shaffer and M. Matthews, "Electrical Shock by Dislodged Spark Gap in Bipolar Electrosurgical Device," *Anest. Analg.* 73:355–357 (1991).

Gordon, L. B., "Electrical Hazards in the High Energy Laboratory," *Institute of Electrical and Electronics Engineers Transactions on Education* 34:231–242 (1991).

Luce, E.A. and S. E. Gottlieb, "'True' High-Tension Electrical Injuries," *Ann. Plast. Surg.* 12:321–326 (1984).

Moritz, A. R. and F. C. Henriques, "Studies in Thermal Injury: The Relative Importance of Time and Surface Temperature in the Cause of Cutaneous Burns," *Am. J. of Pathol.* 23:695–720 (1947).

Nute, R., "Dynamic Aspects of Body Impedance," in *Electrical Shock Safety Criteria: Proceedings of the First International Symposium on Electrical Shock Safety Criteria,* J. E. Bridges et al., eds. (NY: Pergamon Press, 1985), 173–181.

Wright, R. K. and J. H. Davis, "The Investigation of Electrical Deaths: A Report of 220 Fatalities," *J. Forensic Sci.* 25:514–521 (1980).

Chapter 12

Electrical Stimulation of the Heart[*]

Synopsis

Accidental contact with electricity can result in injury or death. However, there are many instances when deliberate electrical stimulation is an effective treatment.

12.1 The Natural Pacemaker and Signal Conduction System of the Heart

In a healthy heart, muscle contractions are initiated and coordinated by a natural "pacemaker" and "conduction system." These are made up of special muscle cells. While many cells in the heart will spontaneously discharge (depolarize), causing a contraction to occur, the pacemaker area of the heart contains cells that spontaneously discharge the fastest. After the pacemaker cells discharge, electrical signals travel throughout the atria

---

[*]An earlier version of this chapter was published as "Medical Uses of Electric Shock," *Radio Electronics*, November 1985. ©1985 Gernsback Publications, Inc. Reprinted with permission.

(the top half of the heart). The atria are electrically insulated from the ventricles (the bottom half of the heart).

The signal from the atria is conducted to the ventricles by a specialized collection of muscle fibers (the AV node and associated fibers) that cause a delay of about a tenth of a second. Thus, after the atria contract to push blood into the ventricles, there is a delay of about a tenth of a second before the ventricles receive the signal to contract. The delay allows blood to fill the ventricles before they start to contract. It is the ventricles that produce the greatest pumping action, giving a pulse that can be felt at the wrist and elsewhere.

12.2 Fibrillation: Atrial and Ventricular

With the rhythm called ventricular fibrillation, the beating of the heart muscle becomes uncoordinated. During fibrillation, the exposed heart can be seen to writhe like a bag of worms, rather than contracting in a useful manner.

If the ventricles beat normally, but there is atrial fibrillation (disorganized motion of the atria), about 20 percent of the efficiency of the heart is lost because blood does not enter the ventricles as well as it should. In addition, the fibrillation signals passing through the AV node usually stimulate the ventricles to contract at a rate of about 170 beats per minute, a condition not well tolerated by many individuals. While many people have atrial fibrillation that cannot be stopped, the rate of the beating of the ventricles can be controlled by medication that slows conduction of impulses through the AV node and decreases the ventricular contraction rate (the effective heart rate).

12.3 Defibrillation

One way to stop fibrillation of the atria and ventricles is to apply an electrical shock or stimulation to the chest. That stimulation is administered through large paddles using a machine called a defibrillator. When that electrical stimulation is applied, all muscle cells in the heart are depolarized, as if they had just discharged. The first cells to recover are those in the pacemaker area of the heart; they send signals to the conduction system, which causes organized contraction of the heart muscles.

Figure 12.1 shows an electrocardiogram of a patient in ventricular fibrillation in the region labeled A. This area has irregular, non-repeating

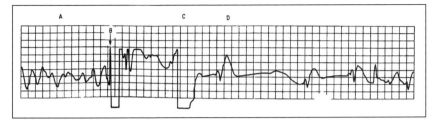

Figure 12.1 Electrocardiogram of a patient with ventricular fibrillation. At point (B) defibrillation (the applying of a voltage) is performed. A heartbeat, although abnormal, slowly begins to appear after several seconds (D).

voltage fluctuations. A defibrillating stimulation of over 1,000 volts (a pulse lasting several milliseconds) is applied at B. That causes the electrocardiogram amplifier to overload. For a period, the electrocardiogram shows overload and movement artifact. Then the amplifier saturates again (C). After a few seconds, the heart begins to beat slowly (D), though not in a normal manner.

A relatively small number of people have recurrent episodes of cardiac rhythm disturbances (dysrhythmias) that are not associated with heart attacks. Many people with recurrent potentially lethal arrhythmias have been treated with surgically implanted defibrillators. When such a unit recognizes a fatal rhythm, a stimulation of about 30 joules is applied to the heart. That is less than the 200 to 360 joules usually applied when the defibrillation stimulation is administered externally. The power requirements are less because the stimulation is applied directly to the heart rather than to the chest wall.

A typical defibrillator output signal is given in the manual for the Lifepak 11 (PhysioControl 1996, table A-1). This instrument is now in use in hospitals and ambulances. The defibrillator waveform roughly resembles half a cycle of a sine wave, with a rise time of one millisecond, and a fall time of three milliseconds; these numbers vary somewhat depending on instrument knob settings and the impedance of the person. The impedance for the short defibrillator pulse, as seen by the large paddles, is normally 25 to 100 ohms. For a 25-ohm load, a peak current of about 90 amps flows.

12.4 Pacemakers for Bradycardia (Slow Heartbeat)

In fibrillation, there are too many signals or depolarizations occurring. With a slow heart rate (bradycardia), there are too few depolarizations. Figure 12.2 shows an electrocardiogram from a patient who has suffered an acute heart attack. The beats are coming much too slowly, about one every two seconds. That gives a pulse rate of about thirty beats per minute. The shape of the waveform shown changes because the lead selector switch on the monitor was turned after every two heartbeats. It was decided that a pacemaker was needed in that case because drugs would not increase the heart rate, and the patient was in cardiogenic shock (the blood pressure was very low due to insufficient heart function). A temporary pacemaker, actually a specially built pulse generator in a small box, was connected to the heart by a catheter with wires built into it. The pacemaker catheter was inserted into a vein in the neck and pushed forward until it reached the heart. (See Figures 12.3 and 12.4.)

A. Transvenous pacemaker insertion

Usually when a pacemaker catheter is inserted, the positioning of the catheter is obtained using fluoroscopy. Fluoroscopy uses a continuous x-ray source and an image intensifier system that permits the physician to see a real-time image of the catheter working its way to the heart. Because veins branch and turn, it is useful to be able to see where the catheter is going and to twist or redirect it when needed.

Because the condition of the patient whose electrocardiogram is shown in Figure 12.2 was so acutely poor, there was not time to set up the

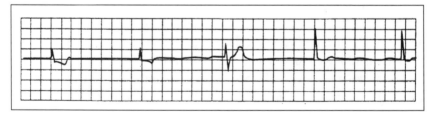

Figure 12.2 This slow heartbeat is the result of a myocardial infarction. In order to restore the heartbeat to normal, a pacemaker had to be implanted. Changes in the waveform are due to the different locations of electrodes used. The monitor was switched from one set of electrodes to another while the tracing was being made.

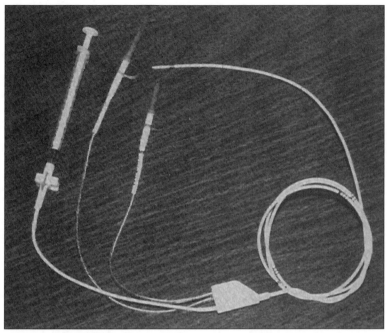

Figure 12.3 A pacemaker catheter, such as the one shown here, is inserted into the body so that the electrodes at its end contact the heart muscle.

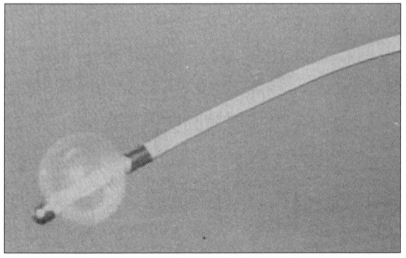

Figure 12.4 If there is any circulation, a balloon at the end of the catheter is inflated so that the catheter tip will be carried to the heart by blood flow.

fluoroscopy equipment or wait for the technicians who run it to come to the hospital. Thus, the catheter was inserted "blindly." That is, the catheter was inserted in the vein through a large needle and pushed forward until small spikes, caused by the signal from the pacemaker, were seen in the patient's electrocardiogram. The presence of those spikes meant that the catheter was near the chest electrodes used to monitor the electrocardiogram. The catheter was further advanced until the small spikes were followed by heartbeats. That was electrical confirmation of the fact that the pacemaker had "captured" (was stimulating) the heart. Later, routine x-rays showed that the pacemaker was in a good location. Because of the type of heart attack, that pacemaker was only needed for a few days. In other cases, a permanent pacemaker must be surgically implanted in the patient and connected to the heart.

B. Types of pacemakers

There are several types of electronic pacemakers. An atrial pacemaker can be used if the atria are not contracting often enough, but the natural conduction between the atria and ventricles is normal. A ventricular pacemaker can be used to stimulate just the ventricles. A sequential pacemaker can sense and stimulate both the atria and the ventricles. This allows stimulation of the ventricles after a delay that simulates the delay normally caused by the AV node. With a sequential pacemaker, the 20 percent boost in cardiac output provided by the atria is retained.

Different pacemakers operate in different manners. Some work only when needed; those are called demand pacemakers. The same wires that stimulate the heart are used to detect heart signals that are spontaneously present. Thus, if the heart is beating adequately, the pacemaker does not fire. If the heart rate gets below a selected rate, the pacemaker fires.

Asynchronous pacemakers are pacemakers that fire regardless of spontaneous heart activity.

C. Outside interference and triggering

Instead of turning off when a heartbeat is detected, some pacemakers fire within milliseconds of each detected heartbeat (with a maximum rate of firing). In that way, externally induced electrical signals cannot trick the pacemaker into shutting off.

Transcutaneous pacemakers use large electrodes applied to the chest. These are now in use in some ambulances and in most emergency departments. If the patient is awake, the process is very uncomfortable, but can be life-saving. This author has seen one salesman demonstrate the external transcutaneous pacer on himself.

D. Programming and controlling pacemakers

External pacemakers have controls that allow the physician to program the stimulus current and heart rate. It is also possible to choose whether or not the pacemaker should be inhibited by spontaneous heart activity. With surgically implanted pacemakers that is not possible unless the pacemaker is remotely programmable. Programmable pacemakers contain a receiver that detects coded signals sent by a hand-held transmitter that looks something like a calculator or small computer. With such a unit, it is possible to control a wide variety of pacemaker parameters.

E. Failure to pace

If a permanently implanted pacemaker is not functioning, troubleshooting can be difficult. However, there are some tests that can be done to help determine the cause of the problem.

Most pacemakers contain a magnetic reed switch. Placing a strong permanent magnet near the pacemaker will activate the switch and convert the pacemaker to an asynchronous mode of operation. As long as the magnet is held in place, the pacemaker will fire at a constant rate regardless of the person's spontaneous heart rate. If a magnet is applied and no pacemaker spikes can be seen on the electrocardiogram, it is possible that the pulse generator or the electrode wire is defective.

If a pacemaker fails within weeks of being implanted, the problem is often with the electrode wire. The wire may have dislodged, or the electrical resistance between the electrode and the heart tissue may have increased.

A failure after years of operation is most often due to weak batteries; placing a magnet over the pacemaker may give a relatively slow heart rate when batteries are weak.

When pacemaker spikes are seen on the electrocardiogram, but there is not capture of the heart, the problem might be with the patient or with electrode placement. Chest x-ray will only in some cases show a break in the electrode wire or indicate that the electrode has moved or perforated the wall of the heart. Listening to heart sounds may reveal a "pericardial rub" that indicates irritation of the lining of the outside of the heart. If the electrode is in the proper location, loss of capture may be due to chemical imbalances (electrolyte abnormalities) in the patient's blood.

Further troubleshooting can be done if the pacemaker is a programmable type. Some such pacemakers allow measurements of lead impedance, sensitivity, and output energy.

12.5 Failure to Detect Cardiac or Respiratory Arrest Because of Pacemaker Signals

The pacemaker produces a signal that is seen as part of the EKG, as in Figure 12.5. The size of the pacemaker signal and the likelihood of its being mistaken for a heartbeat depends on a number of factors, as listed in the Table 12.1. If a patient's heart does stop beating, but the pacemaker continues trying to stimulate the heart, the cardiac monitor may interpret the pacemaker signals as being from the heart itself and thus not recognize the cardiac arrest. Hospital personnel may therefore not be alerted to the fact that the patient needs resuscitation. Steps that can be taken to make cardiac monitoring more effective in patients with pacemakers are listed in Table 12.2 (Brownlee et al. 1989).

The importance of additional types of monitoring. In the patient with a pacemaker, additional means of monitoring, in addition to EKG monitoring, are important because

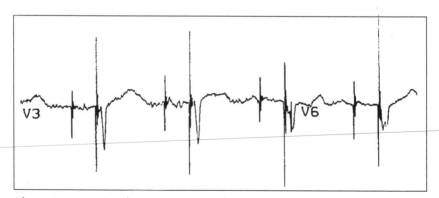

Figure 12.5 *Tracing from a patient with a sequential pacemaker*

- the pacemaker may simulate the electrical activity of the heart (as discussed above), and
- the changes in heart rate usually associated with insufficient respiration may not occur in the patient with a pacemaker. Therefore the heart may continue to beat at a normal rate for some time after oxygen levels have been low enough to cause brain injury.

12.6 MRI (Magnetic Resonance Imaging) for Patients with Pacemakers

A number of patients have undergone MRI examinations with implanted pacemakers with no adverse effects (Gimbel et al. 1996). However, some patients have had problems.

Table 12.1
Factors Affecting the Likelihood of the Pacemaker Signal Being Mistaken for a QRS Complex

- location of monitor leads
- amplitude of the pacemaker signal
- patient size
- rate of rise of the pacemaker signal
- signal filtering of the EKG monitor (its bandwidth)
- EKG monitor sensitivity

Table 12.2
Actions That Can Make Cardiac Monitoring in Patients with Pacemakers More Effective

- Adjust the parameters in Table 12.1 (when possible) to
  - maximize QRS size and detection, and
  - minimize pacemaker signal size and detection.
- Use additional types of monitoring with alarms. Possible types of monitoring include pulse oximetry, carbon dioxide monitoring, and other means of monitoring respirations.

A. MRI-pacemaker interactions

Induction of currents in pacemaker leads can cause inhibition of the pacemaker. Rapid pacing, induction of arrhythmias, and significant heating of electrode tips have also been reported.

B. Lessening the risk

It is suggested by Achenbach et al. (1997) that (1) patients with pacemakers should not have MRI studies unless urgently needed; (2) the pacemaker and electrodes identical to those implanted in each patient should be tested in a phantom study; and (3) temporary reprogramming of the pacemaker (as in the asynchronous mode) can lessen the risk of arrhythmias.

The phantom study recommendation may be difficult to follow. However, weighing the risks versus the benefits of the procedure and reprogramming of the pacemaker are generally applicable suggestions. It is also desirable to have careful monitoring of the patient's status with resuscitation personnel and equipment ready in case there is a cardiac arrest. It does take some time to get a patient out of an MRI machine, making timely resuscitation more difficult than usual.

References

Achenbach, S. et al., "Imaging and Diagnostic Testing: Effects of Magnetic Resonance Imaging on Cardiac Pacemakers and Electrodes," *American Heart Journal* 134(4):467–73 (1997).

Brownlee, J. R. et al., "Failure of Electrocardiographic Monitoring to Detect Cardiac Arrest in Patients with Pacemakers," *American Journal of Diseases of Children* 143:105–107 (1989).

Gimbel, J. R. et al., "Safe Performance of Magnetic Resonance Imaging on Five Patients with Permanent Cardiac Pacemakers," *Pacing Clin. Electrophysiol.* 19(6):913–9 (1996).

PhysioControl, instruction manual for the LIFEPAK® 11 diagnostic cardiac monitor (Redmond, WA: PhysioControl, 1996).

Chapter 13

Understanding the Information in Medical Records

This chapter discusses some of the more interesting items in medical records that can cause confusion for anyone trying to understand what actually happened to a patient. Several factors are described that can cause inaccurate and misleading information to be put into medical records.

13.1 The Importance of Medical Record Information

A. Forensic issues

The information contained in medical records can be of critical importance when one is trying to understand a variety of types of forensic cases. Medical records almost always contain relevant information in cases involving injury, toxic exposure, illness, disability, and medical treatment. Medical information is also useful in many cases involving product liability, life insurance claims, and qualifications for pension and other retirement benefits.

This chapter will describe a number of sources of medical information in addition to the medical record itself. There will be some discussion of what may be contained in each source, and factors that can affect the accuracy of the information. If expected information in a case is not provided, try to obtain it.

B. Biomedical engineering, marketing and health care delivery issues

The information in this chapter is valuable for bioengineers, equipment designers, and persons marketing and providing equipment and services for use in the medical setting. Medical equipment, services, and procedures are designed, made, distributed, and serviced by persons who sometimes have difficulty understanding medical thinking and health care delivery problems. This chapter describes problems and areas of confusion concerning many issues, including medical information systems, resuscitation, mechanism of injury, inaccuracies in vital sign measurement (often by automated equipment), laboratory measurement and reporting problems, and respiratory therapy-related issues.

The orientation of the discussion in this chapter is that of investigating a case involving litigation. This situation is sometimes relevant to the bioengineer and nonmedical members of the healthcare delivery system. More commonly, this information will be of use to the bioengineer in developing and planning medical equipment and services.

13.2 Difficulties in Obtaining Information

There is great variation in how and where records are kept. In hospitals, the medical records department may not keep some items. Fetal heart tracings may be kept in the obstetrics department. Physical therapy records may be kept in the outpatient department. Billing records may be in the business office. Records may be destroyed or lost when charts are converted to microfilm or sent somewhere to be stored. The ability to digitally process, record, and retrieve radiographic studies, printed medical records, and even hand written notes (as in PDF format) is available, but not widely used in hospitals.

13.3 Information That Cannot Be Used

State and federal laws make some sources of information confidential and not discoverable. An attorney should research the current applicable laws when there is a question.

A. Mental health records

Mental health records, including those involving counseling and psychotherapy, often cannot be reviewed without the permission of the patient.

B. Peer review and quality assurance

Peer review and quality assurance activities, and the records they generate, are often not discoverable. Healthcare practitioners would be discouraged from criticizing each other or doing meaningful case reviews if the discussions and the papers they generated were discoverable. In medicine, ongoing review of the nature and quality of care is especially needed because new medications, medical knowledge, and treatments are constantly being developed.

Peer review and quality assurance information should remain confidential because it frequently contains invalid criticisms of care that was given. For example, one physician may state (without researching the topic) that a patient would have done better if a different treatment were given. An exhaustive literature review may show that the treatment given was an acceptable practice, and the expected outcome would not have been significantly different if the alternative treatment had been given. Moreover, a careful review of the case may reveal reasons that the suggested alternative treatment was not suitable for the patient in question because of medication interactions, allergy, inability to tolerate surgery, refusal of the treatment by the patient, or other reasons.

13.4 Sources of Information

In general, it is preferable to examine entire medical records and depositions rather than summaries. Critical issues may be missed by the person making the summaries (Beckmann 1994). If expected information is missing, it is likely important and should be requested. Unexpected information should be examined carefully. For example, a long, handwritten addition to the chart written by a nurse would be worthy of careful reading.

Table 13.1 lists many of the sources of information that may exist concerning a case with medical issues that need to be investigated. In any given case, medical records may range anywhere from a one-page emergency department record to many hundreds of pages of medical records and reports. There are references available that list in extensive detail what should be in medical records (Smith 1991; Roach 1994; Strodel 1988) and what usually can be found in medical records (Rothblatt 1983).

This chapter will not give a complete listing or explanation of all the items listed in these references. Instead, this chapter will discuss some of the more interesting aspects of a few items that are likely to cause confusion when one is trying to understand medical cases and problems through the review of medical records.

Previous medical records. A patient may claim that a medical condition resulted from an event such as an electrical injury, slip and fall, or motor vehicle accident. Medical records from before the time of the accident may document that the patient previously had the supposedly new medical condition. This may be relatively obvious in cases of back pain,

---

Table 13.1
Sources of Medical Information

1. Previous medical records
2. Hospital records
    a. Fire and rescue run sheet
    b. Emergency medical service (ambulance) run sheet
    c. Emergency department
        (1) Triage notes, consent forms
        (2) Nursing notes, including medication, fluid intake and output charting
        (3) Emergency, intern, resident and consultant physician notes: written and dictated
        (4) Physician orders
        (5) Respiratory therapy, obstetric, physical therapy, social service, and other consulting personnel notes
        (6) Preliminary and final reports from: laboratory, radiology, anesthesia, fetal monitoring, ECG
        (7) Hospital security, incident reports, and other police reports
        (8) Records from billing and pharmacy
        (9) Refusal of treatment papers (AMA, or against medical advice)
        (10) Discharge instruction sheets
        (11) Transfer papers: COBRA form, ambulance papers
    d. Inpatient hospital
        (1)–(11) same as from the emergency department plus:
        (12) Admitting nursing notes
        (13) Later nursing notes: written descriptions, charting of vital signs and other ordered data, graphical summaries, care plans, discharge instructions
        (14) Attending physician written and dictated: history and physical, progress
        (15) Notes, discharge summary
        (16) Surgical, recovery room, and pathology records
        (17) Anesthesia records
    e. Extended care facilities, rehabilitation facilities, and nursing homes. Many items similar to emergency department and inpatient hospital records
3. Outpatient records
    a. Pharmacy records
    b. Physician office records: progress notes, letters, memos, reports, bills, reminders sent to the patient, insurance and disability papers
    c. Clinic and therapy visits, including emergency department, physical, speech and occupational therapy, nontraditional medicine practitioners, health club
4. Death certificate
5. Autopsy report

but can be very subtle in cases of slowly progressive dementia and other chronic, psychological, or physical conditions.

Previous medical records can also tell much about a person. The information in old medical records may have relevance to determining why an accident occurred or why later medical treatment was difficult. Issues such as drug or alcohol abuse, obesity, and poor vision or hearing may help explain why the person did not hear or see warnings, or why CPR or other treatment was unusually difficult.

13.5 History of an Accident

Information can be obtained about an accident that caused an injury by looking at many of the items listed in Table 13.1. It is interesting to compare the descriptions of an accident or other event as it is described in the notes written by rescue workers, ambulance personnel, emergency department nurses and physicians, admitting physicians, and consulting physicians. There are often substantial differences in what these written records say. Later testimony by the writers of these notes, the patient, and other witnesses may also be inconsistent with the written records. Be sure to carefully read nursing notes, as well as police and engineering reports.

A. Sources of inaccuracy in histories from witnesses and medical personnel

The history of an incident may be described in a medical record by the writings of EMTs, nurses, physicians, and consultants. However, in most cases, few of these people have any first hand knowledge of what they are writing about, except possibly police and rescue workers who were at the scene of the incident. People writing later histories often try to understand what happened by questioning the patient and any witnesses who may be available. Often they rely on notes previously written in the chart by others. The history of events may, therefore, be based upon the observations or suppositions of witnesses who have no significant medical training.

For example, when a person falls, bystanders may say the person had a "seizure." To some laypersons, a seizure means that the person lost consciousness. To others, it means that the person was shaking. To other laypersons, the word "seizure" may mean the person had labored respirations and foamy fluid in the mouth. Physicians can question people in a way that does bring out accurate information, and this can be evident from the medical record itself. A detailed description of the events during a seizure would be much more informative than simply saying, "The patient had a seizure."

B. Sources of inaccuracy in histories given by patients

Patients sometimes give inaccurate histories. One factor influencing the accuracy of a patient's history is the amount and quality of the patient's medical knowledge. Some patients deliberately or inadvertently give significantly different histories to various people who interview them. There are many reasons for this, as discussed in the paragraphs below.

1. How questions are asked

Some physicians and nurses may ask general questions, such as, "Tell me what happened." Others may limit their area of apparent interest by saying, "What happened after you fell?" Some nurses may fill out a form with dozens of specific questions about the patient's health, but little about recent events. At times, healthcare providers are simply busy and do not want to address some problems.

2. The various meanings of words

Patients and physicians may not understand each other because of a lack of agreement on the meaning of words used. For example, the word "dizziness" is sometimes used to describe a general weakness, a floating feeling, a sensation of the patient himself spinning, or the observation that the room seems to be spinning. The word "sharp" is sometimes used to describe a pain that feels like a needle or knife, but at other times is used to mean that a pain was severe. Physicians may used technical terms, and the patient may answer without asking for the terms to be defined because he is embarrassed to show his lack of knowledge.

3. Organic memory problems

Factors that can cause confusion and trouble with memory itself include head injury, legal and illegal drugs, alcohol, psychiatric conditions, and metabolic disturbances (abnormal temperature, glucose, sodium, blood pressure, oxygen, and many others).

4. Avoiding repetition

Patients may not relate information to a physician because the information was told to the ambulance personnel, a clerk, or the nurse. The patient may be tired of repeating things. The patient may assume that the physician will know everything the clerk and nurse were told because the physician seems to be holding the patient's chart. Because ambulance personnel, clerks, and nurses do not write everything down or discuss everything with the physician, such information may be lost as far as the medial record and physician are concerned.

5. Fear

Some patients are afraid they will be diagnosed with a terrible condition if they give a suggestive answer to the physician. For example, a physician once asked a man how severe his chest pain was. He said, "Oh, it was fairly mild." His wife, who was standing by the bedside said, "Is that why you were laying on the kitchen floor clutching your chest?" Such patients have fear or a strong sense of denial. This influences what they say. Some patients have a fear of the medical and hospital environment. They may be afraid of invasive or costly tests and procedures.

Following accidents, patients may be afraid they will be blamed for the event. This may influence the history they give.

6. Filling in the blanks

Still other patients do not know what happened to them. Instead of saying they do not know what happened, these patients will tell physicians and nurses what they think must have happened. Or, the patient will relate what someone else said about what happened. Many elderly patients who say they tripped on something will change their story if questioned further, such as "Do you remember tripping, or do you just think that must be what happened?" These patients often have a functional or organic basis for their poor memory. Patients who have drank alcohol, even in small amounts, may have similar problems.

7. Unexplained memory loss

In almost all emergency departments, patients are given written discharge instructions. The patient (or another responsible party) will sign the discharge instruction sheet and will be given a copy of it. It is very common for patients to call an emergency department saying they do not know who to follow up with or what to do about certain problems even though the discharge instruction sheet they signed has the needed information. On questioning, they sometimes deny receiving the paper.

Recollection difficulties can occur for several reasons with electrical injury. Events are often unusual, and the events occur quickly. There may be distracting loud noises, flashes of light, or fire. Important events, such as the passage of a current through a person, may not be visually apparent to observers. There is sometimes loss of memory for events close to the time of injury in people with even minor head injury that did not have loss of consciousness. Such head injury can be due to falling or the blast effect of electric arcs. Impaired brain function may occur due to inhalation of carbon monoxide or other substances, impaired breathing, or cardiac dysrhythmias. Carbon monoxide is produced by burning, especially in the setting of poor ventilation or improper function of a furnace or other device.

8. Changing stories associated with abuse

People who have abused children or others frequently give different histories as to what occurred around the time of an injury; the abused patient may give an inaccurate history, or no history at all. This is characteristic of the battered child syndrome (Dix and Calaluce 1998).

9. Memories fade

Memories fade and change with time and other influences. The patient and other witnesses may not accurately remember and keep separate in their minds what symptoms were present before, during, and after an office or emergency department visit. Thus, it is fairly common for written medical records to differ dramatically from patient and family recollections of what happened. A patient or family may remember episodes of severe pain that occurred a few hours before or after seeing a physician. The fact that the pain was mild or gone entirely while being examined may not be clearly remembered months later.

10. The power of suggestion

Experiments have shown that recollections can be changed by later exposure to other information (Wells and Loftus 1984). False information can be introduced into a person's recollection and later this information may be reported as if it actually occurred. Witnesses can pick up new information by talking to other witnesses, being asked questions, or reading or hearing about the events they have witnessed (Loftus and Doyle 1992).

11. Stress affects memory

A little stress may improve a person's ability to remember what is happening at the time. In a stressful situation, people tend to have their attention focused on what is occurring. However, too much stress can be expected to impair memory and other mental functions (Loftus and Doyle 1992, 31–33).

13.6 The Mechanism of Injury

How and why an accident occurred can sometimes be pieced together from information in medical records. The patient's medical records, including rescue and ambulance records, may contain descriptions of the accident scene and other details about the injury. This information should be compared to later statements of all parties and to accident reconstruction information.

13.7 Time Factors
A. Organizing the information in records for analysis

When analyzing medical records, events are easier to understand if put in chronological order. It is difficult to chronologically arrange pieces of paper having physician notes, laboratory tests, nurses notes, vital signs, physician orders, consultant reports, x-ray reports, and so on. It is often best to leave the papers as they are and to type into a word processor each significant event. Each event should be labeled and placed according to the time the event occurred.

B. Medical conditions change over time

With many illnesses and injuries, time plays an important role. With time, there are changes in symptoms (what the patient feels) and signs (things that can be observed by others). The resolution of symptoms with time can influence treatment decisions. Nursing notes, sometimes spread over hours or days and several pages of charting, may indicate the patient's condition better than the physician's notes.

C. Test results

Test results can be affected by treatments given, and the test results can guide further treatment. Therefore, it is often important to recognize when tests were ordered, when they were actually performed, and when the test results were obtained.

D. Inaccurate and inconsistent recording of times

With quickly evolving situations, the times noted on medical records may be misleading. The extreme, but common, example of this is the code situation (respiratory arrest, or cardiac plus respiratory arrest). When someone stops breathing, it can seem like a very long time until things are done to help, even though only a few minutes pass. If one observer records a series of event times, an accurate estimate of time intervals may be obtained. However, a series of times recorded by several different persons is likely to be inaccurate because of differences between the clocks and watches used.

A patient's cardiac rhythm may change several times a minute during a code. A clerk who announced the code, physicians, nurses, and respiratory therapists may make records, and a separate person assigned to take notes of what occurred during the code. In addition, the heart monitor tracings may have times automatically printed on them. People do not normally synchronize their watches daily (or ever). Clocks from one room to another in hospitals are often several minutes apart. Because wall clocks, watches, and heart monitors are not synchronized, times recorded during codes will likely not be accurate or consistent with each other.

There are other reasons for inaccurate charting during codes. If there are too many people present at a code, the record keeper may have trouble hearing what is being said and seeing the monitor screen. If there are too few people, they will be busy trying to save the patient—much too busy to write minute-by-minute records of cardiac rhythm, drugs being given, continuation of bagging and chest compressions, breath sounds, pupil size, and other information.

13.8 Vital Signs

Vital signs are blood pressure, heart rate, respiratory rate, and temperature. Recently, it has been suggested that pulse oximetry be considered to be a fifth vital sign; though, this is not generally accepted (Mower et al.

1998). Vital signs vary over time and have important meaning in some circumstances. Automated equipment may take and record the vital signs (except temperature) every few minutes. A printout of all measurements may be posted in the chart. If the treating physician examines the results of such comprehensive monitoring at the time, the monitoring can point out difficulties such as an unstable blood pressure in a trauma victim. Sometimes it is apparent that the detailed printouts (or vital signs taken manually by a nurse) were not taken into account in clinical decision making. They were simply put in the chart and ignored.

Axillary and tympanic membrane (electronic ear) measurements are relatively unreliable (Brennan et al. 1995; Roth et al. 1996). One consideration is that personnel using the tympanic devices often do not use them properly or even look to see if the ear canal is blocked by wax.

13.9 Preliminary Reports

It is common for preliminary reports to be written out for immediate use while a dictated report is typed some time later. These preliminary reports are sometimes discarded. In one case, a radiologist read spine x-rays as normal. The patient was later sat up for more x-rays and was found to have unstable fractures of the spine. The dictated report of the radiologist mentioned the fractures and made no mention of the initial normal reading. A lawsuit was filed against the radiologist and the treating physician. No one could find the initial handwritten radiology report except for the treating physician who had made a copy of the initial radiology reading for his personal records.

13.10 Who Sees What

Different health care personnel are in positions to see different things. Rescue and ambulance personnel may document information about the scene of an accident as well as giving the earliest observations of the patient's rapidly changing condition.

Physicians, in general, have greater powers of observation and knowledge than other health care personnel. However, other personnel have the advantage of longer and repeated interactions with the patient. For example, in one case several nurses repeatedly charted that a patient's abdomen was becoming distended. A number of physicians seemed to not notice these observations while others disagreed with the observations. The patient suffered serious problems from the great amount of fluid that was eventually documented on a CT scan.

Nurses may spend much more time with patients than anyone else. Nurses often document repeatedly over time: patient complaints; how much pain medication is asked for; mental status; and vital signs. Separate pages of nursing notes may be devoted to a comprehensive past medical history, repeated neurological examinations, subjective complaints, physical observations, amounts and kinds of food eaten, fluid balance, care plans, and medication given. Nursing notes often contain information that is not present anywhere else. Check lists and computer entry systems are sometimes replacing the more meaningful narrative notes that nurses have traditionally made.

13.11 The Methodology of Medical Diagnosis

The method of making a medical diagnosis ideally consists of three steps. These steps are: (1) taking a history, (2) doing a physical examination and (3) performing ancillary studies (Daily 1998; Goldman 1991; Shapiro et al. 1975; Dunphy 1991).

In medical practice, a diagnosis is often made without the benefit of all of these items. Some common examples of working with incomplete information: the patient may be unconscious, and no one else has any information to offer; a consultant may hear about a patient over the telephone and be asked to help determine the diagnosis; there is no time for ancillary studies, or the diagnosis is clear without any studies being done.

13.12 Misleading Test Results

A number of circumstances can result in the misinterpretation of laboratory and other tests that are done. Some of the more interesting misleading medical test situations will be discussed below.

A. Arterial blood gas reports

When trying to draw arterial blood gases, it is common to obtain blood from a vein instead of an artery. The problem is usually recognized and the blood discarded, except during CPR, when it is more difficult to tell where the blood came from. It is sometimes possible to say that the blood must have been arterial because the oxygen reading is high or the carbon dioxide reading is low. Unfortunately, sometimes this is not always possible. The test result is likely to be printed on an "Arterial Blood Gas" report form with no mention of the fact it may have come from a vein.

B. Pulse oximeters

Factors that can make pulse oximeter readings inaccurate include patient movement, not positioning the sensor accurately, not waiting long enough for a steady reading to be obtained, hypotension, the presence of carbon monoxide or other gases, hypothermia, and the fact that the patient was recently put on or taken off supplemental oxygen.

C. Carbon monoxide

Some arterial blood gas machines and some (if not all) pulse oximetry devices will be inaccurate in the presence of carbon monoxide. Carbon monoxide (as from a running car in a closed garage) displaces oxygen from the hemoglobin in the blood. Oxygen readings that are much higher than they should be can result when a large percentage of the oxygen has been displaced by carbon monoxide. Some blood gas machines and other machines that use samples of blood or exhaled breath are available to measure carbon monoxide. These should be used when needed. Although if they have not been used, one should realize it.

D. Radiology reports

Radiology reports must be interpreted with relevant background knowledge. For example, ventilation-perfusion-lung-scans are relatively poor at predicting the presence or absence of the pulmonary emboli they are used to detect. Mammograms miss some breast tumors. Some types of fractures will not show on x-ray in a large percentage of cases (Fish and Ehrhardt 1989).

E. Units

Blood test results are listed with units. A drug level in an overdose case may be listed in nanograms per milliliter or micrograms per milliliter. A result of "45" called to a consultant may be misleading if the units are not known. If one simply looks at the number, mistakes can be expected. When reviewing charts from different institutions, it is, therefore, necessary to look at the units. But, that is not all. Sometimes the ranges of normal are different from one institution to another. Fortunately, the range of normal for each test is usually listed on each laboratory report sheet. If the limits of normal are very different from what is usually seen, one should determine why.

F. Muscle damage

Muscle damage due to electrical injury, blunt trauma, myocardial infarction, and a variety of other causes can be detected by several different blood tests. The usual blood test used to detect heart or skeletal muscle damage is CK (creatine kinase, also called CPK or creatine phosphokinase). CK is found in skeletal and heart muscle and in the brain. Lesser amounts are found in the intestine and lung. CK values are often high in patients with myocardial infarction, progressive muscular dystrophy, alcoholic myopathy, rhabdomyolysis, delirium tremens, moderate exercise, some infections, large bruises, and intramuscular injections (Henry, 1996).

CK exists as a dimer of three possible combinations of M (originally for muscle) and B (originally for brain) chains. About 99 percent of total CK in skeletal muscle is the MM dimer, and a small portion is in the MB form. In cardiac muscle, about 80 percent of the total CK is in the MM form, and 20 percent is in the MB form. Within six hours of the beginning of a myocardial infarction, there will usually be increases in CK-MB, total CK, and the ratio of CB-MB to CK (Henry 1996). Injury to skeletal muscle may release large amounts of CK-MB, but the ratio of CK-MB to total CK should remain normal (usually under 5 percent, depending on units used and the particular laboratory). Increases in total CK and CK-MB are to be expected with contusions, crush injuries, and damage to skeletal muscle due to electrical injury.

G. Respiratory effects of electrical injury

Other new tests are beginning to be used, including serum myoglobin and troponins (Brogan et al. 1996; Gibler et al. 1987). With all these tests, it is important to keep track of the units being used and note the limits of normal for the particular laboratory. Also, it must be remembered that measurements are sometime made of enzyme mass, and at other times of enzyme activity (Bhayana et al. 1990). This may not be obvious because many laboratory tests are reported as so many U (units) or IU (international units). This is much less descriptive than more meaningful notations such as "nanograms per milliliter." Knowing what the "units" are is especially important when calculating the ratio of two different measurements.

If the listed normal range for a measurement is not what one expects, that test may not be what one thinks it is. Another clue: if thinking about the two quantities separately leads to a different conclusion than considering their ratio, then something is wrong. For example, two quantities considered separately suggest no problem, but their ratio indicates severe trouble. If in doubt, obtain information from the laboratory and measurement instruments involved as to what tests were done, the normal ranges of any tests and ratios of interest, and what dimensions (mass, activity and so forth) and units were used.

13.13 Death Certificates and Autopsy Reports

Death certificates are sometimes made without full knowledge of all the evidence in a case and without benefit of an autopsy report. Death certificates are sometimes not helpful and may even be misleading. As stated by Strodel (1988), "To look at a death certificate and ascertain that the cause of death was 'cardiac arrest' is ludicrous. I have yet to find anyone who has not died from cardiac arrest!"

When they are done, as many as 25 percent of autopsies reveal completely unrecognized, perhaps unrelated entities, as well as unsuspected variations in known clinical problems. Some authors believe that this realization has caused a decrease in the number of autopsies ordered by physicians (Blackman and Bailey 1990).

Autopsy reports are often helpful in determining the cause and mechanism of death. The presence of drugs or toxins as well as evidence of damage to vital organs may be of interest. Knowing the mechanism of death may allow one to determine if the victim was consciously suffering pain for some time during and after an injury, or if consciousness was immediately lost.

13.14 Conclusion

Much information can be obtained from medical records. This chapter has discussed some of the more interesting issues that can affect the accuracy of the information contained in medical records and the interpretation of that information.

References

Bhayana, V. et al., "Diagnostic Evaluation of Creatine Kinase-2 Mass and Creatine Kinase-3 and -2 Isoform Ratios in Early Diagnosis of Acute Myocardial Infarction," *Clinical Chemistry* 39:488–495 (1990).

Blackman, N. S. and C. P. Bailey, *Liability in Medical Practice: A Reference for Physicians* (Chur, Switzerland: Harwood Academic Publishers, 1990), 255.

Brennan, D. F. et al., "Reliability of Infrared Tympanic Thermometry in the Detection of Rectal Fever in Children," *Annals of Emergency Medicine* 25: 21–30 (1995).

Brogan, G. X. et al., "Improved Specificity of Myoglobin Plus Carbonic Anhydrase Assay versus That of Creatine Kinase-MB for Early Diagnosis of Acute Myocardial Infarction," *Annals of Emergency Medicine* 27:22–28 (1996)..

Dix, J. and R. Calaluce, *Guide to Forensic Pathology* (St. Louis: Jay Dix, 1998), 99.

Fish, R. M. and M. E. Ehrhardt, *Preventing Emergency Malpractice* (Oradell, NJ: Medical Economics Books, 1989).

Gibler, W. B. et al., "Myoglobin as an Early Indicator of Acute Myocardial Infarction," *Annals of Emergency Medicine* 16:851–856 (1987).

Henry, J. B., *Clinical Diagnosis and Management by Laboratory Methods*, 19th ed. (Philadelphia: W. B. Saunders, 1996).

Loftus, Elizabeth F. and James M. Doyle, *Eyewitness Testimony: Civil and Criminal*, 2nd ed. (Charlottesville, VA: Michie Company, 1992), 65.

Mower, W. R. et al., "Pulse Oximetry as a Fifth Vital Sign in Emergency Geriatric Assessment," *Academic Emergency Medicine* 5:858–865 (1998).

Roach, W. H. Jr., *Medical Records and the Law*, 2nd ed. (Gaithersburg, MD: Aspen, 1994).

Roth, R. N. et al., "Agreement between Rectal and Tympanic Membrane Temperatures in Marathon Runners," *Annals of Emergency Medicine* 28:414–417 (1996).

Rothblatt, H. B., *Handling Health Practitioner Cases* (Rochester, NY: Lawyers Cooperative Publishing, 1983), 183–214.

Smith, James W., *Hospital Liability* (NY: Law Journal Seminars-Press, 1991), sec. 14.

Strodel, Robert C., *Securing and Using Medical Evidence in Personal Injury and Health-Care Cases* (Englewood Cliffs, NJ: Prentice-Hall, 1988), viii, 33–50.

Wells, Gary L. and Elizabeth F. Loftus, *Eyewitness Testimony: Pyschological Perspectives* (Cambridge: Cambridge University Press, 1984), 129–131.

Chapter 14

Determining Whether an Electrical Accident is the Etiology of a Medical Condition

The effects of electrical injury are sometimes readily apparent and objectively demonstrable. There may be death, burns, or neurological injury that can be documented by nerve conduction or radiographic studies. However, sometimes there is no objective relationship between an apparent electrical injury and the physical, neurological, or psychological problems present after the injury.

Studies involving multiple case reports may have inaccurate, if any, estimates of the amount of current that flowed through the persons involved. Epidemiological studies are unlikely to become helpful in linking electrical injury involving less than 240 volts AC to certain sequelae. This is because most of these injuries involve an unknown amount of current flow. The amount of current is small in many, but not all, cases.

14.1 A Previous Evaluation Protocol

Morse and Weiss (1993) have designed an "evaluation protocol for electric shock injury supported by minimal diagnostic evidence." This protocol suggests it is a logical conclusion that electric injury is the cause of a victim's condition, even in the absence of firm diagnostic medical evidence, if certain criteria can be met. First, an evaluation of the electrical source, magnitude of the electric current that went through the person, and other parameters must be done to establish the nature of the electric exposure. Next, an evaluation of medical records predating and postdating the injury must confirm that symptoms did not predate the injury. Also, a complete psychological workup must be conducted to determine if the patient is given to lying, gross exaggeration, or malingering. A clinical review and the Minnesota Multiphasic Personality Inventory are usually adequate. In addition, available case studies from the literature should be used to determine if symptoms are within the confines of what might be viewed as reasonable probability for an electric injury. According to the protocol, when it has been established that an electric shock did occur, the individual is not given to dishonesty, the symptoms are not tied to conditions that predated the incident, and similar types of injuries have yielded similar (although sometimes unexplainable) results, it is a logical conclusion that the electric shock was the cause of the current symptoms, even in the absence of firm diagnostic medical evidence.

14.2 Modifying the Protocol

This author would modify the above criteria slightly, as shown in Table 14.1. The term "causation" is avoided because it has extensive legal meanings and implications.

Item 6 in Table 14.1 raises the issue of whether the electrical accident was probably (more likely than not), or just possibly the cause of the injury. Relevant to this item in Table 14.1 is the discussion of the cause and effect relationship between intrapartum asphyxia and brain injury by Stevenson and Sunshine (1997). They discuss the development of severe brain injury due to events occurring at birth.

> Most individual neurodevelopmental risk factors will not be followed by the disability for which the child is at increased risk . . . additional intervening evidence must exist to reliably link risk to disability and to scien-

---

Table 14.1
**Determining Whether Electrical Injury or Accident Is the
Etiology of a Medical Condition**

1.   There is evidence that an electrical accident did occur.
2.   The person has not been found to be lying, exaggerating, or malingering.
3.   Physical (non-psychological) conditions: Medical or other records from before and after the accident establish that the medical condition was present after, but not before, the accident. If the condition was present before the accident, worsening of the condition as a result of the injury could be substantiated only by clear documentation of the nature of the condition before and after the accident along with a consideration of the natural time course of the condition with respect to spontaneous worsening.
4.   Psychological conditions: the condition did not predate the accident.
5.   Scientific literature demonstrates that:
   a. Similar medical conditions have been associated with electrical injury in the past, OR
   b. A mechanism can be identified by which the electrical accident could cause the medical condition.
6.   The condition does not seem to be due to other causes.
7.   If all the above criteria are met, analysis of the facts of the case and the literature will determine if the electrical accident probably caused the injury, or if the injury is simply consistent with and possibly caused by the electrical accident. Important considerations are:
   a. How common the condition is in the absence of electrical injury
   b. The temporal relationship between the accident and onset of medical signs or symptoms involving the body system or region involved in the sequelae of the accident

---

tifically and mediocolegally convert a possible risk-disability association into a probable cause and effect relationship. In the case of potential acquired brain injuries, it must be demonstrated that the risk agent or event was temporally closely followed by evidence of acute neurologic depression and/or deterioration (such as, reduction in state of consciousness, alterations of muscle tone, autonomic nervous system instability, apnea, seizure activity) which, despite often apparently resolving, eventually evolved, over varying periods of time, into a permanent disability. The presence of relatively immediate neurological abnormalities and signs of acute brain dysfunction following a potential risk, such as, intrapartum asphyxia, provides confirmatory evidence of the gravity of the event and renders causal linkages with a subsequent disability as plausible; conversely, the virtual absence of signs or symptoms of acute neurologic compromise makes risk-disability causal linkages unlikely. (Stevenson and Sunshine 1997, viii-ix)

14.3 Determination of Medical Etiology
Table 14.1 summarizes these issues.

14.4 Epidemiological Studies Are Not Likely to Be Done
A. Injuries are relatively rare
The number of electrical injuries occurring is small, and reporting of sequelae in the medical literature is seldom done. When reporting of sequelae of electrical accidents is done, there are problems with data collection and reporting.

B. The amount of current involved in accidental injuries is not accurately known
Clinical effects in electrical injury are to a great extent determined by the amount of current flow. As discussed below, this quantity is usually not known with great accuracy in accidental injury, making epidemiological studies difficult. For example, many (if not most) persons contacting a 110-VAC power source have dry skin, make contact with a small area of skin, and quickly jerk away from the contact.

C. Experimental studies are difficult to perform
Studies are limited because injury should not be deliberately inflicted on humans for the purposes of experimentation. In animals, nervous system damage may be unobservable, especially as it relates to changes in cognitive and other higher neurological functions.

It would not be obvious, and may be difficult to determine, if an animal were to suffer moderate chronic pain, partial numbness, tinnitus, and many other sequelae characteristics of electric injury and blunt head trauma.

D. Current determines clinical effect or injury
Laboratory studies, including those that have been done on humans, demonstrate that the important parameter to control is current, assuming one is

dealing with 60-Hz AC sine wave power sources. Effects such as burning of tissue or disruption of heart rhythm or breathing depend on a certain amount of current flowing in certain areas of the body. Studies have shown that certain amounts of current cause persons to tightly grasp a conductor and be unable to let go. Certain amounts of current are needed to induce ventricular fibrillation in the heart. The heat produced in tissue per unit time is proportional to the amount of current squared.

With different frequencies or waveforms (such as pulses), the clinical effects are not necessarily related in a simple fashion to the effects of 60-Hz AC sine wave injuries.

E. Current is usually known and well controlled in laboratory studies

In experiments, electronic equipment is usually set up to compensate for differences in electrode or connection resistance and other factors that might affect the current flow.

F. Current is usually not known in clinical reports

In an accidental injury, the actual amount of current that flowed through the person is usually not known with precise accuracy. The voltage of the electrical source is often known. Some studies do report information that is useful in making estimates of the amount of current flow. Such information includes presence of moisture, firmness of contact, anticipation of the injury, and approximate duration of the electrical contact.

Resistance to current flow can vary by a factor of 100 or more depending on the firmness of contact, area of contact, condition of the contact surface, skin lesions or lacerations, and the presence of moisture.

The duration of contact in many accidents is a fraction of a second. Contact may be several minutes if a person has involuntary grasping of the current source, or is otherwise unable to quickly release from the source. Time of current flow can give another factor of 100 or more variation in the total current that actually enters the person over time. Thus, electrical accidents from any given source voltage may differ greatly in amount and duration of current flow through the patient.

High voltage injuries (usually defined as being over 1,000 volts) are somewhat different in that there is arcing with generation of high temperatures and breakdown of skin resistance.

14.5 Autopsy-Related Considerations

There are sometimes inaccuracies in death certificates and the reports of medical examiners and coroners. For example, one study found that the rate of electrocution deaths in Dade County was 50 percent higher than that in the rest of the country (Wright and Davis 1980). The study concluded that this difference was due to the under-reporting of such incidents in the rest of the United States.

A. Medical examiner and coroner systems

In the United States, medical-legal investigations are usually carried out by medical examiner or coroner systems. Medical examiners generally have greater expertise in unnatural death investigations than do coroners. Medical examiners are usually physicians with training in pathology, medicolegal death investigation, and the performance of forensic autopsies. There has been a trend toward replacing coroner systems with medical examiner systems. However, as of 1998, medical examiner systems that operate without coroner involvement served only about 48 percent of the United States population. Furthermore, few state or county medical examiner systems had been implemented between 1990 and 1998 (Hanzlick and Combs 1998).

B. The autopsy

Even when a pathologist with many years of experience does an autopsy, the autopsy and its conclusions may be open to question. There are several reasons for this. For example, the examiner may fail to do such things as: review the medical records; examine statements of witnesses; or describe skin lesions that may have been electrical burns. Some examiners have had no experience in doing autopsies of electrical injury victims. On questioning, the examiner may admit lack of knowledge concerning the nature of electrical injury and the expected autopsy findings.

C. Evolution of rigor mortis

Experiments in animals and observations in human cases have shown that rigor mortis may develop more quickly than usual following fatal electrical injury. Without electrical injury, the body usually begins to stiffen two or three hours after death, with complete stiffness developing in six to twelve hours. With electrical injury, well-developed rigor mortis has been observed within about two hours (Krompecher and Bergerioux 1988).

References

Hanzlick, R. and D. Combs, "Medical Examiner and Coroner Systems," *JAMA* 279(11):870–874 (1998).

Krompecher, T. and C. Bergerioux, "Experimental Evaluation of Rigor Mortis, part 7: Effect of Ante- and Post-Mortem Electrocution on the Evolution of Rigor Mortis," *Forensic Science International* 38:27–35 (1988).

Morse, M. S. and D. K. Weiss, "An Evaluation Protocol for Electric Shock Injury Supported by Minimal Diagnostic Evidence," in *Proceedings of the Annual Conference on Engineering in Medicine and Biology* (Piscataway, NJ: IEEE Service Center, 1993), vol. 15, pt. 3, 1424–1425.

Stevenson, D. K. and P. Sunshine, *Fetal and Neonatal Brain Injury*, 2nd ed. (Oxford: Oxford University Press, 1997), viii–ix.

Wright, R. K. and J. H. Davis, "The Investigation of Electrical Deaths: A Report of 220 Fatalities," *Journal of Forensic Sciences* 25(3):514–521 (1980).

Chapter 15

Accident Reconstruction in Electrical Injury Cases

15.1 Introduction

Accident reconstruction in electrical injury cases involves a number of tasks. The order in which the tasks are done will depend on when information becomes available to the consultant. Several tasks may be done simultaneously. First, data concerning the injury must be obtained to determine whether or not electric current did pass through the person's body. The consultant should correlate the temporal relationship of events during the accident with the medical condition of the person before, during, and after the accident. The medical effects expected from such current flow must be compared to the injuries actually sustained by the person. Next, the consultant should consider the possibility that the person's condition is due to disease or other processes unrelated to the electrical injury. Finally, the consultant should cite references from the scientific literature that support and illustrate the consultant's opinions.

The physiological events that occur during and shortly after the injury can give much information as to the nature of the electrical injury, its effect on the body, and whether or not there really was an electrical injury. For example, a man is grasping a grounded metal railing with one hand and a power tool with the other hand. The tool has a short circuit causing 110 volts AC to be applied to its metal case. The man is seen to stand for about a number of seconds without being able to speak or breathe. In this case, the current flow from hand-to-hand could be 110 milliamperes (110 volts divided by 1,000 ohms). This amount of current passing through the arm is known to cause tightening of the grasp and inability to let go. And, if crossing the chest, it would be expected to paralyze the muscles of respiration (Dalziel 1956; Dalziel and Lee 1968). This amount of current could cause ventricular fibrillation, depending on the person's size and the duration of contact.

15.2 Tasks in Electrical Injury Accident Reconstruction

The tasks listed in Table 15.1 may not be able to be performed in the exact order listed, depending on when information becomes available. In addition, several tasks may be worked on at the same time.

These topics will be discussed below.

A. Task 1: Determine current flow

Document through witness interviews, photographs, police reports, electricians, engineers, technicians, medical records, and other sources, evidence relevant to the information listed in Table 15.2.

1. Consider the meaning of missing information

Those responsible for investigating and preserving evidence concerning the accident may not have done a good job. Or, they may have done little or no investigation because they felt there was no accident or injury. They may claim that the person had a heart attack or seizure, and these events had nothing to do with electricity that may have been applied to the person's head or body. They may believe there was no electrical accident, or that the amount of current was too small to cause injury. It may be claimed that the injury or death had nothing to do with the work site or general

Table 15.1
Tasks in Electrical Injury Accident Reconstruction

1. Determine that electric current did or did not flow through certain parts of the person's body.
2. Analyze the medical effects that would be expected from such current flow.
3. Determine the detailed characteristics of the injuries actually sustained by the person.
4. Compare the expected effects of current flow to the actual injury (compare the results of tasks 2 and 3).
5. Consider the possibility that the person's condition is due to disease or other processes unrelated to the electrical injury. The condition should not predate the injury.
6. Cite references from scientific literature that support and illustrate the consultant's conclusions.

Table 15.2
Information Relevant to Determining Current Flow

A. Electric source
   1. AC or DC
   2. If AC, the frequency (Hz), waveform (such as sine wave) and duty cycle
   3. Voltage, equivalent circuit including impedance, and effective voltage
   4. Condition of the source (if an electrical device)
      a. Defects
      b. Damage
      c. Moisture at the time of the accident
      d. Proper installation, including grounding
      e. Presence, type, and condition of insulation and transformer isolation
B. Current path
   1. Electrical resistance or impedance inside and outside the person's body. The resistance can change over time as materials burn, accumulate moisture, or dry.
   2. Areas of contact with the person's body
C. Duration of current flow
   1. Effects of circuit breakers, fuses, GFI (ground fault interruption), or manual disconnection of source
   2. Movements of the person causing loss of connection
   3. Burning of tissue or other materials changing current flow

environment, so documentation of the particulars of the accident was not necessary.

The failure of such persons to provide adequate information is sometimes a sign that there was inadequate understanding of the dangers at the accident site, inadequate training of personnel, and inadequate safety measures. Lack of information concerning resuscitative procedures may mean that none were done. Questioning the personnel can often discover these inadequacies. Thus, the reasons that information is missing are often significant.

There are other, less informative reasons that information is sometimes missing. Ideally, except as needed for safety reasons, nothing should be moved before documentation, measurements, and photography or videotaping is completed (Rao 1995). However, such evidence preservation is often not possible. Sometimes, the accident itself or a resulting fire will destroy or modify evidence. Construction will continue, power lines will be repaired, and items that were initially preserved will sometimes get lost or be modified during later testing. By the time it is decided an investigation is needed, much time has often passed.

2. Examine electrical devices

Examine any electrical devices involved in the accident. If this is not possible, similar electrical devices are often available for testing. In using such exemplary models, take into account evidence concerning wear and modifications that may have made the devices involved in the accident different than the test models. If the incident involved a modified device, the model device can be similarly changed to demonstrate the effects of such modifications.

If damaged in the accident, an electrical device may yield significant data concerning the accident because of how it was damaged. Therefore, the investigator should attempt to obtain and examine the actual electrical devices present at the time of the accident.

3. Interactions between the electrical environment and the electrical device

The electrical environment and an electrical device may interact to cause injury. This synergy may result from the electrical device providing a voltage at one point on the person's body, with the environment providing a different voltage or ground to another part of the body. Improper wiring in the environment may lead to injury despite the fact that the electrical device itself was in no way defective.

Humidity is an important environmental factor that can cause more current to flow than would occur in dry conditions. Sometimes a history of persons receiving minor shock-like sensations before the accident under investigation occurs. Humidity or individual differences in skin resistance may explain why persons were not injured on previous occasions.

B. Task 2: Determine expected medical effects of the electrical current

The types of injuries that can result from current flow through the body are many and varied (Dalziel 1956; Fish 1993a,b; Wright and Davis 1980; Demun 1993; VanDenburg et al. 1996). Table 15.3 lists some of the immediate effects that can be expected in adults at various current levels. The amount of current needed for any given effect depends on a number of factors, including the weight and sex of the person. The current needed to cause ventricular fibrillation also varies with the duration of current flow.

Index of Effects

Tingling sensation. A tingling sensation, or minimal perception, occurs with currents from 0.5 to 2 milliamperes for men, and at somewhat lower levels for women. With alternating current, the first sensations are tingling; while with direct current, the person will often feel warmth (Dalziel 1956).

Pain. With increasing alternating current levels beyond that required to just cause tingling, muscle contractions start. Sensations of heat and pain develop, and voluntary control of the muscles in the current pathway becomes increasingly difficult (Dalziel 1956).

Let-go current. With still further increases in current, the "let-go" limit is reached. The "let-go" current threshold is measured by having a person hold an electrode in each hand. Above a certain current flow through the forearm muscles, the person cannot let go because of the repetitive (tetanic) stimulation of forearm muscles. Partially responsible for this phenomena is the fact that the forearm flexor muscles are stronger than the extensors. The forearm flexor muscles flex the fingers. This phenomena often keeps victims frozen to the source of electricity and causes a firmer (and lower resistance) contact to be made.

Respiratory paralysis. Respiratory paralysis can be caused by current flow through muscles of respiration. The muscles of respiration (intercostal, pectoral, and diaphragmatic) may be immobilized along with the forearm muscles (described under let-go current above). This respiratory paralysis will happen if the current is on the order of 18 to 30 milliamperes for a limb-to-limb current pathway (Cabanes 1985; Dalziel and Lee 1968 and 1969; Lee 1965).

Paralysis of the muscles of respiration with continued circulation of the blood eventually leads to hypoxia and cyanosis (a blue skin color due

---

Table 15.3
Effects of Various Amounts of Current in Man

Ranges are approximate and depend on a number of factors. The amount of current needed depends on the subject factors (including health, medications, sex, and weight), duration of current flow, and current path (e.g. head-to-foot).

Effect	Effect	Minimum Current, milliamperes, 60 Hz rms AC
Ventricular fibrillation	Through an electrode wire or fluid-filled catheter to the inside surface of a cardiac ventricle	0.06 to 0.43
Tingling sensation, minimal perception	Through intact skin	0.5 to 2
Pain threshold	Through intact skin	1 to 4
Inability to let go. Tetanic contractions of forearm muscles tighten grasp, decreasing contact resistance	From hand, through forearm muscles, into the trunk. (Other pathways will stimulate other muscular contractions.)	6 to 22
Respiratory arrest. Can be fatal if prolonged	Through the chest	18 to 30
Ventricular fibrillation	Through the chest	70[1] to 4,000
Ventricular standstill (asystole) In effect, is a defibrillation. When the current stops, sinus rhythm may resume, sometimes with persistent respiratory arrest.	Through the chest	> 2,000 (> 2 amperes)

[1]A minimum value for a 50-kg man with current applied for three seconds; for the most sensitive 0.5% of the population (Dalziel and Lee, 1968, page 476)

to decreased oxygen in the blood). People dying of ventricular fibrillation without preceding hypoxia will usually not be cyanotic (Polson et al. 1985, 281).

In summary, current levels between the let-go threshold and the current level needed to cause ventricular fibrillation will restrict respiratory movements. If continued long enough, this may result in an asphyxial death due to spasm of the muscles of respiration. The heart continues to beat for some time after the respiratory paralysis. This is similar to traumatic asphyxia and is likely to produce cyanosis. However, the expected petechial (small purple) hemorrhages are not so diffuse and prominent as in other forms of asphyxial deaths, but may be seen in the eyelids, face, and conjunctivae (the thin, transparent mucous membranes over the sclera or white portion of the front of the eye and the insides of the eyelids) (Camps 1976, 362).

Paralysis of the respiratory center. The respiratory center becomes paralyzed when current flows through it. The paralysis often persists after the current ceases. The heart continues to beat, and prolonged support of respiration can be effective in preserving life. Such support is sometimes needed for several hours. Electroconvulsive therapy (EST or ECT) involves passing several hundred milliamperes through the head. However, such current does not pass through the respiratory center (Camps 1976, 362; Knight 1976, 125; Knight 1982, 152). ECT will cause respiratory insufficiency because respirations are greatly decreased during grand mal seizures.

Some authors have said that the hand-to-hand respiratory center paralysis mechanism of death is common and important. In seeking evidence about this assertion, one study found that of 118 deaths occurring with medium voltage exposure, 80 percent involved such limb-to-limb contact (Lee 1965). However, this would not distinguish respiratory center from chest muscle spasm or ventricular fibrillation deaths.

Ventricular fibrillation. For a 70-kg man, the current at 60 Hz required to cause ventricular fibrillation is around 165 milliamperes for a one-second current duration. The current needed is inversely proportional to the square root of the current duration. This is valid over a range of about 8.3 milliseconds to 30 seconds (Dalziel and Lee 1969).

The cardiac effects listed in Table 15.3 will require more current for paths that cause a smaller percentage of the total current to pass through the heart. Ventricular fibrillation is possible from 70 milliamperes up to about four amperes. Thus, there is a range of currents in which either fibrillation or ventricular standstill can occur (Cabanes 1985).

The current required to produce ventricular fibrillation and other effects is proportional to body weight (Dalziel and Lee 1969, 48; Ferris 1936; IEEE 1986). (See Section 5.2, Equation 5.2.) The amount of current to produce apnea and other effects is probably also related to weight. This is an important consideration when considering the effects of electric current on children (See Section 6.5 on electric fences). Women and children generally require smaller amounts of electric current to produce various effects than do men.

Asystole. Asystole refers to a standstill of the heart. There is no pumping of blood, and no motion of the heart. As discussed below, the heart will likely recover from asystole if a brief electric current induced it. There is usually no recovery if asystole results from other medical or traumatic conditions.

Microshock causing ventricular fibrillation. Alternating 50 or 60 Hertz currents as small as 100 microamperes (Kugelberg 1975 and 1976) brought to the heart by a pacemaker wire or catheter can produce ventricular fibrillation. This is true because nearly all of the current carried by the device passes through a small area in the heart. In contrast, with arm- to - arm contact, most of the current goes around the heart, with a fraction of the current going through the heart with a nonconcentrated distribution. Hospital equipment is generally required to pass no more than 100 microamperes of current with patient contact (AAMI 1985).

It has been found that plastic catheters filled with physiological crystalloid (such as normal saline) can conduct electricity and produce fibrillation if the catheter is advanced to the right ventricle. With this arrangement, as little as 253 microamperes can cause ventricular fibrillation in dogs. It is therefore recommended that CVP (central venous pressure) measuring systems be kept as far as possible from electric instruments and conducting materials. Also, personnel should avoid touching electric equipment or electric conducting materials when handling the tubes associated with the CVP system. Medical rubber gloves are effective insulators and provide suitable safeguard in these situations (Monies-Chass et al. 1986).

Fatal injury with no visible burns. An electrothermal burn of the skin is caused by a current flow through the skin resistance, causing heat to be generated. A useful model (Wright and Davis 1980; Moritz and Henriques 1947) has been designed to analyze heating from electric current flow. Using this model, Wright and Davis (1980) performed calculations to determine if a person receiving an electrical injury just adequate to cause ventricular fibrillation would also suffer an electrothermal skin burn. Charring requires a temperature of 90°C. Calculations showed that the fibrillating current would not raise the tissue temperature enough to cause a burn. This explains why persons with fatal electrocution sometimes have no burns.

C. Task 3: Determine the nature of the injury actually sustained

1. Medical events around the time of the accident

Obtain descriptions of what occurred, taking into account the items listed in Table 15.4. Medically important observations made during and after an injury include whether the person was: conscious, having a seizure, breathing, turning colors, walking, talking, or falling. A series of such actions and abnormalities can reveal much about the physiology of the person during and following the accident.

X-ray studies, blood chemistry, urine (for blood, myoglobin, and hemoglobin), and electrocardiographic investigations may reveal relevant abnormalities (Fisher 1980; Fish 1993c; Jensen 1987). This information can provide data concerning what did and did not happen to the person. For example, elevation of serum CPK (CK, or creatine phosphokinase) is an indication of muscle damage. A urine dipstick that is positive for blood in urine, but has no red blood cells on microscopic examination indicates muscle damage or hemolysis (breakdown of red blood cells), both of which can follow electrical injury. In such cases, the dipstick is responding to urine myoglobin or hemoglobin.

2. Medical condition of the person over time

Examine the medical records of the patient from before the alleged injury to determine if the person had the injury or disability before the accident occurred. Examine the medical records from the time of the accident and afterward for information concerning how the medical condition of the patient changed over time.

3. Sources of information

Obtain information from photographs, police reports, and medical records. People who can provide useful information include witnesses and people who are familiar with or examined the electrical devices or the electrical environment where the accident occurred, including electrical engineers and electricians. Obtain information concerning the performance of resuscitation, including CPR and other emergency care, to determine if this was done in a timely and proper fashion (American Heart Association 1992; Fish 1989; Fontanarosa 1993; Moran et al. 1986). Statements, reports, or depositions should be obtained from persons with knowledge of these issues. Medical and EMS (emergency medical system) records should be evaluated.

A variety of other documents may also contain information relevant to an accident. There may be incident reports, insurance papers, memos, routine maintenance and calibration records, wiring plans, police and autopsy reports, repair bills, and invoices.

Medical records, such as ambulance and emergency department charts, usually contain useful information. However, physicians and nurses may not have had the benefit of knowledge concerning the accident scene. Unfortunately, they may not be knowledgeable concerning the effects of electrical injury. Therefore, the forensic consultant must be careful to differentiate between clinical observations and unsupported conclusions in the medical records.

These considerations are summarized in Table 15.4.

D. Task 4: Compare the expected effects of current flow to the actual injury

Table 15.3 lists some of the immediate effects of electric current passage through the body. Less immediate effects of electric current on the body and mind are discussed in the medical and engineering literature, as reviewed in other parts of this book.

Table 15.4
Information Checklist

1. Description of the accident from witnesses.
   A. Was there arcing, an explosion, power failure, or a fire?
   B. Was it in an enclosed space?
   C. What body parts were contacting voltage sources and other objects?
   D. Nature of the ground or floor
   E. Presence of moisture
   F. How did the victim separate from the power source?
2. Medical events and findings over time:
   A. Mental status: consciousness, confusion, ability to talk, seizure activity
   B. Respiratory status: breathing (rate, depth, abnormal sounds), skin color
   C. Cardiovascular status: Palpable pulse, blood pressure
   D. Motor system: voluntary or involuntary movement, falling
3. Pre-hospital treatment
   A. Immediate resuscitation, including CPR and other emergency care
      1. Was the person breathing? If not, how were respirations supported?
      2. Was there a pulse? If not, were chest compressions done?
      3. Narrative description of care given
   B. Fire, police, and rescue run sheets and reports
   C. Emergency medical service (ambulance) run sheet
4. Medical records
   A. Tests especially relevant to detecting traumatic injury: x-ray, CPK, urinalysis, EKG
   B. Emergency department
   C. Inpatient hospital
   D. Outpatient: physician office, therapy
   E. Pharmacy records
5. Other records
   A. Evaluations for insurance, disability, and other claims
   B. Death certificate
   C. Autopsy report

E. Task 5: Consider that the person's condition is due to disease or other processes unrelated to the electrical injury

The person's medical condition before and after the accident needs to be considered. Conditions existing before the accident cannot be attributed to the accident.

F. Task 6: Cite references from the scientific literature that support and illustrate the consultant's opinions

Copies of articles or book sections from the medical or engineering literature should be attached to the consultant's report or testimony to show that opinions are in agreement with accepted scientific knowledge.

One valuable function of the consultant is to review opinion statements of opposing experts. It then becomes possible to obtain articles for one's attorney that will provide the knowledge necessary to understand differences in opinions. Such literature can be especially helpful if it can be obtained before the attorney deposes the opposition's experts.

15.3 Conclusions

Accident reconstruction in cases of electrical injury calls for an analysis that takes into account medical and engineering considerations. The consultant should cite and provide scientific literature that explains issues about the case to everyone who is interested in gaining such understanding. The literature citations should support the consultant's opinions.

References

American Association for the Advancement of Medical Instrumentation (AAMI), ANSI/AAMI ESI. *Safe Current Limits for Electromedical Apparatus* (Arlington, VA: American Association for the Advancement of Medical Instrumentation, 1985).

American Heart Association, "Guidelines for Cardiopulmonary Resuscitation and Emergency Cardiac Care," *JAMA* 268(16):2248 (1992).

Cabanes, J., "Physiological Effects of Electric Currents on Living Organisms, More Particularly Humans," in *Electrical Shock Safety Criteria: Proceedings of the First International Symposium on Electrical Shock Safety Criteria,* J. E. Bridges et al., eds. (NY: Pergamon Press, 1985), 7–24.

Camps, Francis E., Anne E. Robinson and Bernard G. B. Lucas, eds. *Gradwohl's Legal Medicine*, 3rd ed. (Chicago: J. Wright, 1976), 362.

Dalziel, C. F., "Effects of Electric Shock on Man," *IRE Transactions on Medical Electronics* 5:44–62 (1956).

Dalziel, C. F. and W. R. Lee, "Reevaluation of Lethal Electric Currents," *IEEE Transactions on Industry and General Applications* IGA-4(5):467–476, (1968).

Dalziel, C. F. and W. R. Lee, "Lethal Electric Currents," *IEEE Spectrum* (6):44–50 (1969).

Demun, E. M., J. L. Redd and K. A. Buchanan, "Reflex Sympathetic Dystrophy after a Minor Electric Injury," *Journal of Emergency Medicine* 11:393–396 (1993).

Ferris, L. P. et al., "Effect of Electric Shock on the Heart," *Elec. Eng.* 55:498–515 (1936).

Fish, R., *The Resuscitation Handbook* (Oradell, NJ: Medical Economics Books, 1989).

Fish, R., "Electric Injury, part 1: Physics and Pathophysiology," *Journal of Emergency Medicine* 11:309–312 (1993a).

Fish, R., "Electric Injury, part 2: Nature and Mechanisms of Injury," *Journal of Emergency Medicine* 11:457–462 (1993b).

Fish, R., "Electric Injury, part 3: Deliberately Applied Electric Injuries and the Treatment of Electric Injuries," *Journal of Emergency Medicine* 11:599–603 (1993c).

Fisher, R. S., "Electrical and Lightning Injuries," in *Medicolegal Investigation of Death*, 2nd ed., W. U. Spitz and R. S. Fisher, eds. (Springfield: Thomas, 1980), 367.

Fontanarosa, P. B., "Electrical Injury and Lightning Strike," *Annals of Emergency Medicine* 22(2):378–387 (1993).

IEEE Power Engineering Society Substation Committee, *IEEE Guide for Safety in AC Substation Grounding* (Piscataway, NJ: IEEE Press, 1986), 32.

Knight, B., "Electrocution," in *Legal Aspects of Medical Practice*, 2nd ed. (Edinburgh: Churchill Livingston, 1976) 125 (also 3rd ed., 1982, 152).

Jensen, P. J. et al., "Electrical Injury Causing Ventricular Arrhythmias," *British Heart Journal* 57:279–283 (1987).

Kugelberg, J., "Accidental Ventricular Fibrillation of the Human Heart," *Scand. J. Thor. Cardiovasc. Surg.* 9:133–139 (1975).

Kugelberg, J., "Electrical Induction of Ventricular Fibrillation in the Human Heart," *Scand. J. Thor. Cardiovasc. Surg.* 10:237–240 (1976).

Lee, W. R., "The Mechanisms of Death from Electric Shock," *Medicine, Science, and the Law* 5(1):23–28 (1965).

Monies-Chass, I. et al., "Hidden Risk in Operating Room Micro-Shock," *Acta Anesthesiol. Belg.* 37:39–44 (1986).

Moran, K. T., J. N. Thupari and A. M. Munster, "Electric- and Lightning-Induced Cardiac Arrest Reversed by Prompt Cardiopulmonary Resuscitation," *JAMA* 255:2157 (1986).

Moritz, A. R. and F. C. Henriques, "Studies in Thermal Injury: The Relative Importance of Time and Surface Temperature in the Cause of Cutaneous Burns," *American Journal of Pathology* 23(5):695–720 (1947).

Rao, G., "Anatomy of an Accident," *Risk Management*, October 1995, 63–70.

VanDenburg, S., G. M. McCormick and D. B. Young, "Investigation of Deaths Related to Electrical Injury," *Southern Medical Journal* 89:869–872 (1996).

Wright, R. K. and M. D. Davis, "The Investigation of Electrical Deaths: A Report of 220 Fatalities," *Journal of Forensic Sciences* 25(3):514–521 (1980).

Chapter 16

Burns, Muscle, Bone and Joint Injuries from Electricity

16.1 Burns

The severity and depth of electric burns are often difficult or impossible to determine on initial clinical examination. Burns from electric injury have a variety of appearances and may be difficult to distinguish from other skin lesions.

A. The clinical diagnosis of burns

1. Degrees of burns

Burns (electrical or otherwise) can be first-, second-, third- or fourth-degree. First- and second-degree burns are sometimes referred to as being partial skin-thickness, while third- and fourth-degree are full skin-thickness burns.

a. First-degree burns are areas of redness and pain, such as a sunburn without skin blistering.

b. Second-degree burns have pain, redness, or a mottled (having various shades or colors) appearance, and possible swelling. There is blister formation. The blisters may break within minutes or after many days, leaving (if before healing occurs) a wet painful area.

c. Third-degree burns are leathery (firm), dry, and painless; the color may be translucent, white, or dark. If red, third degree burns will not blanch (lose their color) with pressure. The diagnosis of a third-degree burn may be missed initially; a third-degree burn may look like a lesser degree burn, with the only distinguishing characteristic being that there is no pain or blanching with pressure. And, it is not common (or humane) practice to press on all burned areas to see if they blanch and are painful.

d. Fourth-degree burns are those burns that extend into deeper tissues, such as muscle or bone.

Burns are often not uniform; that is, a person can have a mixture of burns of various degrees from the same injury. There are fluid resuscitation formulas (such as the Parkland formula) that estimate how much intravenous fluid will be required by patients with burns of certain sizes. These formulas ignore first-degree burns and make their determinations based on the percent of body surface area suffering second- or higher degrees of burn. These formulas are of limited value with electric injury because deep tissue injury requiring fluids often occurs with deceptively little in the way of surface burns.

2. Difficulty of determining extent of deep injury related to burns

Skin burns are often not good indicators of vascular and other types of deep injury. Edema (swelling) under an eschar (coagulated, crusty tissue) or under tight muscle fascia (fibrous tissue surrounding muscles) can make feeling pulses difficult. And, even if pulses are detected by ultrasound, they are not assurance of the viability of underlying muscle. Arteriography to reveal vascular damage can be useful, but does not always identify important arterial branches. Surgical exploration is sometimes needed to determine the extent of deep injury (Hunt and McManus 1974). Newer imaging methods, such as MRI, can sometimes identify deep muscle necrosis (Nettelblad et al. 1996).

The physiological effects of current may not be well correlated with burn size; in fact, there may not be any surface burn at all in cases of significant injury. Contact resistance will be lower per unit area if the skin is wet. Similarly, a larger contact area (such as being in a bathtub) will give a lower resistance. With lower resistance, there will be less heat produced than with a high resistance contact (such as, a small area of wire touching dry skin) if the same current is flowing in each case. Thus, a current capable of causing deep tissue damage, respiratory arrest, or cardiac arrest may or may not cause skin lesions depending on the resistance of the contact made with the skin. In a study of 108 deaths caused by injury with sources under 1,000 volts, electric burns were absent in over 40 percent of cases (Wright and Davis 1980; Damjanov and Linder 1996).

B. Factors related to the formation of burns

1. Changes in skin resistance over time

When there is enough current flow to cause skin burns, the skin resistance will change over time. Most of the resistance to current flow occurs at the intact, undamaged skin because internal body resistance is lower than skin resistance. Therefore, the total resistance to current flow will often significantly decline as the skin breaks down. With continued burning, however, resistance can increase due to carbonization and destruction of skin and other tissues (Cooper 1984).

For example, a dry hand may have sufficient resistance to avoid passage of significant current from a low-voltage source over a short time period. However, the generation of several thousand degrees at the contact site with a high-voltage source will lead to immediate tissue injury (coagulation). This thermal injury will disrupt the electrical barrier of the skin, allowing current to flow more readily (Lee et al. 1992, 121–124).

The severity of injury is proportional to the duration of current flow. However, even extremely brief exposures to high amperage can produce massive tissue damage. A high-voltage source giving 5 amps or more can cause severe tissue destruction.

Electrical burns sometimes resemble a crush injury in that the damage below the skin is usually far greater than the appearance of overlying skin would indicate. The immediate damage caused by the thermal destruction of cells is usually patchy in distribution along the course of the current. Blood vessels may thrombose (become blocked by blood clots) over four days (Lee et al. 1992, 121–124).

2. Enlargement of burns over time

The size of the primary burn does not change, but burns caused by high voltage may develop a zone of secondary ischemic necrosis (tissue death due to lack of oxygen supply) that enlarges for days or weeks. This is due to thrombosis (clotting) of arterioles and arteries that sustained intimal (internal blood vessel lining) damage due to passage of electric current. Therefore, repeated debridement or amputations are sometimes needed following high-voltage electric injuries (Damjanov and Linder 1996, 107).

C. Types of burns

1. Electrothermal burns

Electrothermal burns are burns caused by the passage of electric current through tissue. Tissue can be thought of as a resistor with a certain resistance, R. Power, in the form of heat, is generated in the tissue having current flow (I) following the equation $P = I^2R$. Thus, power is proportional to the current squared.

A burn from an external hot object may be labeled as being of extrinsic origin. In contrast, an electrothermal (or electrothermic) burn is produced within the tissue itself (intrinsic).

Electrothermal burns may be confused with thermal burns caused by touching an object that has been heated by a short circuit. A short circuit through a metal conductor may cause almost immediate heating to the melting point, even with 110 volts AC or DC (or with less, as in welding).

Contact with such a high temperature conductor may cause severe instantaneous burning even though there is no electric current flow through the skin. A current produced by a 110-volt AC source will rarely cause a large electrothermal injury of the skin unless the contact is maintained for a significant period of time (Damjanov and Linder 1996, 107).

2. Arc burns

Arc burns are due to the intense radiation of heat caused by electric current arcing through the air. Current can arc from one metal conductor to another near a person, causing burns due to heat. A more dangerous situation occurs when current arcs from a conductor to the person. In this situation, there can be thermal burns from the arc, as well as damage due to the passage of electric current thought the person. In one such case, the person did not touch the conductor, but was within the air flashover (or breakdown) distance, which can be several feet in the industrial setting (Jamil et al. 1997). The temperatures generated by arcing current are thought to be in the range of 3,000–20,000°C (Baxter 1970). Heat can cause fatal burns as much as five feet away, and major burns up to ten feet away (Lee 1982). See Section 5.4, for a discussion on power line arc flash hazards.

Gases and droplets of molten metal are expelled by electric arcs, including the arcs from electric arc welding. The gases and droplets have temperatures of 1,000°C or more and can cause burns and ignite clothing. Thus, protective clothing and other devices can be important in preventing injury. These issues are mentioned in OSHA documents (29 CFR 1910.335, subpart S, and 29 CFR 1910.269, subpart R).

a. Case example of arc injury. Moar and Hunt (1987) describe the case of a man who was climbing a high-voltage electric pylon. Before he reached the level of the cable, a blue flash of current was seen, causing him to fall twenty-one feet to the ground. Autopsy found numerous round, crater-like wounds with slightly raised edges and areas of severe charring of the skin and deeper tissues. There were also internal injuries due to the fall. Histology (microscopic examination) of the skin lesions showed changes in the structure and arrangements of cells that are characteristic of electric burns (Fisher 1980, 371).

b. Additional clinical features of arc burns. The high-voltage electrical trauma victim often has burns due to arcing, passage of current through the body with heating, and from burning clothing. Such patients usually have charred skin craters at the contact sites and adjacent area of inflamed, edematous skin. However, there is no correlation between the size of the contact skin injury and the actual total extent of all injuries. The extent of injury is nearly always more extensive than is apparent. Frequently, there is charred tissue surrounding the skin craters; these require debridement (surgical removal of devitalized tissue and foreign material). Flame burns are frequently found in association with electric injury because an arc ignited clothing. The percentage of skin burn is of little value in estimating underlying injury. A black coating on the skin may result from metallic contacts being vaporized by the arc, followed by metal condensation on the epidermis. Such condensation can look like an eschar (a scab) (Lee et al. 1992).

3. Assisted or pseudo-arcing

Moar and Hunt (1987) also describe a variety of situations in which the victim does not actually touch a solid conductor directly. In these cases, current is conducted through liquid, or materials between the victim and the power source initiate arcing. Such sources of current have included: drinking from a water fountain in contact with electrical current from an underground cable, contacting an overhead cable while operating a wire-controlled model airplane, and urinating on an electric railroad line. A report of urinating on a high voltage cable while standing on a bridge has also been reported; the current passes to the victim along the stream of urine. Substances such as salts that are in the liquid influence the conductivity of liquids.

In still another case, a man was unloading a truck. A canvas side cover attached to the truck had a heavy steel wire along its edge. The canvas cover was thrown upward and came into contact with a high voltage cable fifteen to eighteen feet above the ground. There was a flash and explosive sound, as the man was thrown to the ground. The ground around the wheels of the truck was scorched, and the victims clothing was burnt and charred. Autopsy found multiple circumscribed crater-like lesions in some areas, and full thickness skin burns in other areas (Moar and Hunt 1987).

4. Electric cord injuries

Children biting an electric cord or sucking the end of an extension cord can receive burns that may damage the maxilla (bone supporting the upper teeth), mandible (jaw) and growing portions of teeth. Cosmetic surgery and braces to prevent deformity are often necessary. Bleeding from the labial artery is common when the eschar (scab) separates up to two weeks after initial injury. If such patients are treated as outpatients, parents must be shown how to apply direct pressure to the artery to control bleeding. Children are sometimes hospitalized for one or two weeks until the eschar separates (Cooper 1983).

D. Clinical and pathological aspects of burns

Skin lesions caused by electric force are referred to as current marks (Somogyi and Tedeschi 1977). Such marks are frequently not detectable in cases of fatal electrocution. Ventricular fibrillation and death may be caused with no skin damage, because larger currents are needed to burn the skin than are required to disrupt cardiac function (Wright and Davis 1980). Current marks are less likely to occur if the area of contact is larger, as when a person is in a bathtub or other body of water.

It may be difficult to differentiate an intrinsic current (electrothermal) mark from a burn of extrinsic origin (from an external, high temperature object). Generally, electric burns are less uniform than extrinsic burns. Current marks may be limited to the epidermis which will have a grayish-white parchment-like alteration. Alternatively, the burn may extend deeper into the skin and even subjacent tissues, giving a crater-shaped ulcer with curling borders. The lesion may be surrounded by a bright red area and may have vesicles, similar to second degree burns of other causes. The current mark may be the size of a pinhead or a lentil, but rarely larger, usually being the same size as the conductor that was contacted. The size and shape of the wound may correspond to the shape of the contacted object, especially if there was firm contact. Sometimes the skin appears linearly divided, as with an incision. Current marks can occur under intact clothing or hair. A mark may not be visible initially if a body is wet, but may be seen more clearly after drying (Somogyi and Tedeschi 1977).

Current marks may also not be obvious if the current is applied to the genitals or abdomen, or if they occur in the mouth. Children may place a live plug in the mouth and sustain burns that may be overlooked at autopsy (Knight 1991).

If there was not firm contact between the electrical conductor and the skin, there may be small pinpoint areas of burning. Small blisters and grayish-yellow marks may appear if the skin has not been burnt. Burns may develop a blackened core surrounded by a halo of pallor, with a still more peripheral area of redness. With voltages above domestic levels (110–240 volts AC), flash burns and charring become more common (Camps 1976).

With a poor or intermittent contact, a dry pitted lesion (often very small) may occur because of arcing of current from the conductor may occur. A yellow parchment-like scab may form with a surrounding ring of pallor due to capillary contraction. In contrast, if there is firm contact, as with spasmodic muscle contraction, a raised blister containing gas or a little fluid may form (Knight 1976).

Cyanosis may be a generalized finding if death is not instantaneous and respirations have been primarily affected (Camps 1976).

If there has been firm contact with the electrical conductor, current through the high skin resistance heats up the tissue fluids to produce steam. This can split the layers of the epidermis or the epidermal-dermal junction. This can produce a raised blister. If the current continues or the area is large, the blister may rupture. When current ceases, the blister cools and collapses. This gives the appearance often seen at autopsy. Such collapsed blisters are often ring-like (annular) with a raised gray or white ring and an umbilicated (depressed, naval-like) center. The mark may reproduce the shape of the conductor, especially if it was a linear wire or shaped metal object. If the tip of the wire or a rod was a right angles to the skin, a focal pit may be created, sometimes penetrating deeply into the skin (Knight 1991).

If contact is less firm there is a narrow air gap between the skin and conductor. A spark of current jumps the gap, generating a temperature of several thousand degrees. The outer skin keratin melts and fuses on cooling into a hard brownish nodule that is usually raised above the surrounding surface. This is called a spark lesion. Spark lesions may coexist with firm contact-related blisters (Knight 1991, 298).

A surrounding ring, or areola of blanched skin at the periphery of an electric mark commonly occurs. It is presumably due to arteriolar spasm from the current. The pallor can be seen after death. There may be a hyperemic (red) border outside the blanching. Redness may also be seen inside the pale zone as a rim outside of the burn area. With linear burns, as from a bare wire, the areola may appear as a pale zone parallel to the burn (Knight 1991, 298).

Minimal burns may be tiny white discs, representing tiny blisters where the epidermis has split with no redness or areola formation (Knight 1991, 298).

High-voltage electrical trauma often involves burns due to (1) arcing or flash burns, (2) passage of current through the body with heating, and (3) ignition of clothing. Mixed burns are said to occur when two or more types of burn occur together. Thermal burns from burning materials and from splashing of materials heated by electric current (such as metals and oils) may occur alone or in combination with other electric injuries.

High voltage burns can have multiple spark lesions, giving a crocodile-skin effect. Lower voltage burns may resemble high voltage burns, with charring and extensive blistering and deep muscle damage if contact is prolonged (Knight 1991, 298).

Many high voltage injuries leave obvious burns. However, a case reported by Chandrasiri shows that such external injuries are not always obvious (Chandrasiri 1988). This case involved a twenty-seven-year-old man who was holding an aluminum staff for surveying a newly constructed dam in Sri Lanka. His feet were bare. He suddenly fell to the ground and was not resuscitated. A medical officer without formal training in forensic medicine or pathology conducted an autopsy without examining the scene of the incident. He judged that the cause of death was occlusion of a coronary artery. The body was embalmed and buried.

A week later another worker at the same site doing the same task suddenly shouted in pain and "ran amok." He recovered within a few minutes. He had been wearing rubber slippers and was found to have burns on his hands. It was realized that there had been arcing from overhead high tension power lines to the staff the men had been holding.

The body of the first man was exhumed and re-examined three weeks after the death. There was shriveling of the left hand with congestion of its skin and palm. There were several crater-like areas of burned tissue on the balls of the toes of both feet with an average diameter of 2 mm. The right hand had pinhead-sized pits on the skin. There were no other burns on the body. Coronary arteries were normal. The medical officer who conducted the first examination said that he mistook the craters in the balls of the toes for callosities, but histological examination showed classic features of the passage of electric current.

Examination of the scene of the accidents was conducted. The aluminum staff was 63.6 cm long. When standing on the ground vertically directly below the power lines, there was a gap of 1 meter from the upper end of the staff to the overhead cables. There was no melting or destruction of the surface of the staff.

Postmortem burns can be inflicted on a dead body giving blistering and burning. It is generally thought that the red flare of the so-called vital reaction will not be seen if death occurred some time earlier. However, in one experiment involving dead tissue that had been stored in a refrigerator for several days, a reddened zone appeared surrounding an experimental electric mark (Mant 1973, 272).

E. Microscopic examination of current marks

Microscopically, current marks have separation of cells in the form of sharp slits, known as electric channels. Current marks may be induced postmortem; though this is controversial, the detection of vital reaction is needed to say that the exposure occurred before or after death as noted above. Current marks are resistant to postmortem decomposition, and exhumation may be useful in some cases (Somogyi and Tedeschi 1977; Al-Alousi 1990).

Electric arc burn injuries show a sharp demarcation of a damaged area from adjacent tissues on histological examination. Multiple seared or punched out lesions may be formed, as the arc seems to "dance" over the surface (Fisher 1980, 371). In contrast, thermal burns show a progressive gradation in injury from injured to normal tissue. Also with electric arc burns, the high temperatures may produce coagulation necrosis of the underlying dermis and also of small blood vessels far from the skin burn.

F. Skin metallization

Current causes ion migration and electrolysis to occur, causing metal salts to be formed and diffuse into the tissue (Somogyi and Tedeschi 1977). This process depends on the current density (current per unit area in a cross section of tissue), time of current flow, and type of metal contacted.

The color of the metal imprint depends on the electrode material: iron gives brownish black, copper gives reddish brown or bright green, and aluminum gives a silvery color. If present, metallization gives definite evidence that a burn was due to electrical force (Al-Alousi 1990; Mant 1984). See Section 5.2.

The metallized skin desquamates within a few weeks in the living. Metallization may also be present on nails, and it will disappear as the nails grow. Chemical analysis can be done by spectroscopic, histochemical, or polarographic methods. A simple color reaction to demonstrate metal particles on skin surfaces is called the acroreaction test. Small wedges of filter paper are moistened with acid and then applied to current marks on the skin. They are then removed and tested with drops of reagents. The reagents produce color reactions with various metals. Scanning electron microscopy can also detect metallic particles in electric marks (Mant 1984; Adjutantis and Skalos 1962).

Even without contact, metal may be deposited if there is an electric arc from the conductor to the skin (Somogyi and Tedeschi 1977). With arcing, current is transmitted by ionized air and usually lasts a few seconds. Temperatures will be several thousand degrees Celsius. With the arc, metal and gas particles are deposited on the skin. Because of the bright light associated with an electric arc, the victim often shuts the eyes reflexively; the heat and metallic deposits may lead to a crowsfeet-like pattern around the eyes.

G. Skin lesions that may be mistaken for electric marks or burns

First, some definitions (*Stedman's Electronic Medical Dictionary*):

> **bulla** (plural: bullae). A large blister appearing as a circumscribed area of separation of the epidermis from the subepidermal structure (subepidermal bulla) or as a circumscribed area of separation of epidermal cells (intraepidermal bulla) caused by the presence of serum, or occasionally by an injected substance.

> **blister**. A fluid-filled thin-walled structure under the epidermis or within the epidermis (subepidermal or intradermal).

callosity. A circumscribed thickening of the keratin layer of the epidermis as a result of repeated friction or intermittent pressure.

Bullae can by caused by chemical exposures, heat, or prolonged pressure. Heat and some chemicals will cause bullae if applied to the skin immediately after death. These bullae may be surrounded by a red zone. Such bullae with their red areola may be indistinguishable from immediately antemortem or agonal burns. (Camps 1976).

Pressure bullae occur when a deeply unconscious person lays on an area, as in coma caused by barbiturates or carbon monoxide. Pressure bullae can be attributed to burns by physicians unfamiliar with pressure bullae (Camps, 1976). Bullae may be discrete, as over bony prominences, between the knees and in the axilla. Or, bullae may be diffuse, as when they cover one side of a limb or a wide area of the trunk.

Postmortem bullae can appear in the early stages of putrefaction. There can also be postmortem bullae due to heat and chemical burns. If a person dies in front of a fire or has a hot water bottle applied to them soon after death, areas resembling scalds may appear. Unlike scalds, these areas lack fluid beneath the epidermis. There may be desiccation of the skin and discoloration that looks like early charring. This burning may take place through unaffected clothing.

Diffuse superficial bullae may be caused by the postmortem application of paraffin or petrol to the skin. The associated odor often makes the source clear. These burns occur in some cases of murder, arson, and automobile accidents. Soaking of clothes with petrol may lead to burns (Camps 1976).

calluses and corns. Corns and calluses may be mistaken for burns, and vice versa. Calluses and corns are responses to external pressure and friction. Factors intrinsic to a person that can lead to calluses and corns on the feet include deformities such as bunions, claw toes, or abnormal foot biomechanics. Extrinsic factors would include such things as improper shoes or activity level (Brainard 1991).

Calluses on the hands sometimes have characteristic patterns from the type of work or sports activity a person undergoes. Calluses may be seen on the palmar side of the metacarpal heads (knuckles) of the little and ring fingers of weight lifters. Calluses may be seen across the palmar aspect of the metacarpal heads of all four fingers in persons who ride bicycles in the bent-forward position. Rowers may develop what has been called "pulling-boat hands." Calluses can provide a competitive advantage for gymnasts, but can become painful if they become fissured. (Reichel and Laub 1992).

A corn, or clavus, is a thickening of the stratum corneum due to localized increases in pressure. Corns have sharply defined margins, with dermal ridges having contour deviation because of the corn. Corns are hyperkeratotic with a deep central core. Another type of corn is the soft corn; it is white, flat, and macerated. Soft corns can be found between toes, where there is moisture and pressure (Brainard 1991).

Calluses have diffuse thickening of the epidermis and are caused by repetitive direct or sheer stress to an area. They are most commonly found on the palms and soles. Keratin may proliferate, producing a very prominent callus (Brainard 1991).

16.2 Muscle Injury
A. Effects on muscle of direct and alternating current
A direct current (DC) will often produce one brief stimulation of muscle or nervous tissue. Alternating current (AC) repetitively stimulates nerves and muscles, resulting in a tetanic contraction that may last as long as the contact is continued. A person in this situation may be unable to move, with the hand gripping the current source stimulated into a tight grasp on the source. This gives continued electric current flow through the person. Respiratory muscles may be similarly held in tight contraction, causing respiratory arrest. Strong and sometimes prolonged contractions of muscles can give various degrees of muscle strain and even tears of muscle bodies. Thermal damage may coexist with strains (Somogyi and Tedeschi 1977).

Rupture of skeletal muscle cell membranes is a prominent feature of electric injury (Lee 1991). Muscle damage is due to (1) heating and (2) formation of pores in the cell membrane, called electroporation. Electroporation can result in rupture of the cell membrane (Lee 1991; Gaylor 1988).

With high voltage, muscles may be stimulated before actual contact is made with the conductor because of arcing (Davis 1980; Maclachlan 1930). After such stimulation, the muscles may be sore or severely injured. Tearing of muscle is unusual (Davis 1980, 656). Rupture of tendons is also uncommon because the tensile strength of tendons is stronger than that of muscles (Davis 1980, 656).

Several different outcomes may occur when a person grabs a conductor giving 10 kV AC hand-to-hand voltage. It takes over 0.5 second of such contact before most of the distal forearm cells are heat damaged. However, within 10 to 100 milliseconds, muscles in the current path will contract. The person may be stimulated to grasp the conductor more tightly, making a stronger mechanical contact. Or, the person may be propelled away from the contact. Which of these events occurs depends on the position of the hand relative to the conductor. Most eyewitnesses report the victims being propelled from the conductor, possibly because of generalized muscle contractions. The time of contact is estimated to be about 100 milliseconds or less in such cases (Lee et al. 1992, 57).

B. Detection of muscle injury by blood tests

In rhabdomyolysis (breakdown of muscle tissue), the contents of dead muscle cells are released into the circulation. Destruction of 2 cc (2 grams) of skeletal muscle tissue can give a level of CK (CPK) that is ten times normal (Brumback et al. 1995). Potassium release from damaged muscle cells can lead to hyperkalemia. (Brumback et al. 1995).

Muscle injury due to electrical current, blunt trauma, myocardial infarction, and a variety of other causes can be detected by several different blood tests. The usual blood test used to detect heart or skeletal muscle damage is CK (creatine kinase, also called CPK or creatine phosphokinase). CK is found in skeletal and heart muscle and in the brain. Lesser amounts are found in the intestine and lung. CK values are often high in patients with myocardial infarction, progressive muscular dystrophy, alcoholic myopathy, rhabdomyolysis, delirium tremens, moderate exercise, some infections, large bruises, and intramuscular injections (Henry 1996).

CK exists as a dimer of three possible combinations of M (originally for muscle) and B (originally for brain) chains. About 99 percent of total CK in skeletal muscle is the MM dimer, and a small portion is in the MB form. In cardiac muscle, about 80 percent of the total CK is in the MM form, and 20 percent is in the MB form. Within six hours of the beginning of a myocardial infarction, there will usually be increases in CK-MB, total CK, and the ratio of CB-MB to CK (Henry 1996). Injury to skeletal muscle may release large amounts of CK-MB, but the ratio of CK-MB to total CK should remain normal (usually under 5 percent, depending on the laboratory). Increases in total CK and CK-MB are to be expected with contusions, crush injuries, and damage to skeletal muscle due to electrical injury. More discussion of this topic is found in Chapter 18.

Other new tests are beginning to be used, including serum myoglobin and troponins (Brogan et al. 1996; Gibler et al. 1987). With all these tests, it is important to keep track of the units being used and note the limits of normal for the particular laboratory. Also, it must be remembered that measurements are sometime made of enzyme mass, and at other times of enzyme activity (Bhayana et al. 1990). This may not be obvious because many laboratory tests are reported as so many U (units) or IU (international units). This is much less descriptive than more meaningful notations such as "nanograms per milliliter." Knowing what the "units" are is especially important when calculating the ratio of two different measurements.

C. Detecting the location of deep muscle injury
1. Clinical recognition is difficult

Clinical recognition is difficult because there are often few external signs. High voltage vascular lesions often are associated with a limited cutaneous burn. Vascular injury can lead to hypoxic injury of muscle and other tissues. The degree of deep muscle damage is variable and often not clinically apparent. Arterial pulses may not be palpable because of swelling under crusted tissue or under the fascia surrounding muscle bundles (subeschar or subfascial edema). Deep tissue injury is characteristic of high voltage (over 1,000 volts) alternating current source injuries, such as those due to power lines. Deep tissue injury is much less common with lightning injuries.

Muscle layers adjacent to bone seem to be more vulnerable to electrical injury than more superficial muscles. The initial injury may not be visually apparent. Electrically damaged muscle is often normal in appearance at initial surgical exploration, unless there has been severe heat exposure. Repeat inspections, sometimes involving surgical explorations, may be needed every forty-eight hours. Whether the recognition of additional nonviable tissue at serial debridements represents progressive necrosis or progressive recognition of fatally damaged tissue remains an unresolved question. Current through the body can cause skin and deep tissue injury locally and distant from the contact sites (Lee et al. 1992, 65, 68, 85).

Underlying tissue injury may lead to life-threatening sepsis and loss of limb. Morbidity and mortality may be increased by underestimation of the extent of tissue injury and resultant delayed surgical debridement of nonviable tissue.

2. Detection by arteriography

Hunt et al. (1974) studied eleven men who had sustained electric injury from 500 volts AC or more and had an average total body surface burn of 26 percent. Arteriograms were performed after cardiorespiratory stabilization. Complete occlusion was found in four limbs, partial occlusion in four more, and no occlusion in five others. Additional arterial vascular findings included narrowing, irregularity, beading, and decreased nutrient muscle branches. All patients with injured muscle had moderate to massive subeschar or subfascial edema under unburned skin. Hidden muscle injury was thus common. The decision to amputate was guided in part by the findings at arteriography. When complete vascular occlusion existed, massive tissue necrosis was always present. Partial vascular occlusion was also indicative of muscle necrosis. Arteriographic identification of decreased nutrient muscular branches signified local muscle injury and the need for further surgical exploration.

Although abnormal arteriograms are indicative of muscle necrosis, normal arteriograms do not prove absence of muscle damage. Direct injury to muscle can also occur, leading to muscle necrosis in association with vascular patency. In such cases, diagnostic fasciotomies through eschar or unburned skin permit an accurate assessment of the patient's injury (Hunt et al. 1974).

3. Detection by other imaging studies

Newer imaging methods, such as MRI, can sometimes identify deep muscle necrosis (Nettelblad et al. 1996).

16.3 Bone and Joint Injury

Orthopedic injury related to electrical accidents may be due to a variety of mechanisms. Electric current can stimulate muscles to contract strongly enough to cause a fracture. Secondary trauma refers to indirect mechanisms of injury, such as falls and fires. The recognition of orthopedic injury is sometimes delayed.

A. Mechanisms of orthopedic injury

Violent muscular contractions may lead to the fracture of bones (Tompkins 1990; Baxter 1970). Muscular contractions may be due to direct stimulation by electric current passing through the involved muscle. Contraction of muscles may also be due to seizures that were caused by the electric current (Kelly 1954). Falls associated with electrical injury may also cause fractures (Stueland et al. 1989). When caused by muscular contraction, the processes or tubercles where large muscles are inserted may break off. Frequent fracture sites are the head and neck of the humerus, the ulna, the femoral neck, and spinal processes. Subluxation (an incomplete dislocation) of the shoulder joint may occur (Somogyi and Tedeschi 1977).

B. Delayed recognition of fractures following electrical injury
1. Reasons

Fractures and dislocations due to electrical injury are sometimes recognized weeks or months after injury (Somogyi and Tedeschi 1977, 656). Failure to initially diagnose a fracture may be due to a number of factors (Fish and Ehrhardt 1989) as shown in Table 16.2.

2. Case report. Delayed recognition of bilateral hip fractures

A man was standing next to a dump truck when the bed of the truck contacted a power line carrying approximately 40,000 volts AC. The man fell to the ground and lost consciousness. When he woke, he crawled from the truck and was mentally alert. He was taken to a nearby hospital and then transferred to the burn center at a nearby university hospital. He had a full-thickness 3-cm burn on his left forearm. There were superficial burns on the bottoms of both feet. He had myoglobinuria (muscle breakdown products in the urine), and that was treated with hydration. Two days after the injury, he underwent surgery for his wounds. Due to persistent pain in the groin, x-rays were taken on the third day following injury. He was found to have bilateral displaced hip fractures. These were then repaired surgically. These fractures probably resulted from muscle contractions caused by electric current. In this case, the patient's inability to walk might have been attributed to the fact that both his feet were burned (Tompkins et al. 1990).

3. Case report. Delayed recognition of scapular fracture

An example of a brief delay in recognition of a fracture is given by Silversides (1964). A thirty-two-year-old electrician was squatting on his heels when one hand contacted a conduit. The other contacted a machine with a 550-volt AC difference from the conduit. He had a generalized tetanic muscle contraction. He shot up into an erect posture but was unable to let go with his hands. He remained conscious, but could not call out. He could breathe only with great effort and was extremely frightened. He was sure he was going to die. When the current was shut off, he became aware of a severe pain in his left shoulder. He was transiently mute and could not tell anyone of his pain. After a period of observation in the hospital, a fracture of his left scapula was discovered.

Table 16.1
Mechanisms of Orthopedic Injury

1. Muscular contractions
   a. Stimulated by electrical current
   b. Induced by seizures due to the accident (see the chapter in this book on neurological injury)
2. Secondary trauma
   a. Falls
   b. Thermal injury
   c. Blast effects
   d. Other indirect consequences of an electrical accident

Table 16.2
Reasons for Delayed Recognition of Orthopedic Injury

1. Other nearby injuries that seem to explain the signs and symptoms
2. Failure of injured nerves to transmit pain signals to the brain (peripheral nerve or spinal cord)
3. Abnormal mental status of the patient, as with brain injury or alcohol
4. Distraction of the patient by other painful injuries
5. X-ray films that are of poor quality
6. Fractures and dislocations that characteristically do not show on initial x-ray, but may be suspected clinically

C. Melting of bone

In high voltage accidents, electrothermic effects can result in osteonecrosis and melting of bone tissue. Osseous pearls the size of a pea, grayish white and hollow, may be found on the surface of injured bone (Somogyi and Tedeschi 1977, 657).

D. Spinal fractures

Multiple spinal fractures may be caused by electric injury. Spinal fractures should be suspected in patients with back pain or continued loss of consciousness. Vertebral fractures are more common with low voltage (under 1,000 volts) and alternating current (as compared to direct current).

1. Cervical and thoracic spinal fractures

Layton et al. (1984) reported multiple spinal fractures from electrical injury. A thirty-eight-year-old man was welding in a garage in which puddles of water covered the floor. He contacted a 220-AC power source and suffered respiratory arrest. A coworker administered CPR. When the patient woke, he had no memory of the injury, but had severe neck pain. He had 10-percent body surface area partial-thickness burns of the hands, forearms, right thigh, and scrotum. He was neurologically intact but had a fracture of the spinous process of C2 and compression fractures of C5, T7, and T11. Such fractures could result from electrically induced muscle contractions causing strong extension or flexion of the neck and trunk.

2. Lumbar burst fracture

Lumbar burst fracture occurred in a sixty-two-year-old man who was holding a lamp in his left hand connected by an extension cord to 220 volts AC. He crawled under a floor and over the wet ground below a cellar. He became unconscious for a short time after feeling an electrical shock. He could not let go of the lamp until his wife unplugged the wire. He had a burn on the left hand and felt low back pain. His physician suggested bed rest. He did so; and after nine days, he was referred for further investigation. There were no neurological signs, but plain radiographs showed a fracture of L4 with involvement of the dorsal aspect. Computed tomography showed a burst fracture with a small bony fragment in the spinal canal. He was treated with a plaster corset and did well (van den Brink and van Leeuwen 1995).

E. Injury of the skull

Electrical injury of the skull is uncommon. High voltage arcing is usually the cause of an injury to the skull, and this is often associated with serious brain injury (Somogyi and Tedeschi 1977, 657).

F. Fractures and dislocations of the shoulders

Fractures and dislocations of the shoulders have been reported from electrical injuries received from sources of 110 to 440 volts AC (Stueland et al. 1989). These reports have included cases of bilateral scapular fracture (Beswick et al. 1982), bilateral shoulder dislocations (Carew-McColl 1980), and bilateral anterior fracture-dislocation of the shoulder joints (Salem 1982).

Bilateral humeral fractures from electrically induced muscular spasm occurred when a fifty-seven-year-old male was installing a device into an electrical box containing two 110-volt AC lines (Stueland et al. 1989). His arms were slightly above his shoulders and he was unable to release himself from the current source. A witness pulled him off and he suffered no significant fall and no loss of consciousness. He arrived at the emergency department with bilateral shoulder pain radiating into the upper anterior chest, both arms and both hands. He had paresthesias (numbness and tingling) of the hands. There was a small needle-like wound on the thenar eminence of the left hand and redness of the right dorsal wrist where a watch had been worn. Creatinine kinase (CPK or CK) was normal. There was no myoglobin in the urine, though blood myoglobin was elevated at 206 ng/mL (expected value being less than 90). Paresthesias resolved in two days. He had open reduction and internal fixation of the humeral fractures after four days. In this case electrically induced muscle contractions could have caused the fractures.

References

Burns

Adjutantis, G. and G. Skalos, "The Identification of the Electrical Burn in Cases of Electrocution by the Acroreaction Test," *Journal of Forensic Medicine* 9(3):101–105 (1962).

Al-Alousi, L. M., "Homicide by Electrocution," *Medical Science Law* 30(3):239–246 (1990).

Baxter, Charles R., "Present Concepts in the Management of Major Electrical Injury," *Surgical Clinics of North America* 50(6):1401–1418 (1970).

Brainard, B. J., "Managing Corns and Plantar Calluses," *Physician and Sportsmedicine* 19(12):61–67 (1991).

Camps, Francis E., Anne E. Robinson and Bernard G. B. Lucas, eds. *Gradwohl's Legal Medicine*, 3rd ed. (Chicago: J. Wright, 1976).

Chandrasiri, N., "Electrocution by Dielectric Breaking (Arcing) from Overhead High Tension Cables," *Med Sci Law* 28(3):237–240 (1988).

Cooper, M. A., "Electrical and Lightning Injuries," *Emergency Clinics of North America,* August 1984, 489–501.

Damjanov, Ivan and James Linder, eds., *Anderson's Pathology*, 10th ed. (St. Louis: Mosby, 1996), 106.

Fisher, R. S., "Electrical and Lightning Injuries," in *Medicolegal Investigation of Death: Guidelines for the Application of Pathology to Crime Investigation*, 2nd ed., Werner U. Spitz and Russell S. Fisher, eds. (Springfield, IL: Charles C. Thomas, 1980), 371.

Hunt, J. L., et al., "Vascular Lesions in Acute Electrical Injuries," *Journal of Trauma* 14(6):461–473 (1974).

Jamil, S., R. A. Jones and L. B. McClung, "Arc and Flash Burn Hazards at Various Levels of an Electrical System," *IEEE Transactions on Industry Applications* 33(2):359–366 (1997).

Knight, Bernard, "Electrical Fatalities," in *Forensic Pathology* (NY: Oxford University Press, 1991), 294–306.

Knight, Bernard, *Legal Aspects of Medical Practice* (Edinburgh and NY: Churchill Livingstone, 1976), 124.

Lee, R. H., "The Other Electrical Hazard: Electric Arc Blast Burns," *IEEE Transactions on Industry Applications* IA-18:246–251 (1982).

Mant, A. Keith, ed., *Taylor's Principles and Practice of Medical Jurisprudence* (Edinburgh and NY: Churchill Livingstone, 1984), 272.

Moar, J. J. and J. B. Hunt, "Death from Electrical Arc Flash Burns: A Report of Two Cases," *SAMJ* 71:181–182 (1987).

Nettelblad, H., K. A. Thuomas and F. SjAoberg, "Magnetic Resonance Imaging: A New Diagnostic Aid in the Care of High-Voltage Electrical Burns," *Burns* 22(2):117–119 (1996).

Polson, C. J. and D. J. Gee, *Essentials of Forensic Medicine*, 3rd ed. (Oxford: Pergamon Press, 1973).

Lee, R. C., E. G. Cravalho and J. F. Burke, eds., *Electrical Trauma* (Cambridge: Cambridge University Press, 1992), 121–124.

Reichel, M. and D. A. Laub, "From Acne to Black Heel: Common Skin Injuries in Sports," *Physician and Sportsmedicine* 20(2):111–114 (1992).

Somogyi, E. and C. G. Tedeschi, "Injury by Electrical Force," in *Forensic Medicine: A Study in Trauma and Environmental Hazards,* Tedeschi C. G., W. G. Eckert and L. G. Tedeschi, eds. (Philadelphia: W. B. Saunders, 1977), 645–655 .

Stedman's Electronic Medical Dictionary (Hagerstown, MD: Williams & Wilkins, 1996).

Wright, R. K. and J. H. Davis, "The Investigation of Electrical Deaths: A Report of 220 Fatalities," *Journal of Forensic Sciences* 25:514 (1980).

Muscle injury

Bhayana, V. et al.,"Diagnostic Evaluation of Creatine Kinase-2 Mass and Creatine Kinase-3 and -2 Isoform Ratios in Early Diagnosis of Acute Myocardial Infarction," *Clinical Chemistry* 39:488–495 (1990).

Brogan, G. X. et al., "Improved Specificity of Myoglobin Plus Carbonic Anhydrase Assay versus That of Creatine Kinase-MB for Early Diagnosis of Acute Myocardial Infarction," *Annals of Emergency Medicine* 27:22–28 (1996).

Brumback, R. A., D. L. Feeback and R. W. Leech, "Rhabdomyolysis Following Electrical Injury," *Seminars in Neurology* 15(4):329–334 (1995).

Davis, J. H. "Asphyxial Deaths," in *Modern Legal Medicine, Psychiatry, and Forensic Science*, Curran. W. J., A. L. McGarry and C. S. Petty, eds. (Philadelphia: F. A. Davis, 1980), 249–266.

Gaylor, D.C., K. Prakah-Asante and R. C. Lee,. "Significance of Cell Size and Tissue Structure in Electrical Treatment," *J. Theor. Biol.* 3:223–237 (1988).

Gibler, W. B. et al., "Myoglobin as an Early Indicator of Acute Myocardial Infarction," *Annals of Emergency Medicine* 16:851–856 (1987).

Henry, J. B., *Clinical Diagnosis and Management by Laboratory Methods*, 19th ed. (Philadelphia: W. B. Saunders, 1996).

Hunt, J. L. et al., "Vascular Lesions in Acute Electrical Injuries," *Journal of Trauma* 14(6):461–473 (1974).

Lee, R. C., E. G. Cravalho and J. F. Burke, eds., *Electrical Trauma* (Cambridge: Cambridge University Press, 1992). 57.

Maclachlan, W. "Electric Shock: Interpretation of Field Notes," *J. Ind. Hyg.* 12:291 (1930).

Nettelblad, H., K. A. Thuomas and F. SjAoberg, "Magnetic Resonance Imaging: A New Diagnostic Aid in the Care of High-Voltage Electrical Burns," *Burns* 22(2):117–119 (1996).

Bone and joint injury

Beswick, D. R., S. D. Morse and A. U. Barns, "Bilateral Scapular Fractures from Low-Voltage Electrical Injury," *Annals of Emergency Medicine* 11:676–7 (1982).

Carew-McColl, M., "Bilateral Shoulder Dislocations Caused by Electrical Shock," *Br. J. Clin. Pract.* 34:251–4 (1980).

Fish, R. M. and M. E. Ehrhardt, *Preventing Emergency Malpractice* (Oradell, NJ: Medical Economics Books, 1989).

Kelly, J. P., "Fractures Complicating Electro-Convulsive Therapy and Chronic Epilepsy," *J. Bone Joint Surgery* 36B:70–9 (1954).

Layton, T. R. et al., "Multiple Spine Fractures from Electric Injury," *JBCR* 5(5):373–375 (1984).

Salem, M. I., "Bilateral Anterior Fracture-Dislocation of the Shoulder Joints Due to Severe Electrical Shock," *Injury* 14:361–3 (1982).

Silversides, J., "The Neurological Sequelae of Electrical Injury," *Canadian Medical Association Journal* 91:195–204 (1964).

Somogyi, Endre and C. G. Tedeschi, "Injury by Electrical Force," in *Forensic Medicine: A Study in Trauma and Environmental Hazards,* Tedeschi C. G., W. G. Eckert and L. G. Tedeschi, eds. (Philadelphia: W. B. Saunders, 1977).

Stueland, D.T. et al., "Bilateral Humeral Fractures from Electrically Induced Muscular Spasm," *Journal of Emergency Medicine* 7:457–459 (1989).

Tompkins, G. S., R. C. Henderson and Peterson, "Bilateral Simultaneous Fractures of the Femoral Neck: Case Report," *Journal of Trauma* 30(11):1415–1416 (1990).

van den Brink, W. A. and O. van Leeuwen, "Lumbar Burst Fracture due to Low Voltage Shock," *Acta Orthop. Scand.* 66(4):374–375 (1995).

Chapter 17

Electrical Injuries to the Nervous System and Sensory Organs

17.1 Brain Injury

This chapter describes mechanisms of brain injury, movement disorders, and case studies from the medical literature. See also the chapters in this book on fetal injury and psychological effects.

A. Mechanisms of brain injury

The brain can be injured in a variety of ways (Patel and Lo 1993; Stanley and Suss 1985). The case reports and research described below explain and illustrate some of these mechanisms of injury.

B. Involuntary movement disorders

Involuntary movement disorders are rare and have followed lightning and nonlightning electrical injuries (O'Brien 1995). These disorders can be classified as

- psychogenic,
- due to injury of the central nervous system, or
- due to injury of the peripheral nervous system.

Table 17.1
Mechanisms of Brain Injury

1. Thermal destruction of brain tissue from
    A. Current flowing through the head
    B. Fire
2. Hypoxic brain injury from
    A. Temporary respiratory or cardiac dysfunction
    B. Carbon monoxide or other gases
3. Vascular occlusion (blockage giving stroke) from
    A. Immediate vasoconstriction
    B. Intimal injury with later thrombosis
    C. Thrombosis secondary to trauma or systemic changes
    D. Dislodging of thrombus to give an embolus
4. Mechanical trauma to the head
5. Blast effects from nearby electric arc (may be only relevant for currents over 10,000 amperes. See chapter on Psychological Effects).
6. Increased intracranial pressure (sometimes increasing over hours to days) due to
    A. Cerebral edema
    B. Intracranial bleeding
    C. Obstruction of cerebral spinal fluid flow

---

1. Psychogenic cases

In psychogenic cases of involuntary movement disorder, signs and symptoms have characteristics that do not seem to have an anatomic or physiological basis. For example, the frequency and amplitude of a tremor may fluctuate greatly. Similarly, nonanatomic "trigger points" may release flexion deformity in a limb in a patient with tremor or dystonia. In addition, radiographic and electrophysiologic abnormalities will not be found that explain the problem (O'Brien 1995).

2. Central nervous system movement disorders

Central nervous system movement disorders are usually due to abnormal excitation and inhibition within the basal ganglia or their afferent pathways. This can be caused by ischemic damage. Such damage may produce jerky involuntary movements of the proximal limb, called hemiballism. More distal writhing movements are called athetosis. Damage to other areas in the brain can cause slow movements or rigidity

(O'Brien 1995). Abnormalities characteristic of strokes anywhere in the brain can be caused by physical or ischemic damage induced by electrical injury.

3. Peripheral nervous system movement disorders

Peripheral nervous system movement disorders may cause dystonia (postural abnormality) or sensory loss that leads to abnormal movements (O'Brien 1995).

C. High voltage contact to the head

When a high voltage line contacts the head directly or through arcing, physical injury to the brain often shows on CT scan or autopsy. If the contact is brief, there may be little or no injury to the brain. In such cases, loss of consciousness may occur, with or without seizures. Induction of seizures is discussed in the chapter of this book on Conscious Awareness During Fatal Electrical Injury.

D. Case reports

1. Brain injury associated with burns from high voltage contact to the head

Sure and Kleihues report a case of intracerebral venous thrombosis and hematoma secondary to high voltage brain injury (Sure and Kleihues 1997). In this case, a nineteen-year-old male was on top of a railway carriage in Sweden. He was hit by an arc from, and may have directly contacted, a 15,000-volt, 16.67-Hz overhead railway cable. He fell from the top of the carriage and landed on the ground about nine feet below. His clothes were ignited; they were extinguished after about five minutes. He was initially alert and able to communicate. He complained of a severe headache and lost consciousness thirty minutes after the injury. Computed tomography of the brain done four hours after injury showed an 8 cm × 4 cm × 4 cm intercerebral hematoma, subarachnoid hemorrhage, and a subgaleal hematoma. Computed tomography of the brain done one and four days later showed progressive edema of the brain. The patient died eight days after the injury, most likely from brainstem herniation. Autopsy showed thrombosis of both intraparenchymal and subarachnoidal veins, but no thrombosis of the venous sinuses. The authors suggest that the venous thrombosis was a consequence of local high temperature electro-coagulation of vessel.

2. Brain and spinal cord injury associated with burns

Grube et al. (1990) studied ninety patients with burns due to electrical injury. These patients had a variety of brain and spinal cord injuries. Eleven of the twenty-two patients with low voltage injury had neurologic symptoms, usually transient, including: seizures (one), motor weakness (four), decreased sensation (five), left hemiparesis (one), and loss of consciousness (four). In the high voltage group of sixty-four patients, eight required CPR before admission. Of these, three never regained consciousness and died. Loss of consciousness occurred in twenty-nine of the sixty-four high voltage-injured patients. Twenty of these patients became completely asymptomatic, while six had evidence of persistent or delayed central neuropathy ranging from amnesia for the accident to global hyperreflexia with aphasia and bilateral clonus (rapid alternation of contraction and relaxation of muscles).

3. Delayed onset of brain and spinal cord injury following high voltage contact from hand to foot

A ten-year-old boy used fishing line as a kite string (Jackson et al. 1965). This line crossed a 75,000-volt AC transmission cable. The child was spun around and had transient loss of consciousness. His clothes burst into flame, and he suffered second and third-degree burns of the arms, legs, and abdomen. There were electrical wounds in the right hand and left heel. Starting the second week, he received physiotherapy including range of motion exercises. He was able to move all extremities very well.

He continued with burn care, apparently doing well, until seven weeks after the injury. At that time he started to hallucinate, was confused, and became uncooperative. An EEG (electroencephalogram) was diffusely abnormal. A quadriparesis also developed, with motor and sensory loss below the level of C7 (base of the neck). Eyes showed a diffuse retinitis, blurring of disc margins, and haziness of retinae. There was no definite papilledema, hemorrhages, or exudates (fluid accumulation inside the eye). Lumbar puncture was essentially normal. Electrolyte concentrations were abnormal, with sodium at 127 meq/L (moderately low), potassium at

6.9 meq/L (dangerously high) and chloride at 92 meq/L. These were corrected, and hydrocortisone was given. In two days, his mental status improved, but the quadriparesis did not improve. Repeat lumbar puncture nine weeks after the injury showed fine particulate matter in the spinal fluid with an increasing initial pressure. Total protein was 81 mg percent. There were only four white blood cells (WBC) in the spinal fluid. Respiratory insufficiency developed and he was put on a respirator. Despite this he died seventy days after his initial injury.

Pathological examination of the brain showed only diffuse swelling. There was no brain abscess, meningitis, or meningeal inflammation (inflammation of the membranes covering the spinal cord-the dura, arachnoid, and pia). The spinal cord had a segmental level of marked myelopathy (disease) and myelomalacia (softening) at the T4 level; the cord was very soft and even necrotic in places. There was little gross reaction suggesting meningeal inflammation or infection. There was no histological evidence of acute infection or trauma. The changes resembled those seen in recent anoxia of the spinal cord.

4. Intracranial vasospasm and thrombosis

Patel and Lo (1985) describe a thirty-one-year-old man who was repairing a microwave oven. He touched a capacitor (capable of holding an electric charge). The oven had been unplugged for three minutes. The exact voltage on the capacitor was unknown, but it was thought to be 800 volts. The patient reported a shock-like sensation in both arms and his head, though the current pathway was thought to be from the right arm to the legs. He lost consciousness, and a coworker later found him sitting in a dazed condition. The patient had minimal burns, a severe headache, and redness in his right arm. His wife noticed periodic confusion and deterioration of recent memory. Physical examination showed a right visual field defect, right facial numbness, and a mild numbness and weakness of he right arm. The left foot had an abnormal Babinski reflex. The CT scan of the head was normal. An EEG was abnormal, and a cerebral angiogram showed a thrombus (blood clot) at the distal end of the vein of Labbe (a superficial vein traversing the temporoparietal cortex) on the left projecting into the transverse venous sinus. There was also evidence of some thrombus in the left internal cerebral vein and the left vein of Galen. A six-month trial of warfarin (anticoagulant) gave no improvement. Over the next two years, there was some gradual improvement, but the patient continued to have trouble with an ataxic gait, headache, memory problems, poor concentration and personality change (being withdrawn and depressed). The authors discuss a number of mechanisms by which the thrombosis and other problems may have arisen. These mechanisms include hypoxia, vasospasm, and blood vessel (intimal) injury. He may have been thrown back, receiving mechanical trauma to the head.

5. Delayed onset of tremor, rigidity, mental status and memory problems

Alexander (1938) describes a thirty-four-year-old healthy man who contacted 600 volts AC when changing a headlight on a street car. The contact was from hand to hand. At the time of the electrical contact, he became unconscious, fell, and developed myoclonic convulsions of the face. He woke after twelve hours, but he was drowsy, and somewhat disoriented. In addition, at times he was delirious and excited. He had retrograde amnesia for the accident. There was persistence of the myoclonic movements of the face, involving the facial and masticatory muscles, bilateral, but more on the left. During the half year following the injury, the victim gradually developed tremor at rest, rigidity, and some loss of movements of the right hand and arm. During this same half year, the mental changes became more definite and eventually stabilized. He had decrease of spontaneity, mental dullness, slowness, lack of productivity, circumstantiality, disturbance of memory for recent events, and difficulty in finding words. These changes remained essentially unaltered during the next three years of close observation. There were, however, changes in the function of the pupils of the eyes. There were also disturbances of eye movements (convergence abnormalities, nystagmus, and exophoria).

The mechanism of injury is not clear in this case. Possibilities include sequelae of head trauma when he fell and hypoxic injury from an inadequate airway during or after his seizure. The case occurred long before CT scans were available.

E. Conclusions

A variety of mechanisms of brain injury are clearly possible. Still, in some of the cases, it is not clear how or why the injury occurred. Modern imaging techniques, including CT and MRI, will no doubt prove useful in understanding electrical injury to the brain.

17.2 Spinal Cord Injury

Spinal cord injuries from electric accidents are often incomplete and may or may not be associated with vertebral fractures. The level of spinal cord damage often does not correspond to the apparent path of the current. In one series (Baxter 1970), only two of twelve patients with physiologic spinal cord transection had the point of entry of electric current near the spinal column. Spinal cord lesions from electric injury may lead to spastic paresis or motor changes (with or without accompanying sensory deficits), muscle imbalance, abnormal gait, impotence, paraparesis (weakness of the legs), or bladder dysfunction (Baxter 1970; Varghese et al. 1986). Motor involvement may progress for years after injury. Symptoms of spinal cord transection, sympathetic dystrophy, or cerebral dysfunction may appear years after injury (Baxter 1970). The study by Varghese at the end of this chapter describes a 4.3-percent incidence of delayed spinal injury in patients with serious electric burns.

A. Cord lesions from hand-to-hand electric contact

Cord lesions from hand to hand electric contact in humans causes lesions between the fifth and seventh cervical segment: softening with myelin degeneration, small hemorrhages, and cavitating lesions. These lesions give a variety of permanent functional deficits (Somogyi and Tedeschi 1977, 659; Alexander 1938a,b).

B. Delayed onset of spinal cord and brain dysfunction: Multiple case listing

In 1968, Farrell and Starr listed twenty-three previously reported cases of delayed neurological sequelae, plus one case of their own. Information about the twenty-four cases is summarized in Table 17.2. "Extremity dysfunction" refers to atrophy, paralysis, or paresis of an extremity, or part of an extremity. Although not stated for many of the patients, most of the voltages (other than lightning) are probably AC rather than DC.

Table 17.2 Delayed Onset of Spinal Cord and Brain Dysfunction			
Syndrome	**Number of Cases**	**Voltage**	**Delay of Onset**
Extremity dysfunction months (Lightning)	11	120–5,000 V	Days to 4
Atrophy of shoulder muscles	5	500–1,000 V	Days to 1 year
Amyotrophic lateral sclerosis-like picture	2	200 V, 220 V	10 months, 15 months
Right hemiparesis with aphasia	1	Unknown	9 months
Spinal atrophic paralysis	2	110 V 18,000 V	3 weeks 24 months
Left basal ganglion	1	Lightning	3 weeks
Basilar thrombosis	1	Unknown	3 weeks
Transverse myelopathy	1	75,000 V	2 months

C. Case reports

1. Delay (several days) of onset of spinal cord damage from high-voltage injury

A thirty-four-year-old man was working barefoot on the iron roof of a shed. His head contacted an overhead transmission line with 15.5 kV AC to ground (Petty and Parkin 1986). A circuit breaker tripped. The circuit breaker was set to operate on a ground leak of 5 amps for 0.6 second. Thus, the minimal power delivered to the patient was 77.5 kW for 0.6 second, assuming the shed represented a good connection to earth. He was thrown about twelve feet to the ground and was rendered unconscious. Several hours later, he was conscious but disoriented and confused. He had a full-thickness skin burn several inches in diameter at the vertex of the skull as well as burns on the soles of the feet. There were no abnormal focal neurological signs. He had a fracture dislocation of T4 on T5. During the next few days, he developed shortness of breath. On day six he became incontinent of urine and was weak in the legs. Myelography showed no spinal cord compression at the level of the thoracic fracture. The weakness progressed rapidly over several hours and spread to the arms and respiratory muscles. Lumbar puncture was normal. The weakness spread to involve all muscle groups, including those of the face. Mentation was normal. The patient required intubation. Nerve conduction studies showed a neuropathy. Return of strength was first noted on day twenty-six in his neck and facial muscles.

2. Delayed (one week) spinal cord damage

A previously healthy twenty-three-year-old man cut through a cable carrying 33,000 volts with a hacksaw held in his left hand (Holbrook et al. 1970). When he awoke, he was able to move all limbs and get out of bed without assistance. He had superficial burns typical of an electrical flash injury over 15 percent of his body surface. The burn involved the face, front of the neck and chest, and part of the right thigh. There were localized areas of full-thickness burns suggesting direct electrical contact on both hands, the right leg, and the epigastric region. Eight days after the injury, he developed partial anesthesia of the left thumb and index finger. At twelve days following the injury, a spastic paresis (partial paralysis with spasticity) developed in both legs with extensor plantar responses and sensory impairment of all sensory modalities of the legs. By day fourteen, the weakness had spread to the arms.

The patient's condition was its worst twenty-one days after the injury, with almost total paralysis and sensory loss in all limbs. Tendon reflexes were increased in the legs and absent in the arms. There was severe wasting of the intrinsic muscles of the hands (interossei). The patient maintained normal control of bowel, bladder, and breathing. His condition improved, with sensation returning before motor function. At thirty-five days post injury, he could raise his legs from the bed. At fifty-six days, he could stand unsupported. With intensive physical therapy, improvement continued. At four months post injury, he could dress himself unaided. At that time, he complained of blurred vision and was found to have developed bilateral cataracts (not noted on repeated eye examinations earlier following the injury). At 160 days after the injury, he was able to walk with two sticks.

This was a case of delayed myelopathy (spinal cord disorder). Mechanical trauma to the spinal cord was ruled out because of repeated cervical x-rays and the fact that there had been no evidence of a block, red blood cells, or xanthochromia (old dissolved red blood cells) on lumbar puncture.

3. Spinal atrophic paralysis two years after injury

A sixty-seven-year-old man was injured by an 18,000-volt, 60 Hz line The man was a non-insulin dependent diabetic, and the accident occurred in 1964. He was standing on a rock guiding one end of a metal pipe with his right hand. The other end of the pipe hit the high-tension line. He remembers a loud bang, and witnesses told him he was thrown four feet from the rock. He was dazed for a few seconds, but continued working immediately. He felt "shaky" for the rest of the day. The next day he developed right arm and interscapular pain. A physician found burns on the right palm and lateral aspect of the left little toe. These were minor and healed without complications. He received several injections of local anesthetic around the right shoulder. Over the week following the injury, the patient developed minimal weakness of the left leg that did not progress.

Two years after the electric injury, he experienced lightning-like pains starting in the low back, radiating around the left hip, and going down the medial aspect of the left leg to the ankle. The pains lasted twenty minutes and occurred about six times a day. Also, the same area of his leg was numb. An orthopedist noted the left thigh to be smaller than the right. Lumbar spine films revealed minimal osteoarthritis. The weakness progressed to the point of his not being able to completely extend the left knee on stepping forward. Twenty-seven months after the injury, he developed twitching in the muscles of the left thigh. There were no problems with voiding or defecation, and a lumbar myelogram was normal. A diabetic amyotrophy or radiculopathy did not seem likely since the spinal fluid protein was normal and there was no evidence of slowed nerve conduction. It was concluded that this patient had developed spinal atrophic paralysis as a result of the electric injury two years earlier (Farrell and

Starr 1968). However it has been argued that this patient actually had classical unilateral diabetic amyotrophy (Wilbourn 1995).

4. Incomplete delayed (few days to four weeks) quadriparesis and para-paresis

Five electric accident patients developed incomplete delayed quadriparesis and paraparesis (Varghese et al. 1986). The neurological deficits were detected from a few days to four weeks after injury. Motor deficits predominated, but there was also sensory involvement. The cases were found in a sample of 116 cases of electrical accidents among 1,206 burn patients admitted to Kansas University Medical Center. This is an incidence of delayed spinal injury in patients with serious electric burns of about 4.3 percent. All patients had incomplete lesions. Two of them had quadriparesis, and three patients had paraparesis.

5. Thoracic disc herniation with paraplegia

A forty-one-year-old man received an electric injury when moving a scaffold along the ground. The scaffold struck an overhead 11,000-volt transmission line. The man remembered being shaken several times. He was spun around and was transiently unconscious. On admission to the hospital, he was conscious and oriented with a normal neurological examination except for right facial palsy, right miosis (small pupil), and palpebral ptosis (drooping eyelid). His extremities had motor function. There was normal sensation in the extremities except for an area of third-degree burn. There was a full-thickness 15 × 10 cm burn at the right submandibular and lateral cervical area and a penetrating orifice in the submaxillary gland with drainage of saliva. There was edema surrounding this area with displacement of the oral cavity and oropharynx with minor vocal cord edema. There were large wounds of both hands and feet. There was edema and necrosis of the right leg and foot musculature, second and third degree burns on both forearms, the right thigh and knee, and a third degree burn on the anterior chest over which he was wearing a medal. EKG and laboratory tests were normal except for elevated creatine kinase (CPK or CK), leukocytosis (high white blood cell count), and low potassium.

Some hours after admission, he developed airway obstruction requiring intubation and ventilator support. On the seventh day after admission, he became paraplegic. MRI showed posteromedial disc herniation at the T6–T7 level with anterior spinal cord compression. He was treated with intravenous steroids. Two weeks after the injury, he started to regain motor function. One year after the injury, he had almost complete neurologic recovery in both legs although a new MRI showed persistent disc herniation (Vazquez et al., 1994).

17.3 Peripheral Nerves
A. Mechanisms of electric injury to peripheral nerves
Nerve injury from electrical current may be due to several different mechanisms (Dendooven et al. 1990). These mechanisms include thermal injury, mechanical trauma to nerve tissue, vascular injury, and cell membrane injury, including electroporation. Vascular spasm can be caused by heating. Blood vessels can undergo thrombosis, necrosis, or hemorrhage.

1. Direct thermal injury
Direct thermal injury occurs when electrical energy is converted into heat. The amount of heat energy produced is calculated by $Q = I^2(R)(t)$, where Q is the energy in joules, I is the current in amperes, R is the resistance to current flow in ohms, and t is the time in seconds. In reality, these quantities usually change over time. For example, with burning, the resistance may change, leading to changes in the current.

2. Vascular injury can cause delayed peripheral nerve and spinal cord injury
Delayed peripheral nerve lesions can be caused by vascular thrombosis, hemorrhage, and resultant alteration in blood flow. This leads to ischemia (lack of oxygen) with later fibrosis (scarring) of structures around the nerves. This in turn leads to further progressive loss of nerve function. The resulting neurological symptoms develop from a few weeks to several years after the accident. These mechanisms of injury are thought to be especially important in the spinal cord. Medullary lesions (near the center of the spinal cord) can give a clinical picture similar to amyotrophic lateral sclerosis (including progressive development of spastic paralysis), transverse myelitis, or ascending paralysis. Such delayed nerve lesions are usually irreversible (Dendooven 1990).

3. Mechanical trauma

Mechanical trauma to nerves can be due to tetanic muscle spasms, fractures of bones, falls, and other sharp or blunt mechanical forces.

4. Cell membrane injury: Electroporation

Cellular injury is often produced both by (1) heating and (2) electroporation of cell membranes. The relative contributions of these mechanisms are dependent on the duration of electric current passage, the geometry of the cells, their location, and other factors. If the contact is brief with little time for heating, nonthermal mechanisms of cell injury will likely be most important. Thus, tissue can be injured in the absence of burns (Lee et al. 1988). If the contact is much longer, heat injury will predominate (Lee 1991; Lee et al. 1995).

Putting a relatively low voltage across a small area of tissue can injure that tissue because the electric field is concentrated in that area. Electrical injuries are frequently classified as low or high voltage. However, analysis of electrical trauma suggests a sometimes more relevant injury classification (Capelli-Schellpfeffer et al. 1995). This classification takes into account the electric field. The electric field is the spatial gradient of voltage (i.e., volts per unit length). For example, when a line mechanic is in contact with a 20,000-V power line, the magnitude of the electric field in his body is expected to be roughly 10,000 V/m (volts per meter). Using conventional medical terminology, this would be classified as a high-voltage accident based on the exposure to 20,000 volts. By comparison, the electric field established when a child chews on a power cord that allows oral contact with a 120-V household appliance cord is also about 10,000 V/m. Contact points are separated by relatively short distances. Therefore, the imposed field strengths are large. Field strength and mechanism of injury from electricity are similar with the appliance cord contact to a child's lips and a line mechanic's contact with 20,000 V. However, the volume and site of tissue injured are different.

B. Specific peripheral nerve lesions

Some specific peripheral nerve lesions and effects seen following contact with electrical power sources are described by Dendooven et al. (1990). Contact with the palmar side of the wrist most commonly leads to injury of the median and ulnar nerves. Peripheral polyneuropathy may occur with decreased motor nerve conduction velocities due to demyelination. In addition, plexus lesions (injury to a group of nerves) may occur, especially in the brachial plexus (that supplies the arm). Entrapment syndromes involve pressure on nerves caused by factors such as swelling and tissue contracture due to scarring. Appearance of the syndrome may therefore be delayed in some cases. Spinal cord lesions can cause what seems to be peripheral nerve dysfunction.

Partial injury to peripheral nerve sensory axons often has the paradoxical effect of inducing sensory disturbances: paresthesias (numbness or tingling) and chronic neuropathic pain. A partially injured (as compared to completely sectioned) sensory neuron may respond to weak stimulation by causing intense pain. Injured axons can become the source of abnormal spontaneous discharges. Abnormal impulses generated can be conducted through the spinal cord to the brain where they are interpreted as originating in the tissue originally served by the intact nerve (Devor 1991).

C. Case example of delayed peripheral nerve injury

A six-year-old boy inserted an opened metal paper clip into a 220-volt AC electrical outlet using the thumb and index fingers of both hands. Initially, there was "mild erythema and edema," but no burns on the skin. After a few weeks, he developed numbness and weakness in both hands. Nerve conduction studies demonstrated median nerve injury (Parano et al. 1996).

17.4 Reflex Sympathetic Dystrophy and Causalgia
A. RSD is a syndrome

Reflex sympathetic dystrophy (RSD) is a syndrome, or set of signs and symptoms, that occur together. A variety of signs and symptoms can be associated with RSD, with considerable variation from patient to patient. RSD involves injury to different parts of the sympathetic nervous system and sometimes other structures. Exactly which nerves are injured, and where those nerves are, will influence the signs and symptoms that occur.

Signs and symptoms that are not uniform and rigidly defined characterize many, if not most, medical conditions. As a result, most people are familiar with the concept of medical conditions giving different effects in different persons. For example, a patient with a "stroke" may have one or more of the following: weakness of the right side of the body; trouble speaking; a slight limp, trouble swallowing food; or permanent coma. This is because different parts of the nervous system are affected in various persons with strokes.

Even with a condition like appendicitis, where the anatomy and physiology are relatively constant, there are great variations in signs and symptoms. Persons with appendicitis may or may not have each of the following: fever, elevated white blood cell count, vomiting, mid abdominal pain before onset of localized pain, marked tenderness, and loss of appetite.

B. Criteria for diagnosing reflex sympathetic dystrophy

Reflex sympathetic dystrophy (RSD) is a syndrome of posttraumatic pain and sympathetic nervous system aberration (Webster et al. 1991). Signs and symptoms of RSD at various times or stages of the disease can include muscle spasm, rapid or slowed hair and nail growth, vasospasm, muscle atrophy, osteoporosis, hypersensitivity to cold, edema, joint stiffness, and flexor tendon contractions (Hendler et al. 1994; Greipp and Thomas 1994).

The diagnosis of RSD depends primarily on clinical assessment. Unfortunately, laboratory tests are not useful in most cases (Shelton et al. 1990, 517).

Veldman et al. (1993) gave criteria for patients who would be considered to have RSD for the purposes of their study. Their criteria are listed in Table 17.3.

C. Types of nerves affected in reflex sympathetic dystrophy

In RSD, it is mostly nerves in the sympathetic nervous system that are affected. There may also be some influence on RSD from the spinal cord (Teasell et al. 1994), which is part of the central nervous system. RSD usually has little or no direct effect on motor nerves (tested by EMG) or sensory nerves (tested by sensory latency or conduction velocity studies). Nerve conduction studies test sensory and motor nerves, not sympathetic nerves. Therefore, normal nerve conduction studies do not make the diagnosis of RSD less likely.

In RSD, an overactive sympathetic nervous system apparently is involved. Reflex sympathetic dystrophy results from "trauma or endog-

---

Table 17.3
Criteria for Diagnosing Reflex Sympathetic Dystrophy,
According to Veldman et al.

1. Presence of at least four of:
   Unexplained diffuse pain
   Difference in skin color relative to other limb
   Diffuse edema
   Difference in skin temperature relative to other limb
   Limited active range of motion
2. Occurrence or increase of above signs and symptoms after use
3. Above signs and symptoms present in an area larger than the area of primary injury

---

enous irritation of the sympathetic peripheral nervous system and its interaction with somatic afferent fibers" (Shelton et al. 1990, 519).

Teasell et al. (1994) state:

> There are many theories regarding the pathogenesis of Reflex Sympathetic Dystrophy which involve peripheral and central mechanisms. Nevertheless, the disease remains an enigma. Because of the characteristic skin mottling, edema, and vasomotor changes, Reflex Sympathetic Dystrophy has long been considered a manifestation of sympathetic nervous system dysfunction. This relationship is supported by the frequent alleviation of Reflex Sympathetic Dystrophy symptoms by sympathetic blockade, particularly in the initial stage of this disease . . . A positive response to sympathetic nervous system blockade is considered by some to be an important diagnostic criterion, although it may be too variable in Reflex Sympathetic Dystrophy to be considered reliable.

D. Skin lesions in RSD

The most common skin lesion found in RSD is an area that is red and appears to be burnt (Greipp and Thomas 1994). A variety of other skin lesions may occur in RSD. There can be a generalized rash, or small multiple eruptions. Crater-like ulcerations also occur. Wide areas of skin rash on the forearm or leg are characteristic of RSD and may result from trauma to a small area of a finger or toe. Areas that appeared to be infected are also common.

Differentiation of RSD-related skin disorders from infectious conditions may be difficult (Veldman 1993, 1014). Patients may be given antibiotics and undergo surgical procedures such as incision and drainage because of presumed infection. The inflammatory reaction associated with RSD resembles infection and is not accompanied by leucocytosis (high white blood cell count) or fever. However, the same is often true of localized infections.

E. Delayed onset of reflex sympathetic dystrophy
Delayed onset of symptoms in reflex sympathetic dystrophy is usual. The onset may be sudden, but usually occurs several weeks to many months after the initial injury (Webster 1991, 1541; Demun 1993; Bonezzi et al. 1991; Shantha 1991).

F. RSD following electric injury
Rosenberg (1989) describes a nineteen-year-old man received a "jolt" when he touched a phone booth with his right leg and left hand. He reported pain on the volar aspect (palm side) of his left forearm. Electromyography (EMG) studies done two and twenty-one days after the trauma were normal, despite continued pain. Four months after the incident, he was seen because of persistent burning, numbness, hyperpathia, and difficulty in moving the fingers. His left hand was edematous. He improved with stellate ganglion block (injection of anesthetic to block sympathetic nerve fibers).

Demun (1993) describes a thirty-seven-year-old female touching a 120-volt AC appliance. She "immediately" released her grip when she felt the shock. During the next five days, she noted a progressive onset of paresthesia (numbness and tingling) and swelling of her right hand. There was no burn injury. Over the next two months, there was progression of the paresthesia and swelling of her right hand.

Tarsy et al. (1994) describe (in their case number 1) a twenty-nine-year-old man who received an electrical shock, but no skin burns from 110-volt AC power lines. He was diagnosed as having Reflex Sympathetic Dystrophy with problems including pain and edema of the hand. Nerve conduction studies were normal.

Bonezzi et al. (1991) published an article "Reflex Sympathetic Dystrophy Following Electric Shock: Description of a Clinical Case." A forty-seven-year-old man was injured on his left arm by contact with a 380-volt switch. A few hours later, he had burning pain, dysesthesia, weakness, and motor impairment of the arm. During subsequent months the symptoms did not change except for the appearance of signs of autonomic nervous system dysfunction, including hyperhidrosis, edema, atrophy of the skin and nails, and excessive sweating. One year later, he improved with sympathetic nerve blockades.

G. RSD following lightning injury

Autonomic nervous system problems, including RSD, can follow lightning injury (Cohen, 1995). Cases of causalgia and RSD are described in Section 9.6.

H. Causalgia due to electric current

Causalgia is often considered to be a type of RSD. Many of the causes, signs, and symptoms of RSD and causalgia are similar. Causalgia, however, involves definable damage to a nerve. Causalgia is characterized by severe pain, often of a burning character. In a clinical report of forty-five patients with major electric burn injuries, fifteen patients developed causalgia (Baxter 1970, 1415; Demun 1993). This high incidence of causalgia indicates the sensitivity of the autonomic nervous system to injury.

Shantha (1991) reports on two telephone operators who developed severe causalgia after being struck by lightning through their telephone headsets (see Section 9C).

I. Abnormal response to cold in RSD

Limb temperatures, microcirculatory dynamics, and thermoregulatory behavior are altered in reflex sympathetic dystrophy (Cooke et al. 1993). As a result, cold intolerance is characteristic of reflex sympathetic dystrophy. Vasospastic attacks of white or blue digits may also be experienced and suggest a diagnosis of Raynaud's phenomenon that has developed because of the RSD (Fitzpatrick et al. 1993).

J. Edema (swelling) caused by electrical injury and RSD

Edema can be caused by electrical injury in the absence of RSD. Electrical injury to lymphatics (that drain lymph fluid) or veins (that drain blood) from an area would be expected to cause edema.

Edema can be caused by reflex sympathetic dystrophy in two different ways, as explained below: (1) By increasing vascular permeability (allowing fluid and large molecules to enter the tissues from the blood); (2) by impairing vasomotor reflex responses (constriction of blood vessels) that normally prevent swelling.

In reflex sympathetic dystrophy, there is increased vascular permeability for macromolecules, similar to that which occurs in inflammation (Oyen et al. 1993). This means that large molecules leak out of the blood stream into the tissues of the affected area. Water will follow the large molecules. An inflammatory-like process would explain the clinical findings of edema, swelling, erythema, and impaired function sometimes seen in RSD.

Impaired vasomotor reflex responses. These sympathetic dysfunctions could explain the limb edema that occurs in reflex sympathetic dystrophy. In the hand, cutaneous resistance vessels, arterio-venous shunts, and veins are richly innervated with sympathetic vasoconstrictor nerves (Rosen et al. 1987, 307). Some of the actions of these nerves are deficient in patients with reflex sympathetic dystrophy.

The vasoconstrictor response to an increase in venous pressure represents a mechanism to maintain capillary pressure and filtration within normal limits. The oedema formation in patients suffering from the sympathetic dystrophies may partly be due to a defect in this protective mechanism. A normal vasomotor activity will promote optimal fluid balance across the capillary wall, and it may be assumed that this balance is disturbed in patients with sympathetic dystrophies in such a way that oedema is formed (Rosen et al. 1987, 308).

Edema can be caused by sympathetic nerve dysfunction or damage. The effect of venous pressure elevation upon capillary filtration rate in the limb was studied in six chronically sympathectomized patients and compared to five healthy controls. "The results suggested that a local sympathetic veno-arteriolar (axon) reflex plays a dominant role for the reduced increase in net capillary filtration rate during large increases in venous pressure. The local axon reflex may therefore act as an edema protecting factor" (Henriksen et al. 1983).

K. Nerve entrapment: A sometimes-late complication of RSD

Nerve entrapment occurs when a nerve is compressed. This usually occurs in certain anatomic locations where a nerve is in a relatively confined space, such as the carpal tunnel at the wrist and at several other places in the arm (Howard 1986). Edema in an otherwise normal person can precipitate nerve entrapment in such places where there is little room for swelling. Edema is thought to be the reason that carpal tunnel syndrome occurs in pregnancy (Rengachary 1985, 1775), in some patients with burns of the wrist (Rengachary 1985, 1776), and in patients with edema due to mastectomy (Ganel 1979).

Similarly, when the swelling of reflex sympathetic dystrophy leads to distortion of tissue structures, nerves can be compressed. The effect can be delayed by months to years if chronic swelling leads to deep tissue scaring or other anatomical abnormalities.

L. Complex regional pain syndrome: A new name for RSD

CRPS is defined and discussed in the 1994 IASP (International Association for the Study of Pain) *Classification of Chronic Pain*, second edition (Merskey and Bogduk 1994). It states that complex regional pain syndrome type-I (reflex sympathetic dystrophy) is a syndrome that usually develops after an initiating noxious event, and is disproportionate to the inciting event. CRPS is associated at some point with evidence of edema, changes in skin blood flow, abnormal sudomotor activity in the region of the pain, or allodynia or hyperalgesia. Sudomotor refers to the sympathetic nerves that stimulate sweat glands. Complex regional pain syndrome requires the presence of regional pain and sensory changes following a noxious event. Type-I complex regional pain syndrome corresponds to RSD and occurs without a definable nerve lesion.

CRPS, type II, formerly called causalgia, refers to cases where a definable nerve lesion is present. These terms were defined at a IASP "Special Consensus Workshop" was held in Orlando, Florida in 1993 to examine the terms reflex sympathetic dystrophy, causalgia, sympathetically maintained pain (SMP), and sympathetically independent pain (SIP) (Stanton-Hicks et al. 1995).

In CRPS, pain often follows trauma. The trauma is usually mild and is not associated with significant nerve injury. The onset of symptoms usually occurs within one month of the inciting event. Abnormalities of blood flow occur, related to changes in skin temperature and color. Soft or firm edema is usually present. Increased or decreased sweating may appear. The symptoms and signs may spread proximally (Merskey and Bogduk 1994; Stanton-Hicks et al. 1995).

Criteria for complex regional pain syndrome, type I: reflex sympathetic dystrophy. Two authors who organized the IASP conference (Stanton-Hicks et al. 1995) give the criteria as listed in Table 17.4.

Unilateral abandonment of the terms "reflex sympathetic dystrophy" and "RSD" was thought by many of the 1994 IASP conference participants to be unrealistic (Stanton-Hicks et al. 1995, 130).

Although the term "complex regional pain syndrome" itself implies that pain is a sine qua non of the diagnosis, there is a very small group of patients without pain but with many or all of the other criteria for reflex sympathetic dystrophy or causalgia. It was decided that, for the present, these patients will remain outside of the complex regional pain syndrome umbrella but might benefit from analysis in the future (Stanton-Hicks et al. 1995).

Table 17.4
Criteria for Complex Regional Pain Syndrome, Type I:
Reflex Sympathetic Dystrophy

1. It is a syndrome that develops after an initiating noxious event.
2. It involves spontaneous pain or allodynia/hyperalgesia that is not limited to the territory of a single peripheral nerve, and is disproportionate to the inciting event.
3. There is or has been evidence of edema, skin blood flow abnormality, or abnormal sudomotor activity in the region of the pain since the inciting event.
4. This diagnosis is excluded by the existence of conditions that would otherwise account for the degree of pain and dysfunction.

17.5 Ear Injury
A. Incidence
A report of 2,080 work-related electric injuries in France included twenty-nine cases of auditory sequelae (Gourbiere 1994). These resulted from passage of current through the head, arc burns with flame burns of the pinna, and head injury. Sequelae included conductive or sensorineural hearing loss, tinnitus, and vertigo. There were no cases of ruptured eardrums in this study.

B. Mechanisms of injury
The ear, acoustic nerve, and related structures can be injured by current passing through them. Hemorrhage may occur in the tympanic membrane (eardrum), middle ear, cochlea, cochlear duct, and vestibular apparatus. Damage to the structures may lead to a variety of complications and infections, including mastoiditis, venous sinus thrombosis, meningitis, and brain abscess (Somogyi and Tedeschi 1977, 661). Hearing loss may come immediately at the time of injury or later as a result of developing complications.

Otologic and temporal bone injuries include sensorineural hearing loss, conductive deafness, tinnitus, basilar skull fracture, avulsion of the mastoid bone, burns of the external auditory canal, and peripheral facial nerve palsy. Hemorrhages in the tympanic membrane, middle ear, cochlea, vestibular apparatus, and other structures have been reported (Somogyi and Tedeschi 1977). Both direct effects from current flow and blast effects from the acoustic shock wave associated with lightning may each cause damage (Ogren and Edmunds 1995).

Lightning carried to a person through a telephone receiver may lead to injuries such as tympanic membrane perforation, persistent tinnitus, sensorineural deafness, ataxia, vertigo and nystagmus (Frayne 1987; Johnstone 1986). Tympanic membrane rupture occurs in many victims of lightning injury (Frayne 1987).

17.6 Eye Injury
A. Mechanisms of injury
The visual system contains many small, delicate structures. Damage can occur due to heat, ischemia, and intense light. Heat can be due to the passage of electric current through tissues, radiation from nearby arcing, or

from burning of clothes or other objects. Ischemia is lack of oxygen, sometimes due to inadequate blood flow. Ischemia can be due to constriction or damage of blood vessels, hypotension, inadequate breathing, cardiac dysrhythmias, or a combination of these factors. Intense light may be of visual wavelengths, infrared, or ultraviolet.

1. Electrothermal burns

Electrothermal burns may affect any portion of the eye (Johnson et al. 1987; Somogyi and Tedeschi 1977; Baxter 1970; Adam and Klein 1945). Corneal burns can range from temporary irritation to perforation. The cornea may develop transient punctate, striate, or diffuse interstitial opacities, scar formation, loss of corneal sensation, and corneal necrosis. The anterior chamber may have irritation of the iris (colored portion), irregular mydriasis (dilation of the pupil), miosis (constriction of the pupil), Horner's syndrome (drooping eyelid with other signs), and spasm or insufficiency of accommodation (focus) (Johnson, Kline and Skala 1987).

2. Electric arc light injury

Electric arc light is a combination of intense infrared, visible, and ultraviolet light. The ultraviolet component may lead in several hours to burns similar to that experienced by welders. The other light components may penetrate deeper into the eye (Somogyi and Tedeschi 1977).

Electrothermal and arc injuries can each affect any part of the eye. Reported complications include (Somogyi and Tedeschi 1977, 661): strabismus, ptosis, paralysis of ocular muscles, disturbances in accommodation, scotomas, narrowing of the field of vision, intraocular hemorrhage and thrombosis, uveitis, retinal edema and detachment, papillitis, and atrophy of the optic nerve.

3. Lightning injury

Following lightning injury, corneal ulceration and perforation, retinal damage, and optic nerve injuries may occur. Cataracts can appear months to years later, as with alternating current injury. Late onset of optic atrophy has also been reported (Apelberg 1974).

B. Specific injuries

1. Cataracts

Cataracts caused by electrothermal injury are generally unilateral, while cataracts induced by lightning are usually bilateral. Cataract formation has been described with current passing through the body, without current flow through the head or eyes (Somogyi and Tedeschi 1977; Saffle et al. 1985). Similarly, cataracts have been reported after brief exposure to an electric arc without any passage of current through the head or body (Gourbiere 1994).

Saffle et al. (1985) reviewed 113 patients with major electrical injury and found that 7 of these had a total of thirteen cataracts. One man was injured by a 440-volt source, while all the rest were injured by high voltage (over 1,000 volts). Although all patients had wounds, only three involved the head or neck. The patients had a mean age of 24.7 years and presented with cataracts one to twelve months post injury. Surgery was successful in all cases except for the development of a late retinal detachment in one case.

2. Intraocular complications

Intraocular hemorrhage and thrombosis, uveitis, retinal edema and detachment, and optic nerve atrophy have been reported. Cataract formation can occur up to several years after the accident (Johnson, Kline and Skalka 1987; Somogyi and Tedeschi 1977; Baxter 1970; Adam and Klein 1945; Fraunfelder and Hanna 1972).

3. Optic neuropathy, papillopathy, and papilledema

Lightning and nonlightning injuries have led to optic nerve head swelling, retinal hemorrhages, and eventual optic atrophy. Three sometimes related conditions can be defined (Grover and Goodwin 1995):

- **Optic neuropathy** is optic nerve dysfunction following lightning or electrical injury.
- **Papillopathy** refers to swelling of the optic disc.
- **Papilledema** is a term that has been used nonspecifically for many years in referring to any condition in which the optic nerve head is swollen. Grover and Goodwin (1995) believe the term should be reserved for conditions in which increased intracranial pressure is the

cause of the swelling. Papilledema will usually be bilateral with early preservation of the visual function.

References

Brain injury

Alexander, L., "Electrical Injuries to the Central Nervous System," *Medical Clinics of North America* 22:663–688 (1938).

Grube, B. J. et al., "Neurologic consequences of electrical burns," *Journal of Trauma* 30(3):254–258 (1990).

Jackson, F. E., R. Martin and R. Davis, "Delayed Quadriplegia Following Electrical Burn," *Military Medicine,* June 1965, 601–605.

O'Brien, C. F., "Movement Disorders after Lightning Injury," *Seminars in Neurology* 15(3):263–267 (1965).

Patel, A. and R. Lo, "Electric Injury with Cerebral Venous Thrombosis," *Stroke* 24:903–905 (1993).

Stanley, L. D. and R. A. Suss, "Intracerebral Hematoma Secondary to Lighting Stroke: Case Report and Review of the Literature," *Neurosurgery* 16(5): 686–688 (1985).

Sure, U. and P. Kleihues, "Intracerebral Venous Thrombosis and Hematoma Secondary to High Voltage Brain Injury," *Journal of Trauma: Injury, Infection, and Critical Care,* June 1997, 1161–1164.

Spinal injury

Alexander, L., "Clinical and Neuropathological Aspects of Electrical Injuries," *J. Ind. Hygiene. Toxicology* 20:191 (1938a).

Alexander, L., "Electrical Injuries to Central Nervous System," *Medical Clinics of North America* 22:663 (1938b).

Baxter, Charles R. "Present Concepts in the Management of Major Electrical Injury," *Surgical Clinics of North America* 50(6):1401–1418 (1970).

Farrell, D. F. and A. Starr, "Delayed Neurological Sequelae of Electrical Injuries," *Neurology* 18:601–606 (1968).

Holbrook, L. A., F. X. M. Beach and J. R. Silver,. "Delayed Myelopathy: A Rare Complication of Severe Electrical Burns," *British Medical Journal* 4:659–666 (1970).

Petty, P. G. and G. Parkin, "Electrical Injury to the Central Nervous System," *Neurosurgery* 19:282–285 (1986).

Somogyi, Endre and C. G. Tedeschi, "Injury by Electrical Force," in *Forensic Medicine: A Study in Trauma and Environmental Hazards,* vol. 1, Tedeschi C. G., W. G. Eckert and L. G. Tedeschi, eds. (Philadelphia: W. B. Saunders, 1977), 659.

Vazquez, D. et al., "Thoracic Disc Herniation, Cord Compression, and Paraplegia Caused by Electrical Injury: Case Report and Review of the Literature," *Journal of Trauma* 37(2):328–332 (1994).

Varghese, G., M. M. Mani and J. B. Redford, "Spinal Cord Injuries Following Electrical Accidents," *Paraplegia* 24:159–166 (1986).

Nervous system and peripheral nerve injury

Capelli-Schellpfeffer, M. et al., "Advances in the Evaluation and Treatment of Electrical and Thermal Injury Emergencies," *IEEE Transactions on Industry Applications* 31(5):1147–1152 (1995).

Dendooven, A. M. et al., "Electrical Injuries to Peripheral Nerves," *Medica Physica* 13:161–165 (1990).

Devor, M., "Neuropathic Pain and Injured Nerve: Peripheral Mechanisms," *British Medical Bulletin* 47:619–30 (1991).

Lee, R. C., "Physical Measurements of Tissue Injury in Electrical Trauma," *IEEE Transactions on Education* 34(3):223–230 (1991).

Lee, R. C. et al., "Role of Cell Membrane Rupture in the Pathogenesis of Electrical Trauma," *Journal of Surgical Research* 44:709–719 (1988).

Lee, R. C. et al. "Biophysical Mechanisms of Cell Membrane Damage in Electrical Shock," *Seminars in Neurology* 15(4):367–374 (1995).

Parano, E. et al., "Delayed Bilateral Median Nerve Injury due to Low-Tension Electric Current," *Europediatrics* 27:2, 105–7 (1996).

Reflex sympathetic dystrophy and causalgia

Baxter, C. R., "Present Concepts in the Management of Major Electrical Injury," *Surgical Clinics of North America* 50(6):1401–17 (1970).

Bonezzi, C., R. Bettaglio and G. Catenecci, "Reflex Sympathetic Dystrophy following Electric Shock," *Med. Lav.* 82(6):521–6 (1991).

Capelli-Schellpfeffer, M. et al., "Advances in the Evaluation and Treatment of Electrical and Thermal Injury Emergencies," *IEEE Transactions on Industry Applications* 31(5):1147–52 (1995).

Cohen, J. A., "Autonomic Nervous System Disorders and Reflex Sympathetic Dystrophy in Lightning and Electrical Injuries," *Seminars in Neurology* 15(4):387–390 (1995).

Cooke, E. D. et al., "Reflex Sympathetic Dystrophy and Repetitive Strain Injury: Temperature and Microcirculatory Changes following Mild Cold Stress," *J. Roy. Soc. Med.* 86:690–3 (1993).

Demun, E. M. et al., "Reflex Sympathetic Dystrophy after a Minor Electric Shock," *J. Emerg. Med.* 11:393–6 (1993).

Dendooven, A. M. et al., "Electrical Injuries to Peripheral Nerves," *Medica Physica* 13:161–5 (1990).

Devor, M., "Neuropathic Pain and Injured Nerve: Peripheral Mechanisms," *British Medical Bulletin* 47(3):619–30 (1991).

Fiztpatrick, T. B. et al., *Dermatology in General Practice* (McGraw-Hill, New York, 1993), 2091.

Ganel, A. et al., "Nerve Entrapments Associated with Postmastectomy Lymphedema," *Cancer* 44(60):2254–9 (1979).

Greipp, M. E. and A. F. Thomas, "Skin Lesions Occurring in Clients with Reflex Sympathetic Dystrophy Syndrome," *Journal of Neuroscience Nursing* 26(6):342–346 (1994).

Halsey, J. H., "Post-Traumatic Pain Syndromes," in *Merritt's Textbook of Neurology*, 9th ed., Rowland, Lewis P., ed. (Baltimore: Williams & Wilkins, 1995), 486–8

Hendler, N, and N. R. Raja Srinivasa, "Reflex Sympathetic Dystrophy," in *The Handbook of Pain Management,* Tollison, C. D., J. R. Satterhwaite and J. W. Tollison, eds. (Baltimore: Williams & Wilkins, 1994), 484–496.

Henricksen, O. et al., "Effect of Chronic Sympathetic Denervation upon the Transcapillary Filtration Rate Induced by Venous Stasis," *Acta Physiol. Scand.* 117:171–6 (1983).

Howard, F. M., "Controversies in Nerve Entrapment Syndromes in the Forearm and Wrist," *Orthopedic Clinics of North America* 17(3):375–81 (1986).

Merskey, D. M. and N. Bogduk, "Complex Regional Pain Syndrome, Type I (Reflex Sympathetic Dystrophy), Classification of Chronic Pain," (Seattle: International Association for the Study of Pain, IASP Press, 1994), 41–2.

Oyen, W. J. G. et al., "Reflex Sympathetic Dystrophy of the Hand: An Excessive Inflammatory Response?" *Pain* 55:151–7 (1993).

Rengachary, S. S., "Entrapment Neuropathies," in *Neurosurgery*, Wilkins, R. H. and S. S. Rengachary, eds. (NY: McGraw-Hill, 1985), 1771–95.

Rosen, L. et al., "Skin Microvascular Circulation in the Sympathetic Dystrophies Elevated by Videophotometric Capillaroscopy and Laser Doppler Fluxmetry," *European Journal of Clinical Investigation* 18:305–8 (1988).

Rosenberg, D. B., "Neurologic Sequelae of Minor Electric Burns," *Arch. Phys. Med. Rehabil.* 70:914–5 (1993).

Shantha, T. R,. "Causalgia Induced by Telephone-Mediated Lightning Electrical Injury and Treated by Intrapleural Block," *Anesth. Analg.* 73:502–510 (1991).

Shelton, R. M., and C. W. Lewis, "Reflex Sympathetic Dystrophy: A Review," *J. Am. Acad. Dermatol.* 22:513–20 (1990).

Stanton-Hicks, M. et al., "Reflex Sympathetic Dystrophy: Changing Concepts and Taxonomy," *Pain* 63:127–33 (1995).

Stedman's Electronic Medical Dictionary (Hagerstown, MD: Williams & Wilkins, 1996).

Tarsay, D., L. Sudarsky and M. E. Charness, "Limb Dystonia Following Electrical Injury," *Movement Disorders* 9(2):230–2 (1994).

Teasell, R. W., P. Potter and D. Moulin, "Reflex Sympathetic Dystrophy Involving Three Limbs: A Case Study," *Arch. Phys. Med. Rehabil.* 75:1008–1010 (1994).

Treister, M. R. et al., "Entrapment Neuropathies of the Upper Extremities," correspondence, *New England Journal of Medicine* 330:1389-1390 (1994).

Veldman, P. H. et al., "Signs and Symptoms of Reflex Sympathetic Dystrophy: Prospective Study of 829 Patients," *Lancet* 342:1012–6 (1993).

Webster, G. F. et al., "Reflex Sympathetic Dystrophy: Occurrence of Chronic Edema and Nonimmune Bullous Skin Lesions," *J. Am. Acad. Dermatol.* 28(1):29–32 (1993).

Webster, G. F. et al., "Reflex Sympathetic Dystrophy: Occurrence of Inflammatory Skin Lesions in Patients with Stages II and III Disease," *Arch. Dermatol.* 127:1541–4 (1991).

Ear injury

Amy, B. W. et al., "Lightning Injury with Survival in Five Patients," *JAMA* 253(2):243–245 (1985).

Frayne, J. H. and B. S. Gilligan, "Neurological Sequelae of Lightning Stroke," *Clinical and Experimental Neurology* 24:195–200 (1987).

Johnstone, B. R., D. L. Harding and H. Bruce, "Telephone-Related Lightning Injury," *Medical Journal of Australia* 144:706–709 (1986).

Gourbiere, E., J. Corbut and Y. Bazin, "Functional Consequence of Electrical Injury," *Annals of the New York Academy of Sciences* 720:259–271 (1994).

Ogren, F. P. and A. L. Edmunds, "Neuro-Otologic Findings in the Lightning-Injured Patient," *Seminars in Neurology* 15(3):256–262 (1995).

Eye injury

Adam, A. L. and M. Klein, "Electrical Cataract," *Br. J. Ophthalmol.* 29:169 (1945).

Apelberg, D. B., F. W. Masters and D. W. Robinson, "Pathophysiology and Treatment of Lightning Injuries," *Journal of Trauma* 14(6):453–460 (1974).

Baxter, C. R., "Present Concepts in the Management of Major Electrical Injury," *Surg. Clin. North Am.* 50(6):1401–1418 (1970).

Craig, S. R., "When Lightning Strikes," *Postgraduate Medicine* 79(4):109–124 (1968).

Fraunfelder, F. T, and C. Hanna, "Electric Cataracts, part 1: Sequential Changes, Unusual and Prognostic Findings," *Arch. Ophthalmol.* 87:179–183 (1972).

Gourbiere, E. M., J. Corbut and Y. Bazin, "Functional Consequence of Electrical Injury," *Annals of the New York Academy of Sciences* 720:259–271 (1994).

Grover, S. and J. Goodwin, "Lightning and Electrical Injuries: Neuro-Ophthalmologic Aspects," *Seminars in Neurology* 15(4):335–341 (1995).

Johnson, E. V., L. B. Kline and H. W. Skalka, "Electrical Cataracts: A Case Report and Review of the Literature," *Ophthalmic Surg.* 18(4):283–285 (1987).

Saffle, J. R., A. Crandall and G. D. Warden, "Cataracts: A Long-Term Complication of Electrical Injury," *Journal of Trauma* 25(1):17–21 (1985).

Somogyi, Endre and C. G. Tedeschi, "Injury by Electrical Force," in *Forensic Medicine: A Study in Trauma and Environmental Hazards,* vol. 1: *Mechanical Trauma*, Tedeschi C. G., W. G. Eckert and L. G. Tedeschi, eds. (Philadelphia: W. B. Saunders, 1977), 645–676.

Chapter 18

Cardiac and Respiratory Effects of Electrical Injury

18.1 Introduction

This section discusses cardiac and pulmonary injury caused by passage of electric current through the heart and lungs. Application of thousands of volts to the chest, or from arm to arm, is not always fatal; in many cases, normal heart function continues. Immediate effects of electrical injury related to cardiac and respiratory arrest are discussed in Section 18.3. That section discusses mechanisms of sudden death and related topics.

A. Pulmonary injury

Pleural injury can result in effusions (collections of fluid) and lobular pneumonitis (inflammation of the lung) directly adjacent to electric contact areas. These complications are often evident within a week of the injury. A sterile yellowish fluid can be removed by thoracentesis (removal by a needle from the chest cavity). Reaccumulation is unusual. Pulmonary infection following electrical injury to the chest is thought to result from systemic infection or inhalation, rather than from electric current effects. Still, it is possible that electrical injury to pulmonary parenchyma might occur in some cases. (Baxter 1970).

High-voltage injury can cause actual burns of lung tissue (Somogyi and Tedeschi 1977).

B. Myocardial infarction following electrical injury

A fifty-seven-year-old man was standing behind a crane and holding onto a welding torch that may have come into contact with the crane body. The crane boom contacted an overhead 23,000-volt AC line. The crane operator was killed. The man standing behind the crane was thrown six to eight feet in the air. He felt a shock and a momentary paralysis, but did not remember being thrown to the ground. He may have been transiently unconscious. He immediately developed a severe left anterior chest pain. He had burns of the hands and feet. An ECG showed ST elevations in II, III and aVF with reciprocal changes in the remaining leads (an inferior wall myocardial infarction). There were later elevations of the cardiac-specific CPK and LDH isoenzymes (Kinney 1982).

Another case of myocardial infarction due to electrical injury involved a patient who was later found to have normal coronary arteries (Ku 1989). Possible mechanisms of injury in such cases are thought to include occlusion of small coronary arteries not well visualized with coronary arteriograms, coronary artery spasm induced by electricity, and direct injury to the myocardium (Ku 1989).

C. Myocardial dysfunction from electrical injury
1. Direct myocardial injury

Myocardial injury after high-voltage electrical injury is often not recognized clinically because patients with such injury often lack typical ischemic chest discomfort, ECG changes, or dysrhythmias. Chandra (1990) studied patients with high-voltage electrical injury and myocardial injury who did not have suggestive cardiac signs, symptoms, or dysrhythmias. He found that such direct myocardial injury is most likely to occur in patients who have relatively large body surface area burns, an average of 16 percent in patients with myocardial injury as compared to 4 percent in those without. Patients with upper and lower body wounds of exit and entrance are also likely to have direct myocardial injury. Detection of myocardial injury in such patients was by CK (creatine kinase) and CK-MB (creatine kinase, MB isoenzyme) determinations. Patients had CK values of 1373 mU/mL to 52,544 mU/mL with the mean MB fraction being 6.7 percent (normal 0 to 5 percent). Laboratory normal CK values were 0 to 70 mU/mL for females and 0 to 100 mU/ml for males. The MB fraction rises to over 3 percent within nine hours of admission in 69 percent of patients. Patients without myocardial injury have CK elevations as high as 640 mU/mL, but these are MB negative. Patients with myocardial injury should be monitored. Such patients may develop left ventricular dysfunction, but ST elevation seldom occurs because the myocardial necrosis is usually not transmural (across the entire thickness of the wall of the ventricle).

Lewin et al. (1983) believe that electrical injury sometimes produces a patchy necrosis of the myocardium. Electrocardiographic changes, elevation of CK-MB, and left ventricular hypokinesis (decreased movement on ultrasound or other imaging studies) may occur. ECG findings are thought to be nondiagnostic because the pattern of heart injury is patchy rather than following the distribution of a coronary artery. Lewin et al. (1083) report the case of a nineteen-year-old man who contacted 220 volts AC 50Hz and had cardiac arrest. Cardiac enzymes and EKG showed myocardial infarction. There was transient global left ventricular dysfunction, but he made an apparently complete recovery.

2. Myocardial ischemia and pulmonary edema

Alternating current defibrillation is much more likely to produce electrocardiographic changes consistent with myocardial ischemia than DC defibrillation (Lown 1962). Myocardial ischemia secondary to alternating current has been reported as the probable cause of myocardial dysfunction and acute pulmonary edema (Schein et al. 1990). Neurogenic pulmonary edema in association with hemolysis and disseminated intravascular coagulation following contact with 11,000 volts AC has also been reported (Diamond 1982). Neurogenic pulmonary edema is seen in a variety of central nervous system conditions. An alteration in pulmonary vascular permeability mediated by sympathetic nerves is probably involved (Drislane et al. 1994). In this situation, the blood vessels in the lungs leak fluids and other materials from the blood stream into lung tissue.

D. Proof of myocardial (heart muscle) injury

CK-MB, the muscle enzyme long thought to be specific to heart muscle, can be released from noncardiac muscles in small amounts. Therefore, it is the ratio of CKMB to total CK that can lead to a determination of the presence of cardiac injury (Pincus et al. 1996). In addition, other signs of heart muscle injury should be sought. These would include changes in the electrocardiogram, signs of heart dysfunction on ultrasound or other scans that measure cardiac function, and other enzyme assays. The troponin assays are very specific for heart muscle injury. These became widely used in the late 1990s, and they will hopefully be measured in persons with electrical injury.

Questioning the proof. Two articles, one by Housinger et al. (1985) and one by McBride (1984), describe patients with elevated cardiac enzymes, including elevated ratios of CK-MB to total CK, who apparently had no real cardiac injury. However, the articles do not substantiate the claim of no cardiac injury. Functional testing, such as some types of stress testing, would be more convincing. Other cardiac enzymes, introduced in the late 1990s, such as the troponins, would also provide useful information.

The article by Housinger et al. includes pyrophosphate scans to detect cardiac injury. However, the sensitivity of the test is only 32 percent for nontransmural (non-full-wall thickness) cardiac injury. Stress testing and other functional tests would be more definitive. Housinger's article (1985) describes fifteen patients with high-voltage injury (over 1,000 volts AC). All of these persons had burns, and all lived. Of nine patients with elevation of CK-MB, only two had an abnormal ECG. None of the patients had clinical evidence of cardiac dysfunction.

The article by McBride (1984) reports patients who have CK-MB elevations, but no diagnostic ECG abnormalities or LDH isoenzyme increases. He theorizes that skeletal muscle is stimulated to produce and release CK-MB in some cases. As described below, the article contains inconsistencies and inadequate investigation of cardiac function of the involved cases. It is true that skeletal muscle contains CK-MB, but the amounts are such that cardiac injury can be distinguished from skeletal muscle injury by considering the ratio of CK-MB to total CK.

In the McBride study, muscle biopsies were analyzed for CK-MB activity. CK-MB activity was found in apparently normal muscle adjacent to the injury site. However, the same paper discusses the case of a twenty-eight-year-old man who sustained an injury from 115,000 volts AC to both hands and feet and had normal ECGs on the first two postburn days followed by ST segment and T-wave changes on day three. On day four, a classic inferior myocardial infarction pattern evolved. Total serum CK reached 21,396 units/L with 8.3 percent MB. Total LDH level reached 638 units/L. However, the expected cardiac fraction of LDH did not increase as would be expected, and the ratio of cardiac to noncardiac LDH did not increase either. A number of the other patients in the study had elevated CK-MB, but no additional evidence of myocardial injury; though it appears that ultrasound and other modalities to find cardiac dysfunction were not done.

EKGs would not be expected to show global or widespread myocardial injury. LDH isoenzymes were not diagnostic in the patient reported by McBride who most definitely did develop a myocardial infarction, as seen on multiple EKGs; this is an inconsistent result. Therefore, the conclusions of the paper are not well supported.

E. Cardiac muscle injury, with survival of the patient

Despite direct cardiac injury from electric current, resuscitation can often be successful. As described below, the methods of resuscitation are taught to healthcare personnel through the ACLS (Advanced Cardiac Life Support) and other courses; the American Heart Association developed many of these programs.

The articles cited below describe large currents going through the heart, because there were high voltages applied in such a way as to cause significant current flow through the chest. In many cases, cardiac enzymes were elevated. However as discussed in the article by McBride below, this is not definite proof of heart muscle injury.

F. Case examples of survival after current flow through the heart

Chandra (1990) discussed thirteen patients (in their "Group A") who contacted sources of 3,000 to 130,000 volts AC and had significant body burns and elevation of cardiac enzymes. The patients had current paths horizontally or vertically (or both) across the trunk. Only one of the thirteen patients died (following surgery on his eighteenth day in the hospital).

Another article with survivors is by Homma (1990). It describes two young men who went into ventricular fibrillation after contacting electrical power sources. One patient died of hypoxic encephalopathy (brain injury from lack of oxygen). The other recovered with good exercise tolerance two months after injury. Thallium imaging revealed a fixed apical defect consistent with a scar in the patient who survived. It is thought that ischemic insult may have been responsible for the heart injury. This would probably have been due to poor circulation before restoration of a normal cardiac rhythm.

Still another set of case reports is given by Moran et al. (1986). Three persons with high-voltage injury (over 1,000 volts) and one with lightning injury had cardiac arrest. Some had elevated cardiac enzymes, but they all survived.

18.2 Vascular Injury

Vascular injury can be due to thermal effects, trauma, compression of blood vessels, and formation of blood clots inside blood vessels. Blood clots can form due to irregularities inside the blood vessels or a slow rate of blood flow through the vessels. Once a clot (thrombus) forms that totally or even partially occludes the lumen of a blood vessel, pieces of the clot may break off and travel along with the blood flow. Such pieces of clot are called emboli. Emboli in the arterial system will travel to smaller and smaller arteries until they get stuck, often totally occluding blood flow to an area of tissue. Venous emboli will usually go the heart and then the lungs, leading to a pulmonary embolus. Unless large, such pulmonary emboli will cause little injury. If there is a connection between the right and left heart (an atrial or ventricular septal defect), the embolus of venous origin may gain access to the systemic arterial circulation rather than the pulmonary circulation. In that case, the embolus may go to the brain or somewhere in the body. Relatively small emboli in the arterial circulation can cause significant injury.

A. Delayed arterial thrombosis following low-voltage injury

A twenty-four-year-old man touched the wet plug of a 220-volt AC vacuum cleaner (Bongard and Fagrell 1989). He was stuck to the plug for about five seconds until another person was able to disconnect the plug from the socket. He immediately felt numbness and itching of the index, ring, and little fingers of his right hand that lasted a few hours. After two week, he felt similar symptoms. After another two weeks, his symptoms were mild, but then became worse with the addition of pain and development of skin necrosis of the fingertips of the affected fingers. Arteriography showed total occlusion of the radial and ulnar arteries. Thrombolytic therapy with streptokinase was successful in improving circulation and lessening symptoms even though this was eight and one half weeks after the accident. The larger thromboses in the radial and ulnar arteries were not dissolved, but the ones in the digital arteries were dissolved.

B. Vascular injuries from high voltage

High-voltage vascular lesions often are associated with a limited cutaneous burn. The degree of deep muscle damage is variable and often not clinically apparent. Arterial pulses may not be palpable because of subeschar or subfascial edema. Deep tissue damage is characteristic of high-voltage alternating current source injuries, such as those due to power lines. Deeper tissue injury is uncommon with lightning injuries. Underlying tissue injury may lead to life-threatening sepsis and loss of limb.

Hunt (1974) studied eleven men who had sustained electric injury from 500 volts or more and had an average total body surface burn of 26 percent. Arteriograms were performed after cardiorespiratory stabilization. Complete occlusion was found in four limbs, partial occlusion in four more, and no occlusion in five others. Additional findings included narrowing, irregularity, beading, and decreased nutrient muscle branches. All patients with injured muscle had moderate to massive subeschar or subfascial edema under unburned skin. Hidden muscle injury was thus common. The decision to amputate was guided in part by the findings at arteriography. When complete vascular occlusion existed, massive tissue necrosis was always present. Partial vascular occlusion was also indicative of muscle necrosis. Arteriographic identification of decreased nutrient muscular branches signified local muscle injury and the need for further surgical exploration.

Although abnormal arteriograms are indicative of muscle necrosis, normal arteriograms do not prove absence of muscle damage. Direct injury to muscle can also occur, leading to muscle necrosis in association with vascular patency. In such cases, diagnostic fasciotomies through eschar or unburned skin permit an accurate assessment of the patient's injury (Hunt 1974).

C. Modern imaging methods
Newer imaging methods, such as MRI, can sometimes identify deep muscle necrosis (Nettelblad et al. 1996).

18.3 Conscious Awareness During Fatal Electric Injury
A more detailed and thorough treatment of conscious awareness during electric injury can be found in Fish and Geddes (2003, 411–413).

Cardiac, respiratory, and neurological events occur during and following fatal electric injury. These events can be analyzed to see if the person was conscious at various times during and after the passage of electric current through the person. In many cases, loss of consciousness will occur ten to fifteen seconds after the heart stops beating. During respiratory arrest with a continuing normal heart rhythm, consciousness may persist for up to three minutes. Electroconvulsive therapy currents passed through the head can induce grand mal seizures with loss of consciousness in a third of a second; loss of consciousness with large currents through the head probably occurs within one cycle (1/60 second) of the electric current.

A. Immediate cardiac and respiratory effects of various amounts of current
The effects listed in Table 15.3 can be expected from 60 Hz (or 50 Hz) alternating current applied to the skin. In addition, even apparently harmless currents can lead to secondary trauma. For example, while 3 milliamperes will cause no direct harm, it may cause a startle reaction, causing a person to fall or be harmed in some other manner. Thus, 0.5 milliamperes

is often considered the maximum allowable leakage current for household appliances. A smaller current, 100 microamperes, is sometimes considered the limit in the medical equipment environment where current may be carried directly to the heart (Kugelberg 1975 and 1976; Levin 1991). The numbers in Table 15.3 are for adults. Exact values will vary depending on the current path (such as hand-to-hand, right-arm-to-right-leg), and also on the person's size, age, muscular development, and sex.

B. Mechanisms of death

Electric current can cause death in many ways. The more common mechanisms of death are listed in Table 18.1. Some of these were discussed in Chapter 15, and more will be explained below. The list is not complete, since electric current can affect every organ and every part of the body in a variety of ways that may each lead to death.

Table 18.1
Some Mechanisms of Death from Electric Injury

1. Induction of cardiac dysrhythmias
   A. Ventricular fibrillation
   B. Asystole
2. Respiratory arrest
   A. Brain or brainstem stimulation
   B. Paralysis of muscles of respiration
3. Hyperthermia from heating of tissues
4. Fluid loss
5. Metabolic complications
   A. Coagulation abnormalities
   B. Electrolyte and pH abnormalities
   C. Renal failure
6. Direct damage to vital structures
7. Burns
8. Blasts and explosions
9. Secondary trauma
   A. Falls
   B. Fire, including resultant trauma, carbon monoxide and other inhalations
10. Sepsis (infection)

C. Cardiac arrest

Electric current can induce cardiac rhythms that do not adequately pump blood, including ventricular fibrillation and asystole.

Asystole is absence of contractions. There is no electrical activity of the heart and no muscle contractions. There will, therefore, be no blood flow.

Ventricular fibrillation is a chaotic, uncoordinated, rapid contraction of heart muscle. The heart muscle writhes, something like a bag of worms, though faster. It is generally taught and believed that there is no blood pressure during ventricular fibrillation. However, measurements have been made during implantation of cardioverter-defibrillators that show there is a minimal blood pressure during ventricular fibrillation, at least for several seconds. This blood pressure, measured in 277 periods of ventricular fibrillation in thirty-seven patients in one study, was always below 30 mmHg. The curves in the paper show the blood pressure decreasing to 15 mmHg about eleven seconds after onset of ventricular fibrillation. At the same time, blood flow in the brain (as measured by blood flow in the middle cerebral artery) went to zero during ventricular fibrillation. The EEG showed ischemic changes and declined to an isoelectric record (flatline) within eleven (± 2) seconds after induction of ventricular fibrillation (De Vries et al. 1998). The reason that there was no blood flow to the brain with a small blood pressure is that there is normally a pressure in the head (called intracranial pressure). Intracranial pressure is normally up to 15 mmHg, and can be several times this with head injury. For blood to flow, mean arterial pressure must be greater than intracranial pressure. The eleven-second period (± 2) of loss of brain activity agrees with the clinical observation that patients with sudden cardiac arrest are sometimes seen to remain conscious for ten to fifteen seconds.

Respiratory arrest with normal cardiac rhythm. In 1932, Langworthy and Kouwenshoven contrasted the prognosis for electrically induced respiratory arrest with that for cases of electrically induced ventricular fibrillation. They stated, "Prolonged artificial respiration may give time for recovery of the respiratory mechanism but there is no adequate method at the present time for dealing with ventricular fibrillation." This concept is still true in that persons with respiratory arrest and a normal cardiac rhythm can be maintained neurologically intact if artificial respirations are begun soon enough and continued until spontaneous breathing resumes. "Soon enough" means before hypoxic brain damage and other complications arise.

Resuscitation from ventricular fibrillation. The above statement from 1932 is out of date in the sense that ventricular fibrillation can now be treated with defibrillation. Defibrillation involves placing electrodes and conductive jelly on the chest. Over 1,000 volts DC are applied; this results in a current flow of up to a few tens of amperes, but for only several milliseconds. These numbers vary considerably and depend on the instrument, settings, and other factors (Fisher 1980, 367; Tacker 1995; Feinberg 1986). Such defibrillation puts the heart in asystole: a complete stoppage of electrical activity of the heart. Within a few seconds, the heart will usually resume a normal pattern of beating. Thus, ventricular fibrillation can be converted to a normal heart rhythm. Of course, if CPR has not maintained oxygenation and circulation adequately, hypoxic damage to the heart and other organs may have occurred before the defibrillation. In that situation, the inability to restore a normal cardiac rhythm and other problems may result.

Ventricular fibrillation usually does not spontaneously revert to a normal heart rhythm though it may do so (Josephson et al. 1979; Somogyi and Tedeschi 1977, 650).

Prognosis in asystole. As mentioned above under ventricular fibrillation, when the heart is suddenly put into asystole by an external current, the heart will usually return to a normal rhythm when the current is finished. This is what is done during resuscitation from cardiac arrest: the heart is put into asystole to break the cycle of ventricular fibrillation. As also mentioned above, if there has been prolonged loss of adequate oxygenation and circulation of blood, hypoxic damage to the heart and other organs may have resulted. In such cases, a normal rhythm may not be restored.

During the application of several thousand volts DC applied (for example) from arm to leg, several amperes will flow through the trunk. This is likely to put the heart into asystole for the duration of the current flow. If the current flow is not so long as to damage vital structures or heat the body to nonphysiological temperatures, a normal heart rhythm will likely resume within several seconds of current flow termination. The brain will lose consciousness after ten to fifteen seconds of loss of circulation of oxygenated blood. Breathing also stops soon after cardiac arrest. If respiratory support reestablishes oxygenation of the blood and circulation continues, spontaneous respirations will likely result and the person will wake unless other factors have caused brain or other vital tissue damage.

Asystole caused by factors other than a relatively brief electric current flow has a much worse prognosis. When persons have asystole for medical or traumatic reasons, something else is seriously wrong besides passage of electricity though the body. When asystole not due to electric current has been studied, the patients have been found to almost never survive. Reported rates of resuscitation are only 1 to 4 percent, and these may be overestimated because of misclassification (fine ventricular fibrillation is mistaken for asystole). Though there may be rare exceptions, asystole not due to electric current is an indication of a dead heart (Cummins et al. 1993; Cummins 1997).

D. Consciousness and awareness during cardiac arrest

In the condition of no blood flow, consciousness is lost after about ten to fifteen seconds, during which time the person can speak rationally and continue breathing. Patients with acute myocardial infarction who develop ventricular fibrillation while on a cardiac monitor in the emergency department are sometimes seen to remained conscious for over ten seconds. Such patients can continue to talk quite normally, but eventually do lose consciousness unless CPR is started or defibrillation is done. This phenomena is also well-described in the medical literature (Damjanov and Linder 1996, 107; Davis 1980, 252; Walters 1972; Lee 1965). These clinical observations agree with the measurements made during cardioverter-defibrillator implantation discussed above. In such cases, breathing will usually stop after the loss of consciousness has occurred.

The observation that respiration and consciousness can persist for a short while during ventricular fibrillation accounts for accident reports of persons talking and sometimes moving about or walking after receiving a fatal electric shock (Fisher 1980, 372; Lee 1965).

Sensations following electric injury. Survivors of electric injury have described symptoms including severe muscle cramps, a sensation of heat, terror, chest tightness, difficulty breathing, a sensation of strangulation, and a feeling of the heart pounding against the chest wall (Walters 1972). Such sensations and the memories of them may not occur if there is significant and immediate electric current through the head, which occurs in about 10 percent of electrocutions (Walters 1972; Lee 1965).

The heart is likely to recover from asystole that was induced by a brief but large electric current. This is what occurs when a person is defibrillated. In such cases, the person may continue or restart breathing. If breathing does not restart spontaneously, the heart will likely continue beating for ten minutes or longer (Davis 1980). During this time, support of respirations (mouth to mouth breathing or other means) can be done to supply oxygen to the blood that is being circulated by the heart. If this is done soon enough, the person will likely be saved, unless there were other serious effects of the injury.

E. Respiratory arrest

1. Loss of consciousness from cessation of breathing

It has been observed in many cases of submersion in water that consciousness is lost within three minutes of submersion (Pearn 1985). When a person in this setting loses consciousness, this is almost always because of cerebral hypoxia. In cold water accidents, consciousness can also be lost because the body temperature falls too low.

2. Resuscitation after loss of consciousness from respiratory arrest

Craig (1976) conducted a study of swimmers who deliberately held their breath, and thereby lost consciousness. His observations and experimental data suggest that the time between loss of consciousness and certain death is about 2.5 minutes depending on the circumstances of the case. In every case in which the person did survive and could describe his experiences, there was a history of deliberately hyperventilating before the accident in order to prolong breath-holding and underwater swimming times. In thirty-four people who did survive to recount their story, most reported that they had an urge to breathe, but lost consciousness without recognizable warning signs besides the strong urge to breathe.

3. Autopsy findings in death due to respiratory arrest

If the heart continues to beat without respirations, "lack of circulatory assistance" (that chest wall movements usually give) leads to pooling of blood in the lungs. This leads to hemorrhagic, and edematous lungs. This congestion is characteristic of acute asphyxial death (Davis 1980, 252; Knight 1991, 298). Petechial hemorrhages of the conjunctivae and some peripheral and central cyanosis may be present, though this is by no means constant (Al-Alousi 1990). In some cases, acute hypoxia leading to death can result in dilatation of the heart, congestion of internal organs such as the liver, acute pulmonary hypertension, cor pulmonale, and congestion and dilatation of the vessels in the brain (Craig 1976).

The expected pulmonary congestion is not always found in death due to respiratory paralysis due to tetanic chest wall muscle contraction. A possible explanation is given by Lee (1965). He compared autopsy findings of rabbits that had died of respiratory arrest caused by strangulation and by sustained contraction of the respiratory muscles caused by electric current. The electrocuted rabbit in the experiment did not develop the pulmonary congestion seen in the strangulated rabbit. His explanation was that the anoxic tissues on the surface of the lungs of the strangulated rabbit were subjected to strong negative pressures by powerful attempted inspiratory movements; these forces would lead to pulmonary congestion. No such movements were possible in the electrocuted rabbit because the muscles were in tetanic contraction. This explanation ignores the "lack of circulatory assistance" factor in causing edema of the lungs and other internal organs. Ignoring this factor would be appropriate in cases in which cardiac arrest came relatively soon after the respiratory arrest. For example, if ventricular fibrillation developed a few minutes after respiratory arrest, congestion of internal organs might not have time to develop to a significant degree. In Lee's rabbit experiment, the rabbit did go into ventricular fibrillation less than six minutes from the beginning of respiratory arrest. Persons with respiratory arrest, as with judicial hanging, have been observed to continue circulation for much longer periods of time.

For example, Davis (1980) reported that after a hanging with no respiratory activity, peripheral pulses could be felt for seven minutes, and heartbeats were heard for twelve minutes. Heart sounds indicate there is blood circulation, and a palpable peripheral pulse indicates a blood pressure of roughly 80 mmHg or more. Therefore after respiratory arrest from hanging in the reported case, there was a blood pressure of at least 80 mmHg for seven minutes, and a lesser blood pressure for twelve minutes following onset of respiratory arrest and hanging.

The person being hung would probably have an earlier cardiac arrest than persons with respiratory arrest from other causes for two reasons: (1) the upright position of the victim would tend to lower the blood pressure; and (2) vagal effects from pressure on the neck would be expected to lower the blood pressure and would encourage earlier cardiac arrest in the patient with hypoxia and acidosis.

4. Loss of consciousness from electric current passed through the head

Electric current applied to the head can lead to grand mal seizures, with loss of consciousness occurring in a fraction of a second. Consciousness is maintained by large numbers of nerve cells in various areas of the brain firing in certain patterns. Wakefulness depends on activation of the cerebral hemispheres by groups of nerve cells located in the brainstem in an area called the reticular activating system. Suppression of both cerebral hemispheres or of the reticular activating system will lead to loss of consciousness. In clinical practice, this is most often observed with drugs or toxins (Wilson et al. 1991, 194).

Consciousness will also be lost during grand mal (generalized) seizures caused by externally applied electric current or by other factors. The onset of a grand mal seizure is marked by a sudden loss of consciousness (Wilson et al. 1991, p. 969).

a. Types of electric current used to induce seizures. Electroconvulsive therapy involves placing electrodes on the head and applying various electrical stimuli. Stimuli have varied over the years, using different wave forms (sine, square, pulse), voltages, currents, polarities (positive, negative, both), duration of cycles or pulses, intervals between pulses or cycles, and the total stimulus duration. A "usual commercial" electroconvulsive therapy instrument has been described as an AC sine wave of 200 peak volts, 600 mA (milliamperes) peak current, and a stimulus duration of 0.75 second (Weaver et al. 1977).

b. Time to induction of seizures. A voltage of 130 volts AC (183 volts peak) applied for 0.3 second has been used to induce grand mal seizures during electroconvulsive therapy (Kelly 1954). Valentine, Keddie and Dunne (1968) describe EST machines that put out 200 to 300 volts AC for several seconds and another machine that put out 260 volts for one second. Unidirectional (one voltage polarity, or pulsed dc) stimuli were also studied, as were bidirectional (positive and negative pulsed) stimuli. After the ECT was applied and a convulsion achieved, spontaneous respirations resumed in 41 to 98 seconds, and consciousness returned in 97 to 480 seconds. The time periods varied depending on the various electrode positions. Spontaneous respirations came first, with recovery of consciousness tending to take at least twice as long.

c. Time until loss of consciousness from electric current applied to the head. It is likely that when a current large enough to reliably induce seizures is passed through the head, the normal patterns of nerve firings needed to maintain consciousness are lost. The patterns of nerve firings would be lost because so many brain cells are simultaneously stimulated, similar to defibrillation of the heart. Neurons are depolarized, and then epileptiform complexes begin. Consciousness would thus be lost within one cycle of the applied current (1/60 second). Consciousness may return when the current stops unless there is a seizure, hypoxia, or other problem. The person would not regain consciousness during a grand mal seizure. There will be some breathing during the seizure, but it is less than normal.

There is often strong physical movement when electric currents are passed through the head. Therefore, as with any mechanical head injury, consciousness may be lost for quite variable lengths of time because of the mechanical trauma. Observation of the person and analysis of the situation should be able to determine if and when the person regained consciousness.

F. Absence of burns in fatal electric injury

A current capable of causing respiratory or cardiac arrest may not cause skin lesions depending on the resistance of the contact made with the skin, and the amount, and duration of current flow. In a study of 108 deaths involving electric sources under 1,000 volts, electric burns were absent in over 40 percent of cases (Wright and Davis 1980; Damjanov and Linder 1996, 106).

G. Conclusions

This section has described some of the mechanisms of death that can follow electric injury. It has also discussed information relevant to determining if there were periods of consciousness during respiratory and cardiac arrest. Cardiac, respiratory, and neurological events occur simultaneously during and following electric injury. These events must be carefully analyzed to see how the concepts discussed in this paper can be applied to any given case. It can be seen from the above discussion that loss of consciousness is expected ten to fifteen seconds after the heart stops beating. In respiratory arrest with a continuing normal heart rhythm, consciousness may persist for up to three minutes. Electroconvulsive therapy currents passed through the head can induce grand mal seizures with loss of consciousness in a third of a second; loss of consciousness with large currents through the head probably occurs within one cycle (1/60 second) of the electric current.

References

Cardiac and respiratory effects of electrical injury

Baxter, C. R., "Present Concepts in the Management of Major Electrical Injury," *Surg. Clin. North Am.* 50(6):1401–1418 (1970).

Chandra, N. C., C. O. Siu and A. M. Munster, "Clinical Predictors of Myocardial Damage after High Voltage Electrical Injury," *Crit. Care Med.* 18(3):293–297 (1990).

Drislane, F. W. and M. A. Samuels, "Neuropulmonology," in *Internal Medicine*, 4th ed., Stein, J. H., ed. (St. Louis: Mosby, 1994), 1195.

Homma, S., L. D. Gillam and A. E. Weyman, "Echocardiographic Observations in Survivors of Acute Electrical Injury," *Chest* 97:103–105 (1990).

Housinger, T. A. et al. "Prospective Study of Myocardial Damage in Electrical Injuries," *J. Trauma* 25(2):122–124 (1985).

Ku, C. S. et al., "Myocardial Damage Associated with Electrical Injury," *American Heart Journal* 118:621–624 (1989).

Kugelberg, J., "Accidental Ventricular Fibrillation of the Human Heart," *Scand. J. Thor. Cardiovasc. Surg.* 9:133–139 (1975).

Kugelberg, J., "Electrical Induction of Ventricular Fibrillation in the Human Heart," *Scand. J. Thor. Cardiovasc. Surg.* 10:237–240 (1976).

Lewin, R. F., A. Arditti and S. Sclarovsky, "Non-Invasive Evaluation of Electrical Cardiac Injury," *Br. Heart J.* 49:190–192 (1983).

Lown, B. et al., "Comparison of Alternating Current with Direct Current Electroshock across the Closed Chest," *Am. J. Cardiol.* 10:223–233 (1962).

McBride, J. W. et al., "Is Serum Creatine Kinase-MB in Electrically Injured Patients Predictive of Myocardial Injury?" *JAMA* 255:764–768 (1984).

Moran, K. T., J. N. Thupari and A. M. Munster, "Electric- and Lightning-Induced Cardiac Arrest Reversed by Prompt Cardiopulmonary Resuscitation," *JAMA* 255(16):2157 (1986).

Pincus, M. R., H. J. Zimmerman and J. B. Henry, "Clinical Enzymology," in *Clinical Diagnosis and Management by Laboratory Methods*, 19th ed., Henry, J. B., ed. (Philadelphia: W. B. Saunders, 1996), 285.

Schein, R. M. H. et al., "Pulmonary edema associated with electrical injury," *Chest.* 97:1248–1250 (1990).

Somogyi, Endre and C. G. Tedeschi, "Injury by Electrical Force," in *Forensic Medicine: A Study in Trauma and Environmental Hazards,* vol. 1: *Mechanical Trauma*, Tedeschi C. G., W. G. Eckert and L. G. Tedeschi, eds. (Philadelphia: W. B. Saunders, 1977), 645–676.

Vascular injury

Bongard, O. and B. Fagrell B, "Delayed Arterial Thrombosis Following an Apparently Trivial Low-Voltage Electric Injury," *VASA* 18(2):162–166 (1989).

Hunt, J. L. et al., "Vascular Lesions in Acute Electrical Injuries," *Journal of Trauma* 14(6):461–473 (1974).

Nettelblad, H., K. A. Thuomas and F. SjAoberg, "Magnetic Resonance Imaging: A New Diagnostic Aid in the Care of High-Voltage Electrical Burns," *Burns* 22(2):117–119 (1996).

Conscious awareness during fatal electrical injury

Lee, R. C., "Physical Measurements of Tissue Injury in Electrical Trauma," *IEEE Transactions on Education* 34:223–230 (1991).

Dawalibi, F. and R. S. Baishiki, "Intricacies of the Safety Criterion around Power System Structures," in *Electrical Shock Safety Criteria: Proceedings of the*

First International Symposium on Electrical Shock Safety Criteria, Bridges, J. E. et al., eds. (NY: Pergamon Press, 1985), 273–282.

Fisher, Rudolph S., "Electrical and Lightning Injuries," in Spitz, Werner U. and Rudolf S. Fisher, *Medicolegal Investigation of Death*, 2nd ed. (Springfield, IL: Charles C. Thomas, 1980), 367.

Wright, R. K. and J. H. Davis, "The Investigation of Electrical Deaths: A Report of 220 Fatalities," *J. Forensic Sci.* 25:514–521 (1980).

General references

Al-Alousi, L. M., "Homicide by Electrocution," *Med. Sci. Law.* 30(3):239–246 (1990).

Craig, A. B., "Summary of 58 Cases of Loss of Consciousness during Underwater Swimming and Diving," *Medicine and Science in Sports* 8(3):1171–175 (1976).

Cummins, Robert O., ed., *Advanced Cardiac Life Support* (Dallas, TX: American Heart Association 1997), 1–25.

Cummins, Robert O. et al., "Out-of-Hospital Transcutaneous Pacing by Emergency Medical Technicians in Patients with Asystolic Cardiac," *New England Journal of Medicine* 328(19):1377–1382 (1993).

Damjanov, I. and J. Linder, *Anderson's Pathology*, 10th ed. (St. Louis: Mosby, 1996).

Davis, J. H. "Asphyxial Deaths" in *Modern Legal Medicine, Psychiatry, and Forensic Science*, Curran, W. J., A. L. McGarry and C. S. Pety, eds. (Philadelphia: F. A. Davis, 1980), 252.

de Vries, J. W. et al., "Changes in Cerebral Oxygen Uptake and Cerebral Electrical Activity during Defibrillation Threshold Testing," *Anesth. Analg.* 87:16–20 (1998).

Feinberg, B. N. *Applied Clinical Engineering* (Englewood Cliffs, NJ: Prentice-Hall, 1986) 415–420.

Fish, Raymond M. and Leslie A. Geddes, *Medical and Bioengineering Aspects of Electrical Injuries* (Tucson, AZ: Lawyers & Judges Publishing, 2003).

Fisher, Rudolph S., "Electrical and Lightning Injuries," in Spitz, Werner U. and Rudolf S. Fisher, *Medicolegal Investigation of Death*, 2nd ed. (Springfield, IL: Charles C. Thomas, 1980), 367.

IEEE Power Engineering Society Substation Committee. *IEEE Guide for Safety in AC Substation Grounding* (NY: IEEE, 1986), 32.

Josephson, M. E. et al., "Mechanism of Ventricular Fibrillation in Man," *American Journal of Cardiology* 44:623–631 (1979).

Kelly, J. P., "Fractures Complicating Electro-Convulsive Therapy and Chronic Epilepsy," *J. Bone Joint Surgery* 36B:70–79 (1954).

Kugelberg J. "Accidental Ventricular Fibrillation of the Human Heart," *Scand. J. Thor. Cardiovasc. Surg.* 9:133–139 (1975).

Kugelberg J. "Electrical Induction of Ventricular Fibrillation in the Human Heart," *Scand. J. Thor. Cardiovasc. Surg.* 10:237–240 (1976).

Langworthy, O. R. and W. B. Kouwenshoven, "Injuries Produced by Contact with Electric Circuits," *American Journal of Hygiene* 16(3):625–666 (1932).

Lee, W. R., "The Mechanisms of Death from Electric Shock," *Medicine, Science, and the Law* 5(1):23–28 (1965).

Levin, M., "Perception of Chassis Leakage Current," *Biomedical Instrumentation & Technology* 25:135–140 (1991).

Pearn, J., "Pathophysiology of Drowning," *Medical Journal of Australia* 142:586–588 (1985).

Polson, C. F., D. J. Lee and B. Knight, "Electrical Injuries and Lightning Stroke," in *The Essentials of Forensic Medicine*, 4th ed. (NY: Pergamon Press, 1985), 281.

Somogyi, Endre and C. G. Tedeschi, "Injury by Electrical Force," in *Forensic Medicine: A Study in Trauma and Environmental Hazards,* vol. 1: *Mechanical Trauma*, Tedeschi C. G., W. G. Eckert and L. G. Tedeschi, eds. (Philadelphia: W. B. Saunders, 1977), 659.

Tacker, W. A., "External Defibrillators," in *The Biomedical Engineering Handbook*, Bronzino, J. D., ed. (Hartford, CT: CRC Press, 1995), 1275–1283.

Valentine, M., K. M. G. Keddie and D. Dunne, "A Comparison of Techniques in Electro-Convulsive Therapy," *Brit. J. Psychiat.* 114:989–996 (1968).

Walters, C. W., "Is Death from Accidental Electric Shock Instantaneous?" *JAMA* 221(8):922 (1972).

Weaver, L. A. et al., "A Comparison of Standard Alternating Current and Low-Energy Brief Pulse Electrotherapy," *Biological Psychiatry* 12(4):525–543 (1977).

Wilson, J. D. et al., eds., *Harrison's Principles of Internal Medicine*, 12th ed. (NY: McGraw-Hill, 1991), 194.

Wright, R. K. and J. H. Davis, "The Investigation of Electrical Deaths: A Report of 220 Fatalities," *J. Forensic Sci.* 25:514 (1980).

Chapter 19

Electrical Injuries to the Digestive and Urinary Systems

19.1 Gastrointestinal Injury
A. Direct injury of intra-abdominal organs

The most common form of direct gastrointestinal injury from high voltage is widespread necrosis of the colon or small intestine. This is associated in most cases with extensive electric burns of the overlying abdominal wall. Hollow viscus injuries have included perforation or necrosis of the gallbladder, small intestine, stomach, and sigmoid colon. Solid organs damaged by such high-voltage accidents have included the pancreas and liver (Kumar et al. 1993).

A series of forty-five patients with high-voltage injury reported by Baxter (1970) demonstrates the variety of effects electric current can cause. All patients had serious injury from a source of 5,000 volts AC or more. Injuries included direct tissue damage, stress ulcers in the stomach and duodenum, prolonged ileus, development of a mild transient diabetic state, and respiratory arrest and cardiac dysrhythmias from electrolyte imbalance.

Intra-abdominal structures can be directly injured by electric contact on the abdominal wall. On autopsy, submucosal hemorrhages are frequently found scattered throughout the gastrointestinal tract. Therefore, in addition to obvious injury, undetected injury to intra-abdominal structures probably occurs in many cases (Baxter 1970).

B. Indirect effects on the gastrointestinal system
1. Stress ulcers
Stress ulcers (Curling's ulcers) following high voltage electric burns were reported by Baxter (1970). Six patients had massive gastrointestinal hemorrhage from the ulcers in the stomach or duodenum. A subtotal gastrectomy and vagotomy was performed in three of the patients. All three patients developed anastomotic leaks and intra-abdominal abscesses. All three patients died though the leak was the cause of death in only one.

2. Prolonged ileus
Prolonged ileus (blockage or paralysis of bowel function) with elevated serum amylase occurred in four of Baxter's patients. They responded to medical management. Signs and symptoms seen following electric injury that may progress to ileus include nausea, vomiting, intestinal colic, and abdominal distension (Kumar et al. 1993).

3. Pseudodiabetic state
Two patients reported by Baxter developed a pseudodiabetic state. These patients developed high blood sugar and serum ketones about a week after injury. They were treated with small quantities of insulin and reverted to normal.

4. Hypokalemia leading to respiratory arrest and cardiac dysrhythmias
Between the second and fourth weeks after injury, four patients developed severe potassium deficiency. The serum potassium dropped from between 4 to 4.5 mEq per liter to between 1 and 2 mEq per liter in less than forty-eight hours. Respiratory arrest and severe cardiac dysrhythmias led to the diagnosis in two of the patients. These patients had no apparent cause for the hypokalemia. They were eating well and had normal renal

function, gastrointestinal function, and acid-base balance. Urinary excretion of potassium was not high.

5. Delayed effects

Recurrent dysfunction of the upper gastrointestinal tract occurred in about three fourths of the patients within twelve to eighteen months after injury. Six of the forty-five patients developed gallstones (cholelithiasis) within two years after recovery; this is unusual in young males. Multiple small mixed stones were often found. In the remaining patients, the cause of the abdominal symptoms was not understood.

C. Treatment of abdominal electric injuries

The ABCs of trauma and cardiac care apply to the electric injury victim. One must first tend to airway, breathing, and circulation (ABC) with cervical spine control.

Ileus is a cessation or blockage of normal bowel function that can lead to abdominal distention, vomiting, and aspiration. Ileus can occur with a wide variety of conditions including lumbar fractures, abdominal trauma, and generalized body burns. A nasogastric tube is useful in an effort to prevent distention and the resultant vomiting and aspiration, though the NG tube is not 100 percent effective in preventing this problem.

Stress ulcer of the duodenum (Curling's ulcer) can come from burns of any kind. Its occurrence can be made less likely by antacids and medicines that decrease acid production (such as Tagamet, Pepcid, Axid or Zantac). Intra-abdominal injury should be suspected and looked for if there were abdominal burns or if ileus lasts more than two days.

The majority of patients with intra-abdominal hollow viscus injury reported in the literature have had a diagnosis that was either delayed up to two weeks or made at autopsy. Diagnosis of such injury is often difficult. Work-up is indicated if there are burns related to electric contact points over the abdomen. Also, as with trauma of any etiology, work-up of possible intra-abdominal injury is indicated if there is loss of consciousness or other neurological impairment and a history of a fall or other type of blunt trauma (Cooper 1984).

19.2 Metabolic, Renal and Hepatic Complications
A. The liver

Elevations of serum bilirubin and bilirubin in the urine are sometimes detected after electric shock, but there is usually not jaundice (Somogyi and Tedeschi 1977, 660).

B. The kidneys

Renal failure is an expected result of high voltage injury if proper treatment is not given. With electric and other types of injury involving muscles, myoglobin from muscle is released into the blood. The myoglobin travels to and blocks the kidneys. This blockage produces decreased urine output, a rise in BUN and creatinine, and electrolyte imbalance. Renal failure can lead to death (Somogyi and Tedeschi 1977, 661).

C. Blood gas changes due to respiratory arrest

At many places in this book, situations are described in which breathing stops because of electric injury. In some cases, this respiratory arrest is followed by cardiac arrest. When severe enough, the blood gas alterations caused by respiratory arrest lead to circulatory collapse and cardiac arrest (Kristoffersen et al. 1967).

Acid-base imbalance. It is not unusual for patients with electric injury to have serum pH values of 6.8 to 7.2 on admission to emergency departments (Copstead 1995, 1113). This degree of acidosis is dangerous because only a slight worsening of the patient's acid-base status could lead to cardiac arrest.

A number of alterations occur in blood gas parameters as a result of decreased respirations, as explained in Table 19.1. Acute respiratory failure is defined as a drop in pO_2 of 10 to 15 mmHg or more (Wilson et al. 1991).

Table 19.1
Blood Gas Changes Due to Decreased Respirations

1. Arterial blood gases measure levels of oxygen (pO_2) and carbon dioxide (pCO_2). The acid-base balance, or pH, is also measured.
2. Breathing normally brings oxygen into the body and removes carbon dioxide. Therefore, decreased respirations will
   a. Decrease the oxygen level in the blood (decrease pO_2)
   b. Increase the carbon dioxide level in the blood (increase pCO_2)
3. Through a series of chemical reactions, increased carbon dioxide level in the blood (increased pCO_2) causes acidosis of the blood (a decreased pH). This is called a respiratory acidosis.
4. Decreased oxygen supply leads tissues to function using chemical reactions that do not use oxygen (called anaerobic metabolism). This decreases the level of sodium bicarbonate in the blood, leading to a metabolic acidosis.
5. From points 2–4 above, it can be seen that respiratory arrest will directly cause a respiratory acidosis and indirectly cause a metabolic acidosis. The effects on pH are additive in a nonlinear fashion.
6. A decrease in respirations causing a drop in pO_2 of 10 to 15 mmHg or more would be called acute respiratory failure.
7. If severe enough, respiratory failure may cause or contribute to cardiac arrest.
8. Even if cardiac arrest does not occur, hypoxic brain injury may result from prolonged severe respiratory failure.

References

Baxter, C. R., "Present Concepts in the Management of Major Electrical Injury," *Surg. Clin. North. Am.* 50(6):1401–1418 (1970).

Cooper, M. A., "Electrical and Lightning Injuries," *Emergency Clinics of North America*, August 1984, 489–501.

Copstead, L. E. C., *Perspectives on Pathophysiology* (Philadelphia: W. B. Saunders, 1995), 1113.

Kumar, S., S. Thomas and S. Lehri, "Abdominal Wall and Stomach Perforation Following Accidental Electrocution with High Tension Wire: A Unique Case," *Journal of Emergency Medicine* 11:141–145 (1993).

Kristoffersen, M. B., C. C. Rattenborg and D. A. Holaday, "Asphyxial Deaths: The Roles of Acute Anoxia, Hypercarbia and Acidosis," *Anesthesiology* 28(3):488–497 (1967).

Somogyi, Endre and C. G. Tedeschi, "Injury by Electrical Force," in *Forensic Medicine: A Study in Trauma and Environmental Hazards*, Tedeschi C. G., W. G. Eckert and L. G. Tedeschi, eds. (Philadelphia: W. B. Saunders, 1977), sec. 4.

Wilson, J. D. et al., eds., *Harrison's Principles of Internal Medicine*, 12th ed. (NY: McGraw-Hill, 1991), 1080.

Chapter 20

Maternal and Fetal Electrical Injuries

For many years, fetal injury and death have been noted to follow maternal electric injury. Pliny the Elder in his *Natural History* (year 77) recorded lightning hitting a pregnant woman; the child was killed, but the woman survived (Rackhan 1938; Wagner, McCann and Clayton 1950). One prospective study designed to show if electric injury increases the incidence of fetal death has been published, but it did not involve enough cases to address the issue.

This chapter describes reported cases of fetal death and injury following apparently minor material electric injury. Medical information relevant to interpreting the case reports is given at the end of this chapter. This medical information includes statistics about the usual incidence of fetal loss. Oligohydramnios, a condition that often follows electric injury,

437

is also discussed. Oligohydramnios is a risk factor for fetal injury and death.

20.1 Incidence of Fetal Death with Apparently Minor Maternal Electrical Injury

A. A study finding a high probability of injury

A 73-percent fetal mortality was reported by Fatovich (1993). He reviewed case reports in the medical literature of electric injury to the mother in pregnancy. In his series of fifteen patients, eleven involved fetal mortality, and there was only one normal pregnancy following maternal electric injury. The probably of fetal injury is high in this study. The true probability of fetal injury is probably lower, assuming that papers would not have been published about women who had no problems following electric accidents.

B. A study finding a low probability of injury

In contrast, another paper concludes, "In most cases accidental electric shock occurring during the day-to-day life during pregnancy does not pose a major fetal risk" (Einarson et al. 1997). This conclusion has been criticized (Jaffe and Fejgin 1997). In the Einarson study, thirty-one women who had received an electric shock were compared to a control group of thirty-one women who did not receive a shock. A shock involved touching a 110-volt AC source in twenty-six of the thirty-one mothers. Two mothers touched a 220-volt AC source, one a 12-volt telephone source, and two had touched an electric fence (2,000 and 8,000 volts). Only two had tetany (possible prolonged contact), and only one mother had a burn. In the control group, there was one spontaneous abortion.

In the group receiving shock there were twenty-eight normal births, two spontaneous abortions, and a child with a ventricular septal defect. The current path did not cross the uterus in either of the cases of spontaneous abortion, and fetal death occurred before the electric shock in one of the cases; this was determined by the apparent age of the fetus and dates. The study involved only three cases in which there was a current path involving the uterus. The authors contrast their results with past reports they found in the literature; the literature reports gave a 76-percent fetal mortality rate. The authors attribute this to reporting bias: case reports are generally prompted by adverse outcomes, and case reports rarely report on normal outcomes. Einarson et al. also note that the previously published case reports had a 62-percent hand-to-foot current pathway, while it was 10 percent in their study.

The Einarson paper lists the baseline risk of fetal death as 15 percent. The authors suggest that a sample size of ninety-eight would be needed to have 80 percent statistical power to detect a twofold increase in the risk of fetal death. Their study involved only three patients with a current path from hand to foot-much less than the ninety-eight patients the authors say would be needed to detect a doubling in fetal death.

The Einarson study is also insufficient to investigate the mechanism of fetal injury involving dislodging placental clots, a mechanism of fetal injury that would not necessarily involve hand to foot current flow. The mechanical trauma from jerking back from the current source might be enough to dislodge placental clots in patients who have them. Placental clots are an issue in patients with the inherited genetic factor V Leiden mutation, which is associated with APC (activated protein C) resistance (Kraus 1997). However, the incidence in the population of APC resistance is 2–7 percent (Thorarensen 1997). The Einarson study would be expected to have only two or three such patients. Again, this is much less than the ninety-eight patients the authors say would be needed to detect a doubling in fetal death.

It is difficult to do studies with enough cases to obtain statistically significant results. This is because few persons have electrical accidents. Many persons who do have an electrical accident have a very brief, high resistance contact to the source, in other words, current flow is small. It took Einarson and coworkers over ten years to collect the cases they did have.

20.2 Fetal Movements: A Sign of Fetal Well-Being

The fetus responds to chronic hypoxia by attempting to conserve energy, sometimes by reducing body movements. Maternal perception of fetal movements correlates well with ultrasound observations. The small number of women who have trouble perceiving fetal movements often improve after viewing the fetus with real-time ultrasound. Reduced or abnormal fetal movements are associated with stillbirths and poor neonatal condition. Fetal movement recording sometimes correlates with the result of nonstress testing, but in some studies does not (Baskett and Liston 1989).

Effects of electric current on fetal movements. Mothers sometimes notice a change in fetal movements after an apparently minor electric injury. Ianniroberto and Tajani (1981) reported a somewhat quantitative observation of this effect. Sequential ultrasound examinations were done on the fetus of a mother who received a 220-volt AC electric shock at eighteen weeks of gestation. The fetus had become immobile, had a tachycardia, and did not respond to external tactile stimulation. This lasted for forty-eight hours. The child was normal at birth (Ianniroberto and Tajani 1981).

20.3 Causal Relationships and the Temporal Sequence of Events

The quote below refers to the evaluation of the significance of asphyxia around the time of birth. The concept is that brain injury due to alleged brain trauma is unlikely if the neonate seems to have normal brain function immediately following the alleged brain trauma. In applying this thinking to a fetus in earlier pregnancy, one must take into account that it is usually not possible to evaluate brain function of the fetus unless the mother notices changes in fetal movements. Changes in fetal movements were noted in some of the case reports described in this chapter. The ability of mothers to note fetal movements is variable. The quote below concerns neonates who can be seen and evaluated neurologically.

> Most individual neurodevelopmental risk factors will not be followed by the disability for which the child is at increased risk . . . additional intervening evidence must exist to reliably link risk to disability and to scientifically and mediocolegally convert a possible risk-disability association into a probable cause and effect relationship. In the case of potential acquired brain injuries, it must be demonstrated that the risk agent or event was temporally closely followed by evidence of acute neurologic depression and/or deterioration (e.g., reduction in state of consciousness, alterations of muscle tone, autonomic nervous system instability, apnea, seizure activity) which, despite often apparently resolving, eventually evolved, over varying periods of time, into a permanent disability. The presence of relatively immediate neurological abnormalities and signs of acute brain dysfunction following a potential risk, such as intrapartum asphyxia, provides confirmatory evidence of the gravity of the event and renders causal linkages with a subsequent disability as plau-

sible; conversely, the virtual absence of signs or symptoms of acute neurologic compromise makes risk-disability causal linkages unlikely (Stevenson and Sunshine 1997).

Observation of the immediate effects described in the previous paragraph might not be possible in a fetus, as the fetus is not readily observable. Thus, electrical injury during pregnancy might greatly depress the neurologic function of a fetus, but the mother might not notice anything. Induction of a fetal seizure might be recognized as severe jerking motions (Conover et al. 1986; Landy et al. 1989), but other fetal neurological dysfunction will likely go unnoticed. Conditions other than severe brain injury may not have noticeable immediate effects, as is suggested by the reports of delayed spinal cord damage from electrical injury discussed in another chapter of this book. However, when immediate effects of a trauma are noted in a part of the body or brain, even if the effects are transient, it suggests that the trauma had some effect on the affected part.

20.4 Possible Mechanisms of Fetal Injury
See Table 20.1.

20.5 Case Reports of Fetal Death
A. Low voltage (220 volts or less) with minor maternal injury
Lieberman et al. (1986) report on six pregnant women between the ages of twenty-seven and thirty-seven who suffered an apparently minor electrical injury at home during pregnancy. All six patients had a hand-to-foot current path and felt a slight electrical sensation at the time of injury. No patient had loss of consciousness or skin wounds. All felt well after the incident. Gestational ages were from twenty-one to forty weeks. Patients 2 and 5 were seen by a physician on the day of injury, and the others did not seek immediate care. Patients 1 and 3 immediately noticed decreased fetal movements and had stillbirths within a week; their gestational ages were twenty-six and forty weeks. Patient 2 was at twenty-one weeks of gestation and did not notice a change in fetal movements; but twelve weeks after the electric shock, she had a stillborn child showing intrauterine growth retardation that may have started before the electric shock. Patients 4 and 5 were at thirty-two and twenty weeks of gestation and had

normal births except for oligohydramnios. Patient 6 was at forty weeks of gestation and had a normal birth.

The three stillborn infants showed maceration, but no anatomical or pathological lesions suggesting a specific type of injury. It was thought that changes in fetal heart conduction or lesions in the utero-placental bed might have been involved in causing the deaths.

Fatovich (1993) examined case reports of fifteen pregnant electric shock victims. In this series, only one mother was injured, receiving a burn. None had loss of consciousness. Several were thrown back from the

---

Table 20.1
Possible Mechanisms of Fetal Injury

1. Maternal nervous system stimulation
   a. vagal can slow maternal heart rate and lower maternal blood pressure, leading to fetal hypoxia
   b. adrenergic (involving adrenalin or epinephrine) can decrease uterine blood flow by causing constriction of uterine arteries
2. Maternal and/or fetal dysrhythmias (heart rhythm changes near the time of the electric injury)
3. Maternal respiratory abnormalities near the time of the electric injury
4. Mechanical trauma, resulting from:
   a. strong muscle contractions and bodily movements induced by the electric current
   b. falling
   c. being thrown
   d. blast effect, if there was an electric arc or other explosive force
   e. trauma secondary to additional events (fire, flying debris, inhalation injury)
5. Sequelae of mechanical trauma include:
   a. dislodging of a placental thrombus to cause an embolus to the fetus
   b. placental abruption

current source. Eight had moist skin. There was one normal pregnancy, with fetal death occurring in eleven of the fifteen cases (73 percent).

Strong et al. (1987) report a thirty-week pregnant woman who received a 110-volt DC shock and several seemingly milder shocks at eighteen weeks of gestational age. On the day she received the shock at thirty weeks, she came to an emergency department because of decreased fetal movements. Electrical contact had been made with the hands. The patient and coworkers had been thrown clear without loss of consciousness. The patient had no skin lesions. Monitoring showed fetal distress with a fetal heart rate of 120 to 160, no beat-to-beat variation in the baseline heart rate, and repetitive spontaneous fetal heart decelerations to as low as 70 beats per minute. Ultrasound showed a twenty-eight-week fetus with oligohydramnios and no spontaneous fetal movement. Maternal CPK (creatinine phosphokinase) was slightly elevated, and the urine contained myoglobin. Maternal ECG was normal. A Cesarean section was done because of the fetal distress. Apgar scores were 5 and 7, and umbilical artery blood pH was 7.25 (normal 7.25-7.35). Gross and microscopic study of the placenta, cord, and membranes were normal. The child had growth retardation, hyperbilirubinemia, and a patent ductus arteriosus, but did well. The authors conclude that the IUGR (intrauterine growth retardation) and oligohydramnios were due to earlier electric shocks. Ultrasound is useful to assess gestational age, baseline parameters for following fetal growth, and amniotic fluid volume estimation.

A case reported by Peppler et al. (1972) involved a woman who was involved in an unusual accident eleven days before her expected delivery date. The patient was a twenty-one-year-old who was driving along a highway in a rainstorm when an approaching vehicle skidded off the road and severed a utility pole. The power line whipped across the highway and struck the windshield of her Volkswagen. A hole was made in the windshield near the patient's right hand. She felt a jolt in her right arm that forced her to temporarily let go of the steering wheel. She noted a blue color and numbness of the arm from the elbow distally for thirty minutes. An hour later she felt a slight movement in her uterus, but no later fetal movements. Six days later during her regular weekly visit, fetal heart tones could not be heard, though they had been one day before the accident. She delivered a macerated stillborn infant nine days later. Autopsy revealed a fetus with no defect or abnormality to account for the death.

The appearance (degree of maceration) was compatible with death at the time of the electric shock. The authors suggest that the fetal heart and blood vessels are very susceptible to electrical and mechanical stimuli, with mere touching of fetal vessels being able to produce severe spasms (Assali and Morris 1964).

Fetal death at nine weeks of gestation occurred when a woman suffered a hand to foot 220-volt AC electric shock from a washing machine. The day before the accident a sonogram showed a single live fetus with no abnormalities seen. When she received the shock, there were no burns or loss of consciousness. After the electric shock, no fetal heart activity could be detected. She had a spontaneous abortion two days later. The authors commented that an association of events does not constitute proof of cause and effect. However, it seemed reasonable to them to conclude that electric shock caused the fetal death. (Mazor and Leiberman 1987).

B. Cranial nerve and musculoskeletal abnormalities

Neurological damage to the fetus has been discussed by Lipson et al. (1989). They describe (their case number 8) a woman who received a 240-volt AC shock to the hand at sixteen weeks of gestation. She was thrown backwards and was unconscious for an undetermined period of time. There was no definite head injury or burn. The child had unilateral cranial and neurological deficits; there was a left-sided Duane syndrome and left facial nerve palsy. Duane syndrome is a marked limitation of ocular abduction (turning the eye laterally) and retraction of the globe and narrowing of the palpebral fissure (skin fold near the eye) on attempted adduction (bringing the eye toward the nose). The child also had bilateral finger syndactyly (webbing or fusion) and distal deficiencies of the fingers.

This was diagnosed as a case of Möbius' syndrome, a congenital seventh nerve palsy that is often associated with other cranial nerve palsies and musculoskeletal abnormalities. Lipson et al. report that such defects are often associated with events that cause transient uteroplacental vascular insufficiency (decreased blood flow to the uterus). Eight of fifteen cases they studied involved events that could be expected to cause uteroplacental vascular insufficiency, including the electric injury case described above. In addition, a rat model showed that abdominal trauma, uterine vessel clamping, and other events can lead to brainstem lesions in fetal rats.

It is thought that there is a vascular etiology for the Möbius' syndrome that is induced by external trauma, including electric current (Lipson et al. 1989). Control of uterine blood flow is by sympathetic adrenergic vasoconstrictor fibers. There is minimal resting tone of these fibers, giving a widely dilated vascular bed in the normal state. Adrenergic stimulation causes vasoconstriction (closing of blood vessels) and decreased blood flow to the uterus. This effect, along with other possible factors that could cause an episode of fetal hypoxia, is listed in Table 20.1.

C. Vasospasm and focal cerebral ischemia produced experimentally

Electrical stimulation can constrict arteries, arterioles and capillaries over an area of cortex and cause temporary, but possibly complete, ischemia of the underlying brain (Echlin 1942, 85). Vascular constriction occurs with a stimulus just adequate to produce motor movement. Such a stimulus applied for two seconds could cause a blood vessel to constrict up to five minutes (Echlin 1942, 83). This stimulus strength would stimulate intact nerve cells, but would not be strong enough to cause thermal damage to tissues (Echlin 1942).

It is possible the above experiments mean that relatively small electric currents flowing through the fetus can cause prolonged vasoconstriction of vessels supplying blood to the fetal brain. This theory seems less likely in light of the fact that electroconvulsive therapy in the (fully developed) adult does not cause such brain injury (Devanand 1994). The theory seems more likely in light of the fact that many cases of progressive and delayed spinal cord injury have been reported in adults with electric accidents. And many of those accidents did not involve currents that caused burning or thermal damage to the spinal cord (see the chapter in this book on spinal injury).

D. Electric fence contact and fetal death

Steer (1992) reported the case of a thirty-one-year-old who received a shock through her jeans as she was stepping over an electric fence at eleven weeks of gestation.

The electric fence produced pulses of 5,000 volts lasting less than 0.1 second at one second intervals. The current limit set by Australian Standard 3129 was 300 milliamperes being delivered for a maximum of 0.3

millisecond. The charge per pulse was 2.5 milliamp-seconds, or 2.5 millicoulombs.

The patient felt that the shock went from the vulva to the upper abdomen in the midline. She felt well and did not seek medical attention. At her sixteen-week checkup, ultrasound found a dead fetus of twelve weeks' gestation. She was induced and delivered a macerated fetus with foot length of 8 mm, corresponding to a maximum gestational age of twelve weeks plus two days and a minimum of eleven weeks plus one day. There were no external signs of electric injury, dysmorphic fetal features, or specific placental signs.

E. Placental abruption following electric injury

Yoong (1990) describes a twenty-eight-year-old, thirty-two-week pregnant woman in England who was fixing the plug of her iron at home. She received an electric shock and was thrown five meters across the room. She had no loss of consciousness, but felt "tingly" for several minutes. She went to the accident and emergency department and had a normal electrocardiogram. The uterus was soft, and fetal heart rate was 130 beats per minute. She was sent home. The next day she noted decreased fetal movements. She then developed severe abdominal pain, but no vaginal bleeding. Her uterus was hard and tender. Fetal heart rate was 70, falling to 48. An emergency cesarean section was done, revealing a large retroplacental clot. The Apgar score was 0 at nine minutes. The baby was resuscitated and died twenty-four hours following delivery. The parents refused postmortem exam. The mother required transfusion of four units of blood, but made a good recovery. In this case, abruptio placentae is the likely mechanism of injury.

Abruptio placentae is a (usually partial) separation of the placenta from the uterine wall. Abruptio placentae is the most common cause of fetal death following blunt trauma (American College of Surgeons 1997). In the second half of pregnancy, abruption can follow relatively minor injury. Vaginal bleeding will be absent in 30 percent of cases. Signs and symptoms may include abdominal pain, uterine tenderness or rigidity, expanding fundal height, and maternal shock. Uterine ultrasound may or may not show the abruption. Abruption is suggested by frequent uterine activity on monitoring (American College of Surgeons 1997). Even with trivial blunt or indirect abdominal trauma, at least three hours of fetal monitoring is usually recommended (Harwood-Nuss and Luten 1995, 271).

F. Lightning strike in pregnancy

Of eleven pregnant women who survived being struck by lightning, there were five cases of fetal death in utero, abortion, stillbirth, and neonatal deaths. The only fetal autopsy revealed pulmonary interstitial hemorrhage, thought to be explicable by the passage of lightning current (Fatovich 1993).

20.6 Treatment of Electrical Injury in Pregnancy

The pregnant woman who has received an apparently harmless electric injury may suffer later fetal damage or loss. However, there is no proof that any sort of monitoring or treatment can influence the outcome. Einarson et al. (1997) recommend an electrocardiogram for any woman who has had an electric shock of over 220 volts, was wet, had tetany, or a current pathway across the heart. They recommend cardiac monitoring for twenty-four hours if there was an abnormal initial electrocardiogram, loss of consciousness, or cardiovascular disease. They also recommend fetal heart Doppler monitoring. In addition, if it had not been done earlier, they recommend ultrasonography. They also recommend a Doppler assessment of the fetus two weeks later because of possible late fetal death.

Patient disposition and monitoring following electric shock are treated in more detail by Fish in Fish and Geddes (2003, 39–43).

20.7 Information Relevant to Interpreting Case Reports

The following is from the 1993 edition of *Williams' Obstetrics*. It refers to statistics in the United States (Cunningham et al. 1993).

A. Incidence of fetal deaths in the United States

Fetal deaths of twenty-weeks gestation or more were 1.88 percent in 1950 and 0.75 percent in 1989. Neonatal deaths of infants less than twenty-nine days old were 2.05 percent in 1950 and 0.62 percent in 1989. Perinatal mortality is defined as fetal deaths of twenty weeks' gestation or greater and infant deaths of less than twenty-eight days. Thus, perinatal morality is approximately the sum of fetal and neonatal deaths, being 3.9 percent in 1950 and 1.37 percent in 1989 (Cunningham et al. 1993, 5).

Spontaneous abortion (miscarriage) refers to the spontaneous loss of the fetus before twenty weeks of gestation, based upon the date of the first day of the last normal menses. Another definition refers to the fetus or neonate weighing less than 500 grams. The definition is different in some European countries, being less than 1,000 grams. Over 80 percent of spontaneous abortions occur in the first twelve weeks of pregnancy. The risk of spontaneous abortion increases with parity, maternal age, and paternal age. Clinically recognized spontaneous abortion occurs in 12 percent of women under age twenty and in 26 percent of women over the age of forty.

B. Factors affecting the incidence of fetal death

A number of factors affect the rate of spontaneous abortion. One of the most striking is smoking. The risk of euploidic spontaneous abortion is doubled in women who smoke more than fourteen cigarettes a day (Cunningham et al. 1993, 669; Kline et al. 1980, 225).

Oligohydramnios (Cunningham et al. 1993, 738–9) is a decrease in the volume of amniotic fluid. This is relatively common in pregnancies that have continued beyond term, being about 12 percent at forty-one weeks. Causes of oligohydramnios include prematurely ruptured membranes, fetal growth retardation, fetal congenital anomalies, and placental abruption.

Oligohydramnios increases the risk of cord compression, and thus fetal distress, in labor. Oligohydramnios can be caused by lack of fetal urine output, as from obstruction or absence of the fetal urinary tract.

In one study, of thirty-four mid-trimester pregnancies with severe oligohydramnios, there were only seven surviving infants. Twenty-six percent of fetuses had anomalies. Ten of the twenty-five who were phenotypically normal died because of severe maternal hypertension, retarded fetal growth, or placental abruption (Mercer et al. 1986). Oligohydramnios may cause adhesions between fetal parts and the amnion, leading to deformities such as clubfoot and amputation.

References

American College of Surgeons, Committee on Trauma, *Advanced Trauma Life Support for Doctors* (Chicago: American College of Surgeons, 1997), 321.

Assali and Morris, "Maternal and Fetal Circulations and Their Interrelation-ships," *Obstet. Gynec. Survey* 19:923–948 (1964).

Baskett, T. F. and R. M. Liston, "Fetal Movement Monitoring: Clinical Applica-tion," *Clinics in Perinatology* 16(3):613–625 (1989).

Conover et al., "Antenatal Diagnosis of Fetal Seizure Activity with Use of Real-Time Ultrasound," *Am. J. Obstet. Gynecol.* 155:846–7 (1986).

Cunningham et al., eds., *Williams' Obstetrics*, 19th ed. (Norwalk, CT: Appleton & Lange, 1993).

Devanand, D. P. et al., "Does ECT Alter Brain Structure?" *American Journal of Psychiatry* 151(7):957–970 (1994).

Echlin, F. A., "Vasospasm and Focal Cerebral Ischemia: An Experimental Study," *Archives of Neurology and Psychiatry* 47:77–96 (1942).

Einarson, A, et al., "Accidental Electric Shock in Pregnancy: A Prospective Co-hort Study," *Am. J. Obstet. Gynecol.* 176:678–681 (1997).

Fatovich, D. M., "Electric Shock in Pregnancy," *Journal of Emergency Medicine* 11:175–177 (1993).

Fish, Raymond M. and Leslie A. Geddes, *Medical and Bioengineering Aspects of Electrical Injuries* (Tucson, AZ: Lawyers & Judges Publishing, 2003).

Harwood-Nuss, Ann L. and R. C. Luten, *Handbook of Emergency Medicine* (Philadelphia: J. B. Lippincott, 1995), 271.

Ianniroberto, A. and E. Tajani, Ultrasonographic Study of Fetal Movements," *Seminars in Perinatology* 5:175–188 (1981).

Jaffe, Richard and Moshe Fejgin, "Accidental Electric Shock in Pregnancy: A Prospective Cohort Study" (letter to the editor), *Am. J. Obstet. Gynecol.* 174(4):983–984, 1997.

Kline, J. et al., "Environmental Influences on Early Reproductive Loss in a Cur-rent New York City Study," in *Human Embryonic and Fetal Death*, Porter, I. H. and E. B. Hook, eds. (NY: Academic Press, 1980), 225.

Kraus, F. T., "Cerebral Palsy and Thrombi in Placental Vessels of the Fetus: In-sights from Litigation," *Hum. Pathol.* 28:246–248 (1997).

Landy, H. J. et al., "Antenatal Ultrasonographic Diagnosis of Fetal Seizure Activity," *Am. J. Obstet. Gynecol.* 161:308 (1989).

Leiberman, J. R. et al., "Electrical Accidents during Pregnancy," *Obstetrics & Gynecology* 67:861–863 (1986).

Lipson, A. H. et al., "Moebius Syndrome: Animal Model-Human Correlations and Evidence for a Brainstem Vascular Etiology," *Teratology* 40:339–350 (1989).

Mazor, M. and J. R. Leiberman, "Abortion Caused by Electrical Current," *Arch. Gynecol. Obstet.* 241:71–72 (1987).

Mercer, L. J. and L. B. Brown, "Fetal Outcome with Oligohydramnios in the Second Trimester," *Obstet. Gynecol.* 67:840 (1986).

Peppler, R. D., F. J. Labranche and J. J. Comeaux, "Intrauterine Death of a Fetus in a Mother Shocked by an Electric Current: A Case Report," *Journal of the Louisiana State Medical Society* 124(2):37–38 (1972).

Rackham, H., *Pliny's Natural History, Book II*, translated by H. Rackham (Cambridge, MA: Harvard University Press, 1938), 275.

Steer, R. G., "Delayed Fetal Death Following Electrical Injury in the First Trimester," *Australian and New Zealand Journal of Obstetrics and Gynaecology* 32(4):377–378 (1992).

Stevenson, D. K. and P. Sunshine, *Fetal and Neonatal Brain Injury,* 2nd ed. (Oxford: Oxford University Press, 1997), viii–ix.

Strong, T. H. et al., "Electrical Shock in Pregnancy: A Case Report," *Journal of Emergency Medicine* 5:381–383 (1987).

Thorarensen, O. et al., "Mutation: An Unrecognized Cause of Hemiplegic Cerebral Palsy, Neonatal Stroke, and Placental Thrombosis," *Ann. Neurol.* 42:372–375 (1997).

Wagner, C. F., G. D. McCann, and J. M. Clayton, "Lightning Phenomena," in *Electrical Transmission and Distribution Reference Book*, 4th ed. (East Pittsburgh, PA: Westinghouse Electric, 1950).

Yoong, A. F. E., "Electrical Shock Sustained in Pregnancy by Placental Abruption," *Postgraduate Medical Journal* 66:563–564 (1990).

Chapter 21

Psychological Effects of Electrical Injury

Synopsis
21.1 Incidence
21.2 Psychological Effects of Uncertain Etiology
21.3 Similarities Between Depression and Suspected Brain Injury of Uncertain Origin
References

A more thorough treatment of the psychological effects of electrical injury can be found in Fish and Geddes (2003, 329–334) .

21.1 Incidence

A study of 2,080 work-related electric injuries in France reported fifty-one cases of posttraumatic stress disorders and various "postconcussion" syndromes (Gourbiere et al. 1994). In sixteen of these, the symptomatology was similar to criteria described in the *Diagnostic and Statistical Manual of Mental Disorders* of the American Psychiatric Association. In the other thirty-five cases, the symptomatology was incomplete, mild, or did not meet the criteria. The most common symptoms were headaches and dizziness. The majority of posttraumatic disorders occurred gradually after an electrical injury. These were likely to occur after a true electrical injury, defined as electrothermal or mixed burns with contact points on the head, or related to associated head injury. Sometimes, burn injury of any kind was found to be the sole cause of posttraumatic disorder. Other neuropsychic sequelae reported in this study included twenty-two cases of autonomic nervous system disorders, mood disturbances, asymptomatic electroencephalogram abnormalities (thirteen cases), and other central nervous system disorders (five cases, including one tetraplegia and one paraplegia).

21.2 Psychological Effects of Uncertain Etiology

A study of sixty-three electrically injured patients at the University of Chicago involved patients seen for non-lightning electrical injury (Pliskin et al. 1998). The study found a progressive neuropsychological syndrome of electrical injury survival that included physical, cognitive, and emotional complaints. The patients had no evidence of electrical or mechanical injury to the head. However, it is thought that the patients may have been exposed to a blast effect through the air. One theory is that the blast effect may cause brain injury.

High-voltage accidents frequently involve formation of electric arcs. Electric arcs create a blast or explosion effect because the sudden high arc temperatures cause rapid expansion of the air. The blast victim may not have had any burns or physical contact with the current source, yet may have apparent nervous system impairment. A correlation between blast force and injury has not yet been established, though such a correlation may be found in future studies. The blasts under consideration usually involve currents over 10 kA (10,000 amps) (Capelli-Schellpfeffer et al. 1996 and 1998, 28).

Blast injury can cause eardrum rupture and injury to the lung, brain, and other organs. Just how much brain injury seems to result from electric arc blasts of various strengths has not been established.

Early and late signs and symptoms that may indicate brain injury have been listed in a number of articles (see References). Two articles list these signs and symptoms as (Capelli-Schellpfeffer et al. 1996 and 1998):

- loss of hearing,
- irritability,
- confusion,
- unsteady walking,
- loss of concentration,
- memory changes,
- discouragement or depression,
- inability to complete tasks, and
- unexpected family difficulties.

21.3 Similarities Between Depression and Suspected Brain Injury of Uncertain Origin

Depression can cause the signs and symptoms listed above that are said to be indicative of brain injury except for the hearing loss, and possibly, the unsteady walking. The physical effects of the blast may also include hearing loss. Unsteady walking may result from inner ear (balance) difficulties also caused by blast injury. Alternatively, unsteady walking may be equivalent to the slowed body movement listed below as being characteristic of depression.

Except for hearing and balance problems, all of the conditions listed above as possibly indicating brain injury from electrical accidents are characteristic of depression.

Symptoms characteristic of depression are listed below, as described in the *DSM-IV* (1994, 320–322) under features of "major depressive episodes":

- suicidal ideation,
- change in sleep,
- somatic complaints (body aches and pains),
- change in weight,
- irritability,
- fatigue, decreased energy,
- difficulty thinking, concentrating, or making decisions,
- impairment in social, occupational, or other important areas of functioning,
- slowed speech, thinking and body movement,
- increased pauses before answering, and
- memory difficulties.

Depression is often a chronically recurrent condition. Some persons have isolated episodes separated by many years, some have clusters of episodes, and others have increasingly frequent episodes as they get older. Persons who have had one major depressive episode have a 50- to 60-percent chance of having a second episode. Those with two episodes of major depression have a 70-percent chance of having a third episode. Persons with three episodes have a 90-percent chance of further depressive episodes (*DSM-IV* 1994, 341–342). Therefore, persons who have been depressed before are likely to develop depression again, even with no blast or electrical injuries occurring.

It is therefore important to carefully examine the person's past medical and psychiatric histories. It is important to determine if the person claiming new onset of the above symptoms and signs has had depressive episodes in the past. It is not adequate to simply ask the person about past problems, especially when many such patients are complaining of cognitive and memory problems.

Whether or not any given patient has had depression in the past, the fact is that the two lists above are very similar. This similarity makes one wonder if some cases of unexplained brain injury may actually be depression, rather than a physical injury to the brain.

References

American Psychiatric Association, *Diagnostic and Statistical Manual of Mental Disorders*, 4th ed. (DSM-IV) (Washington, DC: American Psychiatric Association, 1994).

Capelli-Schellpfeffer, M. et al., "Correlation between Electrical Accident Parameters and Sustained Injury," in *Proceedings*, IEEE Industry Applications Society 43rd Annual Petroleum and Chemical Industry Conference, 1996, 299–305.

Capelli-Schellpfeffer, M. et al., "Correlation between Electrical Accident Parameters and Injury," *IEEE Industry Applications Magazine*, March-April 1998, 25–41.

Fish, Raymond M. and Leslie A. Geddes, *Medical and Bioengineering Aspects of Electrical Injuries* (Tucson, AZ: Lawyers & Judges Publishing, 2003).

Gourbiere, E., J. Corbut and Y. Bazin, "Functional Consequence of Electrical Injury," *Annals of the New York Academy of Sciences* 720:259–271 (1994).

Pliskin, N. H. et al., "Neurological Symptom Presentation Following Electrical Injury," *Journal of Trauma* 44(4):709–715 (1998).

Primeau. M., G. H. Engelstatter and K. K. Bares, "Behavioral Consequences of Lightning and Electrical Injury," *Seminars in Neurology* 15(3):279–285 (1995).

Part 3

Legal Aspects of Electrical Injuries

Paul F. Hill, Esq.

Chapter 22

Compliance with Codes, Regulations, Statutes and Ordinances

The law recognizes that electricity is an inherently dangerous product and that the producer and supplier of the product owes a high degree of care to the public. The state courts are not uniform with the exact language describing the degree of care. The language ranges from "ordinary care" to "utmost care." We can state generally that a producer must exercise a high degree of care commensurate with the risk and consistent with the practicalities of its business. The law also recognizes the superior knowledge of the power company as compared with the electrical knowledge of the average prudent individual. However, an electrician or linesman who is injured or killed by electricity may be held to the standard of the average prudent worker in those fields.

Electrical codes, regulations, statutes, and ordinances are designed to meet an acceptable standard of care by promoting practices and procedures which enhance safety. This chapter will note some cases in which the courts construed these standards. Is compliance with such standards a complete defense? Is a violation merely evidence of negligence, or is it negligence as a matter of law (negligence per se)? Is the violation related to causation of the accident at all? If not, it may not be relevant. The attorney with an electrical case will want to determine which, if any, code, regulation, state statute or city ordinance might apply to his case. The following case selection is arranged alphabetically by state. Some of the cases annotated below will be mentioned in other chapters.

A 1987 Arizona case involved the construction of a statute which governed activity in close proximity to a power line. The case arose when the boom of a truck contacted an overhead line carrying 13,800 volts and injured a worker. A contractor was moving vacant houses and assumed that the codefendant, a power company, had de-energized appropriate lines. The High Voltage Power Lines and Safety Restrictions Act, Arizona Revised Statute § 40-360.42–.43, prohibits an entity working near a live power line from using any tool or material that could come within six feet of the line, and requires the entity to notify the owner/operator of the line of any activity planned which might impinge on the six-foot rule. The jury awarded over $1 million, and found the utility and the contractor equally at fault. The contractor argued on appeal that it was excused from complying with the notice statute; it had notified the utility, and power to the houses had been disconnected. Apparently no one had thought that the overhead high-voltage line might be a hazard. The appellate court stated that while Arizona holds that violation of a safety regulation is negligence per se, whether the contractor was excused was a jury question. The trial court had granted summary judgment against the contractor on this point. The appellate court cited Restatement (Second) of Torts § 288A as giving a nonexclusive list of possible excuses. The court reversed and remanded for a new trial on this point. *Monares v. Wilcoxson*, 736 P.2d 1171 (Ariz. App. 1987).

The same statute was at issue in another 1987 Arizona case which arose out of an apartment construction site. A lathing worker was injured when a ten-foot piece of metal he was carrying contacted an overhead power line. The worker was on scaffolding at the time. He sued the power company, the general contractor and two subcontractors. All defendants were granted summary judgment. The appellate court reversed and remanded as to the contractors, holding that the power company is not necessarily immune from liability simply because of the lack of formal notice. Its employees were at the site prior to the accident to check on power requirements, but at that time only footers had been completed, and they were not told of the size of the building. Summary judgment was proper as to the power company. The High Voltage Act requires "a person or business entity" planning construction within six feet of a power line to give notice. Rather than impose a rule that would create unnecessary duplication of efforts among contractors, the court held that a jury trial was necessary to determine which contractors were liable for failure of notice. *Cohen v. Salt River Project*, 736 P.2d 809 (Ariz. App. 1987).

Alaska's similar statute, AS 18.60.670(1), prohibits placing any type of equipment that is "capable of lateral, vertical, or swinging motion within ten feet of a high-voltage overhead electrical line or conductor." A 1992 case arose out of the electrocution of a worker. The deceased was holding a tag line of a pile driver as a crane was moving the pile driver. The crane's lift line contacted an overhead power line, and this lethally charged the tag line. The plaintiff's estate sued the power company, HFA. The plaintiff argued that the statute should be construed to mean that it is illegal, and therefore negligent per se, to permit the placement of a crane near a power line if any part of the crane is capable of reaching to within ten feet of the line, and that any other interpretation would render the statute meaningless. The trial judge so ruled, and defendant HFA appealed. HFA argued that the statute permits placing equipment near a power line as long as no part impinges on the ten foot rule. HFA further argued that the plaintiff's interpretation conflicted with similar federal laws, with other state statutes, and with the Alaska Labor Department interpretations. The Alaska Supreme Court observed that most safety rules are a compromise between safety and efficiency. It noted that an expert for HFA, in an affidavit, testified that it is not required for safety, nor is it feasible, to barricade or de-energize all such overhead lines, and that indeed such an interpretation would prevent the use of cranes and backhoes on most construction sites in Alaska. The court ruled that the plaintiff's interpretation was erroneous. The literal meaning is that one may not place equipment within ten feet of a power line, not the placement of equipment where some parts of it may be moved within the ten foot zone. There was a dissent. *Homer Elec. Ass'n v. Towsley,* 841 P.2d 1042 (Alaska 1992).

A 1991 Alaska case shows how provisions of the National Electric Safety Code (NESC) may be relevant to judge the reasonableness of a party's conduct. A contractor, Grasle, upgraded an electric system to 7,200 volts for the Village of Ruby. In rural Alaska it is common for unskilled villagers to maintain the electric system. While Grasle did not undertake to train the villagers on the system, the contractor warned them to turn off the power before working on the system. Specifically, they were told to "kill it before it kills you." Some years later a villager climbed a pole without turning off the power because he was "only going to look at it." He contacted a hot bushing, and because of the burns, had both arms amputated. He sued Grasle. On appeal, the Alaska Supreme Court affirmed a defense jury verdict, holding that it was proper to instruct on the plaintiff's violations of the NESC. The plaintiff's comparative negligence is measured by his conduct, and the code is an objective measure of reasonable conduct when working with electricity. *Keogh v. W.R. Grasle, Inc.*, 816 P.2d 1343 (Alaska 1991).

States may have an ultrahazardous work statute which may be construed in an electrical injury accident, as a 1988 Georgia case illustrates. A painting contractor contracted with a power company to paint transmission towers without the lines being de-energized. One of the painters got too close to a line, and suffered sever burns when arcing occurred. He sued the power company for failure of warning and supervision, and cited the Georgia ultrahazardous work statute. The statute, Ga. Code Ann § 51-2-5(2), states that an employer is liable for the negligence of a contractor if the work "is in its nature dangerous to others however carefully performed." The 11th Circuit held that electricity is not so inherently dangerous that it fits the statute, and reversed a verdict for the plaintiff. *Jenkins v. Georgia Power Co.*, 849 F.2d 507 (11th Cir. 1988).

A 1996 Georgia case involved the High Voltage Safety Act, which requires that a person or business intending to work within ten feet of power lines must notify the utility and take certain precautions. A farm worker who was assembling irrigation pipes lifted one high to clear debris and touched a power line. He was injured and sued the power company and his employer. The pipe was thirty feet long. The appellate court directed that summary judgment be granted to the power company. The act contemplates usual work, and normally irrigation pipes remain close to the ground. *Southern Orchard Supply v. Boyer*, 472 S.E.2d 157 (Ga. App. 1996).

The court in a 1992 Georgia case also construed the High Voltage Safety Act. A cable television installer touched a live wire while working, and sued the premises owner for failure to notify the power company. The appellate court affirmed summary judgment for the owner. The owner was not responsible for the work being done, nor was he an employer of the plaintiff. He did not fit the statutory definition of one who must give notice. *Johnson v. Richardson*, 414 S.E.2d 698 (Ga. App. 1992). A 1998 Georgia Supreme Court decision held that the High Voltage Safety Act was constitutional. The legislature is at liberty to create immunities consistent with due process. The statute is not vague because it does not advise the public that a power line is high voltage. The language of the act is clear: it merely requires persons planning to work near high voltage lines to give notice to the power line owner. The court stated that persons not sure which power lines qualify as high voltage may have to ask. The case arose when painters were injured when their ladder touched a power line, and the court held that summary judgment was proper on the showing that no notice was given. *Santana v. Georgia Power Co.*, 498 S.E.2d 521 (Ga. 1998).

A 2002 Georgia case construed the High Voltage Safety Act. The plaintiffs were the parents of a young man who was electrocuted when his construction equipment contacted a high-voltage power line. They sued the power company and UPC, the agency formed by the utilities to receive notices of intention to work near power lines and pass them on to the proper utility. The plaintiff appealed defense summary judgment, and the court of appeals reversed. Summary judgment was based upon the fact that, when the work was delayed, the contractor did not renew its request by giving a "new notice" to UPC. The High Voltage Safety Act. Unlike work involving underground utilities, it is customary for notices involving overhead lines to be kept open until the contractor says it no longer needs protection. The last request for protection was May 27, and the accident happened May 30. The plaintiffs alleged that a glitch in either CPS's or the utility's computer system caused the danger. Under these circumstances, the court reversed for further proceedings. *Smith v. Jackson Elec. Membership*, 560 S.E.2d 26 (Ga. App. 2002).

Note also a Georgia 2002 case of an electrocuted farm worker operating a cotton picker. For several reasons (old copper wire that stretches with age, and 495 feet between poles) the power line sagged below code standards. The defendant power company had neither inspected nor measured the sage in the line since it was installed in 1949. The lower neutral was only twelve feet high at the point where the picker snagged it. The operator was killed when he climbed up on the picker to free it. Following a jury verdict for the plaintiff, the trial court granted judgment notwithstanding the verdict. The court of appeals affirmed. It was error to base the JNOV on assumption of the risk, but lack of notice to the utility, pursuant to the High Voltage Safety Act, was fatal to the plaintiff's case. *Williams v. Mitchell County Elec. Corp.*, 566 S.E.2d 356 (Ga. App. 2002).

A 1998 Illinois case involved a trespasser who was injured by contact with a power line. The plaintiff was attending homecoming at the University of Illinois. In the wee hours he and a confederate decided to steal a banner hanging from the front roof of a fraternity house. He climbed onto the roof without permission and untied the banner. It caught on a power line, and while trying to dislodge it, the plaintiff was shocked and fell to the ground. The plaintiff alleged that the power line was closer to the building than the fifteen feet required by the Illinois Commerce Commission. The power company moved for summary judgment on the grounds that its only duty to a trespasser was to refrain from willful and wanton conduct. The trial court granted the motion, and the appellate court reversed and remanded the case for trial. It was not clear that the plaintiff was a trespasser as to the defendant. *Knyal v. Illinois Power Co.*, 523 N.E.2d 639 (Ill. App. 1988).

Illinois' Structural Work Act requires that "scaffolds, hoists, cranes, stays, ladders, supports" and the like shall be safe and proper for the protection of workers using them. The act essentially eliminates contributory negligence and assumption of the risk as defenses. A 1992 wrongful death case construed the act. A workman was painting a billboard, standing on the walkway. He put a ladder on the walkway and climbed it to unhook painting hooks, and was electrocuted by a power line which crossed the billboard at one end with twenty-four to thirty inches of clearance. The workman's estate sued the lessee of the billboard for violation of the act. The Illinois Supreme Court held that the ladder was itself not hazardous, and thus the act could not apply. There was a dissent. The court held that a jury question existed as to the negligence of the defendant for failure to warn workers of the power line. *American Natl. Bank v. National Advertising*, 594 N.E.2d 313 (Ill. 1992).

A 1992 Iowa grain mill case dealt with the newer, versus older, version of the NESC. The plaintiff was an employee of the mill. He climbed to the top of the structure to see where the grain flow was plugged. He picked up a metal pole to clear the clog, inadvertently touched an overhead power line, and found himself lying on a lower catwalk. (To show that the injuries are catastrophic in many of these electrical accident cases, the plaintiff suffered a broken neck, burns to hands and feet, cardiac arrhythmia, and a skull fracture.) He sued the power company for insufficient clearance of the line. The line clearance met the NESC standards when installed in 1963, and again when the line was changed in 1975. However, the 1977 standards were not met. The court held that all three codes were admissible as evidence and that the jury could not find the defendant negligent per se for violation of the most recent code, but could consider the code as representing the current safety thinking as evidence of negligence. Merely meeting NESC standards is a minimum obligation. The Iowa Supreme Court affirmed a verdict for the plaintiff, noting that a fair trial does not mean a perfect trial. *Johnson v. Interstate Power Co.*, 481 N.W.2d 310 (Iowa 1992).

The court in a 1988 Kansas case noted that the introduction to the NESC itself states that the code provisions are the minimum considered necessary for the safety of employees and the public. The case arose from the electrocution of a painter who was working at a new building. The deceased was holding a thirty-two-foot ladder away from the wall while another employee, standing on the ladder, attempted to extend it. The ladder leaned back into a 7,200-volt line and the man on the ground was electrocuted. The estate sued the power company and the employer. The jury awarded over $1 million, finding the power company 85 percent at fault and the employer 15 percent. The Kansas Supreme Court affirmed, after reducing punitive damages to $500,000. The power company cannot use NESC compliance as a defense because, in addition to providing only minimum standards, the code does not apply to construction sites with respect to clearance between power lines and adjacent buildings. There was also evidence that the city had violated a local ordinance requiring underground wiring in new areas. The power company sought too late in the trial to bring in the City of Lawrence and the developer/architect as co-defendants on this point. *Folks v. Kansas Power and Light*, 755 P.2d 1319 (Kan. 1988).

A 1987 Louisiana case decided whether electricity is a "hazardous or toxic substance" pursuant to Art. 2315.3, dealing with the award of punitive damages. The plaintiff argued that natural gas, which represented a similar risk, had been so classified. The court, finding that the statute did not define the term "hazardous substance," looked to legislative history and existing law. The court examined state environmental statutes defining hazardous substances and found that all referred to a gas, liquid, or solid. Since electricity is none of these, and has "no particular or definite chemical constitution," it was not a hazardous substance for the purposes of this case. *Vincent v. Southwest Louisiana. Elec. Membership Corp.*, 666 F. Supp. 94 (W.D. La. 1987). (Author's comment: an electric current is a flow of electrons, usually alternating, but one can hardly blame the court for not getting into the subatomic level of matter. In 1990, the legislature amended the punitive damages statute to state that electricity is not a hazardous or toxic substance for the purposes of the statute.)

A 1986 Louisiana case opinion construed the Safe Scaffolding Act, holding that the act refers only to the safety of the scaffolding itself, not the danger of electrocution. A carpenter was electrocuted when scaffolding touched a power line which was less than four feet from a building under construction. The court stated that three feet ten inches is a "far cry" from a proper margin of safety. The defendant power company argued that the lines were properly "insulated by isolation," that is, in an area not readily accessible to people. The court held that the standard which the defendant relied upon referred only to completed buildings with solid walls and no windows facing the power lines. *Snow v. Gulf States Util. Co.*, 492 So.2d 31 (La. App. 1986).

The effect of employer violation of OSHA standards frequently comes up in work accidents. The employee cannot sued his employer because workers' compensation is an exclusive remedy, but a defendant power company may assert that the violation of OSHA standards must be considered in allocating percentages of fault. Such was the claim in a 1994 Louisiana case. A logging truck driver was electrocuted when, attempting to secure his load, he threw a chain over the logs and was electrocuted when the chain touched a power line. The OSHA violations alleged were failure to provide the driver with a safe place to chain, and failure to notify the power company of the line which, to the employer, "looked low." In fact, the line was four inches below code. The appellate court noted that Louisiana law was changed in 1987 to permit such consideration of employer negligence. The court accordingly modified the allocation of fault to the power company from 58 percent to 35 percent, employer 40 percent, and employee 25 percent. This reduced the damages payable by the power company by over $400,000. *Nigreville v. Federated Rural Elec. Co.*, 642 So.2d 216 (La. App. 1994).

In a 1993 Louisiana case in which a shrimper was injured when his boat antenna touched an overhead power line, the court noted that the NESC had not been adopted in any law or ordinance. The court stated that the code may nevertheless be given probative value in determining whether a breach of duty has occurred. The court affirmed a finding that the power company was 33 percent at fault and the plaintiff 67 percent. The defendant's liability was grounded on the fact that a number of boats had had similar accidents at that site. This indicated that the power line was a hazard to navigation, which violated the permit issued to the defendant by the Corps of Engineers, although the line itself met NESC height requirements. *Bourgeois v. Louisiana Power & Light*, 620 So.2d 306 (La. App. 1993).

The reader should know that power lines are strung to permit a sag between poles or towers to permit expansion and contraction of the line, and to better withstand storms. As the temperature rises, lines tend to sag. A 1993 Louisiana case arose when a 15'9" cotton picker snagged a power line. The plaintiff was a worker who climbed on top of the picker and, wearing neoprene gloves, moved the snagged line, which was the neutral line. Somehow he touched the upper high-voltage line and was injured. The minimum code height for the line was sixteen feet, but obviously in the heat of the day it had sagged below the code distance. The jury found the utility negligent, but not the cause of the injury. It found the cause was the plaintiff's own imprudent act. The appellate court reversed, finding the utility 50 percent at fault for the $744,759 damages. The court noted that the utility's duty of "utmost care" is virtually indistinguishable from strict liability. Here, utility employees had helped get the cotton picker into other fields several days before the accident, and knew of the scant clearance. *Weaver v. Elec. Membership Corp.*, 615 So.2d 1375 (La. App. 1993).

The Montana Supreme Court has held that violation of NESC standards is negligence per se, not merely evidence of negligence, as is the rule in some other jurisdictions. The case arose when a trespasser climbed a tower and was permanently injured when he was arced by a 100,000-volt line. He alleged that the tower was not properly barricaded and that proper warning signs were not in place. The court reversed a jury finding that the utility was 25 percent at fault, and remanded the case for a new trial, holding that the jury must be instructed that, even if the utility did not build the facilities in question, violation of NESC standards was negligence as a matter of law. The jury must also be instructed that, to find negligence, the violations must be related to the cause of the accident. *Martel v. Montana Power Co.*, 752 P.2d 140 (Mont. 1988).

New York Labor Law 240(1) requires contractors and owners who employ subcontractors for work in building or demolishing structures to provide a safe workplace, especially for workers at risk. Violations which cause injuries constitute absolute negligence. A 1988 case applied this law. A crane helper was electrocuted when as he sought to hook a crane line to building materials as the line contacted an overhead power line. An appellate court affirmed partial summary judgment against the general contractor. The statute specifically requires that hoists be placed and operated for safe work. The evidence showed that the defendant did not take any of the following steps: having the power line de-energized or insulated; erecting barriers to prevent the crane from entering the danger zone; installing proximity-sensing devices on the crane; or providing workers with insulating clothing and equipment. *Region v. W.J. Woodward Const. Co.*, 527 N.Y.S.2d 641 (N.Y. App. 1988).

In a 1994 New York case, the court construed the High-Voltage Proximity Act. The act requires one about to work near power lines to notify the line owner. The case arose when the plaintiff attempted to cut down an old, rotted red maple tree. He was injured when he contacted a power line. (The case states that he was "injured by electrocution," but this is an oxymoron. The dictionary meaning, and the ordinary usage of the word, means death.) The plaintiff sued the power company and the landowner. The court affirmed summary judgment for the landowner because the landowner did not control or direct the work. Apparently the plaintiff was cutting the tree for firewood, with the landowner's consent and approval. The court held that it was the plaintiff's obligation to notify the power company, but a jury could find he was excused because the law was new, its regulations had not even been promulgated, and the plaintiff was from another state without a similar law. The court held that a jury could find the power company partially liable. There was evidence of splices, indicating that branches of the tree had previously broken the lines, which placed the power company on notice to remove the tree or take other action. *Lane v. New York State Elec. & Gas*, 18 F.3d 172 (2nd Cir. 1994).

A 1986 Ohio case, heard in federal court, involved a sandblaster whose metal ladder lethally contacted or was arced by a power line. The line was seven feet from the building, and the deceased was moving the ladder. The plaintiff argued that evidence that the defendant landowner, the United States, was in compliance with the NESC was irrelevant. However, the court stated that a defendant's compliance with the NESC is significant in deciding the threshold issues of foreseeability and duty of care. The court held that the accident was not reasonably foreseeable and that the deceased's own negligence was the sole cause of his death. *Angel v. United States*, 650 F.Supp. 434 (S.D. Ohio 1986).

The same issue came up in a 1989 Ohio case. This time a repairman was installing a new street lighting pole to replace one damaged in an accident. The pole site was thirteen feet from the nearest power line, which was itself thirty-one feet above the ground. As the pole was being raised by a boom truck, it twisted and its mast arm contacted the power line. The repairman was riding in the truck's bucket and suffered severe injuries, including a leg amputation. He sued the power company and the city. The appellate court held that the city was not liable to this independent contractor, but that summary judgment was improperly granted to the utility. The plaintiff conceded that the utility had complied with the NESC, but the court agreed with the plaintiff that such compliance did not dispose of the claim. The issue was whether the accident was an unusual and unforeseeable occurrence. This question cannot be disposed of by summary judgment. The court remanded for trial. *Brauning v. Cincinnati Gas & Elec. Co.*, 560 N.E.2d 811 (Ohio App. 1989). In *Grabill v. Worthington Ind., Inc.*, 649 N.E.2d 874 (Ohio App. 1994) the court examined a similar issue. Several workmen were electrocuted when a scaffolding they were moving touched a 69,000-volt power line. The appellate court reversed summary judgment for the power company. The company had complied with NESC provisions, and the line was thirty feet from the building with the scaffolding, but the court held that whether the defendant exercised the highest degree of care was an issue on which reasonable minds could differ. The court noted that it is nearly always easy to see how an accident could have been avoided in hindsight. The question was whether the accident could have been reasonably anticipated?

Oklahoma case law holds that if a power company complies with standards of the Oklahoma Corporation Commission and the NESC, that compliance is a prima facie showing of lack of negligence. A plaintiff must prove "exceptional circumstances" to show negligence by the power company, according to a 1996 case. The case arose when a farm grain auger touched a power line, resulting in one death and two injuries. The workers had lowered the auger to move it up to the grain bin, when they again raised it. However, they then decided to move it from the west to the south side, and the top of the auger touched the line some fifty feet away. Their estates sued the electric utility for failure to maintain the power lines in a safe manner, and for failure to warn the workers of the hazard allegedly created by running lines within four or five feet from one side of the bin. The trial court granted the utility's motion for summary judgment on the ground that the plaintiffs had violated the statutory six-foot rule. That rule requires persons working around high voltage equipment to maintain this distance. The court of appeals correctly found that the six-foot rule did not act to relieve the utility of its duty to exercise a high degree of care. That court reversed on a finding that there were unresolved issues of fact. The plaintiffs argued that the utility's employees routinely visited the farm to read and set the meter, and passed by the grain bin. The plaintiffs' theory was that the visits put the utility on notice of an obviously hazardous condition. The supreme court reinstated summary judgment. It found no legal duty on the utility to inspect the lines and no reason to move its lines. The employees had not observed the auger working or being moved. After the accident, the utility's employees stated that closeness of the lines created a dangerous condition. The plaintiffs' cases were hurt by the fact that the contact with the line was fifty feet from the bin. Two judges were just as convinced that the case should have gone to trial. They cited another case in their dissent which held that a power company owes the highest duty of care, and must exercise caution consistent with the peril. *Shelley v. Kiwash Elec. Co-op*, 914 P.2d 669 (Okla. 1996). The author, who grew up on a farm, would comment that power lines close to a grain bin would indeed be a hazardous condition where the use of an auger is necessary.

The court in a 1987 Oregon case construed 437-84-029 of the Occupational Safety & Health Code. The code calls for a "safety watcher" to keep "constant watch" over workers who are required to work in areas where inadvertent movements would violate specified clearances. The plaintiff was shocked as he installed a fence around an electric utility's substation. The operator of the substation acted as the safety watcher. The watcher's attention was diverted momentarily and he turned away from the plaintiff. The plaintiff raised a metal rod to thread it into the fence and touched a live bus bar that was four feet over his head. The trial court directed a verdict for the utility. The question on appeal was what constitutes a constant watch. The appellate court noted that the code provides that if the safety watcher is distracted or must leave, he must order the work stopped until he is replaced. If the watcher looked away, he was in technical violation. The court examined whether his action was reasonable. The watcher remembered looking away for thirty to sixty seconds, but could not recall exactly why. He testified that he had three other workers to watch, and that the most probable explanation would be a "bump in the generator if we were running a rough load." The court noted that the plaintiff did not have the bar in his hands when the watcher turned away, and had been warned several times about the danger. The court held that the actions were reasonable, and affirmed the verdict. A dissent would follow the law literally, and find that there was no constant watch. The dissent noted that its position is not strict liability, but a finding of negligence per se, which would put the burden of proving no negligence on the utility. *Torres v. Pacific Power & Light*, 734 P.2d 364 (Ore. App. 1987).

A Texas statute requires that power lines must be maintained in accordance with the NESC. A case arose in 1990 when a concrete worker was moderately shocked. He was working with a finishing broom with a thirty-foot handle. The broom stuck in the forms, and when the worker tried to free it, the handle touched a power line eighteen feet high. Appealing from a directed verdict for the power company, the worker argued that the trial court improperly took judicial notice of the NESC. The appellate court affirmed. The worker claimed that the line was below the specified height, so whether the defendant had complied with the code was relevant. *Hernandez v. Houston Power & Light*, 795 S.W.2d 775 (Tex. App. 1990).

A 1993 Wisconsin case arose when tree branches caused a high-voltage line to arc across the three lines. The arcing caused a power outage lasting several seconds in a nearby bowling alley. The owner saw smoke, went to the basement, and saw flames and smoke coming from the main distribution panel. The building burned to the ground, and the insurers sued the power company. The supreme court upheld a verdict holding the power company liable for 85 percent of the damages, finding that there was evidence to support the verdict in that an uncommon spike or transient entered the distribution panel caused by the arcing. The arcing was caused by untrimmed trees. The jury found that the defendant violated the

NESC provision that "trees which may interfere with ungrounded supply conductors should be trimmed or removed." The defendant argued that "should" is advisory, not mandatory, and so the provision could not be violated. The court held that NESC 015 states that "where a rule is of an advisory nature, to be followed insofar as practical, it is indicated by the use of the word should." If the trimming is practical, the rule can be violated. *Beacon Bowl v. Wisconsin Elec. Power*, 501 N.W.2d 788 (Wis. 1993).

Chapter 23

Product Liability and Strict Liability

This chapter examines cases in which the plaintiff has asserted a products liability claim against the electricity provider or the maker of a product. Related questions that have come to the appellate courts include whether electricity is a product or a service, and if it is a product, whether electricity is a product from its generation or at some further point in the chain of distribution. Clearly electricity is not a product similar to, for example, a car. A car is made at a manufacturing plant and transported unchanged to a retail dealer. Only then is it for sale. Electricity is generated at a power plant and sent over high-voltage lines many miles before its voltage is reduced and it is "for sale" to the customer. Yet the claim for injury may arise from an incident far from the customer's meter.

Cases have considered whether strict liability can apply to electricity. Strict liability removes the requirement for privity, and may permit punitive damages awards, depending on the jurisdiction. The main issue is whether the product is defective, not whether the consumer was negligent. There is an issue of whether the production and sale of electricity is an abnormally dangerous activity within the meaning of Restatement (Second) of Torts § 519. This section states, "One who carries on an abnormally dangerous activity is subject to liability for harm to the person, land or chattels of another resulting from the activity, although he has exercised the utmost care to prevent the harm." This chapter will also include some cases in which the defendant is not the producer of electricity, but rather is the manufacturer of electrical equipment.

A California house fire case dealt with strict liability. The plaintiff's house caught fire when the service meter attached to the house "exploded." The plaintiff's expert stated that the pole transformer which fed the meter had been modified by the power company so that it could carry up to 200 percent of its normal capacity. This led to degradation of the windings in the transformer, which caused arcing and a voltage surge to the meter, causing it to explode. The power company claimed that the fault was in the house wiring. The appellate court affirmed a jury verdict for the plaintiffs. It held that the instruction on strict liability was proper. The power company argued that electricity does not become a "product" until it passes through the customer's meter. The question is, when does the electricity enter the stream of commerce? The court reviewed cases with similar, but not identical facts. It refused to state a "bright line" rule as being impractical. It was sufficient that the electricity entered the customer's meter. It could not be metered and "sold" only because the surge destroyed the meter. The issue of strict liability was correctly given to the jury, which awarded damages of $390,290. *Stein v. Southern Calif. Edison*, 8 Cal. Rptr.2d 907 (Cal. App. 1992).

In a 1988 California case involving a garage fire, the court concluded that electricity is not a product and therefore is not subject to products liability until it is metered. The plaintiff claimed that the fire was caused by defective insulation of two wires in the weatherhead above the garage, and that arcing caused heat and molten aluminum to drop onto the garage roof. The power company had a very different version of the chain of events. Since the plaintiff's meter was past the weatherhead, the court held that strict liability could not apply and reversed a plaintiff's verdict. *Fong v. Pacific Gas & Elec.*, 245 Cal. Rptr. 436 (Cal. App. 1988).

A 1991 California case dealt with fire caused by lightning. During an unusually intense storm, lightning struck a transformer near the plaintiff's building. In seeking a path to ground, the lightning stroke (probably a positive rather than the more usual negative), which was estimated to be an astounding 400,000 volts and up to 100,000 amperes, traveled through the plaintiff's wires, exploded his meter, and set the building on fire. The power company's transformer was lightning-protected up to 95,000 volts. The power company argued that it was not the generator of the lightning and that strict liability was inappropriate. The plaintiff argued that such an "act of God" defense could not be asserted because lightning is a foreseeable event. The defendant did show that the area where the building was located was a low lightning risk area. The trial judge ruled that strict liability could be asserted, and the jury returned a plaintiff's verdict. The appellate court reversed. It conceded that electricity can be a product, but ruled that lightning-generated electricity is not a product of the defendant. The court also held that an act of God defense is proper if the defendant can show that the event was so unusual that it was not reasonably foreseeable. The court held that a negligence action could have been maintained, but here the defendant had already dropped that count. *Mancuso v. Southern Calif. Edison*, 283 Cal. Rptr. 300 (Cal. App. 1991).

A 1987 Colorado case arose when two dairy farmers were electrocuted. They were moving a grain auger and touched a 7,200-volt uninsulated power line which supplied power to the dairy barn. The families sued the manufacturer of the auger (and settled with that party during trial) and the electric utility for negligence and strict liability. The trial judge granted the utility's motion for summary judgment on the strict liability claim. The jury then found for the utility on the remaining negligence claim. The court of appeals affirmed, and the case came to the supreme court. The court noted that strict liability concepts focus on the nature of the product, not the negligent conduct of producer or consumer. One becomes strictly liable if one places a defective product in the stream of commerce. The court rejected the utility's argument that electricity, because of its intangible nature, is not a product. Rather than focusing on the technical definition of electricity, the court stated that electricity is a form of energy that can be produced, confined, controlled, and transmitted to the consumer. It is a consumable product as far as the ordinary user is concerned. The question is, when does electricity enter the stream of commerce, or when is it sold? When it reaches that point, strict liability can apply. The court found that most courts fix that point at the consumer's meter, when the electricity is available and suitable for its intended use. In this case, even though the power lines were near the barn and extended no farther, the electricity had not yet been stepped down to a suitable voltage for use. The court rejected the plaintiffs' argument that the electricity was released into the stream of commerce when it left the roadside power lines and entered the distribution line that caused the deaths. The court agreed with the court of appeals that the electric system is in the nature of a service, not a product, at this point.

The court summarized with the public policy arguments for its decision. A power company is not in the same position as are most producers of goods. The industry is heavily regulated and must comply with safety statutes and industry codes which are designed to protect the consumer.

The power industry cannot raise its rates without permission, and thus cannot simply raise prices to cover potential awards for strict liability. The distribution lines and related equipment are not products intended for consumption. The industry is not free to cease supplying particular customers. The court affirmed summary judgment for the utility. *Smith v. Home Light & Power*, 734 P.2d 1051 (Colo. 1987).

A 1996 Georgia case arose when a driver towing a shrimp boat stopped when a metal stanchion on the boat contacted an overhead power line. Unfortunately, when the person stepped from his vehicle, he completed a ground and was electrocuted. The supreme court surveyed the law as stated in other jurisdictions, and held with the majority that electricity is indeed a product. It rejected the Ohio case of *Otte* (see below). The court declined to hold that whether there has been a "sale" is controlling, preferring instead a case-by-case analysis. The issue is, has the product been placed in the stream of commerce? Has the product been placed into the hands of the consumer in a usable condition? The court had little difficulty finding that the high voltage which killed the plaintiff and which had not gone through the dock's meter was not in the stream of commerce. The court affirmed summary judgment for the defendant on the strict liability count. *Monroe v. Savannah Elec. and Power*, 471 S.E.2d 854 (Ga. 1996).

A 1996 Indiana case arose when a law firm sued the power company (IPL) for economic loss because of a power surge. The surge was caused by equipment failure somewhere in the city. The plaintiffs claimed a loss of two days of work because they had to close their office. They claimed about $15,000 in economic loss. The appellate court affirmed summary judgment for IPL. The plaintiffs could not base their claim on the Indiana Product Liability Act because electricity is not a product until it is in a marketable stage. Here the equipment failure was in a conduit some distance from the law offices, and the current at that point was not yet in the stream of commerce. The court also affirmed the lower court's finding that the law firm could not recover for economic loss under negligence concepts because there was no physical harm to person or property. *Bamberger & Feibleman v. IPL*, 665 N.E.2d 933 (Ind. App. 1996).

A 1991 Kentucky case raised a different issue. A dairy farmer alleged that stray voltage adversely affected milk production. He worked with an employee of the power company, Princeton Electric, and after the installation of a "ronk blocker," (an isolation transformer) milk production improved. The farmer sued Princeton for negligence and strict liability. The federal district court granted summary judgment to Princeton on strict liability based on two grounds. The defendant did not "manufacture" the electricity, but receives it from the TVA, so it is providing a service, and is not a manufacturer. Second, stray voltage is an inherent by-product of the electrical transmission system; it is neither marketed nor marketable. Whether electricity is "goods" under the Uniform Commercial Code warranties, and it has been held both ways, it is not "goods" until it has reached the customer's meter. Strict liability cannot apply. The court held that the negligence claim may proceed. *G & K Dairy v. Princeton Elec. Plant Bd.*, 781 F. Supp. 485 (W.D. Ky. 1991). There is a 1985 Pennsylvania case involving stray voltage and dairy herds in which the court held that under proper circumstances, a power company could be held strictly liable. Strict liability can apply when the electricity has entered the stream of commerce by passing into the customer's meter. The trial court denied the defendant power company's objections, and the power company appealed. The appellate court did not get into the question of whether stray voltage is a marketed and marketable product. The court remanded the case to the trial court for further action. *Schriner v. Pennsylvania Power & Light*, 501 A.2d 1128 (Pa. App. 1985).

A 1988 Ohio case explored in detail the question of stray voltage affecting dairy herds. The plaintiff's dairy cows exhibited nervousness, kicking, and reluctance to come into contact with milking equipment. Not surprisingly, milk production dropped. The court explained that stray voltage in a dairy herd is the result of the increased use of milking parlors (devices that enable one to milk a number of cows simultaneously) which brought extensive metal parts and electrical equipment into the barn. Neutral-to-earth voltage can stray to these parts and pass into the earth, rather than such voltage being carried on the proper neutral line. The plaintiff eventually solved the problem by installing an isolation transformer. The Ohio Supreme Court affirmed summary judgment for the defendant Dayton Power & Light on the strict liability count. The court found that attempting to define electricity as an ordinary consumer product is an "intellectual disaster." It did not find much logic in holding electricity a service before it reaches the consumer's meter and a product afterward. (The case has a good footnote on cases in other jurisdictions which have held electricity to be a product at some point.) The power company does not manufacture electricity in the usual sense. It sets in motion the necessary elements that allow the flow of electricity. The court found this system to be a service. The court noted that customers do not purchase individual electrically charged particles; rather, they are charged for the time that electricity flows through their own electrical systems. They are buying a service, not a product. The court found that public policy was best served by not finding the DP&L strictly liable for such claims. As a highly-regulated pubic utility, the power company does not operate in a free market. The court did affirm finding the DP&L 51 percent at fault and the plaintiff 49 percent based on ordinary negligence. *Otte v. Dayton Power & Light*, 523 N.E.2d 835 (Ohio 1988).

A 1992 New York case followed the reasoning of Otte. The case arose when a healthy tree limb fell on power lines some two miles from the plaintiff's house. This caused a power surge when the 46,000-volt trans-mission line touched the 4,800-volt distribution line, and the power surge allegedly set the plaintiff's house on fire. The plaintiff alleged that the surge arrestors on his transformer failed. The appellate division cited and followed Otte in holding that strict liability was not available to the plain-tiff, though he may assert his claim in negligence. *Bowen v. Niagra Mohawk Power Corp.*, 590 N.Y.S.2d 628 (N.Y. 1992). The court con-trasted Otte with a Wisconsin case relied upon by the homeowner, *Ransome v. Wisconsin Elec. Power*, 275 N.W.2d 641 (Wis. 1979). The Wisconsin case also was a house fire, apparently caused by a lightning strike on or near the plaintiff's transformer, which destroyed elements in and near the transformer. Four days later, in a rainstorm, the plaintiff's house caught on fire when some 1,000 to 4,000 volts jumped to the 110–240-volt house line. The Wisconsin Supreme Court held that the jury was properly instructed on strict liability. It held that electricity is a product within the meaning of Restatement (Second) of Torts § 402A: "One who sells any product in a defective condition unreasonably dangerous to the user . . . is subject to liability for physical harm . . . ." The court pointed out that under Wisconsin law the plaintiff still must prove that the product was defective, and that the defenses of contributory negligence and mis-use are available to the defendant. We can conclude that courts have taken several positions on this matter. Depending on the jurisdiction, electricity is always a product, is a product only when it is metered at the customer's premises, or it is never a product.

A 1989 Maryland case arose out of the electrocution of a minor. The child was climbing a tree and touched a power line. The parents sued the power company and the tree trimming service which had the contract to keep the trees trimmed. These defendants sued the landowner for failure to supervise and protect the deceased. The parent plaintiffs alleged strict liability on the theory that transmitting high-voltage power through trees in residential areas is a "dangerous and ultrahazardous" activity; that is, abnormally dangerous within the scope of Restatement (Second) of Torts § 519. The federal district court hearing the case noted that while there was no Maryland precedent, generally other jurisdictions have held that such activity is not abnormally dangerous. Rarely is that label applied to acts carried out as a public duty, and the transmission of electricity is a public duty. One of the criteria used to judge such cases is the extent to which value to the community is outweighed by the dangerous attributes of the activity. The court noted that electricity is transmitted through power lines constantly, and such accidents are rare—usually caused by the negligence of the injured or killed individual, the power company, or a third party. The court held that the plaintiffs may proceed with their negligence claims, but not with strict liability. *Voelker v. Delmarva Power & Light*, 727 F. Supp. 991 (D. Md. 1989).

A 1990 South Carolina electrocution case arose as a result of an automobile accident. A drunk driver hit a power line pole. The impact broke the "pole top pin," which attaches the wire to the pole. The unbroken wire fell across the highway at a curve and stopped a few inches from the pavement. An officer, though warned that the line was hot, said that since it was not insulated, it was the neutral. (This belief was incorrect. High-voltage lines are difficult to insulate permanently with coverings, and they rarely are insulated.) He touched it and was electrocuted. His estate sued the power company for negligence and product liability. The appellate court affirmed summary judgment for the defendant. Product liability cannot apply because there was no sale of the product. The facts of the case alone show that the product—electricity—had not been placed in the stream of commerce. The court further held that, while the power company could have installed a stronger line-suspension system at the location, the line met code requirements. In any event, the deceased was clearly contributorily negligent. *Priest v. Brown*, 396 S.E.2d 638 (S.C. App. 1990).

A 1988 Texas case held that electricity is a product for the purposes of product liability. The case shows the devastating injuries that high voltage can inflict. The plaintiff was a sixteen-year-old boy. He intentionally touched a 35,000-volt power line some twenty-six feet high by coupling eight sections of tent poles. His injuries were two amputated legs and one amputated arm. The Texas Supreme Court noted that the question of whether electricity is a product had been before two lower courts, and the results conflicted. The court held that "the better reasoned opinions" of other jurisdictions find that electricity is a product. However, for strict liability to apply, the product must reach the consumer without substantial change. The high voltage must be stepped down to a usable voltage, and accordingly, strict liability cannot apply. The court reversed a multimillion dollar verdict. The court also held that the power company defendant had no duty to warn of high voltage under the facts of the case. The power company had complied with all applicable ordinances and codes. The line was ten feet above the minimum. The plaintiff had proven no other reason why the lines were dangerous. A dissenting judge would hold that once the power company has "released" the electricity to the lines, the company had relinquished control of the electricity forever and that strict liability could apply. The plaintiff was not without remedy, as the court noted that he settled with the developer of the subdivision for $700,000 plus $1,300,000 if the plaintiff got nothing from any other defendant. *Houston Power & Light v. Reynolds,* 765 S.W.2d 784 (Tex. 1988).

The court in a 1993 Washington case held it proper to consider the cost of making high-voltage lines safe from unanticipated contacts with people. A farm worker was electrocuted when he raised a thirty-two foot irrigation pipe and contacted a power line twenty-seven feet overhead. The deceased had raised the pipe because it was blocking vehicle access to a field. The court affirmed a defense verdict. The plaintiff alleged that when the power company knew or should have known that farmers were using pipes up to forty feet long, it had a duty to take steps to protect against the kind of accident that killed the worker. The court held it proper to give the jury evidence of the cost the ratepayers would bear for such changes. Moreover, the steps the plaintiff suggested were not feasible nor effective to accomplish the goals of increased safety. Raising the lines would increase the risk to crop dusters. Burying lines increases the risk to those digging, and buried lines fail more frequently than those in the air. Current methods of insulating overhead lines are ineffective. Purchasing the rights-of-way and fencing off people would create serious access problems. *Martinez v. Grant County Pub. Util.*, 851 P.2d 1248 (Wash. App. 1993).

A 1995 Wyoming case arose out of a roofing accident. A roofer was working on a house, over which ran "house" voltage (110- to 240-volt) lines. The lowest line was three feet above the roof. The roofer contacted a line, fell, and was injured. He sued the power company. One claim was based on strict liability. The Wyoming Supreme Court held that electricity is not a product as contemplated under strict liability concepts. A product is "anything made by human art or industry." Electricity is a flow of electrically charged particles along a conductor. A power generator sets in motion the elements necessary to allow the flow of electricity. The distribution system is a service. There cannot be strict liability for a service. The court affirmed a jury verdict holding the power company 60 percent at fault and the plaintiff 40 percent. It was correct to instruct on ordinary care, since such care depends on the facts. Counsel can point out the hazards of electricity. The court saw little difference in the ordinary care standard and the utmost care that some jurisdictions permit in electrical accident cases. *Wyrulec v. Schutt*, 866 P.2d 756 (Wyo. 1993). Note also a 1991 Maine case in which a painter was electrocuted when the aluminum ladder he was moving touched a 7,200-volt distribution line. The supreme judicial court affirmed a dismissal of the product liability claims. The court stated that there is a strong unanimity among the courts that electricity in that condition is not a product for product liability claims. *Fuller v. Central Maine Power*, 598 A.2d 457 (Me. 1991).

We now turn to cases in which allegedly defective products other than high-voltage lines are the issue. A 1991 Georgia case brings up the special knowledge of an electrician as a defense. A journeyman electronics technician was engaged in cleaning an "AC switchgear compartment" for his employer. (The case does not indicate what the business of the employer was.) The technician was to use "dry cloth" only, rather than "wet" cleaners. Instead, he sprayed an area of high voltage with an aerosol cleaner, Apollo All Purpose (similar to Windex). There was a flash and an explosion. The technician was severely burned, and soon died. His employer concluded that the aerosol provided a conductive plasma for electrical arcing. The widow sued the maker of the aerosol for failure to adequately warn. The plaintiff's expert's affidavit to this effect lacked any factual basis for its conclusions. The appellate court affirmed summary judgment for the defendant. The product was sold only to commercial and industrial users. It was common knowledge among the employer's technicians not to use the spray around high voltage or inside a "live" cubicle. The deceased must be held to the standard of knowledge presumed to be possessed by others in his profession. In fact, he had done similar jobs twenty-five to thirty times in the past. *Brown v. Apollo Industries, Inc.*, 404 S.E.2d 447 (Ga. App. 1991).

A 1990 Pennsylvania case also involved the standard to which an experienced electrician is held. The product was a 4,000-plus voltage capacitor (a device which can accumulate and hold a charge) installed in a hospital. The plaintiff was an electrician with thirty years of experience. A co-worker had unlocked the switchgear room preparatory to installing a capacitor. He removed the lid of the operating capacitor. The lid carried this warning: "This capacitor contains built-in discharge resistors. Caution! Wait five minutes after disconnecting. Then short circuit the terminals and ground the capacitor before handling." The plaintiff began to warn the co-worker of the danger and pointed a screwdriver toward the unit. Electricity arced to the plaintiff and he was severely burned. He sued the manufactured of the capacitor for lack of adequate warnings. The defendant argued assumption of the risk, and the trial judge so instructed the jury. The supreme court affirmed a verdict for the defendant. The trial judge correctly stated the law in instructing that it is sufficient if the plaintiff recognizes the danger, not necessarily the specific danger; here, the arcing. The court opined that an experienced electrician would in fact be aware of the danger of arcing. There was a dissent. *Mackowick v. Westinghouse Elec. Corp.*, 575 A.2d 100 (Pa. 1990).

A 1990 Washington case also dealt with adequate warnings. The defendant company chose to take the voltage from its power company directly as 12,500 volts, and to maintain its own transformers. The plaintiff journeyman electrician was an employee of an independent contractor. The plaintiff was certified to work on lines up to 480 volts only. A high voltage-qualified electrician was sent when required. While the plaintiff was at the defendant's plant, an employee of the defendant asked the plaintiff to come to the transformer room and take some part numbers of fuses. The plant employee thought the plaintiff was the high-voltage man (they had the same first name), while the plaintiff thought the devices in the room were low voltage only. The plaintiff used a mirror to attempt to read numbers, and was severely injured by arcing electricity at 12,500 volts. He lost the use of one arm and most of the use of the other. The appellate court affirmed a jury award of $1.1 million. The warnings on the panels in the transformer room read "Danger. High Voltage," regardless of whether the equipment was low or high voltage. The jury found this to be misleading. There was evidence that high-voltage electricians are trained differently from low-voltage workers. The former are taught to maintain at least a two-foot distance from high-voltage equipment. The plaintiff was asked to get the part numbers of "low-voltage fuses," further misleading him. The court held that the defendant was correctly held to the highest degree of care. *Winfrey v. Rocket Research*, 794 P.2d 1300 (Wash. App. 1990).

There have been some recent cases involving construction cranes. In a 1995 Indiana case, the court applied the "open and obvious" rule. An employee of an advertising firm was classified as a journeyman sign electrician and had a "working knowledge" of electricity. He and another were sent to repair a neon sign. They used a truck-mounted crane and basket, neither insulated. There also was a generator mounted on the truck to supply electricity. The truck was not equipped with a GFI device, a device which senses when the truck or crane is building up a charge and shuts off power automatically. The employee reached into the sign after repairs were completed to retrieve his tools and was electrocuted. The estate sued the crane manufacturer and others. The appellate court affirmed summary judgment for the defendants. The dangers of using an uninsulated crane and basket, having no GFI device, and touching a live electrical sign were open and obvious to one experienced in that area. The court noted that the deceased was initially shocked, and his co-worker shut off the generator. It was turned on to test the sign, and at that point the deceased touched the sign. The court held that the advent of the comparative negligence statute did not abrogate the open and obvious rule. *Anderson v. P.A. Radocy & Sons*, 67 F.3d 619 (7th Cir. 1995).

The Montana Supreme Court affirmed a jury verdict of $815,400 in a 1994 crane electrocution case. The deceased's job was to hook and unhook the crane cable from the loads, in this case, pipes. The line contacted an overhead power line. The estate sued several defendants, and settled with all but the crane manufacturer. The alleged defect was that the crane was defectively designed in that it did not have an insulating link. The defendant raised assumption of the risk and misuse as defenses. Specifically, the defense argued that the crane was "sideloaded." That means that the operator was attempting to drag the pipes out from under the power line and was not hooking directly above the load. The defense argued that it could not be liable for "unreasonable misuse." The workers were well aware of the power line, and had marked a boundary on the ground beyond which the crane would not be driven. There was evidence of the difficulty of the deceased's judging whether the crane's cable would, when tightened, contact the power line. The court held that assumption of the risk was improperly given to the jury. No rational person would assume the risk of electrocution by holding onto a pipe if he though it might become lethally charged. Accordingly, the court reversed the finding of 20 percent deceased's negligence. The court held that some sideloading of a crane is foreseeable, not an unreasonable misuse, and that the verdict was proper under strict liability. The case has a good discussion of the use of insulating links. There are several types, and they generally are not permanently installed. *Lutz v. National Crane Corp.*, 884 P.2d 455 (Mont. 1994). The case noted that there are some 2,300 crane-power line contacts each year, and that such accidents are the fifth leading cause of work-related deaths.

A 1990 Indiana case also arose out of a crane-power line contact. A twenty-eight-year-old laborer was electrocuted when a crane line touched a power line. The deceased was guiding the load. The estate sued the crane manufacturer in strict liability for supplying a defective product; specifically, for not informing the purchaser of the availability of insulating links, and in not making a proximity warning device available. Such a device senses the buildup of electric charges near power lines. The defendant urged open and obvious danger, misuse, and argued that the device alleged would in fact, if installed, make the crane more, not less, dangerous. There was evidence that cranes with insulating links are not involved in electrocution accidents. The supreme court affirmed a verdict for the estate. The deceased left a widow and two children. The court held that the verdict of about $2 million was not excessive. *FMC Corp. v. Brown*, 551 N.E.2d 444 (Ind. 1990).

There have been fatal vending machine electrical accidents, proving that it is not just high voltage that can be dangerous. A 1990 Louisiana case involved a pop machine. A repairman was sent to check on a machine. He attempted to move the machine away from the wall, brushed the adjoining machine, and was electrocuted. The victim did not die immediately, and evidence that he gasped for breath was sufficient to support an award for pain and suffering. It appeared that at some time the premises owner, a golf pro shop owned by the city, had moved the pop machine from its original location and had used a "cheater," or three-pronged plug, to connect the machine to an extension cord, which plugged into the two-pronged wall outlet. This was an improper use, as the cheater plug is supposed to plug into the wall outlet and be grounded on the outlet's center screw. Thus polarity was lost. Also, the city's mechanic had installed a 30-amp fuse into a 20-amp fuse slot because fuses were being blown. The mechanic heard a pop coming from the pop machine when he did this imprudent act, and thus the repairman was called. Finally, the pop machine had a short circuit in its compressor, permitting voltage to travel to the frame of the ungrounded machine. Thus the lethal trap was set, and the unwitting repairman completed the ground. The estate sued the maker of the cheater plug, the city, the vending machine maker, and others. The estate settled with all but the cheater plug maker. The jury found for the defendant, and the appellate court reversed, with a finding that the defendant was liable for 10 percent of the damages of $960,000. The court found liability for inadequate warning. The Underwriters Laboratories suggested warning for such plugs is "CAUTION - Connect tab to grounded screw." The court held that UL guidelines are just that, guidelines, and are not definitive respecting liability. It noted that the warning can hardly be seen by the naked eye. The estate's expert stated that of the three warning words (caution, warning, and danger), caution is the weakest. It might have been true, as the defendant argued, that the plug had been sold with packaging with adequate warnings, but there was no evidence to show that. *Cannon v. Cavalier Co.*, 572 So.2d 299 (La. App. 1990).

In a 1996 Wyoming vending machine case the court found that a plaintiff's *res ipsa loquitur* argument was proper. The plaintiff was delivering baked goods at the defendant's restaurant when he brushed between two pop machines, and received an electric shock. He suffered a broken shoulder and a burn on one wrist. An employee of the restaurant found nothing wrong but took one machine to the dump. When suit was filed a year later, the machine was retrieved. The plaintiff's expert found the power cord plug was missing, so he could give no opinion as to whether it was defective at the time of the accident. The appellate court affirmed an award of $50,000. It noted that the if the missing plug was defective or improperly wired, it was missing because of the action of the defendant. Other likely causes had been eliminated. *Res ipsa loquitur* was applicable and supported the verdict. *Kieffer v. Weston Land, Inc.*, 90 F.3d 1496 (10th Cir. 1996).

I note a 2001 Arkansas case primarily because it is a high-settlement one. A Wal-Mart customer bought a "torchiere style halogen floor lamp." The bulb allegedly exploded and cause an apartment fire that severely burned a minor resident. The buyer negotiated an $11 million settlement with Wal-Mart. (The case itself deals with Wal-Mart's claim against an insurer.) *Wal-Mart Stores, Inc. v. RLI Ins. Co.*, 163 F. Supp.2d 1025 (W.D. Ark. 2001). Note also a 2001 Missouri case that is similar. A four-year-old child was electrocuted after touching a floor lamp. A jury awarded $17,282,054 against the importer of the lamp. On appeal, the court affirmed the award as not excessive, after striking the prejudgment interest award, some $2 million. *Foster v. Catalina Indus., Inc,* 55 S.W.3d 385 (Mo. App. 2001).

Not all plaintiffs are successful, as a 1993 Michigan case shows. An eighteen-year-old farm hand was found electrocuted while using a portable power washer with a defective extension cord. The estate claimed inadequate design and warnings on the part of the washer manufacturer. The washer was supplied with a heavy three-prong plug. Warnings placed on top of the washer stated that the unit must be connected to a grounded power supply only, using no. 12 wire. The unit was connected to power with a defective, ungrounded extension cord. Apparently, the cabinet of the washer became lethally charged. The appellate court affirmed summary judgment for the defendant. The fact that farmers were known to have old wiring systems and were careless was not enough to hold the accident foreseeable. Even if the washer had been built with a plastic instead of a metal wand handle, there was no evidence the wand itself was involved in causation. *Zettle v. Handy Mfg. Co.*, 998 F.2d 358 (6th Cir. 1993).

A 1995 Mississippi case involved a substation circuit breaker. The plaintiff was a power company lineman who responded to a storm-caused power outage. He found a circuit breaker open and closed it. At the request of a co-employee, he opened it and the device exploded. The plaintiff was severely burned. He sued the manufacturer of the circuit breaker for a design defect, and received a jury award of $5 million. The appellate court affirmed, upon condition that the plaintiff accept $3 million or agree to a new trial. The circuit breaker was an oil-filled unit twenty-nine years old. The oil is intended to eliminate arcing when the contact points open or close. It appeared that the arc escaped the "interrupter grid," went through the oil, and contacted the metal side of the tank. The plaintiff's theory in strict liability was that the defendant should have installed an insulating tank liner, which would have prevented arcing to the side of the tank. The defendant asserted that the cause was lack of maintenance, allowing corrosion in the contact points. The court found sufficient evidence for the verdict. The evidence was complex, and the interested reader is urged to read the entire case. There was evidence that other similar breakers had exhibited the same problems, and that within months of when the unit in question was installed, the design was changed to include tank insulators. *Eiland v. Westinghouse Elec. Corp.*, 58 F.3d 176 (5th Cir. 1995).

A 1997 New York case arose when an electrician at a job site suffered injuries when a switchbox exploded as he tried to open it to turn off the power. The box is designed to cut off power when the handle is turned to open the box. This movement pulls the contact blades out of the fuses. The electrician sued the box maker. The plaintiff denied using a screwdriver, as the defendant alleged. The plaintiff put on two lay witnesses, while the defendant's witness testified as to the condition of the box after the accident and the pre-market testing procedure. The appellate division held that there was sufficient evidence for the verdict. The court did reduce the award for past earnings to $175,000 from $340,000. The plaintiff was out of work for three and one-half years and earned $50,000 per year. The trial judge had already struck the award of $255,000 for lost future earnings. *Place v. Federal Pacific Elec.*, 659 N.Y.S.2d 29 (N.Y. A.D. 1997).

In a 1993 Florida case involving injury from electric shock, the court held that electricity is an inherently dangerous product, and manufacturers of related products owe those who may use those products a fair and adequate warning. The product in question was a busway, a device used to distribute electrical service throughout a building. When the busway is installed horizontally, the word "Top" must be on top; but when it is installed vertically, "Top" must be on the right side. Workers improperly installed with "Top" on the left side. This required another worker to install a 100-amp switch upside down, the only way it would fit. This reverses the neutral and hot switches, a very dangerous condition. The plaintiff, relying on the switch, was injured when he began to wire the neutral. The shock entered one arm and passed out his back, and he suffered brain injury. The question was whether the defendant, Square D, had adequately labeled the busway. The appellate court affirmed a verdict for the plaintiff. Some of Square D's competitors had already adopted labeling which could have prevented the mistaken installation of the unit. On another point, the court held that a plaintiff expert witness, a Ph.D. in mechanical engineering who held over forty patents, was qualified even though he possessed only an elementary knowledge of electricity. He was an expert in "failure mode and effects analysis," and the busway was essentially a mechanical unit. *Square D Co. v. Hayson*, 621 So.2d 1373 (Fla. App. 1993).

Square D was also the defendant in a condominium fire in a South Carolina case. A condo was destroyed, and the owner sued Square D as the manufacturer of a circuit breaker that failed to work properly. The plaintiff chose to bring the product liability action in negligence. That meant that he had to prove that the defendant failed to exercise due care. The expert employed by the plaintiff sent the breaker to Square D for analysis. Square D reported that the breaker failed because of water contamination; the water entered with the top lead in wires. The plaintiff's expert thought there was some other cause, but could not identify it. The court granted Square D a directed verdict. The appellate court affirmed. The plaintiff failed to prove negligent design or manufacture. *Sunvillas Homeowners v. Square D*, 391 S.E.2d 868 (S.C. App. 1990).

A 1989 Texas case involved an exploding switchbox at a rock crushing plant. The plaintiff was an employee who was testing two fuses. His hands were severely burned. The switchbox became energized when power cables entering the unit through the punch-out hole became frayed on the sharp edges. No bushing had been installed to prevent this. The plaintiff sued the maker of the switchbox. The defendant argued that the jury's finding of no contributory negligence was against the weight of the evidence. The defendant argued that the plaintiff improperly used a galvanometer rather than a voltmeter, allowed a wire from the galvanometer to touch the wall of the switchbox, failed to disconnect power, and had not removed the fuses to test them. The plaintiff was not a trained electrician. He testified that he had done the job as taught by his employer. The appellate court affirmed a verdict of $350,000 for the plaintiff upon a finding of sufficient evidence to support it. The court did order a remittitur of $142,000 or a new trial. The plaintiff's wage was $5 per hour, but the award was based on a hypothetical of how much the plaintiff would earn to age 70 at $12 to $14 per hour as a heavy-equipment operator. The plaintiff did not possess those qualifications. *Loyd Elec. Co. v. Millett*, 767 S.W.2d 476 (Tex. App. 1989).

A 1986 Louisiana case brought up assumption of the risk as a defense. The product was a switch which exploded when a plant maintenance man was checking it. The plaintiff had to defeat the safety interlock on the switch box because he had to open the door with the power on to check the fuses. The interlock was intended to prevent laymen from opening the switch box. Assumption of the risk is not applicable under these facts. As the plaintiff's actions would not normally result in an explosion, the court affirmed the jury verdict for the plaintiff on the basis of defective manufacture. The award was $350,000, based in part on the explosion aggravating the plaintiff's emphysema. His physician testified that blast in the plaintiff's face had extended into his bronchial tubes. *Howell v. Gould, Inc.*, 800 F.2d 482 (5th Cir. 1986).

A 1990 Illinois case arose from a fatal accident which happened in 1975. The deceased was working in a coal mine and using a Black & Decker impact wrench. The electrocution occurred when an internal screw loosened and contacted the positive terminal of the switch, energizing the wrench. The three-prong plug originally supplied to provide grounding protection had been removed and a two-prong plug installed. The plaintiff sued the wrench manufacturer in strict liability; alleging that the tool should have been double insulated. The plaintiff argued that it was foreseeable that the three-prong plug might be replaced at some time. The appellate court affirmed a defense verdict, holding that the trial court had properly permitted the defendant to prove that federal regulations required the grounding of tools used in coal mines. The court found that such evidence was relevant; that it tended to show that the wrench was not unreasonably dangerous when sold. In addition, the defendant's physician expert was permitted to state that he did not think electrocution was the cause of death, as witnesses saw no sparks. *Jones v. Black & Decker*, 559 N.E.2d 1004 (Ill. App. 1990).

In a case involving an electric arc welder, an Illinois court held that the court properly refused to instruct the jury that a defendant's failure to "adopt any and all safety devices" would render the product not reasonably safe for its intended use. The accident happened when a plant employee driving a piece of equipment found his way blocked by a portable arc welder. He dismounted to move it and was electrocuted when he touched it. The welder is shipped by the maker with an internal grounding system. The purchaser is required to connect input cables to the welder, and warnings on the welder stated that an electrician should be used to make sure the grounding is properly done. The user, Fiat-Allis, had connected the welder with a Crouse-Hinds plug which had the green wire (the internal ground) connected to a live post, while the white wire was cut and unconnected. This apparently lethally charged the welder body. The plaintiff's expert postulated the lack of an external grounding system, but could not show that such lack caused the accident. Thus the instruction about any and all safety devices was not justified. The court affirmed a defense verdict. *Walters v. Lincoln Elec. Co.*, 557 N.E.2d 208 (Ill. App. 1990).

To find strict liability, there must be a defect in the product. This point is made in a 1986 Louisiana electrocution case. The victim was a retired man who had taken some courses in air conditioning, but was not a certified electrician. His air conditioning work was a "paying hobby." He was attempting to install a new motor in an attic air conditioner without cutting off the power to the attic. The homeowner suggested three times that power be disconnected, but the repairman said it wasn't necessary. The repairman called for the fuses to the compressor to be put back in place; there was a scream, and the repairman was found dead, clutching two wires. The estate sued the homeowner, the motor manufacturer, and the retailer which adapted the new motor to fit the installation. The appellate court affirmed defense verdicts for all defendants. The motor in question checked out perfectly. It is up to the individual installing a replacement motor to connect the proper leads (wires) to the house wires, and to insulate and tie off leads not used. The cause of the accident was the failure to turn off the power. Under these facts, *res ipsa loquitur*, argued by the estate, was not applicable. *Carollo v. Newton*, 492 So.2d 205 (La. App. 1986).

A Missouri electrocution case arose from a construction accident. The victim was operating a concrete pump (a long flexible boom which delivers concrete to a site not accessible to a concrete delivery truck) when the boom touched a power line. His estate alleged that the switch lacked insulation in the remote controls. The remote controls are at the end of a 100-foot cable, and permit the operator to move about for better visibility in controlling the boom. The defendant pump maker inserts a flexible cardboard-like material called fish paper between the inside of the control box and the electric wires and switches. The purpose is to keep out moisture and, the estate alleged, to insulate the operator from shock. There was evidence that a co-worker had repaired the switch and removed what he called a gasket, apparently the fish paper. The appellate court affirmed a verdict for the pump maker. There was no evidence that the control box was supplied without the fish paper, which negated the claim of a defective product. The court did hold that it was improper to instruct the jury on the affirmative defense of contributory negligence, but that the error was harmless. The deceased could not be negligent unless he thought the control box lacked the insulation. The defendant argued that the deceased had repeatedly been warned about power lines. *White v. Thomsen Concrete Pump Co.*, 747 S.W.2d 655 (Mo. App. 1988).

A 2002 Mississippi case involved product liability claims against the maker of a telescoping mast used by a TV station. All of us have seen these devices run up at a site to transmit back to the station. Obviously, they must be kept clear of overhead power lines. An electrocution accident happened in 1997 when the crew ran the mast into 8,000-volt lines on a city street. The victim walked to the van and was hit when he touched it. The TV van had been bought ten years earlier from the original buyer, and had been "completely rebuilt" at some point. The mast had highly visible warnings, including: DANGER. WATCH FOR WIRES. YOU CAN BE *KILLED* IF THIS PRODUCT COMES NEAR ELECTRICAL POWER LINES. The court found the plaintiff's arguments on defective design and other matters not persuasive, and affirmed defense summary judgment. *Austin v. Will-Burt Co.*, 232 F. Supp.2d 682 (N.D. Miss. 2002).

For further research, a good source for cases, including older ones, is *American Law of Products Liability*, 3rd ed., ch. 117, "Electricity and Electrical Equipment."

Chapter 24

Power-Line Accidents

24.1 Introduction

High-voltage power lines appear to be the most common instrumentality involved in electrical accidents that ultimately wind up in appellate courts. The injuries often are catastrophic if not deadly. The victim may be injured or killed by the electricity, or may be on a ladder, scaffolding, or otherwise off the ground; fall because of the electrical shock, and be injured or killed by the fall. One with a case involving a high-voltage line will want to check the applicable codes, statutes, and ordinances to see if the lines met standards. The general rule is that compliance is the minimum obligation of the power company, and not a complete defense. All the victims of power-line accidents covered in this chapter had some lawful purpose in working or carrying on some activity near the lines. There is a separate chapter dealing with trespassers. Power companies have a duty to protect the public commensurate with the risk. Since high-voltage electricity is an inherently dangerous product, the duty of care is high. Power companies have the duty to insulate high-voltage lines to minimize the risk to the public. Typically, the insulation is done by isolation of the lines, either by appropriate height from the ground, or by routing lines where they are unlikely to be contacted by ordinary nearby uses of the land. Actual insulation covering high voltage lines does not work well because of the voltage, but there are temporary coverings that can be thrown over the lines for a temporary purpose. Lesser voltage lines may actually be insulated by appropriate wire coverings.

Those who find it necessary to work dangerously close to power lines have a duty to notify the power company, but the power company itself has an obligation to inspect its lines periodically and note when nearby activity, such as construction projects, may require some action. Note a 2003 Georgia case in which a pipeline contractor notified the power company he needed overhead power-line protection until May 2. The contractor failed to renew his request, and his employee was electrocuted on May 30. The Georgia Supreme Court overturned the court of appeals and reinstated summary judgment for the power company. *Jackson Elec. Membership Corp. v. Smith*, 576 S.E.2d Ga. 2003). See also a 2001 case in which a painting contractor working for the National Park Service was held to have the duty to educate his employee on safety and to notify the Park Service if he thought a power line was a hazard and needed to be de-energized. A worker using a twenty-eight-foot ladder was electrocuted. The federal granted summary judgment to the United States. *Robinson v. Geo Licensing Co.*, 173 F. Supp.3d 419 (D. Md. 2001). Notwithstanding the high duty of the power-line owner, most accidents would not occur absent some mistake by the victim or another person. Contributory or comparative negligence is almost always a question and possible defense. The following recent cases are arranged by type of incident.

24.2 Cranes, Cherry Pickers and Grain Augers

A 1986 Louisiana case arose out of use of a crane on a construction site near a power line. The line was forty-five feet from the building under construction and thirty feet high. The lines met NESC provisions. The lines were insulated by isolation, and were not readily accessible to people. The plaintiff was an ironworker who was shocked when he attempted to hook a crane line to a load and the line touched one of the power lines carrying 7,200 volts. The loads were bales of iron mesh which had been stored almost under the power lines. The plaintiff and others were aware of the overhead lines. Ordinarily the mesh would have been moved by hand, but the crane was about to leave the job site and the plaintiff's foreman decided on the spur of the moment to use the crane instead. The injuries were severe burns, including facial, and some loss of vision due to electric shock cataracts. The appellate court affirmed a jury verdict for the power company. Insulation by isolation can be degraded, as in this case, by construction activity near the power lines. However, the accident must be one that is reasonably foreseeable. Here it simply was not foreseeable that the foreman would direct the dangerous use of the crane. One would expect that the mesh bales would have been dragged away from the power lines before lifting them. The plaintiff also argued that meter reader employees of the defendant had visited the site and should have noticed the construction and potential danger. The court noted that the crane was not even on the site when the meters were read, the building under construction was sixty feet away, and most of the materials were near the site, not the power lines. *Frazee v. Gulf State Util. Co.*, 498 So.2d 47 (La. App. 1986).

But note a Montana case also mentioned in the chapter on products liability, *Lutz v. National Crane Corp.*, 884 P.2d 455 (Mont. 1994). As above, workers used the crane to drag loads from under a power line. Such use is called sideloading. The court affirmed a jury verdict in strict liability for the injured worker, reduced 20 percent for contributory negligence. The defendant argued that sideloading is an unforeseeable misuse. The court held that such use is foreseeable, that the workers apparently misjudged the distance between the cable and the power lines. The workers were not intentionally sideloading. Expert testimony showed that visual misperception is not uncommon in such situations. The defendant was held negligent for the lack of an insulating link.

A 1987 Pennsylvania case had a power company and a landowner as defendants. Container General Co., the landowner, had contracted with the plaintiff's employer for the latter to construct a large fuel tank. A panel box (electrical equipment) needed to be connected to the landowner's "batch house" some 147 feet from the construction site to provide electricity for welding. The contractor used a crane to move the panel box. The crane's path went under high-voltage lines forty-seven feet in the air. The plaintiff was walking backwards in front of the crane, holding a wire attached to the panel box. The crane boom touched the wires and the plaintiff was severely injured. In the first trial, the jury found the power company not negligent, and the judge granted a judgment notwithstanding the verdict for the landowner. On remand, the jury found the plaintiff and the landowner equally negligent, and awarded $500,000 less $250,000 for contributory negligence. The appellate court affirmed, holding that the jury could find that the landowner knew that the panel box would have to be moved under the power line. The voltage was 34,500. The court noted that electric lines may be harmless or extremely dangerous, and the difference is not an obvious one to the layman. Here the landowner knew the box would be moved, though not necessarily by crane. The landowner could be found negligent for failure to warn or to insulate. In addition, the landowner could foresee that the plaintiff, while knowing of the danger, could be distracted by guiding the load and forget to watch for the line. High danger creates a high duty. The court held that the plaintiff's expert witness, a professional engineer with forty years of experience, could testify that the wires were "virtually invisible" in any type of weather, especially sunny weather. The expert was not necessarily testifying that it was sunny that day. *Beary v. Container General Corp.*, 533 A.2d 716 (Pa. Super. 1987).

A 2002 New York case also involved a claim against a landowner for failure to warn against a dangerous condition, in this case power lines twenty-eight feet high. Workers were moving grave stones at a cemetery with the use of a boom truck. They contacted the lines, and one worker was injured, another electrocuted. The defendant cemetery was granted summary judgment and the appellate division affirmed. The defendant did not supervise the work, not did it have actual or constructive notice any dangerous condition. *Rosenberg v. Eternal Memorials, Inc.*, 737 N.Y.S.2d 632 (A.D. 2002).

A 1991 Alabama case held a power company not liable for the electrocution of two workers at a construction site. The men were instructed to stand on each end of a steel beam to stabilize it as it was being lifted to a truck. The crane operator raised the boom into overhead uninsulated power lines. The operator himself was not injured. The estates sued the power company for negligence and wanton conduct. The court affirmed a verdict for the defendant and held that the trial court properly refused to instruct on wanton conduct. The plaintiffs' theory was that an employee of the power company was at the construction site thirty minutes before the accident and must have noticed the crane and steel beams. (The employee in fact had insulating material in his truck, and could have insulated the lines in an hour.) The court held that without evidence that the employee knew the crane would be used to move the steel beams, wantonness cannot be inferred. *Bonner v. Electric Power Bd.*, 583 So.2d 260 (Ala. 1991).

The appellate court in a 1991 Tennessee case did hold the power company (the city-owned Memphis Light, Gas & Water) liable for a crane accident resulting in two dead and one injured. A lumber company contracted with a builder to construct a storage shed. The building's planned location was originally under power lines running along the property line, but because of the cost of relocating the lines, the plans were changed and the building was constructed close to other lines running across the lumber company property. The accident happened when a crane got too close to those lines. At a bench trial the court awarded damages. The defendant appealed, arguing that it was not notified of the new location for the building. The appellate court affirmed, finding both actual and constructive knowledge. The court awarded damages to the coverage limits of $1 million. *McGaughy v. City of Memphis*, 823 S.W.2d 209 (Tenn. App. 1991).

In a 1993 Louisiana case the court held the injured plaintiff solely responsible for the accident. The plaintiff was the superintendent of a construction crew on a project. He was directing, by use of a crane, the moving of a horse trailer which served as a tool shed. As the crane moved across a highway, the boom touched a neutral overhead wire, producing a popping noise. At the plaintiff's directions, the operator lowered the crane and they tried again. This time they touched the primary wires, and the plaintiff was shocked when the trailer he was holding became charged. The court affirmed a dismissal of the suit against the power company. The plaintiff was aware of the ten-foot rule (stay at least ten feet away from power lines), and had directed the crane operator to move again after the first attempt. The trial judge was entitled to accept the conclusions of one expert over another. Each had argued a different interpretation of the requirements of the National Electric Safety Code. *Blue v. Louisiana Power & Light*, 619 So.2d 726 (La. App. 1993).

Assumption of the risk can be a viable defense and was successful in a 1994 Alabama case. A company contracted to dismantle a bridge, and at a preconstruction conference with the power company, the company was told to inform the power company if there were going to be any operations near power lines. No such notification was given before the accident. A company truck broke down under a power line, and employees used a crane to unload the truck. The workers were specifically warned of the line and the danger if the crane or a cable touched the line. The crane cable did touch the power line and a worker who was leaning on a trailer in contact with the cable was electrocuted. The supreme court held that the issues of contributory negligence and assumption of the risk were properly given to the jury, and affirmed a verdict for the defendant power company. *Spence v. Southern Pine Elec. Co-op*, 643 So.2d 970 (Ala. 1994). It appears to the author that it is difficult to see any negligence on the part of the power company, given the lack of notification or evidence that the lines did not meet code.

A 1995 Virgin Islands case also found assumption of the risk appropriate. A contractor was constructing a building on a site over which ran live power lines. The workers were well aware of the power lines and the danger of using a crane near them. The plaintiff worker used a tag line or rope (a line attached to a crane load to control it) to install one steel beam. He decided to guide the next beam with his hands for better control. The beam touched a power line, and the worker suffered catastrophic injuries: severe burns led to the amputation of one arm and both legs. He sued the landowner and the power company. The appellate court affirmed summary judgment for both parties. The primary issue was whether assumption of the risk was a viable defense under comparative negligence statutes. The plaintiff argued that the statute implicitly abolished the defense of assumption of the risk. In a scholarly opinion, the court held that the Virgin Islands had adopted the Restatement (Second) of Torts as its law, and the Restatement includes the defense. Since the comparative negligence did not specifically abolish the defense, as some other jurisdictions have, the defense of assumption of the risk is viable. The court noted that this may be a minority view among the states. *Monk v. Virgin Islands Water & Power Auth.*, 53 F.3d 1381 (3rd Cir. 1995).

Work and equipment near a power line can place the line owner on notice that the danger of an accident occurring has increased. A 1994 Oklahoma case presented this question. A county employee was testing a crane that the county had an interest in buying. The crane was located on the premises of the dealer. The employee was electrocuted when the crane touched an overhead power line. Apparently the crane was stored outside the statutory six-foot rule, but was about twelve feet from the line. When the county employee operated the boom, he touched the line, and a co-worker was killed. The estate sued the employer county, the crane dealer, and the power company. The jury found the two employees 71 percent at fault, the county 14.7 percent, the dealer 10.8 percent, and the power company 3.3 percent. The power company appealed on the basis that it had no actual notice that a crane would be operated within six feet of its lines. The court held that actual notice was not required. There was evidence that power company employees had inspected the power lines at the site, and must have seen cranes and dump trucks parked there that could reach the lines. The company had done nothing to insulate, raise, or move the lines. The total award was $283,083, so the power company's share was only $9,506. The court held that the power company was entitled to indemnification as a matter of law from the county because it was the county employee who violated the six-foot rule. *Taylor v. Payne,* 872 P.2d 953 (Okla. App. 1994).

A 1994 Ohio case arose when workers at a construction site were moving scaffolding, which touched a 69,000-volt power line. Three were killed and three seriously injured. The line was located thirty feet east of the building under construction. The defendant power company was granted summary judgment. The appellate court reversed and remanded for trial. The defendant argued that since it had complied with the National Electric Safety Code's distance of thirty feet, or with the ten foot distance permitted when NESC standards are suspended during construction, it had met the obligation of "the highest degree of care" required by Ohio law. The court held that compliance is a factor but not necessarily dispositive of the issue of care. The defendant knew that the building would encroach on the power-line easement. It was foreseeable that equipment would be used that could reach the high-voltage line, and that scaffolding would be used, and presumably moved about. The fact that the wires were "open and obvious" does not determine the case on a motion for summary judgment. The defendant could have marked the wires with streamers, moved them, or installed a mesh fence to guard against encroachment of equipment. *Grabill v. Worthington Industries, Inc.,* 649 N.E.2d 874 (Ohio App. 1994).

There may be a specific statute that can be used to establish liability, as shown by a 1988 New York case. A subcontractor on a new building was erecting steel. An employee was electrocuted while hooking a crane's lifting cable to materials stored under a power line. The boom contacted the line. The estate sued a number of parties, including the general contractor and the employer of the deceased. The plaintiff moved for summary judgment for violation of Labor Law 240(1). That statute directs contractors and owners who contract for, but do not direct the work, to furnish or erect scaffolding, hoists and other devices that give proper protection to employees. Violation of the statute creates absolute liability. The appellate court affirmed. The purpose of the law is to place the responsibility for the protection of workers "in positions of great risk" upon those best suited to provide such safeguards. The operation of a crane under power lines, without any safety measures being taken, violated the statute. *Region v. W.J. Woodward Const, Inc.*, 527 N.Y.S.2d 641 (N.Y. 1988).

We now look at some cases involving raised dump trucks. The Alabama Supreme Court affirmed a 1989 Alabama wrongful death case awarding $1 million. The accident happened when the deceased, standing on wet and muddy ground, raised the trailer dump of his tractor-trailer and touched a distribution line. The deceased was trying to empty water and debris from his truck before taking on a load of asphalt. The line had been installed only a week before the accident at the request of the employer. The defendant power company's representative had observed the site and he and the employer discussed how high a trailer dump could reach, some thirty-six feet. They decided to run the line across the roadway, which was not a dumping area for asphalt. The court noted that there was no designated dumping area for cleaning out trucks, and that the place selected by the deceased had the firmest ground, and thus must have seemed suitable. The court permitted the introduction of evidence that the defendant put orange warning balls on the power lines after the accident. It is important to note that the lines exceeded the minimum NESC provision, but the plaintiff's expert testified that notwithstanding that, "local conditions" must be considered. The court held that the plaintiff was not negligent as a matter of law. There was no evidence that he knew how high the dump could raise. He did know of the installation of the power line, and may have assumed it would pose no risk. The court held that there were sufficient questions of fact to go to a jury. A dissent would hold that contributory negligence was proven by the facts; that the deceased was an experienced driver, that he frequently attended safety meetings at which the subject of power lines was discussed, and that there was a specific warning label on every truck and trailer about power lines and other obstructions.

The opinion includes a discussion of the Alabama punitive damages law. *Central Alabama Elec. Co-op v. Tapley,* 546 So.2d 371 (Ala. 1989).

A 1983 Louisiana case reached a different conclusion on different facts. The victim was the owner of several dump trucks and three long-bed dump trailers. He had arranged to park them on the property of a truck stop business. On the evening of the accident, one of his drivers had parked a trailer somewhat outside of the usual area, and beneath a power line. The owner repaired a malfunction on the trailer the next morning, and raised it to test the repair. The trailer touched the line, and unfortunately the owner tried to enter the cab to lower it. He was electrocuted when he touched the door handle. The line was twenty-eight feet high, eight feet higher than required by code for wires crossing roads, streets, parking lots, and other areas subject to truck traffic. The appellate court affirmed a defense verdict, holding that the jury could find that the accident was not foreseeable. The plaintiff's expert had testified that the power lines did not meet code because they were not suitable "for the service and conditions under which they are to be operated." Unlike Central Alabama above, however, the truck was not in a work situation and it was not foreseeable that the bed would be raised at that location. *Thibodeaux v. Central Louisiana Elec. Co.,* 428 So.2d 1269 (La. App. 1983).

A 1996 Indiana case arose from a natural disaster. Some seven inches of rain fell in an eight hour period in northwest Indiana, and the Little Calumet River began flooding the town of Highland. The town hired a trucking service to haul sand and to build a dike across a parking lot. One of the truck drivers was electrocuted when he drove onto the gravel ramp, raised his truck bed, and touched or was arced by an overhead power line. The estate sued the town, the parking lot owner, and the power company, NIPSCO. The trial court granted summary judgment to the defendants. The appellate court affirmed summary judgment for the town because the Civil Defense and Disaster Law applied. That statute gives a governmental unit power to coordinate and direct measures taken in a natural disaster. The statute grants immunity in such activity, which extended to NIPSCO because its employees were acting under the direction of the town. The town wanted power cut off to the threatened subdivision, but wanted power retained for pumping. The estate contended that NIPSCO's acts or omissions constituted "willful misconduct, gross negligence, or bad faith." The natural disaster statute does not grant immunity for this conduct. The court noted that usually such questions are a matter for the trier of fact, and that NIPSCO had not responded to this allegation in its motion. The court reversed and remanded the case on this point. The court also held that the parking lot owner was not liable because the allegation that the owner had lowered the nearby levee some time earlier was too remote a cause. *Sharp v. Town of Highland*, 665 N.E.2d 610 (Ind. App. 1996).

In a 1994 Texas case, the county of Galveston was held liable for an electrical injury to an employee of a trucking company. The county had hired the company to haul gypsum for road resurfacing. The county provided spotters to watch for dangers and obstructions when the truck dump beds were raised for spreading the gypsum. The accident happened when the front spotter allowed a truck to get to within twenty-two inches of a high-voltage line. Work stopped while the spotters considered what to do. The rear spotter called for a bulldozer to push away material so the truck could back up. A driver in the next truck in line decided to climb up the raised bed to see if the truck could be moved safely. When he had reached six to eight feet from the top, he was shocked, fell to the back of the truck, and was injured both from the electricity and the fall. The appellate court affirmed a verdict finding plaintiff and defendant equally negligent, reducing the award by 50 percent. The court found sufficient evidence that the negligence of the spotter was a proximate cause. The plaintiff was obviously negligent for his imprudent act. *County of Galveston v. Morgan*, 882 S.W.2d 485 (Tex. App. 1994). By contrast in a 1994 Georgia case, the court found a truck driver solely negligent on the basis of assumption of the risk. The driver was towing a trailer carrying a front-end loader on private road. The loader caught on a telephone wire, and when the driver climbed up to free it, came in contact with a power line farther up. The court held summary judgment for the utility companies was proper. *Brown v. Southern Bell*, 432 S.E.2d 675 (Ga. App. 1993).

Cherry pickers are trucks with a boom and a basket which are operated by the worker riding in the basket. They can bring the worker into contact with power lines. A 1990 Alabama case arose when the plaintiff was building a billboard. He had contracted with the defendant company to set the six poles that would support the billboard, and supplied the defendant with a diagram. The pole nearest to a power line was to be ten feet from the line. In fact, the nearest pole was set only three feet from the utility right-of-way. As the plaintiff worked from a cherry picker, he was badly burned when an angle iron carried on the basket touched a power line. The jury awarded $400,000 to the plaintiff and $100,000 to his spouse. The supreme court affirmed, finding that the jury could fairly characterize the plaintiff's actions as heedless, but not contributorily negligent as a matter of law. The plaintiff had used the defendant's services before, and could assume that the poles were set as directed. The plaintiff was not facing the power lines as he operated the boom upwards, and was not aware of the immediate danger from the protruding angle iron. The court wisely noted that deciding cases like this one is not "without difficulty," and the resolution depends on the facts and circumstances unique to each case. *Electric Serv. Co. v. Dyess*, 565 So.2d 244 (Ala. 1990).

A 1986 Colorado case examined whether the degree of care a power company owes the public is modified by a plaintiff's occupation and his familiarity with the danger of overhead power lines. The accident happened when an independent contractor was repairing an irrigation well pump. The workman was using a boom truck to lift the pump when the boom touched an overhead line some twenty-seven feet high, and he was electrocuted. The estate settled with the truck maker for $50,000, and sued the power company. The estate alleged that the power company moved the lines too close to the well, apparently at the request of a landowner. The jury awarded $700,000, less 30 percent for contributory negligence. On appeal, the defendant argued that the jury should not have been instructed that the defendant owed the plaintiff the "highest degree of care" because of the deceased's occupation and his assumed knowledge of the danger of operating the boom near overhead lines. The court did not agree. The federal court hearing the case found that Colorado law supported the instruction. Electricity is inherently dangerous, the utility has expertise in dealing with it, and the general public is not able to recognize the danger in certain situations. The court did direct that the settlement with the truck maker be deducted from the jury award. *Hauser v. Public Serv. Co.*, 797 F.2d 867 (10th Cir. 1986).

A 1990 Montana case involved a boom truck being used to carry steel beams across a construction company's yard. The plaintiff was not an employee of the company. He and the owner hooked a beam to the truck and before moving discussed the danger of the overhead power lines. Nevertheless, the boom touched a line, injuring the worker holding the beam. The victim suffered burns to one hand and one leg, and lost one ring finger to amputation as a result. He sued the yard owner for negligently hitting the line, and the power company for not having the line higher. The jury found the plaintiff 15 percent at fault, the owner 20 percent, and the power company 65 percent. The supreme court affirmed. In essence, the power company argued that the act of the owner was a superseding cause which broke the chain of causation. The court held that there may be more than one cause of an accident, and it did not accept the defendant's argument that the acts of the plaintiff and owner were unforeseeable. Occasional negligence is "one of the ordinary incidents" of life, and can be anticipated. It is foreseeable that boom trucks operated in a construction company's yard might occasionally touch too-low overhead lines. The court noted that, of course, it must construe the evidence in a light most favorable to the prevailing party. *Sizemore v. Montana Power Co.*, 803 P.2d 629 (Mont. 1990).

In a 1994 Georgia case, a court found the power company not liable when the boom of a truck touched a power line because of a malfunctioning switch. The injured worker thought the line was dead because his co-workers were framing a house only eight feet from the line, and power company workers were moving the line. Nevertheless, he conceded that the accident would not have happened but for the malfunction. The court affirmed summary judgment for the defendant because the bad switch was an unforeseeable superseding cause. *Mobley v. Flowers*, 440 S.E.2d 473 (Ga. App. 1994).

Relying on past experience can be a defense. A 1994 Georgia case involved a boom truck delivering grain to a dairy farm. The drive, on his own for the first time, positioned his truck to unload. When finished, he raised the auger boom from the bin and noticed smoke coming from the cab. He went to the cab to check and was shocked when he stepped on the running board. Only then did he notice that the boom was in contact with an overhead line. The appellate court affirmed summary judgment for the power company, holding that it was proper to show that this was the first such accident in twenty years at this site. The lines were seventeen feet from the bin and met code standards. A dissent argued that the court had invaded the province of the jury. The power line was not conspicuous, and it was reasonable to expect equipment to be operating near a grain bin. *Wooten v. Central Georgia Elec.*, 447 S.E.2d 672 (Ga. App. 1994).

A 2001 Indiana case arose from a common holiday activity, that of stringing Christmas lights. An employee of a private company was stringing lights on trees in front of a public building in East Chicago. He was using a cherry picker. He and his employer were aware of power lines above the trees, but did not request assistance from the power company. The employee was injured from electric shock. The court of appeals affirmed summary judgment for the defendant. The plaintiff was held not to be a member of the general public that would not normally come in contact with power lines thirty-eight feet high. Instead, he was in that group of people whose work may require them to work near power lines, and it was his and his employer's responsibility to notify the power company. *Spudich v. Northern Indiana Public Service*, 745 N.E.2d 281 (Ind. App. 2001).

A grain auger is a common piece of farm equipment. It is a long metal tube, six to ten inches in diameter, enclosing a screw or auger which carries grain from a hopper at the bottom up the tube and into a bin or truck. The auger can be raised and lowered with a winch, and is powered by electricity, or by the power take-off of a tractor. The device is mounted on a set of wheels, and normally is moved by a tractor, but can with difficulty be moved manually by several people. It conducts electricity very well, and if it accidentally touches a power line, the results can be lethal. If there is an accident and a suit, the typical defendants will be a power company and the maker of the auger in a products liability claim. Generally, the issues include the following: Which was in place first, the grain bin or the power line? Did the line meet code standards? Did the power company have actual or constructive notice of a potentially dangerous situation?

We now examine several grain auger cases. A 1988 Louisiana case arose when three men, manually attempting to reposition a grain auger, accidentally touched a power line when one of the men stumbled. They suffered severe injuries. One had part of his arm amputated and all went through multiple surgeries. They sued the power company. The line they touched was the distribution line that served the grain bin. The appellate court affirmed a jury defense verdict. The plaintiffs were found to be negligent in attempting to move the auger without lowering it. It had been set at twenty-seven feet in the air when positioned above the bin. The plaintiffs intended to move it so that the distribution (high) end would be over a truck for unloading the bin. Twenty-seven feet was much too high for unloading, and if the plaintiffs had lowered the auger before moving it, no accident would have happened. In addition, the power company had bought an easement to run high-voltage lines nearby, and in that agreement the plaintiff owner of the property had agreed to assume liability for any accident arising from touching the power lines. The court held this agreement was binding on the other two plaintiffs. The power company had specifically warned the plaintiff about the danger of grain augers earlier. The power line itself met code height standards. *Vincent v. Beauregard Elec. Co-op*, 536 So.2d 798 (La. App. 1998).

A 1987 Nebraska case is tragic. Two men were manually moving a grain auger, with one standing by, when they either touched or got arced by a high-voltage line. All three were killed. One person standing at some distance was knocked unconscious, showing that the ground itself was charged. Tiede, the individual in charge of the harvest operations and a neighbor of the landowner, knew of the line, was warned that the bin had always been loaded from the south side because of the danger, but said that he thought there was room to miss the wires without lowering the auger. This mistake cost him his life. Nebraska at that time had not enacted a comparative negligence statute, so contributory negligence was an available defense. The supreme court affirmed a defense verdict as to both the landowner and the power company. The landowner was not present because of illness, and only his sixteen-year-old grandson was present. In any event, the landowner had no duty to warn when the danger was known. The court noted that the power company could be found negligent for not running the power lines along a fence nearby, but that the finding of contributory negligence supported the verdict. Today, with comparative negligence, the power company might well have been found liable for a percentage of the damages. *Tiede v. Loup Power Dist.*, 411 N.W.2d 312 (Neb. 1987).

A 1988 Nebraska case is similar. Farmers attempted manually to move a grain auger without lowering it, and touched a power line. The result was one dead and two injured. One man holding the auger was unaffected because he was wearing gloves and rubber-soled shoes without nails. The court affirmed a directed verdict for the power company. It noted that the auger could have been lowered down to five feet for moving. This case also was decided under traditional contributory negligence concepts. *Engleman v. Nebraska Public Power Dist.*, 424 N.W.2d 596 (Neb. 1988).

A 1991 Missouri grain auger accident left one dead and one injured. A farmer and his son were moving an auger after dark (between 5:30 and 6:00 P.M. in January) and touched or were arced by an overhead 7,200-volt line across the driveway. The farmer was killed and his son knocked unconscious. Evidence showed that the power company had recently moved the transformer to another location, with the result that the power line's voltage went from 120–140 volts to 7,200. Evidence showed that the line was about eighteen feet above the driveway. The plaintiffs' experts alleged a number of violations of the National Electric Safety Code, and in general stated that the line was so low as to be a hazard where farm equipment up to thirty-five feet high might be used. At night the line was practically invisible. The appellate court affirmed an award of $500,000 to the wife, less 30 percent for comparative fault, and $25,000 to the son. The power company argued that one of the plaintiff's experts, William C. Heilman, was not qualified. The court did not agree. Though the expert's bachelor's degree was in social science, he had seventeen years of work as a safety consultant, was a member of several professional organizations, had qualified many times as an expert in similar cases, and had worked for years with rural electric cooperatives to help identify such hazards. *Washburn v. Grundy Elec. Co-op*, 804 S.W.2d 424 (Mo. App. 1991).

In a 1992 Indiana case, the court held that when a power company has knowledge that farm equipment (a grain auger) can be elevated and there are high-voltage power lines near a grain bin, a potential hazard exists, precluding summary judgment for the power company. The accident arose when two men were moving a grain auger. They were unable to lower it because of some malfunction. They chained it to the front of a tractor; one man drove, and the other had his hand on the auger. He was electrocuted when it touched the power line. The appellate court reversed summary judgment for the power company, holding that the deceased could be found to be less than 50 percent at fault, and not contributorily negligent as a matter of law. There were no warnings of bare high-voltage lines, the lines were near the bin, and some of the lines were in fact harmless cable television and telephone wires. Under these circumstances, the case should go to a jury. *Rogers v. Grunden*, 589 N.E.2d 248 (Ind. App. 1992).

The supreme court in a 1996 Oklahoma case arising out of a fatal grain auger power-line accident overruled the court of appeals and held that summary judgment for the power company was proper. The deceased and two others were moving the auger for better access to the bin and touched a power line. The line was fifty feet from the center line of the bin. The plaintiff had alleged that the power company's employees must have noticed the grain bin and the proximity of the power lines, and could foresee the dangers of using a grain auger near the bin. The supreme court found no duty on the power company's part to monitor activities of "third parties" or to discover dangerous conditions such parties might create while working near power lines. A dissent was convinced the case was wrongly decided, and commented on the power company's obligation of the highest duty owed to the public. That duty may well require more than mere code compliance. *Shelley v. Kiwash Elec. Co-op*, 914 P.2d 669 (Okla. 1996).

24.3 Pipes, Poles and Handles

Unlike cranes, booms, and grain augers, irrigation pipes are intended to be used on or near the ground. Nevertheless, there are instances where, for one reason or another, irrigation pipes come into contact with overhead power lines. We begin with a 1983 Kansas case. The plaintiffs were two brothers who were laying irrigation pipe along a corn field. Kansas Power & Light's high-voltage lines ran twenty-three feet overhead along the edge of the field. The pipes were thirty feet long, and are intended to stay near the ground in use with the flood system of irrigation. The men noticed that a gate was loose in one section of pipe, and with one man holding one end down the other walked the pipe into the air. They inadvertently got too close to the power line, and both were injured. The lines met code height standards "absent special hazardous circumstances." The plaintiffs sued KPL on the theory that when irrigation equipment was installed, KPL should have realized that the lines presented a hazard and should have, but failed to mitigate the danger. Specifically, KPL did not physically alter the lines, place warnings on the poles, or inspect regularly. The jury found damages to be over $2 million and found the defendant 60 percent responsible. The supreme court reversed on a finding that KPL was not negligent as a matter of law, and that its motion for a judgment notwithstanding the verdict should have been granted. The court noted that KPL alone had 12,000 miles of power lines in Kansas. Both electricity and irrigation are a necessary fact of life in Kansas. The defendant did not fail to take a precaution that it should have taken. The plaintiffs themselves were aware of the danger. A dissent thought that the jury should not have been overruled; the fact that irrigation has been installed does place a duty of special care on the power company. The dissent noted a similar case some eighteen years previously. *Wilson v. Kansas Power & Light,* 657 P.2d 546 (Kan. 1983).

The court in a 1994 Colorado irrigation pipe case found the power company negligent in failing to warn farm workers of the danger of raising pipes near power lines, but also found that such negligence was not the cause of the accident. The worker who was injured was well aware of the danger, and had in fact warned others of the danger. The plaintiff proffered a jury instruction which would permit the jury to find the plaintiff excused of negligence if he, while aware of the danger, momentarily forgot the danger or was justifiably distracted. Colorado law in precomparative days did permit this doctrine to soften the harsh rule of contributory negligence as a complete bar to recovery. The court affirmed a jury verdict for the power company. It found there was no longer any need for a momentary forgetfulness rule with comparative negligence. *Rodriquez v. Morgan County R.E.A.,* 878 P.2d 77 (Colo. App. 1994).

A Georgia farm worker, who similarly inadvertently touched an overhead power line when he raised an irrigation pipe to clear debris, sued his employer for alleged failure to comply with the High Voltage Safety Act. That act requires an entity to notify the power company at least seventy-two hours in advance of performing work within ten feet of a power line. The appellate court affirmed summary judgment for the defendant. The act applies only to those whose usual business would foreseeably bring employees in close proximity to power lines. In this case, assembling irrigation pipes normally does not bring workers in close proximity to power lines. *Southern Orchard Supply v. Boyer,* 472 S.E.2d 157 (Ga. App. 1996).

In a 1995 Colorado case, the plaintiff did prevail, and was granted a verdict holding the power company 60 percent at fault in an irrigation pipe accident. The accident happened when the plaintiff, a fifteen-year-old boy, was rabbit hunting around a pile of irrigation pipes which were stacked under a power line some twenty feet above. A rabbit ran into one of the pipes, and the plaintiff tilted it upward to get the rabbit out and touched the power line. He suffered serious burns and neurological injuries. He sued the City of Fountain, owner of the power line. His expert witnesses testified that the power lines should have been higher, up to thirty-seven feet, when it was apparent that the fields were occasionally irrigated, and the pipes in use were thirty feet long. The experts stated that the city's hazard mitigation efforts were lacking. There were no effective consumer education programs about the hazard. The city could have either raised the lines or asked the landowner to cease irrigation, and upon a refusal by the landowner, cut off the power, according to the plaintiff's expert. The plaintiff in essence set out a number of actions which he claimed the city could have taken to avoid the accident, any of which, he contended, would support a finding of negligence. The court instructed on the duty of care as: "One carrying on an inherently dangerous activity such as the distribution of electricity must exercise the highest possible degree of skill, care, caution, diligence and foresight with regard to that activity, according to the best technical, mechanical, and scientific knowledge and methods which are practical and available at the time . . . ." The court of appeals reversed on a finding that the city had no duty to raise the power lines. The supreme court reversed that finding and reinstated the verdict, holding that the jury could have found the city 60 percent at fault on any of several theories. There were three dissents. *City of Fountain v. Gast*, 904 P.2d 478 (Colo. 1995).

A 2002 Utah case arose when the victim was electrocuted while moving irrigation pipes and touched or moved the pipe within arcing distance of an overhead power line. The line was owned by the city. The plaintiff family sued, claiming that the lines were too low, were not insulated, and there were no warnings. The city moved for summary judgment on the basis of governmental immunity for discretionary functions. The district court granted the motion, and the case was appealed to the Utah Supreme Court. The court found that the functions in question were indeed discretionary ones for which immunity had not been waived under the Governmental Immunity Act. The court notes that the power line met industry safety standards; if it had not, the city would not have discretionary immunity. However, the court went on to find the immunity act unconstitutional in part as a violation of the open courts provision in Art. 1, § 11 of the state constitution. The problem was that § 63-30-2(4)(a) of the immunity act, enacted in 1987, in granting governmental immunity for upgrading publicly-owned power lines, took away an existing remedy without an adequate legislative reason. The legislative history indicated that the purpose was to make it cheaper for cities to buy liability insurance. *Laney v. Fairview City*, 57 P.3d 1007 (Utah 2002).

We now turn to cases in which workers accidentally touch power lines with handles or poles. Typically the worker is doing an activity, such as painting, which may be expected, somewhat unlike the touching of a power line with an irrigation pipe. The defendant may be the landowner, as well as or instead of, the power company. Also, the area is not necessarily a rural one where lines would not normally be insulated. A 1988 Illinois case arose when a painting contractor undertook to paint several buildings, including a feed bin. A worker, the plaintiff, was injured when his painting wand contacted a 7,200-volt line twelve feet above the bin. He sued the power company and the landowner. He did not contest the dismissal of the power company, but appealed the dismissal of his claim against the land owner. The appellate court affirmed. The wires were open and obvious, and the defendant landowner twice warned the plaintiff about getting too close to them. The wires met code standards in that they were not accessible to people without a ladder, and were at the required ten foot minimum distance. The court noted that the area was a rural one, and that uninsulated power lines are common and are reasonable in that setting. *Icenogle v. Myers*, 521 N.E.2d 163 (Ill. App. 1988).

A 1990 Illinois case also involved a grain bin, and this time the court held that the power company owed a duty to the deceased and reversed summary judgment for the power company. The deceased was engaged in cleaning encrusted grain from the inside of a grain bin seventeen feet high. Power lines ran thirteen feet over the bin. The worker was electrocuted. The court distinguished Icenogle above. There the power lines were on a public right-of-way, and the accident happened while painting, not a usual activity involving a grain bin. The court stated that whether power lines should be insulated or properly located depends on whether the circumstances would indicate that people might come in contact with the lines. Here it was foreseeable that one would need a long pole to clean the inside of a seventeen foot bin, and lines only thirteen feet above represented a hazard and created a duty. *Matter of Estate of Martin*, 559 N.E.2d 1125 (Ill. App. 1990).

A 1991 Ohio case points out that the responsibility to prevent accidents usually rests with an independent contractor who is working on a job. The case arose when an employee of a paving contractor suffered a severe electrical shock. He was a cement finisher, and used a check rod to test the new cement for smoothness. He had lengthened the metal handle to twenty feet. He inadvertently touch or was arced by an overhead power line at least twenty-two feet above. He sued Navistar, the premises owner, alleging failure to warn of uninsulated wires. The appellate court affirmed summary judgment for the defendant. The defendant had not actively participated in nor supervised the work. The plaintiff admitted that he was aware of the lines, as he could hear them humming. He argued that he was unaware of the arcing phenomenon, and that he assumed the lines were insulated. The court noted that it was not proven that arcing did occur, and even if the lines had been insulated the plaintiff would have suffered some injury. *Betzner v. Navistar International Transp.*, 603 N.E.2d 256 (Ohio App. 1991).

The court in a 1988 Illinois case held it at least a jury question as to whether the an independent contractor working on the premises. The plaintiff was hired to process crude oil by the defendant landowner. He was using a metal gauging pole while standing on a catwalk between two oil tanks when he touched a nearby uninsulated power line and fell to the ground. He sued both power company and landowner. The trial judge dismissed both actions, and the appellate court reinstated the action against the landowner. The court found the claims against the power company without merit because it is unreasonable to expect a utility to insulate thousands of miles of lines in rural areas, or to post warning signs at places where it is unlikely that a person may come in contact with them. However, the plaintiff did state a cause of action against the landowner. Restatement (Second) of Torts § 343A states that a landowner is not liable for harm caused by an obvious danger on the land, unless it can be anticipated that harm may come regardless of the obviousness of the danger. One who must work with a long metal pole while standing on a catwalk near power lines seems to fit this scenario. The court pointed out that the tanks were built after the power lines. A dissent wondered just what measures the landowner could have taken, considering the plaintiff was experienced in working around oil tanks. *Watkins v. Mt. Carmel Pub. Util.*, 519 N.E.2d 10 (Ill. App. 1988).

A 1995 Louisiana case also involved oil tanks. This time the high-voltage lines were well within the minimum ten foot distance specified by the National Electrical Safety Code. The wires were as close as two feet. The plaintiff worker was burned when he attempted to treat a tank of oil with an emulsion to separate oil and water. The appellate court reversed a defense verdict and found that the power company was 70 percent at fault and the worker 30 percent. (In Louisiana, a reviewing court may review all the evidence and modify or set aside a verdict it finds clearly wrong.) The court fixed damages at $189,517. The medicals were about $40,000. The defendant argued that the injuries were not thermal burns at all, but were the result of acetic acid the plaintiff spilled on himself. *Ayres v. Beauregard Elec. Co-op*, 663 So.2d 127 (La. App. 1995).

A 1992 Iowa feed mill accident resulted in a jury verdict against the defendant power company. The plaintiff was a D & J feed mill employee who was operating a processing machine called a jetsploder when grain stopped feeding into the machine. He climbed to the top of the mill to an area called the doghouse and noticed that the grain seemed to be clogged at its outlet grate. He noticed a ten-foot metal pole lying on the catwalk nearby and used it to try to free the obstruction. His next recollection was one of lying on the catwalk below. Apparently he had touched an 8000-volt line over his head. He suffered initial cardiac arrhythmia, a broken neck, facial and skull fractures, and burns to the hands and feet. He sued the power company, Interstate, for negligent positioning of the lines. One of Interstate's defenses was that when D & J purchased electricity it impliedly agreed to use the product safely. Interstate alleged that D & J failed in that it did not adequately train the plaintiff and did not warn him of the danger. The trial court correctly ruled against a motion for a directed verdict on this point because there was no evidence of gross negligence which caused the accident. The plaintiff had been trained to run the jetsploder when its operator was on vacation, as was the case when the accident happened. Also, the clogging was not a usual occurrence. The supreme court affirmed a plaintiff's verdict (amount not given). The court referred to a 1917 case in which the court stated that the dangers arising from the production and distribution of electricity are among the greatest and most subtle known, and that its proper control involves technical knowledge, skill and care "which are a sealed book to the great mass of the people." Evidence showed that Interstate employees made annual inspections of the premises, and it was evident that two readily available ladders went almost to the top of the jetsploder. The jury could find that the plaintiff was not more than 50 percent at fault under the comparative negligence law. It was proper to admit evidence of the National Electric Safety Code of 1977. Experts differed on whether meeting the require- ment of the 1973 Code met Interstate's current duty of care. On another point, relative to Interstate's claim for indemnity from D & J, the court ruled that OSHA violations, if any, could not be introduced. *Johnson v. Interstate Power Co.*, 481 N.W.2d 301 (Iowa 1992).

A 1992 Georgia case involved a man in a tree who was harvesting pecans. He was using a long aluminum pole to knock the pecans down, and was injured when he touched a power line. He sued the power com- pany. The company's former manager testified that the nearest branches were seven feet from the power lines. Both parties referred to industry standards but did not introduce evidence of those standards. The appellate court affirmed a denial of summary judgment for the defendant. The court said that usually the foreseeability of the plaintiff's actions leading to an injury in such electrical shock cases is for the jury. No evidence had been presented about whether pecan harvesting in the area was common, whether harvesters usually used metal poles, or whether the defendant had actual or constructive notice of the activity. Without such evidence, sum- mary judgment would be improper. *Buckner v. Colquitt Elec. Member- ship*, 424 S.E.2d 299 (Ga. App. 1992).

A 1984 Georgia case held a power company liable to a chicken farmer who used a hoe to reach up and clean feed bins and touched a power line. A metal conduit pipe had been clamped to the handle of the hoe to in- crease its reach. There was evidence that when the farmer built the chicken houses under the power lines, he had a power company employee come out and inspect the premises. The farmer asked that the lines be moved, and offered to pay half the cost. The power company declined to move the lines, and in fact added three more after the chicken buildings were built. The court held that an accident of this type was foreseeable. *Habersham Elec. Membership v. Dalton*, 317 S.E.2d 312 (Ga. App. 1984).

Power companies have a high duty to protect the public, but the risk must be reasonably foreseeable. Attempting to rescue a cat up a tree is not that kind of risk. A nineteen-year-old Louisiana man volunteered to res- cue a cat on the property of another. He propped a twenty foot ladder against the tree, climbed the ladder, and attempted to hook the cat's collar with a twenty-two-foot metal pole. Naturally the cat did not cooperate, and as the volunteer started down he touched a wire. He fell to the ground and injured his back. The appellate court affirmed a defense verdict. The power line was ten feet from the ladder and 27.5 feet high. It was effectively insulated by isolation. The court also affirmed a directed verdict for the property owner and his insurer. *LeBlanc v. Wall*, 430 So.2d 1130 (La. App. 1983).

24.4 Ladders and Scaffolding

We will now deal with ladder cases, followed by scaffolding cases. Ladder cases can involve ordinary persons who are not professional painters, or others who reasonably should be more aware of the risk of high-voltage power lines than the average person. A 1993 Michigan case involved a homeowner painting his own house. The victim was a friend helping the homeowner. An uninsulated power line installed in 1937 ran twenty-four feet high and fifteen feet away from the house. The house was older than the power line. The painters used a twenty-seven foot extension ladder to reach the peak, and when finished, attempted to lower the ladder. The homeowner said that there was a "brilliant flash" and the friend was electrocuted and the homeowner injured. The estate sued the power company. The jury found the deceased was not negligent, and awarded $750,000. The court of appeals reversed on a finding that the defendant owned no duty to the decedent, and the case came before the supreme court. There was sharp disagreement at trial about how close the ladder came to the wire. It was assumed that the power arced, as there were no marks on the ladder that would indicate physical contact. The plaintiff's expert testified that, depending on conditions of ionized and moist air such as prevailed at the time, electricity could arc several feet, though the plaintiff did not claim any particular distance. The court of appeals based its reversal partly on testimony that it would be impossible for the power to arc farther than one inch. The supreme court reinstated the verdict. It found sufficient evidence of the defendant's negligence in failure of inspection which allowed frayed wires to present a hazard. The defendant is not excused by compliance with industry codes when a reasonable person in the industry would have taken additional precautions. The introduction to the NESC guidelines states that the guidelines state minimum provisions for the

safety of employees and the public. They are not intended as design specifications or instruction manuals. A concurring judge suggested that the
basis of negligence was stringing the lines too close to existing dwellings
when a sixty foot right-of-way was available to the power company. A
long dissent would affirm, finding the danger open and obvious. The
judge found the majority's holding tantamount to strict liability. *Schultz v.
Consumers Power Co.*, 506 N.W.2d 175 (Mich. 1993).

The Michigan Supreme Court revisited the issue in 1996, *Groncki v.
Detroit Edison,* 557 N.W.2d 289 (Mich. 1996). Apparently the court
wanted to make a further statement on this point of law. It combined three
cases in one decision. In one case a maintenance supervisor at a condominium attempted to move a twenty-four-foot ladder by himself and
touched a power line twenty-one feet high and fourteen feet from the
building. He suffered cardiac arrest, burns, a toe amputation, and he alleged brain injury. He was aware of the power line and had warned other
workers about it. The trial court granted summary judgment to the utility
and the court of appeals reversed. In the second case, a worker at a super-
market construction site was moving a twenty-nine-foot high scaffold by
means of a forklift and, while reversing around some debris, touched a
power line thirty-five feet high and sixty-five feet from the building. He
was electrocuted. The trial judge granted summary judgment to the utility
and the court of appeals affirmed. In the third case, a worker was delivering a load of cement blocks to a house construction site. He operated his
boom lift into a power line twenty-six feet high and twelve feet from the
house. He was also electrocuted. The court of appeals reversed summary
judgment for the utility. It is obvious that the intermediate appellate courts
were, perhaps understandably, confused about the common law on this
point, so it was very appropriate for the supreme court to consolidate and
take these cases. The case is a good one for our analysis because it points
up the problems in deciding such cases, and whether the liability decisions should be made by a jury or made by a court on a motion for summary judgment.

The court found that the defendant Detroit Edison had not violated a
duty in each case and that it was entitled to summary judgment. Three
judges concurred in part and dissented in part and each wrote an opinion.
A fourth judge dissented and wrote an opinion. The majority noted
Schultz in articulating the central issue: should the defendant have fore-

seen the probability that injury might result from any reasonable activity done on the premises for work, business, or pleasure? It is not necessary that the defendant should have foreseen a particular act that led to the accident. The majority distinguished Schultz by noting that there was an allegation that the lines running near the house were frayed and pitted; in other words, in a state of disrepair. In the three cases here there was no similar allegation. The plaintiffs argued that the power company had a duty to relocate, insulate, de-energize, warn or erect barriers around the lines at the site of the accidents. The costs of these mitigating measures would, as a matter of public policy, outweigh the risks. The majority emphasized that all the accident victims were experienced workmen who were aware of the dangers of power lines, and were aware of the specific lines they inadvertently touched.

The dissenting opinions made several points. The majority appeared to restrict the utility's obligations to homeowners. The dissent saw little difference between the homeowner painting his house in Schultz and the deceased in Groncki working on a condominium roof with lines even closer. Both activities are routine maintenance that are to be expected. Justice Levin's dissent found it improper to grant summary judgment on an inadequate record and incomplete factual assessment in finding that the defendant "could not have been expected to do anything to protect the injured and deceased workmen who, further, could have avoided injury had they been more alert and careful." Most workplace injuries can be avoided if the persons involved at all times are alert, careful, and never make a mistake in years of work from fatigue, distraction, or momentary lapse. As we know, that does not describe the real world. The defendant in these three cases is not asked to relocate or bury thousands of miles of lines. Simple measures such as warning streamers, orange balls, temporary insulation, or temporary de-energizing of lines at construction sites may not be unreasonable. Justice Levin would vote to hold the defendant to a duty to take reasonable-not ruinous-precautions to protect the public. *Groncki v. Detroit Edison*, 557 N.W.2d 289 (Mich. 1996).

In connection with worker alertness throughout the day's work, see a 1986 Florida case. The plaintiff was a roofer who was removing metal items from the roof. He touched a power line that ran six feet diagonally from the roof. The trial court held inadmissible testimony by the plaintiff's expert witness that a person's concentration and ability to remain aware of all of one's surroundings diminish as the day wears on. The appellate court reversed a finding that the power company was 95 percent at fault and ordered a new trial. The expert's testimony referred to a matter that is within the common understanding of the average layman. The court held it possible that the jury gave undue importance to the expert's statement on a matter it could determine for itself. *Florida Power Corp. v. Barron*, 481 So.2d 1309 (Fla. App. 1986).

A 1986 Minnesota case arose from the electrocution deaths of two painters. The victims were school teachers who painted during the summer breaks. They contracted to paint a large farmhouse. There were no witnesses, but they were found dead. It was apparent that their forty-foot extension ladder had contacted a 7,200-volt line located twenty-one feet from the house. The jury found the power company 58.4 percent at fault and each painter 20.8 percent, and awarded amounts before reduction of $1,112,650 and $858,535. (The trial court improperly reduced each award by not only that deceased's negligence, but also by the fault of the other, and the appellate court ordered that only 20.8 percent be taken off.) The power company argued on appeal that it had exceeded the distances from the house required by code for the routing of the power line. It argued that it had complied with Minn. Stat. § 326.243, and that statute stated that compliance is prima facie evidence of accepted standards. The appellate court noted that NESC provision, section 20, provided that "construction shall be made according to accepted good practice for the given local conditions . . . .", and the "all electric supply and communication lines and equipment shall be installed and maintained so as to reduce hazards to life as far as practicable." Accordingly, whether an uninsulated 7,200-volt line needed to be run in the middle of a farmyard was properly a jury question. The court declined to hold the deceased painters to the standards of professional painters because the group is too diverse. Painters run the gamut from union professionals to college students to persons working on their own property. There was testimony that the victims would have had the power shut off, as they had done in the past, if they had suspected the lines were of high voltage. Thus it was proper to hold the victims to a standard of ordinary care of reasonable persons, not of professionals. *Steinbrecher v. McLeod Co-op*, 392 N.W.2d 709 (Minn. App. 1986).

The Virginia Supreme Court had no problem in holding a professional painter to a higher standard. The plaintiff was severely injured when an aluminum ladder he was moving touched an uninsulated 19,900-volt line. He was painting the gutter of an apartment building and was required to move the ladder every four feet as he progressed. The power line was ten feet from the building and twenty-four feet high. The plaintiff was using a thirty-two-foot extension ladder. He sued the power company for negligently positioning and maintaining the line. The jury awarded $1.5 million, and the trial judge then granted the defendant's motion to set aside the verdict on finding that the plaintiff was contributorily negligent as a matter of law, and that the plaintiff had not established that the defendant was primarily negligent. The supreme court affirmed the motion. The plaintiff's theory of negligence was that, while he was well aware of the danger of power lines, he had no special knowledge of electricity. He said that he thought that the line was a telephone wire. Otherwise he would have either borrowed a fiberglass ladder or asked for help from other workmen. The court found that the plaintiff, as a professional painter, could be charged with knowledge of the danger involved. A person handling a metal ladder in close proximity to lines strung between poles should ascertain if they are power lines. A dissent would find that the jury properly had the issue of contributory negligence and should not have been overruled. The dissent pointed out that the power line in question had oxidized over the years and had the appearance of an insulated wire. *Kelly v. Virginia Elec. and Power*, 381 S.E.2d 219 (Va. 1989).

A 1991 Nebraska case is almost identical to Kelly. The plaintiff was a small business owner who was using an aluminum ladder to paint his building. The 120-volt lines attached to the building were insulated and wound about an uninsulated ground wire for support. The wires were spliced at the building. The splices were not insulated, but again, because of oxidation, they might have appeared insulated to the average person. The plaintiff touched one of the splices and fell to the ground. The supreme court reversed a bench trial judgment for the plaintiff on the finding that the plaintiff's negligence was more than slight, which before the comparative negligence statute, would bar his claim. The court found that the plaintiff's "cavalier assumption" that it was safe to work around the wires was negligence. The court noted that the plaintiff was a college graduate and had operated an arc welder. A dissent simply stated that the court ignored its own standard of review and improperly invaded the province of the trial judge. *Fetty v. Seward City Rural Pub. Power Dist.*, 471 N.W.2d 756 (N.W.2d 1991).

A 1993 Maryland case is similar, again decided under traditional contributory negligence concepts. A siding installer was seriously injured when he and a co-worker were raising an extension ladder and it touched an overhead high-voltage line which they had not noticed. When the job was bid, the supervisor noticed a cluster of 110-volt lines which he thought were far enough away so that it was not necessary to have them de-energized. The high-voltage line was higher and ran nearer the house. After an almost $5 million verdict, the trial judge granted a judgment notwithstanding the verdict. The appellate court affirmed. It found that the danger was open and obvious, and that the plaintiff could not rely on whatever assurances he had from his employer about safety. The court agreed that the plaintiff was negligent as a matter of law. *Campbell v. Baltimore Gas & Elec.*, 619 A.2d 213 (A.2d 1993).

A 1992 Louisiana case decision emphasized the fact that the power company exceeded code requirements and weighed the slight risk of accident against the cost of taking further precautions, such as insulating or relocating the lines. The case arose when an apartment complex painter was injured when he moved his aluminum extension ladder against a high-voltage line. The power line was five feet above the minimum fifteen-foot vertical clearance for pedestrian areas, and had thirteen feet of horizontal clearance rather than the five feet specified by the code. That alone does not preclude negligence, but here the danger was open and obvious and the plaintiff was a professional painter. The painters were conscious of the danger and repeatedly warned each other. In fact, the plaintiff broke one of their rules by attempting to move the ladder by himself. *Davis v. Louisiana Power & Light*, 612 So.2d 235 (La. App. 1992).

A 1997 Louisiana case held that a plaintiff who was replacing gutters at an apartment complex was subject to summary judgment. He was injured when he attempted to move an extension ladder and touched a power line. By affidavit, he alleged that he was told by apartment residents that he was not the first such workman shocked by the lines, and also that the utility had advised the complex to have the lines moved. The defendant complex submitted an affidavit which was contrary. The appellate court affirmed summary judgment for the complex. The plaintiff's affidavit was hearsay, and such an affidavit aimed at impeaching the defendant's affidavit cannot be used to defeat summary judgment. *Butzman v. Louisiana Power & Light*, 694 So.2d 514 (La. App. 1997).

A 1993 Missouri case arose from an ice storm. The plaintiff, who lived in the country, was without power for several days. When he discovered that his neighbors' power came back on, he looked at his transformer pole and noticed something dangling. Upon calling the power company, he was told it was a fuse, and someone would run by and "slap one in." After some time he became impatient, placed an aluminum ladder on the cab of his pickup and climbed the pole. He removed the blown fuse and took it to the power company's warehouse. A person never identified helped him find a fuse. When he tried to install it, he was shocked and fell to the ground. He sued the power company for failure to warn of the danger of installing the fuse and for failure to warn of the danger of working on the transformer. The jury found the power company 75 percent at fault. The appellate court ordered a new trial. It agreed that the plaintiff had made a submissible case. Someone in the defendant's warehouse had apparent authority to give the fuse to the plaintiff. This gave rise to the implication that the customer would likely try to install the fuse, and the deposition of the warehouseman was that it would be dangerous for a customer to try to install such a fuse. Thus, foreseeability was shown. However, the instruction on duty to warn about the transformer was error. The facts in this case did not support it. Incidentally, the plaintiff was held not to be a trespasser. Handing him the fuse was an implicit invitation to install it. *Mobley v. Webster Co-op*, 859 S.W.2d 923 (Mo. App. 1993).

A 1997 Missouri case arose from an electrocution of a workman when his ladder touched a power line as he was attempting to get to the roof of a building. The appellate court affirmed a judgment for the defendant power company. Evidence of an alternative access site to the roof, away from power lines, was properly admitted. The evidence went to the foreseeability issue and to the affirmative defenses of negligence by the plaintiff and assumption of the risk. *Liszewski v. Union Elec. Co.*, 941 S.W.2d 748 (Mo. App. 1997).

A 1993 Colorado case arose when a homeowner was using an aluminum ladder to do maintenance work on his house. He contacted a high-voltage line and was electrocuted. The estate sued the power company. The plaintiff appealed a defense verdict. The appeal was centered on Instruction 20, which was offered by the defendant. The instruction stated in part, "If you find by a preponderance of the evidence that the Telecky electric distribution line was constructed, installed and maintained in accordance with the applicable National Electric Safety Code, then the law presumes that the line complied with accepted good engineering practice in the electric industry." Both parties agreed that Public Utilities Commission had accepted the code for the purpose of regulating the industry. Instruction 1 correctly stated that compliance is not an absolute defense, but is an indication of due care. It does not preclude a finding of negligence where a reasonable person would have taken additional precautions under the circumstances. The supreme court reversed for a new trial. The problem with Instruction 20 was the language "presumes that the line complied with good engineering practice," and with the fact that it was held to be a rebuttable presumption against the plaintiff. Whether compliance in a particular case embodied good engineering practice is best determined by the jury after hearing evidence (usually from expert witnesses). *Yampa Valley Elec. v. Telecky*, 862 P.2d 252 (Colo. 1993).

A 1998 Massachusetts case found a utility not negligent in the electrocution death of a person moving a ladder. The deceased was visiting her parents. Her father was painting the house and asked for help in moving his extension ladder. Four family members responded. The ladder touched power lines sixteen to eighteen feet from the porch and twenty-five and thirty-five feet high. All were injured by the shock, and the deceased died five days later. The wires were in plain view and were not insulated. The power company was in compliance with all applicable code provisions. The appellate court affirmed summary judgment for the power company. The power company would not reasonably anticipate that a homeowner would attempt to move an extended ladder on the sidewalk in front of his house, and near power lines. No rational view of the evidence would support a verdict for the plaintiff, so summary judgment is proper. *Bergendahl v. Massachusetts Elec. Co.*, 701 N.E.2d 656 (Mass. App. 1998).

In a 1986 Ohio case heard in federal court, the court held that code compliance does not "end an inquiry into foreseeability," but that it is significant in deciding threshold issues of foreseeability and duty of care. The case arose when a sandblaster working from a ladder was electrocuted when his equipment touched a nearby high-voltage line. The estate sued the owner of the building, the United States. The district court judge found that the deceased's own negligence was the sole proximate cause and dismissed the complaint. The court held that the United States did not actively participate in the work. It neither gave nor denied permission for the critical acts that led to the death; primarily, the placing of an aluminum ladder near power lines. The court also found that the reservation by the defendant of the right to inspect the safety of the work did not constitute active participation. The court found that depositions from coworkers showed that sandblasting is inherently dangerous work. The worker must position ladders or other equipment on the sides of buildings, carry up the sandblasting equipment, and stand high enough so that he is pointing the nozzle downwards to observe the effect of the blasting. A work that is inherently dangerous requires appropriate caution. High-voltage lines are one of the common dangers. In this case, there was no duty to warn of obvious dangers. *Angel v. United States*, 650 F. Supp. 434 (Ohio 1986).

A 2001 West Virginia case has a surprising result, and, as shown by the dissenting opinion, controversial. A homeowner hired an unlicensed electrician to upgrade the wiring at his mother's home. The dissent points out the electrician had worked as an electrician for twenty-three years, so if he was currently unlicensed, he was not necessarily incompetent. His pay was either $40 or a case of beer. He hooked up a breaker box and apparently failed to connect the ground wire. A cable company employee working on a pole at the premises and was shocked, falling to the ground and sustaining multiple fractures. He sued the power company (later dismissed from the suit) and the homeowner who hired the electrician. The theory of the plaintiff was that the homeowner negligently hired an unlicensed electrician to do inherently dangerous work, and that the homeowner could not escape liability as providing a safe workplace was a nondelegable duty. The jury awarded damages of $1,299,000 apportioned as follows: Appalachian Power 90 percent, CableComm 9 percent, and homeowner one percent. Under the rules of joint and several liability, the homeowner was liable for the entire amount. (The West Virginia Supreme Court noted that this seemed unfair, but the court would not overturn one of the principles of tort law.) The supreme court affirmed. The long dissent thought that decision now makes the typical homeowner liable for the negligent work of an independent contractor performing inherently dangerous work. Heretofore, the doctrine has not applied to homeowners. *Kizer v. Harper*, 561 S.E.2d 368 (W. Va. 2001).

We now turn to several cases involving scaffolding. Scaffolding generally is erected in a commercial setting and not used by homeowners. Often there is a general contractor and subcontractors. A 1986 Louisiana case was one in which the injured workman recovered damages from the utility company. A general contractor was constructing new apartment buildings. One building was sited so as to run only three-feet ten-inches from a power line. There were three lines. The lowest was a grounded guy wire carrying no current. The middle carried 7,620 volts, and the top was the ground wire. Scaffolding was erected for the siding of the building. The initial scaffolding touched the guy wire, and the workmen pulled it aside. The next section of scaffolding touched the live wire, and the plaintiff, who was assembling the scaffolding, suffered numerous electric burns. He was an employee of a subcontractor. He sued the power company and the general contractor. The appellate court affirmed an award of $200,000 against the power company. The line had been put in a year earlier, and the power company knew that the subdivision was to be developed, and that the lot owner had the right to build up to the servitude line. In addition, the defendant's employees had installed a temporary connection after the foundations had been poured and should have noticed how close the building would be to the power line. The court rejected the argument that code requirements were met with insulation by isolation; that is, not readily accessible to people. Less than four feet from a building is far from isolation. The court also rejected the argument of contributory negligence and assumption of the risk. The plaintiff and his coworkers were not warned of the live line and they testified that they of course would not have touched it had they known it was energized. They might reasonably assume that since the bottom wire was not live, neither were the others. In any event, their only remedy would have been "to tell their supervisors how to run the job or quit." (The author finds this assertion not to ring true. A worker who notifies his supervisor of a possibly dangerous work situation is more likely to be thanked than fired.) The plaintiff had some right to expect that his employers would provide a safe workplace. One defense the author finds interesting was embodied in an instruction offered by the defendant. It said that electric lines announce their danger by their mere presence. The court properly rejected the instruction as being based on dictum in a case and not an accurate statement of the law. As to the general contractor defendant, the court held it to be the statutory employer of the plaintiff and thus worker's compensation was the only remedy as to it. *Snow v. Gulf States Util. Co.*, 492 So.2d 31 (La. App. 1986).

A 1988 Louisiana case arose when a bridge painter was electrocuted when the scaffolding the painting crew was moving contacted a high-voltage line. The estate sued the maker of a rented scaffolding for product liability. The appellate court affirmed summary judgment for the manufacturer. Not only was the danger of power lines common knowledge among construction crews, the user's manual supplied with the scaffolding and warning labels on the unit was a defense. The crew foreman had specifically read the manual. The crew simply misjudged the location of, or did not notice, the power line. *Duncan v. Louisiana Power & Light*, 532 So.2d 968 (La. App. 1988).

Duncan's widow also sued his employer, the power company, and the Louisiana Department of Transportation. The court affirmed awards for the widow and for a co-employee who was injured by the contact with the wire. The court held that even though the victims were doing their work as directed by their foreman, and the employer's conduct was gross and wantonly negligent, it was not intentional. Obviously the foreman would not have intentionally directed the men to walk the cable into a power line. Therefore the employer was not liable for contribution to the two parties found negligent, the DOT and the power company. There was no question that permitting the work to go on near a power line was negligence. The cost to move the line would have been less than $6,000. Duncan's widow received about $833,000. There was some interesting medical testimony. The widow sought damages for conscious pain and suffering. The medical expert testified that while electricity passes through the body almost instantaneously, the victim would feel a violent contraction of his muscles, and to some degree would understand what was happening. The victim would be unconscious within a minute. The appellate court also gave some credence to the injured workman's claim of lingering disability. He was cleared to return to work a week after the accident, but did not begin working for three years because of "pain and nervousness." Then he suffered a heart attack. The court held that damages for lost wages were proper for this period of time. *Fannin v. Louisiana Power & Light*, 594 So.2d 1119 (La. App. 1992).

We can contrast this case with a 1988 Kansas case which is similar. Two ironworkers were injured when they came in contact with a live power line on a bridge construction project. The court held that the power company (Board of Public Utilities) was not negligent and that summary judgment was proper. All parties knew the line would remain energized, and it was of a distance that complied with the code. *Slater v. Board of Pub. Util.*, 703 F. Sup. 893 (Kan. 1988).

One should keep in mind that there can be defendants other than a power company. An employee of a subcontractor may sue the general contractor for failure to provide a safe common work area. This was the finding in the Michigan *Gronki* case noted above. Also, state statute may require a person or business entity to notify the power company if it contemplates working near a power line, and the precise distance will be stated in the statute. An Arizona case dealt with which of possible entities should have been responsible for notice to the power company. The court reversed summary judgment for the general contractor and held it to be a jury question to determine who had agreed to do what. *Cohen v. Salt River Project*, 736 P.2d 809 (Ariz. App. 1987).

A 1983 Illinois case involved a hoist and a high-voltage line which appeared to be insulated. The plaintiff was an experienced roofer, but was on his first job as an independent contractor. He was repairing the roof of a three-story warehouse. He set up a hoist for materials, noticed power lines six feet away, and knew that the hoist boom set the lifting cable four feet out. However, the lines were covered with what he thought was insulation, and he thought they were low voltage. They carried 12,000 volts. The lines were installed in 1929, and were wrapped with weatherproofing. Such weatherproofing wrapping is no longer used because it looks like insulation. A gust of wind blew the hoist cable into the line, and the plaintiff was severely injured. The appellate court affirmed an award of $1,125.000, less 50 percent for contributory negligence. The court noted that supervisory employees of the defendant themselves thought the lines were insulated. *German v. Illinois Power Co.*, 451 N.E.2d 903 (Ill App. 1983).

Note that there may be a statutory exception to the scaffolding statutes. In a 2002 New York case, an electrician was injured while upgrading the service at a house when he was shocked and fell. He was employed by the homeowner. The cause of the accident was the electrician's own sloppy work methods. The homeowner was entitled to the one-or two-family exception to Labor Law § 240(1). *Angelucci v. Sands*, 748 N.Y.S.2d 757 (A.D. 2002).

24.5 TV and CB Antennas

We now turn to cases involving citizens band and television antennas touching power lines. Usually such devices are installed by a homeowner himself at his own property. The antennas are made of light metals and unfortunately are very good conductors of electricity. The issues presented are whether the power lines presented an unreasonable risk of injury, whether the activity could be reasonably anticipated by the power company, and whether the injured or deceased person was aware or should have been aware of the danger, and was negligent. A limited number of such cases have come before the appellate courts, and usually the verdict is for the defendant. A 1993 Georgia case involved a TV antenna. A family was moving into a new home, and the two sons (ages not given) tried to put up a thirty-three foot mast and antenna. The mast could be telescoped to a shorter length. The sons decided to fully extend the mast and walk it up. They touched a power line twenty-six feet high and both were electrocuted. The parents filed separate actions, so our case deals with son Craig only. The jury found the full value of Craig's life to be $225,000, and awarded that amount less 25 percent for comparative fault. The trial judge then granted the plaintiffs' motion for judgment notwithstanding the verdict and ordered the full amount paid. The appellate court reversed this motion, and directed that the jury verdict be reinstated. There was some evidence of comparative negligence. The father, upon discovering the bodies, looked up and saw the power line, so the line was clearly visible. Craig himself had worked around electricity from an early age and had been specifically warned about the danger when putting up the mast. *Three Notch Elec. v. Simpson,* 430 S.E.2d 52 (Ga. App. 1993).

A 1986 Louisiana case arose out of the sale of a CB antenna. The defendant here is the homeowner (and his insurer), not the power company. The plaintiff was the buyer, and the seller was the defendant's eighteen-year-old son. As they were lowering the antenna, it came in contact with a power line. The son was electrocuted and the buyer-plaintiff was severely shocked and suffered burns to both hands and "blow-out" burns to his feet. The blow-out burns, up to the size of a fifty-cent piece, required the plaintiff to give up his job as a welder and he found a desk job. The jury awarded damages of $182,550, reduced 50 percent for contributory negligence. The appellate court affirmed. The homeowner could be found negligent for not maintaining his property in a safe condition. He was aware of the power line and had installed the antenna himself. He was aware that his son had sold the antenna, and that the plaintiff, an invitee, would come onto the property to remove it. There was a failure to warn. The plaintiff was aware of the wire, but did not assume the risk. Only the top two inches of the antenna touched the wire, so the risk was not entirely apparent. A dissent would not find the homeowner negligent because, while he knew of the sale, he was not aware of when and how the antenna would be taken down. *Deville v. Louisiana Farm Bureau Ins.*, 492 So.2d 895 (La. App. 1986).

A 1988 Louisiana case found some negligence on the part of two defendants, the power company and the owner of a mobile home park. A man who was installing a TV antenna was seriously injured when the antenna touched a 13,800-volt power line directly above the trailer. The fully extended antenna was a foot higher than the line. Power company employees were aware that the trailer was parked directly under the line and took no action, which was proof of some negligence. By the same token the park owner should have known of the hazard. The court reversed a defense verdict as to both defendants, and made a finding of plaintiff's negligence 70 percent, and 15 percent for each defendant. The award before reduction was $200,000 plus $29,669 for medical expenses. The plaintiff suffered third-degree burns of the hands, feet, back, and abdomen. *Casanova v. Ballard*, 533 So.2d 1005 (La. App. 1988).

The remaining antenna cases found for the defendant. A 1987 Louisiana case arose when a homeowner attempted to take down his TV antenna without a ladder or help. The antenna was supported by a tripod. The plaintiff loosened the set screw holding the antenna pipe in the tripod, lifted the antenna, lost his balance backward, and the antenna contacted a high-voltage line. The plaintiff admitted he could have taken down the antenna safely by untaping and telescoping it. His theory of liability was that the power company should have anticipated this kind of accident and should have insulated the line. (The power company's expert testified that rarely are high-voltage lines insulated because the insulation tends to break down under static charges.) The jury found the defendant negligent, but not the proximate cause. The appellate court affirmed. The trial judge correctly ruled inadmissible reports of other similar incidents. The bare reports without details of the circumstances would not necessarily show similarity to the case in question. On a rather novel point, an expert for the defendant did concede that it was foreseeable that when cable television becomes available to a neighborhood that residents might want to take down their TV antennas. *Creppel v. Louisiana Power & Light*, 514 So.2d 239 (La. App. 1987).

Note a 1990 Louisiana case in which the supreme court applied a public policy approach. An older adult man was electrocuted when he was moving his citizens band radio antenna and touched a high-voltage line which spanned his back yard. The jury found for the estate. The court of appeals reversed, and the supreme court affirmed. The court noted that the deceased had narrowly escaped injury or death five years earlier while moving the antenna. On the fatal day, he had for no apparent good reason picked up the antenna from the ground, held it erect, and walked into the power line. The court held that the burden of protecting from this accident exceeded the risk. The court noted that there is "an essential balancing process that lies at the heart of negligence." Here the balance favored the defendant. (The jury had awarded $500,000.) *Washington v. Louisiana Power & Light*, 555 So.2d 1350 (La. 1990). (The author has no ready explanation of why most of these antenna cases are from Louisiana.)

A 1987 Illinois case was brought on a theory of product liability. Two boys were attempting to erect a radio mast when it touched a power line, and one boy was electrocuted. The estate sued the maker of the antenna for selling a dangerous product and for failure to warn. The appellate court affirmed a defense verdict. The surviving boy testified that they had noticed the power lines, along with lower and more visible telephone wires, but thought the antenna would clear as they walked it up. The plaintiff's expert testified that the antenna could have been made safe from shock either by coating the entire antenna with insulation or by installing an insulating plug in the middle of the antenna. The defendant testified that it had tried to insulate antennas, and the experiment had not been successful. The court stated that lack of warning labels and printed matter was not relevant. There is no duty to warn of an obvious danger. *In re Estate of Dickens*, 515 N.E.2d 208 (Ill. App. 1987).

A 2001 Illinois case arose when a homeowner attempted to take down a CB antenna that was attached to his detached garage. The antenna was over fifty feet high to get better reception. The homeowner and a helper discussed how to get the antenna down safely, but it touched the 120–240 power line and the homeowner was electrocuted. The court of appeals, after discussing prior case law, affirmed summary judgment for the power company. It is essential that there be one rule about the issue of insulating power lines. Since electricity is a basic necessity, it is reasonable not to require such insulation in locations, such as this alley, where the general public may come into contact with them occasionally. The court noted that power lines are often weatherproofed to protect them from atmospheric conditions, and that might lead one to think that they had been insulation. In this case, it was clear that the deceased knew of the danger. *Tinder v. Illinois Power*, 758 N.E.2d 483 (Ill. App. 2001).

Note a 1990 Pennsylvania case with almost identical facts in which one was killed and another injured. Again the maker of the antenna was sued in strict liability, along with the premises owner and the power company. The jury found the seller of the antenna, Tandy Corporation, not liable. The lack of Consumer Product Safety Commission-required labels was excused because the antenna was manufactured or sold before those regulations were in force. The jury found the premises owner 36 percent at fault, the power company 15 percent, and each victim 49 percent. The jury's findings were affirmed on appeal. *Dunkle v. West Penn. Power Co.*, 538 A.2d 814 (Pa. App. 1990).

24.6 Boats, Aircraft and Balloons

We have examined cases in which people have contacted power lines from the ground. Now let's turn to contact from the air. A hot air balloon case arose in Illinois from an incident in 1981. A balloon carrying six passengers and a pilot and operating near Route 14 in Barrington Hills contacted high-voltage power lines. One passenger escaped by jumping out; all the others perished. Many suits were filed against a variety of defendants, including the power company, the balloon owner, and various manufacturers of the balloon and its components. Those suits were settled or dismissed. This case deals with the power company only. The trial court granted summary judgment to the power company and the appellate court affirmed. (The power company failed to file its appellate brief, and there was no oral argument, so the court decided the case on the record before it.) The evidence revealed that the crash took place one and one-half miles from the balloon port, that a storm was approaching with winds up to 37 mph, that the balloon owner believed that the accident was caused by pilot error and "a timing problem and an optical illusion," that the balloon pilot knew of the acute danger of power lines and that contact is usually fatal, and that the balloon pilots were well aware of the power line and used it as a reference point. The plaintiffs argued that the accident site was an area where it was foreseeable that people might come in contact with power lines, and that whether the accident was foreseeable must be a jury question. The appellate court held that there is not a jury question of fact unless there is also a legal duty. In the context of this case, whether there is a legal duty on the defendant depends on an analysis of the risk versus the burden on the defendant of guarding against that risk. This issue can be decided by a trial judge on a motion for summary judgment. The trial judge found that the defendant had no legal duty to warn of an obvious and known danger. *Coleman v. Windy City Balloon Port*, 513 N.E.2 506 (Ill. App. 1987).

A South Dakota helicopter passenger was injured when the helicopter struck power lines. The men were inspecting power lines for their employer, a power company. They flew into the lines of another power company (the defendant) which crossed over their own lines. The passenger was seriously injured and sued the defendant for failure to mark the lines at that point with signs or "spherical line markers." The trial judge found no legal duty and directed a verdict for the defendant. The supreme court affirmed. The defendant routinely marks its own lines where they cross other of its own lines, but when they cross a foreign line, it installs warning markers only at the request of the foreign line. There was no request here. Also, the defendant need not assume other power companies will inspect their lines from the air. In fact, the plaintiff's own employer's flight operations manual stated that the area around the Fort Thompson substation was a dangerous one, with "numerous lines in all directions." Finally, the negligence of the pilot was a superseding cause. *Poelstra v. Basin Elec. Power Co-op*, 545 N.W.2d 823 (S.D. 1996).

In a case similar to Poelstra, a Pennsylvania appellate court affirmed a jury verdict finding the power company at fault and awarding damages. Again a helicopter pilot and passenger were inspecting power lines and struck an intersecting line. Both lines were owned by the same power company. The pilot and passenger were employees of an independent contractor hired to make such inspection flights. One was killed and the other severely injured. They sued the power company. Citing a 1956 case, *Yoffee v. Pennsylvania Power & Light*, 123 A.2d 636, the trial court correctly found that the defendant had a high duty to warn pilots where air activity may be expected near power lines. Such warnings may be highly visible markings on poles or towers, and orange balls on lines. The fact that the defendant engaged the services of the plaintiffs' employer indicates knowledge of the activity. The jury could find that the warnings were inadequate. Both sides offered the jury extensive evidence, including video reenactment by helicopter. The jury could find that the danger was not open and obvious. The jury did find the pilot 35 percent at fault. *Bailey v. Pennsylvania Elec. Co.*, 598 A.2d 41 (Pa. App. 1991).

A 2002 Missouri case involved Army Reserve helicopter pilots on a training mission. They flew down the Osage River at an altitude below 100 feet and struck power lines that were not marked with marker balls. Two were killed, and the jury awarded $10 million and $11 million. The court of appeals affirmed. Construing the evidence favorably to support the verdict, the jury could find that the crew's mission was to fly down the river low and fast. The defendant either knew or should have known of the lack of marker balls. An Army report on the accident was properly excluded under 10 U.S.C. § 2254 as not a safety investigation. *Lopez v. Three Rivers Elec. Co-op*, 92 S.W.3d 165 (Mo. App. E.D. 2002).

A 1993 Colorado case arose out of a helicopter accident. The pilot and a passenger struck power lines and both were killed. The appellate case does not indicate the circumstances. The court consolidated both wrongful death actions and the property damage claim of the helicopter owner. The jury made awards totaling $2.9 million against the defendant power company. The key point at trial was the admission of evidence that the defendant intended to mark the lines with orange balls but had not yet done so. The appellate court affirmed the verdicts. It was proper to admit the evidence about the warnings because there was a pre-existing common law duty to warn. The jury found the defendant 65 percent at fault. The pilot was found 35 percent at fault as to his claim, and the helicopter owner likewise 35 percent at fault on it's claim. The court rejected the defendant's claim for setoff as to social security and workers' compensation benefits paid. Those payments arose out of the deceased's employment contracts and had nothing to do with the defendant. *Combined Communications Corp. v. Public Serv. Co.*, 865 P.2d 893 (Colo. App. 1993).

It is obvious that power lines are not marked with warning balls at every point to warn pilots. FFA regulations require pilots to maintain minimum altitudes which will place them well above power lines. A 1992 Oklahoma case noted that pilots of small planes are required to maintain at least 1,000 feet over any congested area of a city, town, or settlement, and 500 feet over other areas except over open water or sparsely populated areas. In any case, the aircraft may not be flown closer than 500 feet to any person, vessel, vehicle, or structure except when necessary for takeoff or landing. A case arose when the pilot and passenger of a small plane were helping to search for a missing elderly man and flew into power lines which were 180 feet high. Both were injured. The lines were in a rural area, but spanned a four lane, heavily used highway. There were some forty houses within a half mile area. The pilot was clearly operating lower than the required 500 feet because he would have been within 500 feet of a vehicle and a building (a garage). Even if he were in minimum compliance, it was not foreseeable that this kind of accident would happen at this place. The appellate court affirmed judgment for the defendant power company. It had no legal duty to mark its lines with warning devices at this place. The pilot argued that he was exempt from FAA regulations by the emergency doctrine. However, the emergency contemplated by the regulations refers to an in-flight emergency, not the search for a missing person. *Blaine v. Oklahoma Gas & Elec.*, 850 P.2d 346 (Okla. App. 1992).

A 1993 Kentucky case reached the same result. A pilot flying a small plane was killed when he flew into a static nonenergized line 233 feet high. The area was mountainous. There were no warning markers on the line. The widow sued the power company. The federal district court granted summary judgment to the defendant. The plaintiff theorized that the deceased was flying low because of engine trouble, but her initial statement was that he carrying out a plan to "buzz" the flea market they were attending as a signal to his family that he was to be picked up at the airport. The accident site was under the control of the Kentucky Airport Zoning Commission. It was five miles from an airport. KAZC regulations relate to marking and lighting structures. However, a grandfather provision excluded pre-existing power lines "so long as such lines are not subsequently determined to be a hazard to air navigation." The defendant's lines had not been so identified, and consequently there was no duty to mark. *Pike v. Kentucky Power Co.*, 876 F. Supp. 143 (E.D. Ky. 1993).

A 1994 Arizona case arose when a pilot and two passengers were killed when their plane struck power lines along I-17, near several airports, including one within a mile of the crash site. The plaintiffs alleged that the engine failed and the pilot was trying to make an emergency landing on I-17, while the defendants claimed that the pilot was buzzing I-17. The defendants were the power company, the plane manufacturer, and the engine maker. The appellate court affirmed summary judgment for the power company. The court found that the power company did owe a duty to the plaintiffs, but whether that duty was breached depends on whether it was a foreseeable and unreasonable risk that the accident would happen. While this determination is ordinarily a jury question, the courts can set "outer limits." The courts can act as a gatekeeper to keep the question of what is an unreasonable risk from the jury. The court held that the power company did not have a duty to mark the lines where the accident occurred. The unmarked lines were reasonably safe and the power company did not have to guard against the possibility that a pilot would choose to attempt an emergency landing at that place. *Davis v. Cessna Aircraft Corp.*, 893 P.2d 26 (Ariz. App. 1994). There are several treatises on aircraft accidents that one with a case would wish to consult. These few cases noted above are the ones that the author found dealing with power lines in the last few years.

Under a comparative negligence statute, a federal court jury found the pilot of a small plane 60 percent at fault in a power-line accident. The pilot was seriously injured. The accident came about when the pilot was approaching an airport and was forced downward, as the pilot claimed, by a windshear burst. He recovered control near the ground and near the defendant's power lines. He attempted to fly under them but the top of his tail struck the lines, and he crashed just short of the runway. He sued the power company, the former owner of the airport, and the current owner. The jury found the pilot 60 percent at fault, the original owner 20 percent, the current owner 10 percent, and the power company 10 percent. The pilot was found negligent for approaching too low and too close to a hedgerow which might have caused a windshear effect. An expert testified that windshear as described by the pilot was not possible under the weather conditions. Because the pilot was more than 50 percent at fault, he was not awarded damages. *Cox v. Kansas Gas & Elec.*, 630 F.Supp. 95 (D. Kan. 1986).

A 1985 Florida case shows the difficulty in reaching a consensus on the just outcome of these cases. A pilot and a passenger took off from the North Perry Airport and encountered a fuel starvation problem. The pilot managed to regain power and found himself eight miles from the airport and approaching a power line one-quarter mile away at an altitude of 100 feet. The line was under construction and was not energized. The power lines were sagging thirty or forty feet above the ground. The towers themselves were 102 feet high. The pilot decided to fly between the towers. What he didn't know was that three-eighths-inch static lines (used to absorb lightning) were strung high between the towers, and he struck these and crashed. Damages were agreed upon as $500,000 and the trial was held on liability only. The jury found for the plaintiff. A three judge panel affirmed. The appellate court reversed and ordered judgment for the defendant power company, with a strong dissent. The court found no duty on the defendant; specifically, no duty to mark the static lines to make them more visible to pilots who might encounter problems eight miles from an airport. The court relied on the common knowledge that one should never fly between towers, and that the defendant had complied with all applicable FAA regulations. Structures at the accident site may be as tall as 1,620 feet, and only those above 200 feet need to be marked. The court found it nonsensical to require, in order to escape liability, the marking of all transmission lines regardless of height or location. The dissent was equally convinced that the jury verdict should have been affirmed. The dissent would not require all lines marked, but here the accident site was in the westerly approach zone of the Miami International Airport, was in an open area, and one in which a pilot in trouble may make an emergency landing. Moreover, the static lines were strung in a "trap-like" fashion, making it appear safe to fly between the towers. *Florida Power & Light v. Lively*, 465 So.2d 120 (Fla. App. 1985).

Several years ago small model planes controlled by a wire were popular. The author can't say if they are common today. The operator apparently controlled the altitude, but otherwise the plane flew around the operator. We note two cases in which the wire contacted a power line. In a Michigan case, the accident site was a private picnic grounds which was often rented by private parties. For several years a wire-controlled model plane demonstration was put on by a club. An area was marked off away from power lines where the craft could be flown safely. Two club members were demonstrating a dogfight. Because of some difficulties, they walked into the forbidden area and their lines became tangled. One plane touched a 4,800-volt power line, and one of the participants was electrocuted and the other injured. The estate sued Detroit Edison and others and the trial judge granted summary judgment to all defendants. The appellate court affirmed as to the power company, the picnic organizing committee, and the landowner. The power lines were thirty-three feet above the ground and had been in place many years when the area was a pasture. It was not reasonably foreseeable that this accident would happen. The deceased was a mature individual who was well aware of the dangers of power lines. The court did reverse as to the other participant. There was some evidence that he led the way into the danger zone, and his negligence is a jury question. *Ransford v. Detroit Edison Co.*, 335 N.W.2d 211 (Mich. App. 1983). The second case is from Illinois. The soon-to-be-deceased bought a wire-controlled plane and the following day flew it into a 345,000-volt line near his home. He died a couple of weeks later, but did say that he thought the lines were higher than they apparently were. The estate sued the hobby store and the manufacturer for selling a dangerous product and for failure to warn. The appellate court affirmed judgment for the defendants. The court noted that each case of electrical accident must be decided on its on facts, and here the product was not defective and there was no duty to warn of this obvious danger. *Holecek v. E-Z Just*, 464 N.E.2d 696 (Ill. App. 1984).

We now take up watercraft accidents. A 1992 Kansas case is a good one to begin with. The boat in question was a Coast Catamaran with a twenty-eight-foot aluminum mast. The mast contacted a 7,200-volt power line, which was twenty-six feet five inches above the water, while sailing on Council Grove City Lake. The wife was electrocuted and the plaintiff husband was injured. The three children on board were not touching any part of the rigging and were not injured. They sued the power company and the boat maker. The boat maker settled before trial. The jury found the power company 94 percent at fault and the husband and wife 3 percent each at fault. It awarded over one million dollars in damages, including $75,000 in punitive damages. The supreme court affirmed. The court began by saying that high-voltage power lines are one of the most dangerous things known to man, and the average person does not know if such lines are carrying a deadly current or are harmless. The power company is held to the highest duty of care. A power company has a duty to foresee that injury might result from any reasonable activity that might be carried out by persons who have a right to be on the land. The court held that the jury had sufficient evidence to find that under the standards of the power industry or the NESC, the power lines should have been marked or altered for the safety of those sailing on the lake. The power company unsuccessfully argued that it should have been granted a directed verdict at the close of evidence because the plaintiff's own witness testified that the manufacturer was at fault for selling the boat with an aluminum mast. There was evidence that the manufacturer had begun a retrofit program to supply masts with composition tips. The trial judge denied the motion, finding that the power lines, not the aluminum mast, was the hazardous object. *Cerretti v. Flint Hills Rural Elec.*, 837 P.2d 330 (Kan. 1992).

A 1986 Illinois case also involved a Coast Catamaran. Two women were electrocuted when the mast caught on an overhead power line as the boat passed through a channel. When the boat repeatedly contacted the power line, two persons jumped into the water and were electrocuted. The person steering stayed on the boat and survived. The plaintiffs sued the manufacturer and the City of Springfield. They settled with the city. The supreme court affirmed an award. Evidence of previous Hobie Cat power line accidents was properly admitted. It was not necessary, as the court of appeals had ruled, that each incident had to be exactly the same. The reports of past accidents showed that the all-metal Hobie Cat conducted electricity, and if electrified by touching a power line, can electrocute people in contact with the boat and in the water up to 100 feet distant. The court also overruled the court of appeal's finding that pain and suffering was not shown. A dissent would hold that an instruction assumed that the defendant was the sole proximate cause. It would find that the person who was controlling the boat, and the city as owner of the power lines, were proximate causes. The city settled for the comparatively small sum of $37,500. The jury awarded $304,388 compensatory damages and over $1 million punitive. The supreme court disallowed the punitive damages as not awardable in cases under the Survival Act (Ill. Rev. Stat. 1977). *Ballweg v. City of Springfield*, 499 N.E.2d 1373 (Ill. 1986).

A Coast Catamaran was also involved in an electrocution accident in a 1986 Georgia case. A day before this accident on Lake Hartwell, another boat's mast had struck the line in the same place and had knocked down a neutral line which carried the warning devices. The power company re-energized the line, but did not put up the downed line. The accident happened when the plaintiff and his brother sailed on the lake and struck the energized line. The brother, who was at the tiller, was electrocuted and the plaintiff suffered burns which caused the amputation of one arm. He sued the power company and, in a separate action, the boat maker. The appellate court affirmed summary judgment for the power company. Even if the power company was negligent in failing to restore the line with the markers, the deceased's negligence was the cause of the accident. Family members of the deceased and the plaintiff had discussed the power line and its danger. There was evidence that the deceased had said that he would tilt the boat if necessary to clear the line. *Mann v. Hart County Elec. Membership Corp.*, 349 S.E.2d 215 (Ga. App. 1996).

We now look at a 1993 Maryland case in which the federal district court hearing the case ruled as a matter of law that the boaters were contributorily negligent and granted the power company summary judgment. The plaintiffs were picnicking at St. George's Creek Beach along the Potomac River. They attempted to take a catamaran from the river and load it on a trailer. The boat had a thirty- foot mast. The plaintiffs noticed an overhead power line, but decided they did not need to take down the mast. The line was thirty-two feet high. The mast touched it and one man was electrocuted and three were injured. The plaintiffs' expert testified by deposition that the power company should have been on notice that its lines were dangerous near a recreational waterway. The defendant said that the lines had been in place thirty years, were in plain view, and there had been no previous such accidents. The court of appeals decided that Maryland case law held a plaintiff with constructive knowledge of power lines that are in plain view. The plaintiffs failed to make a case of gross negligence against the power company sufficient to overcome their own negligence. Apparently Maryland has not adopted comparative negligence. *Ramos v. Southern Maryland Elec. Co-op*, 996 F.2d 52 (4th Cir. 1993).

Commercial as well as recreational boaters, can be injured by power lines. A 1993 Louisiana case arose when a shrimper touched a power line. The crew had shrimped until midnight and then anchored for the night about fifteen feet from an overhead power line. As the men slept, the tide came in and pushed the boat under power line. When the crew awoke, they discovered they were on the wrong side of the power line on a rising tide. When they attempted to navigate under the line, the antenna touched the line or was arced and the plaintiff at the helm was seriously injured. A bench trial was held, and the judge found the plaintiff two-thirds at fault and the defendant power company one- third. The award of $216,745 was reduced by two thirds. The appellate court affirmed. The court found that the defendant did maintain the line at the required thirty-eight-foot height, as required by its permit to string lines across the bay. The permit was issued by the U.S. Army Corps of Engineers. The NESC requires forty-two feet, but no Louisiana legislative or administrative body had adopted that code. There was evidence that other similar incidents had happened, and that was sufficient to show constructive knowledge that the power lines were an unreasonable interference with navigation and supported the finding of negligence. The plaintiff was the more negligent party in picking a hazardous place to anchor, in failing to consider lowering the antenna, and failing to take the advice of his deck hand who knew the antenna would not clear the line and who warned the plaintiff. *Bourgeois v. Louisiana Power & Light*, 620 So.2d 306 (La. App. 1993).

A California power company unsuccessfully attempted to plead the recreational land use statute. Most states have such statutes. They encourage landowners to open their land to public recreation by granting immunity from liability for accidents on the land. The case arose when the plaintiff launched his catamaran from a U.S. Forest Service boat ramp at Lake Shasta. The boat drifted into a power line and injury resulted. The appellate court held that the recreational land use statute, Civ.Code § 846, did not apply. The public has a constitutional right to use navigable waterways. Since the defendant did not have the right to limit or prohibit the plaintiff's use, the act cannot apply. *Pacific Gas and Elec. v. Superior Court*, 193 Cal. Rptr. 336 (Cal. App. 1983).

24.7 Tree Trimmers and Climbers

Tree trimming and cutting would strike most of us as inherently dangerous work. When trees are near or in power lines, the danger is increased. The National Electrical Safety Code has a provision dealing with the duty of power companies to properly trim or cut trees which impinge on the lines. The utility may engage a tree service to regularly inspect and trim or cut as needed. Companies will have a policy for regular inspections, and should maintain a record of customer complaints about particular trees. The company may perform necessary work, or offer to do it for a fee, or suggest the customer hire a tree service company. The attorney with a tree trimmer case will want to document exactly what contact the client had with the power company. The duty of care is not all one way, of course. Tree trimmers range from professionals with all the appropriate equipment and expertise, to part-timers, to homeowners and volunteers helping them. The nonprofessionals may not realize the high danger of working near power lines that have not been de-energized. They may mistake wrapping on the lines for insulation. The probably do not know that tree limbs are good conductors of electricity, especially when the weather is cloudy and moist. Frequently they become engrossed in the task and forget the lines, or simply misjudge the distance between cut limbs and the lines. It is probably true that most men love to get their hands on a chainsaw and go to work.

Most of the cases annotated below hold that the power company was not negligent, but we begin with two that found some fault attributable to the power company. A 1992 Louisiana case involved dead branches of a hackberry tree. The tree was located in a back yard and was not itself in the power-line servitude, but dead and rotten branches did impinge on the servitude. The tenant residing at the house decided to remove some branches, and using a ladder and an extension cord as a rope, pulled down a branch. The cord contacted a high-voltage line and the tenant was severely burned. The trial judge made findings of fact that the property owner had made several complaints to the power company. The power company denied any record of such complaints and said that the tree was not in the servitude, and was not a "danger tree." The judge fixed damages at $259,488 and reduced them by two-thirds for the plaintiff's negligence. The appellate court affirmed, holding that the findings of fact were not clearly wrong. It noted that the defendant has the duty of utmost care. *Astredo v. Louisiana Power & Light*, 612 So.2d 283 (La. App. 1992).

In a 1989 case, an appellate court in Arizona affirmed an award of $1,500,000 for wrongful death of a tree trimmer. The deceased had a full-time job and did tree trimming on the side. Arizona requires power companies to comply with a provision of the National Electrical Safety Code which states that trees which may interfere with ungrounded supply conductors should be trimmed or removed. The tree in question was a large elm with at least one branch over the power lines in the alley. The adjoining neighbor made complaints to the power company with no results, except that a crew in the area said it would cost $200. The neighbor then hired the deceased. He climbed the tree and used an electric chainsaw. He cut the overhanging branch. While it was still attached to the tree, it hit and broke the power line and electrocuted him. The jury found the deceased 5 percent at fault. The defendant argued that the deceased violated safety precautions, including the use of an electric chainsaw and use of a chain rather than a rope to tie the cut branch to an overhanging branch, and in general a lack of expertise in the work. The trial court did not err in admitting photographs taken after the accident showing other trees with branches close to power lines in the area. The photographs were admissible for the purpose of rebutting the defendant's claim of diligently patrolling for tree branches near lines. *Gonzales v. Arizona Pub. Serv. Co.*, 775 P.2d 1148 (Ariz. App. 1989).

An appellate court decided a tragic 1993 Wisconsin case on the concept of open and obvious danger as overwhelming contributory negligence. A man was helping his father cut a tree at the latter's cottage. The tree was twenty feet from a power line at the road. Contrary to their plans, after the initial cuts the tree fell the wrong way and landed on the power line but was still attached at the trunk. Then they cut off four feet and the tree swung free on the line perpendicular to the ground. The tree began burning and arcing at the ground as well as the line. A state employee stopped and told the men not to touch the tree, but they tried to pull it off the line with a rope and the father was electrocuted and the son burned. The son sued his father's homeowners insurer. The appellate court affirmed a finding of contributory negligence of more than 50 percent, which precluded any liability by the defendant under comparative negligence. The defendant may still be negligent to a degree, but here there could hardly be a more clear case of open and obvious danger. *Hertelendy v. Agway Ins. Co.*, 501 N.W.2d 903 (Wis. App. 1993).

A 1993 Georgia case had the common outcome. The deceased was a professional tree trimmer who was hired to remove a tree. A 11,400-volt line ran twenty-four feet high and only seventeen inches from the trunk. The deceased and his employer saw the power line. The deceased climbed the tree and was electrocuted when he touched the line. The appellate court affirmed summary judgment for the defendant. While it was common for tree workers to have the power shut off for such tasks, no request was made to Georgia Power. The court held that even if the defendant was negligent to some degree, the negligence of the deceased was the proximate cause. Assumption of the risk would also apply to this case. *Leonardson v. Georgia Power Co.*, 436 S.E.2d 690 (Ga. App. 1993).

A 1991 Alabama case held the plaintiff contributorily negligent as a matter of law, and declined to apply comparative negligence. The plaintiff was not a professional tree worker, but was an electrician by trade. He requested the power company to trim his backyard tree to prevent it from shading his swimming pool. The company declined because it worked on a set five to seven year cycle for tree trimming. The plaintiff then did his own trimming and was shocked by a branch that he thought would not reach the power line. He also thought the line was insulated because it was black. The supreme court held that the plaintiff was an experienced electrician and made an erroneous guess about the distance to the line. *Knight v. Alabama Power Co.*, 580 So.2d 576 (Ala. 1991).

An injured tree trimmer who is an employee of a tree service contractor ordinarily cannot sue his employer because workers' compensation is an exclusive remedy. He can try to hold the power line owner liable. This was the situation in a 1992 South Dakota case. The plaintiff worked for a tree service who contracted with the power company for tree trimming. The cherry picker used broke a power line and the line dropped, still live, and coiled around the plaintiff who was picking up branches on the ground. The supreme court affirmed summary judgment for the power company. The only duty the defendant owed the plaintiff was to refrain from any active acts of negligence. The workmen were experienced tree workers and could have requested to have the line de-energized, had they chosen. The contractor's own rule was to keep all equipment at least six feet from power lines. As the contractor's own crew were the cause of the accident, the court declined to permit an "end-run" around the worker's compensation law. *Ashby v. Northwestern Pub. Serv. Co.*, 490 N.W.2d 286 (S.D. 1992)

A 1994 New York case, heard in federal court, held that a plaintiff presented a jury question and reversed summary judgment for the power company. The tree was an old red maple which stood six to seven feet from a utility pole carrying high voltage, as well as other lines. The plaintiff wanted to cut the tree for firewood. It was disputed whether the lot owner asked him to take the tree. The plaintiff, who was not an experienced tree worker, noticed the power line running through the branches and climbed the tree to attach a rope to cause the tree to fall away from the line when cut. He touched a wire and was severely injured and underwent amputative and reconstructive surgery. A forestry expert testified that the tree was almost totally rotten and presented a hazard to the power lines, the road, and anyone nearby. There was evidence that some branches had been cut from the lines. This would indicate that the power company knew or should have known of the condition of the tree. Under these facts, it was improper to hold the plaintiff solely responsible for his injuries. New York has a purely comparative negligence law, so even if the plaintiff were to be found more than 50 percent at fault, he still could receive any damages attributable to the power company. *Lane v. New York State Elec. & Gas*, 18 F.3d 172 (2nd Cir. 1994).

A 1984 New York case is quite interesting because it held that the plaintiff tree trimmer would not be expected to know that electricity can arc quite a distance from power line to tree. The tree was a pine and the top was estimated to be three to five feet below the power line and five to seven feet south of it. The plaintiff was trimming the tree on the property of another. He stood on the bucket of a tractor and handsawed the tree in the middle. As the top fell, electricity arced into the tree and injured the plaintiff. He sued the landowner and the power company, settling with the former. The jury found all three negligent, which prior to comparative negligence barred any damages. The appellate court reversed on a finding that the plaintiff was not negligent, and ordered a trial on damages only. The plaintiff was well aware of the power lines, but had no idea the power could arc at that distance. His expert gave this explanation:

> Now, as to the needles those, of course, have very sharp points and electrically they act as corona points which produces a tiny electric discharge right at the tip of the needle before any major discharge, and initially it actually boils off some of the organic material and helps to make a carbonaceous plasma in the area in that region and will help the electricity jump to an even greater distance that it could to a metallic point.

The court held that the average reasonable man would not expect electricity to jump that distance and travel ten feet down the tree and into his body. The power company could be found negligent in not meeting code clearances and in failing to maintain the right-of-way. *Sundt v. New York State Elec. & Gas*, 478 N.Y.S.2d 417 (N.Y. App. 1984).

A 2001 New York case involved a sixteen-year-old boy invited to a barbeque. The rented house had a single pine tree in the back, and electric wires passed through the tree. The power company had an easement and maintained the tree by trimming as needed. The boy climbed to a height of twenty-five feet (above the wires), touched the line, was shocked and fell to the ground. He lived. The plaintiff sued the property owner, Jakob, for failure to warn the tenant of this hazard. The Court of Appeals held that the owner had no duty of warn of the wires, which were open and obvious, and further no duty to trim as needed. That would be a dangerous job indeed for any property owner. *Tagle v. Jakob*, 737 N.Y.S.2d 331 (Ct. App. 2001).

A 2001 Florida case arose when a seventeen-year-old man was electrocuted while picking avocados. The picker was hired by an elderly neighbor. They would go about the neighborhood getting permission to pick the fruit from residential yards, by climbing the trees, using a pole, or climbing a ladder. The deceased climbed the ladder into a tree, and suddenly fell to the ground dead. The ladder apparently had touched an electric wire or a branch that touched the wire. The family sued the power company the homeowner of the accident site. The evidence was disputed on how visible the wires were, and how close tree branches were. Apparently the wires were visible "if you looked for them." The court of appeals reversed defense summary judgment. There were genuine issues of material fact that precluded summary judgment. *Estate of Marimon v. Florida Power*, 787 So.2d 887 (Fla. App. 2001).

We briefly note a few more tree cases. The court in a 1982 California wrongful death case reversed a jury verdict for the utility. A homeowner was electrocuted while trying to trim his tree. The jury was improperly instructed on superseding cause which ignored the foreseeability of the risk of harm. The court ordered a new trial. *Pappert v. San Diego Gas & Elec.*, 186 Cal. Rptr. 847 (Cal. App. 1982). Three Georgia men were injured when, while trimming a tree in their front yard, a limb did not clear the power line when it was cut. The appellate court affirmed summary judgment for the power company. Even if the defendant breached a duty to maintain its lines no closer than fifteen feet from adjacent trees, the negligent acts of the defendants was the cause of their injuries. *Matthews v. Georgia Power Co.*, 333 S.e.2d 631 (Ga. App. 1985). A 1982 Wyoming case involved a double arm amputee. The victim worked for a tree service which had a contract with Pacific Power & Light for trimming along the power lines. He only had a couple of days actually working around lines, and while in a boom bucket he touched or was arced by lines. The appellate court held it error to grant summary judgment to the power company. The defendant had a nondelegable duty to provide a safe workplace around power lines to its employees and to the public. Whether the defendant complied with the NESC is a question of material fact. *Ruhs v. Pacific Power & Light*, 671 F.2d 1268 (1982). In a short New York case, the court held that where a child climbed a tree and touched a 7,200-volt line raised a triable issue as to whether the power company properly insulated the line or failed to exercise reasonable care in maintaining the line. *Trapani v. Rochester Gas & Elec.*, 645 N.Y.S.2d 229 (N.Y. App. 1996). A 1988 Illinois case held that where a fourteen-year-old boy climbed a tree to conceal marijuana planters and was shocked by high-voltage wires, neither the power company nor the homeowner were liable. The plaintiff was of an age to be aware of the danger. *Bonder v. Commonwealth Edison Co.*, 522 N.E.2d 227 (Ill. App. 1988). A 2002 Texas case involved the fireman's rule. (The fireman's rule in Texas exempts a premises owner from ordinary negligence as to firefighters fighting a fire on the premises.) Firefighters were injured fighting a grass fire that was ignited by a tree limb rubbing on electric wires. At a bench trial, the judge awarded damages to two firefighters and a city. The court of appeals refused to extend the fireman's rule to non-premises, and affirmed. *Greenbelt Elec. Coop. v. Mills*, 2002 WL 440990 (Tex. App.).

24.8 Buried Cables

Buried power lines present a risk precisely because they are not visible to the individual working around them. There is a procedure to follow before digging in such areas. Most of us have seen the signs utilities put up stating that before digging one needs to call a telephone number. A 1992 Florida case came before the supreme court to resolve conflicting lower court decisions. The plaintiff was the operator of a trencher and struck a buried power line. He allegedly suffered an electrical shock. I say allegedly because the power company argued that this was not possible. There is a fuse designed to protect against this kind of accident. The instant a buried line is severed, the fuse is supposed to blow. The defendant power company's witness testified that he knew of more than fifty such cuts, and none of them caused a shock to equipment operators. The jury awarded the plaintiff $175,000 less 30 percent for negligence. The court of appeals reversed on its finding that no duty was breached. The defendant had discharged its duty by fuse-protecting the lines, even though the power company may have negligently marked the area safe for digging. The supreme court reinstated the verdict. The fact that the power company marked out an area indicates that the plaintiff was operating in a risk of injury zone. Even if the plaintiff could point to no other instance of a failure of a fuse, "Human experience teaches us that safety equipment can fail and that the severing of any energized cable is a dangerous event likely to lead to an electrical shock, even if the safety equipment fails for only a split second." Whether a specific injury was foreseeable is generally a jury question. *McCain v. Florida Power Corp.*, 593 So.2d 500 (Fla. 1992).

A 1994 Nebraska case involved an injury caused when a post hole digger struck a power line while working on a fence installation. It is common for utility companies to form a one-call service for contractors to call. In this case the service was called Hotline. The utilities finance the service. In this case the contractor called Hotline and gave the location of the work. Hotline then notified the electric utility, OPPD, and an employee marked OPPD's primary underground line. The worker struck an unmarked line on a different part of the property which was a service line running from a transformer to a neighboring business. The injured worker sued Hotline and OPPD, and the trial court granted them summary judgment. The supreme court reversed and remanded for trial. There was a question about whether the required notice of claim was properly made to OPPD, a political subdivision. The worker alleged that Hotline negligently led him to believe that all buried lines would be located and marked. The court held that it was foreseeable the worker would assume that it was safe to dig. Hotline might have discharged its duty by warning the worker that OPPD would only mark it's primary lines, for instance. Whether the duty was breached depends on such facts as whether the worker knew and appreciated the peril. These matters must be determined by the trier of fact. *Schmidt v. Omaha Public Power Dist.*, 515 N.W.2d 756 (Neb. 1994).

A 1994 Massachusetts jury awarded an injured worker $5.5 million, less 20 percent for his own negligence. The appellate court affirmed. A contractor was called to repair a water main break, and notified the electric utility under the "dig safe" statute. The utility arranged for the work to be done safely. Then the contractor discovered that only one water pipe supplied the nearby building, instead of the code-required two. The building owner hired the contractor to install the second line. To do this, the contractor dug close to the original repair, and uncovered a 13,800-volt line. While working around this line, one of the workers was severely shocked and injured when his "chipping gun" penetrated the power-line cable. The court held that there was evidence that the utility knew of the work in the area, and that the cable was not separated from an old brick sewer line at the code-required distance. (The worker was chipping away the top of the old sewer line to make room.) *Commonwealth v. Fallon*, 648 N.E.2d 767 (Mass. App. 1995).

Chapter 25

More Power-Line Accidents and Some Miscellaneous Cases

25.1 Roofers, House Movers and Others Working around Power Lines

A 1989 Alabama case was tried three times. The plaintiff was a roofer and was part of a crew working in a residential area of Brookley Field in Mobile. His job was to raise buckets of hot tar as needed with a rope. Two power lines ran overhead. The lower was the neutral line and the upper the 7,200-volt line. The lines exceeded the height requirements of the NESC. The plaintiff's version of the accident was that he was on the roof and blacked out when he got the call for more tar. Other workers' version was that the plaintiff reached up and grabbed the neutral line, and then grabbed the primary line with his other hand. Both hands had to be amputated. The plaintiff sued the power company. There was no dispute that the crew foreman had inspected the site, seen the power lines, warned the crew to stay away from them, and had not asked the power company to de-energize them. The first trial ended in a mistrial. The second found no liability, but a new trial was granted solely because one juror owned stock in the power company. The third jury also found for the defendant, but the trial judge set aside the verdict and granted a new trial without specifying the grounds. In such cases, Alabama presumes that the new trial was granted because the verdict was against the great weight of the evidence. The case arrived in the supreme court. Alabama's rule is that a jury verdict will not be overturned if it is supported by the evidence. The court made a thorough review of the record and found the verdict was supported. It reversed and ordered judgment be entered for the defendant. *Alabama Power Co. v. Wallace*, 548 So.2d 1372 (Ala. 1989).

A 1987 Indiana case held an experienced roofer contributorily negligent as a matter of law. The facts were that a shopping center owner contracted with a roofing contractor to repair a theater roof. The owner and the crew supervisor inspected the area. The owner pointed out low power lines near the east side of the theater. The owner made arrangements for the roofers to gain access to the roof from the north end by using a bank drive-through lane. Unfortunately, the supervisor was late on the first day of the job and the crew arrived on time. One of the roofers put up an aluminum ladder on the east side and climbed up. His head touched the 7,200-volt line and he was electrocuted. His estate sued the premises owner for failure to warn. The appellate court affirmed summary judgment for the defendant. The danger was clearly visible, and the defendant did not own or control the power lines. The deceased was negligent as a matter of law in exposing himself to the danger. A concurrence would hold that the defendant acted with reasonable care, but that the majority improperly usurped the province of the trier of fact in resorting to photographs and other evidence in arriving at its conclusion. *Howard v. H. J. Ricks Const. Co.*, 509 N.E.2d 201 (Ind. App. 1987).

A 2003 Indiana case also involved a roofer. He was the crew foreman of a job on a two-story house. He was standing on a platform and a worker handed him a ten-foot piece of aluminum drip edge. The piece touched a 7,200 volt overhead line and the roofer was shocked. He fell and was made a paraplegic. He sued the power company. The jury found the defendant not at fault, the roofer 10 percent at fault, and North Central Roofing 90 percent. The court of appeals noted that the lines were twenty-three feet high between two residences over a grassy alley that was kept mowed. The court found that a utility is not required to insulate its lines if the general public is not normally expected to come into contact with such lines, nor to protect those whose work may be expected to bring them closer to the lines. (The plaintiff would fall into the latter category, and are charged with exercising due care.) The court affirmed the verdict. A concurrence would find a duty to individuals such as the plaintiff, but respected the jury's verdict. *Goodrich v. Indiana Michigan Power Co.*, 783 N.E. 2d 793 (Ind. App. 2003).

In a short 1990 Missouri case, the court found a homeowner who fell from a ladder after making some repairs did not make a convincing case against the power company. He alleged that he fell after being shocked by an uninsulated power line that brought service to his house. The defendant suffered back and wrist injuries. The court affirmed a jury verdict for the defendant. Improper references to alcohol did not require a mistrial. The defendant contended that the supposed electrical shock injury was an afterthought to justify the lawsuit, as it is not mentioned in the medical records for the first six months. The court found this to be a legitimate defense tactic. The court did comment that it was "perplexed" that the case was brought on a duty-to-warn theory. The power company has a duty to isolate or insulate power lines. If this duty is met (which it wasn't here), the company is not liable. If it has not insulated or isolated, it is liable. Duty to warn then relates only to comparative negligence. *Hawk v. Union Elec. Co.*, 798 S.W.2d 173 (Mo. App. 1990).

A 1993 Georgia case construed the duty of a consultant in a roofing accident. The consultant was hired by a state board to prepare specifications for the reroofing and repair of a building on a college campus. The consultant's contract with the board included a disclaimer of responsibility for safety precautions or for a contractor's failure to carry out the work as specified. A contractor was hired, and the contractor hired a subcontractor to do the roofing. Their agreement required the subcontractor to assume the obligations the contractor had to the building owner. There was an understanding that the power would be turned off when the workers had to work near power lines, and that the contractor would give the owner four days notice when de-energizing became necessary. A day before work was to begin in the dangerous area, the foreman did make a request to the campus building and grounds office, but was told the school needed the power and that insulating covers would be provided. Nothing was done. The next day the plaintiff, a roofer, was shocked and injured when his mop handle touched an overhead line. He sued a number of parties, but eventually dropped all complaints except as to the consultant. The court held that summary judgment should have been granted to the consultant. Any responsibility he might have had for safe work practices were effectively delegated to the contractor. *Henry Roy Portwood, Inc. v. Smith*, 429 S.E.2d 143 (Ga. App. 1993).

I briefly note a 2002 Georgia case. A gutter installer was working from a ladder at an apartment complex with a partner on the ground. The partner passed up a long piece of gutter. The gutter apparently touched a live power line among the several lines and cables above. There was a shock, and the man on the ladder fell off. He sued building owner, the general contractor, and the power company (later dismissed without prejudice.) The court of appeals reversed summary judgment for trial. There were genuine issues of material fact as to whether the plaintiff knew or should have known of the dangers. The court did affirm summary judgment as to the general contractor, who was protected by the worker's compensation insurance of the subcontractor. A dissent felt that case law generally assumed that individuals such as the plaintiff are held to knowledge of electric lines around their workplace, and would affirm summary judgment. *Bossard v. Atlanta Neighborhood Develop.*, 564 S.E,2d 31 (Ga. App. 2002).

A 2001 North Carolina case was a ladder accident. A cable technician went to a house where the last tenants had moved out to disconnect the cable. He leaned his fiberglass ladder against a wire support on a telephone pole and climbed up. He felt electric shock and jumped off, injuring his leg. He sued the city for negligent maintenance of its electric service, alleging a bare or broken wire. The court of appeals affirmed summary judgment for the city. The plaintiff had not pointed to any specific condition that caused the accident other than he felt electric shock. The court also found that res ipsa loquitur did not apply. A dissent would have reversed. *Campbell v. City of High Point*, 551 S.E.2d 443 (N.C. App. 2001).

The court in a 1993 Wyoming case construed the High Voltage Power Lines and Safety Restriction Act. The case arose when a roofer was working on a roof and fell when he raised up and touched two low-voltage electric lines. He fractured two vertebrae. Four low voltage lines ran to the house, carrying 110–240 volts. The lowest of these lines was three feet above the roof. The roofer sued the power company. The jury awarded $368,584 in damages and found the defendant liable for 60 percent. The plaintiff was held to be 40 percent at fault. The supreme court affirmed, holding that the High Voltage Act did not apply. The Act refers to "high voltage" only, so the requirement of notice to the power company does not apply to contemplated work around low-voltage lines. High voltage is statutorily defined as 600 volts or more. The court held that product liability would not apply to electricity, citing the Ohio case of *Otte v. Dayton Power & Light*, 523 N.E.2d 835. The court also held that ordinary care is the proper standard even in a case involving electricity, because what is ordinary care depends on the facts of each case. Plaintiff's counsel had the opportunity to argue to the jury that the inherently dangerous nature of electricity requires appropriate care. *Wyrulec Co. v. Schutt*, 866 P.2d 757 (Wyo. 1993).

We now turn to three house mover cases. A house is a rather large object to be moving, and some conflict with power lines may be expected. A 1989 Georgia case arose from such an incident. The plaintiff was riding on top of the house, and was severely burned when he touched a high voltage line. He sued a number of persons and governmental entities, and finally received a judgment against the Georgia Public Service Commission and its employee, McGuirt. McGuirt was at the scene, and the plaintiff's theory of liability was that McGuirt should have stopped the house and measured the house and so on. The plaintiff asserted that the house movement was in violation of several PSC and Department of Transportation regulations, and that McGuirt should have stepped in and taken action. The appellate court reversed the judgment, holding that the defendants were not liable. The court found that McGuirt was present but was not on duty at the time. The court makes an analogy to a hypothetical situation in which a police officer notices that a car has defective brake lights. If another driver then runs into the back of the car, the police officer is not liable to him. McGuirt did nothing to increase the danger in which the plaintiff's employer had placed him. *McGuirt v. Lawrence*, 389 S.E.2d 2 (Ga. App. 1990).

A 1991 Ohio case involved two houses being moved. The owners arranged for both to be moved to new locations. The owner contacted the city to remove traffic lights and contacted one power company about its lines. He did not contact another power company, Dayton Power, which had lines on the route of the move. The two houses were hooked together, and a sheriff escort, workers and observers headed down Route 47. They came upon power lines too low for the houses. The owner climbed to the roof of the first house and pushed up the lower line-an uninsulated neutral-and while holding it, stood up and touched his head on another line. He was shocked and injured. He sued Logan County Coop, but it developed that the lines in question were owned by Dayton Power. The plaintiff's theory was that he was told by a Logan County Coop employee that the company owned all the lines on the route and would take care of them. This assertion was contradicted by others. Witnesses testified that the plaintiff saw a bucket truck nearby but said it would do no good to call them because the lines were Dayton's. Finally, the plaintiff deposed that he had a four day memory lapse. The appellate court found this not believable and dismissed the case. The plaintiff himself was responsible for his injuries. *Williams v. Logan County Coop*, 594 N.E.2d 195 (Ohio App. 1991).

A 1992 Alabama case involved a house being moved that was, on the street, eighteen feet high at the peak. One man was driving the truck and one riding the roof. They encountered a TV cable fourteen feet high and a secondary 110-volt power line seventeen feet, two inches. The roof rider, according to a witness, first placed the cable on the roof, and then the secondary line. He "straightened up" and was electrocuted when his head touched the third 7,200-volt line. His widow sued the town of Slocomb, the power company, and the cable TV company. At the close of the plaintiff's evidence, the court directed a verdict for the cable company. Then the remaining defendants put on evidence that the deceased's urine sample showed traces of cocaine, and put an "addictionologist" on the stand to testify how cocaine might affect the deceased's behavior. The jury then returned a defense verdict. The supreme court affirmed as to the cable company. It admittedly used an existing pole and had its line too low, but this did not cause the accident. The court reversed for a new trial as to the remaining defendants. It found chain-of-custody irregularities in the introduction of the cocaine evidence. *Green v. Alabama Power Co.*, 597 So.2d 1325 (Ala. 1992).

We now look at several cases of people working around electrical equipment and lines. An Illinois lightning rod installer was injured when he was working on a newly constructed shed and was shocked by high-voltage lines nearby. The installer was self-employed. He normally drove about looking for buildings without lightning rods and would then solicit the job, which was how he found the job in question. He sued the power company, the building owner, and the builder. He eventually settled with the power company. The other defendants were granted summary judgment. The appellate court affirmed. The plaintiff appealed the dismissal as to the owner. He contended that the owner failed to warn him of the danger, citing Restatement (Second) of Torts § 343A. That section states that a possessor of land is not liable to invitees for a known danger or condition on the land, unless the possessor should anticipate the harm despite such knowledge or obviousness. The court notes that there was no evidence that the plaintiff was distracted or otherwise might come to harm. The plaintiff's own deposition showed that he saw the power line, and that he knew it carried electricity. *Carroll v. Commonwealth Edison Co.*, 498 N.E.2d 645 (Ill. App. 1986).

A 1990 Alabama case turned on the plaintiff's understanding of what "everything is ready for you to change the bolts" meant. The plaintiff was an experienced electrician hired to construct and install a new transformer to supplement the two already in use at a chemical company. He was an employee of an electrical contractor on the job. At the time of the injury, the plaintiff was working under the direction of Bagwell, the chemical company's maintenance supervisor, who was also in charge of electrical safety. Bagwell had previously told the plaintiff that the rusty bolts needed to be changed on the transformer, and on the day of the accident, Bagwell told the plaintiff that when he finished his current task, "Everything is ready for you to change the bolts." The plaintiff thought this meant to change rusty bolts on one of the older transformers and that it was de-energized, while Bagwell meant for the plaintiff to change bolts on the new transformer. The plaintiff was injured, and sued the chemical company. The trial court granted summary judgment for the defendant on a finding that the plaintiff was contributorily negligent as a matter of law. This was based on the argument that the plaintiff knew the older transformers were working and if power were cut off, plant operations would have been severely curtailed. The Fifth Circuit, applying Alabama law, reversed. To find negligence as a matter of law, the plaintiff would have to be found to have appreciated the danger and to have put himself in harm's way. Mere heedlessness is not enough. On another point, the court did affirm that the defendant's conduct was not wanton. *Jackson v. Stauffer Chemical Co.*, 896 F.2d 915 (5th Cir. 1990).

A 1988 Mississippi case is somewhat similar. Two workers were electrocuted when they attempted to put in place a concrete pole and it came in contact with a power line. The City of Greenwood contracted with Hensley-Schmidt for consulting and supervising relocation and installation of traffic lights. The deceased workers were employees of a contractor hired to do the work. The job on the day of the accident was to install the pole. When placed in its six foot hole, it would be twenty-nine feet high and within two feet of a power line. Supervisors for Hensley, the city, and the contractor were present at various times that day, and it was agreed that the pole would not be installed until the power company covered the nearby line. For whatever reason, Goodbar, the crew foreman, ordered that the pole be installed. He said he looked across the street to some of the supervisors who were gathered there and thought he got a "thumbs-up" sign. The estates sued the city, the power company, and Hensley. The first two defendants settled. The jury found Hensley negligent, but also held the workers comparatively negligent. The supreme court found that to be error, and reversed and remanded for a new trial, solely to determine damages. The deceased workers did not raise the pole on their own. They could reasonably assume that their supervisor, Goodbar, was competent. *Anderson v. Hensley-Schmidt, Inc.*, 530 So.2d 181 (Miss. 1988).

A 1990 Missouri case considered whether some electrical work is inherently dangerous. The case arose from a job to re-phase a power line. Old poles would be replaced with new ones, and additional lines would be installed. The job was to be done hot, which meant that the original single phase line would remain energized. Eazy Construction Co. was hired by the main contractor, Tel-Elec, to do the work. The plaintiff was an employee of Eazy, and was a groundman. The plaintiff's job was to roll up the slack in a new line as it was being pulled by a truck to tighten it. As the line was being tightened, it contacted the hot line and the plaintiff was severely shocked and burned. He survived and sued the power company and Tel-Elec. The plaintiff's theory of liability was that the accident was caused by Eazy's negligence, and that both defendants were vicariously liable because the work was inherently dangerous. There is a negligence concept that one cannot by contract avoid liability for inherently dangerous work. The concept is embodied in Restatement (Second) of Torts §§ 416-429. There are some situations where, for matters of public policy, an entity cannot shift responsibility for the conduct of the work to a contractor. The jury returned a verdict of $1.5 million. The supreme court found that vicarious liability applied. It did not find persuasive the power company's argument that hot re-phasing is commonly done and can be done safely. The court found that stringing wires near hot lines is inherently dangerous. It compared this to digging narrow trenches as also inherently dangerous. On another point, Tel-Elec argued that it was immune because of worker's compensation. The court ordered a remand to determine the precise relationship between Eazy and Tel-Elec. *Ballinger v. Gascosage Elec. Co-op*, 788 S.W.2d 506 (Mo. 1990).

One thing we can count on with the common law is that it not changeless. Just one year after *Ballinger*, the Missouri Supreme Court overruled itself and held that the inherently dangerous work exception of immunity of a landowner would no longer be recognized. The common law in Missouri on this point dates back to a 1928 case, *Mallory v. Louisiana Pure Ice*, 6 S.W.2d 617. The vehicle for overruling *Mallory* and *Ballinger* was a painter injury case. In 1992 the court applied the new rule to an electrical injury case. The victim was an electrician who worked for an independent contractor. The contractor contracted with the power company for the installation of lightning arresters and squirrel-proofing transformers. This work is done with the power on, and thus it is inherently dangerous work. The worker had closed the fuse to de-energize the bottom of a transformer. His wrench slipped and contacted the top part of the fuse, and he was electrocuted. The estate went to trial on the same theory as *Ballinger*, and the jury awarded $2 million, less 35 percent for contributory negligence. The supreme court reversed. It found that the dangerous work doctrine sent the wrong signal (to use an overworked term) to landowners. If the landowner was faced with a dangerous task for which he lacked expertise and did not wish to risk his own employees and contracted with another, he could be vicariously liable for damages. He was penalized for doing the right thing. If on the other hand, his employees did the work and there was an accident, he was protected by workers' compensation. *Prayson v. Kansas City Power & Light*, 847 S.W.2d 852 (Mo. App. 1992). The author would point out that there is another side to this question. The traditional view is that it is against public policy to permit one to contract away liability for inherently dangerous work. The author's view is that those who are willing to perform such work deserve all the legal protection that is practicable. One with a case with similar facts will want to see what the law is in one's jurisdiction.

A 1993 Ohio case involved the question of inherently dangerous work. An independent contractor was hired by a building owner to connect service to a new air-conditioning unit in the computer center of an office building. Two electricians who were feeding an electric wire through a conduit accidentally shorted a circuit and blew out three limiters. This cut off the overhead lighting. As employees expected to work in the center that night, the electricians voluntarily decided to "jump the breaker," that is, wire around the blown fuses and limiters. Computer center employees questioned the safety of the procedure. One electrician said that he had done it many times. He donned long rubber gloves and stood on a piece of cardboard. As he connected the wire, the panel exploded and burned. He was killed and the other electrician burned. There was evidence that bypassing a 480-volt circuit is not a complex job, but it must be done very carefully. The estate and the injured worker sued the various parties, and the trial judge granted summary judgment to all defendants. The plaintiffs appealed on the argument that a landowner cannot contract away liability for inherently dangerous work. The appellate court affirmed. The court admitted that usually unresolved questions of fact should not be disposed by summary judgment, but here the court found no authority for the plaintiff's position. The rule in Ohio is that one who retains an independent contractor is not liable for mishaps even if the work is dangerous, unless he participates in the work or fails to eliminate a hazard. The court found that there were no questions of fact for a jury. It was not clear exactly how the electricians gained access to the electrical room, but even if the owner's employees let them in, that is not active participation in the work. *Gross v. Western-Southern Life Ins. Co.*, 621 N.E.2d 412 (Ohio App. 1993).

A 1991 West Virginia case arose out of a guy wire attached to an electric pole. The pole was on the property of Hester Industries, Inc. The plaintiff was an employee of a contractor hired by Hester to do some construction work. The guy wire was attached on the same side as the electrical equipment on the pole. The guy wire had to be moved temporarily several times during construction, and the employer had attached a come-along to it which employees of the power company, Potomac Edison, must have observed. Potomac itself declined a request to move the guy wire or relocate the pole. The accident happened when the plaintiff and other employees were attempting to move the guy wire. This time it became energized and the plaintiff suffered burns to his left forearm and to the soles of both feet. Eventually the arm was amputated, and the plaintiff was able to walk after skin grafts to his feet. He sued the power company, and the jury found the plaintiff not negligent, the employer 60 percent, and Potomac 40 percent. It found the plaintiff totally unable to work and awarded $515,622. The supreme court affirmed. Potomac was held liable for the entire award with no setoff for workers compensation or the employer's 60 percent fault. The court held that the "deliberate intention" (to injure the employee) exception could not be applied to the plaintiff's employer. The rule is designed to punish the malicious employer, not the stupid one. The court had some plain words about Potomac's claim that the plaintiff was not totally disabled. His IQ was in the low eighties, and the court noted that there were few jobs for one-armed ditch diggers. *Helmick v. Potomac Edison Co.*, 406 S.E.2d 700 (W. Va. 1991).

A short 2002 New York case also involved a guy wire. The plaintiff had installed the guy wire, running horizontally between two buildings. The plaintiff then coiled a coaxial cable around the guy wire. Some seven years later, the plaintiff attempted to replace the coaxial cable. The wire was thirteen feet above the ground, and the overhead power line, twenty-five feet. The plaintiff threw the cable over the guy and was arced by the power line, suffering a severely burned hand. He was awarded damages and the appellate division affirmed. The defendant power company argued that the plaintiff voluntarily exposed himself to a known danger. The appellate court did not agree. The defendant had several years in which to discover the danger during regular inspections of the line. *Pomichter v. Niagara Mohawk Power Corp.*, 744 N.Y.S.2d 280 (N.Y.A.D. 2002).

A 2002 Louisiana involved a horse worth $35,000. A guy line (a pole support) apparently extended into the pasture. The pole itself was outside the fence, was titled 15 or 20 degrees, and one time served an abandoned house. The mare somehow became entangled in the guy line, and her kicking caused the pole to rock. This caused the energized line to contact the neutral, and in accordance to custom, the neutral was grounded on the guy line. This sent an electrical shock into the horse repeatedly and she was found dead, still entangled. The plaintiff's experts found that a second guy was broken or missing, and theorized that, if installed, there would be less sag in the energized line and there would not have been contact. The case was heard at a bench trial, and the judge found that the defendant had breached its high duty to protect the public. The court of appeals affirmed. *Pillow v. Entergy Corp.*, 828 So.2d 83 (La. App. 2002).

In a case involving a painting accident, the West Virginia Supreme Court affirmed a $500,000 award against the power company. The plaintiff was a painter who was employed by an independent contractor. He was painting a railroad bridge which spanned the Ohio River. High voltage lines ran some eight feet below the bridge. As he was descending from the top of the bridge, his hose contacted the power lines. High voltage energized the painting spray gun, and the painter fell into the lines, and then to the ground. He was permanently and totally disabled. The painter settled with the railroad for $35,000. He sued the power company. Liability was claimed on the fact that the defendant knew in advance that the bridge was to be painted. There was some conflicting evidence. The painter's foreman contacted the power company and was told that the line could not be de-energized, while there was evidence that it had been de-energized for a day a month earlier. The defendant sought to introduce evidence of several prior de-energizings to show that it could be and was done when necessary. The trial court correctly rejected this evidence because it was based on logbook entries and did not show who asked or why the lines were de-energized. The plaintiff's expert also testified as to other steps the defendant could have taken to prevent the accident. *Grillis v. Monongahela Power Co.*, 346 S.E.2d 812 (W. Va. 1986).

A 1987 Arizona case points up the consequences of the failure of a contractor to notify the power company if the contemplated activity will come within six feet of a high-voltage line. The statute requires such an entity to notify the utility, to make arrangements for safety measures to be taken, and to agree to pay any of the utility's expenses. A contractor did not follow these steps, and a surveyor using a twelve-foot survey rod contacted a power line. The pole is normally inserted in a two-foot tripod. Conflicting testimony gave the required height of the power line at that point as fifteen, eighteen, or twenty feet, according to the National Electric Safety Code. The surveyor sued the power company, and the company asked the court to order the contractor to indemnify it for any judgment it might have to pay. The trial court granted summary judgment to the power company, and the appellate court affirmed. There was no compliance with the statute, and no evidence that the power company knew of the contractor's activities around the power line. *Tucson Elec. Power v. Dooley-Jones and Assoc.*, 746 P.2d 510 (Ariz. App. 1987).

A 1995 South Dakota case involved electrocution. The victim was the owner of land on which he was building a pole shed. The shed was built on a former railroad right-of-way, and there were overhead high voltage lines some twenty-six feet high. The roof of the shed at one point came to within five feet of the line. There were no witnesses, but apparently the deceased raised up and was arced. The estate sued the power company on the basis of an a 1959 agreement between the company and the former landowner, a railroad. The estate argued that the agreement was binding as to the new landowner. The agreement had a save harmless clause as to the railroad, and the estate argued that it was essentially a contract of insurance. The supreme court held that the agreement would not be so held. It was silent as to any negligence on the part of the railroad. Additionally, the jury could properly find that the deceased knowingly assumed the risk of injury. He had warned others about getting too near the line. Finally, the court held that the agreement clause about requiring a power line clearance of thirty-two feet above rails did not apply. There were no longer rails on the property. *Bell v. East River Elec. Power Co-op*, 535 N.W.2d 750 (S.D. 1995).

25.2 Stray Voltage on Dairy Farms

It perhaps is not very likely that readers will have cases involving stray voltage and dairy cows, but it has some similarity to the claims of electromagnetic radiation and its possible effects on humans. (The author deals with those claims in the chapter on the power line-cancer controversy in a previous edition. That controversy has faded as legal claims failed, and is not reprinted in this edition) The author grew up on a dairy farm and can state that dairy cows are easily upset if their routine is not followed. For example, if a stranger walks into the dairy barn at milking time some cows will not let down their milk as long as that person is visible. Incomplete milking can cause a disease or infection called mastitis that is very troublesome for dairy operators. If the cows are being lightly shocked by stray voltage at milking time, they would indeed become upset. Farmers and county extension agents themselves learned about stray voltage, and the problem was discussed in dairy journals. It became a problem with the increasing introduction of mechanized milking equipment. This equipment brought metal milking parlors into the barns and the chance for stray voltage, or more properly neutral-to-earth voltage, to seek the ground by going through these metal parts. Electric distribution systems have a primary or hot wire and a secondary or neutral wire. The neutral wires are grounded as required by code, but this does not always prevent a low current from seeking the ground through parts of the milking system. Eventually farmers learned that an isolation transformer, or ronk blocker, sometimes solved the problem. We look at the cases in chronological order.

The first case is from Indiana. The plaintiff was a farmer who went into debt to build a barn and began dairying. Employees of the power company visited the site and discussed the electrical needs for the operation. Milking began in 1979, and the plaintiff soon noticed that the herd was not producing well, and that the cows seemed nervous and developed mastitis. The feed salesman suggested that the problem was stray voltage. The power company was called to investigate, and discovered that stray voltage was coming from the neutral line. The company attempted to solve the problem by separating the hot and neutral lines. The company neglected to tell the plaintiff that this lack of proper grounding created dangers of fire and electrocution. Upon discovering this fact, the plaintiff had the grounds connected again and asked the company to solve the problem another way. The company took the position that it had done all it was obligated or permitted to do. By 1981, the dairy was ruined and the plaintiff had to file for bankruptcy. He sued the power company, and the jury awarded $343,000. The appellate court affirmed the verdict. The court rejected the defendant's argument that only the Public Service Commission had jurisdiction. The PSC is the proper agency for questions of whether the utility provides "constant, reliable and efficient service." Its authorizing statute makes no provision for an award of damages for harm caused by inadequate service. (This is the typical finding on this point.) It would be pointless for the plaintiff to apply to the PUC if it could not redress the complaint. The court held that strict liability could apply because the electricity was on the customer's side of the meter. The fact that the product was stray voltage does not matter. Finally, the court held that it was proper for the plaintiff to introduce expert testimony. The problem of stray voltage is a complex area of electricity requiring special knowledge to understand the cause and solutions available. It is outside the general knowledge of the typical juror, and it was proper for the expert to give his opinion on the adequacy of the steps taken by the power company. *Public Serv. Indiana, Inc. v. Nichols*, 494 N.E.2d 349 (1986).

The court in a 1988 Ohio case held that strict liability does not apply to stray voltage. This case is cited also in the chapter on products liability. It probably represents a minority view in holding that strict liability cannot apply to electricity for public policy reasons and because of its view that electricity is a service, not a product. The plaintiff was a dairyman who alleged that stray voltage (neutral-to-ground) caused mastitis. The cows were dancing, kicking, urinating, and vomiting in the milking parlor. The plaintiff installed an isolation transformer to solve the problem. The plaintiff sued the power company on several grounds. After dismissals of some grounds, the case went to the jury on the merged counts of failure to warn and negligence. The jury found the power company 51 percent at fault and awarded $36,500 before reduction of 49 percent. The supreme court affirmed, primarily reversing the appellate court's finding that strict liability applied. There was scant discussion of the negligence, and no discussion of exactly how the plaintiff was comparatively negligent. *Otte v. Dayton Power & Light*, 523 N.E.2d 835 (Ohio 1988).

In a 1989 Pennsylvania case, the court affirmed an award of $81,374 in damages to a dairy farmer with no reduction for contributory negligence and with an additional award of $27,340 in delay damages. The dairyman noticed a reluctance of the cows to enter the barn. (This alone would be a warning that something was wrong, because cows are fed their high-protein meals while being milked, and like the rest of us do not like to miss meals.) The power company was notified, and its employee inspected the premises, found stray voltage, and suggested some steps be taken at the dairyman's expense. These measures were not effective. Finally, the defendant, at the plaintiff's request, isolated its ground wire from the neutral, and that solved the problem. It was obvious that the power company was slow in detecting the cause and cure of the problem. The dairyman sued the power company, and the jury agreed that the power company was slow in solving the problem even after it had inspected the premises. The plaintiff provided his production records to show the decline in milk production before the problem was solved. Also, he mitigated damages by selling affected cows for slaughter. The appellate court affirmed in all respects. The damages awarded were not speculative, and the defendant offered no contradictory evidence. *Slater v. Pennsylvania Power Co.*, 557 A.2d 368 (Pa. App. 1989).

A Kentucky farmer suspected stray voltage in his dairy barn, and in April 1987 had an electrician check. The electrician detected .7 volts at various points in the milking parlor. He notified the power company, and the measures its employees took were ineffective. In the spring of 1988 the herd suffered a severe outbreak of mastitis. That October, the power company checked and found stray voltage up to 1.4 volts. The dairyman meanwhile had learned about ronk blockers, and had one installed at his expense. Production returned to normal. The federal district court, applying Kentucky law, granted the defendant power company summary judgment on the product liability count. It held that electricity is not a product. The negligence count was permitted to stand. The power company owes the public the utmost care because of the nature of electricity. The defendant argued that it could not reasonably have foreseen the danger of stray voltage to a dairy herd. The court pointed out that the power industry had known of the danger since the late 1970s. *G & K Dairy v. Princeton Elec. Plant Bd.*, 781 F. Supp. 485 (W.D. Ky. 1991).

A 1991 Wisconsin case made an important finding concerning the effect of a statute of limitations. The nature of these stray voltage cases make it difficult to pinpoint a specific time when the damage begins, and, more important, when the farmer discovers or should have discovered the problem. As is typical in these cases, the farmer noticed the behavior problems and a high incidence of mastitis shortly after moving into a new milking parlor in 1977. The plaintiff began reading about the problem in a farm magazine a couple of years later, and he contacted the power company in 1980. Its employees put in twenty additional grounding rods. This reduced the measurable stray voltage, but problems with the cows continued. In 1984 the plaintiff installed an electronic grounding device (apparently a ronk blocker) at a cost of $1,500, and production returned to normal. The plaintiff did not contact the power company again until he filed suit in 1987 for negligence, nuisance, and strict liability. The applicable statute of limitations for damage to real or personal property is six years. The jury found for the plaintiff on all three counts and awarded $133,326, but also found that the cause accrued more than six years before suit. The trial judge overruled the jury on this point on a finding of continuous negligence. The court of appeals reversed. The supreme court ordered the jury award be reinstated. The court emphasized the difficulty the plaintiff had in pinpointing the cause of his problems. He had lots of advice about how the problem could be on the farm, off the farm, or just an inherent phenomena of electricity. He learned about the ronk blocker from a neighbor, not the power company, on a date well within the statute of limitations. *Koplin v. Pioneer Power & Light*, 469 N.W.2d 595 (Wis. 1991).

An Iowa dairyman was not successful in his claim against the power company in that a jury found him to be 80 percent responsible for the loss of milk production. Under Iowa law, a claimant who is found at least 51 percent at fault recovers no damages. The plaintiff began dairying in 1981. His cows had bouts of mastitis. In 1987 an electrician told him that the problem could be stray voltage, and a ronk blocker was installed by the power company in 1987. The plaintiff sued the power company for damages from 1981 to the date of the installation. Expert testimony gave three sources for stray voltage: primary to earth neutral, voltage drop in the secondary neutral, or faulty equipment. Plaintiff and defense experts disagreed on the source of the stray voltage in this case. More persuasive, the defendant put on veterinarian testimony that mastitis can be caused by poor dairy practices, such as preventing the spread of bacteria by proper washing of equipment, hands, and udders. The appellate court held that the jury could reasonably find that the plaintiff did not follow good practices and was primarily at fault. Poor record keeping was one factor which hurt the plaintiff's claim. *Fox v. Interstate Power Co.*, 521 N.W.2d 762 (Iowa App. 1994).

A 2002 decision of the Iowa Supreme Court affirmed a jury award to a dairy farmer of $700,000 in a stray voltage claim. A dairy farmer, whose farm was one quarter of a mile from a power company substation, called a veterinarian about the cows' reluctance to enter the barn. The veterinarian diagnosed the problem as stray voltage. The power company separated the farm's neutral wires from the utility's neutrals, and that solved the problem for a time, but it returned. Eventually the farmer bought a farm four miles away and resumed normal dairy operation. He sued the power company for nuisance, after dropping claims based on strict liability, negligence, and trespass. The jury awarded as noted above. The issue on appeal was whether a private nuisance award could be sustained without an allegation and proof of negligence. The defendant urged the court to adopt the rule of Restatement (Second) of Torts § 822. That section predicates liability for private nuisance to be based on, part (b), "Unintentional and otherwise actionable conduct under the rules controlling liability for negligent or reckless conduct." The court noted cases from other jurisdictions where that rule was applied, but declined to apply it here. The key was that the plaintiff did not assert negligence. The court noted that unlike some other states, Iowa statutory law does not exempt nuisance claims against public utilities. A dissent thought the decision imposed, in effect, strict liability on the defendant against the intent of the legislature. *Martins v. Interstate Power Co.*, 652 N.W.2d 657 (Iowa 2002). The case cited and article: Peter G. Yelkovac, "Homogenizing the Law of Stray Voltage: An Electrifying Attempt to Corral the Controversy," 28 Val. U.L.Rev. 1111 (Spring 1994).

In a 1996 Wisconsin case of stray voltage in the dairy barn, the jury awarded economic damages of $240,000 and $60,000 for private nuisance (invasion of one's private use and enjoyment of one's land) less one-third for contributory negligence. The plaintiff dairyman built a new milking facility in 1970, and promptly noticed erratic and nervous behavior in the herd while milking. There was excessive and chronic mastitis, which caused frequent culling of the herd. The appellate court reversed the award for private nuisance, and the plaintiff appealed both that holding and the finding of contributory negligence. The supreme court reinstated the award for private nuisance. The court of appeals was in error in finding that nuisance could not apply because the plaintiff requested and purchased the electricity. The plaintiff bought electrical service, not harmful (to the cows) stray voltage. Whether the stray voltage is a nuisance in a particular claim is properly up to the trier of fact. *Vogel v. Grant-Lafayette Elec. Co-op*, 548 N.W.2d 829 (Wis. 1996).

A 1996 South Dakota case of stray voltage on a dairy farm resulted in a jury award of $573,792 for damages for the period 1988-1995, and $129,081 in prejudgment interest. It is not clear from the extensive record in the case if the source of the stray voltage was ever found and neutralized, even though both the power company and an electrician employed by the farmer worked on the problem. The supreme court reversed and remanded for a new trial. The trial court erred in an instruction, giving the defendant's standard of care as the highest. It is proper to instruct that electrical energy is a dangerous entity, but the proper degree of care involving the provider of electricity is one of ordinary and reasonable care under the circumstances. Perhaps more important, the court held that it was improper to submit the theory of nuisance to the jury. A public utility cannot be designated a nuisance, because the utility is regulated by a state agency. Stray voltage is a normal condition which is common to all power distribution systems. Many public utilities emit byproducts which may be troublesome for some, but that is outweighed by the public's need for power. There was a dissent on this point. *Kuper v. Lincoln-Union Elec. Co.*, 557 N.E.2d 748 (S.D. 1996).

In a 1997 Missouri case, the jury awarded $783,333. The dairy was a state-of-the-art operation of some 200 cows. The power company installed a used transformer, and the dairy farmer began to notice problems with his herd. Mastitis increased, hundreds of cows died, and the farmer sold the rest in 1993. The electrical problem is not called stray voltage, but apparently there was inconsistent voltage and abnormally high electric bills. The jury was instructed on strict liability. The case has a good summary of those jurisdictions imposing strict liability in the provision of electric service and those which do not. The matter was one of first impression in Missouri, and the appellate court held that strict liability would not apply. Nor would *res ipsa loquitur* apply. The court remanded for a new trial on the negligence count. *Balke v. Central Missouri Elec. Co-op*, 966 S.W.2d 15 (Mo. App. 1997).

A jury award of $1,683,800 was affirmed in a 1998 Indiana case. The plaintiff put on two experts. One had tested for stray voltage on more than 800 farms and had caused corrective measures to be taken. He testified that voltage above 0.5 would cause problems in dairy animals. He found voltages between 0.5 and 1 volt. He found somatic cells counts of over one million, which would indicate mastitis. Since the plaintiff followed good practices, the expert attributed the problems to stray voltage. The court found sufficient evidence for the verdict. On the issue of excessive damages, the court also affirmed. Damages are generally the province of the jury. There was no evidence that the jury was attempting to award punitive damages in the guise of general damages. *Tipmont Rural Elec. Membership v. Fisher*, 697 N.E.2d 83 (Ind. App. 1998).

The court in a 1998 Michigan case affirmed an award for several farmers in a case which consolidated several plaintiffs. The court found that the power company has a duty to inspect and repair its facilities to discover and remedy hazards, and this applies to cases of dairy herd stray voltage. Production increased when the condition was remedied. The power company apparently had a policy to waiting for complaints before taking any action. The jury found that the plaintiffs were themselves 55 percent at fault, and reduced the awards to $1,951,029. The trial judge further reduced the awards as based on speculation. (One plaintiff watered the milk on the day the milk was tested to inflate his production figures.) *Carpenter v. Consumers Power,* 584 N.W.2d 375 (Mich. App. 1998).

Stray voltage continues to vex some dairy farmers, and its solution is still not obvious. In a 2001 Washington case, a dairy farmer began milking in the early '90s. His herd exhibited the usual characteristics of stray voltage, and his production dropped. His power company, PUD, sent an employee, who with the farmer identified the problem poor insulators on the secondary neutral between the transformer and the barn. Milk production began to improve. The farmer sued for losses, and the jury awarded $1,089,000 in damages over approximately a two year period. The court of appeals affirmed the award as to negligence, but reversed for a new trial on damages only based on errors in the calculations. *Kaech v. Lewis County PUD,* 23 P.3d 529 (Wash. App. 2001).

25.3 Miscellaneous Duties of a Power Company

A 1996 Georgia case involved the question of whether an intervening act of a third person absolves a power company of any negligent act which it might have done. A family moved into a mobile home and promptly noticed that they received small electric shocks when, for example, they touched two metals simultaneously. The mother notified the mobile home owner from whom the structure was rented with no result. She then called the power company. Its technician, Yost, inspected the premises and found it improperly grounded, and found evidence of dangerous voltage. He discovered that if he shut off one circuit breaker the problem vanished. Yost told the mother that the voltage was lethally dangerous and not to turn on the circuit breaker until an electrician (which Yost was not) had made repairs. The power company did have a policy requiring all employees to notify their supervisors of unsafe conditions. Yost testified later that he thought the policy applied only to lines and equipment outside the homes of customers. The owner made some ineffective repairs, and a few weeks later a six-month-old child was electrocuted. The circuit breaker had been turned on to run the air conditioner. The appellate court held that summary judgment was properly granted to the power company. The mother had been adequately warned of the dangers by Yost. There was evidence that a man (qualifications as to electricity not given) hired by the owner told the mother she could run the air conditioner but to stay away from it. *Stegall v. Central Georgia E.M.C.*, 470 S.E.2d 782 (Ga. App. 1996).

In contrast to Stegall, the court in a 1995 Idaho case held that dismissal was improperly granted to a power company. The company had cut off service to the plaintiff's farm, and the plaintiff believed that the termination was wrongful. The case does not give the details on the reason for the termination of service. The plaintiff attempted to reconnect the service and tragically was shocked and wound up with both legs amputated and with other permanent injuries. The supreme court found that it could not say that, based on the complaint, there was no conceivable set of facts which would permit recovery of damages. The court notes that a power company is held to the highest degree of care. The complaint charged that it was foreseeable that one in the plaintiff's position might resort to self help. Finally, the court found it unlikely that the plaintiff's actions would be viewed as an intervening cause because he was not a third party. *Orthman v. Idaho Power Co.*, 895 P.2d 561 (Idaho 1995).

In a 1992 West Virginia case, the supreme court affirmed a plaintiff's verdict upon a finding that a premises owner, here a power company, owes the employees of an independent contractor a reasonably safe place to work. The accident site was a coal-fired power plant. A short circuit developed in the basement in the "condenser pit." The defective cable and a number of other high voltage cables were carried in trays above the floor. The short needed to be repaired immediately, and the power company called on an independent contractor. Neal, the contractor's foreman, was shown the wiring diagrams in the blueprint room but was not allowed to take a copy with him. The company had de-energized the cable and placed tags on each end, but there was evidence that the pit was poorly lighted, and that someone in the pit could not see the tags. Neal took the employee who was to do the work into the pit and pointed out the cable. Then Neal left, and another employee brought some tools. The worker told the other employee that he knew which cable to cut. It was the wrong one, and he was electrocuted. His widow sued the power company. At trial, the plaintiff's expert pointed out a number of safety measures that could have been taken. For example, if the deceased had been standing on a rubber mat and been wearing insulated gloves and boots, he would not have been harmed. There was finger-pointing about which party was responsible for providing such equipment. The defendant's expert blamed the contractor's foreman. The jury awarded $6,175,000, finding the deceased not negligent, the contractor 85 percent at fault, and the power company 15 percent. The supreme court affirmed. *Pasquale v. Ohio Power Co.*, 418 S.E.2d 738 (W. Va. 1992).

An Arkansas man who was fishing in a pond owned by the city of Plumerville was unpleasantly surprised when he was shocked by a sagging electric line. The line had served a pump at the pond when it was a part of the city's active water supply system. The city had not used the pump for several years, and the pond was open to recreation. The city owned the line that went to the pump. The fisherman sued the power company, which moved for summary judgment. There were conflicting affidavits. The former mayor said that he had requested the line to be de-energized, and was told that it had been done. Power company employees denied this. The trial court granted the motion, and the supreme court reversed for trial on a finding that a genuine issue of fact existed. Whether the defendant had a duty to cut off power, and whether the accident was foreseeable are questions for the trier of fact. The defendant knew or should have known that the pond was being used for recreation and would attract people. A dissent pointed out that the line was owned by the city and it had the responsibility for safe use of the pond. *Stacks v. Arkansas Power & Light*, 771 S.W.2d 754 (Ark. 1989).

A California power company successfully used the Recreational Land Use Act, Civ. Code § 846, as a defense in a 1987 case. The plaintiff was a fourteen-year-old boy who was shocked when the guy wire he was holding contacted an energized line. The plaintiff had been riding his bicycle along a creek and noticed a dangling guy wire. It had washed out the night before. The plaintiff was standing in water when he pulled on the line. The power company had an easement to use the land. The company asserted the act. It had to prove that it owned the easement and that the land was suitable for recreation, and that the plaintiff was on the land for that purpose. The jury found for the defendant, and the trial judge granted a new trial on the grounds that the land was not the premises of the defendant. The appellate court reversed. While it was true that the power company's equipment on the land was not suitable for recreation, the easement itself was open to anyone hiking, cycling and roaming about. Such recreational use was foreseeable. There was no question that the site of the accident was within the easement. *Colvin v. Southern Calif. Edison*, 240 Cal. Rptr. 142 (Cal. App. 1987).

The court in a 1988 Louisiana case found a power company not negligent in a crane accident which was related to a storm. The storm caused downed wires on 600 of the 800 miles of power lines owned by the company. Hundreds of temporary workers were called in to restore power. At one point a temporary pole was erected to replace a down pole, but because of debris and water, the new pole was erected twenty-four feet from the adjacent highway center line, some seventeen feet closer to the road than the old pole. The plaintiff was a highway worker helping clear debris from a bridge reconstruction site. He was resting on a truck-mounted crane bumper when the lifting cable became entangled in vines, snapped loose and swung into the power line. The plaintiff was electrically shocked. He sued the power company, and the jury returned a defense verdict. The appellate court affirmed. The accident was not reasonably foreseeable. The plaintiff's expert had testified that the temporary pole was left too close to the road for too long a period. (The accident happened four months after the storm.) He admitted that he did not know what the local conditions were when the pole was put up. The court stated that even the temporary pole met NESC requirements, and that the jury had ample evidence for its verdict. *Coleman v. Louisiana Power & Light*, 535 So.2d 955 (La. App. 1988).

A 1990 Arkansas case also is related to a storm. A rural family returned home after dark and found trees, branches and other debris blocking the road following a storm. The plaintiff, a sixteen-year-old boy, and his brother started walking to their house while the father stayed behind to clear debris. In the darkness, the plaintiff walked into a downed 7.200-volt line and suffered second and third degree burns over 40 percent of his body. Eventually his right leg was amputated. He sued the power company on the theory that the pole was rotten and the company was negligent in maintenance. The plaintiff also sued Osmose Wood Preserving Co., which contracted with the power company to inspect and treat the poles. The power company filed a third-party complaint against Osmose for failure to inspect. The plaintiff's expert testified that poles are supposed to be replaced if they are reduced to 75 percent of their strength. He said the pole was at only 25 percent strength. If so, this would violate NESC provisions and would be evidence of negligence. The trial court directed a ver-

dict for Osmose. The jury found the power company negligent in maintenance and awarded damages. The supreme court affirmed. It rejected the
defendant's argument that the proximate cause was an act of God as a
matter of law. The fact that the storm was an F-1 class tornado justified an
act-of-God instruction, but the jury was properly instructed that if an act-
of-God concurs with negligence, the negligence is not excused. *Arkansas
Valley Elec. Co-op. v. Davis*, 800 S.W.2d 420 (Ark. 1990).

A 1991 Ohio case also involved a storm. A nine-year-old boy was
electrocuted when he grabbed a downed power line. He was observed by
an emergency worker to be violently shaking until the wire burned free.
He was then unconscious and soon was pronounced dead. A violent thunderstorm had hit Cleveland at 4:00 P.M., causing damage and downed
power lines. The power line in question came down at 4:23. A police officer noticed it burning at 4:35 and called his dispatcher to have it reported
to the power company. (These details may seem irrelevant, but they are
necessary to understand the decision.) At 5:00 the officer left to attend to
other duties. At 6:25 a child walking with his mother touched the line and
was shocked. The police were called, and they called for an ambulance,
which arrived at 6:34. The child had already been taken to a nearby hospital. While the ambulance crew was still on the scene, the nine-year-old
was electrocuted. The mother and siblings sued the power company, and
the jury awarded $500,000. The appellate court affirmed. The question for
the jury was whether the defendant responded to the emergency within a
reasonable time. The power company argued that it believed that a police
officer was guarding the scene, and that the number of downed wire reports exceeded the number of crews. However, there was evidence that
some crews were working to restore power, and were thus available to
deal with this hazardous condition. The defendant's own manual called
for it to repair all hazardous conditions before moving on to merely restor-
ing power. Also, the defendant believed, but did not know, if the hazard
was being guarded. *Wilburn v. Cleveland Elec. Illum. Co.*, 599 N.E.2d 301
(Ohio App. 1991).

Power company customers have to wait their turns for power to be
restored. Note a 2001 Texas case. Lightning struck a church that was
meeting for evening services, and the lights went out. No damage was
apparent, and the building was vacated and secured. The following day
power was still off, so a church member called the power company, and a

repair crew arrived that evening. It found lightning damage, and replaced the pole transformer and a fuse. Voltage at the customer's meter was proper, and the lights came on. The crew left, but the church caught on fire in the wee hours of the morning. The defendant power company moved for summary judgment, asserting the Tariff for Electric Service clause. The effect of the tariff is to hold the company blameless for faulting wiring on the customer's side of the meter. The appellate court affirmed summary judgment for the defendant. The company exercised ordinary care in performing repairs, and was not responsible for whatever caused the fire. The plaintiffs failed to show that any act of the defendant was the sole proximate cause. *First Assembly of God v. Texas Utilities*, 52 S.W.3d 482 (Tex. App. 2001).

In a short 1991 Iowa case, the court gave effect to a hold harmless clause in a contract between a power company and a contractor. The contractor won the bid to replace underground electric lines. The contract included what the court subsequently called a clear and unequivocal clause requiring the contractor to indemnify the power company for any claims, damages or loses. The contract included detailed safety procedures to be followed by the contractor. The contract stated that since the workmen would be at ground potential at all times, special precautions were necessary to avoid electrical shock. The plaintiff was an employee of the contractor and was injured when working on a power line that should have been de-energized. The jury found damages to be $400,000. It found the contractor to be negligent in many respects and found its negligence to be the proximate cause. The power company admitted its own negligence but asserted the indemnity clause. Both parties agreed that the trial judge would decide that question, not the jury. The trial judge granted the contractor's motion for judgment notwithstanding the verdict and held the clause not valid. The supreme court reversed and ordered judgment against the contractor and for the power company. The court noted that it looks with disfavor on such hold harmless clauses, but if sufficiently clear and unequivocal, they must be enforced. *Thornton v. Guthrie County Rural Elec.*, 467 N.W.2d 574 (Iowa 1991).

The final case is from Pennsylvania. A painting contractor was hired by a power company to paint several de-energized substations. After completing five of the substations, the crew moved on to one in Easton. The substation had been de-energized except for a 4,800-volt capacitor. The capacitor had not been roped off, nor were there any warning signs. The painter climbed onto the capacitor's structural housing and was working when he was knocked off by a large electrical shock. He fell ten feet to the ground. He suffered broken ribs, entrance and exit electrical burns, and a finger amputation. The jury awarded $1,460,414 in compensatory damages and $3 million in punitive. The power company appealed the award of punitive damages. The appellate court reversed the trial court and found that the defendant had preserved the issue of punitive damages. The supreme court found that it had not, and held that the error alleged in the punitive damages charge to the jury had not been preserved for appeal. *Takes v. Metropolitan Edison Co.*, 695 A.2d 397 (Pa. 1997).

Chapter 26

Trespassing Adults and Minors

A landowner generally owes a trespasser nothing more than to refrain from willfully injuring him (Restatement of Torts § 333). A landowner owes a greater duty of care to constant trespassers who intrude on a limited part of the land and may be injured by some artificial condition maintained by the landowner, especially if the artificial condition is highly dangerous. This would certainly describe high-voltage lines and equipment (Restatement of Torts §§ 334 and 335). A landowner also has a duty to take care not to injure a known trespasser (Restatement of Torts §§ 336 to 338). Finally, there is a special duty to children with respect to artificial conditions on the land (Restatement of Torts § 339). Section 339 is termed the attractive nuisance doctrine, and where it has been recognized it can be implemented by statute or common law; that is, the decision of the highest court in the state. Even in states which have not recognized the doctrine, children are not held to an adult standard of care.

High-voltage power lines crisscross the country. They often run along easements or power company property which are accessible to trespassers. It is not required or feasible to fence or otherwise protect power lines in most cases, but where trespassing is common and obvious, there may be a duty, expressed in codes, rules, or statutes to protect poles and towers. Poles are generally protected because one must have special equipment to climb them. Any nearby object which would enable a climbing trespasser may have to be protected. Towers have permanent climbing rungs, but these are required to begin at a certain height, and in some circumstances the tower may have to be fenced. One with this kind of case will want to investigate all applicable rules. Poles and towers seem to have a strong attraction for individuals who like to live dangerously. Power companies have a special responsibility and duty because electricity is an inherently dangerous thing, especially high voltage.

As we will see from some of the cases below, the nature of the danger may not be fully known. A tower climber knows of the danger of falling, and should know of the danger of being shocked by electricity. However, he may not know of the danger of arcing, or at what distance arcing is likely in that situation. Also, a trespasser may assume wires are harmless telephone or cable lines, or may assume any dark-colored line is insulated. Trespassers may be on other places such as roofs of buildings and come into contact with power lines. Then the landowner as well as the power company is a likely defendant.

We will deal first with adult trespasser cases. The author has decided to make age sixteen the dividing line between the two groups. Without knowing anything about the cases, we can guess that adult trespassers rarely succeed in court. A typical jury instruction defining a trespasser is one from Arizona, and reads as follows: "A trespasser is defined as a person who enters or remains on another's land without a privilege to do so. A privilege can be created by the possessor's consent or otherwise. A landowner owes no duty to trespassers except neither to willfully nor intentionally inflict injury upon them." (See *Rodriguez*, below, at p. 448) A landowner may owe a duty to a constant trespasser if the landowner negligently carries on an activity involving a risk of death or serious bodily injury.

A 1989 Arizona case dealt with an alleged constant trespasser. The accident site was an oasis-type area called the Moras. It consisted of a pond, several trees, an irrigation pump, and three transformers used to reduce the voltage for a nearby pump. The transformers were on a platform and were not fenced. In spite of a no trespassing sign and a skull and crossbones symbol affixed near the transformers, the place was a popular swimming and picnic area. The plaintiff was a nineteen-year-old man visiting the area with three others. He decided to hide from them as a joke, climbed the platform and suffered severe burns when he contacted a wire. The trial court instructed on trespasser, constant trespasser, and recreational user. The trial judge instructed the jury that to find that the plaintiff was a constant trespasser, the jury would have to find that the use of the transformers in pumping water was an activity involving a risk of death or serious injury. The jury did not so conclude. The jury found for all defendants, including the landowner and the power company. The appellate court affirmed. *Rodriquez v. Schlittenhart,* 780 P.2d 442 (Ariz. App. 1989).

A trespasser who comes onto the land to commit a crime is in a poor position to sue for damages. A 1990 Alabama case arose when two men came to a closed mine to "strip out"—in other words, steal—metals. They came to a fenced switch rack (substation) which had the gate open and had already been partially stripped out. One of them touched a 44,000-volt line and died after lingering a few days. The estate sued the landowner for failing to refrain from reckless and wanton conduct. The estate argued that there had been two previous deaths from the same cause. The supreme court affirmed summary judgment for the defendant. The unlocked gate to a fenced area with a sign nearby warning of high voltage would not imperil a trespasser unless that trespasser chose to disregard the obvious danger. A concurrence would not emphasize the criminal intent of the deceased. Suppose the criminal act was hunting on posted land? Would the only duty to a landowner then be to refrain from intentionally injuring such a person? *Ryals v. U.S. Steel Corp.,* 562 So.2d 192 (Ala. 1990).

A Pennsylvania sixteen-year-old boy and two companions illegally entered the premises of a steel company's closed furnace to steal copper. They used a mallet to smash a steel guard which had been welded around the ladder of a transmission tower and climbed to a platform at the 140-foot level. One of them began to hacksaw a live high-voltage line. That was the last thing he ever did. The estate sued the steel company and two scrap metal dealers. The appellate court affirmed summary judgment for all defendants. The steel company had a right to maintain the energized lines because they supplied power to a working facility. Reasonable steps were taken to secure the property, including hiring a security service. There was not enough evidence of wanton conduct to go to a jury. The court also affirmed as to the scrap dealers. Even if they knowingly bought stolen copper, they would not reasonably anticipate the theft would be attempted in this imprudent manner. *Dudley v. USX Corp.,* 606 A.2d 916 (Pa. App. 1992).

A 1986 California case also dealt with trespassing thieves. The site was an unused missile test facility on a remote part of the Miramar Naval Air Station. Though posted with no trespassing signs (bullet-ridden), it was common for trespassers to enter through holes in the fences. Picnicking, beer parties, vandalism, and theft were common trespasser activities. This case arose when two men attempted to steal copper wire. One used climbing spikes to climb a pole and was electrocuted when he discovered, too late, that the wires were live. The other climbed to retrieve the body, also touched a wire, fell to the ground and was paralyzed. This case was brought by the second man. Under the Federal Tort Claims Act, the land-owner, the United States, would be liable if a private person would be li-able in the same circumstances under California law. One concurring judge called the area of duty and foreseeability a "convoluted and com-plex" area of the law, a statement the author would agree with. The district court entered judgment for the defendant on a finding that the accident was not foreseeable. A panel of the Ninth Circuit reversed with orders to reconsider whether the defendant owed a duty to the trespasser independent of foreseeability. On rehearing, the same panel, with the same judge writing the opinion, reversed itself and affirmed the district court. The court read the entire eighteen volume district court transcript and found no duty. Most of the relevant factors, including foreseeabliity, moral blame, prevention of future harm, and consequences to the community weighed heavily against duty. More specifically, in the area of the accident, there was little evidence of trespasser activity, especially cut wires, to put the defendant on notice of the danger to trespassers. The average layman might well wonder how this seemingly obvious result could consume so much judicial energy. *Henderson v. United States*, 846 F.2d 1233 (9th Cir. 1988).

A 1990 Illinois case involved four trespassing young people who gained access to a catwalk connecting the flat roofs of warehouses. Fol-lowing an earlier incident, the ladders leading to the catwalk had been cut to begin some eight feet above ground level. The plaintiff was one of the group, and in the darkness she walked into high-voltage lines five feet above the catwalk and was injured. The court affirmed summary judgment for the defendant warehouse owner. There was no willful or wanton mis-conduct by the defendant. The danger was open and obvious. The tres-passers did not use a light to conceal themselves. The youth of the plaintiff was no excuse, as even a younger child could comprehend the danger. *Hansen v. Goodyear Tire & Rubber*, 551 N.E.2d 253 (Ill. App. 1990)

We now move on to trespassers with more innocent motives. A twenty-seven-year-old Missouri man was playing frisbee on land adjacent to high-voltage power lines. The frisbee became lodged on a transmission tower. The plaintiff climbed the tower to retrieve it. He passed a sign reading "Danger. Electric Wires. Keep Off." However, the plaintiff had climbed such towers many times in the past. The towers were on land owned in fee by the power company. The plaintiff went out on the metal arm and was shocked and fell forty-three feet, but survived. The plaintiff waived a jury trial on the understanding that the judge would direct a verdict at the close of the opening statement. The judge directed a verdict for the power company, and the appellate court affirmed. The plaintiff's expert would have testified that the defendant was in violation of the NESC and did not adequately guard against tower climbers. Also, the plaintiff would have called his brother to testify that others had climbed the towers and had been observed by power company employees and were not warned. However, those alleged incidents were not recent. The appellate court noted that the defendant is not obligated to maintain his land in a safe condition for trespassers. The plaintiff was not injured by some hidden trap, rather the danger was obvious and the plaintiff climbed directly over the warning sign. *Politte v. Union Elec. Co.*, 988 S.W.2d 590 (Mo. App. 1995).

A 1987 Georgia case arose when a sixteen-year-old boy climbed a pole carrying high-voltage lines to retrieve his rocket-propelled parachute. There were no climbing pegs, but somehow the boy managed to climb by using a fiberglass rod which permitted the electricians to de-energize the line when necessary. He used the rod to gain access to bolts beginning ten feet up to climb. He touched a wire and was electrocuted. The appellate court affirmed summary judgment for the power company. The facts did not support attractive nuisance because they did not meet the five conditions required: knowledge of trespassing children, an unreasonable risk of harm, children not likely to discover or realize the danger, the balance between duty and risk must favor the child, and reasonable care was not evident. Most children could not manage four-foot steps, and the deceased was not climbing for a lark but to recover a toy. *Lewis v. Georgia Power Co.*, 355 S.E.2d 731 (Ga. App. 1987). See also a 1993 New York case in which the plaintiff, at three in the morning, came upon an eight-foot chain link fence, climbed it, then attempted to climb a ten-foot fence and grabbed a live wire. She was trying to get back to her car after swimming. The fences protected a hydroelectric station. The court found that the power company met its obligation of reasonable care with the fencing. *White v. Niagara Mohawk Power Corp.*, 602 N.Y.S.2d 263 (N.Y. App. 1993).

Note a 2001 California case in which a ten-year-old boy was seriously injured when he used an aluminum pole to try to dislodge a kite that got stuck on a power line. The defendant power company asserted a rather unusual defense in these cases, that of recreational lands immunity. The defense was successful. There was no question that kite flying is a recreational use. The power company's right-of-way qualifies as private land that can and is used for recreation. Under Code Civ. Proc. § 846, the landowner is not liable to a recreational user. The plaintiff argued that he was expressly invited onto the land (his grandmother's property). In any event, the court found that the "express invitee" exception to immunity pertained to personal guests of the landowner, and here the defendant's status was an easement holder only. The plaintiff obviously was not a personal guest of the power company. The defendant was entitled to summary judgment. *Jackson v. Pacific Gas & Elec.*, 114 Cal. Rptr.2d 831 (Cal. App. 2001).

A 1989 Florida case came about when a disturbed sixteen-year-old girl climbed a power line tower at night with the intention of committing suicide. She had to climb over a twelve-foot fence first. Her screams attracted attention, but rescue was difficult because she threatened to jump if rescuers approached. She asked for her high school principal, who came to the scene and climbed part way up the forty-foot tower. The principal was told that the power was off, but that there was a danger from residual power and to stay on the east side. The girl was severely injured by an arc as she climbed down. She sued the power company for failure to turn off all the power and for failure to warn. The jury found the plaintiff 90 percent at fault and awarded past medical bills only. Then the judge granted a judgment notwithstanding the verdict. The appellate court reversed for a new trial. Since there was some evidence that the defendant's employee was uncertain as to which switch controlled the power, a jury could find evidence of wanton conduct in permitting the principal to ascend and encourage the plaintiff to come down. *Molinari v. Florida Key Electronic Co-op*, 545 So.2d 322 (Fla. App. 1989).

A very interesting case arose in West Virginia. The site was a transmission tower in a public park within the city limits. The tower was forty feet high and carried three high-voltage lines. It could be climbed by pegs on one leg of the tower beginning four feet nine inches from the ground, with the next peg being four feet higher. The plaintiff was an eighteen-year-old high school student and a known climber. The plaintiff climbed the tower to enjoy the view, was shocked, and fell to the ground, incurring severe and permanent injuries. He sued the power company and the jury awarded $1.5 million, reduced 22 percent for contributory negligence. The supreme court reversed and ordered that the defendant's motion for judgment notwithstanding the verdict be granted. The court found that the plaintiff was not a "technical"—that is, an inadvertent—trespasser. Therefore the only duty the defendant owed was to refrain from willfully injuring the plaintiff. Even though a power company is held to a high standard as being in control of a dangerous instrumentality, it would not expect that a trespasser would climb forty feet and contact electricity. The fact that the tower was in a public park made no difference. The plaintiff became a trespasser when he left the ground. The case is excellent in citing many other jurisdictions on particular points, such as whether the mere existence of climbing pegs on towers constitutes an invitation to climb. One dissent thought it unfair to adopt a new rule (that a plaintiff in such cases must present sufficient evidence of constant and persistent tower climbers) in the case and then not give the plaintiff the opportunity to do that. A second dissenting-in-part opinion thought there was too much "excess fat," or dicta, in the majority opinion regarding speculations of when a landowner might be liable to constant trespassers. This is almost the attractive nuisance doctrine for adults, when West Virginia does not recognize it even for children. The dissent commented that all courts, beginning with the U.S. Supreme Court, would better serve the bar if they decided more cases with shorter opinions. *Huffman v. Appalachian Power Co.*, 415 S.E.2d 145 (W.Va. 1991).

A 1994 Louisiana case came up when a trespasser entered an abandoned building in a strip shopping center. He gained access through a hole in the wall. There was a vault in the building which housed a transformer servicing power lines to other structures. The vault was locked but the hasp was broken. It was not known who broke the hasp. Apparently the trespasser touched live lines, and was electrocuted. The estate sued the building owner and the utility. The trial court granted summary judgment to the premises owner. His duty to maintain the building against trespassers did not extend to the unforeseeable risk that such a person would enter the vault. The appellate court affirmed. The case gives no indication of what happened to the claim against the utility. *Wiggins v. Ledet*, 643 So.2d 796 (La. App. 1994).

A 1982 Louisiana case arose out of an imprudent wager. The plaintiff had been drinking at a bar, and bet another that he could climb to the top of a nearby utility pole which carried a telephone line and, at a higher level, a high-voltage line. Though intoxicated, the plaintiff managed to climb past the telephone wires and shinny to the top. He was shocked, and as a result had one arm and one leg amputated. The plaintiff's case rested on the fact that the first step on the pole was one and one-half inches below the NESC standard. Also, the plaintiff argued that alcoholism was an excuse. The court held that the plaintiff's own negligence superseded any possible negligence of the power company. *Martin v. Louisiana Power & Light*, 546 F.Supp. 780 (E.D. La. 1982).

A Villanova University student decided to climb to the top of a boxcar when a train was stopped for at least an hour on the campus. When he reached the top, he touched a power line used for electric locomotives and was injured. He sued the university and the railroad. The area was not fenced, but provision was made for students to cross via an underpass. The land was owned by the railroad. The court granted summary judgment to both the university and the railroad. The university had no duty to fence its land to prevent students from trespassing on the land of another. The railroad was not guilty of willful and wanton conduct in failing to prevent the trespass and injury. The only two railroad employees present were the two crew in the locomotive. It would be unreasonable for them to leave their posts and patrol a ninety-car train for a temporary stop. The plaintiff's own negligence was the cause of his injury. He left his dorm room specifically to see what the top a boxcar looked like. *Heller v. Consolidated Rail Corp.*, 576 F. Supp. 6 (E.D. Pa. 1982).

A Pennsylvania eighteen-year-old man was held to be a trespasser when he climbed to the roof of a school to retrieve a tennis ball. He had been hitting balls against the wall. As he climbed, his foot touched a lighting fixture and he was electrocuted. The estate sued the fixture manufacturer, who cross-claimed against the school district. The appellate court affirmed summary judgment for the district. The deceased was a licensee when he entered the school grounds to hit balls, but became a trespasser when he climbed. School officials depositions showed that the school took reasonable steps to protect against roof trespassers. *Ellis v. Chester Upland School Dist.*, 651 A.2d 616 (Pa. App. 1994).

A 1991 Massachusetts case applied the attractive nuisance doctrine (which was enacted into law as the Child Trespasser Statute) to a case involving a sixteen-year-old trespasser. The plaintiff decided to climb a utility pole to impress his friends. He climbed past several telephone, television cable, and electrical wires without harm, but when he reached the top he grabbed the primary electrical wire and suffered severe injuries. The jury applied comparative negligence to the case and found the plaintiff 75 percent at fault, and found the defendant utility 25 percent at fault for breaching its duty to foreseeable child trespassers. This barred any damages because the plaintiff's fault was more than 50 percent. The plaintiff argued on appeal that since the defendant failed on one or more duties under the child trespasser law, it is strictly liable. The appellate court held that the verdict was not inconsistent. The plaintiff in a child trespassing case is owed ordinary care, not strict liability. *Mathis v. Massachusetts Elec. Co.*, 565 N.E.2d 1180 (Mass. 1991).

A 1988 Texas case (also noted in the chapter on strict liability) involved a sixteen-year-old boy. While not technically a trespasser, the concepts are similar. The boy put eight tent pole sections together and intentionally touched an overhead power line. His injuries required the amputation of both legs and one arm. The power line ran across an easement in his friend's backyard. The line was at the required height. The plaintiff settled with the home builder and the developer of the subdivision before trial. The case against the power company was based solely on product liability. The jury returned a multimillion dollar verdict. The supreme court reversed on a finding that high-voltage electricity is not a product. The power line was ten feet above the minimum height required, and the power company could not reasonably anticipate this "totally bizarre" use of the product. A dissent worried that the majority's opinion would "cut off in its infancy the development of an area of law speaking to new compelling and terrifying evidence" in reference to a Texas case on power lines and cancer. (The science has not supported the power line-cancer link, and the cases have been lost or abandoned.) *Houston Lighting & Power v. Reynolds*, 765 S.W.2d 784 (Tex. 1988).

Now we turn to minor trespassers, and will discover that sometimes there are grounds for liability. We first report cases where a plaintiff's verdict was affirmed, or at least a defendant's motion for summary judgment was reversed. A 1986 North Carolina case involved an outdoor "cabinet," a metal box 3.5 by 4 by 4.5 feet. The cabinet contained high-voltage wires. The entering and exiting wires apparently were underground. It was installed in a wooded residential area. It was marked only to the extent that the locks on the two doors were identified as being owned by Duke Power Co. The reason for no markings, including high voltage signs, was that the power company did not wish to alarm the neighbors. A child entered the unlocked cabinet and was electrocuted. There was conflicting evidence on how the cabinet came to be unlocked. The jury awarded $1.5 million in compensatory damages and $1.5 million in punitive. The appellate court affirmed in every respect. Even if a malicious person or one of the children had sawed off the lock, the defendant could be held liable for gross negligence for having no warnings of the danger of the cabinet. This negligence will not be negated by the acts of another. The defendant had only an easement, and the landowner had given permission for the children to play on the land. *Cole v. Duke Power*, 344 S.E.2d 130 (N.C. App. 1986).

A fifteen-year-old Oklahoma boy climbed a power line transmission tower at night and was electrocuted when the electricity arced to him as he reached the crossbar near the top of the fifty-foot tower. The parents alleged that the power company failed to make the tower more difficult for an unauthorized person to climb. The supreme court, with four dissents, affirmed a jury verdict for the parents, less 35 percent for contributory negligence. The case does not specifically state that the deceased had a special status as a minor. The court held that there was evidence of a breach of safety regulations which was negligence per se. The first step of the tower, according to NESC regulations, must be six and one-half feet above the ground or other readily accessible place. The court did state that the deceased was a trespasser. The trial judge instructed that the defendant owed a high degree of care. The dissent argued that the judge should have given the defendant's instruction that the only duty was to refrain from willful and wanton conduct, as contemplated by Restatement (Second) of Torts § 386. That section states that the duty of care is ordinary, not a high degree of care. *Woodis v. Oklahoma Gas & Elec.*, 704 P.2d 483 (Okla. 1985).

The court in a 1990 Arizona case construed the doctrine of attractive nuisance. The doctrine is expressed in Restatement of Torts 339. It subjects one to liability for injuries to trespassing children who are attracted by a structure or other artificial thing on the land if the landowner knows children are likely to trespass, knows there is an unreasonable risk of harm to such trespassers, the children do not realize or discover the danger because of their youth, and the cost of maintaining the condition in a safe manner is slight compared with the risk of harm. The case came about when a sixteen-year-old boy climbed a power line pole, was shocked, and fell. He climbed partly to rescue a cat and partly to see if he could do it and to enjoy the view. He was able to climb the pole because of a vertical pipe attached to the pole which provided steps. The trial judge granted summary judgment to the defendant because the hazard was not the attraction which attracted the plaintiff. The appellate court reversed and remanded, because current Arizona law clearly holds that the attraction need not be the hazard. The court reversed, but expressed no opinion as to ultimate liability or whether attractive nuisance applied to this case. *Brown v. Arizona Pub. Serv. Co.*, 790 P.2d 290 (Ariz. App. 1990).

A 1989 Maryland case held that even if the only duty was to refrain from willfully or wantonly injuring the plaintiff, evidence indicated that the power company failed this duty. The victim was a fifteen-year-old girl who was walking along the power company's easement. There were no fences around the easement, and the public used it for walking, jogging, and to access a school. A 7,600-volt power line had sagged from its minimum required height of twenty-five feet, down to two or three feet, for a distance of twenty or so feet in close proximity to the path. Even the paramedics called to the accident scene did not recognize the line as a live wire until they traced it to its poles. It sagged because a wooden cross arm had broken. Some three days before the fatal accident, the power company received a complaint about the line, but for several reasons the employee who checked did not find the particular sag. (He thought he found it when he noticed another, higher sag.) The court affirmed punitive damages of over $7 million plus compensatory damages to the statutory cap of $350,000. In view of the reporting of the defect to the power company, the company's actions could be held as willful and wanton. The court held that the trial court properly did not instruct on assumption of the risk. There was evidence that the line looked like a rope or railing, and the victim had not been on the path before the accident. There was no eyewitness as to why or how the victim touched the line. When her companion turned around to look, she saw the victim lying dead with her hand on the line. *Potomac Elec. v. Smith*, 558 A.2d 768 (Md. App. 1989).

A controversial Pennsylvania case involved how the doctrine of attractive nuisance applied to a fourteen-year-old boy. The accident site was a partially closed steel mill, the same place as in the Dudley case above. (In Dudley, a sixteen-year-old broke a metal guard to get access to a tower.) Here the tower was unprotected and had a ladder from ground level. Two boys had been trespassing and on this occasion climbed to the 135-foot level platform. The plaintiff ducked under "four grayish-colored insulated wires" to get to the edge of the platform for a better view. The plaintiff suffered severe shock and burns, eventually having his left forearm amputated. Somehow his companion got him down the tower before going for help. He sued the steel company, and the jury awarded $1.5 million less 20 percent for his own negligence. The defendant appealed a refusal to grant a judgment notwithstanding the verdict. The appellate court affirmed, finding that reasonable minds could disagree on the verdict. The company's security was roving patrols twice a day. The tower could have been fenced at small cost, and there were scant warnings of the danger. The dissents would have granted the defendant's motion. The two boys well understood the danger of electricity, and stopped several times to listen for buzzing, which they thought would indicate that the wires were hot. They thought the power must be off because that part of the complex was closed. One of the requirements of attractive nuisance as given in Restatement of Torts § 339 is that the child does not discover or apprehend the risk. Here they did understand the arcing risk of high-voltage wires. *Carter v. U.S. Steel Corp.*, 568 A.2d 646 (Pa. App. 1990). Note that the supreme court affirmed the case on other grounds, 604 A.2d 1010 (Pa. 1992).

The court in a 1993 Alabama case found the power company liable for wantonness for failing to prevent children from climbing a tower carrying 44,000-volt lines. The tower was erected in a residential area near Tuscaloosa. Originally it had been fenced to keep trespassers off, but a switching pole was later installed which was outside the fence. The pole came to within three feet of the ground. The plaintiff twelve-year-old child used the pole to get around the fence, climbed the tower, and received a severe shock and injuries. The jury awarded special damages plus $500,000 in punitive damages. The supreme court affirmed. Wantoness could be found by evidence that the tower could have been secured at minimal cost. Footpaths showed that pedestrians frequented the easement, and it was common knowledge in the industry that children do climb and play on towers unless prevented. The National Electrical Safety Code, section 280A.1.b, states that such towers which are adjacent to roads, regularly traveled pedestrian thoroughfares, or places where persons frequently gather shall be equipped with barriers to inhibit climbing. Three dissents disagreed that wantoness was proven. *Henderson v. Alabama Power*, 627 So.2d 878 (Ala. 1993).

We now turn to case of minor trespassers who did not recover damages. As the author has noted above, most of these cases have dissenting opinions. This shows that the cases could have gone either way. We begin with the wrong way to cook an eel. In a 1993 Maine case, the injured plaintiff was a nine-year-old boy. After catching an eel, he climbed to the top of a fence of a nearby substation and leaned over to reach a live wire to cook his eel. He suffered severe burns. Maine has adopted the attractive nuisance doctrine, but nevertheless the supreme judicial court affirmed summary judgment for the power company. The attractive nuisance doctrine requires that the child not discover or realize the danger. In his deposition, the plaintiff admitted that what he did was a "dumb thing." The court held that he did appreciate the danger. There were no dissents. *Merrill v. Central Maine Power Co.*, 628 A.2d 1062 (Me. 1993).

In a 1988 Kentucky case, the court held that a fifteen-year-old honor student who climbed an unprotected tower and was injured by arcing electricity was a trespasser, and affirmed summary judgment for the power company. The tower was in an open area frequented by the neighborhood children. The tower had climbing steps from the bottom. The plaintiff and friends carried a piece of plywood up to create a platform. The plaintiff was standing on this, and when he waved to people below, electricity arced from the power lines about six feet away. The attractive nuisance doctrine did not apply because that covers those under fifteen. As a trespasser, he was owed only the duty to refrain from traps or concealed dangers. Here the danger was open and obvious. One dissent insisted that there were issues of fact, such as acquiescence to trespassing, which required a trial. The other dissent thought the majority opinion belonged in feudal England where "protection of the property of the privileged class was more important than the lives of the common people." It surely was a question whether the defendant knew or should have know of the danger of trespassing minors in this case. Also, arcing electricity is not an obvious hazard. *Kirschner v. Louisville Gas & Elec.*, 743 S.W.2d 840 (Ky. 1988).

A 1988 Arizona case arose when a fourteen-year-old boy, a serial climber who had previously climbed the bell tower and television antenna at the University of Arizona, climbed the guy wires of a utility pole located in an alley and was injured by electricity. He fell to the ground unconscious. The plaintiff was unusual in that he was highly intelligent and excelled in science and math. He climbed the pole by using two guy wires which ran at a 45 degree angle. He walked out on the two electric wires with a belief that he would not get "zapped," as he had performed this stunt a month previously. (Perhaps a case of a little knowledge is a dangerous thing?) The appellate court affirmed a defense verdict for the power company. Attractive nuisance did not apply, although it was instructed on, because here the poles would be very difficult for a typical young person to climb. The defendant met its obligation of care to this trespasser. *Moore v. Tucson Power Co.*, 761 P.2d 1091 (Ariz. App. 1988).

The plaintiff in a 1997 Texas case is quite the opposite from the plaintiff in Moore above. He also was fourteen, but was in special education classes, received poor grades, and was immature and impulsive for his age. After an evening of drinking beer, he decided to climb a power line tower in spite of pleas from others to come down. The tower was fenced, but poor maintenance led to defects and persons from time to time did climb to the lower reaches. The plaintiff climbed to the top. When he began to descend at 1:18 A.M., there was a flash of light and the power went off in the neighborhood. The plaintiff's body fell to the ground. It was determined that arcing caused his death. The trial court granted summary judgment to the power company, the court of appeals reversed, and the supreme court reinstated the summary judgment. The court declined to apply attractive nuisance to this claim. The court held that the deceased knew of the danger, and even if he specifically did not know of the danger of arcing, he knew that high-voltage lines were dangerous. If considered as a mere trespasser, the power company did not willfully kill the plaintiff. A dissenting opinion held that there were triable issues. The tower was defectively protected and it presented a climbing attraction, and previous court of appeals cases applied attractive nuisance when the child did not know of the danger of arcing. *Texas Utilities Elec. Co. v. Timmons*, 947 S.W.2d. 191 (Tex. 1997).

A 1992 Illinois case arose from a trespassing thirteen-year-old boy who allegedly was mentally disabled. The boy climbed a ladder from street level to the roof of a warehouse. He then climbed to the roof of an enclosed catwalk to another building and was injured when he touched a city-owned power line. He sued the city, the building owner, and the tenant. The appellate court affirmed a dismissal of all claims. The court noted that this case is almost identical to *Hansen v. Goodyear Tire & Rubber*, 551 N.E.2d 253 (Ill. App. 1990). There the plaintiff was sixteen, and the ladder was some eight feet above street level. The court held that the plaintiff had not established that there was a dangerous condition likely to cause injury to children, who because of their immaturity, might not appreciate the danger. The court held that the risk here was obvious, and that the plaintiff exposed himself to a host of dangers when he climbed to the roof. He must be held to have appreciated those dangers. *Booth v. Goodyear Tire & Rubber*, 587 N.E.2d 9 (Ill. App. 1992).

A 1990 Illinois case also involved climbing to the roof. A minor, age not given, was playing ball and one was thrown or hit onto the top of a commercial building. To retrieve the ball, the minor climbed on top of trash barrels under a window of the building. From there he climbed up the horizontal bars of a grate protecting the window, then to the climbing pegs of a nearby utility pole. He found the roof was fenced, went part way down, and when he tried to move to another pole he grabbed a transformer was severely burned. He sued the utility company and the building owner. The appellate court affirmed summary judgment for the building owner on a finding that the owner owed no duty to the plaintiff. The accident was not a foreseeable risk. The trash barrels did not belong to the owner, the roof was fenced in an attempt to prevent roof trespassers, and the instrumentalities that caused the injury belonged to another. Oddly, a similar accident happened five years earlier, and at that time the building owner suggested to the utility that the poles be fenced. *Johnston v. Illinois Bell Telephone Co.*, 553 N.E.2d 11 (Ill. App. 1990).

Chapter 27

Liability for Power Surges, Outages and Fires

Power surges and spikes are a fact of life in the world of electricity transmission. Electricity is not a product like water or gas. Variations in the electric current can come from the starting of a large electric motor, or even from the domestic use of energy hogs such as microwave ovens, especially in older houses. Lightning can transfer a huge voltage to power lines and cause a surge for customers. Tree limbs tossed about by winds can press on power lines and cause arcing, which can produce a surge. A severed electric line on the customer's own premises can cause a surge. In this day of computers, most people are aware of power surges and try to protect their sensitive equipment with surge protectors. The writer has been told that the typical inexpensive surge protector is of little value. Better protectors are available at an appropriate cost. Building fires can be caused by power surges which travel to the customer's premises. Normally if the customer's distribution panel is properly grounded and fused, there will be no danger of fire. Frequently, the electrician who did the electrical work will be a defendant, in addition to a power company. It is not uncommon for the jury to be faced with conflicting expert testimony.

Few surge cases reach the appellate courts. We can speculate that generally the only damage is to equipment, and that the responsible entity comes to an agreement with the equipment owner on damages. A 1990 Minnesota case brought to light a defense that many power company customers probably are not familiar with. The case arose when telephone company workmen were installing underground wires in a residential development and severed two power lines. The resulting power surge damaged computer equipment of a nearby business. The business sued both utilities, and the utilities cross-claimed against each other. The trial judge granted the power company's motion for a directed verdict on the basis of the rate tariff. The rate tariff states that the company will try to provide uninterrupted electrical service but does not guarantee that service, and will not be liable for loss or damage absent gross negligence. The appellate court affirmed the directed verdict. The limitation of liability was approved by the Public Service Commission, which has broad legislative-granted authority to set rates. Limiting liability involves balancing the public's need for efficient and reasonable electric service with the need to provide the utility sufficient profit. Rates would rise without the limitation. The court affirmed the jury verdict against the telephone company, but also held it proper for the jury to consider the comparative negligence of the plaintiff's business. The business was aware of the danger of power surges to computers and did nothing to protect them when low cost surge protectors were available. (The court does not indicate whether comparative negligence was applied to the damages.) *Computer Tool & Engineering v. Northern States Power Co.*, 453 N.W.2d 559 (Minn. App. 1990).

A plaintiff with a surge complaint may have to go to the public service commission (PSC) before going to court, as a 2002 Michigan case indicates. A business alleged that it was getting spikes and surges from Detroit Edison that above acceptable standards, and that its equipment was thereby damaged. The company filed suit in the circuit court of Wayne County. Detroit Edison claimed the dispute must go to the Michigan Public Service Commission. The court of appeals agreed. The complaint was essentially one of power surges and spikes, and the plaintiff may not avoid the MPSC merely by alleging torts. The rate tariff specifically states that the power company will not be liable for interruption of service or for "frequency variations." If it is found that the causes of the surges is negligence, the plaintiff may be able to return to civil court. But first the expertise of the MPSC is needed. *Durcon Co. v. Detroit Edison*, 655 N.W.2d 304 (Mich. App. 2002).

A 1994 Ohio case makes no mention of a rate tariff. A barn caught on fire at night and was destroyed. Livestock, including sixteen thoroughbred horses, also perished, so the damages were substantial. The owner sued the power company. The plaintiff's expert testified that there were five possible causes of power surges. He ruled out lightning and accidents (vehicles striking power line poles, for example). Of the remaining three, not described, all were under the control of the defendant. The plaintiff's wiring was "up to code." The fire could not have begun absent some negligence by the defendant, and the instrumentalities were under the defendant's control. Therefore, the plaintiff argued, *res ipsa loquitur* applied. The defendant countered with several experts. The gist of their testimony was that no surge occurred, that in the alternative if there had been a surge, it could not have caused the fire, and that the fire broke out in the breaker panel in the barn because of a failure to insulate the panel. The appellate court affirmed a jury verdict for the plaintiff. It held that the instruction on res ipsa loquitur was correct. The plaintiff met the requirements by presenting evidence that the instrumentality was under the defendant's control and by evidence that the power surge on the neutral line would not have occurred without some negligence on the defendant's part. The jury could reasonably find from the evidence that it was more probable than not that the negligence of the defendant caused the damages. If one cause is not more probable than another, then of course res ipsa loquitur is not applicable. On another issue, the court held that the Public Utilities Commission did not have exclusive jurisdiction over this tort action. *Gayheart v. Dayton Power & Light*, 648 N.E.2d 72 (Ohio App. 1994).

In a 1994 Louisiana case the plaintiff pleaded res ipsa loquitur, but in this case the court held he had not met its requirements. The facts were that a small fire broke out in the plaintiff's attic. It was quickly put out, and the firemen disconnected the electric service and told the homeowner to call an electrician. The electrician made repairs and connected the power. A second attic fire broke out and caused over $90,000 in damages. The plaintiff sued the electrician and claimed res ipsa loquitur. He reasoned that there could be only three causes of the fire: arson, reignition of the first fire, or negligence by the electrician. Since the first two could be ruled out, that left the third as the only explanation. Sherlock Holmes fans will find this argument familiar. On several occasions Holmes explained to Watson that when one has ruled out the impossible, whatever remains—however improbable—must be the truth. Unfortunately for the plaintiff, the jury did not find this principle applicable, and found for the defendant. The expert witnesses could not pinpoint a single cause, and there were a number of reasonable hypotheses as to the cause. The appellate court affirmed. The trial judge correctly refused to charge on res ipsa loquitur. On another point, the court found that a defense expert witness, Dr. Leonard Adams, former head of the LSU Electrical Engineering Department, was properly qualified. The plaintiff had objected because he was not a working electrician. Although he had not been a hands-on electrician for fifty years, he supervised the electricians in his building and clearly had extensive knowledge of electricity. *Aetna Life v. AMI-Electrical & Hoist*, 673 So.2d 173 (La. App. 1994).

In a 2001 Louisiana case, the cause of a power surge was obvious, but the issue was what entity was legally liable. A dump truck owned by the defendant backed into a power pole. This caused some wire ties to break, plus one of the conductor supports snapped, and the result was a voltage surge that damaged electrical equipment of customers of the utility. The utility paid $94,020 to settle the damage claims and sued the dump truck owner for that amount. The case has a complicated history, but eventually the court of appeals held that the utility's only claim could be for damage to its pole, but that neither the utility nor its customers may recover against the truck owner for damage to customers' equipment. The Louisiana Supreme Court reversed for further proceedings in the trial court. The court of appeals was following an earlier supreme court case, *Professional Answering Service v. Central Louisiana Elec. Co.*, 521 So.2d 549), which held that one who damages power lines does not owe a duty to customers of the power company. The supreme court overturned (according to a dissent) twenty years of law holding that such claims are too remote, that there is no "ease of association" between the party who caused the damage and the party who suffered the loss. The court held that the customers have a claim against the defendant, and that if the utility is subrogated to the customers, it also has a claim. *Cleco Corp. v. Johnson*, 795 So.2d 3302 (La. 2001).

A 2001 Nebraska case did find that res ipsa loquitur applied, and reversed a defense directed verdict for a new trial in which the jury must be properly instructed on the doctrine. The case a rose after a power line fell onto a farm field and caused a fire resulting in at least $41,243 in damages. The two-wire power line was held by wooden poles, and photographs showed that the lines had visible splice repairs. The plaintiff farmer testified that the wind was blowing 40 mph, and that he noticed a grain bin fan was not running, and that he saw smoke in the field. He did not know what caused the line to break, and his attorney argued that res ipsa loquitur applied. The defendant power company's engineer noted that it was dove and squirrel season, and that perhaps a hunter's bullet hit the line, or that a vandal had caused the break. He knew of instances of a bullet breaking a line, but admitted that it could not be so determined in this case because of fire damage to the break. The trial judge agreed and directed a verdict for the defendant. The court of appeals reversed for a new trial. The trial judge found that the plaintiff must have evidence that no third party could have caused the break. Of course, the plaintiff could not do that. However, all elements of *res ipsa* must be applied. Power lines do not ordinarily fall, nor are them expected to fail in ordinary extreme weather. Forty mph winds are far from rare in the Great Plains. If the lines do come down, a jury may find some negligence in their maintenance or a flaw in their manufacture. *Koch v. Norris Public Power Dist.*, 632 N.W.2d 391 (Neb. App. 2001).

An Alabama 2001 case also involved res ipsa. A homeowner collected damages on his homeowner's policy for a house fire, and the insurer claimed against an electrical contractor who had done some repair work after an earlier fire. The original fire was in 1994. The homeowner had repairs made by Mobile Power, a private company. Early in 1996, another fire broke out and caused damage, and an unidentified party replaced the "fused disconnect." Then the final fire in August 1996 destroyed the home. The insurer sued Mobile Power for negligent repair. The trial court granted summary judgment to Mobile Power, and the appellate court reversed. The Alabama Supreme Court reversed again. *Res ipsa loquitur* did not control because Mobil Power did not do the later repair, and moreover, the insurer's theories of causation were speculative. *Ex parte Mobile power and Light*, 810 So.2d 756 (Ala. 2001).

Res ipsa loquitur is not the only theory available to a plaintiff in a fire caused by electricity. There is always simple negligence if the cause can be supported by some evidence. It is often difficult to pinpoint the exact cause of an electrical fire. A 1992 Oregon case is an example. The plaintiff was a tenant in a building. The building owner was having renovation work done, and a fire started in a room adjacent to the tenant's rooms. The tenant sued the owner and several other parties. The tenant argued *res ipsa loquitur*. The trial court granted summary judgment for the defendants. The appellate court reversed and remanded. The tenant did not met the first prong of *res ipsa loquitur* (the fire could not have started unless someone was negligent), but the tenant may have evidence of ordinary negligence. The summary judgment was based on *res ipsa loquitur* only. *Umpqua Aquaculture v. Ron's Welding*, 826 P.2d 31 (Ore. App. 1992).

A West Virginia jury in a house fire case found the homeowner-plaintiff and the electric company equally at fault. The plaintiff called no experts, but testified himself that he thought the fire was caused by a broken pole guy wire which caused the service drop to his house to be too tight. While fleeing the house after being awakened by the smoke alarm, he noticed sparks coming from the service drop. The power company's expert, a Ph.D. engineer and an expert in fire causation, put the likely cause on numerous defects in the house wiring which were in violation of the NEC. The supreme court affirmed. No one could state the exact cause of the fire, and when the evidence is conflicting and the case fairly tried under proper instructions, the verdict must be affirmed. This case shows the common problem of the difficulty of pinpointing the exact cause after the building is destroyed. The defendant will usually move for summary judgment or a directed verdict, while the plaintiff will want to get to a jury and present some evidence. *Birdsell v. Monongahela Power Co.*, 382 S.E.2d 60 (W. Va. 1989).

A 1992 Missouri case involved the question of an intervening force breaking the chain of causation. A homeowner hired a tree service to do some trimming. The service had the power company de-energize the service line running to the house. A large limb "got away" from the trimmers and fell on a 2,400-volt line. That line broke and contacted the service line, which caused a surge to flow into the house wiring. The surge caused a fire which damaged the house. The homeowner sued the power company, and the jury found against the company. The appellate court affirmed. It was proper to admit evidence that the defendant trimmed all tree limbs that were over the power line after the accident. The city's negligence was based on not de-energizing the 2,400-volt line. The acts of the trimmers were not a superseding cause. *Matthews v. City of Farmington*, 828 S.W.2d 693 (Mo. App. 1992).

A 1988 Missouri case had an interesting theory of liability. A charcoal manufacturing plant caught fire and was extensively damaged. For a reason not disclosed, live power lines were down around the plant, and firefighters were unable to get close safely and put out the fire until the power was cut off. The origin of the fire itself was not known. (The original plaintiff owned charcoal stored in the plant, and sued the plant owner for the value of the lost charcoal. The plant owner settled, and brought in the power company as third-party defendant. In this case, the plant owner is the plaintiff and the power company the defendant.) The allegation was that the power company was unreasonably late in cutting off the power. The jury found the power company negligent. The claimed damages were $5 million. The jury awarded $375,000. The appellate court affirmed as to negligence but remanded for a new trial on damages. Fire losses traditionally are not apportionable between more than one cause. It would be improper for the jury to attempt to determine to what extent damages would have been lessened if the power had been shut off earlier. Also, the question of insurance was improperly injected into the trial. *Rozak Farms, Inc. v. Ozark Border Elec. Co-op*, 849 F.2d 306 (8th Cir. 1988).

In a 1991 Texas case, the jury found two defendants each 50 percent at fault in a warehouse fire. The plaintiffs were the owners of pecans and peanuts that were stored in the warehouse. The fire began when a truck struck a guy line, causing the power lines to vibrate and arc. They fell onto the roof of the warehouse and set it on fire. The defendants were the trucking company and the power company. The trucking company settled before trial. The guy line was unmarked and was exposed to traffic. The guy and pole were shown to be deficient in that an ordinary person could push on the guy and cause the power lines to shake and arc. It was proper to admit, as excited utterance, the statement of the trucking company's traffic manager that "I have told T.P. & L. a dozen times to move that damn guy wire." The appellate court affirmed, and directed that the power company was entitled to a dollar-for-dollar credit for the amount of the other defendant's settlement. *Texas Util. Elec. v. Gold Kist*, 817 S.W.2d 749 (Tex. App. 1991).

The court in a 1988 Montana case held a power company liable for a building fire. The appellate court affirmed a jury verdict for the building owner. There was sufficient evidence of negligence for the case to go to the jury. Building residents noticed lights dimming and radio static on the day of the fire. A delivery man noticed arcing within the joints of the tin siding. An expert witness testified that from studying depositions and photographs it appeared that the fire was caused when the upper roof knob pulled loose and swung into the tin siding. He testified that arcing temperature could range between two to four thousand degrees or higher, and this was what set the inflammable materials on fire in the building. The defendant argued that a fireman at the scene did not see any loose roof knobs, so the plaintiff's expert's theory was incorrect. The court held that

conflicting evidence is a question for the jury and it was proper to reject
the defendant's motion for a directed verdict. *Stout v. Montana Power Co.*,
762 P.2d 875 (Mont. 1988).

A 1989 Alabama case involved the duties of a general and a subcontractor. The plaintiffs hired the general contractor to rebuild their house
after a fire. The general contractor hired a subcontractor for the electrical
work. The plaintiffs notified the sub several times of popping noises in a
hallway switch. The day before the sub was to examine the switch, the
house burned again. The plaintiffs sued the general and the subcontractors, as well as the maker of the switch. They settled with the maker. The
trial court granted the remaining defendants summary judgment. The appellate court affirmed as to the general contractor. A general is not liable
for the acts of a subcontractor absent two exceptions: inherently dangerous work and nondelegable duties. Neither applied here. However, there
were questions about the negligence of the subcontractor to be resolved,
so summary judgment was not proper as to that party. *Clark v. Jackson*,
549 So.2d 85 (Ala. 1989).

A 2001 Alabama case also involved a house fire, but also a fatality as
a result, a two-year-old child. The plaintiff moved into a new house in
1991, and began to have electrical problems. The lights would blink, bulbs
would burn out, the air conditioning unit would not cool, and so on. The
plaintiff notified the builder, Jim Walter Homes, but not the power company or the subcontractor who did the electrical work. Twice Jim Walter
Homes sent someone to check these problems. The house burned at 11:00
A.M. in 1996. The plaintiff sued the power company, Jim Walter Homes,
the supplier of the electrical items, and the subcontractor, and all moved
for summary judgment. The state fire marshal investigated and concluded
that the fire started in a bedroom, and that the most likely cause was "children playing with matches." The plaintiff contended that the fire started in
the attic above the bedroom and was caused by some negligence by one or
all of the parties. The trial court granted summary judgment to all. The
Alabama Supreme Court reversed for trial as to the builder and subcontractor. The fact that the builder sent someone to inspect the electrical system several times, when perhaps he should have referred the plaintiff to
the subcontractor, and voluntarily undertook to inspect the house, involves a claim of negligence that may not be resolved by summary judgment. As for the subcontractor, expert differed as to the cause of the fire,

and thus summary judgment is not appropriate. *McGinnis v. Jim Walter Homes, Inc.*, 800 So.2d 140 (Ala. 2001).

In a 1995 Pennsylvania case, the court held that a dispute between a public utility and a customer alleging a tort belonged in court and not before the Public Utility Commission. The customer's barn was set on fire when a storm caused a subtransmission and a distribution line to touch. The customer alleged negligent splicing and other negligent acts. The common pleas judge transferred the matter to the PUC. The PUC then decided that the power company had met its obligations of providing electric service as contemplated by the Utility Code. The customer appealed to the appellate court, and that court ordered the PUC to relinquish jurisdiction back to common pleas. The matter was not a complex one which required the special expertise of the PUC. It was an allegation of failure to protect one customer from a damaging power surge on one occasion. The court system, with the assistance of expert witness, could decide the dispute. *Poorbaugh v. Public Utility Comm.*, 666 N.E.2d 744 (Pa. App. 1995).

We move on to Arkansas and the 9,000 chickens. The plaintiffs raised chickens. A severe storm caused power outages to the chicken houses. Apparently, a tree blew down onto a phase wire and caused it to sag to within inches of the neutral wire, rather then maintaining the four foot clearance. The following day was hot, and that plus high usage made the line sag more. This tripped the circuit breakers, and outages occurred from time to time. The plaintiffs lost their cooling equipment and 9,000 chickens perished. There was a bench trial, and the judge found the defendant 51 percent at fault and the plaintiffs 49 percent. There was evidence that the power company crews checked the eight or ten miles of lines several times, resetting the circuit breakers, before they noticed the sagging. The judge found the plaintiffs comparatively negligent in not having backup generators on chicken farms in Arkansas. The supreme court affirmed. Power outages happen. *Rich Mountain Elec. Co-op v. Revels*, 841 S.W.2d 151 (Ark. 1992).

The court in a 1994 Arkansas case held that summary judgment was improperly granted to a power company in a mobile home fire. The facts are quite simple. The mobile home owner requested the power company to turn on the power at the pole. He was making electrical repairs to the premises at the time. The company employee activated the power at the pole and also turned on the customer's breaker switches. This caused a fire and damage in the mobile home. The trial court found no duty was breached and granted summary judgment. The appellate court found there were issues of material fact to be resolved and reversed for trial. State statutes require public utilities to act with reasonable care in the delivery of their services. Whether turning on the breaker switches without inspecting the premises breaches this duty is a question of fact. *Bellanca v. Arkansas Power & Light*, 870 S.W.2d 735 (Ark. 1994).

In a short 1994 New York case the court held a power company grossly negligent for a power surge. The surge happened when a ceramic insulator holding a wire broke. The surge caused a fire at the pole and damaged three appliances in the plaintiff's house. The court found a reckless disregard for the plaintiff's safety. The judge based his finding on the defendant's admission that it installed the insulator in 1979 and had not inspected or maintained it since. It did not inspect such installations absent a complaint. *Ricciardi v. Consolidated Edison*, 615 N.Y.S.2d 854 (N.Y. City Ct. 1994). (The author notes that this case is absolutely the most trivial in terms of damages he has ever annotated for this and similar books. The judge awarded $1,382 in damages and $5.86 in costs. Needless to say, the plaintiff appeared pro se.)

We might quibble with the Ricciardi decision holding a power company liable for gross negligence for not inspecting insulators. A 1991 Louisiana case is an example of more active negligence. The city of Lafayette had been without power because of Hurricane Danny. When the city tried to energize the lines in the plaintiff's residential area, fuses blew. Employees canvassed the area for down lines and found no primary lines down. Early the following morning the lines were again energized. Several residents noticed a down line and informed an unidentified person who represented that he worked for the city. He tried without success to use a cellular phone to report the problem. The power came on and the line, which was severed, arced and flashed around a gas stub. Apparently it energized the gas line and that set the plaintiff's house on fire. The appellate court affirmed a jury verdict finding the city solely liable. The testimony concerning the unidentified city employee was admissible. The city alleged that the fire was caused by a lightning strike because persons heard a loud boom, but that noise could have been the result of a transformer explosion. The city also suggested that the cause of the fire might have been faulty wiring in the attic, and since those wires were destroyed, they cannot be ruled out as the cause. The court held that the plaintiff proved his case. *Valiant Ins. Co. v. City of Lafayette*, 574 So.2d 505 (La. App. 1991).

A 2001 Mississippi case involved a pine tree farm of 315 acres. A power line crossed the farm, and the farmer sued the power company on the theory that the power line must have caused the fire by failing to keep the power line right of way clear of trees. The jury thought otherwise, and the appellate court affirmed. There was evidence that the fire began at some place other than near the power line, the line was rubber-coated where it crossed the forest, and there were safety devices that would shut down the line within 1/100th of a second if the line had contacted a tree. *Redhead v. Entergy Mississippi, Inc.*, 828 So.2d 801 (Miss. App. 2001).

A 2001 Louisiana case arose from a brief power outage in a hospital. A neighborhood power outage triggered the hospital doors to close. The plaintiff was standing in the hallway at doors and was struck within three seconds in the darkness by the door. The lights came back on within several second to a minute. The injury claimed was to the ulnar nerve of the right arm. The plaintiff sued the hospital. At trial the plaintiff herself admitted that she was struck within three seconds of the outage. The trial judge agreed with the defendant that this was not proof of an unreasonable risk and directed a defense verdict. The plaintiff simply had not proven here case. The appellate court affirmed. *Reed v. Coumbia/HCA*, 786 So.2d 142 (La. App. 2001).

The court held in a 1988 New York case held that a contractor who installed circuit breakers, which allegedly were the cause of a house fire, could not be held liable for negligence. The breakers were encased in hard plastic and the interiors were not accessible. They were labeled with a UL sticker. The installation was approved by city inspectors. The court ordered summary judgment for the contractor, but held that there were conflicting expert opinions as to whether the other defendant, the manufacturer, was negligent and that action could proceed. *Wilson v. Woodward Builders*, 530 N.Y.S.2d 343 (N.Y. App. 1988).

A 1996 District of Columbia case focused on arcing in a watt-hour meter. This device is installed by the power company; lines past that point are the customer's. A department store manager arrived to open the store and turned on various lights. He noticed that the lights in the girls' department flickered and went out, followed by a humming noise. He told another employee he would check the breakers and fuses after breakfast. As he was returning to the building, he saw it was on fire. When the fire department arrived, the building was engulfed in flames. The plaintiff, the insurer of the lessor, sued the power company, claiming that arcing in the meter caused the fire. The plaintiff's expert, a retired electrical engineering professor, determined the cause of the fire was arcing in the meter. The humming sound the manager heard was the meter arcing in the basement below the girls' department. This would produce heat sufficient to melt copper and steel. No other combustibles would produce that much heat. The fire department investigator reached the same conclusion. The probable cause was corrosion or contamination between blades and slots in the meter. The district court judge assumed the report was accurate as to the cause of the fire, but held that the power company was not negligent. The meter met code standards, was not negligently installed, and was inspected regularly. While the plaintiff had abandoned its res ipsa loquitur claim, the court held that it would not apply anyhow. The fire was one that could have happened absent some negligent act. *Hartford Cas. Ins. Co. v. Potomac Elec. Power Co.*, 927 F. Supp. 473 (D.D.C. 1996).

A 2001 Georgia case involved the duty of a landlord to maintain and repair the premises. The site was an eight unit apartment, building 1700. A fire in 1997 destroyed all units, and the tenants, who lost their personal property, sued the property manager (TGM), alleging that TGM knew of the electrical problems and failed to repair them. The fire broke out in unit 1709 in the wall between the porch and living room. Fire inspectors found the fire to be consistent with electrical malfunction, but could pinpoint no particular cause other than a sparking light switch where the fire apparently began.. Residents of five of the eight units had reported malfunctions, such as popping noises and lights going off and on for no apparent reason. Using hair dryers would throw the circuit breaker. The tenants expert found systemic electrical problems, but could state no certain cause other than the switch. The court of appeals affirmed summary judgment for TGM. Since there was no prior sparking, TGM would have no reason to inspect behind the switches. *Villareal v. TGM*, 547 S.E.2d 351 (Ga. App. 2001).

A 2001 Georgia house fire case involved a skittish portable generator. A homeowner bought a portable electric generator following a hurricane from the defendant, Farmer's Supply Store. The homeowner's employee picked up the unit, and was briefed by a salesperson on how to add oil, gasoline, and how to hook up the electric cables. He was not told that the unit might move about from vibration. The homeowner set the unit two or three feet from the house and started it. Later he noticed that the unit had moved two inches closer to the house. He merely moved it back. Later that evening the generator moved nearer and set the house on fire. The court of appeals affirmed summary judgment for the store. Its employees had no duty to discover a latent product defect, and here the plaintiff himself had knowledge that he should have staked the unit down. *Federal Ins. Co. v. Farmer's Supply Store*, 555 S.E.2d 238 (Ga. App. 2001).

We now turn to several cases with remote causes. A 1988 Louisiana case arose when a lightning arrestor, located some forty-two feet high on a pole, exploded. The plaintiff was nearby and alleged that the force of the explosion knocked him against a wall, injuring his neck, and burning fragments touched his leg. He sued the power company in strict liability. At trial, the judge limited his claims to first and second-degree burns on his lower right leg. A few weeks after the arrestor accident, the plaintiff allegedly was injured in a streetcar accident and complained of back injures from that. The trial judge believed the testimony of the defendant's expert witness, who testified that the explosion forty-two feet above street level would not cause the plaintiff to be flung against a wall. The judge awarded $4,496 in damages. The appellate court affirmed. *Dyer v. New Orleans Pub. Serv.*, 530 So.2d 628 (La. App. 1988).

A 1994 Louisiana case is somewhat similar. A large transformer containing 1,400 gallons of mineral oil exploded and sent out a large cloud of smoke. The plaintiff was about to enter a McDonald's a block away. She quickly returned to her car and fled the scene. She sued the power company in strict liability for physical and psychological injuries. The plaintiff was initially under the impression that the restaurant had exploded, and she felt guilty about leaving without attempting to rescue children inside. She then learned the cause of the explosion, and heard that anyone exposed to the smoke should wash thoroughly and seek medical help if there were breathing problems. She claimed that her face, arms, and eyes were burning, and she went to a hospital for emergency treatment. The jury awarded $5,600. The appellate court affirmed, and increased the award to $25,000. It was correct to charge the jury on *res ipsa loquitur*.

The transformer was under the control of the defendant, and the only reasonable explanation for the explosion was a defect in the transformer or its connecting lines. The court doubted that the other two possibilities, small animals or an act of God, caused the accident. The defendant's expert testified that the flaw could have been a bad weld, a winding problem, or any number of other causes. The plaintiff had had asthma from childhood, and had often been treated for mental illness. The court mentions the usual rule that the defendant takes the plaintiff as he finds him, and ordered the increased award as a minimum for similar cases. *Presstenbach v. Louisiana Power & Light*, 638 So.2d 234 (La. App. 1994). In a 1992 Pennsylvania case, a curious spectator at a house fire was injured by flying debris when propane tanks exploded. The injured person sued the electric utility, among other defendants. The court held that the plaintiff's injuries were not the result of any negligence by the utility. Even if the fire was caused by some electrical flaw, the injuries were not foreseeable consequence. *Burman v. Golay and Co, Inc.*, 616 A.2d 657 (Pa. Super. 1992).

A remote cause case from Maine found for the defendants. A motel guest fell in his room and was injured during a power outage. He sued the motel owner and the power company. The supreme court affirmed a directed verdict for both defendants. The outage was caused when an elm tree located twenty feet from the power line at an embankment fell on the line during a heavy rain storm. The court found that the power company maintained a regular cycle of trimming and cutting trees to keep the lines clear. The plaintiff's expert's opinion was that if the tree had been damaged from a previous storm, it should have been cut. There was no evidence offered as to prior damage, however. The court declined to speculate what duty a utility has to a non-customer. As to the motel owner, the court found that it met its obligation of reasonable care. No witnesses could identify any motels that provided emergency lighting in rooms. Such lighting was provided in hallways, and flashlights were available at the desk. *LaVallee v. Vermont Motor Inns*, 569 A.2d 1073 (Vt. 1989).

One of the most famous power blackouts ever was the one that left most of New York City without electrical power from 9:36 P.M. on July 13, 1977 until 10:40 P.M. the next evening. Numerous suits were filed. One claim was similar to that of the Vermont case above. An apartment tenant was without water because the electric pump could not operate. He went to the basement to get water and fell on the darkened and defective basement stairs. He sued his landlord and Consolidated Edison. The court of appeals held that Con Ed did not owe a duty to the tenant. There was no contractual relationship between them. Even though an earlier decision had held that Con Ed was grossly negligent, the court did not believe that the defendant's conduct was reckless and wanton. The court found it necessary to set a limit to liability in this system-wide power failure, and the tenant of an apartment building fell outside the line. *Strauss v. Belle Realty Co.*, 65 N.Y.S.2d 399 (N.Y. App. 1985). The blackout was caused by two lightning strikes within eighteen minutes of each other. This caused two outages, and there were allegations that a power plant was unnecessarily out of service, and that the defendant failed to properly inspect and maintain components of the system. Plaintiffs also alleged that the employee responsible at the key point in the system was not properly trained and qualified. A grocery company sued for spoilage of food and loss of business. The jury found Con Ed grossly negligent and awarded damages, and the appellate court affirmed. *Food Pageant v. Consolidated Edison*, 429 N.Y.S.2d 738 (N.Y. App. 1981). A later decision held Food Pageant binding on Con Ed, and awarded damages to the city of New York for certain expenses incurred during the blackout. It is somewhat remarkable that the primary case determining liability related to the blackout involved only some $40,000 in damages, while subsequent claims reached $200 million. *Koch v. Consolidated Edison*, 468 N.E.2d 1 (N.Y. 1984).

The most recent notable power blackout in the United States occurred on August 14, 2003. On September 12, the U.S. Department of Energy released a report prepared by a U.S.-Canadian expert team. The failure of many lines and the self-protective tripping of some generators at 4:10 P.M. EDT led to a condition in which the eastern Michigan and northern Ohio systems had little available generation left, while voltage was declining throughout the areas. When a main transmission life running east from northeast Ohio failed, power that had been flowing west into Ohio reversed direction. The resulting surge started to literally flood grids around Lake Erie through northwest New York state and Ontario, as power sought to find its way into northern Michigan to satisfy unmet load in that region. With the transmission system to the east and northeast of Ohio becoming severely overloaded, the northeast system unraveled at a breathtaking pace. By 4:13 P.M. the cascading sequence was essentially complete. As of this writing, no lawsuits related to this power blackout have been identified. One can be sure, however, that a search for liability for this massive blackout is underway, and that the resulting litigation will prove thought-provoking for lawyers and electrical engineers.

A plaintiff in an electrical fire case can bring an action alleging strict liability, as well as other theories of negligence. We have seen from the chapter on products liability that most courts have held that electricity is not a product within the meaning of strict liability until it reaches the customer's meter. A 1993 Wisconsin fire case held that a jury verdict for the plaintiff could be supported by strict liability as well as ordinary negligence. The plaintiff was the owner of a bowling alley and restaurant. One midafternoon there was a momentary power outage which caused flickering lights. Then smoke poured out of two ball-setting machines. The owner checked the basement and found his main distribution panel hissing and sparking. Molten particles fell on nearby combustibles and the building burned. At the same time, witnesses outside the building heard an explosion and noticed the power line across the street arcing and burning. A power company lineman checked and found one line "locked out." The lines showed evidence of arcing. It was apparent that overgrown trees had touched the lines. The building owner sued the power company and Pinky Electrical Corp. The claim against Pinky was that it had not properly grounded the distribution panel and left a loose connection in one circuit breaker. Pinky cross-claimed against the city of New Berlin, alleging that the city inspector was negligent in approving Pinky's negligent work. During trial the plaintiff settled with all defendants except the power company. The jury found the power company 85 percent at fault, Pinky 10 percent, and the city 5 percent. (The releases did not cover the power company.) The court of appeals reversed. The supreme court heard the case and reinstated the jury verdict.

The plaintiff's expert testified that the high voltage spikes and the lack of grounding were the causes. The spikes or transients finally damaged the insulation in the circuit breaker box, and this permitted arcing in the box. The lack of grounding delayed the operation of a fuse. The power company's expert put all the blame on the customer's electric panel and breakers. The power company made a public policy argument that power surges such as the one in this case that caused the fire were rare events, and it would not serve public policy to hold a public utility liable. The supreme court noted that the plaintiff's expert knew of a similar event in

Wisconsin, and had read of others. Both expert witnesses agreed that ordinary voltage spikes are common phenomena in overhead electrical lines. However, the surges which caused this fire were not common. It was foreseeable that failure to trim trees near power lines could lead to this kind of incident. The power company is not required to prevent all power surges; rather, the duty here is to maintain the lines near trees. Regarding strict liability, the court held that the consumer's expectations play a part. Here the customer would not expect to receive the product in powerful surges. *Beacon Bowl v. Wisconsin Elec. Power*, 501 N.W.2d 788 (Wis. 1993).

A 1992 New York case also involved a house fire caused by a power surge. The surge was caused when a healthy tree limb fell on power lines about two miles from the house. Apparently the surge arresters did not properly prevent the surge from entering the customer's house line. The appellate court held that products liability would not apply, but that there were questions of fact about whether the tree limb was under the control of the power company, and whether the arresters were functioning properly. On another point, the power company was not absolved of liability under Tariff 207. That section states that the power company shall not be liable for damages resulting from interruption of service. The company can still be liable for ordinary negligence. *Bowen v. Niagara Mohawk Power Corp.*, 590 N.Y.S.2d 628 (N.Y. App. 1992).

A 1996 Indiana case dealt with damages claimed as a result of interruption of service. An equipment failure in the electric distribution system some distance from the plaintiff's business (a law firm) resulted in loss of power. The law firm claimed it had to close its office for two days, and it claimed economic loss of about $10,000. The appellate court affirmed summary judgment for the power company. Strict product liability did not apply because the electricity was not a product until it reached the plaintiff's meter. The court applied the economic loss rule. There cannot be recovery of economic damages unless there was physical injury to a person or property damage to the plaintiff's property. The only claim here was that the product failed to perform as expected. *Bamberger & Feibleman v. IPL*, 665 N.E.2d 933 (Ind. App. 1996).

We note three California house fire cases. In the first case, lightning struck a transformer and caused it to explode in flames. A massive voltage surge traveled along the plaintiff's lines and exploded his meter, and that set the building on fire. The trial judge held that the power company was liable to the plaintiff in strict product liability. The jury determined damages, and the plaintiff dismissed his alternate theory of ordinary negligence. The appellate court reversed on a finding that lightning-generated electricity is simply not a product. The court remanded with an order to reinstate the plaintiff's negligence count. The plaintiff not unreasonably dropped this count when he appeared to have recovered in product liability. *Mancuso v. Southern Calif. Edison Co.*, 283 Cal. Rptr. 300 (Cal. App. 1991). A 1992 case was very similar, except that the power surge was not caused by lightning. Instead, a transformer exploded and sent a sent a power surge to the customer's meter, and that set the house on fire. The court held that strict product liability was properly applied and affirmed the award of damages. *Stein v. Southern Calif. Edison Co.*, 7 Cal. Rptr.2d 907 (Cal. App. 1992). In the third case, the fire was started by arcing lines on the power company's side of the meter. The arcing set the roof of the building on fire. Since the defect was located beyond the customer's meter, strict liability did not apply. *Fong v. Pacific Gas & Elec.*, 245 Cal. Rptr. 436 (Cal. App. 1988).

About the Authors

Robert E. Nabours, Ph.D., PE, has been involved in the construction industry for more than fifty-five years. During the early 1960s, he was an instructor in electrical engineering at the University of Arizona, a research engineer in advanced communications systems, and the chief engineer for an Arizona electronics manufacturer. Since 1968, he has been engaged full time in the private practice of design electrical engineering, serving clients in the construction industry and providing forensic electrical engineering services to the legal profession.

He received his B.S. in electrical engineering from the University of Arizona in 1957, his M.S. in electrical engineering from Stanford University in 1959, and his Ph.D. in electrical engineering from the University of Arizona in 1965. He is a registered professional engineer in Arizona, California and New Mexico and is a member of the National Society of Professional Engineers, a life senior member of the Institute of Electrical and Electronics Engineers, and is a Fellow of the National Academy of Forensic Engineers. He is also a member of the technical honorary societies of Sigma Pi Sigma (physics) and Tau Beta Pi (engineering).

Raymond Fish, Ph.D., M.D., received his B.S. and M.S. degrees in electrical engineering from the UIUC (University of Illinois in Urbana-Champaign). He received his Ph.D. in biomedical engineering from Worcester Polytechnic Institute and Clark University, and his M.D. from the University of Chicago. Dr. Fish is board-certified in emergency medicine, which he has practiced for twenty-five years. Before entering medical practice he worked for three and a half years in electrical engineering and research, most of which was at the National Institute of Neurological Diseases and Stroke at NIH. Dr. Fish has appointments at the UIUC in the

Medical School and in Biomedical, Electrical and Computer Engineering. In addition to practicing medicine, he is presently teaching a course at the UIUC entitled "The Physiology of Electrical Injury." That course is based on much of the material in this book. Dr. Fish is a Fellow of the American College of Emergency Physicians.

Paul F. Hill is a retired law school librarian and a member of the Nebraska Bar. He lives in Omaha, Nebraska. He is an experienced legal researcher and writer, and has coauthored books published by Lawyers and Judges Publishing Company on bicycle, motorcycle, pedestrian, and bus accidents.

Index

K

Falls and Related Injuries: Slips, Trips, Missteps and Their Consequences, #5430

Alvin S. Hyde, M.D., Ph.D., Gary Bakken, Ph.D., CPE, John R. Abele, Esq., H. Harvey Cohen, Ph.D., CPE, and Cindy A. LaRue, M.S., CPE

It is important for healthcare professionals, attorneys, writers of building codes and anyone who cares for children or the elderly to understand how falls happen and how they can be prevented. This book was written with this in mind.

Falls and Related Injuries will help you gain an understanding of who is most likely to fall and the types of injuries that are sustained. The authors point out environmental factors and hazards that can cause falls and how you can determine liability. Of course, this text also provides important information on how falls can be prevented. The last section of this book, the *Falls Prevention Manual,* contains forms that will assist you in finding potential trouble areas around buildings before an accident occurs. For your convenience, a CD-ROM of printable forms from the *Falls Prevention Manual* is included with this text. 6 $^1/_8$" × 9 $^1/_4$", casebound, 548 pages, with CD-ROM of printable forms from the *Falls Prevention Manual*.

Elevator and Escalator Accident Reconstruction and Litigation, #6249

James Filippone, PE, Joel D. Feldman, Esq., Ronald D. Schloss and David A. Cooper

As you are aware, many questions arise when accidents occur. Was the equipment inspected? Were repairs completed properly? Where signs and warnings posted? This book examines all aspects of an elevator or escalator accident and helps you find the answers to these questions. You will learn about elevator and escalator codes and regulations, how the equipment is designed to work and statistics of the types of accidents that can occur.

The authors of this book used their diverse backgrounds as mechanical engineers, electrical engineers and attorneys to investigate numerous elevator and escalator accidents and have compiled their findings into this comprehensive resource. This one book will give you the information you need to know if you are litigating or reconstructing these types of accidents. 6" × 9", casebound, 366 pages.

Workplace Injury Litigation, #6125

Edited by Todd McFarren, Esq. and Glen J. Grossman, Esq.

Workers' compensation law is a complex field in which even a seasoned litigator may occasionally need the guidance of an expert. The compensibility of on-the-job injuries and death varies from state to state, many genuine injuries are subjective (i.e., with little or no physical evidence of damage), insurance companies can and do vigorously resist the payment of benefits, the bureaucracy of the appeals process can be a tangle . . . .

Editors McFarren and Grossman have gathered chapters from leading medical and legal experts in the field. Attorneys and judges—as well as healthcare providers, employers, insurance company representatives and vocational consultants—will find new ideas, fresh perspectives and just plain good advice in this volume. Put their expertise to work for you and order your copy today. 6" × 9", casebound.

Warnings, Instructions, and Technical Communications, #5619

George A. Peters, J.D., PE, CSP, CPE, FIOSH, FRSH and Barbara J. Peters, J.D.

This is the first comprehensive book on warnings that provides immediately useful information for design engineers, lawyers, professors and hazard communication specialists. Failure to warn and provide appropriate safety information is often alleged in product liability lawsuits, toxic tort claims, and ethical drug cases. Some allegations and supporting proof seem simple, but failure-to-warn cases can easily become complex. The counsel who proceeds on basic common sense and a case-law approach can be unpleasantly surprised, especially when expert testimony and legal arguments are not effectively rebutted because the counsel considered warning issues elemental.

When you have consulted *Warnings, Instructions, and Technical Communications*, you will be prepared to encounter the most complex situations. You will learn how warnings are distinctive from product defects or deficiencies, and how the analysis of warnings or their absence differs from accident reconstruction. 6 $\frac{1}{8}$" × 9 $\frac{1}{4}$", casebound, 450 pages.

Aircraft Accident Reconstruction and Litigation, Third Edition, #5155

Barnes W. McCormick, Ph.D., P.E. and M. P. Papadakis, Esq.

This book will be helpful to lawyers and accident reconstructionists involved in aircraft accident litigation or investigation. It provides a basic source of technical and legal information that will help you search for probable cause and intelligently litigate your case. It can even be considered a postgraduate guide for the hardware-oriented aircraft accident investigator, especially the sections on human errors and human factors.

Readers will appreciate the book's refreshing review of the elements of aerodynamics, structural design, aircraft control techniques and the nuances of applicable law. The third edition contains new chapters on the Freedom of Information Act, safety, discovery, spoliation of evidence, Death on the High Seas Act, tort litigation and more. 8 ½" × 11", casebound, 702 pages.

Boat Accident Reconstruction and Litigation, Second Edition, #5082

Roy Scott Hickman, PE and Michael M. Sampsel, PE
Contributing author: Jeanne-Marie D. Van Hemmen

This updated and revised edition has even more information to help you understand the complexities of boating accidents. In this edition are expanded chapters on boat accident reconstruction, an entirely new chapter on personal watercraft, and sections on modern developments in steering. Whether you are a beginner or experienced litigator or any expert dealing with a boat accident, the information contained in this excellent resource will save you hours of research time hunting through less complete texts and online services.

If you are a lawyer or an accident reconstructionist, this book will help you find appropriate data, analyze it, and determine cause and effects in a boat accident. The book is a compendium of information useful in litigation dealing with activities in and on the water. 6" × 9", casebound, 360 pages.

Medical-Legal Aspects of Drugs, #6192

Marcelline Burns, Ph.D.

Drugs are not a new phenomenon but the problems associated with them take on new dimensions in the conditions of modern society. Written by a group of knowledgeable individuals, including, law enforcement personnel, attorneys, and healthcare professionals, this book covers a wide range of issues concerning the use and abuse of both prescription and illicit drugs.

Study the seven classifications of drugs, why they are abused and their common side effects.See how the side effects of drugs can impair the user's ability to drive, work and function in society.

This book also covers the legal aspects of drug use in our society. You will read about the lab technology used to test blood, hair and breath samples and the complications associated with using the results as evidence in trial. You will also see how law enforcement agencies identify drugged drivers and how these cases are prosecuted or defended. 6" × 9", casebound, 480 pages

Medical-Legal Aspects of Alcohol, Fourth Edition, #0888

Edited by James C. Garriott, Ph.D.

Forensic alcohol analysis is the most frequently performed of all analyses in forensic laboratories, and is the most commonly used laboratory result in courts of law. Even still, the medical and legal aspects of alcohol are complex topics because so many different components are present in drunk-driving cases. This book is designed to fill your need for an authoritative text on the various scientific and legal aspects of alcohol determination in biological specimens.

Medicolegal Aspects of Alcohol, now in its fourth edition, has been a classic text on the forensic science of alcohol for the last fifteen years. The authors include some of the foremost scientists in the field of alcohol research in the world. Chapters on pharmacology and toxicology, disposition of alcohol in the body, psychomotor performance, test procedures, postmortem testing, workplace testing, specimen handling, quality assurance in the laboratory and legal aspects have been revised and updated to provide current information. 8 ½" × 11", casebound, 544 pages.

Emotional Distress—Proving Damages, #6508

Jon R. Abele, Esq.

Litigating a case involving emotional distress damages can be very difficult because many jurisdictions limit the ways in which these cases can be presented. It is important for attorneys that handle these cases to understand how courts in various jurisdictions have ruled in this area and why.

Emotional Distress provides a summary of emotional distress cases that have been litigated in jurisdictions through out the country. You will read about the different categories of emotional distress and which categories are most accepted by courts and jurors. You will also learn about the limitations that the plaintiffs have in claiming emotional distress, such as their relationship to the victim and being in the "zone of danger." After reading this book you will understand why some cases were successful and others failed. 6" × 9", softbound, 164 pages, 2003.

Sunbear III:
Precise Sun-Moon Positioning Software, #6567

George Alexander

This unique software will give you the ability to determine the exact location of the sun and the moon from anywhere within the United States and eastern Canada at any time and date from 1752 to 2900 A.D. The program is designed to give you the ability to accurately calculate where the sun or moon was at the time of the accident. All you need to know is the zip code, date, and time the accident occurred, and this program will do the rest.

Sunbear III features accurate calculations that adjust for time zones and daylight saving time, calculations from magnetic north and true north so you can use a compass at the scene of an accident to determine the positions and a comprehensive zip code database that covers the longitude and latitude for over 32,000 USPS Zip Codes.

CD-ROM. Sunbear III runs under Win95, Win 98, WinME, WinNT, Win2000 and WinXP. Minumum CPU requirement is a 90 MHz Pentium®. 32 MB of RAM and 17 MB of free disc space are needed. The display works with 16 color minimum, 256 color recommended, true color is supported. Software is nonreturnable.

Elements of Trial Practice, #6060

Peter D. Polchinski, Esq.

Short and persuasive, this book wastes no words.

To win at trial, you must present your case clearly, simply, persuasively, and fairly while you undermine your adversary's case in the same manner. Achieving excellence in trial advocacy is a lifelong pursuit. Nevertheless, trial skills and a basic understanding of this art can be learned quickly.

You'll discover how to select a favorable jury, prepare your witnesses, deliver powerful opening statements, conduct an effective direct examination, cross-examine any witness, introduce exhibits, impeach their witnesses, control consulting experts, and win the case on summation. *Elements of Trial Practice* will become your essential, instant-access reference for trial. Armed with its many valuable techniques, you will approach trial practice with new enthusiasm and confidence. 6" × 9", softbound, 123 pages.

Evaluating and Reserving Wrongful Death and Personal Injury Cases, #5996

Mark Dombroff, Esq.

This book is the ideal step-by-step guide for defense attorneys involved in a catastrophic death suit. For defense attorneys litigating a wrongful death suit, it is a "must have" reference.

A casino bus traveling from New York City to Atlantic City has just crashed, killing everyone including the driver. A witness reported that she saw the bus swerving from lane to lane. Another witness stated that the bus passed him at approximately 20 mph over the speed limit. Worse yet, the driver's record indicates a previous suspension for reckless driving. The file has just landed on your desk. Now what? In the face of clear liability on the part of your client, how do you defend your case? With Mr. Dombroff's concise guide to explain all the issues you must consider and his handy worksheets in the appendix, you will find everything you need to skillfully protect your client to the best of your ability. 8 ½" × 11", softbound, 88 pages (includes forms).